MW01040687

The Creativity Reader

The Creativity Reader

EDITED BY

Vlad P. Glăveanu

Webster University Geneva, Switzerland

OXFORD
UNIVERSITY PRESS

OXFORD
UNIVERSITY PRESS

Oxford University Press is a department of the University of Oxford. It furthers
the University's objective of excellence in research, scholarship, and education
by publishing worldwide. Oxford is a registered trade mark of Oxford University
Press in the UK and certain other countries.

Published in the United States of America by Oxford University Press
198 Madison Avenue, New York, NY 10016, United States of America.

© Oxford University Press 2019

All rights reserved. No part of this publication may be reproduced, stored in
a retrieval system, or transmitted, in any form or by any means, without the
prior permission in writing of Oxford University Press, or as expressly permitted
by law, by license, or under terms agreed with the appropriate reproduction
rights organization. Inquiries concerning reproduction outside the scope of the
above should be sent to the Rights Department, Oxford University Press, at the
address above.

You must not circulate this work in any other form
and you must impose this same condition on any acquirer.

Library of Congress Cataloging-in-Publication Data
Names: Glăveanu, Vlad Petre, editor.
Title: The creativity reader / edited by Vlad P. Glăveanu.
Description: New York : Oxford University Press, [2019]
Identifiers: LCCN 2018029772 | ISBN 9780190841706 (hardcover : alk. paper)
Subjects: LCSH: Creative ability. | Imagination.
Classification: LCC BF408 .C7554 2018 | DDC 153.3/5—dc23
LC record available at https://lccn.loc.gov/2018029772

1 3 5 7 9 8 6 4 2

Printed by Sheridan Books, Inc., United States of America

Contents

Contributors

Teresa M. Amabile
Harvard Business School
Boston, MA, USA

Baptiste Barbot
Pace University
New York, NY, USA;
Yale University
New Haven, CT, USA

Ronald A. Beghetto
University of Connecticut
Storrs, CT, USA

Edward P. Clapp
Harvard Graduate School of Education
Cambridge, MA, USA

Giovanni Emanuele Corazza
University of Bologna
Bologna, Italy

David H. Cropley
University of South Australia
Adelaide, Australia

Vlad P. Glăveanu
Webster University
Geneva, Switzerland

Jacques-Henri Guignard
Université de Nantes
Nantes, France

Michael Hanchett Hanson
Teacher's College, Columbia University
New York, NY, USA

Beth A. Hennessey
Wellesley College
Wellesley, MA, USA

Jessica D. Hoffmann
Yale University
New Haven, CT, USA

Dorota M. Jankowska
The Maria Grzegorzewska University
Warsaw, Poland

Vera John-Steiner
University of New Mexico
Albuquerque, NM, USA

Maciej Karwowski
University of Wroclaw
Wroclaw, Poland

James C. Kaufman
University of Connecticut
Storrs, CT, USA

Salvatore Leone
University of Nebraska
at Omaha
Omaha, NE, USA

Todd Lubart
Université Paris Descartes
Paris, France

Rose H. Miller
Yale University
New Haven, CT, USA

Alfonso Montuori
California Institute of Integral Studies
San Francisco, CA, USA

Seana Moran
Clark University
Worcester, MA, USA

Christophe Mouchiroud
Université Paris Descartes
Paris, France

Roni Reiter-Palmon
University of Nebraska at Omaha
Omaha, NE, USA

Mark A. Runco
American Institute for Behavioral Research
and Technology
La Jolla, CA, USA

Keith Sawyer
University of North Carolina at Chapel Hill
Chapel Hill, NC, USA

Dean Keith Simonton
University of California, Davis
Davis, CA, USA

Tania Zittoun
University of Neuchâtel
Neuchâtel, Switzerland

The Creativity Reader

Revisiting the Foundations of Creativity Studies

Vlad P. Glăveanu

Summary

Creativity research is often considered to have, using Ebbinghaus's formulation, a long past but a short history. This introduction aims to problematize this claim by questioning the "myth" of origin of creativity studies: the fact that it starts with Guilford's American Psychological Association address in 1950. By reflecting on the choice of founding fathers—and what this kind of choice means for how we envision and study creativity nowadays—I am proposing here an expanded history of the discipline. This history considers the continuities and ruptures in the way creativity (also called by different names, e.g., genius, imagination, fantasy) was conceived of and practiced over the centuries. It shows us the great importance of the texts written on this topic in the century that preceded Guilford's address. The present *reader* represents a collection of seminar literature from the period 1850–1950, chosen and commented on by key figures in creativity studies today. This broad yet selective account of the foundations of the field aims to be at once retrospective and prospective, explaining the present and shaping the future of creativity research.

Introduction

Creativity certainly attracts considerable attention. As one of the defining features of the current zeitgeist (Mason, 2003), creativity shapes the way we think about society, about education, about our work as well as family life, the way we think about ourselves. However, the fact that we tend, today, on a global scale, to value creativity and want more of it is a historical novelty (see Glăveanu & Kaufman, 2019). The term "creativity" itself can be traced back, in English, to the end of the 19th century (Weiner, 2000). And yet creativity as a phenomenon and our efforts to understand it go well beyond this time frame. The past several decades in particular have shown a sharp increase in the number of articles, book chapters, books, handbooks, and journals dedicated to creativity and connected processes, such as innovation, imagination, and improvisation; three annual reviews document this upward trajectory (Barron & Harrington, 1981; Hennessey & Amabile, 2010; Runco, 2001). The latest of these reviews points also to the main side effect of this trend: the risk of fragmentation. As Hennessey and Amabile (2010) rightfully argue, what we today call creativity studies is a highly heterogeneous field in which colleagues working in one area know little about what others are doing and even less about what colleagues from other disciplines are discussing. This makes overviews of the entire field more and more difficult to write and handbooks all the more important for trying to take stock of what was done and where we are heading.

A special category of editorial projects in this regard is represented by "retrospective" books. These are either authored or edited volumes dedicated to the history of creativity, recent or centuries long. There are several notable examples of historical accounts, among them Weiner's (2000) *Creativity and Beyond*, Mason's (2003) *The Value of Creativity*, and Pope's (2005) *Creativity: Theory, History, Practice*. Added to these are a handful of chapters (e.g., Runco & Albert, 2010) and articles (e.g., Simonton, 2001). Each of them considers the present in view of the past, an essential exercise. It is not only the case that current developments can be fully understood only when placed in a wider historical context, but also the future of a discipline—including creativity studies—grows out of what came before. This past is not the one of five years ago, a randomly chosen expiration date of scholarship for a lot of literature reviews, but spans decades and centuries. The *stories* we tell about creativity nowadays are not new, for as much as we would like to think that we are living special or unique times. These are in fact old stories—oftentimes going back to ancient mythologies and religions—that are appropriated, transformed, adapted to the place and age we live in. And they are also stories that circulate across groups and cultures, beliefs that migrate between science and common sense, between philosophy and politics, between professional and everyday life. Creativity might appear to be a modern value, but this way of constructing it took many centuries to emerge and its reconstruction is ongoing.

As a matter of fact, historical accounts of what we call creativity are key landmarks in this process. And each author tackling the difficult task of (re)telling the story of creativity is faced with several important *choices*. One of them—the choice of founding fathers and the starting date of the discipline—will be discussed more at length later in this introduction. Since there is no single and ultimate history of creativity, or creativity research, readily available (see Glăveanu, 2017), each account will contribute to one historical line of thinking or another. It is therefore especially interesting, instead of re-presenting past scholarship, to have an opportunity to read the actual words of past authors. Reproductions of original texts, even if in abbreviated form, are extremely rare, though. To my knowledge, the best example of such an exercise is Rothenberg and Hausman's book from 1976, *The Creativity Question*, in which the editors selected seminal texts in the history of creativity from various centuries and organized them by general themes. It is certainly the case that these primary sources have been filtered through the conceptions and views of the two editors, as well as the particular context of the 1970s, a moment in which creativity studies was gaining ground. Still, what this book achieved in the long term was to familiarize a wider audience with the richness of ideas specific for the study of creativity across time and across disciplines (with a focus on philosophical and psychological accounts). The editors merely offered short summaries and further contextual information regarding each text.

The present *Creativity Reader* continues this legacy. Its first aim is to bring together seminal texts for creativity studies from the period 1850–1950. Second, it does so by asking reputable international experts to choose these texts, based on the authors and writings that influence their own work, and comment on them. This is certainly something that disturbs the classic definition of a reader. Unlike Rothenberg and Hausman's (1976) book, this volume doesn't strive to be comprehensive; in fact it is explicitly *selective*. The whole history of thinking of creativity is not presented here, nor is an exhaustive account of the century before 1950. This volume contains a selection of key authors and texts that shaped today's creativity research through the activity of the creativity, innovation, and imagination experts who chose them. It is, in a way, the "living" history of the field without the resonance of a popularity contest. In fact, many of the authors included in this reader have rarely been mentioned or used by the community of creativity scholars. And yet, as the contributors strive to show, their ideas should be recognized and revisited. The reader tries therefore to be, at the same time, *retrospective and prospective*. It recovers the past with a view toward the present and the future. Third, by focusing on the foundations of creativity studies in a future-oriented manner, this book is meant to point us to the origin (or, rather, the origins) of the discipline and its old ideas and help us reflect on where these ideas took us, where they might have taken us, and where they could lead us still.

Before outlining in more detail the structure of the reader, an important detour is needed. Perhaps one of the first questions about this collection is why the period 1850–1950 was chosen. It makes pragmatic sense to offer a time frame, and a century is certainly long enough to fill up a (considerably large) book. Also, this period was fundamental for the emergence of contemporary science, not only creativity research. Why not choose though the 20th century as a whole, or the 19th? The answer to this lies in what happened in 1950 and takes us directly to the complex issue of founding figures.

Founding Father(s)

Deciding on the starting point of a discipline or field of research is never as straightforward as it may seem (de Saint-Laurent, 2015; Farr, 1996). While one would expect that facts and key events matter the most, it is actually their *interpretation* or the *meaning* given to them that decides who the founding father or fathers are. (Sadly, this common expression is gender-biased, reflecting a more general ideological bias when it comes to scientific activities.) In the case of creativity research, the conventional starting point is considered to be 1950, and the leading figure associated with it is that of Joy Paul Guilford (1897–1987). Guilford is widely remembered in psychology for his model of the intellect and the psychometric tools and factorial analyses used to study it (e.g., Guilford, 1967b). When it comes to creativity, this interest led him to propose divergent thinking as a key component (although not the only one; see Guilford, 1970) and to formulate measurements for it (e.g., the alternative uses test). However, what placed both author and year irrevocably on the map of creativity researchers is Guilford's American Psychological Association (APA) presidential address at Pennsylvania State College on September 5, 1950. The fact that, as APA president, Guilford chose to focus on a topic of relatively little interest—creativity—was surprising at the time (Plucker, 2001), yet it makes perfect sense in historical context. His call to focus on creativity and especially its education came at a time in the cold war when the US was witnessing Soviet advances into space and feared losing the arms race (Pope, 2005). In addition, building on the psychometric advances occasioned by World War II, Guilford's work made great contributions to the systematic, standardized study of complex cognitive processes. The time was right, then, for creativity to emerge as a scientific research topic and as a societal concern for educators, parents, and the wider public.

Numerous historical accounts of creativity studies over the past decades start their chronology with Guilford and his 1950 landmark address (see Barron & Harrington, 1981; Runco, 2004; Simonton, 2000; Sternberg & Dess, 2001). Guilford (1967a, 1970) himself, in his later writings on creativity, takes this year as a starting point in order to assess the progress made by the discipline. Importantly, all these authors do acknowledge, in passing, that there were other texts written and research conducted on this topic before the middle of the 20th century, but they catalog these sources of scholarship as *nonsystematic, unfocused,* or even *unscientific.* A more balanced point of view regarding this longer history is offered by Kaufman (2016, p. 9):

> It is not true to say that Guilford single-handedly brought creativity from the realm of esoterica to prominence. On the other hand, it can often feel this way. What Guilford did was to galvanize the field and make it acceptable to study creativity. Many of the ideas and studies that were published in the decade that followed his speech are still widely cited and respected. In contrast, there are only a handful of papers that are still commonly used from the decade before his seminal address.

The fact remains, however, that his "handful of papers" is commonly disregarded by a field keen on celebrating Guilford as the founding father of modern creativity research (see Plucker, 2001; Runco, 2001). Very few authors look before 1950 for the foundations of creativity studies (for a rare example, see Becker, 1995). The important question here is not whether this is right or wrong, whether or not, before Guilford, research was scientific, but what this choice means for the discipline and for how we understand creativity today. In other words, *what does it mean to start our short history with Guilford instead of any of his predecessors or, equally, those who followed him?* Whether intentional or not, this choice is meant to favor a certain view of creativity and of scientific research into creativity. At least at first sight, it validates the link between creativity and cognition and supports the use of psychometrics to investigate both. It also celebrates, for better or worse, a certain democratic and yet highly individualistic view of creating (the birth of what I have called the I-paradigm of creativity; see Glăveanu, 2010a, 2010b). In order to see why this is the case, let us take a closer look at what Guilford actually proposed.

From the beginning, Guilford (1950, p. 444) notes his own hesitation at choosing an area of psychology in which psychologists have generally "feared to tread," yet he announces that it has been one of his "long-standing ambitions" to "undertake an investigation of creativity." He further writes that the neglect of this subject by fellow psychologists has been appalling. He calculates that less than two-tenths of 1 percent of books and articles indexed by *Psychological Abstracts* over the past 25 years has dealt with creativity. Why this state of affairs? Guilford concludes there are multiple reasons for this neglect: the complexity of the topic itself and its associated methodological difficulties, and the presumed association between intelligence and creativity whereby "many believe that creative talent is to be accounted for in terms of high intelligence or IQ" (p. 454). Interestingly, later research largely confirmed Guilford's intuition that, although related, intelligence and creativity are neither one and the same nor do they determine one another (see Karwowski et al., 2016). He used this opportunity to outline his own view about what creativity is:

> Creative abilities determine whether the individual has the power to exhibit creative behavior to a noteworthy degree. Whether or not the individual who has the requisite abilities will actually produce results of a creative nature will depend upon his

motivational and temperamental traits. To the psychologist, the problem is as broad as the qualities that contribute significantly to creative productivity. In other words, the psychologist's problem is that of creative personality. (Guilford, 1950, p. 444)

There are several things worth noticing in this formulation: first, the fact that creativity is defined almost exclusively in *individual, psychological terms*. Creative behavior has to do with abilities and with motivational and temperamental traits, in sum, with what Guilford calls "creative personality." Also important, he differentiates here between creative potential ("requisite abilities") and creative achievement ("creative productivity"), a pervasive dichotomy within creativity research (for its negative consequences, see Glăveanu, 2016). This distinction allowed him, and generations of psychologists afterward, to focus almost exclusively on *creative potential*, or the set of abilities required by the person to be creative. On the bright side, this led to a general democratization of creativity—the idea that creative potential is universal and characterizes each and every person, to various degrees—which is very clearly expressed in Guilford's (1950, p. 446) writing:

> It is probably only a layman's idea that the creative person is peculiarly gifted with a certain quality that ordinary people do not have. This conception can be dismissed by psychologists, very likely by common consent. The general psychological conviction seems to be that all individuals possess to some degree all abilities, except for the occurrence of pathologies. Creative acts can therefore be expected, no matter how feeble or how infrequent, of almost all individuals. The important consideration here is the concept of continuity. Whatever the nature of creative talent may be, those persons who are recognized as creative merely have more of what all of us have. It is this principle of continuity that makes possible the investigation of creativity in people who are not necessarily distinguished.

Such a conception not only generates more open and empowering views of creativity but, as noted at the end of this quote, it also has important methodological consequences. Researchers are encouraged to study creativity empirically using a "normal" population and thus are no longer restricted to studying geniuses or eminent people alone. This conceptual move has important practical implications, and indeed Guilford's aim was twofold in giving his address. As he notes, "The more immediate and more explorable problem is a double one: (1) How can we discover creative promise in our children and our youth? and (2) How can we promote the development of creative personalities?" (p. 445). The educational component is the pragmatic end for a new generation of creativity researchers, a goal that is easier to conceive of and reach now that "we revise our standards, accepting examples of lower degrees of excellence" (p. 445). How do we go about doing this? Guilford proposed more than a democratic view of creativity, he also argued for a *factorial approach* to it. In line with this previous studies of the human intellect, he advanced a systematic way of studying creativity that breaks it down into "primary abilities" that need to be measured and confirmed (or disconfirmed) through factorial analysis before knowing what to educate and how (p. 454). The psychometric push behind his research agenda is obvious.

To be fair, though, Guilford was critical of what he called "the quest for easily objectifiable testing and scoring" (p. 445) and suggested practical criteria for creativity used to this day: fluency (number of ideas per unit of time), flexibility (the ease with which the participant changes set), novelty or originality (frequency of uncommon responses), and complexity or elaboration (intricacy of the conceptual structure the individual is capable of). He also offered concrete examples of creativity test items, such as the following:

> One kind of fluency test would consist of asking the examinee to name as many objects as he can in a given time, the objects having some specified property; for example, things round, things red, or things to eat. In another test, the ideas might be more complex, as in naming a list of appropriate titles for a picture or for a short story. Still more demanding and also more restricting would be the task of naming exceptions to a given statement. . . . The statement might be: A new invention makes it unnecessary for people to eat; what will the consequences be? This type of test has been previously proposed by several investigators. (Guilford, 1950, p. 452)

Nonetheless, despite his dynamic and largely domain-specific account of creativity, Guilford's vision remains firmly focused on the individual and on quantitative measurement. These are, in many ways, limitations intrinsic to many creativity theories since it is particularly difficult to develop a systemic approach to this phenomenon *and* propose measurement tools that would satisfy "scientific" criteria (or, at least, the criteria we associate with doing science in our historical context). And yet, it is important to ask why Guilford is a founding father of creativity studies. The fact that his call was, in the end, successful is undeniable. But it was not only his enthusiasm for studying creativity that makes him stand out; it is also the fact that the scientific community still resonates with his way of thinking and the measures he proposed back in 1950. Despite a variety of possible research methods used to study creativity (e.g., Gruber & Wallace, 1999), the ideal in creativity studies remains closely associated with the experimental and psychometric logic defended by Guilford. What else are we missing from this picture? For one, the *environment*. When it comes to both studying and educating creativity, the focus remains on the individual. The consequences of this partial view were carried over, in the decades that followed, to personality studies of creativity and creative cognition, up to today's interest in the neuroscience of creativity. Could things have been different?

History is said to be written with the pen of the victors, and undeniably Guilford's conception prevailed and shaped what we call creativity studies, at least in psychology. But a careful study of history reveals many (alternative) stories that came, in turn, to complement, oppose, and even transform the dominant narrative. These stories are those of other prominent figures in the field, who either preceded Guilford (e.g., Freud, Wallas), were his contemporaries (e.g., Rogers), or followed him (e.g., Stein, Torrance). Each one of these authors could be considered foundational in his own right, and Torrance is certainly celebrated by many for continuing the path set by Guilford (see Kaufman & Baer, 2006). The interesting questions, especially from the perspective of a creativity reader, are *What does it mean to choose a starting point for an entire field, what might be left out, and why?*

By and large, the reason for choosing Guilford as a founding figure has to do with the fact that he encouraged the *scientific* study of creativity; in contrast, what came before is considered less scientific, at least according to contemporary standards (see Runco & Albert, 2010). But, as we know, these standards themselves are a historical product and, as such, subject to revision. The key role of a reader, in my view, is to contribute to this kind of *historical contextualization and critical appraisal* of founding figures. I am not suggesting we replace Guilford or dismiss his obvious achievements. What I would like this volume to do is to open new horizons for what we consider foundational in creativity studies beyond (and before) the year 1950. By choosing to focus on the century preceding this date, I hope to bring to our attention an essential, and often forgotten, phase within the longer history of thinking about creativity and explore its reverberations today and its lessons for the future.

An Expanded History of Creativity

Ebbinghaus (1908) is credited with saying about psychology that it has a long past but a short history. The same applies to creativity research. Its history seems to start for many in 1950, as just noted. Its past goes back to the beginnings of history itself, and further, into prehistory. There were undeniable acts of creativity that led to the invention of the alphabet, the first cave paintings, and the birth of ancient cities (Festinger, 1983). But nowadays these first achievements are too old and too common to be thought of as creative. Moreover, they are the outcome of centuries of adaptive, gradual evolution rather than moments of rupture we now take as a mark of pure creativity. And yet our lives as not only biological but also social and cultural beings would be unimaginable without them. Immersed like fish in the waters of culture (Cole, 1996), we are oblivious to the fact that everything we use in the everyday—from objects to buildings, from technology to language—is a *product of culture* and, at least initially, a product of human creativity. The story of *Homo creativus* (Lubart et al., in press) is much older than 1950 and the modern cities and technologies we enjoy today.

What about the study of creativity? As a species, we might have been creative for millennia, arguably since the emergence of our capacity to use tools and signs (Vygotsky, 1978), but the systematic study of what it means to create began much later, though certainly not as late as the mid-20th century. Even if the word "creativity" itself was not in use, humans have wondered for a long time, at least since the beginning of written history, about their capacity to create. In antiquity this ability was initially attributed to the gods, to divine inspiration (Sternberg, 2003); then, particularly in the Middle Ages, monotheistic religions credited God. It was the Renaissance in Europe that marked the beginning of a new era of thinking about creativity (Glăveanu & Kaufman, 2019; Weiner, 2000): once considered external to humans, creative powers became internalized; from divine they became eminently human. This Copernican revolution paved the way to modern conceptions of creativity, including Guilford's speech. It was because we started thinking of ourselves as creative that we could start examining what makes us so.

Some of the first answers to what makes us creative pointed to genetics and special forms of heredity (Galton, 1874). From God the Creator the first move—at least in Western culture—was toward geniuses and eminent people. The rarity of this kind of creativity made us think of it as a very special gift bestowed on very few people and made us view these people as different, as standing apart from society and often having to fight against it (Montuori & Purser, 1995). The great value of Guilford's address—even if he was not the initiator of this movement—was to promote a more inclusive definition of creativity as widespread potential waiting to be enhanced through educational means. But the historical novelty of this kind of view should not be overestimated. Greek Antiquity gave us Prometheus, the titan who stole fire (an ancient metaphor of creativity, or the creative spark) from the gods and gave it to mankind. He was severely punished for it, according to legend, but he accomplished his mission: with the help of fire, humans could defend themselves, keep warm, build cities, and advance their civilization. It would be naive to believe that, historically, people didn't think of themselves as potentially creative, ingenious, imaginative, or spontaneous. Turning this into a dominant discourse about the self and about society is, however, a *modern invention* (Mason, 2003).

The immediate roots of this invention are to be found in the rapid industrialization and the development of science and technology in the late 19th and early 20th century (Agar, 2012; Bernal, 2006), which are themselves the product of wider historical forces set in motion by the discovery of the New World, the Industrial Revolution, and the birth of modern science. The short history of psychology is intimately related to these developments. The world wars, in particular, saw the first psychological tests being used on a wide scale, and in the aftermath of World War II, there was a pressing need to understand what made the Holocaust possible and how psychology could help to avoid such atrocities in the future. More than this, in the ensuing cold war, psychologists on both sides of the Iron Curtain were eager to harness the creative potential of scientists, inventors, and the population at large. This, as mentioned earlier, is the historical context that made Guilford's speech possible and his audience highly receptive to it (Pope, 2005). This review is not, though, meant as an exercise in determinism. The events set in motion after 1950 cannot be reduced to the politics of war. In the case of Guilford, they also build on the development of science and methodology, as well as his own, idiosyncratic life history, his interests and agenda. At the same time, there is no denying that each one of these contexts grows out of the fertile ground set up by the century before 1950.

It is precisely this period that the present collection of seminal texts focuses on. The period 1850–1950 was highly complex at social, political, and scientific levels. It witnessed a reversal of the world order, from European hegemony to a bipolar domination of the US and USSR. It saw Alfred Nobel invent dynamite, the Wright brothers produce the first fixed-wing airplane, and Alexander Graham Bell make the first telephone. It was also a century in which modern art was born, cinema was invented, and numerous philosophical currents, from pragmatism to existentialism and psychoanalysis, emerged. Most of all, it was a period in which psychology began to be recognized as a science and introspectionism gave way to behaviorism, preparing the ground for the cognitive revolution. The century between 1850 and 1950 is thus crucial for understanding modern science, contemporary psychology, and current trends in creativity studies.

L. P. Hartley famously wrote in his novel *The Go-Between*, "The past is a foreign country; they do things differently there." This is certainly the case here, and the authors and texts collected in the pages of this *Reader* will certainly testify to it. Reading original scholarship produced more than seventy years ago will most probably leave readers with a sense of *both familiarity and strangeness*. The writing style, the sources used, the statistics (if present), the general logic of the argument are at times strikingly different from the kinds we encounter in creativity journals today. For instance, many of the texts reproduced here develop theoretical, even philosophical arguments about creativity. Many of these authors had the ambition of constructing all-encompassing models that explain creativity rather than simply describe it. They aimed to take us beyond limited empirical examples and toward the basic principles behind the creative process. Such theoretical aspirations are seldom found today (see Glăveanu, 2014). Critics might say that these constructions lack the methodological rigor of "real" science, that they express personal intuitions, at best, and were often disconfirmed by the "proper" research conducted after 1950. In some cases this is correct, but the value of this older body of scholarship is equally undeniable. I contend that there is nothing in today's literature on creativity that doesn't have its roots in a scientific or philosophical movement from the period 1850–1950, if not from before. Ideas about associationism and combinatorial logic, evolutionary principles, phenomenological accounts of creating: they all precede the short history of creativity studies as we know it. This longer past is a different country on many accounts, but it is certainly one *worth visiting*. Without such an excursion we would not be able to place current theories and research in their proper context or understand where they come from and, in many ways, what they take us back to.

The *Creativity Reader*

These are the considerations at the origin of this editorial project. The *Creativity Reader* is envisioned as a necessary companion for all those creativity, innovation, and imagination researchers who want to explore the roots of the ideas they develop today. Having leading experts in the field select, introduce, and comment on seminal texts offers the perfect example of a deeply reflective and scholarly exercise. The seminal accounts included here might seem forgotten, but they are not; they *live on* through the thinking and the work of eminent researchers, their colleagues, and their students. This is a crucial, almost a subversive type of exercise in a day and age when the focus is mainly on the latest empirical research and little else, when literature reviews stop at what has been written five years ago, and old authors are, at best, relegated to the footnotes. To highlight their work means to revitalize it, to give credit where credit is due, and to form a new generation of creativity and innovation researchers who are mindful of the past and unafraid to explore and use it. It is also an exercise that can help us detect more easily when old wine is sold to us in new bottles and when the wheel is periodically rediscovered. Last but not least, this reader testifies to the incredible richness of our discipline and celebrates it. By taking a closer look at the past we are not only able to better understand the present but also to peer into the future. It is within the nature of things that any *retrospective* account is equally *prospective* (see de Saint-Laurent, 2018). We need to know the history of our domain in order to repeat what is valuable from it, dismiss what is not, and create what is needed for its advancement.

The contributors to this reader were invited to choose one (or more) authors and texts from the period 1850–1950 that they considered important to the discipline. This importance was not to be measured in terms of how many times a work or author was cited or how many theories they inspired. In fact contributors were encouraged to focus on sources that might have been neglected by fellow creativity researchers. More than this, the texts selected should be significant for the future of the field as well and contribute to or open up new areas of investigation. The contributors would then introduce their choice of author and text(s), reproduce the original either partially or fully, and offer a commentary pointing to the reception of the ideas, their historical trajectory, and their potential for the future. The call resulted in 33 chapters covering an impressive number of authors and themes. Many key thinkers in the history of creativity studies are certainly missing (among them, Henri Bergson, Lewis Terman, Maurice Merleau-Ponty, Alfred North Whitehead, Catherine Patrick, Otto Rank). Others are included twice, each time with a different contribution (Francis Galton, John Dewey, Alfred Binet). Taken together, the chapters included here showcase a vibrant, transdisciplinary field of investigation that existed before 1950 and continues to inform work done up to this day. I did not follow a chronological but rather a thematic order, grouping chapters into sections. Each one of these sections deals with an area that is prominent nowadays in creativity studies: processes of creativity, assessment, creative thinking and noncognitive factors, development and education, genius, imagination, art, groups and interactions, society and culture, and critical accounts of creativity and its role.

This reader is not meant to be a comprehensive history of creativity research. It is deliberately selective in its account of the period 1850–1950. It should be used to *critically reflect* on this period, its contributors, and the legacy they left us. For instance, it is interesting—and troubling—to notice that the writings of only three women and one nonwhite author are featured within these pages. A deeper reflection about why this is the case and what impact it has on the field—and on science in general—is certainly needed. Also, it is interesting to notice that typically seminal texts come from single authors rather than represent collaborative work, with a few exceptions. And yet, as we know, none of these scholars worked alone, and, in some cases, teachers' or colleagues' work is presented in other parts of the reader (see, e.g., the chapters on Wertheimer and Köhler or those on Peirce, James, and Dewey). This invisible network of collaboration is important to highlight precisely because it contributes to the philosophy underpinning the *Creativity Reader*. One of its most meaningful lessons is that great ideas are never produced in solitude and are never disconnected from each other. We are all standing on the shoulders of giants, and giants themselves have other shoulders to stand on (to be discovered, perhaps, in another volume focused on the period before 1850). Frank Barron (1995) offered an inspiring title to one of his creativity books, *No Rootless Flower*; indeed creative acts do not come out of nowhere but effectively grow out of the fertile soil of communication and interaction between people. Equally, creativity research is not a floating island but a discipline deeply steeped in history, firmly rooted within society, and essential for the transmission and the future of both.

Acknowledgments

I would like to express my deep gratitude toward each one of the contributors for their patience and commitment to this project, which was not the easiest to accomplish. It goes without saying that the present volume would have been impossible without them. I am also extremely grateful to Courtney McCarroll and Abby Gross from Oxford University Press for their guidance and their invaluable support. Throughout the entire process I relied, as always, on the advice, encouragement, and affection of Constance de Saint-Laurent. Thank you for this.

References

Agar, J. (2012). *Science in the twentieth century and beyond*. Cambridge, UK: Polity Press.
Barron, F. (1995). *No rootless flower: An ecology of creativity*. Cresskill, NJ: Hampton Press.
Barron, F., & Harrington, D. (1981). Creativity, intelligence, and personality. *Annual Review of Psychology, 32*, 439–476.
Becker, M. (1995). Nineteenth-century foundations of creativity research. *Creativity Research Journal, 8*(3), 219–229.
Bernal, J. D. (2006). Science and industry in the nineteenth century. London: Routledge.
Cole, M. (1996). Cultural psychology: A once and future discipline. Cambridge, MA: Belknap Press.
de Saint-Laurent, C. (2015). Dialogue and debate in psychology: Commentary on the foundational myth of psychology as a science. In J. Cresswell, A. Haye, A. Larrain, M. Morgan, & G. Sullivan (Eds.), *Dialogue and debate in the making of theoretical psychology* (pp. 231–239). Concord, Ontario: Captus.

de Saint-Laurent, C. (2018). Thinking through time: From collective memories to collective futures. In C. de Saint-Laurent, S. Obradovic, & K. Carriere (Eds.), *Imagining collective futures: Perspectives from social, cultural and political psychology* (pp. 59–81). London: Palgrave.

Ebbinghaus, H. (1908). *Psychology: An elementary textbook.* New York, NY: Arno Press.

Farr, R. (1996). *The roots of modern social psychology, 1872–1954.* Cambridge, MA: Blackwell.

Festinger, L. (1983). *The human legacy.* New York, NY: Columbia University Press.

Galton, F. (1874). *English men of science: Their nature and nurture.* London: Macmillan.

Glăveanu, V. P. (2010a). Paradigms in the study of creativity: Introducing the perspective of cultural psychology. *New Ideas in Psychology, 28*(1), 79–93.

Glăveanu, V. P. (2010b). Principles for a cultural psychology of creativity. *Culture & Psychology, 16*(2), 147–163.

Glăveanu, V. P. (2014). The psychology of creativity: A critical reading. *Creativity: Theories—Research—Applications, 1*(1), 10–32.

Glăveanu, V. P. (2016). The psychology of creating: A cultural-developmental approach to key dichotomies within creativity studies. In V. P. Glăveanu (Ed.), *The Palgrave handbook of creativity and culture research* (pp. 205–224). London: Palgrave.

Glăveanu, V. P. (2017). Creativity in perspective: A socio-cultural and critical account. *Journal of Constructivist Psychology, 31*(2), 118–129.

Glăveanu, V. P., & Kaufman, J. C. (2019). Creativity: A historical perspective. In R. J. Sternberg & J. C. Kaufman (Eds.), *The Cambridge handbook of creativity.* Cambridge: Cambridge University Press.

Gruber, H., & Wallace, D. (1999). The case study method and evolving systems approach for understanding unique creative people at work. In R. Sternberg (Ed.), *Handbook of creativity* (pp. 93–115). Cambridge, UK: Cambridge University Press.

Guilford, J. P. (1950). Creativity. *American Psychologist, 5,* 444–454.

Guilford, J. P. (1967a). Creativity: Yesterday, today, and tomorrow. *Journal of Creative Behavior, 1,* 3–14.

Guilford, J. P. (1967b). *The nature of human intelligence.* New York, NY: McGraw-Hill.

Guilford, J. P. (1970). Creativity: Retrospect and prospect. *Journal of Creative Behavior, 4*(3), 149–168.

Hennessey, B. A., & Amabile, T. (2010). Creativity. *Annual Review of Psychology, 61,* 569–598.

Karwowski, M., Dul, J., Gralewski, J., Jauk, E., Jankowska, D. M., Gajda, A., Chruszczewski, M. H., & Benedek, M. (2016). Is creativity without intelligence possible? A necessary condition analysis. *Intelligence, 57,* 105–117.

Kaufman, J. C. (2016). *Creativity 101* (2nd ed.). New York, NY: Springer.

Kaufman, J. C., & Baer, J. (2006). An introduction to the special issue: A tribute to E. Paul Torrance. *Creativity Research Journal, 18*(1), 1–2.

Lubart, T., Botella, M., Caroff, X., Mouchiroud, C., Nelson, J., & Zenasni, F. (Eds.). (in press). *Homo creativus: The 7 C's of human creativity.* Singapore: Springer.

Mason, J. H. (2003). *The value of creativity: The origins and emergence of a modern belief.* Aldershot, Hampshire, UK: Ashgate.

Montuori, A., & Purser, R. (1995). Deconstructing the lone genius myth: Toward a contextual view of creativity. *Journal of Humanistic Psychology, 35*(3), 69–112.

Plucker, J. A. (2001). Introduction to the special issue: Commemorating Guilford's 1950 presidential address. *Creativity Research Journal, 13*(3–4), 247.

Pope, R. (2005). *Creativity: Theory, history, practice.* London: Routledge.

Rothenberg, A., & Hausman, C. (1976). *The creativity question.* Durham, NC: Duke University Press.

Runco, M. A. (2001). Introduction to the special issue: Commemorating Guilford's 1950 presidential address. *Creativity Research Journal, 13*(3–4), 249.

Runco, M. A. (2004). Creativity. *Annual Review of Psychology, 55,* 657–687.

Runco, M. A., & Albert, R. S. (2010). Creativity research: A historical view. In J. C. Kaufman & R. J. Sternberg (Eds.), *The Cambridge handbook of creativity* (pp. 3–19). Cambridge, UK: Cambridge University Press.

Simonton, D. K. (2000). Creativity: Cognitive, personal, developmental, and social aspects. *American Psychologist, 55*(1), 151–158.

Simonton, D. K. (2001). *The psychology of creativity: A historical perspective.* Paper presented at Green College Lecture Series on the Nature of Creativity: Biology, History, and Socio-Cultural Dimensions, University of British Columbia. Retrieved from https://simonton.faculty.ucdavis.edu/wp-content/uploads/sites/243/2015/08/HistoryCreativity.pdf.

Sternberg, R. (2003). *Wisdom, intelligence, and creativity synthesized.* New York, NY: Cambridge University Press.

Sternberg, R. J., & Dess, N. K. (2001). Creativity for the new millennium. *American Psychologist, 56*(4), 332.

Vygotsky, L. S. (1978). *Mind in society: The development of higher psychological processes* (M. Cole, V. John-Steiner, S. Scribner, & E. Souberman, Eds.). Cambridge, MA: Harvard University Press.

Weiner, R. P. (2000). *Creativity and beyond: Cultures, values, and change.* New York, NY: State University of New York Press.

PART ONE

The Creative Process

2

The Art of (Creative) Thought
Graham Wallas on the Creative Process

TERESA M. AMABILE

Summary

The Art of Thought, published in 1926 by the classicist and political scientist Graham Wallas, includes a detailed description of stages in the creative process. Despite being based almost exclusively on self-introspection and the introspective accounts of well-known creative individuals, the simple, plausible process that Wallas described has shaped a great deal of subsequent empirical research and theorizing in the psychology of creativity. The four stages that Wallas articulated are Preparation (consciously amassing knowledge and applying that knowledge to some problem); Incubation (a period of unconscious work on any problem that remains unsolved after initial efforts); Illumination (a sudden flash of insight); and Verification (the conscious articulation and checking of the insight against existing knowledge). Although many subsequent theorists have elaborated on Wallas's model, others have challenged the very existence of unconscious incubation and sudden illumination. Recent neuropsychological evidence, however, suggests the operation of both incubation and illumination. Nonetheless, considerable future research will be required to enable a comprehensive understanding of how the creative process unfolds and what might influence it.

Introduction

The year 1926 was a particularly fruitful one for the psychology of creativity. Whether due to zeitgeist or coincidence or both, not only did Catharine Cox publish her massive study of 301 geniuses (see Chapter 19, this volume) in that year, but, also, Graham Wallas included in his book *The Art of Thought* a detailed discussion of the creative process that has influenced generations of creativity scholars.

Never formally trained in psychology, Wallas was clearly fascinated with it. A review of his basic biographical facts yields few hints as to why he might have been so psychologically minded.[1] Born in England in 1858, Wallas was educated and earned an advanced degree in classics at Oxford. He taught at Highgate School in London until 1885, when he resigned in protest of enforced participation in religious ceremonies. The following year, he joined—and became a leader in—the Fabian Society, a British socialist organization whose founding purpose was to advance democratic socialism not through revolution but through an incremental, systematic reform of government. In his role in the Fabian Society, in 1895 he became a cofounder of the London School of Economics (LSE) for "the betterment of society." In 1914 he became the first professor of political science at LSE, a position from which he retired in 1923. Besides *The Art of Thought*, other books that Wallas published, most notably *Human Nature in Politics* (1908) and *The Great Society* (1914), revealed that this political scientist had a strong interest in human development, education, and psychology. Wallas's wife, the socialist Ada Radford, and daughter, May Wallas, both attended Newnham College, which has retained the copyright to *The Art of Thought* since Wallas's death in England in 1932.

Although Wallas was deeply intellectual, he combined that bent with a decidedly practical orientation. Above all else, he seems to have been concerned, in *The Art of Thought*, with practical tactics for individuals to improve their own thought processes. The "Art" in his book title refers to the disciplined practice that he believed an "educated man" could use to vastly increase the likelihood that he would discover the solution to a complex problem, invent something great, or produce a notable work of art. For that reason, Wallas concerned himself with only one possible influence on the thought process: voluntary control of the process by such means as putting oneself in the proper frame of mind, setting aside conscious work on a problem at the right point in the process, and paying close attention to one's own mental activity.

In the selection that follows, I have retained most of the key chapter in Wallas's (1926) book, "Stages of Control" (chapter 4), but I have skipped a few extended explanations and examples. Also, I have excised material that betrays prejudices of Wallas's social class and historical place and time. For example, he speaks disparagingly of "uneducated man" (p. 83) and relays disdainful anecdotes about men, such as an "omnibus conductor" (p. 85) he encountered in 1917, who—in Wallas's view—clearly had no idea how to use their brains. In addition, throughout the chapter, Wallas's language and many examples of great thinkers reveal that, to him, "those whose work in life is thought" (p. 101) are men, and only men. To my mind, these anachronistic tics of Wallas's own thought processes in no way diminish the value of his ideas.

Reading: *The Art of Thought*

Source: Wallas, G. (1926). *The art of thought*. New York: Harcourt, Brace. Excerpts from Chapter 4, "Stages of Control" (pp. 79–107). Reprinted with the permission of Newnham College, UK.

---

1. See Fabien Society, n.d.; Graham Wallas, n.d.; Sadler-Smith, 2015.

So far, in this book, I have discussed two problems which are preliminary to any formulation of an art of thought: first, what conception of the human organism and human consciousness best indicates the general facts with which such an art must deal; and, secondly, what is the "natural" thought-process which such an art must attempt to modify. In this chapter, I shall ask at what stages in that thought-process the thinker should bring the conscious and voluntary effort of his art to bear. Here we at once meet the difficulty that unless we can recognize a psychological event, and distinguish it from other events, we cannot bring conscious effort to bear directly upon it; and that our mental life is a stream of intermingled psychological events, all of which affect each other, any of which, at any given moment, may be beginning or continuing or ending, and which, therefore, are extremely hard to distinguish from each other.

We can, to some degree, avoid this difficulty if we take a single achievement of thought—the making of a new generalization or invention, or the poetical expression of a new idea—and ask how it was brought about. We can then roughly dissect out a continuous process, with a beginning and a middle and an end of its own. Helmholtz, for instance, the great German physicist, speaking in 1891 at a banquet on his seventieth birthday, described the way in which his most important new thoughts had come to him. He said that after previous investigation of the problem "in all directions . . . happy ideas come unexpectedly without effort, like an inspiration. So far as I am concerned, they have never come to me when my mind was fatigued, or when I was at my working table. . . . They came particularly readily during the slow ascent of wooded hills on a sunny day."[1] Helmholtz here gives us three stages in the formation of a new thought. The first in time I shall call Preparation, the stage during which the problem was "investigated . . . in all directions"; the second is the stage during which he was not consciously thinking about the problem, which I shall call Incubation; the third, consisting of the appearance of the "happy idea" together with the psychological events which immediately preceded and accompanied that appearance, I shall call Illumination.

And I shall add a fourth stage, of Verification, which Helmholtz does not here mention. Henri Poincaré, for instance, in the book *Science and Method*, which I have already quoted (p. 75), describes in vivid detail the successive stages of two of his great mathematical discoveries. Both of them came to him after a period of Incubation (due in one case to his military service as a reservist, and in the other case to a journey), during which no conscious mathematical thinking was done, but, as Poincaré believed, much unconscious mental exploration took place. In both cases Incubation was preceded by a Preparation stage of hard, conscious, systematic, and fruitless analysis of the problem. In both cases the final idea came to him "with the same characteristics of conciseness, suddenness, and immediate certainty" (p. 54). Each was followed by a period of Verification, in which both the validity of the idea was tested, and the idea itself was reduced to exact form. "It never happens," says Poincaré, in his description of the Verification stage, "that unconscious work supplies *ready-made* the result of a lengthy calculation in which we have only to apply fixed rules. . . . All that we can hope from these inspirations, which are the fruit of unconscious work, is to obtain points of departure for such calculations. As for the calculations themselves, they must be made in the second period of conscious work which follows the inspiration, and in which the results of the inspiration are verified and the consequences deduced. The rules of these calculations are strict and complicated; they demand discipline, attention, will, and consequently, consciousness" (pp. 62, 63). In the daily stream of thought these four different stages constantly overlap each other as we explore different problems. An economist reading a Blue Book, a physiologist watching an experiment, or a business man going through his morning's letters, may at the same time be "incubating" on a problem which he proposed to himself a few days ago, be accumulating knowledge in "preparation" for a second problem, and be "verifying" his conclusions on a third problem. Even in exploring the same problem, the mind may be unconsciously incubating on one aspect of it, while it is consciously employed in preparing for or verifying another aspect. And it must always be remembered that much very important thinking, done for instance by a poet exploring his own memories, or by a man trying to see clearly his emotional relation to his country or his party, resembles musical composition in that the stages leading to success are not very easily fitted into a "problem and solution" scheme. Yet, even when success in thought means the creation of something felt to be beautiful and true rather than the solution of a prescribed problem, the four stages of Preparation, Incubation, Illumination, and the Verification of the final result can generally be distinguished from each other.

If we accept this analysis, we are in a position to ask to what degree, and by what means, we can bring conscious effort, and the habits which arise from conscious effort, to bear upon each of the four stages. I shall not, in this chapter, deal at any length with the stage of Preparation. It includes the whole process of intellectual education. Men have known for thousands of years that conscious effort and its resulting habits can be used to improve the thought-processes of young persons, and have formulated for that purpose an elaborate art of education. The "educated" man can, in consequence, "put his mind on" to a chosen subject, and "turn his mind off"[2] in a way which is impossible to an uneducated man. The educated man has also acquired, by the effort of observation and memorizing, a body of remembered facts and words which gives him a wider range in the final moment of association, as well as a number of those habitual tracks of association which constitute "thought-systems" like "French policy" or "scholastic philosophy" or "biological evolution," and which present themselves as units in the process of thought.

The educated man has, again, learnt, and can, in the Preparation stage, voluntarily or habitually follow out, rules as to the order in which he shall direct his attention to the successive elements in a problem. . . .

Included in these rules for the preliminary "regulation" of our thought, are the whole traditional art of logic, the mathematical forms which are the logic of the modern experimental sciences, and the methods of systematic and continuous examination of present or recorded phenomena which are the basis of astronomy, sociology and other "observational" sciences. Closely connected with this voluntary use of logical methods is the voluntary choice of a "problem-attitude" (Aufgabe). Our mind is not likely to give us a clear answer to any particular problem unless we set it a clear question, and we are more likely to notice the significance of any new piece of evidence, or new association of ideas, if we have formed a definite conception of a case to be proved or disproved. A very successful thinker in natural science told me that he owed much of his success to his practice of following up, when he felt his mind confused, the implications of two propositions, both of which he had hitherto accepted as true, until he had discovered that one of them *must* be untrue. . . .

And though I have assumed, for the sake of clearness, that the thinker is preparing him-self for the solution of a single problem, he will often (particularly if he is working on the very complex material of the social sciences) have several kindred problems in his mind, on all of which the voluntary work of preparation has been, or is being done, and for any of which at the Illumination stage, a solution may present itself.

The fourth stage, of Verification, closely resembles the first stage, of Preparation. It is normally, as Poincaré points out, fully conscious, and men have worked out much the same series of mathematical and logical rules for controlling Verification by conscious effort as those which are used in the control of Preparation.

There remain the second and third stages, Incubation and Illumination. The Incubation stage covers two different things, of which the first is the negative fact that during Incubation we do not voluntarily or consciously think on a particular problem, and the second is the pos-itive fact that a series of unconscious and involuntary (or foreconscious and forevoluntary) mental events may take place during that period. It is the first fact about Incubation which I shall now discuss, leaving the second fact—of subconscious thought during Incubation, and the relation of such thought to Illumination—to be more fully discussed in connection with the Illumination stage. Voluntary abstention from conscious thought on any particular problem may, itself, take two forms: the period of abstention may be spent either in conscious mental work on other problems, or in a relaxation from all conscious mental work. The first kind of Incubation economizes time, and is therefore often the better. We can often get more result in the same time by beginning several problems in succession, and voluntarily leaving them unfinished while we turn to others, than by finishing our work on each problem at one sitting. A well-known academic psychologist, for instance, who was also a preacher, told me that he found by experience that his Sunday sermon was much better if he posed the problem on Monday, than if he did so later in the week, although he might give the same number of hours of conscious work to it in each case. It seems to be a tradition among practising barristers to put off any consideration of each brief to the latest possible moment before they have to deal with it, and to forget the whole matter as rapidly as possible after dealing with it. This fact may help to explain a certain want of depth which has often been noticed in the typ-ical lawyer-statesman, and which may be due to his conscious thought not being sufficiently extended and enriched by subconscious thought.

But, in the case of the more difficult forms of creative thought, the making, for instance, of a scientific discovery, or the writing of a poem or play or the formulation of an important political decision, it is desirable not only that there should be an interval free from conscious thought on the particular problem concerned, but also that that interval should be so spent that nothing should interfere with the free working of the unconscious or partially conscious processes of the mind. In those cases, the stage of Incubation should include a large amount of actual mental relaxation. It would, indeed, be interesting to examine from that point of view, the biographies of a couple of hundred original thinkers and writers. A. R. Wallace, for instance, hit upon the theory of evolution by natural selection in his berth during an attack of malarial fever at sea; and Darwin was compelled by ill-health to spend the greater part of his waking hours in physical and mental relaxation. Sometimes a thinker has been able to get a sufficiency of relaxation owing to a disposition to idleness, against which he has vainly struggled. More often, perhaps, what he has thought to be idleness is really that urgent craving for intense and uninterrupted day-dreaming which Anthony Trollope describes in his account of his boyhood.

One effect of such a comparative biographical study might be the formulation of a few rules as to the relation between original intellectual work and the virtue of industry. There are thousands of idle "geniuses" who require to learn that, without a degree of industry in Preparation and Verification, of which many of them have no conception, no great intellectual work can be done, and that the habit of procrastination may be even more disastrous to a professional thinker than it is to a man of business. And yet a thinker of good health and naturally fertile mind may have to be told that mere industry is for him, as it was for Trollope in his later years, the worst temptation of the devil. . . .

Mental relaxation during the Incubation stage may of course include, and sometimes requires, a certain amount of physical exercise. I have already quoted Helmholtz's reference to "the ascent of wooded hills on a sunny day." A. Carrel, the great New York physiologist, is said to receive all his really important thoughts while quietly walking during the summer vacation in his native Brittany. Jastrow says that "thinkers have at all times resorted to the restful inspiration of a walk in the woods or a stroll over hill and dale."[3] When I once discussed this fact with an athletic Cambridge friend, he expressed his gratitude for any evidence which would prove that it was the duty of all intellectual workers to spend their vacations in Alpine climbing. Alpine climbing has undoubtedly much to give both to health and to imagination, but it would be an interesting quantitative problem whether Goethe, while riding a mule over the Gemmi Pass, and Wordsworth, while walking over the Simplon, were in a more or in a less fruitful condition of Incubation than are a modern Alpine Club party ascending, with hands and feet and rope and ice-axe, the Finster-Aar-horn. In this, however, as in many other respects, it may be that the human organism gains more from the alternation of various forms of activity than from a consistent devotion to one form. . . .

But perhaps the most dangerous substitute for bodily and mental relaxation during the stage of Incubation is neither violent exercise nor routine administration, but the habit of industrious passive reading. . . . Carlyle once told Anthony Trollope that a man, when travelling, "should not read, but sit still and label his thoughts."[4] . . .

So far in this chapter I have inquired how far we can voluntarily improve our methods of thought at those stages—Preparation, Incubation (in its negative sense of abstention from voluntary thought on a particular problem), and Verification—over which our conscious will has comparatively full control. I shall now discuss the much more difficult question of the degree to which our will can influence the less controllable stage which I have called Illumination. Helmholtz and Poincaré, in the passages which I quoted above, both speak of the appearance of a new idea as instantaneous and unexpected. If we so define the Illumination stage as to restrict it to this instantaneous "flash," it is obvious that we cannot influence it by a direct effort of will; because we can only bring our will to bear upon psychological events which last for an appreciable time. On the other hand, the final "flash," or "click," as I pointed out in Chapter III, is the culmination of a successful train of association, which may have lasted for an appreciable time, and which has probably been preceded by a series of tentative and unsuccessful trains. The series of unsuccessful trains of association may last for periods varying from a few seconds to several hours. H. Poincaré, who describes the tentative and unsuccessful trains as being, in his case, almost entirely unconscious, believed that they

THE ART OF (CREATIVE) THOUGHT

occupied a considerable proportion of the whole Incubation stage. "We might," he wrote, "say that the conscious work, [i.e., what I have called the Preparation stage], proved more fruitful because it was interrupted [by the Incubation stage], and that the rest restored freshness to the mind. But it is more probable that the rest was occupied with unconscious work, and that the result of this work was afterwards revealed."[5]

Different thinkers, and the same thinkers at different times, must, of course, vary greatly as to the time occupied by their unsuccessful trains of association; and the same variation must exist in the duration of the final and successful train of association. Sometimes the successful train seems to consist of a single leap of association, or of successive leaps which are so rapid as to be almost instantaneous. Hobbes's "Roman penny" train of association occurred between two remarks in an ordinary conversation, and Hobbes, as I have said, ends his description of it with the words, "and all this in a moment of time, for thought is quick" (*Leviathan,* Chap. III). Hobbes himself was probably an exceptionally rapid thinker, and Aubrey may have been quoting Hobbes's own phrase when he says that Hobbes used to take out his note-book "as soon as a thought darted."[6]

But if our will is to control a psychological process, it is necessary that that process should not only last for an appreciable time, but should also be, during that time, sufficiently conscious for the thinker to be at least aware that something is happening to him. On this point, the evidence seems to show that both the unsuccessful trains of association, which might have led to the "flash" of success, and the final and successful train are normally either unconscious, or take place (with "risings" and "fallings" of consciousness as success seems to approach or retire), in that periphery or "fringe" of consciousness which surrounds our "focal" consciousness as the sun's "corona" surrounds the disk of full luminosity.[7] This "fringe-consciousness" may last up to the "flash" instant, may accompany it, and in some cases may continue beyond it. But, just as it is very difficult to see the sun's corona unless the disk is hidden by a total eclipse, so it is very difficult to observe our "fringe-consciousness" at the instant of full Illumination, or to remember the preceding "fringe" after full Illumination has taken place. As William James says, "When the conclusion is there, we have always forgotten most of the steps preceding its attainment" (*Principles,* Volume I, p. 260).

It is obvious that both Helmholtz and Poincaré had either not noticed, or had forgotten any "fringe-conscious" psychological events which may have preceded and have been connected with the "sudden" and "unexpected" appearance of their new ideas. But other thinkers have observed and afterwards remembered their "fringe-conscious" experiences both before and even at the moment of full Illumination. William James himself, in that beautiful and touching, though sometimes confused introspective account of his own thinking which forms Chapter IX of his *Principles,* says: "Every definite image in the mind is steeped and dyed in the free water that flows round it. With it goes the sense of its relations, near and remote, the dying echo of whence it came to us, the dawning sense of whither it is to lead. The significance, the value, of the image is all in this halo or penumbra that surrounds and escorts it" (*Principles,* Vol. I, p. 255).

I find it convenient to use the term "Intimation" for that moment in the Illumination stage when our fringe-consciousness of an association train is in the state of rising consciousness which indicates that the fully conscious flash of success is coming. A high English civil servant described his experience of Intimation to me by saying that when he is working at a difficult problem, "I often know that the solution is coming, though I don't know what the solution will be," and a very able university student gave me a description of the same fact in his case almost in the same words. Many thinkers, indeed, would recognize the experience which Varendonck describes when he says that on one occasion: "When I became aware that my mind was simmering over something, I had a dim feeling which is very difficult to describe; it was like a vague impression of mental activity. But when the association had risen to the surface, it expanded into an impression of joy."[8] His phrase "expanded into an impression of joy," clearly describes the rising of consciousness as the "flash" approaches.

Most introspective observers speak, as I have done, of Intimation as a "feeling," and the ambiguity of that word creates its usual crop of difficulties. It is often hard to discover in descriptions of Intimation whether the observer is describing a bare awareness of mental activity with no emotional colouring, or an awareness of mental activity coloured by an emotion which may either have originally helped to stimulate the train of thought, or may have been stimulated by the train of thought during its course. Mr. F. M. McMurry seems to refer to little more than awareness when he says, in his useful text-book, *How to Study* (p. 278), "Many of the best thoughts, probably most of them, do not come, like a flash, fully into being but find their beginnings in dim feelings, faint intuitions that need to be encouraged and coaxed before they can be surely felt and defined." Dewey, on the other hand, is obviously describing awareness coloured by emotion when he says that a problem may present itself "as a more or less vague feeling of the unexpected, of something queer, strange, funny, or disconcerting."[9] Wundt was more ambiguous when he said (in perhaps the earliest description of Intimation) that feeling is the pioneer of knowledge, and that a novel thought may come to consciousness first of all in the form of a feeling.[10] My own students have described the Intimation preceding a new thought as being sometimes coloured by a slight feeling of discomfort arising from a sense of separation from one's accustomed self. A student, for instance, told me that his first recognition that he was reaching a new political outlook came from a feeling, when, in answer to a question, he was stating his habitual political opinions, that he "was listening to himself." I can just remember that a good many years ago, in a period preceding an important change of my own political position, I had a vague, almost physical, recurrent feeling as if my clothes did not quite fit me. If this feeling of Intimation lasts for an appreciable time, and is either sufficiently conscious or can by an effort of attention be made sufficiently conscious, it is obvious that our will can be brought directly to bear on it. We can at least attempt to inhibit, or prolong, or divert, the brain-activity which Intimation shows to be going on. And, if Intimation accompanies a rising train of association which the brain accepts, so to speak, as plausible, but would not, without the effort of attention, automatically push to the "flash" of conscious success, we can attempt to hold on to such a train on the chance that it may succeed.

It is a more difficult and more important question whether such an exercise of will is likely to improve our thinking. Many people would argue that any attempt to control the thought-process at this point will always do more harm than good. A schoolboy sitting down to do an algebra sum, a civil servant composing a minute, Shakespeare re-writing a speech in an old play, will, they would say, gain no more by interfering with the ideas whose coming is vaguely indicated to them, before they come, than would a child by digging up a sprouting bean, or a hungry man in front of a good meal, by bringing his will to bear on the intimations of activity in his stomach or his salivary glands. A born runner, they would say, achieves a much more successful co-ordination of those physiological and psychological factors in his organism which are concerned in running by concentrating his will on his purpose of catching the man in front of him, than by troubling about the factors themselves. And a born orator will use better gestures if, as he speaks, he is conscious of his audience than if he is conscious of his hands. This objection might be fatal to the whole conception of an art of thought if it did not neglect two facts, first that we are not all "born" runners or orators or thinkers, and that a good deal of the necessary work of the world has to be done by men who in such respects have to achieve skill instead of receiving it at birth; and, secondly, that the process of learning an art should, even in the case of those who have the finest natural endowment for it, be more conscious than its practice. Mr. Harry Vardon, when he is acquiring a new grip, is wise to make himself more conscious of the relation between his will and his wrists than when he is addressing himself to his approach-shot at the decisive hole of a championship. The violinist with the most magnificent natural temperament has to think of his fingers when he is acquiring a new way of bowing; though on the concert-platform that acquirement may sink beneath the level of full consciousness. And, since the use of our upper brain for the discovery of new truth depends on more recent and less perfect evolutionary factors than does the use of our wrists for hitting small objects with a stick, or for causing catgut to vibrate in emotional patterns, conscious art may prove [to] be even more important, as compared to spontaneous gift, in thought than in golf or violin-playing. Here, again, individual thinkers, and the same thinker at different times and when engaged on different tasks, must differ greatly. But my general conclusion is that there are few or none among those whose work in life is thought who will not gain by directing their attention from time to time to the feeling of Intimation, and by bringing their will to bear upon the cerebral processes which it indicates. . . .

The interference of our will should, finally, vary—with the variations of the subject-matter of our thought—not only in respect of the point in time at which it should take place, but also in respect to the element in a complex thought-process with which we should interfere. A novelist who had just finished a long novel, and who must constantly have employed his conscious will while writing it, to make sure of a good idea or phrase, or to improve a sentence, or rearrange an incident, told me that he had spoilt his book by interfering with the automatic development of his main story and of its chief characters, in order to follow out a pre-conceived plot. Dramatists and poets constantly speak of the need of allowing their characters to "speak for themselves"; and a creative artist often reaches maturity only when he has learnt so to use his conscious craftsmanship in the expression of his thought as not to silence the promptings of that imperfectly co-ordinated whole which is called his personality. It is indeed at the stage of Illumination with its fringe of Intimation that the thinker should most constantly realize that the rules of his art will be of little effect unless they are applied with artistic delicacy of apprehension.

---

1. See Rignano, *Psychology of Reasoning* (1923), pp. 267–8. See also Plato, *Symposium* (210): "He who has been instructed thus far in the things of love, and has learned to see beautiful things in due order and succession, when he comes to the end, will suddenly perceive a beauty wonderful in its nature"; and Remy de

Goncourt: "My conceptions rise into the field of consciousness like a flash of lightning or the flight of a bird" (quoted by H. A. Bruce, *Psychology and Parenthood*, 1919, p. 89).

2. See Sir H. Taylor in my *Our Social Heritage*, Chap. II.
3. J. Jastrow, *The Subconscious* (1906), p. 94.
4. Trollope's *Autobiography* (edition of 1921), p. 94.
5. H. Poincaré, *Science and Method* (trans., pp. 54 and 55). On the other hand, one of the ablest of modern mathematical thinkers told me that he believed that his Incubation period was, as a rule, spent in a state of actual mental repose for all or part of his brain, which made the later explosion of intense and successful thought possible. His belief may have been partly due to the fact that his brain started fewer unsuccessful and more successful association-trains than the brains of other men.
6. See my *The Great Society* (1914), p. 201.
7. I take the word "fringe" from William James, who says in his *Principles*, Vol. I, p. 258: "Let us use the words *psychic overtone, suffusion,* or *fringe*, to designate the influence of a faint brain-process upon our thought, as it makes it aware of relations and objects but dimly perceived." The characteristics of our "fringe-consciousness" may be a result of the "hormic" character of the human organism which I discussed in Chapter I. The "over" and "under" tones of a piano indicate the simultaneous vibration of other strings under the influence of the string which was originally struck. The "fringe-consciousness" of a human being may sometimes indicate that the activity of the main centre of his consciousness is being accompanied by the imperfectly coordinated activity of other factors in his organism.
8. *The Psychology of Day Dreams*, p. 282.
9. *How We Think* (1910), p. 74.
10. Wundt (quoted by E. B. Titchener, *Experimental Psychology of the Thought Processes*, p. 103). Wundt's words are "In diesem Sinn ist das Gefühl der Pionier der Erkenntniss" (*Grundzüge der Physiologischen Psychologie*, Vol. II, 1893, p. 521).

Commentary

The first thing to notice about Wallas's theory of the creative process is that he uses the word "creative" only twice in his key chapter "Stages of Control" and never uses the word "creativity" at all. This is curious and, although it might reflect only historical differences in use of the word, it does raise the question of whether psychologists who have drawn on or cited his theory to describe the stages of the creative process (and there are many of us in the field) have been deluded. Indeed, a close reading of Wallas suggests that he is attempting to describe thought processes quite generally, ranging from "a schoolboy sitting down to do an algebra sum" to "the more difficult forms of creative thought, the making, for instance, of a scientific discovery, or the writing of a poem or play." At the same time, it is clear that Wallas (1926) was most concerned with thought processes that result in "new ideas," (p. 96) and "original intellectual work" (p. 88)—processes that most contemporary scholars in the field would label creative. Nonetheless, it is theoretically useful that Wallas essentially treated creative thinking—thinking that results in an original, valuable idea or product—as a special case of the more general thought process. At least, it was theoretically useful for me.

In the early 1980s, when I set out to articulate a theoretical framework for the social psychology of creativity that I was attempting to build, I was struck by the theoretical fragmentation that existed in the creativity literature at that time. There were interesting and compelling conceptualizations, to be sure, of creative personality, the cognitive skills necessary for creativity, and other aspects of the phenomenon (e.g., Bruner, 1962; Cropley, 1967; Guilford, 1950; MacKinnon, 1975), but there was no theory (that I could find) that attempted to describe creativity comprehensively. With this realization, I faced a dilemma. I could either contribute to the fragmentation by articulating a relatively narrow theory of how the social environment influences creativity, adhering quite closely to my own research findings and those of the few others who had examined such influences, or

I could be much more speculative but much more comprehensive, developing a theory to explain how and why creative thought and behavior differ from noncreative thought and behavior—and explicating the role that the social environment might play in the process. I decided to reach for the latter, larger goal. For this purpose, there was Wallas. And only Wallas.

For me, the appeal of Wallas's theory was that it presented a simple, plausible framework on which to develop ideas. Although it was based almost purely on introspection and anecdotal evidence, it had a compelling logic. The creative thought process that it outlined—Preparation, Incubation, Illumination, and Verification—seemed entirely possible. Beyond its inherent logic and plausibility, Wallas's conceptualization allowed me, an aspiring creativity theorist, to consider what might influence the process at each stage and, thus, the novelty and/or appropriateness of its outcomes—the two hallmarks of creativity, as typically defined—influences beyond the disciplined self-control of thought that so clearly obsessed Wallas.

Through my own experimental research and a review of the then-extant creativity literature, I had identified three essential components of creativity—three sets of intra-individual elements that are all necessary for generating novel, appropriate ideas, products, or problem solutions (Amabile, 1983a, 1983b). Domain-relevant skills constitute the basis for any performance in a given domain and include factual knowledge, technical skills, and special talents in the domain in question. Prior research (e.g., Getzels & Jackson, 1962; Newell, Shaw & Simon, 1962; Newell & Simon, 1972; Schank & Abelson, 1977) had pointed to the importance of domain-relevant skills. Creativity-relevant skills (later renamed creativity-relevant processes; Amabile, 1996) include cognitive style, working style, heuristics for exploring new cognitive pathways, and personality processes conducive to such exploration. A great many previous researchers had, collectively, discovered several creativity-relevant processes that play a role in creativity (e.g., Barron, 1963; Crutchfield, 1962; Duncker, 1945; Getzels & Csikszentmihalyi, 1976; Hogarth, 1980; Langer, 1978; MacKinnon, 1965; Newell et al., 1962; Parnes & Meadow, 1963; Simonton, 1980; Stein, 1974, 1975; Torrance, 1967; Wallach & Kogan, 1965; Wertheimer, 1959; Wickelgren, 1979). Task motivation, the individual's motivation to engage in the particular problem or task at hand, includes both trait motivation (the individual's baseline level of intrinsic interest in the task) and state motivation (alterations above or below the individual's baseline as a function of the immediate social environment).

A focus on this third component, task motivation, had been the contribution of my own work to that point. In a series of experiments testing what I had termed *the intrinsic motivation hypothesis of creativity*, I had discovered that a number of social-environmental factors can undermine intrinsic motivation and creativity (Amabile, 1983a). Those factors included expected evaluation (Amabile, 1979), contracted-for reward (Amabile, Hennessey, & Grossman, 1986), constrained choice (Amabile & Gitomer, 1984), and competition (Amabile, 1982). The general finding of these studies was that extrinsic motivators and extrinsic constraints (factors extrinsic to an activity) can undermine both intrinsic motivation and creativity. As evidence mounted in the ensuing years, from my laboratory and those of other researchers, I came to call this phenomenon *the intrinsic motivation principle of creativity*.

Not only did Wallas's articulation of stages of the creative process provide the scaffolding for me to build my componential theory of creativity, but it already explicitly included two of the three components that I had identified. Although he didn't use the term "domain-relevant skills," Wallas clearly talked about amassing these skills as part of the Preparation stage and deploying these skills during the Verification stage of the creative process. Moreover, his tactics for controlling and facilitating the thought process are, essentially, creativity-relevant skills. Wallas didn't directly discuss motivation, the third component of my theory. However, he implicitly suggested that intrinsic motivation may be more conducive to creativity than extrinsic motivation, in his insistence on the importance of "mental relaxation" punctuating work on "the more difficult forms of creative thought" (1926, p. 87). It isn't too great an inferential leap to assume that, under the pressure of extrinsic motivators like expected evaluation, contracted-for reward, or competition, such mental relaxation could be difficult to achieve.

Despite the appeal of Wallas's stage model as a basic framework on which to build, however, I was uncomfortable with certain aspects of it. Most important, based on my reading of the extant empirical creativity literature at the time I was developing my theory, I was unconvinced that Incubation and, especially, Illumination are necessary elements of the creative process. Wallas's evidence consisted solely of introspection into his own experience and the first-person accounts of well-known creative thinkers—which, of course, were based on their own introspective (and retrospective) musings. Although such accounts can legitimately serve as sources of hypotheses to test with rigorous methods, I was sufficiently suspicious of them that I felt it necessary to alter certain aspects of Wallas's stage model as I adapted it for my purposes. I finessed the issue of the shaky empirical basis for Incubation and Illumination by implicitly including both in my third stage, Response Generation.[2] This hedge allowed me to claim that, although unconscious Incubation and sudden flashes of conscious insight were possible, they were not necessary elements of the creative process.

A second important departure of my theory from Wallas's was that I adopted the language of the information-processing models of problem-solving current in the cognitive psychology of the 1960s, 1970s, and 1980s (e.g., Simon, 1966, 1967a, 1967b, 1978). Even though these models sounded rather mechanistic, they did occasionally use language seeming to refer to the unconscious processes that are so prominent in Wallas's conceptualization. For example, Newell et al. (1962) describe the sense of "getting warmer" during the problem-solving process. That "getting warmer," as discussed by Newell and colleagues, sounds quite like Wallas's (1926, pp. 80, 97) description of "Intimation," the initial rising of an idea into "fringe consciousness"—a state somewhere between the unconscious and the fully conscious.

A third way in which I departed from Wallas was in proposing a new first stage, preceding Preparation: Problem or Task Identification. I did this because some intriguing evidence had emerged that identifying and appropriately articulating an interesting problem could be an important aspect of a successful creative process (Getzels & Csikszentmihalyi, 1976). Despite these changes, however, Wallas's stages are clearly evident in my original componential theory (Amabile, 1983a, 1983b) as well as all subsequent modifications of it (Amabile, 1988, 1993, 1996; Amabile & Mueller, 2008, Amabile & Pratt, 2016).

---

2. The stages in my model (Amabile, 1983a, 1983b, 1996) are: (1) Problem or Task Identification; (2) Preparation; (3) Response Generation; and (4) Response Validation and Communication. Recently, Sadler-Smith (2015), in a close re-examination of Wallas's "Stages of Control" chapter, proposed that Wallas really describes five stages, if we take seriously his description of "Intimation," the initial rising of an idea into "fringe consciousness" (p. 346). Wallas (1926, pp. 80, 97) himself described Intimation as belonging partly to Incubation but mostly to Illumination.

ELABORATIONS ON AND CHALLENGES TO WALLAS'S THEORY

Wallas's ideas about the Preparation and Verification stages were incorporated, in some form, in virtually all subsequent theories of the creative process. Even though his Incubation and Illumination stages generated considerable disagreement and wide divergence in later works, he is referenced (either favorably or critically) by nearly all theorists who propose process models of creativity. Interestingly, Wallas himself was rather vague on the actual process. He presented his four stages as descriptive of all thought that is directed at "exploring . . . problems" (1926, p. 81), emphasizing that the model also applies to endeavors involving "the creation of something felt to be beautiful and true," like poetry, music, and political discernment, which "are not very easily fitted into a 'problem and solution' scheme" (p. 82). In other words, he claimed that the four stages—including Incubation and Illumination—occur in all instances of productive thought. However, because Wallas's main purpose was to provide practical advice on how to corral each of the stages for ever greater productivity ("success"), he devoted scant attention to speculating on how the process might actually happen—except to assert that Illumination involves "the culmination of a successful train of association" (p. 94) that is almost completely unconscious.

Subsequent theorists nicely filled that gap. Donald Campbell's (1960) seminal paper, "Blind Variation and Selective Retention in Creative Thought as in Other Knowledge Processes," provided an elaborated and compelling account of what might happen during Incubation and Illumination—interestingly, without once referencing Wallas and including the words "incubate" and "illumination" only in quotes from Bain (1874) and Poincaré (1970). Nonetheless, Campbell does describe a process of idea combinations and recombinations that take place out of the conscious realm and can result in brilliant creative ideas—an unconscious process and a result that bear considerable similarity to what Wallas termed Incubation and Illumination. Moreover, like Wallas, Campbell presents his model as a general explanation of all forms of productive thought. Campbell bases his conceptualization on the biological evolutionary theory of Charles Darwin (surprisingly, without citing Darwin, either), asserting that a similar evolutionary process takes place when humans think: various ideas and idea combinations arise in an essentially blind process (though not a completely random one) and vie for survival, mostly out of conscious awareness, with one eventually being chosen and thrust into consciousness. Wallas would likely object vigorously to the notion of a blind process that the individual cannot control or even nudge, but he would likely approve of Campbell's description of the seemingly instantaneous appearance of the solution after a period during which the thinker is not consciously thinking.

Dean K. Simonton (1999) elaborated Campbell's evolutionary conceptualization into an intricate, well-argued, book-length "Darwinian theory" (p. 33) of creativity, supported by three types of detailed evidence: biographical and autobiographical accounts of "notable creators" (p. 27); experimental research into insight, imagery, and intuition; and computer programs designed to emulate the creative process. For example, Simonton argues persuasively that experiments on human insight provide powerful evidence of the role of unconscious incubation in creative thought. In these experiments, nearly all people fail in their initial attempts to solve the problem presented to them because the obvious solutions are all wrong. Because a mental reframing of the problem is necessary, the problem-solvers need a period in which they are not consciously trying to solve the problem but rather are attending to other sorts of external stimuli (whatever happens to be present in their immediate environment) and internal stimuli (including memories and mind-wanderings). As Simonton explains:

> Whatever the specific source, this bombardment is constantly "priming," or exciting, different aspects of the mnemonic and semantic networks surrounding a given problem. This largely random influx of priming stimuli produces a series of alternative formulations, some more fruitful than others, but with only one leading the individual down the correct path to solution. In other words, during incubation the mind is engaged in an inadvertent blind-variation process. (p. 44; see pp. 43–45)

As additional evidence that the process is essentially blind, Simonton describes experiments on the "Geneplore" (generate and explore) model of creative thinking (Finke, Ward, & Smith, 1992). Participants in these experiments produced more creative work not when they chose materials to work with or the category of object they would invent with those materials, but when both of those aspects of the problem had been randomly selected for them. Although, like Wallas, Simonton acknowledges that conscious logical and analytical processes play a crucial role in the selection and verification of novel ideas, he lays out a great deal of evidence and argument to support the view of creativity as fundamentally dependent on nonconscious, nonrational, and largely random mental processes—and, in that way, as fundamentally different from noncreative thought. Moreover Simonton goes one step beyond Wallas by arguing that true creative insights are the products of minds so great, so unusual, that they deserve the label of "genius."

Robert Weisberg (1986, 1993) could hardly disagree more. In a book elaborating the first major statement of his viewpoint, Weisberg (1986) argued that creative problem-solving—which he defined as a process that results in a novel and correct solution—is not different in kind from other problem-solving processes. He dismissed the notion of sudden creative insight as a myth, explaining the many anecdotal examples of such moments, as well as the self-perception of them, as misperceptions resulting from other mental processes. Moreover, he dismissed the notion that creativity is the province of genius, by rejecting the very idea of genius as a quality of a person. Rather, he argued, creativity is "an activity resulting from the ordinary thought processes of ordinary individuals" (p. 12), and genius is "a characteristic that society bestows upon an individual in response to his or her work" (p. 88).

Most important for the purposes of this essay, after explicitly citing and describing the four stages of Wallas's model, Weisberg rejected both unconscious Incubation (Wallas's second stage) and sudden Illumination (Wallas's third stage) as myths. Citing a great deal of experimental evidence throughout his book, Weisberg (1986, p. 50) summarized his alternative view in this way: "People create solutions to new problems by starting with what they know and later modify it to meet the specific problem at hand. At every step of the way, the process involves a small movement away from what is known, and even these small tentative movements into the unknown are firmly anchored in past experience." For Weisberg, the great leaps of Illumination described by Wallas, the "Eureka" moments explicated by Campbell (1960, p. 5) and Simonton (1999, p. 35), simply do not exist.

More recently, the cognitive neuroscientists John Kounios and Mark Beeman (2015) have proposed a conceptualization of creativity that resolves these competing perspectives on Wallas's model. Defining creativity as "the ability to reinterpret something by breaking it down into its elements and recombining these elements in a surprising way to achieve some goal" (p. 9), they say that creative recombinations can result from either the gradual, conscious processes of analytical thought or from sudden flashes of insight. It is the latter they focus on in their own theorizing. Citing and retelling (with obvious relish) stories of momentous Eureka-type discoveries in history, they readily admit that firm conclusions cannot rely on subjective, introspective anecdotes because such accounts are subject to so many alternative explanations. Instead they describe experimental evidence produced in their laboratories, as well as the work of other researchers, to support the view that insight truly does arise from unconscious processes and that insight truly does appear quite suddenly. They argue convincingly that the incubation and insight processes (as well as the analytical processes) that lead to creative outcomes do not operate only in geniuses; they operate in ordinary individuals as well.

The clever experiments of Kounios and Beeman (2015) involved the use of both EEG and fMRI to observe brain activity as research participants (ordinary people) worked on difficult problems that could be solved through either analytical thought or insight. The researchers discovered that, on those trials in which participants reported that they solved a problem analytically, their brain activity was markedly different from the trials in which they reported solving the problem in a sudden flash of insight. Moreover, the researchers were able to show that whatever mental processes led to the insight were indeed unconscious; even a fraction of a second before the insight appeared, participants had no idea what the solution was. Kounios and Beeman go on to cite considerable evidence from other researchers, including a meta-analysis (Sio & Ormerod, 2009) that supports the existence of incubation. In other words, it appears that not only do incubation and illumination exist, but they have a distinct neural signature. We can only guess at how Wallas would react to news of these findings, but it is likely that he would feel great satisfaction.

A recent revision of my componential theory of creativity (Amabile & Pratt, 2016) includes a number of changes based on empirical findings since the theory was first articulated (Amabile 1983a, 1983b, 1988, 1996). Affect has been added to the model, not as a necessary component contributing to creativity but as a factor that can importantly influence the creative process either positively or negatively. Motivational forces are now described in a more nuanced fashion, including the possibility that extrinsic motivation can, under some circumstances, not only leave intrinsic motivation intact but actually augment it, resulting in elevated levels of creativity. And there are changes in the creative process itself. Dynamic elements have been added, describing ways in which progress toward a creative solution or product—and even failure, under certain conditions—can lead to reengagement at various points in the process. Yet even with these revisions, the basic skeleton of Wallas's four stages still serves as the underlying foundation—and incubation and illumination are still considered to be possible, though not necessary, subprocesses of response generation.

FUTURE DIRECTIONS: HOW MIGHT WALLAS BE USEFUL?

Wallas's ideas are still useful for sparking new research, in conjunction with the more recent theorizing and empirical work that has been done on the creative process, because many unanswered questions remain—even if we consider only his original description of the stages of the creative process and set aside the debates that have arisen since that time. For example, Wallas speculated on conditions that "the educated man" could establish for himself that would facilitate fruitful incubation and illumination, conditions such as being well-rested and relaxed and engaging in moderate physical exercise. Kounios and Beeman (2015, p. 109) cite research on some of these points and refer to anecdotal evidence on others to suggest that it does indeed make sense to take a break and relax after working hard and getting stuck on a difficult problem, "to cleanse your mental palate." My own research suggests that overnight incubation can facilitate creative problem-solving (Amabile, Barsade, Mueller, & Staw, 2005).

Nearly a century after Wallas's book appeared, we still do not know whether other stages might be involved in the creative process, whether the stages he described do tend to occur in the sequence he proposed, or how alternative sequences might influence the nature of creative outcomes. Recent methodological advances, such as a digital technique for studying the behaviors involved in the adult learning process (Rigolizzo, 2017), could be useful in dissecting the creative process as well as examining it holistically. Most fundamentally, perhaps, it remains for future researchers to discover the extent to which Wallas's model and those that have built on it apply to the various domains in which human creativity appears: the arts, the sciences, business, government, education, social interaction—and theorizing on the art of thought itself.

Acknowledgment

I am grateful for the helpful comments and suggestions made on an earlier version by John Kounios and Vlad Glăveanu.

References

Amabile, T. M. (1979). Effects of external evaluation on artistic creativity. *Journal of Personality and Social Psychology, 37*, 221–233.

Amabile, T. M. (1982). Children's artistic creativity: Detrimental effects of competition in field setting. *Personality and Social Psychology Bulletin, 8*, 573–578.

Amabile, T. M. (1983a). *The social psychology of creativity.* New York: Springer-Verlag.

Amabile, T. M. (1983b). Social psychology of creativity: A componential conceptualization. *Journal of Personality and Social Psychology, 45*, 357–377.

Amabile, T. M. (1988). A model of creativity and innovation in organizations. In B. M. Staw and L. L. Cummings (Eds.), *Research in organizational behavior* (Vol. 10, pp. 123–167). Greenwich, CT: JAI Press.

Amabile, T. M. (1993). Motivational synergy: Toward new conceptualizations of intrinsic and extrinsic motivation in the workplace. *Human Resource Management Review, 3*, 185–201.

Amabile, T. M. (1996). *Creativity in context.* Boulder, CO: Westview Press.

Amabile, T. M., Barsade, S. G., Mueller, J. S., & Staw, B. M. (2005). Affect and creativity at work. *Administrative Science Quarterly, 50*, 367–403.

Amabile, T. M., & Gitomer, J. (1984). Children's artistic creativity: Effects of choice in task materials. *Personality and Social Psychology Bulletin, 10*, 209–215.

Amabile, T. M., Hennessey, B. A., & Grossman, B. S. (1986). Social influences on creativity: The effects of contracted-for reward. *Journal of Personality and Social Psychology, 50*, 14–23.

Amabile, T. M., & Mueller, J. S. (2008). Studying creativity, its processes, and its antecedents: An exploration of the componential theory of creativity. In J. Zhou & C. E. Shalley (Eds.), *Handbook of organizational creativity* (pp. 33–63). New York: Lawrence Erlbaum Associates.

Amabile, T. M., & Pratt, M. G. (2016) The dynamic componential model of creativity and innovation in organizations: Making progress, making meaning. *Research in Organizational Behavior, 36*, 157–183.

Bain, A. (1874). *The senses and the intellect* (3rd ed.). New York: Appleton.

Barron, F. (1963). *Creativity and psychological health.* New York: Van Nostrand.

Bruner, J. (1962). The conditions of creativity. In H. Gruber, G. Terrell, & M. Wertheimer (Eds.), *Contemporary approaches to creative thinking: A symposium held at the University of Colorado.* (pp. 1–30). New York: Atherton Press.

Campbell, D. (1960). Blind variation and selective retention in creative thought as in other knowledge processes. *Psychological Review, 67*, 380–400.

Cropley, A. (1967). *Creativity*. London: Longmans, Green.

Crutchfield, R. (1962). Conformity and creative thinking. In H. Gruber, G. Terrell, & M. Wertheimer (Eds.), *Contemporary approaches to creative thinking: A symposium held at the University of Colorado.* (pp. 120–140). New York: Atherton Press.

Duncker, K. (1945). On problem solving. *Psychological Monographs, 58*(270).

Fabien Society. (n.d.). Wikipedia. Retrieved February 5, 2017, from https://en.wikipedia.org/w/index.php?title=Fabian_Society&oldid=767165819.

Finke, R. A., Ward, T. B., & Smith, S. M. (1992). *Creative cognition: Theory, research, applications.* Cambridge, MA: MIT Press.

Getzels, J., & Csikszentmihalyi, M. (1976). *The creative vision: A longitudinal study of problem-finding in art.* New York: Wiley-Interscience.

Getzels, J., & Jackson, P. (1962). *Creativity and intelligence: Explorations with gifted students.* New York: Wiley.

Graham Wallas. (n.d.). Wikipedia. Retrieved February 5, 2017, from https://en.wikipedia.org/w/index.php?title=Graham_Wallas&oldid-762068117.

Gruber, H., Terrell, G., & Wertheimer, M. (Eds.). (1962). *Contemporary approaches to creative thinking: A symposium held at the University of Colorado.* New York: Atherton Press.

Guilford, J. P. (1950). Creativity. *American Psychologist, 5,* 444–454.

Hogarth, R. (1980). *Judgement and choice.* Chichester, UK: Wiley.

Kounios, J., & Beeman, Mark. (2015). *The Eureka factor: Aha moments, creative insight, and the brain* (1st ed.). New York: Random House.

Langer, E. (1978). Rethinking the role of thought in social interaction. In J. Harvey, W. Ickes, & R. Kidd (Eds.), *New directions in attribution research* (pp. 35–58). Hillsdale, NJ: Lawrence Erlbaum Associates.

MacKinnon, D. W. (1965). Personality and the realization of creative potential. *American Psychologist, 20,* 273–281.

MacKinnon, D. W. (1975). IPAR's contribution to the conceptualization and study of creativity. In I. Taylor & J. Getzels (Eds.), *Perspectives in creativity* (pp. 60–89). Chicago: Aldine.

Newell, A., Shaw, J., & Simon, H. (1962). The process of creative thinking. In H. Gruber, G. Terrell, & M. Wertheimer (Eds.), *Contemporary approaches to creative thinking* (pp. 63–119). New York: Atherton Press.

Newell, A., & Simon, H. (1972). *Human problem solving.* Englewood Cliffs, NJ: Prentice-Hall.

Parnes, S. J., & Meadow, A. (1963). Development of individual creative talent. In C. W. Taylor & F. Barron (Eds.), *Scientific creativity* (pp. 311–320). New York: Wiley.

Poincaré, H. (1970). Mathematical creation. Excerpt from Poincare (1913), *The Foundations of Science.* In P. E. Vernon (Ed.), *Creativity* (pp. 77–88). Middlesex, UK: Penguin Books.

Rigolizzo, M. (2017). *Self-directed learning behaviors: A measure, model, and field experiment of how working adults learn.* Unpublished doctoral dissertation, Harvard University.

Sadler-Smith, E. (2015). Wallas' four-stage model of the creative process: More than meets the eye? *Creativity Research Journal, 27*(4), 342–352.

Schank, R., & Abelson, R. (1977). *Scripts, plans, goals, and understanding.* Hillsdale, NJ: Erlbaum.

Simon, H. (1966). Scientific discovery and the psychology of problem solving. In R. G. Colodny (Ed.), *Mind and cosmos: Essays in contemporary science and philosophy* (pp. 22–40). Pittsburgh: University of Pittsburgh Press.

Simon, H. (1967a). Motivational and emotional controls of cognition. *Psychological Review, 74,* 29–39.

Simon, H. (1967b). Understanding creativity. In J. C. Gowan, G. D. Demos, & E. P. Torrance (Eds.), *Creativity: Its educational implications* (pp. 43–53). New York: Wiley.

Simon, H. (1978). Information-processing theory of human problem solving. In W. K. Estes, (Ed.), *Handbook of learning and cognitive processes: Vol. 5. Human information processing* (pp. 271–295). Hillsdale, NJ: Lawrence Erlbaum Associates.

Simonton, D. K. (1980). Thematic fame, melodic originality, and musical zeitgeist: A biographical and transhistorical content analysis. *Journal of Personality and Social Psychology, 38,* 972–983.

Simonton, D. K. (1999). *Origins of genius: Darwinian perspectives on creativity.* New York: Oxford University Press.

Sio, U. N., & Ormerod, T. C. (2009). Does incubation enhance problem solving? A meta-analytic review. *Psychological Bulletin, 135,* 94–120.

Stein, M. I. (1974). *Stimulating creativity* (Vol. 1). New York: Academic Press.

Stein, M. I. (1975). *Stimulating creativity* (Vol. 2). New York: Academic Press.

Torrance, E. P. (1967). *Understanding the fourth grade slump in creative thinking: Final report.* Athens: University of Georgia Press.

Wallach, M., & Kogan, N. (1965). *Modes of thinking in young children.* New York: Holt, Rinehart & Winston.

Wallas, G. (1908). *Human nature in politics.* London: A. Constable.

Wallas, G. (1914). *The great society: A psychological analysis.* New York: Macmillan.

Wallas, G. (1926). *The art of thought.* New York: Harcourt, Brace.

Weisberg, R. (1986). *Creativity: Genius and other myths.* New York: W. H. Freeman.

Weisberg, R. (1993). *Creativity: Beyond the myth of genius.* New York: W. H. Freeman.

Wertheimer, M. (1959). *Productive thinking.* New York: Harper & Row.

Wickelgren, W. A. (1979). *Cognitive psychology.* Englewood Cliffs, NJ: Prentice-Hall.

3

Science and Method
Henri Poincaré

GIOVANNI EMANUELE CORAZZA AND TODD LUBART

Summary

Henri Poincaré holds a unique place in the history of science, as one of the greatest mathematicians and physicist of all times who contributed to many disciplines at the highest level. Not less important is the fact that he is one of the few who wrote extensively and with great detail on the methodologies he used to generate his creative contributions, as reported in particular in *Science and Method*, the book from which this reading is extracted. Poincaré influenced directly the "preparation, incubation, illumination, verification" model for the creative thinking process, later adopted by Wallas and with an impact that extends to our day. Also of note are his contributions in recognizing combinations as a key to the creative process, aesthetic choice as a selective mechanism (also in science), and problem selection as a critical starting point for all creative endeavors. Poincaré can therefore be considered a fundamental figure in the development of creativity as a scientific discipline.

Introduction

Poincaré contributed at the highest level to numerous and diversified fields, including non-Euclidean geometry, arithmetic, thermodynamics, and celestial mechanics. And he was undoubtedly a philosopher of science. At the same time, we believe Poincaré should be considered a reference figure in the study of the mental processes that lead to the generation of novel ideas, that is, in creativity studies. This is because he made a concentrated effort to describe the conditions and steps that led him to original solutions of very complex scientific problems, and his writings had a very significant influence on the four-stages model for creative thinking (Wallas, 1926; see Chapter 2, this volume). It is relatively rare that the creative process is observed and subjected to a detailed introspective description and analysis by someone who had very significant creative achievements. The value of Poincaré's thoughts was recognized in his own times: his lecture "L'invention mathématique" (Mathematical invention) to the Société de Psychologie in Paris in 1908, as well as many insights on his processes exposed in his colloquia with a French psychiatrist, Dr. Eduard Toulouse, published in 1909 (Toulouse, 1909), are noteworthy.

Although no historically proper biography of Poincaré has been published, many elements of his life may be put together by the writings of his fellow scientists (Weinstein, 2012). Jules Henri Poincaré was born in Nancy on April 29, 1854, in a relatively wealthy and highly educated family, among whose close relatives were a neurologist, a pharmacist, an engineer, a philosopher, as well as the rector of the University of Paris (his cousin Lucian). He was considered extremely gifted in school, particularly in mathematics. Legendary stories report that he started to talk at nine months, and at the very same age he watched the stars intensely with excitement. He was ambidextrous and spoke several languages. Thanks to his many contributions, he was famous in his time, teaching in the best universities and delivering keynote speeches at the most important conferences.

In his many writings, his results went beyond the content to discuss the methodologies that led to the result and to the significance of the latter in the greater realm of science and metaphysics. In this sense, his books *La science et l'hypothése* (1902), *La valeur de la science* (1905), and *Science et méthode* (1908) stand out. The latter was translated in English in 1914 by Francis Maitland, and it is from this version that we extract the most important passages in terms of their relevance to creativity studies. Let's conclude this short introduction with the words of Bertrand Russell, who wrote the preface to that book after Poincaré died prematurely in 1912:

> Henri Poincaré was, by general agreement, the most eminent scientific man of his generation—more eminent, one is tempted to think, than any man of science now living. . . . Poincare's writing, . . . as the reader of this book may see in his account of mathematical invention, has the freshness of actual experience, of vivid, intimate contact with what he is describing. There results a certain richness and resonance in his words: the sound emitted is not hollow, but comes from a great mass of which only the polished surface appears. . . . It is not results, which are what mainly interests the man in the street, that are what is essential in a science: what is essential is its method, and it is with method that Poincaré's philosophical writings are concerned. (in Poincaré, 1914, pp. 5–6)

Reading: *Science and Method*

Source: Poincaré, H. (1914). *Science and method* (Francis Maitland, Trans.). Preface by Bertrand Russell. London: Thomas Nelson & Sons. Selection of passages. Work in the public domain.

Book 1. The Scientist and Science

CHAPTER 1. THE SELECTION OF FACTS

(p. 17) The most interesting facts are those which can be used several times, those which have a chance of recurring.

(p. 20) It is with regular facts . . . that we ought to begin; but as soon as the rule is well established, as soon as it is no longer in doubt, the facts which are in complete conformity with it lose their interest, since they can teach us nothing new. Then it is the exception which becomes important. We cease to look for resemblances, and apply ourselves before all else to differences, and of these differences we select first those that are most accentuated, not only because they are the most striking, but because they will be the most instructive.

(p. 22) The scientist does not study nature because it is useful to do so. He studies it because he takes pleasure in it, and he takes pleasure in it because it is beautiful. If nature were not beautiful it would not be worth knowing, and life would not be worth living. I am not speaking, of course, of that beauty which strikes the senses, of the beauty of qualities and appearances. I am far from despising this, but it has nothing to do with science. What I mean is that more intimate beauty which comes from the harmonious order of its parts, and which a pure intelligence can grasp. . . . Intellectual beauty . . . is self-sufficing, and it is for it, more perhaps than for the future good of humanity, that the scientist condemns himself to long and painful labours.

CHAPTER 2. THE FUTURE OF MATHEMATICS

(p. 25) If we wish to foresee the future of mathematics, our proper course is to study the history and present condition of the science. For us mathematicians, is not this procedure to some extent professional? We are accustomed to extrapolation, which is a method of deducing the future from the past and the present; and since we are well aware of its limitations, we run no risk of deluding ourselves as to the scope of the results it gives us. In the past there have been prophets of ill. They took pleasure in repeating that all problems susceptible of being solved had already been solved, and that after them there would be nothing left but gleanings. Happily we are reassured by the example of the past. Many times already men have thought that they had solved all the problems, or at least that they had made an inventory of all that admit of solution. And then the meaning of the word solution has been extended; the insoluble problems have become the most interesting of all, and other problems hitherto undreamed of have presented themselves. For the Greeks a good solution was one that employed only rule and compass; later it became one obtained by the extraction of radicals, then one in which algebraical functions and radicals alone figured. Thus the pessimists found themselves continually passed over, continually forced to retreat, so that at present I verily believe there are none left.

(p. 27) Physicists do not wait to study a phenomenon until some pressing need of material life makes it an absolute necessity, and they are quite right. If the scientists of the eighteenth century had disregarded electricity, because it appeared to them merely a curiosity having no practical interest, we should not have, in the twentieth century, either telegraphy or electro-chemistry or electro-traction. Physicists forced to select are not guided in their selection solely by utility. What method, then, do they pursue in making a selection between the different natural facts? I have explained this in the preceding chapter. The facts that interest them are those that may lead to the discovery of a law, those that have an analogy with many other facts and do not appear to us as isolated, but as closely grouped with others. The isolated fact attracts the attention of all, of the layman as well as the scientist. But what the true scientist alone can see is the link that unites several facts which have a deep but hidden analogy. The anecdote of Newton's apple is probably not true, but it is symbolical, so we will treat it as if it were true. Well, we must suppose that before Newton's day many men had seen apples fall, but none had been able to draw any conclusion. Facts would be barren if there were not minds capable of selecting between them and distinguishing those which have something hidden behind them and recognizing what is hidden—minds which, behind the bare fact, can detect the soul of the fact. In mathematics we do exactly the same thing. Of the various elements at our disposal we can form millions of different combinations, but any one of these combinations, so long as it is isolated, is absolutely without value; often we have taken great trouble to construct it, but it is of absolutely no use, unless it be, perhaps, to supply a subject for an exercise in secondary schools. It will be quite different as soon as this combination takes its place in a class of analogous combinations whose analogy we have recognized; we shall then be no longer in [the] presence of a fact, but of a law. And then the true discoverer will not be the workman who has patiently built up some of these combinations, but the man who has brought out their relation. The former has only seen the bare fact, the latter alone has detected the soul of the fact. The invention of a new word will often be sufficient to bring out the relation, and the word will be creative.

(p. 29) Thus the importance of a fact is measured by the return it gives—that is, by the amount of thought it enables us to economize. In physics, the facts which give a large return are those which take their place in a very general law, because they enable us to foresee a very large number of others, and it is exactly the same in mathematics. Suppose I apply myself to a complicated calculation and with much difficulty arrive at a result, I shall have gained nothing by my trouble if it has not enabled me to foresee the results of other analogous calculations, and to direct them with certainty, avoiding the blind groping with which I had to be contented the first time. On the contrary, my time will not have been lost if this very groping has succeeded in revealing to me the profound analogy between the problem just dealt with and a much more extensive class of other problems; if it has shown me at once their resemblances and their differences; if, in a word, it has enabled me to perceive the possibility of a generalization. Then it will not be merely a new result that I have acquired, but a new force.

(pp. 30–31) If a new result is to have any value, it must unite elements long since known, but till then scattered and seemingly foreign to each other, and suddenly introduce order where the appearance of disorder reigned. Then it enables us to see at a glance each of these elements in the place it occupies in the whole. Not only is the new fact valuable on its own account, but it alone gives a value to the old facts it unites. Our mind is frail as our senses are; it would lose itself in the complexity of the world if that complexity were not harmonious; like the short-sighted, it would only see the details, and would be obliged to forget each of these details before examining the next, because it would be incapable of taking in the whole. The only facts worthy of our attention are those which introduce order into this complexity and so make it accessible to us. Mathematicians attach a great importance to the elegance of their methods and of their results, and this is not mere dilettantism. What is it that gives us the feeling of elegance in a solution or a demonstration? It is the harmony of the different parts, their symmetry, and their happy adjustment; it is, in a word, all that introduces order, all that gives them unity, that enables us to obtain a clear comprehension of the whole as well as of the parts. But that is also precisely what causes it to give a large return; and in fact the more we see this whole clearly and at a single glance, the better we shall perceive the analogies with other neighbouring objects, and consequently the better chance we shall have of guessing the possible generalizations. Elegance may result from the feeling of surprise caused by the un-looked-for occurrence together of objects not habitually associated. In this, again, it is fruitful, since it thus discloses relations till then unrecognized. It is also fruitful even when it only results from the contrast between the simplicity of the means and the complexity of the problem presented, for it then causes us to reflect on the reason for this contrast, and generally shows us that this reason is not chance, but is to be found in some unsuspected law. Briefly stated, the sentiment of mathematical elegance is nothing but the satisfaction due to some conformity between the solution we wish to discover and the necessities of our mind, and it is on account of this very conformity that the solution can be an instrument for us. This aesthetic satisfaction is consequently connected with the economy of thought.

(p. 32) What I have just said is sufficient to show how vain it would be to attempt to replace the mathematician's free initiative by a mechanical process of any kind. In order to obtain a result having any real value, it is not enough to grind out calculations, or to have a machine for putting things in order: it is not order only, but unexpected order, that has a value. A machine can take hold of the bare fact, but the soul of the fact will always escape it.

(p. 34) I think I have already said somewhere that mathematics is the art of giving the same name to different things. It is enough that these things, though differing in matter, should be similar in form, to permit of their being, so to speak, run in the same mould. When language has been well chosen, one is astonished to find that all demonstrations made for a known object apply immediately to many new objects: nothing requires to be changed, not even the terms, since the names have become the same. A well-chosen term is very often sufficient to remove the exceptions permitted by the rules as stated in the old phraseology. This accounts for the invention of negative quantities, imaginary quantities, decimals to infinity, and I know not what else. And we must never forget that exceptions are pernicious, because they conceal laws. This is one of the characteristics by which we recognize facts which give a great return: they are the facts which permit of these happy innovations of language. The bare fact, then, has sometimes no great interest: it may have been noted many times without rendering any great service to science; it only acquires a value when some more careful thinker perceives the connexion it brings out, and symbolizes it by a term.

(p. 39) In proportion as the science develops, it becomes more difficult to take it in in its entirety. Then an attempt is made to cut it in pieces and to be satisfied with one of these pieces—in a word, to specialize. Too great a movement in this direction would constitute a serious obstacle to the progress of the science. As I have said, it is by unexpected concurrences between its different parts that it can make progress. Too much specializing would prohibit these concurrences. Let us hope that congresses, such as those of Heidelberg and Rome, by putting us in touch with each other, will open up a view of our neighbours' territory, and force us to compare it with our own, and so escape in a measure from our own little village. In this way they will be the best remedy against the danger I have just noted.

CHAPTER 3. MATHEMATICAL DISCOVERY

(p. 46) The genesis of mathematical discovery is a problem which must inspire the psychologist with the keenest interest. For this is the process in which the human mind seems to borrow least from the exterior world, in which it acts, or appears to act, only by itself and on itself, so that by studying the process of geometric thought we may hope to arrive at what is most essential in the human mind.

(p. 49) My memory is not bad, but it would be insufficient to make me a good chess player. Why, then, does it not fail me in a difficult mathematical argument in which the majority of chess players would be lost? Clearly because it is guided by the general trend of the argument. A mathematical demonstration is not a simple juxtaposition of syllogisms; it consists of syllogisms placed in a certain order, and the order in which these elements are placed is much more important than the elements themselves. If I have the feeling, so to speak the intuition, of this order, so that I can perceive the whole of the argument at a glance, I need no longer to be afraid of forgetting one of the elements; each of them will place itself naturally in the position prepared for it, without my having to make any effort of memory. It seems to me, then, as I repeat an argument I have learnt, that I could have discovered it. This is often only an illusion; but even then, even if I am not clever enough to create for myself, I rediscover it myself as I repeat it. We can understand that this feeling, this intuition of mathematical order, which enables us to guess hidden harmonies and relations, cannot belong to every one. Some have neither this delicate feeling that is difficult to define, nor a power of memory and attention above the common, and so they are absolutely incapable of understanding even the first steps of higher mathematics. This applies to the majority of people. Others have the feeling only in a slight degree, but they are gifted with an uncommon memory and a great capacity for attention. They learn the details one after the other by heart, they can understand mathematics and sometimes apply them, but they are not in a condition to create. Lastly, others possess the special intuition I have spoken of more or less highly developed, and they can not only understand mathematics, even though their memory is in no way extraordinary, but they can become creators, and seek to make discovery with more or less chance of success, according as their intuition is more or less developed.

(p. 50) What, in fact, is mathematical discovery? It does not consist in making new combinations with mathematical entities that are already known. That can be done by any one, and the combinations that could be so formed would be infinite in number, and the greater part of them would be absolutely devoid of interest. Discovery consists precisely in not constructing useless combinations, but in constructing those that are useful, which are an infinitely small minority. Discovery is discernment, selection. How this selection is to be made I have explained above. Mathematical facts worthy of being studied are those which, by their analogy with other facts, are capable of conducting us to the knowledge of a mathematical law, in the same way that experimental facts conduct us to the knowledge of a physical law. They are those which reveal unsuspected relations between other facts, long since known, but wrongly believed to be unrelated to each other. Among the combinations we choose, the most fruitful are often those which are formed of elements borrowed from widely separated domains. I do not mean to say that for discovery it is sufficient to bring together objects that are as incongruous as possible. The greater part of the combinations so formed would be entirely fruitless, but some among them, though very rare, are the most fruitful of all. Discovery, as I have said, is selection. But this is perhaps not quite the right word. It suggests a purchaser who has been shown a large number of samples, and examines them one after the other in order to make his selection. In our case the samples would be so numerous that a whole life would not give sufficient time to examine them. Things do not happen in this way. Unfruitful combinations do not so much as present themselves to the mind of the discoverer. In the field of his consciousness there never appear any but really useful combinations, and some that he rejects, which, however, partake to some extent of the character of useful combinations. Everything happens as if the discoverer were a secondary examiner who had only to interrogate candidates declared eligible after passing a preliminary test.

(p. 52) But what I have said up to now is only what can be observed or inferred by reading the works of geometricians, provided they are read with some reflection. It is time to penetrate further, and to see what happens in the very soul of the mathematician. For this purpose I think I cannot do better than recount my personal recollections. Only I am going to confine myself to relating how I wrote my first treatise on Fuchsian functions. I must apologize, for I am going to introduce some technical expressions, but they need not alarm the reader, for he has no need to understand them. I shall say, for instance, that I found the demonstration of such and such a theorem under such and such circumstances; the theorem will have a barbarous name that many will not know, but that is of no importance. What is interesting for the psychologist is not the theorem but the circumstances.

(p. 52) For a fortnight I had been attempting to prove that there could not be any function analogous to what I have since called Fuchsian functions. I was at that time very ignorant. Every day I sat down at my table and spent an hour or two trying a great number of combinations, and I arrived at no result. One night I took some black coffee, contrary to my custom, and was unable to sleep. A host of ideas kept surging in my head; I could almost feel them jostling one another, until two of them coalesced, so to speak, to form a stable combination. When morning came, I had established the existence of one class of Fuchsian functions, those that are derived from the hypergeometric series. I had only to verify the results, which only took a few hours. Then I wished to represent these functions by the quotient of two series. This idea was perfectly conscious and deliberate; I was guided by the analogy with elliptical functions. I asked myself what must be the properties of these series, if they existed, and I succeeded without difficulty in forming the series that I have called Theta-Fuchsian. At this moment I left Caen, where I was then living, to take part in a geological conference arranged by the School of Mines. The incidents of the journey made me forget my mathematical work. When we arrived at Coutances, we got into a break to go for a drive, and, just as I put my foot on the step, the idea came to me, though nothing in my former thoughts seemed to have prepared me for it, that the transformations I had used to define Fuchsian functions were identical with those of non-Euclidian geometry. I made no verification, and had no time to do so, since I took up the conversation again as soon as I had sat down in the break, but I felt absolute certainty at once. When I got back to Caen I verified the result at my leisure to satisfy my conscience.

(pp. 53–54) I then began to study arithmetical questions without any great apparent result, and without suspecting that they could have the least connexion with my previous researches. Disgusted at my want of success, I went away to spend a few days at the seaside, and thought of entirely different things. One day, as I was walking on the cliff, the idea came to me, again with the same characteristics of conciseness, suddenness, and immediate certainty, that arithmetical transformations of indefinite ternary quadratic forms are identical with those of non-Euclidian geometry. Returning to Caen, I reflected on this result and deduced its consequences. The example of quadratic forms showed me that there are Fuchsian groups other than those which correspond with the hypergeometric series; I saw that I could apply to them the theory of the Theta-Fuchsian series, and that, consequently, there are Fuchsian functions other than those which are derived from the hypergeometric series, the only ones I knew up to that time. Naturally, I proposed to form all these functions. I laid siege to them systematically and captured all the outworks one after the other. There was one, however, which still held out, whose fall would carry with it that of the central fortress. But all my efforts were of no avail at first, except to make me better understand the difficulty, which was already something. All this work was perfectly conscious. Thereupon I left for Mont-Valerien, where I had to serve my time in the army, and so my mind was preoccupied with very different matters. One day, as I was crossing the street, the solution of the difficulty which had brought me to a standstill came to me all at once. I did not try to fathom it immediately, and it was only after my service was finished that I returned to the question. I had all the elements, and had only to assemble and arrange them. Accordingly I composed my definitive treatise at a sitting and without any difficulty. It is useless to multiply examples, and I will content myself with this one alone. As regards my other researches, the accounts I should give would be exactly similar.

(p. 55) One is at once struck by these appearances of sudden illumination, obvious indications of a long course of previous unconscious work. The part played by this unconscious work in mathematical discovery seems to me indisputable, and we shall find traces of it in other cases where it is less evident. Often when a man is working at a difficult question, he accomplishes nothing the first time he sets to work. Then he takes more or less of a rest, and sits down again at his table. During the first half-hour he still finds nothing, and then all at once the decisive idea presents itself to his mind. We might say that the conscious work proved more fruitful because it was interrupted and the rest restored force and freshness to the mind. But it is more probable that the rest was occupied with unconscious work, and that the result of this work was afterwards revealed to the geometrician exactly as in the cases I have quoted, except that the revelation, instead of coming to light during a walk or a journey, came during a period of conscious work, but independently of that work, which at most only performs the unlocking process, as if it were the spur that excited into conscious form the results already acquired during the rest, which till then remained unconscious.

(p. 56) There is another remark to be made regarding the conditions of this unconscious work, which is, that it is not possible, or in any case not fruitful, unless it is first preceded and then followed by a period of conscious work. These sudden inspirations are never produced (and this is sufficiently proved already by the examples I have quoted) except after some days of voluntary efforts which appeared absolutely fruitless, in which one thought one had accomplished nothing, and seemed to be on a totally wrong track. These efforts, however, were not as barren as one thought; they set the unconscious machine in motion, and without them it would not have worked at all, and would not have produced anything. The necessity for the second period of conscious work can be even more readily understood. It is necessary to work out the results of the inspiration, to deduce the immediate consequences and put them in order and to set out the demonstrations; but, above all, it is necessary to *verify* [italics added] them. I have spoken of the feeling of absolute certainty which accompanies the inspiration; in the cases quoted this feeling was not deceptive, and more often than not this will be the case. But we must beware of thinking that this is a rule without exceptions. Often the feeling deceives us without being any less distinct on that account, and we only detect it when we attempt to establish the demonstration. I have observed this fact most notably with regard to ideas that have come to me in the morning or at night when I have been in bed in a semi-somnolent condition.

(pp. 56–57) Such are the facts of the case, and they suggest the following reflections. The result of all that precedes is to show that the unconscious ego, or, as it is called, the subliminal ego, plays a most important part in mathematical discovery. But the subliminal ego is generally thought of as purely automatic. Now we have seen that mathematical work is not a simple mechanical work, and that it could not be entrusted to any machine, whatever the degree of perfection we suppose it to have been brought to. It is not merely a question of applying certain rules, of manufacturing as many combinations as possible according to certain fixed laws. The combinations so obtained would be extremely numerous, useless, and encumbering. The real work of the discoverer consists in choosing between these combinations with a view to eliminating those that are useless, or rather not giving himself the trouble of making them at all. The rules which must guide this choice are extremely subtle and delicate, and it is practically impossible to state them in precise language; they must be felt rather than formulated. Under these conditions, how can we imagine a sieve capable of applying them mechanically? The following, then, presents itself as a first hypothesis. The subliminal ego is in no way inferior to the conscious ego; it is not purely automatic; it is capable of discernment; it has tact and lightness of touch; it can select, and it can divine. More than that, it can divine better than the conscious ego, since it succeeds where the latter fails. In a word, is not the subliminal ego superior to the conscious ego? The importance of this question will be readily understood. In a recent lecture, M. Boutroux showed how it had arisen on entirely different occasions, and what consequences would be involved by an answer in the affirmative. (See also the same author's *Science et Religion*, pp. 313ff.) Are we forced to give this affirmative answer by the facts I have just stated? I confess that, for my part, I should be loth to accept it. Let us, then, return to the facts, and see if they do not admit of some other explanation. It is certain that the combinations which present themselves to the mind in a kind of sudden illumination after a somewhat prolonged period of unconscious work are generally useful and fruitful combinations, which appear to be the result of a preliminary sifting. Does it follow from this that the subliminal ego, having divined by a delicate intuition that these combinations could be useful, has formed none but these, or has it formed a great many others which were devoid of interest, and remained unconscious? Under this second aspect, all the combinations are formed as a result of the automatic action of the subliminal ego, but those only which are interesting find their way into the field of consciousness. This, too, is most mysterious. How can we explain the fact that, of the thousand products of our unconscious activity, some are invited to cross the threshold, while others remain outside? Is it mere chance that gives them this privilege? Evidently not. For instance, of all the excitements of our senses, it is only the most intense that retain our attention, unless it has been directed upon them by other causes.

More commonly the privileged unconscious phenomena, those that are capable of becoming conscious, are those which, directly or indirectly, most deeply affect our sensibility.

(p. 59) It may appear surprising that sensibility should be introduced in connexion with mathematical demonstrations, which, it would seem, can only interest the intellect. But not if we bear in mind the feeling of mathematical beauty, of the harmony of numbers and forms and of geometric elegance. It is a real aesthetic feeling that all true mathematicians recognize, and this is truly sensibility. Now, what are the mathematical entities to which we attribute this character of beauty and elegance, which are capable of developing in us a kind of aesthetic emotion? Those whose elements are harmoniously arranged so that the mind can, without effort, take in the whole without neglecting the details. This harmony is at once a satisfaction to our aesthetic requirements, and an assistance to the mind which it supports and guides. At the same time, by setting before our eyes a well-ordered whole, it gives us a presentiment of a mathematical law. Now, as I have said above, the only mathematical facts worthy of retaining our attention and capable of being useful are those which can make us acquainted with a mathematical law. Accordingly we arrive at the following conclusion. The useful combinations are precisely the most beautiful, I mean those that can most charm that special sensibility that all mathematicians know, but of which laymen are so ignorant that they are often tempted to smile at it. What follows, then? Of the very large number of combinations which the subliminal ego blindly forms, almost all are without interest and without utility. But, for that very reason, they are without action on the aesthetic sensibility; the consciousness will never know them. A few only are harmonious, and consequently at once useful and beautiful, and they will be capable of affecting the geometrician's special sensibility I have been speaking of; which, once aroused, will direct our attention upon them, and will thus give them the opportunity of becoming conscious.

(p. 60) This is only a hypothesis, and yet there is an observation which tends to confirm it. When a sudden illumination invades the mathematician's mind, it most frequently happens that it does not mislead him. But it also happens sometimes, as I have said, that it will not stand the test of verification. Well, it is to be observed almost always that this false idea, if it had been correct, would have flattered our natural instinct for mathematical elegance. Thus it is this special aesthetic sensibility that plays the part of the delicate sieve of which I spoke above, and this makes it sufficiently clear why the man who has it not will never be a real discoverer. All the difficulties, however, have not disappeared. The conscious ego is strictly limited, but as regards the subliminal ego, we do not know its limitations, and that is why we are not too loth to suppose that in a brief space of time it can form more different combinations than could be comprised in the whole life of a conscient being. These limitations do exist, however. Is it conceivable that it can form all the possible combinations, whose number staggers the imagination? Nevertheless this would seem to be necessary, for if it produces only a small portion of the combinations, and that by chance, there will be very small likelihood of the right one, the one that must be selected, being found among them. Perhaps we must look for the explanation in that period of preliminary conscious work which always precedes all fruitful unconscious work.

(p. 61) If I may be permitted a crude comparison, let us represent the future elements of our combinations as something resembling Epicurus's hooked atoms. When the mind is in complete repose these atoms are immovable; they are, so to speak, attached to the wall. This complete repose may continue indefinitely without the atoms meeting, and, consequently, without the possibility of the formation of any combination. On the other hand, during a period of apparent repose, but of unconscious work, some of them are detached from the wall and set in motion. They plough through space in all directions, like a swarm of gnats, for instance, or, if we prefer a more learned comparison, like the gaseous molecules in the kinetic theory of gases. Their mutual collisions may then produce new combinations.

What is the part to be played by the preliminary conscious work? Clearly it is to liberate some of these atoms, to detach them from the wall and set them in motion. We think we have accomplished nothing, when we have stirred up the elements in a thousand different ways to try to arrange them, and have not succeeded in finding a satisfactory arrangement. But after this agitation imparted to them by our will, they do not return to their original repose, but continue to circulate freely. Now our will did not select them at random, but in pursuit of a perfectly definite aim. Those it has liberated are not, therefore, chance atoms; they are those from which we may reasonably expect the desired solution. The liberated atoms will then experience collisions, either with each other or with the atoms that have remained stationary, which they will run against in their course. I apologize once more. My comparison is very crude, but I cannot well see how I could explain my thought in any other way.

(p. 62) However it be, the only combinations that have any chance of being formed are those in which one at least of the elements is one of the atoms deliberately selected by our will. Now it is evidently among these that what I called just now the right combination is to be found. Perhaps there is here a means of modifying what was paradoxical in the original hypothesis. Yet another observation. It never happens that unconscious work supplies ready-made the result of a lengthy calculation in which we have only to apply fixed rules. It might be supposed that the subliminal ego, purely automatic as it is, was peculiarly fitted for this kind of work, which is, in a sense, exclusively mechanical. It would seem that, by thinking overnight of the factors of a multiplication sum, we might hope to find the product ready-made for us on waking; or, again, that an algebraical calculation, for instance, or a verification could be made unconsciously. Observation proves that such is by no means the case. All that we can hope from these inspirations, which are the fruits of unconscious work, is to obtain points of departure for such calculations. As for the calculations themselves, they must be made in the second period of conscious work which follows the inspiration, and in which the results of the inspiration are verified and the consequences deduced. The rules of these calculations are strict and complicated; they demand discipline, attention, will, and consequently consciousness. In the subliminal ego, on the contrary, there reigns what I would call liberty, if one could give this name to the mere absence of discipline and to disorder born of chance. Only, this very disorder permits of unexpected couplings.

(p. 63) I will make one last remark. When I related above some personal observations, I spoke of a night of excitement, on which I worked as though in spite of myself. The cases of this are frequent, and it is not necessary that the abnormal cerebral activity should be caused by a physical stimulant, as in the case quoted. Well, it appears that, in these cases, we are ourselves assisting at our own unconscious work, which becomes partly perceptible to the overexcited consciousness, but does not on that account change its nature. We then become vaguely aware of what distinguishes the two mechanisms, or, if you will, of the methods of working of the two egos. The psychological observations I have thus succeeded in making appear to me, in their general characteristics, to confirm the views I have been enunciating. Truly there is great need of this, for in spite of everything they are and remain largely hypothetical. The interest of the question is so great that I do not regret having submitted them to the reader.

Commentary

As the reader surely realized, Henri Poincaré describes the creative thinking process from the point of view of personal experience, with vivid words and a clear mind, certainly influenced by the intellectual turmoil existing at the turn of the 20th century, a time in which many paradigms were being shifted. We will comment on the selected text by following the order in which Poincaré himself presented the material.

PROBLEM SELECTION

In Chapters 1 and 2, Poincaré (1914) analyzes how a scientist comes to the decision of working on some specific facts, which we can interpret as the fundamental step of problem selection and definition of an attentive focus (Corazza & Agnoli, 2016, 2018). It is very interesting to note that even in those times there where "prophets of ill," that is, those who believed that all problems worthy of effort had been solved, and that "after them there would be nothing left but gleanings" (Poincaré, 1914, p. 25). This is a recurring illusion in the human species, the somewhat pessimistic belief that everything has been discovered, invented, artistically produced, and the future is much poorer than the past in terms of opportunities. Luckily this is never true, and Poincaré himself shows great confidence in the progress of humanity's cumulative culture by stating that "the pessimists found themselves continually passed over" (p. 26). So what are the problems which are worth tackling by the scientist? On page 27 Poincaré sets a clear demarcation between science and engineering (see also Corazza & Agnoli, 2018). declaring that "physicists do not study a phenomenon until some pressing need of material life makes it an absolute necessity, and they are quite right." Also, in Chapter 1 at page 22: "The scientist does not study nature because it is useful. . . . He takes pleasure in it because it is beautiful." Aesthetic value becomes the driving force in problem selection, but it is not a generic sense of beauty that Poincaré is referring to. He makes this very clear on page 31 of Chapter 2: "This aesthetic satisfaction is . . . connected with the economy of thought." Beautiful discoveries are those that "introduce order into . . . complexity, and so make it accessible to us" (p. 30). And on page 32: "It is not order only, but unexpected order, that has a value." This is a clear reference to the fact that the important problems are ill-defined in some form, so that the solution is necessarily nonobvious and unexpected in some form. Also, it is very interesting to note that, by discussing the order that emerges out of complexity, Poincaré appears to be anticipating the modern theory of complex systems. Further, Poincaré notes another important characteristic of facts which are worthy of the scientist's attention: "They are the facts which permit . . . innovations of language. The bare fact . . . has sometimes no great interest. . . ; it only acquires a value when some more careful thinker perceives the connection it brings out, and symbolizes it by a term" (p. 34). Finally, Chapter 2 closes with considerations that Poincaré makes about the fact that science is becoming more and more specialized, with the danger of building walls between territories, hopefully overcome by exchange of information. One cannot help but notice the prophetic value of Poincaré's statements.

PROCESS PHASES: PREPARATION, INCUBATION, ILLUMINATION, VERIFICATION

Without a doubt, Chapter 3 of *Science and Method* is by far the most relevant contribution by Poincaré to creativity studies. Indeed in the landmark book *The Art of Thought* by Graham Wallas (1926), Poincaré is cited eight times and *Science and Method* three times. For example, on page 80, Wallas discusses how

> Henri Poincaré . . . in the book *Science and Method* . . . describes in vivid detail the successive stages of two of his great mathematical discoveries. Both of them came to him after a period of Incubation . . . during which no conscious mathematical thinking was done, but, as Poincaré believed, much unconscious mental exploration took place. In both cases Incubation was preceded by a Preparation stage of hard, conscious, systematic, and fruitless analysis of the problem. In both cases the final idea came to him "with the same characteristics of conciseness, suddenness, and immediate certainty" (Poincaré, 1914, p. 54). Each was followed by a period of Verification, in which both the validity of the idea was tested, and the idea itself was reduced to exact form.

In essence, the four-stage model for the creative thinking process by Wallas (1926, p. 79) can be considered an almost direct derivation from Chapter 3 of *Science and Method*, and also supported by the reported speech by the German physicist Helmholtz at the banquet for his seventieth birthday.

This four-stage model, or Wallas' model, as it became to be known, has had a great influence on the creativity literature, both scientific and practice-oriented. For example, some of the first empirical studies of artists and writers engaged in the creative process, conducted by Catherine Patrick (1935, 1937), are based on the Poincaré-Wallas stages. Several decades passed before alternative models would appear, such as those proposed by Guilford (1950, 1967) and later by Mumford et al. (1991). This is both interesting and surprising, if one considers the fact that the contemporary fellow scientist Jacques Hadamard, an acclaimed mathematician in his own right, comments in his book *The Mathematical Mind* (Hadamard, 1945):

> Conditions of invention have been investigated by the greatest genius which our science has known during the last half century. . . . But that extraordinary fact of watching passively, as it from the outside, the evolution of subconscious ideas seems to be quite special to [Poincaré]. I have never experienced that marvellous sensation, nor have I ever heard of its happening to others.

A similar limiting disclaimer was reported by Toulouse (1909, p. 187): "This method of work is not common in science matters, and constitutes a very special mental activity of M. Henri Poincaré." This raises a question in the scientific literature, which is relevant here for creativity studies: how to navigate between introspective reports (with Poincaré's experience contested by Hadamard's and Toulouse's observations) and explicit scientific models of the creative thinking process (see Lubart, 2001).

IDEATION AND SELECTION
THROUGH COMBINATION AND AESTHETICS

Another aspect that is certainly worth mentioning is that Poincaré points clearly to a mechanism for the generation of candidate ideas, which is the combination of elements that have been elicited in the preparation stage. However:

> mathematical discovery . . . does not [simply] consist in making new combinations. . . . [T]he combinations that could be formed would be infinite in number, and the greater part of them would be absolutely of no interest. Discovery . . . consists in constructing those that are useful, which are an infinitely small minority. Discovery is discernment, selection. (p. 49)

Poincaré's specification on page 51 is noteworthy: "Among the combinations we choose, the most fruitful are often those which are formed of elements borrowed from widely separate domains." And in Poincaré's model, the unfruitful combinations remain below the level of awareness, whereas only those that satisfy the aesthetic criteria that the scientist appreciates emerge to the level of conscience. Note that the picture drawn by Poincaré of the evolution taking place in the creative thinking process is very much in line with the dynamic definition of creativity (Corazza, 2016), whereby the process involves a wide search in general characterized by creative inconclusiveness, and only a few events (an infinitely small minority, in Poincaré's words) can correspond to a creative achievement once properly verified. This somewhat random combination of mathematical ideas and aesthetically guided selection is a predecessor to the later blind variation and selective retention model (Campbell, 1960; Simonton, 2011) of the creative process.

DIRECTIONS FOR THE FUTURE

Poincaré's text is a major historical source for two main issues that have fostered and continue to attract attention in creativity research. First, Poincaré highlighted the domains of science and mathematics as creative endeavors. This conception, even today, is not frequently found in societal conceptions nor in educational programs concerning science and math. Second, Poincaré set the stage for most of the work on the creative process in the past century. The "four-stage" and "blind variation and selective retention" models continue to be investigated. Indeed, Poincaré's text offers us the opportunity to reflect on the role and importance of introspective accounts in scientific reflection. Future research will benefit from further discussion on Poincaré's text and might explore in greater detail some issues raised by Poincaré, such as the special nature of mathematical creativity, which has received relatively little attention, and further debates on the basic nature of the creative process in math, science, and numerous other disciplines.

References

Campbell, D. T. (1960). Blind variation and selective retention in creative thought as in other knowledge processes. *Psychological Review, 67*, 380–400.

Corazza, G. E. (2016). Potential originality and effectiveness: The dynamic definition of creativity. *Creativity Research Journal, 28*(3), 258–267.

Corazza, G. E., & Agnoli, S. (2016). On the path towards the science of creative thinking. In G. E. Corazza & S. Agnoli (Eds.), *Multidisciplinary contributions to the science of creative thinking* (pp. 3–19). Singapore: Springer.

Corazza, G.E., & Agnoli, S. (2018). The creative process in science and engineering. In T. Lubart (Ed.), *The Creative Process* (pp. 155–180). London: Palgrave Macmillan.

Guilford, J. P. (1950). Creativity. *American Psychologist, 5,* 444–454.

Guilford, J. P (1967). *The nature of human intelligence.* New York: McGraw-Hill.

Hadamard, J. (1945). *The mathematical mind.* Princeton, NJ: Princeton Science Library.

Lubart, T. (2001). Models of the creative process: Past, present and future, *Creativity Research Journal, 13*(3–4), 295–308.

Mumford, M. D., Mobley, M. I., Uhlman, C. E., Reiter-Palmon, R., & Doares, L. M. (1991). Process analytic models of creative capacities. *Creativity Research Journal, 4,* 91–122.

Patrick, C. (1935). Creative thought in poets. *Archives of Psychology, 178,* 1–74.

Patrick, C. (1937). Creative thought in artists. *Journal of Psychology, 4,* 35–73.

Poincaré, H. (1902). *La science et l'hypothése.* Paris: Flammarion.

Poincaré, H. (1905). *La valeur de la science.* Paris: Flammarion.

Poincaré, H. (1908). *Science et méthode.* Paris: Flammarion.

Poincaré, H., (1914). *Science and method* (Francis Maitland, Trans.). Preface by Bertrand Russell. London: Thomas Nelson & Sons. Original archived at Cornell University Library.

Simonton, D. K. (2011). Creativity and discovery as blind variation: Campbell's (1960) BVSR model after the half-century mark. *Review of General Psychology, 15*(2), 158–174.

Toulouse, E. (1909). *Henri Poincaré.* Paris: Flammarion.

Wallas, G. (1926). *The art of thought.* New York: Harcourt, Brace.

Weinstein, G. (2012). A biography of Henri Poincaré: 2012 centenary of the death of Poincaré. arXiv preprint, Cornell University Library, arXiv:1207.0759. https://arxiv.org/abs/1207.0759.

Inspiration or Perspiration? Reflections on Edwin Prindle's "The Art of Inventing"

David H. Cropley

Summary

Edwin Prindle was both a mechanical engineer and a patent lawyer. The publication under consideration here is a paper presented at the 23rd annual convention of the American Institute of Electrical Engineers, one of the forerunners of today's Institute of Electrical and Electronics Engineers, which boasts more than 150,000 members around the world. It is fair to say, then, that Prindle wrote on the subject of inventing with some authority. His contribution, however, lies not so much in the extent that he influenced others in the field—indeed his paper has been cited a mere 21 times in over 100 years (including a number by this author)—but in what it says about a general failure to integrate closely related concepts across disciplines and thereby advance each more rapidly.

Introduction

Edwin Prindle (1868–1948) practiced patent law, first as an employee of the US Patent Office (until 1899) and then in a private capacity from 1905. He held senior posts on patent committees in both the National Research Council and the American Chemical Society. Perhaps the most striking thing about his work in relation to creativity is the primacy of the concept of *commercial value*: inventions are of interest only insofar as they are patentable, and patentable inventions must have, first and foremost, commercial value.

It would be unfair to Prindle to present this driving mindset in a negative light. His business, after all, was patents and the role these play in the creation of wealth. Nevertheless there is a sense, detectable in his writing, that creativity is merely a means to an end—and not even simply the goal of making money from inventions but of stopping others from doing so.

Prindle (1906, p. 465) tells us that "the engineer is concerned with things having a commercial value." I would argue strongly—supported by the Accreditation Board for Engineering and Technology—that engineers are concerned, principally, with developing "ways to utilize, economically, the materials and forces of nature for the benefit of mankind" (Cropley, 2017, p. 213). Commercial value is a secondary motivation and a happy byproduct. The earliest, prehistoric "engineers" did not fashion tools from stone or build shelters from mud bricks because they thought they could corner a market. They did so out of necessity—to satisfy a need or solve a problem. I believe (Cropley, 2015) that this same fundamental impetus remains the underpinning motivation for creativity and innovation, today as much as it was thousands of years ago.

Prindle's chief motivation for understanding the art of invention therefore was economic. "Patents are the best and most effective ways of controlling competition" (Noble, 1979, p. 89). Does this really matter? Probably not, because Prindle (1906, p. 466) *does* state one of the key concerns of all creativity research: regardless of the motivation, "it becomes a matter of much interest to know how inventions are produced." Indeed after flirting with the question of why we invent (to control competition, to benefit the human race), Prindle spends the majority of his paper addressing the question of how.

Prindle's contribution, in fact, is (at least) threefold. First, he identifies the fact that invention is a *process*. More than that, he hints at stages of the process that are recognizably convergent and divergent in nature. Second, he suggests that there are psychological factors at play over the course of this process. Third, he understands that knowledge is, in the words of Sternberg (2007), a double-edged sword: too much can constrain the inventor, while too little may make invention impossible.

For this reason, and notwithstanding his very commercial motivations, Prindle's work is an important and early signpost in our understanding not only of creativity but also of the role creativity plays in the broader process of innovation.

Reading: "The Art of Inventing"

Source: Prindle, E. J. (1906). The art of inventing. *Transactions of the American Institute for Engineering Education, 25,* 519–547. Reproduced in whole with the permission of the Institute of Electrical and Electronics Engineers.

There are many kinds of invention. The poet, the artist, the playwright, the novelist all exercise or may exercise invention in the production of their works. The merchant may exercise invention in the devising of a new method of selling goods. The department store was an invention of this class.

The subject of my paper is, however, the art of making technical inventions, and particularly patentable inventions. And, first, of its commercial importance; for the engineer is concerned with things having a commercial value. By the art of inventing, wealth is created absolutely out of ideas alone. It usually takes capital to develop an invention and make it productive, but not always. A notable recent example is Professor Pupin's loaded telephone line. He received a very large sum of money, and his expenditures, as I understand, were comparatively trivial.

The certificate of ownership of an invention is a patent, and the importance of the art of invention will be made apparent from a brief consideration of what rights a patent confers and of the part that patents play in the industries.

A patent is the most perfect form of monopoly recognized by the law. As was said in a recent decision:

> Within his domain, the patentee is czar. The people must take the invention on the terms he dictates or let it alone for seventeen years. This is a necessity from the nature of the grant. Cries of restraint of trade and impairment of the freedom of sales are unavailing, because for the promotion of the useful arts the constitution and statutes authorize this very monopoly.

There is an enormous amount of wealth in this country that is based upon patents. As an instance, might be mentioned the fact that the United Shoe Machinery Company is, by means of patents, able to control the sewing machines upon which ninety per cent of the welt shoes in the United States are sewed. The Bell Telephone Company, and the Westinghouse Air Brake Company and many other corporations of the first importance built themselves up on patents. Patents have become so well recognized a factor in commerce that, in many lines of manufacture, concerns do not depend simply upon cheapness of manufacture, or quality of product, to maintain their trade, but they count on always having a product which is at least slightly better than that of their competitors, and which is covered by patents, so that they do not have to compete with an article of equal merit. And they keep a corps of inventors at work in a constant effort to improve the product, so that, when the patents now giving protection have expired, they will have a better article to offer, which shall also be protected by patents.

Inventing has become almost a recognized profession. Many large concerns constantly employ a large corps of inventors, at liberal salaries. Besides the inventors employed by large corporations, there are many inventors who have maintained their independence, and are free lances, so to speak. Some inventors have become wealthy almost solely by their inventions, such as Edison, Bell, Westinghouse, Marconi, Pupin, Tesla, and Sprague. A considerable number of the smaller manufacturing concerns are built largely or wholly upon the inventions of their principal owners.

Aside from the question of financial returns from inventing, the inventor has the satisfaction of knowing that he is a producer of the most fundamental kind. All material progress has involved the production of inventions. Inventors are universally conceded to be among the greatest benefactors of the human race.

The art of invention is therefore one of great commercial and economical importance, and it becomes a matter of much interest to know how inventions are produced. It is my object to attempt an explanation of the manner of their production.

If it be inquired on what grounds I offer an explanation of this apparently most difficult subject, I reply that, in the practice of patent law, I have often had occasion and opportunity to inquire into the mental processes of inventors, and that the subject is one to which I have given considerable attention.

It seems to be popularly believed that the inventor must be born to his work, and that such people are born only occasionally. This is true, to a certain extent, but I am convinced there are many people who, without suspecting it, have latent inventive abilities, which could be put to work if they only knew how to go about it. The large percentage of inventors in this country compared with all other countries, shows that the inventive faculty is one which can be cultivated to some extent. The difference in ingenuity is not wholly a matter of race, for substantially the same blood exists in some other countries, but it is the encouragement of our patent laws that has stimulated the cultivation of this faculty.

The popular idea seems to be that an invention is produced by its inventor at a single effort of the imagination and complete, as Minerva sprang full-grown and fully armed from the mind of Jove.

It is, undoubtedly, true that every inventor must have some imagination or creative faculty, but, as I shall seek to show, this faculty may be greatly assisted by method. While reasoning does not constitute the whole of an inventive act, it can, so to speak, clear the way and render the inventive act easier of accomplishment.

Invention has been defined as "In the nature of a guess; the mind leaps across a logical chasm. Instead of working out a conclusion, it imagines it." The courts have repeatedly held that that which could be produced *purely* by the process of reasoning or inference, on the part of one ordinarily skilled in the art is not patentable, but that the imaginative or creative faculty must somewhere be used in the process. The mind must somewhere leap from the known to the unknown by means of the imagination, and not by mere inference in making the invention. But the inventor, consciously or unconsciously, by proper method, reduces the length of this leap to much more moderate proportions than is popularly supposed.

That reasoning and research frequently enter very largely into the inventive act in aid of the creative faculty is the opinion of Dr. Trowbridge, of Columbia University, who said:

> Important inventions leading to widespread improvements in the arts or to new industries do not come by chance, or as sudden inspiration, but are in almost every instance the result of long and exhaustive researches by men whose thorough familiarity with their subjects enables them to see clearly the way to improvements. Almost all important and successful inventions which have found their way into general use and acceptance have been the products of well-balanced and thoughtful minds, capable of patient laborious investigation.

Judge Drummond, in a decision many years ago, said:

> Most inventions are the result of experiment, trial, and effort, are few of them are worked out by mere will.

Most inventions are an evolution from some previously invented form. It has been said:

> We know exactly how the human mind works. The unknown—or unknowable—it always conceives in terms of the known.

Even the imagination conceives in terms of what is already known; that is, the product of the imagination is a transformation of material already possessed. Imagination is the association in new relations of ideas already possessed by the mind. It is impossible to imagine that, the elements of which are not already known to us. We cannot conceive of a color which does not consist of a blending of one or more colors with which we are already familiar. This evolution of an invention is more or less logical, and is often worked out by logical processes to such an extent that the steps or efforts of imagination are greatly reduced as compared with the effort of producing the invention solely by the imagination.

Edison is quoted as having said that "any man can become an inventor if he has imagination and pertinacity," that "invention is not so much inspiration as perspiration."

There are four classes of protectable inventions. These are
Arts,
Machines,
Manufactures, and
Compositions of matter.

In popular language an art may be said to be any process or series of steps or operations for accomplishing a physical or chemical result. Examples are the art of telephoning by causing undulations of the electric current corresponding to the sound waves of the spoken voice. The art of casting car wheels, which consists in directing the metal into the mold in a stream running tangentially instead of radially, so that the metal in the mold is given a rotary movement, and the heavy, sound metal flows out to the rim of the wheel, while the light and defective metal is displaced toward the centre, where it is not subjected to wear.

The term machine hardly needs any explanation. It may be said to be an assemblage of two or more mechanical elements, having a law of action of its own.

A manufacture is anything made by the hand of man, which is neither a machine nor a composition of matter; such as, a chisel, a match, or a pencil.

The term composition of matter covers all combinations of two or more substances, whether by mechanical mixture or chemical union, and whether they be gases, fluids, powders or solids; such as, a new cement or paint.

These definitions are not legally exact, but serve to illustrate the meaning.

In the making of all inventions which do not consist in the discovery of the adaptability of some means to an end not intentionally being sought after, the first step is the selection of a problem. The inventor should first make certain that the problem is based upon a real need. Much time and money is sometimes spent in an effort to invent something that is not really needed. What already exists is good enough or is so good that no additional cost or complication would justify anything better. The new invention might be objectionable because it would involve counter disadvantages more important than its own advantages, so that a really desirable object is the first thing to be sure of.

Having selected a problem, the next step should be a thorough analysis of the old situation, getting at the reasons for the faults which exist, and in fact discovering the presence of faults which are not obvious to others, because of the tendency to believe that whatever is, is right.

Then the qualities of the material, and the laws of action under which one must operate should be exhaustively considered. It should be considered whether these laws are really or only apparently inflexible. It should be carefully considered whether further improvement is possible for the same direction, and such consideration will often suggest the direction in which further improvement must go; if a change of direction is necessary sometimes the only possible improvement is in an opposite direction. A glance at the accounts of how James Watt invented the condensing steam-engine will show what a large part profound study of the old engine and of the laws of steam played in his invention, and how strongly they suggested the directions of the solutions of his difficulties.

We now come to the constructive part of inventing, in order to illustrate which, I will seek to explain how several inventions were, or could have been, produced.

The way in which the first automatic steam engine was produced was undoubtedly this—and it shows how comparatively easily a really great invention may sometimes be made. It was the duty of Humphrey Potter, a *boy*, to turn a stopcock to let the steam into the cylinder and one to let in water to condense it at certain periods of each stroke of the engine, and if this were not done at the right time, the engine would stop. He noticed that these movements of the stopcock handles took place in unison with the movements of certain portions of the beam of the engine. He simply connected the valve handles with the proper portions of the beam by strings, and the engine became automatic—a most eventful result.

As one example of the evolution of an invention, I will take an instrument for measuring and recording a period of time, known as the calculograph, because it lends itself with facility, to an explanation from a platform and because my duties as a lawyer have necessitated my becoming very familiar with the invention, and have caused me to consider how it was probably produced.

And first the problem: There was much occasion to determine and record the values of periods of elapsed time; such as, the length of time of a telephone conversation; as the revenue of the telephone companies depended upon the accuracy of the determination. All the previous methods involved the recording in hours and minutes the times of day marking the initial and the final limits of the period to be measured, and then the subtraction of the one time of day from the other. This subtraction was found to be very unreliable as well as expensive. The problem then was to devise some way by which the value of the period could be arrived at directly and without subtraction and also by which such value could be mechanically recorded.

The prior machine from which the calculograph was evolved is the time-stamp, a printing machine having a stationary die like a clock dial and having a rotating die like the hand of the clock, as in Figure 4.1. The small triangle outside the dial is the hour hand, it being placed outside the dial because it is necessary that the two hands shall be at the level of the face of the dial and yet be able to pass each other. The hour hand may be disregarded here, as the records needed are almost never an hour long. The manner of using the time stamp to determine the value of an interval was to stamp the time of day at the beginning of the period, and then to stamp the time of day at the close of the period at another place on the paper, as shown in Figure 4.2, and finally mentally to subtract the one time of day from the other to get the value of the period.

The inventor of the new machine conceived the idea that, if the time-stamp were provided with guides or gauges so that the card could be placed both times in the same position, and the two records of the time stamp thus be superimposed concentrically (as illustrated

FIGURE 4.1 **Time stamp record.**

in Figure 4.3), the value of the period would be represented by the arc marked off by the initial and final imprints of the minute hand, so that, instead of subtracting one record from another, he had only to find the value of the arc marked off by counting the corresponding number of minutes along the dial.

The inventor had thus gotten rid of the subtraction, but there were several desirable qualities not yet obtained. First, he could not tell from the record alone, whether it was the longer or the shorter arc marked off that was the measure of the period. For instance, he could not tell whether the period was 7 or 53 minutes. This was because the two hand or pointer imprints were exactly alike except in position. So he conceived the idea of making the pointer imprints different in appearance, by providing the pointer die with a mark in line with the pointer, as illustrated in Figure 4.4.

The mark and pointer revolve together, and either the dies or the platen are so arranged that the mark can be printed without the pointer at the initial imprint and the pointer at the final imprint as in Figure 4.5, the mark being printed or not at the final imprint, as desired. This could be done either by allowing the pointer die or the corresponding portion of the platen to remain retracted from the paper during the first printing.

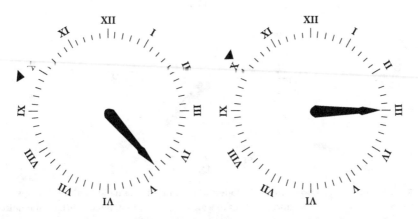

FIGURE 4.2 **To read this record, hours and minutes must be subtracted from hours and minutes, an operation liable to much error.**

FIGURE 4.3 Subtraction eliminated but counting still required and uncertainty whether elapsed period is 7 or 53 minutes.

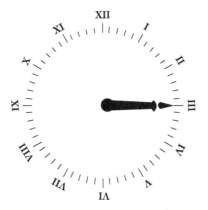

FIGURE 4.4 Hand and zero mark revolving within stationary dial.

FIGURE 4.5 Initial imprint of zero mark alone and final imprint of hand (and zero). Elapsed time, 8 minutes. No subtraction and no uncertainty as to which imprint is first, but counting still required.

It could thus be told with certainty from the record alone whether the longer or the shorter arc is the measure of the period, because the beginning of the arc is that indicated by the imprint of the mark without the pointer.

There was still something to be desired. The counting of the minutes along the measuring arc was a waste of time, if the value of the arc could in some way be directly indicated. If the hand were set back to 12 o'clock for the initial imprint, the final imprint would show the hand pointing directly at the minute whose number on the dial is the value of the period, and it would not even be necessary to count. But the setting of the hand back to zero would prevent its making the final imprint of any previously begun record, so that the machine could only be used for one record at a time.

It was desirable to have a machine that would record any number of overlapping intervals at the same time, so that one machine would record the intervals of all the telephone conversations under the control of a single operator, or rather of two operators, because both of them could reach the same machine.

So it wouldn't do to set the hand back to zero, as the hand must rotate constantly and uniformly. Then why not set the zero up to the hand at each initial imprint? This meant making the dial rotatable, as well as the hand. It gave an initial record like that shown in Figure 4.6.

The inventor then thought of securing the dial to the pointer die so that they would revolve together, the zero of the dial being in line with the pointer, as illustrated in Figure 4.7. This would obviate the necessity of setting the zero of the dial up to the pointer at the initial imprint.

But again the improvement involved a difficulty. As the dial rotated, its final impressions would never register with its initial impressions and would therefore always destroy them.

As the first imprint of the dial was the only useful one, and as the second imprint only made trouble, the inventor conceived the idea of not making any imprint of the dial at the close of the period, and this he accomplished by making the annular portion of the platen covering the dial so that it could be advanced to print or not as desired. As the zero of the dial always marked the beginning of the measuring arc, it served the same purpose as the mark in line with the pointer, and the latter could now be omitted.

FIGURE 4.6 **Dial moved up to initial position of zero mark. Elapsed time, 11 minutes. No subtraction, no counting, no uncertainty, but only one record possible at a time.**

FIGURE 4.7 **Dial with pointer at zero revolving together.**

The final machine then consists simply of a revolving die which, as shown in Figure 4.8, consists of a graduated and progressively numbered dial, having a pointer revolving in line with the zero, and the machine has a platen consisting of an inner circular portion over the pointer and an annular portion over the dial, each portion being operated by a separate handle so that the dial can be printed at the beginning of the period and the pointer alone, at its close.

The final record has an initial imprint of the dial, Figure 4.9a, the zero of the dial showing the position of the pointer at the beginning of the period, and a final imprint of the pointer alone, as shown in Figure 4.9b, the complete final record, Figure 4.9c, consisting of the superimposition of these two records, and showing the pointer in line with that graduation whose number is the value of the period. Here is a record not only involving no subtraction and no uncertainty but not even, counting in its record, and, as it was made without disturbing the motions either of the pointer or dial, any number of records of other periods could have been begun or finished while the machine was measuring the period in question.

Hiding all the intermediate steps in the evolution of this invention, it seems the result of spontaneous creation, but considering the steps in their successive order, it will be seen that the invention is an evolution from the time-stamp; that logic rendered the effort of the imagination at any one step small by comparison, and that the individual steps might be

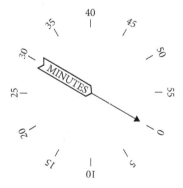

FIGURE 4.8 **Dial with pointer at zero revolving together, zero mark on pointer being replaced by zero of dial.**

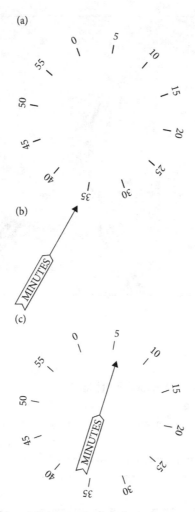

FIGURE 4.9A-C **Simple, direct-reading record. No subtraction, no counting, no uncertainty. Any number of overlapping periods recorded on one machine.**

well within the capacity of a person to whom the spontaneous creation of the final invention might be utterly impossible.

A most interesting example of the evolution of an invention is that of the cord-knotter of the self-binding harvester.

The problem here was to devise a mechanism which would take place of the human hands in tying a knot in a cord whose ends had mechanically been brought together around a bundle of grain.

The first step was to select the knot which could be tied by the simplest motions.

The knot which the inventor selected is that shown in Figure 4.10, and is a form of bow-knot.

The problem was to find how this knot could be tied with the smallest number of fingers, making the smallest number of simple movements. As anyone would ordinarily tie even this simple knot, the movements would be so numerous and complex as to seem impossible

FIGURE 4.10

of performance by mechanism. The inventor, by study of his problem, found that this knot could be tied by the use of only two fingers of one hand, and by very simple movements.

The knot will best be understood by following the motions of these fingers in tying the knot. Using the first and second fingers of the right hand, they are first swept outward and backward in a circular path against the two strands of the cord to be tied, as shown in Figure 4.11.

The fingers continue in their circular motion backward, so that the strands of the cord are wrapped around these fingers, as shown in Figure 4.12.

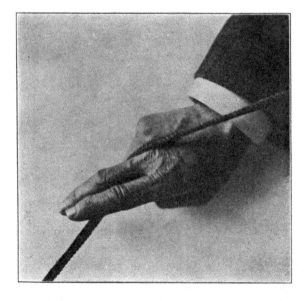

FIGURE 4.11

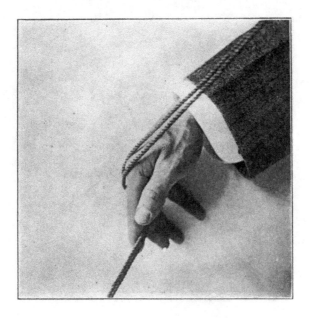

FIGURE 4.12

Continuing their circular motion, the fingers approach the strands of the cord between the twisted portion and a part of the machine which holds the ends of the cord, and the fingers spread apart as shown in Figure 4.13, so that they can pass over and grasp the strands thus approached, as shown in Figure 4.14.

The fingers then draw back through the loop which has been formed about them, the fingers holding the grasped portion of the strands, as shown in Figure 4.15.

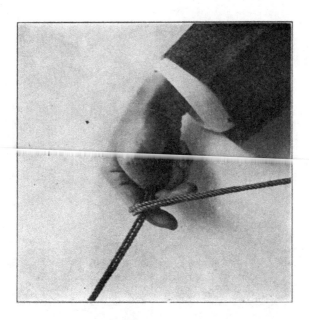

FIGURE 4.13

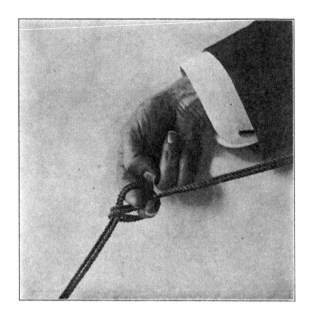

FIGURE 4.14

The knot is finished by the completion of the retracting movement of the fingers through the loop, thus forming the bow of the knot as shown in Figure 4.16.

The inventor found that one finger could have a purely rotary movement, as if it were fixed on the arm and unable to move independently of the arm, and the movement being as if the arm rotated like a shaft, but the second finger must be further capable of moving toward and from the first finger to perform the opening movement of Figure 4.13, and the closing movement of Figure 4.14 by which it grasps the cord. The inventor accordingly, from

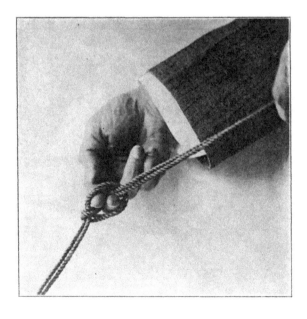

FIGURE 4.15

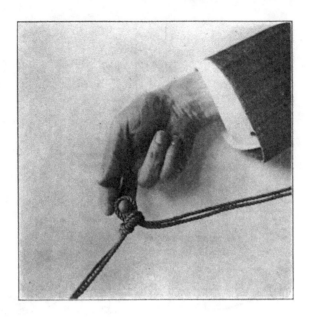

FIGURE 4.16

his exhaustive analysis of his problem, and his invention or discovery of the proper finger motions, had further only to devise the very simple mechanical device illustrated in Figure 4.17 to replace his fingers.

The index finger of the hand is represented by the finger *S,* which is integral with the shaft *V.* The second finger of the hand is represented by the finger *0,* which is pivoted to the first finger by the pins. The grasping movement of the finger *U* is accomplished by a spring *V'* bearing on the shank *U',* and its opening movement is caused by the travel of an antifriction roll *U",* on the rear end of the pivoted finger, over a cam *V",* on the bearing of the shaft. The shaft is rotated by the turning of a bevel pinion *W* on the shaft through the action of an intermittent gear. The necessity of drawing the fingers backward to accomplish the movement between Figures 4.14 and 4.16 was avoided by causing the tied bundle to have a motion away from the fingers as it is expelled from the machine, the relative motion between the fingers and the knot being the same as if the fingers drew back.

Thus the accomplishment of a seemingly almost impossible function was rendered mechanically simple by an evolution from the human hand, after an exhaustive and ingenious analysis of the conditions involved.

It will be seen from the examples I have given that the constructive part of inventing consists of evolution, and it is the association of previously known elements in new relations (using the term elements in its broadest sense). The results of such new association may, themselves, be treated as elements of the next stage of development, but in the last analysis nothing is invented or created absolutely out of nothing.

It must also be apparent, that pure reason and method, while not taking the place of the inventive faculty, can clear the way for the exercise of that faculty and very greatly reduce the demands upon it.

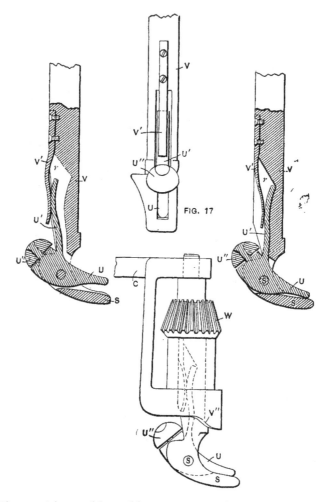

FIGURE 4.17 The essential parts of the cord-knotter.

Where it is desired to make a broadly new invention on fundamentally different lines from those before, having first studied the art to find the results needed, the qualities of the material or other absolutely controlling conditions should be exhaustively considered; but at the time of making the inventive effort, the details should be dismissed from the mind of how results already obtained in the art were gotten. One should endeavor to conceive how he would accomplish the desired result if he were attempting the problem before anyone else had ever solved it.

In other words, he should endeavor to provide himself with the idea [of] elements on which the imagination will operate, but to dismiss from his mind as much as possible the old ways in which these elements have been associated, and thus leave his imagination free to associate them in original and, as to be hoped, better relations than before. He should invent all the means he can possibly invent to accomplish the desired result, and should then, before experimenting, go to the art to see whether or not these means have before been invented. He would probably find that some of the elements, at least, have been better worked out than he has worked them out. Of course, mechanical dictionaries, and other sources of mechanical elements and movements will be found useful in arriving at means for accomplishing certain of the motions, if the invention be a machine.

Many important inventions have been made by persons whose occupation is wholly disconnected with the art in which they are inventing, because their minds were not prejudiced by what had already been done. While such an effort is likely to possess more originality than that on the part of a person in the art, there is, of course, less probability of its being thoroughly practical. The mind well stored with the old ways of solving the problem will, of course, be less likely to repeat any of the mistakes of the earlier inventors, but it will also not be as apt to strike out on distinctly original lines. It is so full, already, of the old forms of association of the elements as to be less likely to think of associating them in broadly new relations.

Nothing should be considered impossible until it has been conclusively worked out or tried by experiments which leave no room for doubt. It is no sufficient reason for believing a thing won't work because immemorial tradition, or those skilled in the art, say it will not work.

Many an important improvement has been condemned as impracticable, by those in the art, before it has been tried.

A conception which an inventor has been striving for unsuccessfully will sometimes come to him at a time of unaccustomed mental stimulation. The slight stimulation of the movement of [a] train of cars, and the sound of music, have been known to produce this effect. The sub-conscious mind, after having been prepared by a full consideration of the problem to be solved, will sometimes solve the problem without conscious effort, on the part of the inventor.

In inventing a machine to operate upon any given material, the logical way is to work from the tool to the power. The tool or tools should first be invented, and the motions determined which are to be given to them. The proper gearing or parts to produce from the power each motion for each tool should then be invented. It should then be considered if parts of each train of gearing cannot be combined, so as to make one part do the work of a part in each train; in short, to reduce the machine to its lowest terms. Occasionally a mechanism will be invented which is exceedingly ingenious, but which it is afterwards seen how to simplify, greatly at the expense of its apparent ingenuity. This simplification will be at the sacrifice of the pride of the inventor, but such considerations as cheapness, durability and certainty of action leave no choice in the matter. It will sometimes be found that a single part can be made to actuate several parts, by the interposition of elements which reverse the motion taken from such part, or which take only a component of the motion of such part, or the resultant of the motion of such part and some other part. Where a machine involves the conjoint action of several forces, it can be more thoroughly studied, if it is found there are positions of the machine in which one force or motion only is in operation, the effect of the others in such position being eliminated, and thus the elements making up the resultant effect can be intelligently controlled.

The drawing board can be made a great source of economy in producing inventions. If the three principal views of all the essentially different positions of the parts of a machine are drawn, it will often be found that defects will be brought to light which would not otherwise have been observed until the machine was put into the metal.

It is desirable to see the whole invention clearly in the mind before beginning to draw, but if that cannot be done, it is often of great assistance to draw what can be seen, and the clearer perception given by the study of the parts already drawn, assists the mind in the conception of the remaining parts.

If the improvement which it is sought to make is a process, it should first be considered whether any radically different process can be conceived of, and if so, whether or not it is better than the old process, and the reason for its defects, and whether it is possible to cure those defects. If the old process appears to be in the right general direction, it should be considered whether one of the old steps cannot with advantage be replaced by a new one, or whether the order of performing the steps cannot be changed to advantage. I have in mind one process in which a reversal of the order of steps resulted in giving the product certain desirable qualities which had before been sought for, but could not be obtained.

It is sometimes desirable not only to invent a good process of producing a product, but to control all feasible processes of producing the product. Such a case occurred where the product itself had been patented, and it was desirable to extend the monopoly beyond the time when the patent on the product should expire. There were two steps or operations which were essential to the production of the product, and the inventor, by reference to permutations, saw that there were but three orders in which those steps could be performed; first, the order A-B, then the order B-A, and then both steps together. The order A-B was the old order, which did not produce an article having the desired qualities. The inventor therefore, proceeded to invent ways by which the steps could be performed together, and then by which they could be performed in the reverse order, and the patenting such two processes would cover generically all possible ways of making the article and secure the desired result of putting himself in position to control the monopoly after the patent on the article had expired, because no one could make the article without using one of his two processes.

In inventing compositions of matter there is one inventor who, if he is seeking for a certain result, will take a chemical dictionary and make every possible combination of every substance that could by any possibility be an ingredient of that which he desires to produce. It is as if he were seeking to locate a vein of mineral in a given territory, and, instead of observing the geographical and geological formation, and thus seeking to arrive at the most probable location of the vein, he should dig up every foot of earth throughout the whole territory, in order finally to locate the vein. This method is exceedingly exhaustive, but does not appeal to one as involving much exercise of the inventive faculties.

Inventing has become so much of a science, that if one is willing to spend sufficient time and money to enable a competent corps of inventors to go at the matter exhaustively, almost any possible invention involving but a reasonable advance in the art can be perfected.

Commentary

What Prindle describes as *inventing* unequivocally encompasses what modern thinkers mean by creativity, and there can be little doubt that if one were to talk to him about "the interaction among *aptitude, process, and environment* by which an individual or group produces a *perceptible product* that is both *novel and useful* as defined within a *social context*" (Plucker, Beghetto, & Dow, 2004, p. 90), he would immediately recognize this as familiar territory. Prindle's work, however, goes further than simply the production of novel and useful products and extends to the exploitation of the same, making his description of inventing as much about *innovation* as it is about creativity. Regardless of the exact span of his focus, however, is that fact that he begins by asking a question of inventing that is all too frequently overlooked in modern discussions of both creativity and innovation, and that is the question "Why?" Why do individuals and organizations engage in invention?

Prindle's answer is twofold. What seems to be his principal reason for *why we invent* is rather disappointingly, and pragmatically, capitalistic in nature. The art of inventing, we are told, is about creating wealth out of ideas. More to the point, once conceived, these valuable ideas must be protected, not so much for the good of society as to preserve the financial interests of the owners of the ideas.

Creativity is the source of ideas, and ideas can be exploited—principally for financial gain. This exploitation is made all the more certain if the ideas can be monopolized through the legal protection of patents.

This rather bleak notion of innovation is perhaps a little unfair to Prindle (1906, p. 466), who also acknowledges that "the inventor has the satisfaction of knowing that he is a producer of the most fundamental kind." He accepts that society has benefited immeasurably from inventions, quite apart from the financial concerns of patentees.

Prindle's real contribution is to attempt to explain *how* inventions are produced, quite apart from *why*. In tackling this question, we are also reminded of a recurring pattern in the history of creativity and innovation, one that reflects a failure to build on the lessons of the past and integrate knowledge from engineering and psychology. Beginning at least with Prindle (1906), moving through Wallas (1926), spanning the era of the *Sputnik* Shock (Buhl, 1960), and still today (Cropley, 2015), engineering, as a discipline, has addressed issues of creativity and innovation, not least from a psychological perspective, and yet the profession still struggles to come to terms with the processes, personal qualities, characteristics, and climates that make invention possible. Even with a somewhat misplaced emphasis on economics, Prindle understood that inventors—the individuals—engage in certain processes and behaviors that can be developed and nurtured, and that invention is not, by any stretch of the imagination, a mysterious and random art restricted to a few lucky individuals.

Prindle's discussion of the *how* of invention begins by addressing two myths that even today still need to be stated and debunked. Prindle lamented, in 1906, that popular belief held that inventors were born with the capacity, and born only infrequently. He noted, much as creativity researchers have done in the century since (e.g., Amabile, 1983; Cropley, 2015; Torrance, 1972), that many people possess "latent inventive abilities, which could be put to work if they only knew how to go about it" (Prindle, 1906, p. 467). He also offered an interesting perspective on why this is the case. Prindle argued that the high numbers of inventors in the United States at that time, compared to other nations, was evidence that inventive ability could be nurtured. He suggested that this was largely a result of the US patent laws. Whether or not that is correct, it fits neatly with modern frameworks, in which the *climate* or *culture* (both organizational and societal) play an important role in stimulating creativity.

The second myth that Prindle addressed is no less influential and is familiar to modern creativity researchers. Drawing on a Roman analogy (Minerva springing fully grown and armed from the mind of Jove), Prindle (1906, p. 467) indicates that inventions *do not* emerge fully formed from the mind of the inventor in a single step, but instead "may be greatly assisted by method." In other words, creativity and innovation—inventions—occur as a result of a sequence of stages. This is a theme that permeates Wallas (1926), Osborn (1953), Guilford (1959), and Cropley & Cropley (2008) and continues to define creative problem-solving (e.g., Puccio & Cabra, 2010) and other variants, such as design thinking (see Puccio & Cabra, 2010).

One consequence of Prindle's identification of *phases* in creativity and innovation is his recognition of the qualitative nature of those phases. In particular, he notes that there is a distinction between the kinds of reasoning that may be applied in different phases. "Reasoning or inference" is contrasted with "the imaginative or creative faculty" (1906, p. 467)—what we would now label as convergent and divergent thinking, respectively. In this manner, Prindle in effect defines *process* (in the sense of cognitive process) alongside *process* (in the sense of the phases of creativity or innovation). More important, it might be said that Prindle was the first to identify the *paradoxical* nature of creativity and innovation— the idea that contradictory reasoning styles must apparently coexist—a characteristic later discussed in detail by, for example, McMullan (1978) and Haner (2005) and which has been a central pillar of my own research in both engineering creativity (Cropley, 2015) and organizational innovation (Cropley & Cropley, 2015).

Somewhat more controversially, an extension of Prindle's (1906, p. 468) discussion of the general process of invention is his belief that "most inventions are an evolution from some previously invented form." This fundamentally *incremental* view of invention seems to limit creativity merely to improvements of what already exists—making things better, faster, and/or cheaper—but rules out paradigm shifts of a kind recognized by Buhl (1960, p. 10), who asserts that "locomotives were not displaced by modified locomotives but by a *new approach* to transportation needs—the car." Prindle calls on Edison for support in this view, citing the latter's famous dictum that "invention is not so much inspiration as perspiration." Prindle seems to interpret this to mean that through the exhaustive (but convergent) search for new combinations of existing forms, inventions emerge; however, I believe that Edison in fact simply acknowledged that the inventive process—both the convergent and the divergent elements—requires deliberate effort.

Prindle's next contribution to the framework of invention reinforces—or perhaps explains—his incremental mindset. In developing his concept of the *process* of invention— the stages involved in realizing an invention—he first dismisses *discovery*. This, he defines, in contrast to invention, as "the adaptability of some means to an end not intentionally being sought after" (1906, p. 469). In modern parlance, this makes the important distinction between two fundamental drivers of creativity and innovation—the reasons why we engage in these processes in the first place.

Change—technological, demographic, economic, and so on—occurs constantly and ubiquitously. Furthermore, change has two main effects. On the one hand, it defines new problems that require new solutions (what is frequently termed "market pull"; e.g., Cropley & Cropley, 2015)—and what Prindle seems to mean with his incremental view of invention. On the other hand, change leads to new solutions (discoveries) that can then be matched to new problems. Prindle thus sees invention almost exclusively in terms of market pull. Change creates an impetus for incremental improvements to existing solutions, and inventors—whose output is to be protected by patents, so that it can be profitably exploited—respond to this need through a predominantly convergent, and exhaustive, search for incremental improvements.

At this point in his paper, Prindle embarks on a rather laborious illustration of this convergent, incremental problem-solving process, and yet even this reveals insights that are ahead of his time. He notes, for example, the vital importance of problem selection: "The inventor should first make certain that the problem is based upon a real need" (1906, p. 469). More modern accounts of the process of creativity and innovation have discussed problem *recognition* and problem *construction* extensively—in simple terms, identifying the real problem, and not merely a symptom of the problem—noting that these are fundamental to success in the latter stages of creativity and innovation.

At this point, Prindle also touches on another key element of modern concepts of creativity and innovation—namely, the role of knowledge in problem-solving. Wallas (1926) called this *preparation*, and in Prindle's discussion of *analysis* as the second step in his inventive process, it becomes clear that a deep and thorough familiarity with the particular field in which the inventor is working is a prerequisite to success. It also lays the groundwork for Pasteur's famous statement "Chance favors only the prepared mind" (in Peterson, 1954, p. 493).

Prindle's lengthy explanation of the stages of development of a device for timestamping telephone calls, while unimportant for present purposes, nevertheless makes one important point. Many inventions, when viewed in their final form, may seem to suggest that this form was arrived at in a single, almost miraculous step. Prindle's point, even in his more convergent, incremental world, is well made: the end result frequently obscures the means by which it was obtained. Perhaps this is why the myth of divine inspiration persists, even in modern times?

Prindle gives a second, equally exhaustive example of his incremental inventive process. This case describes the development of a mechanical device for knotting cords around bundles of grain in a mechanical harvester. Here Prindle delves into another element of the psychology of creativity that is familiar to modern readers. Notwithstanding his incremental focus, Prindle recognizes that even the process of improving what already exists is greatly aided by removing cognitive constraints from the process. Prindle (1906, p. 482) talks about dismissing "from his mind as much as possible the old ways in which these elements have been associated." At the same time, he notes that "many important inventions have been made by persons whose occupation is wholly disconnected with the art in which they are inventing" (p. 482)—a principle frequently applied in modern problem-solving processes with the use of "outsiders" to offer fresh perspectives. Yet Prindle also recognizes that the qualities of the creative solution—originality and practicality—may be present in different proportions, depending on the prior knowledge of the inventor. Thus while an outsider might come up with highly original solutions, Prindle warns that these are typically low on practicality.

Prindle identifies two further stages of the inventive process that resonate with modern creativity and innovation concepts. First is the vital importance of trial and error. "Nothing should be considered impossible until it has been conclusively worked out or tried by experiments" (1906, p. 484). Second is what is now commonly referred to as *incubation*. Prindle understood that "unaccustomed mental stimulation" (p. 484)—in his words "the slight stimulation of the movement of a train of cars" (p. 484)—will sometimes result in the solution of a problem without apparent effort.

In drawing to a close, Prindle touches on one final notion that is important to modern views of creativity and innovation, albeit for reasons that Noble (1979) has suggested are largely selfish in nature. Prindle notes that inventions are not limited to tangible products but that fertile ground may be found in applying his incremental, inventive concepts to processes—that is, the manner in which a product is realized. While this is absolutely true— creativity and innovation are not limited only to products but encompass processes and even *services*—Noble suggests that Prindle's interest in process creativity was as much about locking out competitors as thoroughly as possible as it was about the search for new solutions to society's needs. We can appreciate Prindle's contributions, however, regardless of his motivation.

Conclusions

"The Art of Inventing" by Edwin J. Prindle (1906) is noteworthy for the range of concepts of creativity and innovation that it covers. To what extent it influenced that which has followed it is hard to say. With only a handful of citations, its influence in purely quantitative terms is perhaps low. Qualitatively, however, it is clear that Prindle was, at the very least, ahead of his time in defining and discussing the role of elements of the Person, the Process, the Press, and the Product (the now well-known Four Ps usually attributed to a combination of Rhodes [1961] and Barron [1969]). With the benefit of hindsight, Prindle's work could be seen to inform Wallas (1926), Osborn (1953), Guilford (1959), and other pioneers of the modern, post-*Sputnik* creativity era. Perhaps more significant, it is also a precursor to more modern discussions that have sought to integrate the psychology of creativity with the more pragmatic business of innovation, and not least in a broadly technological framework.

References

Amabile, T. M. (1983). *The social psychology of creativity*. New York, NY: Springer.

Barron, F. X. (1969). *Creative person and creative process*. New York, NY: Holt, Rinehart & Winston.

Buhl, H. R. (1960). *Creative engineering design*. Ames: Iowa State University Press.

Cropley, A. J., & Cropley, D. H. (2008). Resolving the paradoxes of creativity: An extended phase model. *Cambridge Journal of Education, 38*(3), 355–373.

Cropley, D. H. (2015). *Creativity in engineering: Novel solutions to complex problems*. San Diego, CA: Academic Press.

Cropley, D. H. (2017). Nurturing creativity in the engineering classroom. In R. Beghetto & J. C. Kaufman (Eds.), *Nurturing creativity in the classroom* (pp. 212–226). New York, NY: Cambridge University Press.

Cropley, D. H., & Cropley, A. J. (2015). *The psychology of innovation in organizations*. New York, NY: Cambridge University Press.

Guilford, J. P. (1959). Traits of creativity. In H. H. Anderson (Ed.), *Creativity and its cultivation* (pp. 142–161). New York, NY: Harper.

Haner, U.-E. (2005). Spaces for creativity and innovation in two established organizations. *Creativity and Innovation Management, 14*, 288–298.

McMullan, W. E. (1978). Creative individuals: Paradoxical personages. *Journal of Creative Behavior, 10*, 265–275.

Noble, D. F. (1979). *America by design: Science, technology, and the rise of corporate capitalism*. Oxford: Oxford University Press.

Osborn, A. F. (1953). *Applied imagination*. New York, NY: Scribner's.

Peterson, H. (Ed.) (1954). *A treasury of the world's great speeches*. Danbury, CT: Grolier.

Plucker, J. A., Beghetto, R. A., & Dow, G. T. (2004). Why isn't creativity more important to educational psychologists? Potentials, pitfalls, and future directions in creativity research. *Educational Psychologist, 39*(2), 83–96.

Prindle, E. J. (1906). The art of inventing. *Transactions of the American Institute for Engineering Education, 25*, 519–547.

Puccio, G. J., & Cabra, J. F. (2010). Organizational creativity: A systems approach. In J. C. Kaufman & R. J. Sternberg (Eds.), *The Cambridge handbook of creativity* (pp. 145–173). Cambridge, UK: Cambridge University Press.

Rhodes, M. (1961). An analysis of creativity. *Phi Delta Kappan, 42*(7), 305–310.

Sternberg, R. J. (2007). Creativity as a habit. In A.-G. Tan (Ed.), *Creativity: A handbook for teachers* (pp. 3–25). Singapore: World Scientific.

Torrance, E. P. (1972). Can we teach children to think creatively? *Journal of Creative Behavior, 6*(2), 114–143.

Wallas, G. (1926). *The art of thought*. New York, NY: Harcourt Brace.

PART TWO

Creativity Assessment

5

Dr. Laura M. Chassell Toops

Forgotten Pioneer of Creativity Assessment

JAMES C. KAUFMAN

Summary

This chapter highlights the overlooked contributions of Laura Chassell, whose 1916 paper "Tests of Originality," published in the *Journal of Educational Psychology*, included precursors of what are now standard creativity assessments. Chassell's paper includes key concepts that would later evolve into the Remote Associates Test, the consensual assessment technique, and (especially) divergent thinking. Although recognized as an important work in the decades after its publication, current awareness of Chassell's pioneering study is relatively low.

Introduction

In 1916, a 23-year-old teacher in Iowa published an article based on research she conducted as a master's student at Northwestern University. In this paper, Laura M. Chassell pioneered precursors to divergent thinking, remote associations, insight problems, and the consensual assessment technique. Somehow though, it is nearly forgotten a century later.

Her paper made a quick impression; Freeman (1917, p. 246), in a review for *Psychological Bulletin*, described her work as "a variety of ingenious tests for originality and initiative." It briefly seemed like it might be remembered as a pioneering contribution. As late as 1963, Golann wrote in a separate *Psychological Bulletin* review, "Since the

Acknowledgments: Very special thanks to Laura Chassell's relatives, Christine M. Abrell, Nona Toops Raines, Deborah Toops, and—especially—Laurence Toops for their generosity in offering advice, information, and stories. Thank you to Allison B. Kaufman for editorial assistance.

publication of Chassell's (1916) paper numerous investigators have attempted to devise or adapt tests that would measure creative abilities. Although the types of tests have not changed very much over the past 55 years, the methods of analysis have become more complex" (p. 551). What is fascinating is that this exact sentence might be written today, except crediting Guilford or Torrance. Chassell's article has been cited fewer than 10 times in the past decade.

Who was this scholar who was ahead of her time in so many ways? Building off of the Chassell Family Papers, 1821–1999 (1999), and reaching out to her surviving relatives, I was able to find out a bit about her. Chassell was born in 1893 to successful parents. Her father was a pastor who founded a church, and her mother would serve as a school superintendent. Chassell had a twin, Clara, who was also academically accomplished. When Laura Chassell was teaching in Iowa, her sister excitedly called and suggested that she quit her job and go back to school to get her PhD. Laura asked her sister, "What's a PhD?" She was soon convinced and on a train to New York City.

Laura and Clara both received their doctoral degrees in educational psychology from Columbia University in 1920. Laura's dissertation focused on the relationship between success in one's institution and success in one's field of study. Before embarking on the next stage of their academic careers, Laura and Clara had a double wedding in New York City on December 31, 1922. Laura Chassell and her husband, Dr. Herbert Toops, both applied for professorships at Ohio State University. He was offered a tenured professorship; because of her gender, and despite having equally impressive credentials, she was hired only as an instructor.

Chassell published a few more papers on teaching and measurement, sometimes with her sister, and also received a patent for a combined children's seat and toilet (Toops, 1932). While at Ohio State, she started several university organizations, including one for international professors and their wives; she also began a group to study child development. However, as her husband's career flourished, her own writing and work slowed down as she raised their five children (Mathison, 2000). Their first child was named Thorndike, after the legendary psychologist Edward Thorndike (a mentor to her at Columbia).

One of her last known professional appearances was giving a talk at the American Council of Guidance and Personnel Association; excerpts from her speech made the Associated Press wire and appeared in several local papers (such as the Arizona Republic). "Why not a six-hour day for mother?" she was quoted as asking. "Along with the movement to shorten working hours for men, women should not be forgotten. A system of mother apprentices would go a long way toward effecting this step and give otherwise idle children something useful and gainful to do" ("Briefer mothers' work day urged," n.p.). The Interior Journal (Stanford, Kentucky), provided an answer: "We know the answer. Because motherhood is a 24-hour day job. What would you think of a woman who staged a sit-down strike when hungry hubby came home?" ("Why not a six-hour day for mother?," 1937, n.p.).

Her intellectual spirit and teaching instincts continued through the years; her granddaughter remembers getting a letter sent back to her with the spelling errors circled in red. Dr. Laura Merrill Chassell Toops lived to be 101 (nearly 102), passing away in 1995. I will let her take the floor with her 1916 paper, "Tests of Originality," and then I will offer my own commentary and thoughts.

Reading: "Tests for Originality"

Source: Chassell, L. M. (1916). Tests for originality. *Journal of Educational Psychology,* 7(6), 317–328. This content is now in the public domain. It was originally published by the American Psychological Association in the *Journal of Educational Psychology*.

General Plan of the Experiment

The purpose of the investigation was (1) to adapt and devise tests for originality, and (2) to determine by trial the relative value of these tests as a means of ranking the members of a group in terms of originality. The selected tests were applied to 100 students drawn from all classes in Northwestern University and also to one inventor of international reputation.

After preliminary experimentation with a variety of tests, the following twelve were selected and modified for subsequent use: (1) Word-Building; (2) Picture Writing; (3) Analogues; (4) Original Analogues; (5) the Chain Puzzle; (6) the Triangle Puzzle; (7) Royce's Ring; (8) the Completion Test; (9) Economic Prophecies; (10) the Code Test; (11) the Invention for Sheet Music; and (12) Novel Situations. Of these, Picture Writing, Original Analogues, Economic Prophecies, the Invention for Sheet Music, and Novel Situations were devised in the Psychological Laboratory of Northwestern University; the remainder were adaptations or modifications of tests previously used elsewhere.

A time-keeping device, which made it possible for the subjects to record their own time, was constructed. The "minute hand" was a series of cards numbered from 0 to 10. These were suspended on a rod, and removed one by one at intervals of sixty seconds. The "second hand" was a placard upon which had been pasted numerals from 1 to 60, inclusive. Each succeeding second was indicated with a pointer by the experimenter.

There follows a description of the twelve tests.

1. WORD-BUILDING

The test followed the directions given in Whipple's *Manual of Mental and Physical Tests,* 2d edition, page 641, save that the time was reduced from five to three minutes, that only the *AEOMBT-form* was used and that *A* and *0* were not counted as words. The instructions to the subjects were first given orally with illustrations, then given again by means of a large placard on which they were displayed.

2. PICTURE WRITING

For this test five specially prepared cards were used. The first card was shown with this explanation: "These characters are picture writing and have actually been used by a people to express the meaning written after them. The third word is made up of the elements contained in the other two." After this first card had been explained, the four remaining cards were exhibited for a period of two minutes each. A score of 1 was credited for each card correctly solved.

The actual characters used were Chinese: in the following description of the cards the original symbols are replaced, for convenience in reproduction, by Roman letters. The original cards showed clearly that the third character represented in each case a combination of the first and second character.

SAMPLE CARD

A means *country*
B means *people*
AB means *democracy*

CARD 2

C means *enclosure*
D means *man*
CD means what ? (noun)

CARD 3

E means *to take*
F means *woman*
EF means what ? (verb)

CARD 4

G means *sun*
H means *horizon*
GH means what ? (noun)

CARD 5

I means *to quiet*
J means *heart*
IJ means what ? (verb)

3. ANALOGUES

This test was suggested by the analogies test used by Wyatt.

The material, however, was entirely new. Papers on which were the following analogues were distributed face downward:

Illustrations:

1. a hoe: a gardener:: scissors: (a tailor).
2. a county: (a state):: a room: a house.
3. a ring: the finger:: (a bracelet): the arm.

In the following, supply in the brackets the word needed to complete the relationship:

1. a cat: a mouse:: a hawk: ( ).
2. a consistent worker: a spasmodic worker:: ( ): a geyser.
3. an automobile: ( ):: a safety match: flint.
4. a common pen: a fountain pen:: odd jobs: ( ).
5. a caterpillar changes to a cocoon, then changes to ( ), as ice changes to ( ), then changes to steam.
6. *ab:bc*:: democracy: ( ).
   N. B.[1] a is the picture writing for people.
          b is the picture writing for king,
          c is the picture writing for enclosure or country,
          ab is the picture writing for democracy.

Before the subjects looked at the papers the experimenter explained that analogues were "word-ratios," and illustrated this statement by placing several upon the blackboard. Those who completed the test within the allotted eight minutes were instructed to record their time.

The scoring was complicated because of errors, omissions, and lack of uniformity in time. The final score was calculated by adding to the time recorded by the subject, a fine of one-sixth of this time, plus an additional minute for each error or omission save that in the fifth analogue, in which two terms were to be supplied, each error or omission counted one-half the usual fine.

4. ORIGINAL ANALOGUES

The instructions for this test were first given orally, then shown on a placard, which read:

> Make two original analogues.
> Record the time.

In scoring the recorded time was (1) decreased one-fourth for excellent quality, increased one-half for poor, and left unaltered for good; and (2) decreased one-sixth for each analogue given beyond the required two, and increased one-half for failure to give more than one. This arbitrary evaluation of quantity seemed justified because of the probability that less time is required to write a second or a third analogue than to write the first.

5. THE CHAIN PUZZLE

The instructions for this test were as follows: "A farmer had four pairs of links which he wished to have united into a continuous chain. Each cut was to cost ten cents and each weld ten cents. Show how this could be accomplished at a total cost of forty cents." Links of paper were prepared so that there could be no misunderstanding as to the relation of the various links to one another. They were then drawn and numbered as in the accompanying illustration.

    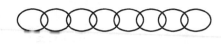

On the placard of instructions was written:
Each cut—10¢.
Each weld—10¢.
Total cost—40¢.
It can be done.
Ten minutes was allowed for the solution of the problem.
The time recorded by the students determined their score.

6. THE TRIANGLE PUZZLE

These instructions were presented on a placard:

> Out of six toothpicks make four equilateral triangles, each side of which shall be as long as a toothpick. It can be done. Record the time.

In order that the solution might depend upon constructive thinking alone, as was explained, no actual materials were supplied.

The time-limit was ten minutes. The score was the time required.

7. ROYCE'S RING

Royce's ring is made from a narrow strip of paper, the ends of which are pasted together after a twist of 180 degrees. A red line marked the longitudinal center of either side of our ring.

The experimenter explained the construction of the figure by preparing a similar ring before the class. The experiment was then conducted in three distinct parts. The first direction was as follows: "Describe fully the figure which would result if the ring were cut along the central line, including in your answer these three points: (1) the number of rings; (2) their interconnection; (3) the number of degrees of twist." After the descriptions had been written, the ring was cut. The resulting figure, a ring with a twist of 720 degrees, was then shown to the class and very carefully explained. The second direction was to describe the figure which would result if the ring were again cut.

Then, when the ring had been cut and the resulting figure, two interlocked rings, each with a twist of 720 degrees, had been explained, the last direction, to describe the figure which would result if the rings should be similarly cut, was given. Again the rings were cut as previously, producing four rings each with a twist of 720 degrees.

In the grading of the first part, a score of 9 was given for a correct solution, a score of 6 for the answer: "one ring twisted 360 degrees." Because of the decreasing difficulty of the problem, a score of 6 was given for the correct solution of the second part and one of 3 for the third. Less value was given to partially correct answers. The final score was the total of these gradings.

8. THE COMPLETION TEST

Completion Test No. 1 (Whipple's *Manual,* p. 652) used with the instructions:

> Supply all missing words or letters. Try first of all to "make sense"; second, to fill in every omission; third, to work as rapidly as possible. The length of each dotted line shows approximately the length of the word or portion of a word to be supplied.

The time-limit was 7 minutes in scoring, each omission filled correctly was given full credit; each one filled partially correctly, one-half credit. The score was the total credits.

9. ECONOMIC PROPHECIES

The experimenter spoke preliminarily to this effect:

> Five hundred years ago the automobile, the air-ship, and the steam railroad were entirely unknown means of locomotion. If any one then had said that today we should be traveling by these means, his statement would have been an economic prophecy.
>
> At that time, also, the present methods of heating by furnace and steam radiators were unheard of. Advertising was an undeveloped science. Skyscrapers had not yet been constructed.
>
> You are now to be asked to make some economic prophecies.

The subjects were then directed to suggest as many entirely original means as possible of (1) locomotion, (2) heating, (3) introducing the product to the consumer, (4) housing for people. These topics were announced by four placards and two minutes were allowed for each one. The suggestions were graded on a scale from 0 to 5 in proportion to their originality. The final score was the total of these gradings.

10. THE CODE TEST

The civil war code described by Healy and Fernald[2] made the basis of this test.

The placard upon which the code was written was displayed for fifteen seconds to give the subjects an idea as to its nature.

To illustrate its use the experimenter then showed a second placard on which was written the word *celery* and its code translation.

The code placard was again displayed, in juxtaposition with the second placard, while the experimenter indicated from what portion of the code the symbols were taken. Then the subjects were told that the code would again be shown for a period of sixty seconds, after which they would be given (1) a message to translate into the code language, and (2) one in the code language to read. These two messages were printed upon placards thus: (1) Come quickly. (2) (in the symbol of the code) "Foe near at hand; beware!" The subjects recorded their own time. The time-limits were three minutes first, and three and a half minutes for the second message.

In scoring, since there were eleven letters in the first message, a fine of one-eleventh of the allotted time was imposed for each error or omission; similarly for the second message, of one-nineteenth.

Disregard of a dot was fined one-half the usual amount. The final score was the sum of the time recorded in each portion, plus the fine.

11. THE INVENTION FOR SHEET MUSIC

For this test the following instructions were displayed on a placard:

> Numbering each, suggest as many details as possible for an invention to turn the pages of sheet music.

In judging the papers, the experimenter first placed in one group those suggesting inventions which would actually turn several pages of sheet music; in a second, those suggesting a means for turning one page; in a third, those suggesting less complete devices; and so on. She then arranged the papers within the groups in order of merit. The final score was determined by the rank-order of the subjects.

12. NOVEL SITUATIONS

The following questions were handed, face downward, to the subjects:

1. If some inexpensive metal should be discovered which, when put in cables, could transmit light at slight cost, what results would follow?
2. If trusts should get control of the surface of all oceans, what competition could arise which would offer means of transportation?
3. If all water, because of some change in its chemical constitution, should contract instead of expand upon freezing, what would be the effect upon animal life, including man?
4. If the prophecies that the earth is going to cool down should come true, what could man do to keep from becoming extinct for a time at least?
5. If the possession of money or wealth in any form should come to be regarded as dishonorable, what significant changes would result?
6. If, because of the exhaustion of materials from which paper is made, its manufacture should absolutely cease, what substitutions could be made?

The instructions were as follows: "Please read and answer only the first question at this time. You will be given two minutes and thirty seconds for this. Stop writing when the experimenter calls time; then pass to the second one; and so on, until the entire six have been answered."

The method of scoring was similar to that employed in Economic Prophecies, i.e., the final score was the sum of the gradings.

The Results

In this article it has been necessary to omit the original scores.

On the basis of these scores there was calculated the rank-order of the 100 students in each test, and also [their] final group rank, which was determined by the median of [their] several ranks (unless the medians were tied, in which case the averages were used).

In the summary tables that follow these abbreviations are used: W.B., Word-Building; P.W., Picture-Writing; Ana., Analogues; O.A., Original Analogues; Cha., the Chain Puzzle; Tri., the Triangle Puzzle; Roy., Royce's Ring; Com., the Completion Test; E.P., Economic Prophecies; Code, the Code Test; I.M., the Invention for Sheet Music; N.S., Novel Situations.

1. RANGE OF PERFORMANCE

A general idea of the performances of the students in the several tests may be gained from Table 5.1, in which is shown the best, the median, and the poorest score in each test. The symbol *F* in the third line means "failed to accomplish the test within the time-limit set."

TABLE 5.1 **Limiting and Median Scores**

Test	W.B.	P.W.	Ana.	O.A.	Cha.	Tri.	Roy.	Com.	E.P.	Code	I.M.	N.S.
Best Median	23	4	104″	37″	50″	50″	15	99	60	162″	1	76
Worst 7	0	760″	405″	F	F	0	12	0	F	96	8	

2. CORRELATIONS

In Table 5.2 there are shown the correlations existing between the rank-order of the 100 subjects in the several tests and their amalgamated rank-order for all the tests combined. These correlations, which were computed by the Spearman "foot-rule" method with R converted into r,[3] indicate the relative degree to which the outcome of each test agrees with the general outcome of all the tests. The probable error of r for 100 cases may be taken as approximately 0.04.

TABLE 5.2 **Correlations between the Several Tests and the Final Rank-Order**

W.B.	P.W.	Ana.	O.A.	Cha.	Tri.	Roy.	Com.	E.P.	Code	I.M.	N.S.
.25	.40	.57	.54	.54	.54	.41	.44	.55	.26	.52	.56

3. RELIABILITY OF THE SINGLE TESTS

In Table 5.3, an indication of its reliability is given for each test by adding the percent of subjects among the first twenty-five of the group of one hundred whose rank in the test under consideration is greater than that of the median rank of the last subject in the group, 37 +, and the percent of subjects among the last twenty-five whose rank is less than the median rank of the first subject in the group, 60.5. This method shows, then, the percent of subjects in the first and the last quarter of the group who would have been thrown out of their respective divisions had but the one test been used in ranking them.

TABLE 5.3 **Reliability**

W.B.	P.W.	Ana.	O.A.	Cha.	Tri.	Roy.	Com.	E.P.	Code	I.M.	N.S.
59	84	29	28	20	74	46	30	32	42	25	36

4. RANK OF EACH TEST AS A PROBABLE MEASURE OF ORIGINALITY

Table 5.4 gives the ranking of the tests upon the basis (1) of their correlation "with the final group rank, (2) of the percent of subjects among the first and the last twenty-five who would have been thrown out of their respective groups had but the test under consideration been used in ranking them, and (3) of the sum of (1) and (2).

TABLE 5.4

W.B.	P.W.	Ana.	C.A.	Cha.	Tri.	Roy.	Com.	E.P.	Code	IM.	N.S.
12	10	1	4	5	6	9	8	3	11	7	2
8	12	4	3	1	11	10	5	6	9	2	7
10.5	12	1	3	2	8	9	7	5	10.5	5	5

The correlation, obtained by the Pearson method adapted to rank-differences, is .50.

Comment on the Tests

The tabulated results alone are not sufficient basis for evaluating the tests because of inadequacies in the method of giving the test or in the system of scoring. Supplementary observations may, therefore, assist in reaching a fairer judgment. *Word-Building* has the lowest correlation with the amalgamated rank-order. This is probably due to the fact that about one-half of the subjects had played anagrams, as was ascertained by means of a questionnaire, and these subjects consequently had some advantage over other members of the group.

The test would doubtless have been fairer, therefore, had a fore-exercise been given. The rank correlation between word-building and the completion test, the one seemingly most closely related to it, is only .28, which is less than would have been anticipated except for the interference of this factor.[4] Terman found the use of a rational plan an important element in the procedure of those subjects who succeeded best in these tests.

Whipple used word-building to test imagination and invention, but did not report the finding of any significant correlations. *Picture Writing* gives promise of becoming a very valuable test if a few slight changes in the method are made, since its correlation with the final group rank is considerably higher than might be expected from the large number of "ties"—a factor tending to reduce correlation. Since but one subject in the first group failed to determine the correct word to be supplied, as compared with eight subjects in the fourth group, it is clear that the test differentiates the good group and that the addition of more cards would yield still better results. Probably the length of time allowed for each card could be shortened, also, since many of the subjects did not require the full two minutes.

Analogues ranks first among the tests. It might have been even more valuable, however, if the "picture writing" analogue (No. 6), which was by far the most difficult, had been replaced by one more nearly like the others, or if the time required for the solution of the five similar analogues and that for the solution of the sixth had been separately recorded. Wyatt found that his analogies test gave a very high correlation with subjective estimations of intelligence, as did also the completion test.

Original Analogues is likewise very successful.

The Chain Puzzle can be modified so as to become a very effective test. Since but five subjects of those ranking among the first twenty-five of the group, nine among the second, twenty among the third, and twenty among the fourth, failed to solve it; and since thirty-one of the forty subjects who succeeded in solving the puzzle are within the first half, it is evident that this test differentiates the good subjects quite successfully. Indeed, of all tests, this best determines the first and the last groups of twenty-five. The fact that the correlation with the final group rank is relatively high, notwithstanding the large number of ties, is another proof of its value. A greater differentiation and possibly a still higher correlation would be secured if the time allowed for solution were increased to fifteen minutes.

Similar observations may be made regarding the *Triangle Puzzle*. Of the fourteen subjects who gave a correct solution within the ten minutes allowed for the test, ten were ranked among the first twenty-five of the group, three among the second, none among the third, and one among the fourth. Since so few subjects succeeded in solving the problem, it is evident that the allotted time was entirely too short; even twenty minutes might with profit have been allowed for the solution. Our results support the conclusions of Lindley and of Terman that puzzles are valuable test material.

Since no one answered the entire test correctly, it is apparent that *Royce's Ring* presents an unusually difficult problem—a conclusion further confirmed by the results of Royce and Johnson and Gregg. The value of the test, especially of the last two parts, is questionable, because most of the students were so surprised at the outcome of the first cutting that their subsequent answers were mere guesses.

The efficiency of the *Completion Test* would in all probability be increased if a fore-exercise were given, as has been suggested in the case of Word-Building, since some of the subjects did not pause to read the instructions carefully.

Economic Prophecies is among the most reliable tests of the twelve from the standpoint of the extent of correlation with the final group rank. Its low correlation with the Chain Puzzle, .24, is not surprising in view of the large number of ties in the latter test.

The *Code Test* seemed to be much enjoyed by many subjects, but the results do not indicate that it is of especial merit in testing originality, although it necessitates, as Healy states, close attention and steadiness of purpose.

The *Invention for Sheet Music* ranks second in its differentiation of the entire group in respect to the first and the last twenty-five subjects. Some of the inventions suggested were exceptionally well planned and seemed to be entirely practicable.

Novel Situations is second in extent of correlation with the final group rank. Since the mental activities required in response to the tests are similar to those involved in Economic Prophecies and the Invention for Sheet Music, it is interesting to note that the three tie in average merit and are among the most effective tests. This result is gratifying, since they were among those devised in our laboratory.

It is evident that the tests, because of their varied nature, could not possess equal value as tests for originality, yet all would appear to test some phase of this trait.

Inspection of the original scores reveals the fact that if three very typical tests, namely, Analogues, the Chain Puzzle, and Economic Prophecies, had been employed, only three subjects would have been thrown out of the group of the first twenty-five, and only four out of the group of the fourth, twenty-five in the amalgamated rank-order. It is thus evident that the employment of these tests alone would have differentiated the group in a manner similar to that accomplished by the use of all the tests.

Finally, it is interesting to note that the inventor did not give exceptional evidence of originality in his response to the tests, though he ranked within the first half of the group. While it would have been most gratifying if his record had been high in every instance, for two reasons his showing in the tests does not invalidate their claim to be tests for originality. In the first place, his age may have prevented his making an unusual record; he was a man past middle life, while the students were all, with a possible exception, under thirty. In the second place, it may very well be that innately he is not unusually original, that his success in invention has come partly as a result of circumstance, and partly as a result of persistence and exhaustiveness of method.

He says: "I do not know that I am particularly original; needs have accidentally been brought to my attention, and I have sought to meet them." He made no important invention until his twenty-eighth year, when his attention was called to the need for a practicable time stamp, which he very shortly devised; another success some time later encouraged Him to devote much of his time to invention. Thus, accident appears to have been influential in stimulating his inventiveness, while industry and perseverance have contributed to his success.

This article represents in a condensed form the material submitted by the author as a master's thesis at Northwestern University in 1914. Credit for general arrangement and oversight of the work should be given to Professor W. D. Scott, under whom the investigation was conducted.

---

1. Here the letters *a, b,* and *c* have been substituted for the Chinese symbols actually used.
2. W. Healy and Grace Fernald, Tests for Practical Mental Classification. *Psychol. Monog.* March, 1911, Whole No. 54, pp. 33f.
3. For the method see Whipple, *Manual of Mental and Physical Tests,* 2d edition, pages 43–44, Formulas 33 and 35.
4. Wyatt has reported raw correlations of .36 and .70, and a corrected correlation of .97, between these two tests.—*Editor.*

Commentary

I remember the first time I read this paper. I was finishing up *Creativity 101* (J. Kaufman, 2009; now J. Kaufman, 2016) and in the midst of obsessive PsycINFO searches in the hopeless quest to not overlook key works. On a whim, after one of my searches for academic articles with creativity, I changed the filter to list the oldest papers. I was primarily hoping to find silly or outdated views on the subject to contrast our progress. Instead, one of the first ones I found was Dr. Chassell's (1916) "Tests of Originality." As I read it, I shifted from anticipated condescension to absolute awe.

Chassell worked before Wallas. Before Guilford. Before Barron, Torrance, Mednick, and modern giants such as Amabile, Sternberg, and Simonton. Not only that, she worked before the United States had yet to enter World War I. Why is this fact relevant? Before World War I, IQ was still very rooted in the Binet tradition of verbal reasoning. It was not until World War I that intelligence tests were developed by the US Army to assess mental abilities in other ways, such as using nonverbal tasks. David Wechsler would build off this work to develop the modern IQ test (A. Kaufman, 2009). Meanwhile Chassell already saw the importance of administering not only verbal measures but also including nonverbal ones (such as using or adapting the Chain Puzzle and Triangle Puzzle).

Chassell describes 12 tests. Seven of them existed before her study; I would argue that they are much more assessments of intelligence than creativity (J. Kaufman, 2010, 2015). Their inclusion may indicate the influence of her master's thesis adviser, Walter Scott, an applied psychologist, one of whose interests was intelligence. Five tests, however, were created for her thesis. These five—Picture Writing, Original Analogues, Economic Prophecies, Invention of Sheet Music, and Novel Situations—are clearly different from the existing seven. These five are measures of creativity, and it is entirely possible that they were the first five to ever exist. I will examine each of these in turn.

Picture Writing required merging two conceptual words to form a third word that combined the first two. It is clearly distinct from Mednick's (1968) Remote Associates Test, which presents three words that can be used as compounds with a fourth word. However, the underlying skill set (being able to make associations between discrepant concepts; Mednick, 1962) is similar, as is the idea of this type of creativity-related task having a "correct" answer.

Original Analogues asks people to create their own analogues. It was administered following the Analogues test, which is comparable to what would today be called Matrix Analogies. The Original Analogues test clearly required the examiner to score the analogues with, at the very least, a score of poor-good-excellent. Much further developed techniques rooted in analogy or metaphor production (e.g., Silvia & Beaty, 2012) are still in use.

The next three subtests are so reminiscent of how we currently measure divergent thinking that it is almost eerie. In Economic Prophesies, participants were asked to make original predictions for the future about scientific energy developments, comparable to some of the Just Suppose questions on the eventual Torrance Tests of Creative Thinking (TTCT; Torrance, 1974, 2008). They were instructed to give as many answers as possible within a time limit (indicating a value of a person's fluency). Invention for Sheet Music asks participants to suggest multiple details for a possible invention to turn the pages of sheet music, which echoes aspects of the TTCT's Product Improvement and using the level of detail provided as an indicator of creativity (as with elaboration). Scoring incorporated a categorization method similar to how flexibility can be calculated. Novel Situations is identical in nature to many of the Just Suppose items (although requiring more intellectual abilities to answer completely).

Unlike the TTCT, the decisions of item quality were not rooted in carefully established protocols, formulas, or trained responses. Chassell herself served as sole rater, using her judgment of a response's quality or originality. Nearly 100 years later, this method was suggested for scoring divergent thinking (Silvia, Martin, & Nusbaum, 2009), although using more raters and much more sophisticated statistics. Years later, too, the idea of a qualified expert being able to use her own judgment to score creativity products would also catch on (also with more raters and much better statistics) as the Consensual Assessment Technique (Amabile, 1996; Kaufman & Baer, 2012).

Am I trying to impugn the work of any of the modern scholars whose work was similar? Of course not—most may have been unaware of Chassell's work in a pre-internet world. Further, current assessments have significant and substantial improvements. My larger point is what might have been. We credit Guilford (1950) with establishing the modern creativity field—and he did. But, taking our cue from Chassell—let's imagine some different situations. What if Chassell's Columbia advisers had encouraged her established interest and proficiency in creativity studies? What if Ohio State (along with most other universities of that time) allowed female research professors? Perhaps Chassell could have followed up her work on developing creativity assessments. Maybe she would have linked it to education and child development, or else examined creativity and professional success.

In some different world, Guilford's powerful APA presidential address wouldn't have been questioning why no one was focused on such an important topic as creativity. Instead he might have delivered an equally influential speech about how the 57-year-old Chassell and the students she mentored had already established that creativity was a meaningful construct. Guilford's own Structure of Intellect model might have incorporated and built on the years of preexisting research. Consider what Barron, Torrance, and everyone else might have further accomplished if their field had deeper roots. It is even possible that Guilford might have used Chassell's body of work and her loving children as an example to argue that Boring (1951) and other psychological leaders of the day were wrong when they argued that women were incapable of being professionally successful while also being loving wives and mothers.

In the world we live in right now, what can we learn from Chassell's work? She certainly built on existing work, using or adapting measures of cognitive ability. But she also was not afraid to invent something completely different. So many "new" creativity measures (including many of my own) are rehashes of Guilford, Torrance, or Amabile—or, as it turns out, Chassell. I would love to see more people walk her fine balance between showing proper awareness for past work and demonstrating the fearlessness of doing something truly original. I only wish that this volume had been proposed two decades earlier, so we could have had the insights of Dr. Laura Merrill Chassell Toops herself.

References

Amabile, T. M. (1996). *Creativity in context: Update to "The social psychology of creativity."* Boulder, CO: Westview Press.

Boring, E. G. (1951). The woman problem. *American Psychologist, 6*, 679–682.

"Briefer mothers' work day urged." (1937, March 6). *Arizona Republic.* Retrieved from https://www.newspapers.com/newspage/116895995/.

Chassell, L. M. (1916). Tests for originality. *Journal of Educational Psychology, 7*, 317–328.

Chassell Family Papers, 1821–1999 (1999). Retrieved from https://www.library.uni.edu/collections/special-collections/university-archives/classification-schedule/chassell-family-papers.

Freeman, F. N. (1917). General reviews and summaries: Tests. *Psychological Bulletin, 14*, 245–249.

Golann, S. E. (1963). Psychological study of creativity. *Psychological Bulletin, 60*, 548–565.

Guilford, J. P. (1950). Creativity. *American Psychologist, 5*, 444–454.

Kaufman, A. S. (2009). *IQ Testing 101.* New York: Springer.

Kaufman, J. C. (2009). *Creativity 101.* New York: Springer.

Kaufman, J. C. (2010). Using creativity to reduce ethnic bias in college admissions. *Review of General Psychology, 14*, 189–203.

Kaufman, J. C. (2015). Why creativity isn't in IQ tests, why it matters, and why it won't change anytime soon . . . probably. *Journal of Intelligence 3*, 59–72.

Kaufman, J. C. (2016). *Creativity 101* (2nd Ed). New York: Springer.

Kaufman, J. C., & Baer, J. (2012). Beyond new and appropriate: Who decides what is creative? *Creativity Research Journal, 24*, 83–91.

Mathison, K. (2000). Toops, Laura Chassell (Merrill). In M. Ogilvie, J. Harvey, & M. Rossitor (Eds.), *The biographical dictionary of women in science: Pioneering lives from ancient times to the mid-20th century* (p. 1298). London: Routledge.

Mednick, S. A. (1962). The associative basis of the creative process. *Psychological Review, 69*, 220–232.

Mednick, S. A. (1968). The Remote Associates Test. *Journal of Creative Behavior, 2*, 213–214.

Pretz, J. E., & Kaufman, J. C. (2017). Do traditional admissions criteria reflect applicant creativity? *Journal of Creative Behavior, 51*, 240–251.

Silvia, P. J., & Beaty, R. E. (2012). Making creative metaphors: The importance of fluid intelligence for creative thought. *Intelligence, 40*, 343–351.

Silvia, P. J., Martin C., & Nusbaum, E. C. (2009). A snapshot of creativity: Evaluating a quick and simple method for assessing divergent thinking. *Thinking Skills and Creativity, 4*, 79–85.

Toops, L. C. (1932). *U.S. patent no. 1,848,443.* Washington, DC: US Patent and Trademark Office.

Torrance, E. P. (1974). *Torrance tests of creative thinking: Directions manual and scoring guide, verbal test booklet B.* Bensenville, IL: Scholastic Testing Service.

Torrance, E. P. (2008). *The Torrance tests of creative thinking norms-technical manual.* Bensenville, IL: Scholastic Testing Service.

"Why not a six-hour day for mother?" (1937, March 16). *Interior Journal from Stanford, Kentucky.* Retrieved from https://www.newspapers.com/newspage/221211038/.

6

Sir Francis Galton and the "Statistics of Mental Imagery"

Maciej Karwowski and Dorota M. Jankowska

Summary

Francis Galton is one of the fathers of contemporary creativity science. His ideas about the role of the interplay of intellectual, motivational, and personality characteristics for creative accomplishments are still timely; his works on heritability—even if outdated in light of today's molecular and behavioral genetics—still inspire new scholars. But do his conclusions regarding the role of specific mental processes for creative thought hold? Here we present and discuss the first attempt to empirically study mental imagery—a famous "breakfast table study" (Galton, 1880b). Are eminent scientists—or creative people in general—indeed deficient in imagery, as Galton suggested? What is the role imagery might play for creative thought? How has our understanding of mechanisms played by imagery changed in the past century? These questions inform our inquiry here.

Introduction

It would be neither controversial nor exaggeration to call Sir Francis Galton one of the founding fathers of creativity science, but also one of the most creative men of his time. Galton significantly contributed to several lines of inquiry within pre-Guilfordian creativity literature; he not only conducted one of the very first empirical studies on Pro-C and Big-C creativity levels (Kaufman & Beghetto, 2009); he also laid the foundations for biographical and historiometric analyses of creativity (Galton, 1869); posed the "nature versus nurture"

Maciej Karwowski, Institute of Psychology, University of Wrocław. Dorota M. Jankowska, Department of Educational Sciences, The Maria Grzegorzewska University. Address correspondence to Maciej Karwowski, Institute of Psychology, University of Wrocław, Dawida 1, 50-527 Wrocław, Poland, email: maciej.karwowski@uwr.edu.pl controversy and provided empirical findings showing the inherited character of creative skills; and highlighted the role of effective synergy between intellectual characteristics and personality and motivational traits (Galton, 1869). Although creativity was not central in his work, he offered a number of intriguing observations regarding men of science. And even if today some of his claims seem clearly sexist or even racist (see Simonton, 2015; this volume, chap. 17), others might still form an inspiration for creativity scholars and researchers interested in genius-level creativity.

Galton himself was considered a genius. Born in 1822, in his 89-year life he published more than 300 scientific papers and books. His works heavily influenced statistics (concepts of correlation and regression to the mean), as well as psychology and sociology, anthropology, geography and meteorology, and a number of other disciplines. Being a cousin of Charles Darwin, Galton was keenly interested in evolutionary theorizing and in the potentially adaptive functions of human abilities. This informed his works on the heritability of abilities and genius, first presented in a short article (Galton, 1865) and then in a now-classic book (Galton, 1869). Galton's intelligence, estimated with the use of historiometric methods (Cox, 1926; see also Simonton, this volume, chap. 19), was clearly extraordinary; according to Lewis Terman (1917), Galton performed at almost twice his chronological age (hence his IQ was close to 200 points; Forrest, 1974).[1] But his accomplishments in a number of domains were clearly even more impressive than his intelligence; the observation that people have unique fingerprints and a method to classify them, development of the first mental tests and questionnaires, input into statistics (the very idea of now classic standard deviation), just to name a few, secured his position as one of the most influential scientists of his time.

Although Galton rarely focused explicitly on creativity as a construct (rather he perceived it as an effect of brilliant intelligence, zeal, and dedication to hard work), it would likely be fair to say that he took quite a generalist perspective on creativity. A combination of intellectual (high intelligence), motivational (zeal), and personality (persistence and perseverance) characteristics was perceived as a sufficient condition to achieve a lot in any domain, be it science or art. However, observing the relatively low heritability of achievement in poetry, Galton (1869, p. 220) concluded:

> The reason is, I think, simple, and it applies to artists generally. To be a great artist, requires a rare and, so to speak, unnatural correlation of qualities. A poet, besides his genius, must have the severity and steadfast earnestness of those whose dispositions afford few temptations to pleasure, and he must, at the same time, have the utmost delight in the exercise of his senses and affections. This is a rare character, only to be formed by some happy accident, and is therefore unstable in inheritance.

This claim suggests that he clearly did not perceive science and art as the same type of creative domain, sharing too much in common. Quite the opposite, the perceived different antecedents of creative genius in science and arts do suggest that Galton himself would agree that creativity is domain-specific and that certain domains are not only heritable to a different extent, but also require specific skills and abilities.

---

1. Terman's estimated IQ of Galton was based on an early concept of IQ as a ratio of mental to chronological age, multiplied by 100. A day before his fifth birthday, Galton wrote in a letter to his sister, Adele, "I am 4 years old and I can read any English book. I can say all the Latin Substantives and Adjectives and active verbs besides 52 lines of Latin poetry. I can cast up any sum in addition and can multiply by 2, 3, 4, 5, 6, 7, 8, [9], 10, [11]. I can also say the pence table. I read French a little and I know the clock. Francis Galton, February 15, 1827" (cited in Terman, 1917, p. 210).

What is the role played by imagination and imagery abilities for creative functioning? Contemporary theorizing does highlight the benefits that stem from fantasies and daydreaming (Zedelius & Schooler, 2015), from the positive functions of mind-wandering (Baird et al., 2012), and the role of visual imagery for creative thought (Jankowska & Karwowski, 2015). Galton was clearly convinced that intellectual creative work is ordered, elegant, and hugely analytic. He seemed not to value such play-like mechanisms as creating mental pictures, playing with concepts, or exploring new combinations of different perceived or mind-created images. But, consistent with his philosophy, he took an empirical approach to the question of whether brilliant minds use their imagery differently than do less creative individuals. This study is widely known as the "breakfast table study," first described in 1880 (Galton, 1880b).

Reading: "Statistics of Mental Imagery"

Source: Galton, F. (1880b). Statistics of mental imagery. *Mind*, 5, 301–318. Work in the public domain.

An outline is given in the following memoir of some of the earlier results of an inquiry which I am still prosecuting, and a comparatively new statistical process will be used in it for the first time in dealings with psychological data. It is that which I described under the title of "Statistics by Intercomparison" in the *Philosophical Magazine* of Jany., 1875.

The larger object of my inquiry is to elicit facts that shall define the natural varieties of mental disposition in the two sexes and in different races, and afford trustworthy data as to the relative frequency with which different faculties are inherited in different degrees. The particular branch of the inquiry to which this memoir refers, is Mental Imagery; that is to say, I desire to define the different degrees of vividness with which different persons have the faculty of recalling familiar scenes under the form of mental pictures, and the peculiarities of the mental visions of different persons. The first questions that I put referred to the illumination, definition and colouring of the mental image, and they were framed as follows (I quote from my second and revised schedule of questions):

> Before addressing yourself to any of the Questions on the opposite page, think of some definite object—suppose it is your breakfast-table as you sat down to it this morning— and consider carefully the picture that rises before your mind's eye. [p. 302]
>
> 1. *Illumination.* — Is the image dim or fairly clear? Is its brightness comparable to that of the actual scene?
>
> 2. *Definition.* — Are all the objects pretty well defined at the same time, or is the place of sharpest definition at any one moment more contracted than it is in a real scene?
>
> 3. *Colouring.* — Are the colours of the china, of the toast, bread-crust, mustard, meat, parsley, or whatever may have been on the table, quite distinct and natural?

There were many other questions besides these, of which I defer mention for the moment.

The first results of my inquiry amazed me. I had begun by questioning friends in the scientific world, as they were the most likely class of men to give accurate answers concerning this faculty of visualising, to which novelists and poets continually allude, which has left an abiding mark on the vocabularies of every language, and which supplies the material out of which dreams and the well-known hallucinations of sick people are built up.

To my astonishment, I found that the great majority of the men of science to whom I first applied, protested that mental imagery was unknown to them, and they looked on me as fanciful and fantastic in supposing that the words 'mental imagery' really expressed what I believed everybody supposed them to mean. They had no more notion of its true nature than a colour-blind man who has not discerned his defect has of the nature of colour. They had a mental deficiency of which they were unaware, and naturally enough supposed that those who were normally endowed, were romancing. To illustrate their mental attitude it will be sufficient to quote a few lines from the letter of one of my correspondents, who writes:

> These questions presuppose assent to some sort of a proposition regarding the 'mind's eye' and the 'images' which it sees. . . . This points to some initial fallacy. . . . It is only by a figure of speech that I can describe my recollection of a scene as a 'mental image' which I can 'see' with my 'mind's eye.' . . . I do not see it . . . any more than a man sees the thousand lines of Sophocles which under due pressure he is ready to repeat. The memory possesses it, &c.

Much the same result followed some inquiries made for me by a friend among members of the French Institute.

On the other hand, when I spoke to persons whom I met in general society, I found an entirely different disposition to prevail. Many men and a yet larger number of women, and many boys and girls, declared that they habitually saw mental imagery, and that it was perfectly distinct to them and full of colour. [p. 303] The more I pressed and cross-questioned them, professing myself to be incredulous, the more obvious was the truth of their first assertions. They described their imagery in minute detail, and they spoke in a tone of surprise at my apparent hesitation in accepting what they said. I felt that I myself should have spoken exactly as they did if I had been describing a scene that lay before my eyes, in broad daylight, to a blind man who persisted in doubting the reality of vision. Reassured by this, I recommended to inquire among scientific men, and soon found scattered instances of what I sought, though in by no means the same abundance as elsewhere. I then circulated my questions more generally among my friends, and so obtained the replies that are the main subject of this memoir. The replies were from persons of both sexes and of various ages, but I shall confine my remarks in this necessarily brief memoir to the experiences derived from the male sex alone.

I have also received batches of answers from various educational establishments, and shall here make use of those sent by the Science Master of the Charterhouse, Mr. W. H. Poole, which he obtained from all the boys who attended his classes, after fully explaining the meaning of the questions, and interesting the boys in them. They have the merit of returns derived from a general census, which my other data lack, because I cannot for a moment suppose that the writers of them are a haphazard proportion of those to whom they were sent. Indeed, I know some men who, disavowing all possession of the power, cared to send no returns at all, and many more who possessed it in too faint a degree to enable them to express what their experiences really were, in a manner satisfactory to themselves. Considerable similarity in the general style of the replies will however be observed between the two sets of returns, and I may add that they accord in this respect with the oral information I have elsewhere obtained. The conformity of replies from so many different sources, the fact of their apparent trustworthiness being on the whole much increased by cross-examination (though I could give one or two amusing instances of break-down), and the evident effort made to give accurate answers, have convinced me that it is a much easier matter than I had anticipated to obtain trustworthy replies to psychological questions. Many persons, especially women and intelligent children, take pleasure in introspection and strive their very best to explain their mental processes, I think that a delight in self-dissection must be a strong ingredient in the pleasure that many are said to take in confessing themselves to priests.

Here then are two rather notable results: the one is the proved facility of obtaining statistical insight into the processes of other [p. 304] persons' minds; and the other is that scientific men as a class have feeble powers of visual representation. There is no doubt whatever on the latter point, however it may be accounted for. My own conclusion is, that an over-readiness to perceive clear mental pictures is antagonistic to the acquirement of habits of highly generalised and abstract thought, and that if the faculty of producing them was ever possessed by men who think hard, it is very apt to be lost by disuse. The highest minds are probably those in which it is not lost, but subordinated, and is ready for use on suitable occasions. I am however bound to say, that the missing faculty seems to be replaced so serviceably by other modes of conception, chiefly I believe connected with the motor sense, that men who declare themselves entirely deficient in the power of seeing mental pictures can nevertheless give life-like descriptions of what they have seen, and [can] otherwise express themselves as if they were gifted with a vivid visual imagination They can also become painters of the rank of Royal Academicians.

The facts I am now about to relate, are obtained from the returns of 100 adult men, of whom 19 are Fellows of the Royal Society, mostly of very high repute, and at least twice, and I think I may say three times, as many more are persons of distinction in various kinds of intellectual work. As already remarked, these returns taken by themselves, do not profess to be of service in a *general* statistical sense, but they are of much importance in showing how men of exceptional accuracy express themselves when they are speaking of mental imagery. They also testify to the variety of experiences to be met with in a moderately large circle. I will begin by giving a few cases of the highest, of the medium, and of the lowest order of the faculty of visualising. The hundred returns were first classified according to the order of the faculty, as judged from the whole of what was said in them, and all I knew from other sources of the writers; and the number prefixed to each quotation shows its place in the class-list.

Vividness of Mental Imagery

(From returns furnished by 100 men, at least half of whom are distinguished in science or in other fields of intellectual work.)

CASES WHERE THE FACULTY IS VERY HIGH

1. Brilliant, distinct, never blotchy.
2. Quite comparable to the real object. I feel as though I was dazzled, *e.g.*, when recalling the sun to my mental vision.
3. In some instances quite as bright as an actual scene.
4. Brightness as in the actual scene.
5. Thinking of the breakfast table this morning, all the objects in my mental picture are as bright as the actual scene. [p. 305]
6. The image once seen is perfectly clear and bright.
7. Brightness at first quite comparable to actual scene.
8. The mental image appears to correspond in all respects with reality. I think it is as clear as the actual scene.
9. The brightness is perfectly comparable to that of the real scene.
10. I think the illumination of the imaginary image is nearly equal to that of the real one.
11. All clear and bright; all the objects seem to me well defined at the same time.
12. I can see my breakfast table or any equally familiar thing with my mind's eye, quite as well in all particulars as I can do if the reality is before me.

CASES WHERE THE FACULTY IS MEDIOCRE

46. Fairly clear and not incomparable in illumination with that of the real scene, especially when I first catch it. Apt to become fainter when more particularly attended to.
47. Fairly clear, not quite comparable to that of the actual scene. Some objects are more sharply defined than others, the more familiar objects coming more distinctly in my mind.
48. Fairly clear as a general image; details rather misty.
49. Fairly clear, but not equal to the scene. Defined, but not sharply; not all seen with equal clearness.
50. Fairly clear. Brightness probably at least one-half to two-thirds of original. [The writer is a physiologist.] Definition varies very much, one or two objects being much more distinct than the others, but the latter come out clearly if attention be paid to them.
51. Image of my breakfast table fairly clear, but not quite so bright as the reality. Altogether it is pretty well defined; the part where I sit and its surroundings are pretty well so.
52. Fairly clear, but brightness not comparable to that of the actual scene. The objects are sharply defined; some of them are salient, and others insignificant and dim, but by separate efforts I can take a visualised inventory of the whole table.
53. Details of breakfast table *when the scene* is *reflected* on, are fairly defined and complete, but I have had a familiarity of many years with my own breakfast table, and the above would not be the case with a table seen casually unless there were some striking peculiarity in it.
54. I can recall any single object or group of objects, but not the whole table at once. The things recalled are generally clearly defined. Our table is a long one; I can in my mind pass my eyes all down the table and see the different things distinctly, but not the whole table at once.

CASES WHERE THE FACULTY IS AT THE LOWEST

89. Dim and indistinct, yet I can give an account of this morning's breakfast table; — split herrings, broiled chickens, bacon, rolls, rather light coloured marmalade, faint green plates with stiff pink flowers, the girls' dresses, &c., &c. I can also tell where all the dishes were, and where the people sat (I was on a visit). But my imagination is seldom pictorial except between sleeping and waking, when I sometimes see rather vivid forms.

90. Dim and not comparable in brightness to the real scene. Badly defined with blotches of light; very incomplete.

91. Dim, poor definition; could not sketch from it. I have a difficulty in seeing two images together.

92. Usually very dim. I cannot speak of its brightness, but only of its faintness. Not well defined and very incomplete. [p. 306]

93. Dim, imperfect.

94. I am very rarely able to recall any object whatever with any sort of distinctness. Very occasionally an object or image will recall itself, but even then it is more like a generalised image than an individual image. I seem to be almost destitute of visualising power, as under control.

95. No power of visualising. Between sleeping and waking, in illness and in health, with eyes closed, some remarkable scenes have occasionally presented themselves, but I cannot recall them when awake with eyes open, and by daylight, or under any circumstances whatever when a copy could be made of them on paper. I have drawn both men and places many days or weeks after seeing them, but it was by an effort of memory acting on study at the time, and assisted by trial and error on the paper or canvas, whether in black, yellow or colour, afterwards.

96. It is only as a figure of speech that I can describe my recollection of a scene as a "mental image" which I can "see" with my "mind's eye". The memory possesses it, and the mind can at will roam over the whole, or study minutely any part.

97. No individual objects, only a general idea of a very uncertain kind.

98. No. My memory is not of the nature of a spontaneous vision, though I remember well where a word occurs in a page, how furniture looks in a room, &c. The ideas are not felt to be mental pictures, but rather the symbols of facts.

99. Extremely dim. The impressions are in all respects so dim, vague and transient, that I doubt whether they can reasonably be called images. They are incomparably less than those of dreams.

100. My powers are zero. To my consciousness there is almost no association of memory with objective visual impressions. I recollect the breakfast table, but do not see it.

These quotations clearly show the great variety of natural powers of visual representation. I will proceed to examine the subject more closely, and to compare the returns from the 100 men with those from the Charterhouse boys, on the principle of my "Statistics by Intercomparison," which I must first explain at sufficient length.

There are many who deny to statistics the title of a science, and say that it is a mere collection of facts. For my part I think that there is such a thing as a science of statistics, though its field is narrowed almost to a point. Its object is to *discover methods* of epitomising a great, even an infinite, amount of variation in a compact form. To fix the ideas, it is well to take as an example the heights of men, in which case the science of statistics enables us to specify, by means of a very few figures, the conditions of stature that characterise the whole of the adult male inhabitants, say of the British Isles. These figures will suffice to inform us that there are so many percent between such and such heights, and so many between such other heights, giving us material whence we can answer any such question as this: Out of 1,000 men how many are we likely to find between 5 feet and 6 feet in height? If the figures do not give the answer directly, we can find it by interpolation and easy calculation from them. So again, if we wish to compare the heights of [p. 307] Englishmen and Frenchmen, statistics show how to obtain the average height of the two races, and the two averages may be readily compared, which goes a considerable way towards answering the question; or, if we wish it, we may compare very much more in detail, all the facts that are needed for the purpose being contained in the few figures of which I spoke.

But all these operations require the use of an *external standard*. The men must be separately measured by a foot-rule before their measurements can be classified, and the same need of an external standard of measurement is felt in every case with which the ordinary methods of statistics profess to deal. The standard of measurement may be that of time, weight, length, price, temperature, &c., but without the almanack or watch, the scales, the foot-rule, the coin, the thermometer, &c., statistics of the ordinary form to which I refer, cannot be made.

In my process, there is no necessity for an external standard. It clearly comes to the same thing whether I take eleven men and, measuring them one against another, range them in order, beginning with the highest and ending with the lowest, or if I measure them separately with a foot-measure, and range them in the order of the magnitude of the measurements recorded in my note-book. In each case the tallest man will stand first, the next tallest second, and so on to the last. In each case the same man will occupy the sixth or *middlemost* place, and will therefore represent the *medium* height of the whole of them. I do not wish to imply that 'medium' is identical with 'mean' or 'average,' for it is not necessarily so. But I do say that the word medium may be strictly defined, and therefore if we wish to compare the heights of Englishmen with Frenchmen, we shall proceed just as scientifically if we compare their medium heights as if we compare their average heights. Now it will be observed that we have got the medium heights without a foot-rule or any external standard; we have done so altogether by the method of intercomparison. In the particular question with which we are dealing I have classified the answers according to the degree of vividness of mental imagery to which they depose, and I pick out the middlemost answer and say that the description given in it describes the medium vividness of mental imagery in the group under discussion. If I want to compare two such groups I compare their respective middlemost answers, and judge which of the two implies the higher faculty.

Thus much is a great gain, yet I claim to effect more; but in order to explain what that is I must return to the illustration of heights of men. Suppose them as before to be all arranged in order of their stature, at equal distances apart on a long line A B, with their backs

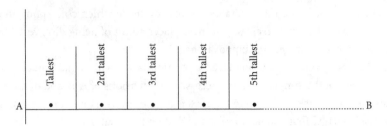

FIGURE 6.1

turned towards us. If there [p. 308] be a thousand men, we must suppose A B to be divided into 1,000 equal parts, and a man to be set in the middle of each part. The tallest man will have A close to his left, and the shortest man will have B close to his right. They will form a series as shewn in Figure 6.1, where the subdivisions of A B are indicated by the vertical lines, and the positions where the men are standing are shown by the dots half-way between those lines.

Owing to the continuity of every statistical series, the imaginary line drawn along the tops of the heads of the men will form a regular curve, and if we can record this curve we shall be furnished with data whereby to ascertain the height of every man in the whole series. Drawing such a curve for Englishmen and another for Frenchmen, and superimposing the two, we should be able to compare the statures of the two nations in the minutest particulars.

A curve is recorded by measuring its ordinates. If we divide A B by a sufficient number of equi-distant subdivisions and measure the ordinates at each of them as has been done in Figure 6.2 [p. 309] (where the ordinates only are shewn, and not the curve), we can at any time plot them to scale, and by tracing a free line touching their tops, we can with more or less precision, reproduce the curve. It happens, however, from the peculiar character of all statistical curves, that ordinates at equal distances apart are by no means the most suitable. The mediocre cases are always so numerous that the curve flows in a steady and almost straight line about its middle, and it becomes a waste of effort to take many measurements thereabouts. On the other hand its shape varies rapidly at either end, and there the observations

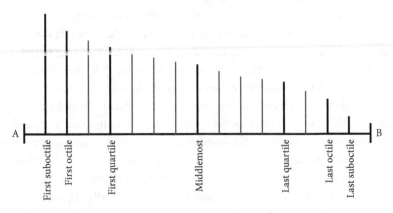

FIGURE 6.2

ought to be numerous. The most suitable stations are those which correspond to ordinates that differ in height by *equal degrees*, and these places admit of being discovered by *a priori* considerations on certain general suppositions.[1]

We shall however do well to ignore those minutiæ on which I laid much stress in the Memoir, and adopt the simpler plan of successive subdivisions of A B, and of measuring the ordinates shown by darkened lines in Figure 6.2, and severally named there as 'middlemost,' first and last 'quartile,' first and last 'octile,' and first and last 'suboctile'. This is far enough for our present wants, though the system admits of indefinite extension. By measuring the 'ordinate,' I mean measuring the 'man' whose place in the series is nearest to the true position of that ordinate. Absolute coincidence is not needed in such rude work as this; thus in a series of 100 men either the 50th or the 51st will do duty for the middlemost. The places I have actually taken in the series of 100 men for the several stations, are, the 6th and 94th for the first and last suboctile, the 12th and 88th for the octiles, the 25th and 75th for the quartiles, and the 50th for the middlemost.

Seven men thus become the efficient representatives of a very large class. It will be found as a general rule that these seven selected representatives will differ each from the next by approximately *equal intervals*, the difference between the suboctile and the octile being usually about the same as that between the octile and quartile, and between the quartile and the middlemost. [p. 310]

As a matter of interest, and for the chance of finding very exceptional cases, I also record the highest and the lowest of the series, but it must be clearly understood that these have no solid value for purposes of comparison. In the first place, their position as ordinates is uncertain unless the number of the group of cases is given, for when the number is large the position of the highest and lowest will be nearer to A and B respectively than when it is small. In the second place, the highest and lowest being outside cases, they are more liable to be of an exceptional character than any of those which stand between neighbours, one on either hand of it.

The comparison of any two groups is made by collating their seven representatives each to each, the first suboctile of the one with the first suboctile of the other, the first octile with the first octile, the first quartile with the first quartile, and so on. I also collate the highest of each, and again the lowest of each, as a mere matter of interest, but not as an accurate statistical operation, for the reasons already given.

It is possible that I may be thought to have somewhat loosely expressed myself under the necessity of foregoing the use of technical terms, but the mathematical reader who demands precision of statement will understand me, while it would require a treatise and much study to make the mathematical substratum of my method perfectly intelligible to a person who was not familiar with the laws of 'Probabilities' and 'Frequency of Error'

In the following comparison between the 100 Adult Englishmen and the 172 Charterhouse boys, I have divided the latter into two groups, to serve as a check upon one another. Group A includes boys of the four upper classes in the school, group B those of the five lower classes. I have combined their replies as to Illumination and Definition under the single head of 'Vividness,' and have taken no editorial liberties whatever except of the most pardonable description. It is wonderful how well and graphically the boys write, and how much individual character is shown in their answers.

Vividness of Imagery

HIGHEST

Adult Males. Brilliant, distinct, never blotchy.

Charterhouse A. The image is perfectly clear. I can see every feature in every one's face and everything on the table with great clearness. The light is quite as bright as reality.

Charterhouse B. The image that arises in my mind is perfectly clear. The brightness is decidedly comparable to that of the real scene, for I can see in my mind's eye just as well as if I was beholding the scene with my real eye. [p. 311]

FIRST SUBOCTILE

Adult Males. The image once seen is perfectly clear and bright.

Charterhouse A. It is very clear and is as bright as it actually was. Everything occurs most distinctly. I can imagine everything at once, but can think a great deal more clearly by thinking more on a particular object.

Charterhouse B. I see it exactly as it was, all clearly defined just as it was.

FIRST OCTILE

Adult Males. I can see my breakfast table or any equally familiar thing with my mind's eye quite as well in all particulars as I can do if the reality is before me.

Charterhouse A. To me the picture seems quite clear and the brightness equal to the real scene. I cannot see the whole scene at the same instant, but I see one thing at once and can turn my eye mentally to another object very quickly so that I soon get the whole scene before my mind.

Charterhouse B. Fairly clear, I cannot see everything at the same time, but what I do see seems almost real.

FIRST QUARTILE

Adult Males. Fairly clear; illumination of actual scene is fairly represented. Well defined. Parts do not obtrude themselves, but attention has to be directed to different points in succession to call up the whole.

Charterhouse A. The image is fairly clear but its brightness is dimmer than the actual. The objects are mostly defined clearly and at the same time.

Charterhouse B. Fairly clear, the objects are pretty well defined at the same time.

MIDDLEMOST

Adult Males. Fairly clear. Brightness probably at least one-half to two-thirds of the original. Definition varies very much, one or two objects being much more distinct than the others, but the latter come out clearly if attention be paid to them.

Charterhouse A. The image is fairly clear, but its brightness is not comparable to that of the actual scene. The objects are pretty well defined at the same time.

Charterhouse B. The image is pretty clear, but not so clear as the actual thing. I cannot take in the whole table at once, and I cannot see more than three plates at once, and when I try to see both ends of the table I cannot see anything of the middle. I can see nothing beyond the table, but the table itself seems to stand out from the distance beyond.

LAST QUARTILE

Adult Males. Dim, certainly not comparable to the actual scene. I have to think separately of the several things on the table to bring them clearly before the mind's eye, and when I think of some things the others fade away in confusion.

Charterhouse A. The image is fairly clear. I cannot see everything at once, but as I think of them they come clearly before me. The objects are not all defined at the same time, and the place of sharpest definition is more contracted than in real scene.

Charterhouse B.— If I think of any particular thing without the others, it seems clear; all at once, are not clear.

LAST OCTILE

Adult Males. Dim and not comparable in brightness to the real scene. [p. 312] Badly defined with blotches of light; very incomplete; very little of one object is seen at one time.

Charterhouse A. I can call up to my mind the picture of the breakfast table in every detail, but seem to see everything through a darkened pane of glass. I see just the same number of people, plates, &c., the whole time, provided of course that I do not change my idea of the scene to any great degree.

Charterhouse B. Rather dim; the objects are pretty well defined.

LAST SUBOCTILE

Adult Males. I am very rarely able to recall any object whatever with any sort of distinctness. Very occasionally an object or image will recall itself, but even then it is more like a genereralised image than an individual one. I seem to be almost destitute of visualising power as under control.

Charterhouse A. The image is dim, dark, and smaller than the actual scene, and the objects nearest to me show most distinctly. The whole picture is more or less of a dark green tint.

Charterhouse B. Dim. The place of sharpest definition is more contracted than in a real scene.

LOWEST

Adult Males. My powers are zero. To my consciousness there is almost no association of memory with objective visual impressions. I recollect the table, but do not see it.

Charterhouse A. Image dim, the brightness much less than in the real scene. Only one object is very clearly visible at the same time.

Charterhouse B. Very dim. I can only see one part at a time.

I gather from the foregoing paragraphs that the A and B boys are alike in mental imagery, and that the adult males are not very dissimilar to them; but the latter do not seem to form so regular a series as the boys. They are avowedly not members of a true statistical group, being an aggregate of one class of persons who replied because they had remarkable powers of imagery and had much to say, of another class of persons, the scientific, who on the whole are very deficient in that gift, and of a third class who may justly be considered as fair samples of adult males.

I next proceed to colour, and annex the returns to the third of the above questions, which I have classified on the same principle as before.

Colour Representation

HIGHEST

Adult Males. Perfectly distinct, bright, and natural.

Charterhouse A. Yes, *perfectly* distinct and natural.

Charterhouse B. The colours look more clear than they really are.

FIRST SUBOCTILE

Adult Males. White cloth, blue china, argand coffee pot, buff stand with sienna drawing, toast, — all clear.

Charterhouse A. I see the colours just as if they were before me, and perfectly natural.

Charterhouse B. The colours are especially distinct in every case. [p. 313]

FIRST OCTILE

Adult Males. All details seen perfectly.

Charterhouse A. Quite distinct and natural.

Charterhouse B. All colours are perfectly distinct to me in my mind's eye, in whatever scene or shape they appear to me.

FIRST QUARTILE

Adult Male. Colours distinct and natural till I begin to puzzle over them.

Charterhouse A. Quite distinct and natural.

Charterhouse B. The colours of the china, &c., are quite distinct and natural.

MIDDLEMOST

Adult Males. Fairly distinct, though not certain that they are accurately recalled.

Charterhouse A. They are all distinct after a little thought, and are natural.

Charterhouse B. Yes, quite distinct and natural.

LAST QUARTILE

Adult Males. Natural, but very indistinct.

Charterhouse A. The colours of the most pronounced things on the table are distinct, as the white tablecloth and yellow mustard.

Charterhouse B. Some are; china, mustard, toast, the others are not.

LAST OCTILE

Adult Males. Faint, can only recall colours by a special effort for each.

Charterhouse A. Colours not very distinct.

Charterhouse B. They are natural, but not very distinct.

LAST SUBOCTILE

Adult Males. (Power is nil.)

Charterhouse A. The colours are very dim.

Charterhouse B. The colours seem to be more like shades, but they have some colour in them.

LOWEST

Adult Males. (Power is nil.)

Charterhouse A. (Power is nil.)

Charterhouse B. (Power is nil.)

The same general remarks may be made about the distribution of the faculty of colour representation as about that of the vividness of imagery. It seems that on the whole, colour is more easily recalled than form, and especially so by the young. As the faculty of visual representation is being dropped by disuse, colour disappears earlier than form. This I may remark, was the case with the often quoted hallucinations of Nicolai, which, in his progress to recovery, faded in colour before they faded in outline.

One of my correspondents, an eminent engineer, who has a highly developed power of recalling form, but who described himself as deficient in the power of recalling colour, tells me that since receiving and answering my questions he has practised [p. 314] himself in visualising colours and has succeeded perfectly in doing so. It now gives him great pleasure to recall them.

It will be of interest to extract the few instances from the returns of the Adult Males in which peculiarities were noticed in connexion with colour representation, other than in its degree of vividness. Each sentence is taken from a different return.

Light colours quite distinct, darker ones less so.
Patchy.

Generally hueless, unless excited.

Mostly neutral.

Brown colour, *e.g.* of the gravy, is difficult to visualise.

Another question that I put was as follows:

Extent of field of view. Call up the image of some panoramic view (the walls of your room might suffice); can you force yourself to see mentally a wider range of it than could be taken in by any single glance of the eyes? Can you mentally see more than three faces of a die, or more than one hemisphere of a globe at the same instant of time?

It would have been possible to classify the Charterhouse returns, but the answers were not so generally good as to make it advisable to spend pains upon them. I therefore content myself with the replies of the Adult Males, but shall subsequently add a few facts taken from those of the boys, in a separate paragraph.

Extent of Field of Mental View

Highest. My mental field of vision is larger than the normal one. In the former I appear to see everything from some commanding point of view, which at once embraces every object and all sides of every object.

First Suboctile. A wider range. A faint perception *I think* of more than three sides of a room. Rather more *I think* than one hemisphere, but am not quite sure about this.

First Octile. Field of view corresponding to reality.

First Quartile. Field of view corresponding to reality.

Middlemost. Field of view corresponding to reality.

Last Quartile. I think the field of view is distinctly smaller than the reality. The object I picture starts out distinct with a hazy outline.

Last Octile. Much smaller than the real. I seem only to see what is straight in front as it were.

Last Suboctile. No field of view at all Lowest. It may seem strange to some that the field of mental vision should occasionally be wider than reality, but I have sufficient [p. 315] testimony to the fact from correspondents of unquestionable accuracy. Here are cases from the returns:

I seem to see the whole room as though my eye was everywhere. I can see all around objects that I have handled.

I can see three walls of a room easily, and with an effort the fourth. I can see all the faces of a die and the whole globe, but die and globe seem transparent.

[An eminent mineralogist told me that familiarity with crystals gave him the power of mentally seeing all their facets simultaneously.]

This subject is of interest to myself on account of a weird nightmare by which I am occasionally plagued. In my dream, a small ball appears inside my eye. I speak in the singular, because the two eyes then seem fused into a single organ of vision, and I see by a kind of touch-sight all round the ball at once. Then the ball grows, and still my vision embraces the whole of it; it continues growing to an enormous size, and at the instant when the brain is ready to burst, I awake in a fright. Now, what I see in an occasional nightmare, others may be able to represent to themselves when awake and in health.

From the foregoing statistical record it will be seen that in one quarter of the cases, that is to say, in the last quartile and in all below, the field of mental view is decidedly contracted. The Charterhouse returns (A and B combined) give a higher ratio. They show that in at least 74 out of the 172 cases, or in 43 percent of them, it is so; indeed, the ratio may be much larger, as I hardly know what to say about 51 cases, owing to insufficient description. I am inclined to believe that habits of thought render the mental field of view more *comprehensive* in the man than in the boy, though at the same time it causes the images contained in it to become fainter.

A few of the boys' answers are much to the point. I append some of them:

The part I look at is much smaller than reality, with a haze of black all round it. It is like a small picture.

I have to fix my eyes on one spot in my imagination, and that alone is fairly defined.

I cannot see anything unless I look specially at it, which is not the case with my real eyes. I have to move my mental eyes a good deal about. The objects are not defined at the same time, but I think of them one at a time; also, if I am thinking of anything, as a map for instance, I can only imagine one name at a time.

The next question that I put referred to the apparent position of the image. It was as follows:

Distance of images. Where do mental images appear to be situated? within the head, within the eye-ball, just in front of [p. 316] the eyes, or at a distance corresponding to reality? Can you project an image upon a piece of paper?

Unfortunately this question was not included among those that I first issued, and I have not a sufficient number of answers to it from adult males to justify a statistical dependence on them even on that ground alone. It is better in this case to rely on the Charterhouse boys, of whom only twelve failed to answer the question. Reducing to percentages, I find:

POSITION OF MENTAL IMAGES.

	Percent
Further than the real scene	9
Corresponding to reality	39
Just in front of the eyes	22
In eye-ball	6
In head	15
Partly at one distance, partly at another	9
	100

The more closely the image resembles in its vividness the result of actual vision the more nearly should we expect its distance to appear to coincide with that of the real object, and this as a matter of fact I find to be the case. The meaning of the word *reflection* is bending backwards, and those who reflect have the sense of a turning back from without to within the head. When a mental scene arises vividly and without any effort, the position of the vision is more frequently external, as it is in an hallucination.

I will next give the results of the latter part of the question, about the ability to project images on paper.

For the same reason as in the last case the returns from the adult males are insufficient. I have five clear cases only among them of an affirmative answer, out of which I will quote the following:—

Ability to Project an Image

Holding a blank piece of paper in my hand, I can imagine on it a photograph or any object that it will hold.

The Charterhouse boys in at least 18 cases, or in ten percent of them, appear to have this power. The following are a few of their answers:

I can think things to be upon [a] blank piece of paper.

I can place a mental image wherever I like, outside the head, either in the air or upon any substance.

After looking at a blank wall for some time, I can imagine what I am thinking of. [p. 317]

I can half project an image upon paper, but could not draw round it, it being too indistinct. I see the effect, but not the details of it.

I find it very hard to project an image on a piece of paper, but if I think for some time and look very hard at the paper, I sometimes can.

I can project an image on to anything, but the longer I keep it the fainter it gets, and I don't think I could keep it long enough to trace it.

I find indirectly from the answers to other questions that visual representations are by no means invariably of the same apparent size as the real objects. The change is usually on the side of reduction, not of enlargement. Among the Charterhouse boys there are thirteen of the one to two cases of the other, and I think, but I have not yet properly worked it out, that the returns from adults generally, male and female, show somewhat similar results. The following are extracts from the reports of the boys:

Images Larger Than Reality

The place and objects in a mental picture seem to be larger altogether than the reality; thus a room seems loftier and broader, and the objects in it taller.

They look larger than the objects [? such objects as may be handled] really are, and seem much further off, they look about five yards off, they look about five yards off.

Images Smaller Than Reality

Very small and close.

Much smaller and very far off.

All the objects are clearly defined, but the image appears much smaller.

The difference that I see is, that everything I call up in my mind seems to be a long way off.

The difference is that it is much smaller.

Space does not admit, neither is this the most suitable opportunity of analysing more of the numerous data which I have in hand, but before concluding I would say a few words on the "Visualised Numerals" which I described first in *Nature*, Jan. 15, 1880, but very much more fully and advisedly in a memoir read before the Anthropological Institute in March, 1880, which will be published in its *Transactions* a few weeks later than the present memoir. It will contain not only my own memoir and numerous illustrations, but the remarks made on it at the meeting by gentlemen who had this curious habit of invariably associating numbers with definite forms of mental imagery. It is a habit that is quite automatic, the form is frequently very vivid and sometimes very elaborate and highly coloured, and its origin is always earlier than those who see it can recollect. Those who visualise numerals in number-forms are apt to see the letters of the alphabet, the months of the year, dates, &c., also in forms; but whereas they nearly always can suggest some clue to the origin of the latter, they never can, or [p. 318] hardly ever can, to that of the numerals. I have argued in the memoir just mentioned, partly from this fact and partly because some of the number-forms twist and plunge and run out of sight in the strangest ways, unlike anything the child has ever seen, that these are his natural, self-developed lines of mnemonic thought, and are survivals of the earliest of his mental processes, and a clue to much that is individual in the constitution of his mind. I found that only about one in thirty adult males saw these forms, but suspected that they were more common in early life, and subsequently lost by disuse. This idea is abundantly confirmed by the returns of the Charterhouse boys. Nearly one in four has the habit of referring numbers to some visual mental form or other; often it is only a straight line, sometimes more elaborate. No doubt as the years go by, most of these will be wholly forgotten as useless and even cumbrous, but the rest will serve some useful turn in arithmetic and become fixed by long habit, and will gradually and insensibly develop themselves. For want of space I must here close my statement of facts; and, my data being thus imperfectly before the reader, it would be premature in me to generalise. I trust, however, that what has been adduced is enough to give a fair knowledge of the variability of the visualising faculty in the English male sex, and I hope that the examples of the use of my "Statistics by Intercomparison" will convince psychologists that the relative development of various mental qualities in different races admits of being pretty accurately defined.

---

1. These are discussed in the Memoir already referred to, "Statistics by Intercomparison," by myself, in *Phil. Mag.*, Jan., 1876, but there are some errors, and also some appearances of error owing to faults of expression, in that article, which were first pointed out to me by Mr. J. W. L. Glaisher. There is a full mathematical discussion bearing on the matter in a memoir by Mr. D. McAlister in the *Proceedings of the Royal Society*, 1879, on the "Law of the Geometric Mean," to which and to the immediately preceding paper by myself on the "Geometric Mean," I would refer the mathematical reader. Mr. J. W. L. Glaisher has also taken the subject in hand and calculated tables, and I trust that his memoir thereon may before long be published.

Commentary

For good reasons, Galton is perceived as a pioneer of the study of imagery—indeed he was the first to take an empirical approach, instead of speculations, in exploring the role, mechanisms, and different levels of imagery. It should be noted, however, that it was 20 years earlier when Gustav Fechner (1860/1996) in his *Elements of Psychophysics* raised the question of differences in mental imagery across populations and called for rigorous, empirical studies that would answer these questions (Burbridge, 1994; Isaac & Marks, 1994). Although Galton does not cite Fechner, it is very likely that "his study of mental imagery was initially prompted by his reading" (Burbridge, 1994, p. 445). Nevertheless Galton's study was recognized as innovative and attracted attention from scholars around the world. Late in the 19th century, when psychology emerged as a scientific discipline, the role of imagery in mental life was not a leading topic of research. Galton (1880a, 1880b, 1883) claimed then that acts of imagining could be quantified and evaluated with the use of the techniques of experimental psychology and should thus be acclaimed for carrying out the first study of this sort. Less than 20 years later, his measure, "the breakfast-table questionnaire," inspired the first fully quantitative questionnaire for measuring mental imagery (Questionnaire upon Mental Imagery; Betts, 1909). But most important, Galton's study was among the very first empirical researches focused on individual differences and psychological processes.

Galton's main conclusions with regard to mental imagery, which at this time are extensively discussed by psychologists worldwide, may be summarized in five main points.

First, regarding the definition, mental imagery is understood as "different degrees of vividness with which different persons have the faculty of recalling familiar scenes under the form of mental pictures, and the peculiarities of the mental visions of different persons" (Galton, 1880b, p. 301). Second, there is an epistemological assumption that it is possible to gain insight into a mental process, such as visual imagery, using introspective methods and quantitative statistical techniques. "Here, then, are two rather notable results: the one is the proved facility of obtaining statistical insight into the processes of other persons' minds, whatever a priori objection may have been made as to its possibility" (Galton, 1883, p. 60). Third, there is wide variability in the capacity for mental imagery within the general population.

> There are great differences in the power of forming pictures of objects in the mind's eye; in other words of visualizing them. In some persons the faculty of perceiving these images is so feeble that they hardly visualize at all. . . . Other persons perceive past scenes with a distinctness and an appearance of reality that differ little from actual vision. Between these wide extremes I have met with a mass of intermediate cases extending in an unbroken series. (Galton, 1880a, p. 312)

Fourth, many intellectuals, and scientists in particular, have very weak visual mental imagery because it is antagonistic to abstract thinking. "Scientific men as a class have feeble powers of visual representation" (Galton, 1880b, p. 304). Fifth, females had higher powers of visualizing than males, and this ability increased with age in both sexes. "The power of visualizing is higher in the female sex than in the male, and is somewhat, but not much, higher in public school-boys than in men. I have, however, a few clear cases in which its power has greatly increased with advancing years" (Galton, 1880a, p. 314).

Do these conclusions hold today, after more than a century of scientific inquiry into imagery studies? Is scientists' imagery really deficient? Are there convincing and robust sex differences in imagery? Let's look at some of Galton's claims in light of more contemporary findings.

Did Galton really measure imagery? First, although there is no doubt that Galton (1880a, 1883) carried out an extremely innovative study, the fair question is whether and to what extent it was a study of mental imagery. It seems that Galton's primary interest was indeed in mental imagining: "I desire to define the different degrees of vividness with which different persons have the faculty of recalling familiar scenes under the form of mental pictures, and the peculiarities of the mental visions of different persons" (Galton, 1880b, p. 21). But the validity of the measure applied seems questionable. Brewer (e.g., 1986, 1996) consistently argued that the breakfast-table questionnaire should be considered a test of recollective memory rather than imagery. Indeed Galton (1880b, p. 21) directed participants' attention to memories and their representations: "Think of some definite object—suppose it is your breakfast-table as you sat down to it this morning—and consider carefully the picture that rises before your mind's eye." Then the results were scored in terms of brightness, definition, completeness, coloring, and the extent of the field of view. These questions were clearly closer to a request to recall the events that happened a few hours earlier than to a task that activates visualization. Mental images are not only based on the recollection of previously perceived objects or events, but are actively created and based on the modification of stored perceptual information in novel ways (Kosslyn, Ganis, & Thompson, 2001). If Galton's participants had been asked to visualize a breakfast they had had with anyone, anywhere, then such a task could be considered a task of mental imagining. Obviously, even in cases of this type of task, it is very likely that a great majority of participants' responses would echo or reconstruct actual perceptual experiences from the past; anyway, such a task would activate imagery processing as well rather than memory alone.

Since the days of Galton's work, research on mental imagery continued to expand. Already in 1909 Betts improved Galton's method and created the more comprehensive scale of the vividness to assess imagery in seven modalities (Questionnaire upon Mental Imagery). Today there are many new measures that allow for assessing imagery abilities and explore not only vividness (e.g., Blajenkova, Kozhevnikov, & Motes, 2006; Jankowska & Karwowski, 2015; Marks, 1995) but also control imagery (e.g., LeBoutillier & Marks, 2002), imagery-processing style (e.g., Kozhevnikov, Kosslyn, & Shephard, 2005), and imagery content (e.g., Hackmann, Clark, & McManus, 2000). Moreover introspective self-report instruments are consistently replaced with tests and experimental tasks created to analyze the very process of imagining. Over time, mental imagery has been linked with many different areas of psychological research, including clinical psychology (Pearson, Deeprose, Wallace-Hadrill, Heyes, & Holmes, 2013) and neuropsychology (e.g., Kosslyn, 2005). This interdisciplinary approach has resulted in a growing number of studies devoted to mental imagery.

Is scientists' imagery really deficient? Galton's finding that scientists show weak or no visual imagery during the recollective memory task was accepted by many leading early and contemporary psychologists, including James, Bradford Titchener, Miller, Paivio, and Kosslyn (see Brewer & Schommer-Aikins, 2006). However, in an excellent overview and comment, Brewer and Schommer-Aikins (2006) showed several problems with Galton's conclusions and were unable to replicate his findings. They found that, in fact, modern scientists tended to show relatively rich and vivid imagery. In their study there were no single scientists who reported a total absence of imagery, while almost all (94 percent) showed moderate or high mental imagery on the breakfast-table questionnaire. Moreover Brewer and Schommer-Aikins reanalyzed Galton's data and showed that the results were far less strong and not consistent with Galton's conclusion. They posited that his interpretation of his findings was primarily driven by a number of outliers—prominent scientists in his pilot sample who indeed reported some very dim images (see Burbridge, 1994, p. 455). But even Brewer and Schommer-Aikins partially agreed with Galton in that scientists have a slightly less vivid imagery than a group of university undergraduates.

Are there robust gender differences in mental imagery? Galton's result concerning the apparently limited imagery of scientists is the most often cited take-home message from his breakfast-table study. Less attention was given to his speculations regarding gender differences. This is surprising, as researchers are still arguing about the gender differences noted by Galton (1883), not about poor vividness in the case of scientists (e.g., Richardson, 1995). For example, reviews of imagery literature (see Campos, 2014; McKelvie, 1995) revealed no significant gender differences on the Vividness of Visual Imagery Questionnaire, while Richardson's (1995) meta-analysis showed that female participants obtained slightly higher scores on this questionnaire than males. Similarly studies that explored potential differences on the Betts Questionnaire upon Mental Imagery bring equivocal findings. On the one hand, White, Ashton, and Brown (1977) found higher scores for women than for men, yet on the other hand, Campos and Pérez-Fabello (2005) showed no significant sex differences in this area. Such examples can be multiplied, and although it seems to be well established that men usually outperform women in terms of mental rotation tasks (Voyer, Voyer, & Bryden, 1995), the results regarding mental imagery, and especially aspects of creative visual imagery, point to a relative equality between men and women (Jankowska & Karwowski, 2015).

FINAL CONSIDERATIONS

It goes without saying that Galton's breakfast-table study was highly creative. Relying on empirical data obtained from accomplished scholars, Galton was able to posit several claims related to the functioning of imagery in general and the level of imagery among scholars in particular. As we illustrated, today these claims are problematic for two main reasons. First, it is questionable whether Galton's measure should be considered a valid instrument of mental imagery. Second, his findings do not necessarily support his strong conclusions regarding scientists' imagery deficiency.

The breakfast-table task, especially when we consider the instruction presented by Galton, very likely activated recollective memory rather than imagery (Brewer & Schommer-Aikins, 2006). That is not to say that memory plays no role for imagery. Obviously imagery is embedded within memory, attention, and thinking-related processes (Dziedziewicz & Karwowski, 2015), so studying imagery in isolation is neither possible nor fruitful. The devil is in the details, however, so there is the question of relative rather than absolute activation of imagery by a certain task. We can easily imagine how the breakfast-table task and instruction might be modified to focus more on imagery—including more creative imagery processes (Finke, Ward, & Smith, 1992; Jankowska & Karwowski, 2015) than memory alone. Would it not be informative and interesting to ask participants (be they scientists or students) to not only recall images but also to transform them (see Gordon Test of Imagery Control; Gordon, 1949)? Is it not possible to call for superposition of elements placed on the breakfast table or their multiplication? Why not call for the hyperbolization of individual image elements (e.g., playing with their proportions) or their selective majorization? All these mechanisms were described as vital for transforming abilities—crucial for creative imagery (see e.g., Dziedziewicz & Karwowski, 2015; Jankowska & Karwowski, 2015). Studies inspired by the creative cognition perspective (Finke et al., 1992) provide a large number of similar mechanisms that might activate more creative functioning of people's imagery; they seem applicable to the breakfast-table task as well. Therefore current and future creativity scholars should consider further works using the modified breakfast-table task to better understand the functioning of creative imagery.

The other important point that deserves discussion is the role mental imagery plays for creativity. Although simple transformation of available images is not creative by definition, and there is a convincing distinction between (creative) imagery and (creative) imagination (see Glăveanu, Karwowski, Jankowska, & Saint-Laurent, 2017, for a discussion), it seems safe to posit that imagery might be considered a necessary yet not sufficient condition of creative imagination and creative achievement in—at least—certain domains. Aside from anecdotal examples of famous creators relying extensively on their imagery (Poincaré, Kekulé, and Einstein, to name only a few), there is also growing empirical evidence that it is indeed hard to imagine (*sic!*) efficient creativity without imagery and imagination. Complex creativity processes are not solely based on analytical, step-by-step, highly verbalized thinking, but also on more chaotic, intuition, and image-based processing. Biographies and studies on scholars convincingly demonstrate clear benefits of the effective use of imagination for their creativity. Hence it seems justified to conclude that Sir Francis Galton was wrong to underestimate the role and power of imaginative abilities.

References

Baird, B., Smallwood, J., Mrazek, M. D., Kam, J. W., Franklin, M. S., & Schooler, J. W. (2012). Inspired by distraction: Mind wandering facilitates creative incubation. *Psychological Science, 23*, 1117–1122.

Betts, G. H. (1909). The distribution and functions of mental imagery. *Teachers' College Columbia University Contributions to Education, 26*, 1–99.

Blajenkova, O., Kozhevnikov, M., & Motes, M. (2006). Object-spatial imagery: A new self-report imagery questionnaire. *Applied Cognitive Psychology, 20*, 239–263.

Brewer, W. F. (1986). What is autobiographical memory? In D. C. Rubin (Ed.), *Autobiographical memory* (pp. 25–49). Cambridge, UK: Cambridge University Press.

Brewer, W. F. (1996). What is recollective memory? In D. C. Rubin (Ed.), *Remembering our past: Studies in autobiographical memory* (pp. 19–66). Cambridge, UK: Cambridge University Press.

Brewer, W. F., & Schommer-Aikins, M. (2006). Scientists are not deficient in mental imagery: Galton revised. *Review of General Psychology, 10*, 130–146.

Burbridge, D. (1994). Galton's 100: An exploration of Francis Galton's imagery studies. *British Journal for the History of Science, 27*(4), 443–463.

Dziedziewicz, D., & Karwowski, M. (2015). Development of children's creative visual imagination: A theoretical model and enhancement programmes. *Education 3–13, 43*, 382–392.

Campos, A. (2014). Gender differences in imagery. *Personality and Individual Differences, 59*, 107–111.

Campos, A., & Pérez-Fabello, M. J. (2005). The Spanish version of the Betts' questionnaire upon mental imagery. *Psychological Reports, 96*, 51–56.

Cox, C. M. (1926). *The early mental traits of three hundred geniuses.* Stanford, CA: Stanford University Press.

Fechner, G. T. (1860/1966). *Elements of psychophysics.* English edition. D. H. Howes & E. G. Boring (Eds.). New York: Holt, Rinehart and Winston.

Finke, R. A., Ward, T. B., & Smith, S. M. (1992). *Creative cognition: Theory, research, and applications.* Cambridge, MA: MIT Press.

Forrest, D. W. (1974). *Francis Galton: The life and work of a Victorian genius.* London: Taplinger.

Galton, F. (1865). Hereditary talent and character. *Macmillan's Magazine, 12*, 157–166 (Part 1) and 318–327 (Part 2).

Galton, F. (1869). *Hereditary genius: An inquiry into its laws and consequences.* London: Macmillan.

Galton, F. (1880a). Mental Imagery. *Fortnightly Review, 28,* 312–24.

Galton, F. (1880b). Statistics of mental imagery. *Mind, 5,* 301–318.

Galton, F. (1883). *Inquiries into the human faculty and its development.* London: Macmillan.

Glăveanu, V. P., Karwowski, M., Jankowska, D. M., & Saint-Laurent, C. (2017). Creative imagination. In V. P. Glăveanu & T. Zittoun (Eds.), *Oxford handbook of culture and imagination* (pp. 61–86). New York: Oxford University Press.

Gordon, R. (1949). An investigation into some of the factors that favour the formation of stereotyped images. *British Journal of Psychology, 39,* 156–167.

Hackmann, A., Clark, D. M., & McManus, F. (2000). Recurrent images and early memories in social phobia. *Behaviour Research and Therapy, 38,* 601–610.

Isaac, A. R., & Marks, D. F. (1994). Individual differences in mental imagery experience: Developmental changes and specialization. *British Journal of Psychology, 85*(4), 479–500.

Jankowska, D. M., & Karwowski, M. (2015). Measuring creative imagery abilities. *Frontiers in Psychology* 6:1591, doi: 10.3389/fpsyg.2015.01591.

Kaufman, J. C., & Beghetto, R. A. (2009). Beyond big and little: The four c model of creativity. *Review of General Psychology, 13,* 1–12.

Kosslyn, S. M. (2005). Mental images and the brain. *Cognitive Neuropsychology, 22,* 333–347.

Kosslyn, S. M., Ganis, G., & Thompson, W. L. (2001). Neural foundations of imagery. *Nature Reviews Neuroscience, 2,* 635–642.

Kozhevnikov, M., Kosslyn, S., & Shephard, J. (2005). Spatial versus object visualizers: A new characterization of visual cognitive style. *Memory & Cognition, 33,* 710–726.

LeBoutillier, N., & Marks, D. (2002). Inherent response leniency in the Modified Gordon Test of Visual Imagery Control Questionnaire. *Imagination, Cognition and Personality, 21,* 311–318.

Marks, D. F. (1995). New directions for mental imagery research. *Journal of Mental Imagery, 19,*153–167.

McKelvie, S. J. (1995). The VVIQ as a psychometric test of individual differences in visual imagery vividness: A critical quantitative review and plea for direction. *Journal of Mental Imagery, 19,* 1–106.

Pearson, D. G., Deeprose, C., Wallace-Hadrill, S. M., Heyes, S. B., & Holmes, E. A. (2013). Assessing mental imagery in clinical psychology: A review of imagery measures and a guiding framework. *Clinical Psychology Review, 33*(1), 1–23.

Richardson, J. T. E. (1995). Gender differences in the vividness of visual imagery questionnaire: A meta-analysis. *Journal of Mental Imagery, 19,* 177–187.

Simonton, D. K. (2015). *The psychology of creativity: A historical perspective.* Paper presented at the Green College Lecture Series on The Nature of Creativity: History, Biology, and Socio-Cultural Dimensions, University of British Columbia, 2001. Available at http://simonton.faculty.ucdavis.edu/wp-content/uploads/sites/243/2015/08/HistoryCreativity.pdf.

Terman, L. M. (1917). The intelligence quotient of Francis Galton in childhood. *American Journal of Psychology, 28,* 209–215.

Voyer, D., Voyer, S., & Bryden, M. P. (1995). Magnitude of sex differences in spatial abilities: A meta-analysis and consideration of critical variables. *Psychological Bulletin, 117,* 250–270.

White, K. D., Ashton, R., & Brown, M. D. (1977). The measurement of imagery vividness: Normative data and their relationship to sex, age, and modality differences. *British Journal of Psychology, 68,* 203–211.

Zedelius, C. M., & Schooler, J. W. (2015). The richness of inner experience: Relating styles of daydreaming to creative processes. *Frontiers in Psychology, 6,* 2063, doi: 10.3389/fpsyg.2015.02063.

Measuring Ideation in the 1900s

The Contribution of Alfred Binet

BAPTISTE BARBOT AND JACQUES-HENRI GUIGNARD

Summary

Prior to formulating his famous test battery for the measurement of intelligence, Binet was a fine observer of imaginative processes and one of the pioneers of its experimental study in the context of thorough case-by-case observation (idiographic approach), through which he was able to formalize an incredibly accurate description of the phenomenon. This chapter presents and discusses two texts of the "pre Binet-Simon era" that reflect Binet's early operationalization of one of the key thinking processes involved in imagination and creativity, namely, ideation. After contextualizing these texts and discussing how they are greatly compatible with current views of the construct of ideation, we highlight how his approach of the time, decidedly clinical and idiographic, could inspire important future lines of work in the field.

Introduction

For well over a century, the French psychologist Alfred Binet has been known for his work on intelligence and the elaboration of the first concept scale for its assessment. But before conceiving what became a powerful tool, his work contrasted strikingly with what the psychology of intelligence was at that time. At the end of the 19th century, the scientific approach to psychology was at its beginning and strove to elucidate mental phenomena using experimental methods. Psychologists of that era were fundamentally inspired by scientific work in the natural sciences—such as physics, chemistry, and biology—to offer new investigative tools in order to quantify mental phenomena. They studied extensively the quality of basic sensations triggered by experimentally induced physiological stimulations, seeking to highlight links among sensations, perceptions, and representations.

This pioneering psychometric approach was mostly in line with the associationist school, derived from the empiricist English philosophy that was introduced in France by Theophile Ribot. According to this perspective, mental activity lies on the association of images that are produced by external stimulations. Sensations are seen as elementary particles of intelligence that combine into higher-order cognitive processes. Binet considered this view to be reductionist as it evacuates the question of how higher-order states of consciousness lead individuals to solve problems and engage in complex productions.

Although associationism was dominant at the very end of the 19th century, another line of research focused on cognitive functions such as memory and mental imagery. Binet and his research assistant Henri (e.g., Binet & Henri, 1896) followed this line by arguing that individual differences in intelligence had to be detected through the expression of complex mental processes, such as imagination. They dedicated their work to *individual psychology*, the psychology of individual differences, also known as differential psychology. Binet (1897) argued that there is not only memory of sensations but also memory of abstract concepts and ideas, with extensive individual differences (Nicolas, Coubart, & Lubart, 2014). In reaching such a conclusion, Binet's methodology was ingeniously simple and relied on accurate reports of what people say about the strategies they operate to perform a wide range of tasks. For example, he asked participants to describe a simple or a complex object (a pin, a coin, a newspaper, or a flower). Binet then observed that each individual used a personal way to explore and represent an object. This methodology relying on introspection led him to quantify the nature of objects' descriptions and to establish different types of approaches to describe objects, further associated with specific intellectual typologies. Illustrating these individual differences from the prolonged observation of his two daughters, Madeleine and Alice (aka "Marguerite and Armande," born in 1885 and 1887, respectively), Binet (1903) published an innovative work, *L'étude expérimentale de l'intelligence* (The experimental study of intelligence), in which he showed that intellectual styles were consistent (i.e., stable) within an individual and were, in sum, an expression of one's individuality. This idiosyncratic approach led him to sketch portraits of his two daughters' mode of thinking using a set of 20 simple tasks.

The first text we present, "L'observateur et l'imaginatif" (The observational and the imaginative types, 1900), was published prior to *The Experimental Study of Intelligence* and provides a brief teaser to the later volume. It introduces the distinction between the "observational" and the "imaginative" cognitive styles. The text is almost an experiential self-report of Binet's discovery of these styles from a battery of specially designed tasks. Through his report, we follow Binet's efforts to describe his daughters' thinking styles and the very idiographic method he develops to do so. By a "fortunate coincidence" (as directly quoted from Binet), for the sake of illustration, one of his subjects (Marguerite, 14 years old at the time of the evaluation) belonged to the observer type, whereas the other (Armande, 12 years old) belonged to the imaginative type, although, as discussed in our commentary, these styles are not mutually exclusive in Binet's thinking.

The second text is a chapter from *The Experimental Study of Intelligence* that compiles Binet's three-year longitudinal study of Marguerite and Armande. This chapter, "Comment la pensée se développe" (How the thought develops), is particularly relevant here as it describes an ideation task in which he asked the girls to provide a list of 20 words, in a multitrial approach. With this method, Binet sought to understand the underlying mechanism of the sequence of these words, that is, how his daughters moved from one word to another in their 20-word sequence. He showed that this sequence was not arbitrary but driven by associations of ideas. Moreover the nature of these associations differentiated the two sisters, according to their intellectual style. Thus the contrast outlined by Binet is holistic, in that it is based on individual differences relying on global mental functioning (including personality) rather than on pure cognitive performances.

After presenting these complementary texts, our discussion focuses on how Binet's ideas in those texts have influenced today's research on ideation and our understanding of cognitive styles, and how his specific methodology may prove useful in future studies of creative ideation.

Reading 1: "L'observateur et L'imaginatif"

Source: Binet, A. (1900). L'observateur et l'imaginatif [The observational and the imaginative types]. *L'année Psychologique, 7*, 519–523. Original translation by Serge Nicolas.

I intended to publish in *L'Année* a set of experiments that I have just completed on a question that appears to me as important for psychology, the question of the typical orientation of the mind; I have insufficient space here to include these investigations, which are long and detailed, and I hope to publish them soon in a volume. *I will only provide a very short summary here.*

One will undoubtedly remember the experiments that I conducted, three or four years ago, on the description of objects.[1] When asking someone to describe a simple or a complex object, a pin, a coin, a cigarette, a violet, a newspaper, a book, an engraving, etc., we notice that each person inspects and understands the object in their own way; the comparison of the written descriptions allows us to classify them according to a number of distinct types of description, among which there are two that I want to note, the observational and the imaginative. The observational person is attentive to the slightest material details of the object, and he notes them with the greatest care; in the end product, this person has the quality of accuracy—and the drawback of mundaneness. In contrast, the imaginative person casts a cursory glance at the object itself; the object is for him only a suggestion, then he detaches himself from it and gives us a literary development, or a general development, or an emotionally nuanced development; this type too has a quality—originality—and a drawback, inaccuracy. When I published the first observations that I made about these two mental types, I thought that I was dealing with a specific small point of limited interest, such as the analysis of some kind of tactile sensation. I glimpsed only very vaguely that this distinction between the two types, the observational and the imaginative, formed the germ of a classification of minds that could hold an important place in experimental psychology. I could have remembered that in the history of politics, religion and even science, we saw these two conflicting trends occurring continuously. One trend was down-to-earth, accurate and slow, and the other speculative, fearless, eccentric and quite adventurous; and at certain times these two trends were embodied in two competing viewpoints. But experimental psychology, rightly or wrongly, is cautious about literature and history; incidentally, my personal taste does not lead me towards studies of this kind, and that is probably why I lost sight of the interest of the question. However, I always remembered my first experiments and I reproduced them when the opportunity arose. I did some research, three years ago, with several of my students at the teachers' training college in Versailles and then in Melun; I asked teacher students at these colleges to describe different objects, and I was struck to see how much some descriptions carried a strong individual imprint. I gave them a penny and a pen to describe. Most of them, I have to say, behaved as simple observers, and gave me exact, full and down-to-earth descriptions. However, three or four of those young people belonged to the imaginative type; one told a story, another one was sentimental, a third had ideas of a dramatic form. I consulted the school director without giving him those papers, and I asked him for some particular information about those three young people. He told me that the first one had substantial literary gifts—he was moreover almost entirely unfit for mathematics; the second one was emotional; and the third one had an adventurous mind, and loved travel and danger. These assessments fitted very well with the papers and the types of description. Later again, in primary schools, I asked for descriptions of engravings, and I also obtained interesting results. Meanwhile several colleagues, Dwelshauvers in Belgium and Sharp in America, repeated these experiments and took some interest in the topic. But I would not have thought of resuming the experiments, nor indeed of generalizing them, without one of those happy coincidences that we often search for and sometimes meet.

I have been observing two young girls in my family.[2] They have already served as my subjects for some experiments which I published recently on tactile sensitivity, and for other research, which I published around ten years ago when they were children, on color and number perception and on the definition of objects. Recently I undertook the project of administer[ing] to these two subjects a set of tests that I devised on individual psychology. I was especially captivated by the occasion when I had to put the set of daily observations that I made on these two girls next to the result of each test; the daily observations were confusing but often quite suggestive, while the test results were accurate but a little narrow. I began this work methodically last July, and I conducted experiments almost every morning during the next 5 months, while trying only to renew their attractiveness with a little variety. No preconceived idea was driving me. Each experiment was analyzed just after it was completed. I continually compared the two sisters together, aiming above all to bring out their mental characteristics, as we have to do in individual psychology. When the experiment did not yield anything significant, I put it aside; but when it was on course to some interesting point, I repeated, verified and modified it. When the result was new, important and accurate, and moreover, seemed to agree with my daily observations, I searched for a theoretical development, and I drafted a theory which I then tried to verify with new experiments. The documents I assembled day by day with this method are extremely abundant; and, although they are concerned with only two subjects, I assume that they do not lack general relevance. By collecting them, I realized that the individual psychology of my two subjects was not constructed from "bits and pieces" (pardon the phrasing); it is not a juxtaposition of disparate mental qualities, as we could imagine when we only do quick tests and summaries on persons we do not know. I noticed that the individual psychology of my subjects is governed by a small number of **dominant characteristics**, to employ a zoological expression. There are—or at least, I have identified so far—three or four of these dominant characteristics; including these, we can link them with a whole collection of qualities and aptitudes that logically stem from them. This is how, in my view, the mental unit of the person is constructed. While untidying the thus far inextricable tangle of mental phenomena that represents a particular person, this observation, which I think important, gave my research a new direction. I gave up the idea of studying the entire individual psychology of my two subjects in a rather random and erratic manner, and I preferred to develop more widely everything that concerns one of these dominant characteristics.

The one that first struck my attention was the usual type of orientation of ideas. By a really fortunate coincidence, it happened that one of my two subjects belonged to the observational type and the other to the imaginative type; the contrast between the two girls is extreme, although they have been brought up in the same family and have received exactly the same education and the same instruction. The contrast is extreme, but I am eager to add that there is no consistency here: while one of these girls is exclusively of the imaginative type, the other is not exclusively of the observational type. The latter girl belongs mostly to the observational type, but on occasions, in special experiments, she can show a certain imaginative development. I admit that I hardly thought of investigating the girls for the existence of those types of orientation of ideas that I have described in the past, and I did not even make use of the experiment of describing objects, which highlights these two types so well. For about a month, I took my time over investigations that were longer, more monotonous, and more elementary. These investigations were equivalent to those whose results my excellent colleague M. Flournoy has published under the title "The influence of the psychological environment on ideation." They consist simply in making the subject write words; the mental analysis of these words helps us to understand the natural ideation of the persons. I had each of my subjects write at least 300 words in several sessions, and that is how I noticed eventually, that one of these young girls showed a trend to observation in the choice of words, and the second one showed an imaginative trend. This was nevertheless not enlightening for me. I continued with studies on the representation of objects and the association of ideas, by using methods similar to those of Bourdon, Aschaffenburg and Ziehen; and here again the two opposed mental types emerged. I pursued my investigations on less elementary phenomena. I studied a development of thought that was narrower and more logical, by finishing sentences, and by filling the gap created by the deletion of some words, according to the methods of Ebbinghaus. The two types appeared again with a perfect clarity. However, to establish their existence in an irrefutable manner, I needed the test on the description of objects. In that case, the difference between the two young girls became completely striking, and it held up in a series of more than twenty descriptions. I then acquired a keystone; and with this starting point I investigated how the observational and imaginative types mark their imprints on the other mental abilities. In other words, I tried to find out if my two young girls possessed a special way of reasoning, remembering and focusing their attention. I believe I found some characteristic differences for these capacities, although I did not know yet whether or not these differences were directly related to the two extreme types of orientation of ideas that my two subjects showed so clearly. The fact that two abilities are combined in a single person does not necessarily mean that one of these abilities depends on the other. This is indeed one aspect of my research for which I wanted to leave a brief report interesting in itself. Besides, in a summary as short as this, I cannot show all the complexity of the question or consider all the various facets. I shall only, for now, affirm that the observational and imaginative types have an importance in individual psychology that was not suspected up till now—an importance that has now been made clear to me through a very large number of precise experiments.

---

1. *L'Année psychologique*, III, p. 296.
2. It is interesting to note how Binet introduce his two daughters.—*Barbot and Guignard*

Reading 2: "Comment la pensée se développe"

Source: Binet, A. (1903). Comment la pensée se développe [How the thought develops]. Chap. 4 in *L'étude expérimentale de l'intelligence* [The experimental study of intelligence]. Paris: Schleicher, pp. 59–69. Original translation by Serge Nicolas.

We will now test our two subjects' association of ideas using this test which involves writing a series of 20 words. I think this is a suitable test for the analysis of association of ideas, maybe even more appropriate than the classic procedure; with this classic procedure, which consists in saying a word, then asking the participant to answer with another word, we only create one association at a time, an isolated, unique association, whereas the 20 words test allows the creation of 20 chained associations. This is a truly important advantage as the 20 word procedure comes closer to the natural conditions than the single association procedure. When our thought grows naturally, it takes its course, and a great deal of ideas succeed one another, running one after another just like a crowd. However, the immediate succession of two ideas does not necessarily give a precise idea of this stream of ideas; it is possible that this stream is subject to a kind of rhythm that does not appear between two ideas, but that can expand to a large number of ideas. This is not a costless hypothesis. We will see by looking further at this stream of thoughts in a 20 words series that some distributions of words cannot simply be explained by the association of ideas, and that the usual process of inquiry, too fractioned, cannot capture this fact.

Our method involving written words has another advantage; the participant who writes 20 words is more free, more spontaneous, more autonomous than the one who has to associate immediately a word to the previous one; in the first case, the participant is forced to make artificial associations, and one could fear that s/he's diverted from her/his natural thinking. Ideation is a very fragile, impressionable phenomenon; it is like a child who stops playing naturally once he/she is being observed.

It would be fair to complete these critiques of the usual procedure by highlighting its advantages; introspection follows directly the formation of every association, which averts errors and memory lapses; the association is evoked by words chosen by the experimenter, which allows to gauge the ideation of the participant by forcing him/her to work with specific words, which makes easier comparisons of psychological reactions of two individuals who were presented with the same words. In short, when balancing every aspect, the two procedures are not redundant, and one could use them cumulatively. I will thus study how my two participants linked the 20 words I made them write. It is normal to expect some inconsistencies. To be honest, if such a large inconsistency was to be found in a letter or any kind of essay, one could think of its author as intellectually-challenged. Let us keep in mind that the series of 20 words cannot be compared to a well-prepared work, written for a specific purpose: the subject is asked to write 20 words of her/his choosing; s/he is not invited to produce any logic or meaningful piece of work.

Here is how I asked my participants to explain their associations of idea. When the 20 words have been written, I used to begin my questioning with a pen in hand, writing questions and answers completely. I would ask firstly for each word its meaning; then I would ask as a second question on how this word followed the previous one; the two questions followed each other, and I only went to the next word once these two questions were answered.

Keeping in mind that I made Marguerite write 320 words in series of 20; I regret not to have questioned her on her association of ideas for all those words; I only questioned her for the last 60. However, I questioned Armande on the 300 words she wrote. These would be really limited data if I only took into account the 60 words associations written by Marguerite; I will take advantage of some series I made her write recently to increase the number of my observations.

The first question that I would like to ask is whether the mind notices associations with the same degree of awareness as its ideas. *A priori*, it does not seem to be the case. The linkage is a transition, a hiatus; it has no substantial nature; it is a way to have an idea, but it is not an idea in itself; for all these reasons, the link is something difficult to perceive. Let us see what the observation tells us in this regard.

Marguerite is not able to explain 13 transitions among the 60 words she wrote: in the first series of 20 words, there are 8 unexplained transitions; in the second series, on the same day, there are 4 of them and in the last series, only one word remains unexplained. This rapid decrease can be understood easily. Marguerite didn't know the first time she wrote a series that she would be questioned on the transitions later on, thus she didn't pay attention; as soon as she was told, and when she was confronted with many precise questions, her quick mind made her pay attention to these transitions, which made them appear more consciously. Perhaps she even altered their nature somehow or made them more systematic. In order to know whether the transitions are less conscious than the ideas, we need to compare this number of 13 unexplained transitions to the number of unexplained words that she wrote in the first series. These three first series contained 9 unexplained words in total. We can see that the transitions are a little bit more frequent, but the difference is not large.

A few days later, I ask Marguerite to write 20 words slowly, and then rapidly.

For the fast series, I count almost 7 unexplained transitions, and two unexplained words; for the slow series, the two figures are smaller, there are only 2 or 3 unconscious transitions and no unconscious words. This way we can see that unconscious words are always fewer in number. But Marguerite is not a good subject for this kind of experiment, her tendency to figure out what she's doing while she's writing the series of words is too strong to give us a good occasion to study the phenomenon of unconsciousness carefully.

For Armande, unconscious transitions are very common; on average, 30 of 60 remain unexplained.

This profusion of ignored associations—regardless of how it is explained—(it could be forgetting the mental associations that were really playing a role, or an inconsistency of these associations, it could also be a complete lack of associations) is not surprising for Armande, who frequently writes words whose meaning she cannot remember or represent to herself. This is an important feature demonstrating the semi-unconsciousness of her ideation. We will notice that these results allow us to answer a question we just formulated. The unconscious transitions are far more frequent than the unconscious words in Armande's series. The number of her unconscious words within a session (that is 60 words) never reached 30; it was 23 for the first session; during the following sessions, it oscillated around 15. There would be, to keep things approximative, twice as many unconscious transitions as unconscious ideas. This proportion should probably not be generalized in its exact figure; but I am inclined to believe it expresses a rather constant fact.

We meet here with W. James who, describing the course of thought, distinguishes its substantial from transitive aspects; the mind is like a bird that sometimes flies, sometimes tilts; James says that transitions, i.e. flights, are accompanied by a lower awareness than landings.[1]

Let us now see what these transitions are, and examine how children who have no theoretical knowledge about associations realize them, and how a systematic exercise of mental analysis made them able to read within themselves.

What struck me first was to find a general picture within their chains of ideas.

The 20 words series is not like a rosary with equally shaped and equally spaced beads; there are clusters of them: a series of words is predominated by a common idea; it forms a unity; then begins another series which comes from a different inspiration, either from a new idea, either evoked by the view of a surrounding object, or from some external noise.

These changes in the direction of the mind, these swerves, are most likely to be conscious. The subject will say, for instance, while analyzing the written words: "All of this is the same idea; but here, I've changed idea." I did not expect these specific groupings, thus I could not help my subjects on their way, nor did I make any suggestion.

I will call these groups *themes,* a word that suits them particularly well since these groups are made of a written form. The themes of Marguerite are very clear, well defined, and well developed. I will quote some of them: she wrote the words *meadows, bridge, water, wash house, poplar tree* [*prés, pont, eau, lavoir, peuplier*]. All these words have some commonalities; from the information given by Marguerite, they represent the same thing: the banks of the river Seine near S——; around this place, there are poplar trees, a bridge, a wash-house, meadows and water; all these items are part of the same landscape, they are so close that one could make them fit in a single picture. So the theme is a description of real objects relived in memory.

In another series, Marguerite wrote the word *furnace*; she thought of the furnace that is in the kitchen of an old farmer from S—— whom she knows; then she wrote the words *kitchen, closet, plate, bedroom, bed, ice, fireplace, lamp, window, table, chair, green couch, bed curtains, door, rabbits*; these words do not have an abstract or vague meaning; they all represent the house of the old farmer, and Marguerite thinks of each named object with its features; then, at *rabbits,* she leaves the house and names other houses from the surrounding area, hence a new series of words: *coal, bags, liquors, haberdashery, glaziery*; coal and bags represent the coal merchant, who lives right next to the old farmer, and the last three words indicate the shops of the wine merchant, the haberdasher and the glazier, which are almost adjacent on the town's main road. Nothing is easier to understand than this type of ideation.

The crucial feature to pinpoint here is the prevalence of spatial contiguity of Marguerite; on 60 links, 42 are spatial.

Of the 60 words written by Marguerite, I picked up a kind of association by resemblance only once; she just wrote the words *duvet, pillow, toilet, hair*, which all apply to Miss X——, and she thought about the bedroom of Miss X—— to write these words, with everything the room contained; then after the word *hair*, she said "*hair* made me think of *pins*, then for a change I wrote *pins* of L. (the maid)." By association of resemblance, she went from a person to another. This case is unique within the series, thus insignificant.

To sum up, Marguerite's ideation develops through memories tied together by spatial contiguity associations. It may be difficult to guess how, for the other series of words that Marguerite wrote, she went from a word to another, since I did not ask her. However, because she indicated the meaning she gave to the words each time, one can have a probable opinion on the question. I said that almost all of her ideation is composed by personal memories and names of surrounding objects; the surrounding objects, as we saw many times, are obtained when Marguerite, embarrassed, takes a look around, their succession mirrors the spatial contiguity. As for the memories, succeeding each other in general by more or less long series, they refer usually to several objects being part of a whole, apartment, garden and street; it is again spatial contiguity. This type of association dominates Marguerite's associations. I find this way of creating ideas lacking unexpectedness and originality; it can be easily understood since association by spatial contiguity is essentially a conservative strength; it revives previous conscious states, in the order that they initially appeared, without any addition.

However, if we remember that Wundt called these associations *external associations*, in opposition to resemblance associations, which are called *internal associations*, one could understand that it is natural to find a lot of external associations within Marguerite's ideation, who belong so clearly to the observant type.

Armande's ideation, being full of imagery and more diversified than Marguerite's, we shall expect her associations to be also more varied. The data I have at hand allow me to do this study in a complete manner; Armande explained her associations for the 300 words she wrote.

But I think that, since we simply compare two subjects here, it will be enough to take a series of 60 words from Armande and to scrutinize them. I already said that half of these associations remain unconscious.

Another feature of her ideation is the complete, or almost complete, absence of associations by spatial contiguity.

When Armande evokes a memory, this memory does not suggest several words; it vanishes in a single word, then there is right away a change in the direction of the thought; that is why we cannot find within the series she wrote some words that revive parts of the same memory or picture. The association she uses the most is the enumeration of objects from the same kind; she writes *house*, without thinking of a particular house, then assumes that she makes her task easier by using all words associated to the word house; another time, she writes the word *disdain*, and she has the intention to write other names for facial expression; but, in general, this enumeration project doesn't take her very far; she doesn't have Marguerite's methodology; she writes two or three words, at best, then she switches to something else. The number of these associations by enumeration was only 7 of the 60 words written.

The other associations are of very different kinds; within the same series, there are:

4 associations by verbal resemblance: "Chien–Chenil; Chêne–Chaine; Terrain–Terrasse; Tiroir–Air" [e.g., earth–birth]. These are not absolute verbal associations; there is generally something more, a reason that makes these associations more suitable than others; Hence, she went from chêne [oak] to chaîne [chain] because she wrote several tree names and she felt the need to change; the word chêne wasn't written. In the same vein, the word tiroir [drawer] doesn't evoke directly the word air [air], which is written right after; the subject, after having written the word tiroir, doubts about the spelling of the word, then wonders whether the word is spelled with one r or two, then she thinks of writing the word air, which sounds alike. In similar fashion, the word terrain [field] comes to the mind because it was written in the previous series, but the subject rejects this word and replaces it by the word terrace [terrace].

1 verbal association, mine–gold.

3 logical associations, at times difficult to define: fox–chicken; paper–nettle; matchstick–fire.

To sum up, Marguerite's ideation is composed of rather broad themes, which develop by association of spatial contiguity; she is consistent, not diversified, even monotonous, and very aware; Armande's ideation, composed of short themes, develops through a more complex mechanism and [is] less conscious; few associations by contiguity, but several enumerations of classification, some logical associations, word resemblance, and more importantly, what appears as a prevalent feature, the constant change of the direction of the thought, a zigzag walk by small broken steps, of new, surprising and original associations.

Conclusions and Hypothesis

The present study suggests many conclusions which I think do not deserve to insist upon; it is for example, the semi-consciousness of the links between ideas, already suggested by authors, but well highlighted in our research; or further, the description, that seems novel to me, of two types of associations, different from the point of view of the individual psychology; what I already said on these questions would suffice for the reader to understand their importance. I will make better use of the last sentences of this chapter by discussing how the facts highlighted above force us to change our current conception of the association of ideas.

According to the lessons of the British Associationists' school, which exerted a strong and legitimate influence on French psychology—I myself must recognize all the veneration I owe to Stuart Mill, my only master in psychology—the association of ideas would be the key, the ultimate explanation of all the mental phenomena; Mill described it in his own terms; and regarding the association of ideas itself, it could be explained by an inherent property of the mental states.

Taine emphasized what is automatic, external to our thought, in this process, using this phrasing to explain the revival of ideas: "A picture emerges when it is already started to emerge."

With these words, Taine was loyal to his wonderful theory of Intelligence, so similar to a clockwork mechanism, where nothing represents effort, direction, adaptation, choice, and where attention itself is reduced to the intensity of the picture. I cannot handle this question with all the attention that it deserves; I only want to show, anecdotally, that the existence of themes of thought cannot be explained by the automatism of associations; because, on the one hand, it happens in Marguerite's series that the transition between two words, although being made by means of conscious association, does not prevent the subject from noticing a change in idea at that point, that is, the appearance of a new theme, a fact that association cannot explain; and, on the other hand, when words are inspired by a same theme, they cannot be given simply by the mere set of associations of ideas; for a theme to develop, one needs to embrace the ideas, a work of choice and rejection that requires far beyond the re-sources of association. The latter is intelligent only when it is directed; all by itself, association makes use of any resemblance or contiguity; it can only then produce incoherence; at best, it could explain the words of a maniac or the kaleidoscopic images of a dream.[2]

---

1. James, *Psychology*, I, ch. IV, p. 243.
2. By the way, Paulhan defended the same thesis a long time ago. See his interesting book *L'Activité mentale et les éléments de l'esprit* (Paris, 1889). I do not intend to make here a bibliography and I refer the reader to the recent work, so accurate and documented, of Claparède, *L'Association des idées* (Paris, Doin, 1903).

Commentary

In this commentary, our discussion focuses on (1) how Binet's ideas in these two texts have influenced (or are still compatible with) today's ideation research, and (2) how his specific ideas and method focusing on intensive observations of a few cases (rather than sparse observation of numerous cases) may prove useful in future studies of creative ideation.

INFLUENCE

Whether the ideas in the selected text have influenced or are still in line with today's general understanding of ideation processes, here we highlight a number of ideas that seem to be still current after well over a century of conceptualization, debates, and research in the field. One critical feature of Binet's thinking is that imagination is compatible with (a) a dimensional view and (b) a multivariate view, which combine into the concept of types or "styles."

Dimensional View

In "L'observateur et l'imaginatif," Binet (1900, p. 522) notes that "while one of these girls is exclusively of the imaginative type, the other is not exclusively of the observational type." Further, he notes that "the latter girl belongs mostly to the observational type, but on occasions, in special experiments, she can show a certain imaginative development" (p. 522). In the first statement, Binet acknowledges implicitly that both styles can coexist, and in the second, that imaginative development can occur to "some degree." On that note, Binet (1903, p. 298) reports in the last pages of the *Experimental Study of Intelligence* how his two daughters changed during the observation period (1900 to 1903), presaging, according to him, many more changes to come: "The psychological portraits I have drawn of them have now become less similar than they were three years ago; And it seems to me probable that in ten years other more important changes will have occurred." In his thinking, Binet takes into account developmental weights in the structuration of cognitive styles. That is, the girls are described as if they were using a preferential style to tackle the tasks. However, the elder showed a preference for the "observational" style, while, in some instances, being able to switch to the imaginative style. According to the specialization-differentiation hypothesis (Barbot & Tinio, 2015), adolescence is a time when creativity begins to specialize into specific domains of interest and relies less on a general factor of abilities. Accordingly, it is plausible that Marguerite, more advanced in adolescence, is more likely to be able to "specialize" her mode of thinking according to the specific constraints of the task. Armande, who has just entered adolescence, uses only one style, regardless of the type of task she has to complete. This interpretation in terms of specialization of the mode of thinking according to the type of task is consistent with recent neurodevelopmental studies of cognitive development (e.g., Kleibeuker, De Dreu, & Crone, 2016).

Although "dimensional" thinking is now well established in the field of creativity and imagination, and more broadly in the field of individual differences psychology, Binet's thinking at the time might often appear to be a "categorical" view, which is even more evident in his later published intelligence scale (e.g., one is imaginative or is not; one meets the developmental milestones of one's age group or does not). Dimensional views of individual differences were already well conceptualized and operationalized at that time, notably with the influence of Galton, but Binet had a far more practical operationalization of individual differences, which often translated into the identifications of "types" or categories of individuals (e.g., subnormal vs. normal), perhaps in an effort to offer an alternative where others had failed. While this view was not incompatible with the notion of variability (within and between individuals, as illustrated in the chosen example) and thus dimensionality, it also insisted on a critical feature that remains relevant in the current thinking: a multivariate view supposing the contribution of multiple factors of diverse nature and their combination to make the creative thought happen.

Multivariate View

When Binet describes "types," he refers to contrastable entities on a number of characteristics (not just a single one), often including cognitive and conative aspects. Specifically, Binet emphasizes the difficulty of summarizing one's ideation style into an all-inclusive word. In the target texts, he mentions that whenever a typological category seems to differentiate the ideational styles of the two sisters in one task, their observation in another task leads him to review his interpretation with a new typological category that replaces the previous one, and so on until a constellation of personal traits (corresponding more to multivariate profiles rather than a simple dichotomy) was gradually built. He thus provides sketches of the ideational processes of his daughters, assembling traits belonging to several psychological arenas which he names: will, intelligence, emotivity, physiology (Binet, 1903, p. 305). In the concluding notes of the *Experimental Study of Intelligence*, Binet established a list of traits (or individual "resources") observed in Armande and Marguerite across the various tasks he employed with them. As illustrated below, these traits are very much in line with modern multivariate and componential theories of creativity and imagination (e.g., Amabile, 1983; Lubart, 2001).

Regarding cognitive dimensions associated with both thinking styles, Binet notes that with the 20-words task, Marguerite uses a systematic and "economic" strategy to produce her ideas. Her ideation is based on the description of real objects retrieved from recent everyday life memories. The transitions between the ideas are obvious and ordered, with a concern for details. As such, it is easy for her to explain the transitions between ideas. Armande, in contrast, does not seem to apply a salient strategy to generate words. Her research strategy is not systematic and the links between the words provided, if any, are far from obvious. As noted by Binet, this "erratic" production may increase her chances of making original associations, which is now widely acknowledged and valued in brainstorming sessions. Indeed Armande exhibits a floating attention that seems to favor the development of her imagination, as it leads to unexpected word associations. This observation was also supported by recent work on the links between cognitive inhibition and creative potential (Benedek, Franz, Heene, & Neubauer, 2012; Radel, Davranche, Fournier, & Dietrich, 2015), although the role of cognitive control as a critical mechanism to inhibit prepotent associations or ideas is becoming increasingly acknowledged (e.g., Beaty & Silvia, 2012; Cassotti, Agogué, Camarda, Houdé, & Borst, 2016).

Regarding personality features, Binet notes that Marguerite's ideation is "self-centered" because she refers to her own experience. Her approach to this task is somewhat rational, with a recessed imagination. Binet also describes her poor daydreaming abilities, which together map onto the description of a character with low openness. In contrast, Armande tends to focus her attention on her internal world, with a nonsystematic deployment of her thought. She demonstrates imagination not only on the content of her production (i.e., reported words) but also on the way she rationalizes the path of her ideation (i.e., the links between each word). In all, these features reflect Armande's higher openness. Relatedly, because the words reported by Armande seem to be particularly unrelated (far remote association), her thought process may at times appear overinclusive (i.e., inability to preserve conceptual boundaries), which is also a key personality characteristic of creative individuals (Eysenck, 1993), often associated with schizotypal thought disorder (Payne & Friedlander, 1962).

Among other key features relevant here as possible elements that distinguish both the observational and the imaginative types, Binet outlines his daughters' differences with respect to daydreaming tendency, fantasy proneness, or complexity and abstractness of ideas. Although he does not directly characterize them as influences of the environment, Binet also implicitly outlines various environmental features (classically incorporated in modern multivariate models of creativity) that may underline the sisters' thinking style or simply be called upon in their thinking process. For example, he notes that Marguerite's ideation is characterized by external associations: when she runs out of ideas, she tends to rely on her immediate environment to find new ideas. In contrast, the ideation of Armande is not underpinned by her concrete environment as her ideas often involve more abstract concepts.

In all, Binet's observations provide a great account of the various important resources involved in ideation and how they tend to co-occur within the same person, supporting the notion of types or "styles." Further, Binet (1900, p. 523) states that "the fact that two abilities are combined in a single person does not necessarily mean that one of these abilities depends on the other." In this statement, Binet suggests that if several components are involved in complex activities, these are not interdependent, nor are they underlined by a common factor. This view is very much in line with classic componential models of creativity (e.g., Amabile, 1983; Sternberg & Lubart, 1995) and current hybrid models that emphasize the combined contribution of domain-general, domain-specific, and task- or content-specific resources in creative ideation, suggesting the existence of multivariate profiles of independent resources (e.g., Barbot, Besançon, & Lubart, 2016; Barbot & Tinio, 2015).

DIRECTIONS FOR CURRENT AND FUTURE RESEARCH ON IDEATION

Binet (1903, p. 60) is aware of the flimsiness of the phenomenon he is trying to study and the difficulty of devising a method to capture its subtleties: "Ideation is a very fragile, impressionable phenomenon; it is like a child who stops playing naturally once he/she is being observed." In fact, by initiating the observation and testing of his own children, Binet is a precursor of what will become Piaget's famous clinical method. His approach emphasizes the importance of qualitative data obtained through the subject's discourse on his or her own mental processes.

Research on creativity has a substantial tradition of studies that focus on microprocesses (i.e., the processes involved in the generation of original ideas). However, in the past few decades there has been renewed interest in the understanding of macroprocesses (i.e., the main stages of the creative process that result in a production). In this line of work, qualitative methods are often used in order to track the steps of the creative process. This can be a retrospective interview of renowned creative individuals about their productions, or an introspective self-report during the production of ideas and decisions that will lead to a creative product (e.g., Botella, Nelson, & Zenasni, 2017; Glaveanu et al., 2013).

Binet intuitively adopted this qualitative approach to tackle the study of higher-order mental processes. Contrary to most contemporary approaches, he focuses as much on the content (the ideas themselves) as on the process (mechanisms that underlie the transition from one idea to the next). As a starting point, he wonders whether both aspects can be studied with the same degree of precision, as he assumes that one may not be as much aware of the process as of the content: "The first question that I would like to ask is whether the mind notices associations with the same degree of awareness as its ideas" (Binet, 1903, p. 61). He elaborates on this distinction by proposing a simple methodology to address this question, illustrated as follows: Among the 60 words that she wrote across her first 3 series of 20 words, Marguerite is unable to explain why she came up with 9 words, and when asked to explain her transitions between words, she fails to explain 13 of them. From this observation, Binet suggests that

> in order to know whether the transitions are less conscious than the ideas, we need to compare this number of 13 unexplained transitions to the number of unexplained words that she wrote in the first series. These three first series contained 9 unexplained words in all. We can see that the unexplained transitions are a little bit more frequent, but the difference is not large. (Binet, 1903, p. 62)

This focus on the transition between words resembles a renewed interest in the notion of sequence of ideas, as illustrated by the "serial order effect" in divergent thinking production or why ideas get increasingly original in a divergent thinking production sequence (e.g., Beaty & Silvia, 2012). It also resembles related work in the field of neuroscience of creativity focusing on the role of semantic memory in creativity typically investigated via quantitative measures of connectivity, distance, and structure of semantic networks of responses in divergent thinking or free association production tasks (e.g., Kenett, 2018). While these recent approaches have greatly advanced and open new directions in the field of creative ideation (e.g., Acar & Runco, 2014), they generally fail to capture the idiosyncratic dynamic that underlies one's ideational sequence and notably the abrupt "switch" of ideas described by Binet and later recognized as an important feature of creative and flexible thinking. Indeed, in reference to the "imaginative type"

(Armande), Binet (1903, p. 68) describes this flexible thinking as "the constant change of the direction of the thought, a zigzag walk by small broken steps, of new, surprising and original associations." In contrast, the observational type, which often produces a sequence of ideas following a "spatial contingency" strategy, is described as "lacking unexpectedness and originality." Future work in this area could combine modern network analysis techniques to quantitatively study the role of semantic memory in creativity (e.g., Kenett, 2018), with a more qualitative approach to elicit how individuals navigate within their own semantic network in the context of creative ideation.

Another important line of work indirectly illuminated by Binet's methodological approach is the study of the specificity or generality of cognitive styles, which has been a critical issue in creativity research (e.g., Baer, 1998). He transposed into the word-production task a typology elaborated on the basis of his work on the strategies used to describe an object. Rather than pointing out quantitative individual differences, he showed that one's *ideation style* is constant across different tasks or domains *in extenso*. Contemporary research on the generality-specificity of ideation has widely focused on correlational approach, that is, on the study of interindividual stability or differences in performance across various tasks. The work of Binet might trigger a new perspective on this problematic that goes beyond the variable-centered approach and even the person-centered approach, which focuses on typical profiles of an individual's performance across various domains or tasks (e.g., Silvia, Kaufman, & Pretz, 2009), by exploring intra-individual differences in the micro-ideational processes as they apply to different creative domains or tasks. Hence Binet's idiographic perspective has much to offer in understanding the microprocesses of creative ideation as they apply to different tasks and contexts, which could be powerfully extended if intensive repeated observations of few subjects were more systematically recorded and analyzed using advanced idiographic analyses (e.g., Barbot & Perchec, 2015).

CONCLUSION

Binet's undeniable contribution within the field of intelligence and its measurement has somewhat obscured his early work on ideation and imagination, perhaps because he himself struggled to legitimate his decidedly clinical, qualitative, and idiographic approach in a prevailing context of experimentalism. However, the early work presented here, together with several other of his contributions of this era, has profoundly shaped the current psychological landscape. One of the most obvious illustrations of this is that his method fundamentally inspired Piaget's work and, therefore, the field of developmental psychology. Through very careful, intensive, and repeated observations and experimentations with his two daughters, Binet was also able to formalize an incredibly thorough and accurate description of the thinking processes involved in ideation. Combined with current idiographic and network science methodologies, future research following Binet's simple introspective and qualitative methods could prove extremely fruitful in eliciting ideational navigation processes.

References

Acar, S., & Runco, M. A. (2014). Assessing associative distance among ideas elicited by tests of divergent thinking. *Creativity Research Journal, 26*(2), 229–238.

Amabile, T. M. (1983). The social psychology of creativity: A componential conceptualization. *Journal of Personality and Social Psychology, 45*(2), 357–376. https://doi.org/10.1037/0022-3514.45.2.357.

Baer, J. (1998). The case for domain specificity of creativity. *Creativity Research Journal, 11*(2), 173–177.

Barbot, B., Besançon, M., & Lubart, T. (2016). The generality-specificity of creativity: Exploring the structure of creative potential with EPoC. *Learning and Individual Differences, 52*, 178–187.

Barbot, B., & Perchec, C. (2015). New directions for the study of within-individual variability in development: The power of "N=1." *New Directions for Child and Adolescent Development, 2015*(147), 57–67.

Barbot, B., & Tinio, P. P. (2015). Where is the "g" in creativity? A specialization-differentiation hypothesis. *Frontiers in Human Neuroscience, 8*, 1041. https://doi.org/doi:10.3389/fnhum.2014.01041.

Beaty, R. E., & Silvia, P. J. (2012). Why do ideas get more creative across time? An executive interpretation of the serial order effect in divergent thinking tasks. *Psychology of Aesthetics, Creativity, and the Arts, 6*(4), 309.

Benedek, M., Franz, F., Heene, M., & Neubauer, A. C. (2012). Differential effects of cognitive inhibition and intelligence on creativity. *Personality and Individual Differences, 53*(4), 480–485.

Binet, A. (1897). Psychologie individuelle: La description d'un objet. *L'année Psychologique, 3*, 296–332.

Binet, A. (1900). L'observateur et l'imaginatif. *L'année Psychologique, 7*, 524–536.

Binet, A. (1903). *L'étude expérimentale de l'intelligence.* Paris: Schleicher.

Binet, A., & Henri, V. (1896). La psychologie individuelle. *L'Année Psychologique, 2*, 411–465.

Botella, M., Nelson, J., & Zenasni, F. (2017). It is time to observe the creative process: How to use a creative process report diary (CRD). *Journal of Creative Behavior.* Retrieved from http://onlinelibrary.wiley.com/doi/10.1002/jocb.172/full.

Cassotti, M., Agogué, M., Camarda, A., Houdé, O., & Borst, G. (2016). Inhibitory control as a core process of creative problem solving and idea generation from childhood to adulthood. *New Directions for Child and Adolescent Development, 2016*(151), 61–72.

Eysenck, H. J. (1993). Creativity and personality: Suggestions for a theory. *Psychological Inquiry, 4*(3), 147–178. https://doi.org/10.1207/s15327965pli0403_1.

Glăveanu, V., Lubart, T. I., Bonnardel, N., Botella, M., Biaisi, P.-M. de, Desainte-Catherine, M., et al. (2013). Creativity as action: Findings from five creative domains. *Frontiers in Educational Psychology, 4*, 176. https://doi.org/10.3389/fpsyg.2013.00176.

Kenett, Y. N. (2018). Investigating creativity from a semantic network perspective. In *Exploring transdisciplinarity in art and sciences* (pp. 49–75). New York, NY: Springer.

Kleibeuker, S. W., De Dreu, C. K., & Crone, E. A. (2016). Creativity development in adolescence: Insight from behavior, brain, and training studies. *New Directions for Child and Adolescent Development, 2016*(151), 73–84.

Lubart, T. I. (2001). Models of the creative process: Past, present and future. *Creativity Research Journal, 13*(3–4), 295–308. https://doi.org/10.1207/S15326934CRJ1334_07.

Nicolas, S., Coubart, A., & Lubart, T. (2014). The program of individual psychology (1895–1896) by Alfred Binet and Victor Henri. *L'Année Psychologique, 114*(1), 5–60.

Payne, R. W., & Friedlander, D. (1962). A short battery of simple tests for measuring overinclusive thinking. *British Journal of Psychiatry, 108*(454), 362–367.

Radel, R., Davranche, K., Fournier, M., & Dietrich, A. (2015). The role of (dis)inhibition in creativity: Decreased inhibition improves idea generation. *Cognition, 134*, 110–120.

Silvia, P. J., Kaufman, J. C., & Pretz, J. E. (2009). Is creativity domain-specific? Latent class models of creative accomplishments and creative self-descriptions. *Psychology of Aesthetics, Creativity, and the Arts, 3*(3), 139–148. https://doi.org/10.1037/a0014940.

Sternberg, R. J., & Lubart, T. I. (1995). *Defying the crowd: Cultivating creativity in a culture of conformity* (1st ed.). New York, NY: Free Press.

PART THREE

Creative Thinking

8

The Impact and Pitfalls
of "Real Thinking"

Wertheimer's Continuing Influence

MICHAEL HANCHETT HANSON

Summary

Max Wertheimer played several roles in creativity research, laying foundations for insight research, mentoring students, inspiring colleagues, and promoting the importance of productive thinking. Among the most influential of his publications is the small book he wrote at the end of his life: *Productive Thinking*. There he promoted a holistic view of thought and laid out challenges that continue to face creativity research today. The general approaches to thinking that Wertheimer described in this book have characterized much of the research into creativity over the subsequent 60-plus years. Cognitive problem-solving research, divergent thinking research, and holistic developmental approaches have reflected the theoretical terrain Wertheimer described. He also defined productive thinking as "real thinking," a position later adopted by humanistic psychology. Wertheimer's bold vision came at a cost, however. In lionizing one way of thinking, which happened to closely resemble his own, he explicitly devalued others. Inspired by both the strengths and weaknesses of Wertheimer's arguments, later theorists have built on his holistic vision. *Productive Thinking* has, thereby, taken on multiple layers of meaning, a theory of generative thought as well as the stimulus to generative thought through both the inspiration of its strengths and the affordances of its limitations.

Introduction

Although Max Wertheimer (1880–1943) did not publish a great deal, his personal and intellectual influence on his contemporaries and on future generations of psychologists has been vast (King & Wertheimer, 2005). In particular, the Gestalt views of perception, insight, and productive thinking that Wertheimer championed have contributed substantially to later creativity theories. Among the most influential of his publications is the small book he wrote at the end of his life: *Productive Thinking* (1945).

Wertheimer was one of the founders of Gestalt psychology, a theory that emerged in the early 20th century, which was at once holistic and empirically based. Gestalt focused on perception and, in relation to creativity, insight. Wertheimer's (1923/2012) experiments in perception led to the laws of *prägnanz*, tendencies to perceive wholes that are different from the sums of their parts. Examples include the law of proximity (perceptual grouping of objects that are near to one another as a whole) and the law of closure (seeing a form with missing parts as a whole). Perception, in the Gestalt view, was not simply a process of building information from stimuli but a dynamic matching of stimuli to expectations, a systemic process of relating parts to wholes. Wertheimer's colleagues (e.g., Koffka, 1924/2002, 1935; Köhler, 1920/1938, 1925) and his student Karl Duncker (e.g., 1926, 1939) looked at moments of insight as restructuring of perceptions. For example, Duncker's (1945) famous "candle problem" asked people to find a way to attach a candle to a door, given just a box of tacks. The answer requires perceiving the box in a new way, using it as a stand for the candle rather than container for the tacks. Wolfgang Köhler's (1925) famous work with primates also looked at how the reorganization of perception produced insight, for example, a chimpanzee suddenly realizing that a stick can be used to reach a banana. Extending this tradition of inquiry, later researchers on problem-solving have often used insight problems in experiments, both within Gestalt theory and outside of it (Weisberg, 2006). One famous example is the nine-dot problem (Scheerer, 1963): how to connect nine dots in a 3 x 3 grid with four straight lines without picking up the pencil. The solution requires drawing outside the nine-dot square. This problem is generally credited as the basis of the "thinking outside the box" metaphor.

The overall influence of Gestalt research and Wertheimer's personal influence also went beyond Gestalt theory. Kurt Lewin's groundbreaking work in social psychology was heavily influenced by Wertheimer and Gestalt theory. For Lewin, the life space of human dynamics was a field of varying forces, the totality of which was perceived as a gestalt. Wertheimer also worked with, and strongly influenced, Rudolph Arnheim (1974), who applied principles of Gestalt psychology to the arts.

Further afield, Gestalt theory had substantial impact on views of creativity in both humanistic and cognitive psychology. Both Kurt Goldstein and Adémar Gelb worked directly with Wertheimer in Frankfurt (King & Wertheimer, 2005). Goldstein and Gelb also worked closely together at the Institute for Research into the Consequences of Brain Injuries (Stahnisch & Hoffman, 2010). Based in part on that work, Goldstein (1935/1995) would later propose the concept of self-actualization as the single drive of all living organisms. Self-actualization would then be central to the work of humanistic psychology, especially the work of Carl Rogers (1961/1989) and Abraham Maslow (1943/2013). After Wertheimer came to the US, escaping Nazi Germany, he directly knew and influenced Maslow (1954/1970), who presented Wertheimer as a case example of self-actualization. As will be discussed later, the manuscript of *Productive Thinking* also had a profound effect on Howard Gruber's (1981, 1989; Gruber & Wallace, 1999) systemic view of creative development.

Wertheimer thus contributed to later creativity theory as researcher, theorist, teacher, colleague, and inspiration. He was a remarkable and challenging teacher by many accounts (King & Wertheimer, 2009). Arnheim described him as a man of "belligerent and sometimes almost reckless optimism" (quoted in King & Wertheimer, 2009, p. 5). As a synthesis of his life's work and the challenges Wertheimer saw ahead, *Productive Thinking* took on a big question—What is thinking?—and offered a polemical answer. "Real thinking" (Wertheimer, 1945, p. 2) was productive thinking as opposed to (a) reproduction of learned facts or processes, (b) blind trial and error from cognitive associations, or (c) the potentially "empty and senseless" (p. 11) reduction of thought to just logic. In spite of the heady topic, the book was written to be accessible to a broad audience and overtly avoided psychological jargon. Given the subject and the depth of Wertheimer's work and knowledge, his longtime colleague Kurt Koffka found the tone disconcerting—a "mixture of the scientist, the prophet and the reformer" (quoted in King & Wertheimer, 2005, p. 348).

Wertheimer did indeed take on these roles in the book's carefully structured argument. The introduction set out the need to consider productive thinking separately from other forms of thought and laid out Wertheimer's criticism of the reduction of thought to just logic or ideational association. Wertheimer the prophet thus set the discursive terrain. Wertheimer the scientist then produced the carefully structured analysis of thinking, moving from insight in learning basic geometric proofs to examples of great minds in math and physics: Gauss, Galileo, and Einstein. Throughout Wertheimer the reformer was seeking to change more than just psychological theory. As would be echoed by so many creativity theorists still to come (e.g., Beghetto & Kaufman, 2010; Craft, 2005; Guilford, 1950; Hanchett Hanson, 2013; Rogers, 1969; Sawyer, 2011), Wertheimer focused on education. Toward the end of World War II, as a German Jewish immigrant who had fled the Nazis, Wertheimer saw education as the path to our becoming a society of "real thinkers" with human dignity.

Reading: Introduction, *Productive Thinking*

Source: Wertheimer, M. (1945). *Productive thinking.* New York, NY: Harper & Brothers. Excerpts from pp. 1–5, 10–13 from *Productive thinking* by Max Wertheimer and edited by Michael Wertheimer. Copyright © 1945, 1959 by Valentin Wertheimer; renewed © 1987 by Michael Wertheimer. Reprinted by permission of HarperCollins Publishers.

What occurs when, now and then, thinking really works productively? What happens when, now and then, thinking forges ahead? What is really going on in such a process?

If we look for answers in books, we often find apparently easy ones. But confronted by actual processes of this kind—when one has just had a creative idea, however modest the issue, when one has begun really to grasp an issue, when one has enjoyed a clean, productive process of thought—those answers often seem to cover up the real problems rather than to face them squarely. The flesh and blood of what has happened seem to be lacking in those answers.

Surely in the course of your life you have been curious about a lot of things, sometimes seriously. Have you been equally serious about what this thing called thinking may be? There are, in this world of ours, eating, thunderstorms, blossoms, crystals. Various sciences deal with them; they attempt by great effort to get real understanding, to grasp what these things really are. Are we equally serious when we ask what productive thinking is?

There are fine cases. You can find them often, even in daily life. If you have had your eyes open, you have probably encountered somewhere in your life—if nowhere else, then in children—this surprising event, the birth of a genuine idea, of a productive development, the transition from a blind attitude to understanding in a productive process. If you have not been fortunate enough to experience it yourself, you may have encountered it in others; or you may—fascinated—have glimpsed it when reading good books.

Many are of the opinion that men do not like to think; that they will do much to avoid it; that they prefer to repeat instead. But in spite of many factors that are inimical to real thinking, that suffocate it, here and there it emerges and flourishes. And often one gets the strong impression that men, even children, long for it.

What really takes place in such processes? What happens if one really thinks, and thinks productively? What may be the decisive features and the steps? How do they come about? Whence the flash, the spark? What are the conditions, the attitudes, favorable or unfavorable to such remarkable events? What is the real difference between good and bad thinking? And in connection with all of these questions: how improve thinking [sic]? your thinking? thinking itself? Suppose we were to make an inventory of basic operations in thinking—how would it look? What, basically is at hand? Could the basic operations themselves be enlarged and improved, and thus be made more productive?

For more than two thousand years some of the best brains in philosophy, in logic, in psychology, in education, have worked hard to find real answers to these questions. The history of these efforts, the brilliant ideas brought forward, the hard work done in research and in theoretical discussion, present on the whole a rich, dramatic picture. Much has been achieved. In a large number of special questions solid contributions to understanding have been made. At the same time there is something tragic in the history of these efforts. Again and again when great thinkers compared the ready answers with actual, fine, thinking, they were troubled and deeply dissatisfied—they felt that what had been done had merits, but that in fact it had perhaps not touched the core of the problem at all.

The situation is still somewhat of this kind. To be sure, many books deal with these questions as if, fundamentally, everything were settled—in one way or another. For there are basically different ideas about what thinking is, each with serious consequences for behavior, for education. When observing a teacher we may often realize how serious the consequences of such ideas about thinking can be.

Although there are good teachers, with a natural feeling for what genuine thinking means, the situation in schools is often not good. How teachers act, how a subject matter is taught, how textbooks are written, all this is widely determined by two traditional views about the nature of thinking: the view of traditional logic and the view of association theory.

This book has been written because the traditional views have ignored important characteristics of thought processes, because in many other books those views are taken for granted without real investigation, because in such books the discussion of thinking runs largely in mere generalities, and because, for the most part, the gestalt view is only superficially known. Much is at stake and it seems proper to bring these neglected issues to the fore, to examine the traditional views, to discuss the crucial problems in concrete instances of fine, productive thought, and in doing so, to give the gestalt interpretation of thinking. . . .

As a kind of background for the following discussions, I present first a very short characterization of the two traditional approaches. They surpass all others in the rigor and completeness with which they consider operations and establish basic concepts, standards, criteria, laws and rules. Other approaches—even if they seem at first in strong opposition to these two—often still contain as their very meat, in one way or another, precisely the operations, the rules of those two. Modern research in thinking is largely determined by one or the other, or both at the same time. I shall indicate their main lines, but shall omit some points which appear as additions of another nature and which, besides, are not clear in themselves. . . .

Consider first traditional logic. In the course of the centuries there arose again and again a deep-felt dissatisfaction with the manner in which traditional logic handles such processes.[1] In comparison with actual, sensible and productive processes, the topics as well as the customary examples of traditional logic often look dull, insipid, lifeless. To be sure, the treatment is rigorous enough, yet often it seems barren, boring, empty, unproductive. If one tries to describe processes of genuine thinking in terms of formal traditional logic, the result is often unsatisfactory: one has, then, a series of correct operations, but the sense of the process and what was vital, forceful, creative in it seems somehow to have evaporated in the foundations. On the other hand it is possible to have a chain of logical operations, each perfectly correct in itself, which does not form a sensible train of thought. Indeed there are people with logical training who in certain situations produce series of correct operations which, viewed as a whole, nevertheless form something akin to a flight of ideas. Training in traditional logic is not to be disparaged: it leads to stringency and rigor in each step, it contributes to critical-mindedness; but it does not, in itself, seem to give rise to productive thinking.[2] In short, there is the danger of being empty and senseless, though exact; and there is always the difficulty with regard to real productiveness.

Realization of the latter point—among others—led in fact to the emphatic declaration by some logicians that logic, interested in correctness and validity, has nothing at all to do with factual thinking or with questions of productivity. A reason was also given for this: logic, it was said, has timeless implications and is, therefore, in principle, divorced from questions of actual thought processes which are merely factual and, of necessity, processes in time. This separation was certainly meritorious for certain problems; from a broader view, however, such assertions often look somehow like the declaration of the fox that the grapes were sour.

Similar difficulties arose in association theory: the fact that we have to distinguish between sensible thought and senseless combinations, and the difficulty of dealing with the *productive* side of thinking.[3]

If a problem is solved by recall, by mechanical repetition of what has been drilled, by sheer chance discovery in a succession of blind trials, one would hesitate to call such a process sensible thinking, and it seems doubtful whether the piling up of such factors only even in large numbers, can lead to an adequate picture of sensible processes. In order to deal somehow with processes which reach new solutions, a number of auxiliary hypotheses were proposed (for instance, Selz's constellation theory, or the concept of the habit-family-hierarchy) which, by their very nature, do not seem to give decisive help.

In the past decades other views originated which brought new conceptions, new directions in the theory of thinking: e.g., the approach of Hegelian and Marxist dialectics, which emphasize dynamic development in their doctrines of "inherent contradictions" with three steps of thesis, antithesis, and synthesis; the broad development of logistics or mathematical logic (Whitehead, Russell *et al.*) which enriches the topics and operations of traditional logic by the study of the logic of relations, of relational networks, considers forms of conclusion other than syllogisms; phenomenology (Husserl) which stresses the viewing of essentials in "phenomenological reduction"; pragmatism (especially John Dewey) with its emphasis on doing and acting, instead of mere ghostlike thinking, on future and on actual progress; also in psychology—starting about the same time as the approach developed in this book—the "Denkpsychologie" of the Würzburg school (Kuelpe, Ach, Buehler, Selz, *et al.*) which centers on the conditions that start actual thinking in a given situation.

Most of these approaches are important in their philosophical and psychological aspects. Although in these developments the situation with regard to our main problem and the crucial points mentioned still seems far from satisfactory, some of them made really new contributions. Some again show the influence of the two classical approaches. In other words, if one penetrates through the new formulations to the nature of the operations which are actually posited *in concreto*, one finds to one's surprise that they are essentially operations of those two traditional approaches. This reminds one of the cases that have frequently occurred in the history of logic. In the introduction or in some early chapter a book may seem to start a new approach, altogether different from the customary treatment of logic; in fact, certain formulations may also appear akin to those of gestalt theory. And yet, when it comes to dealing concretely with a problem, the old operations, old rules, old attitudes appear again.

I have been able to do no more than briefly mention these approaches here. The expert will, I think, see in the text what in them is in line with and what is basically different in nature from the approach in this book.

This book focuses on some elementary, basic issues. The nature of the topics discussed permits us to deal with thought in terms of "relatively closed systems," as though thinking about a problem were a process that occurred independently of larger issues. Only occasionally shall we refer to the place, role, and function of such a process within the personality structure of the subject and within the structure of his social field. For the moment it will suffice if I remark that the same field principles discussed in this book also seem basic to an adequate treatment of processes within such larger regions.

---

1. Cf., for instance, certain movements against traditional logic at the end of the Middle Ages, or the marvelous fragment of young Spinoza, "Improvement of the Understanding." Tragic movements these were, prompted by a feeling of some basic inadequacy, but at the same time unable to achieve a really positive approach.
2. The discussions of methodology in traditional logic, though meritorious in various respects, do not give real help at this point. Cf. the heuristic ideas (or also veritable logical machines) of Buridanus, of Raimundus Lullus, of Jevons.
3. Characteristics in the former respect was the brilliant book of Hugo Liepmann on the flight of ideas (*Über Ideenflucht,* 1904). Discussing concrete examples of flight of ideas in mental patients, he found that the criteria offered by association theory do not really suffice to discriminate even between certain kinds of flight of ideas and reasonable talk.

    A recent formulation exhibits the basic character of the modern form of association theory in a nutshell. I am referring to Clark Hull's paper on "Mind, Mechanism and Adaptive Behavior," *Psychological Review,* 1937, Vol. 44, pp. 1–32: "A *correct* or 'right' reaction is a behavior sequence which results in the reenforcement. An *incorrect* or 'wrong' reaction is a behavior sequence which results in experimental extinction" (p. 15). One sees that the question of repetition is *the* issue. These basic definitions are no doubt in line with the spirit of association theory.

Commentary

Although Koffka noted that Wertheimer's tone in *Productive Thinking* was that of a prophet, and his enduring influence might fit that role, Wertheimer was not a lone voice in the wilderness nor a solitary genius. He was, rather, a man of his times, an enthusiastic collaborator, teacher, and mentor who contributed a prominent voice at a pivotal juncture. Remember that *Productive Thinking* was written during World War II and published posthumously in the final year of the war. This final work of a groundbreaking theorist's life, a Jewish psychologist who had been forced to flee the Nazis, aimed high in an effort to address the needs of his times. In the effort he marshalled resources that came from a broad and rich intellectual life.

Wertheimer came from a time and from schools in which the study of psychology and philosophy were crucially linked. Indeed he taught both (King & Wertheimer, 2005). In his life, his work, and his influence, Wertheimer fully embodied this marriage of disciplines. Like any marriage, the promises of the psychology-philosophy relationship are large and important—arguably life sustaining to each discipline—but filled with pitfalls and requiring constant recalibration.

Wertheimer received his doctorate from the University of Würzburg, but much of his formation had come earlier, in Berlin under Carl Stumpf, who also taught many of his colleagues, including Kurt Koffka, Wolfgang Köhler, Kurt Lewin, and Adémar Gelb (King & Wertheimer, 2005). At the University of Berlin Stumpf emphasized the holism of thought. Wertheimer himself taught in Berlin but later took a position in Frankfurt. Creativity studies has considered how the social and intellectual dynamics of a time can influence thinkers (*zeitgeist*) and how those dynamics can be distinctly generative in certain places at a given time (*ortgeist*; Simonton, 2003). Frankfurt in Weimar Germany was such a place. There Wertheimer worked closely with Gestalt and Gestalt-leaning colleagues, including Gelb, Koffka, Köhler, Kurt Goldstein, and Kurt Riezler, as well as philosophers, especially Paul Tillich and Martin Buber. Wertheimer was also, of course, aware of the work of the famous Frankfurt Institute for Social Research, whose scholars included Max Horkheimer, Herbert Marcuse, Erich Fromm, and Theodor Adorno. Coming out of this fertile intellectual ground, Wertheimer saw his perception research as inherently linked to the questions of what it is to be human and, of course, what it is to think. He was bringing rigorous empirical standards to his work but always with philosophical grounding and philosophical implications in sight.

The marriage of psychology and philosophy also helped guard against the reductions that psychological methodologies can promote. Furthermore Wertheimer's critiques remain important in the face of continued temptations toward reductionism. For example, leading divergent thinking researchers have not claimed that divergent thinking today's best known association theory, is equivalent to creativity (Guilford, 1950; Runco, 2010). Some researchers working in more holistic approaches do not even see divergent thinking as particularly important to creativity (Gruber, 1989; Weisberg, 2006). Even so, today it is all too common for creativity researchers to say that in using divergent thinking tests they are directly measuring creativity (see discussions in Hanchett Hanson, 2015). Wertheimer's work, grounded in both empirical research and philosophy, warned against both the direction of such analyses and the reductionism they promote.

The relations of philosophy and psychology are not simply cautionary, though. The issues go deeper than the discourse *between* philosophers and psychologists. Psychology itself carries philosophical commitments within its assumptions and methods. As creativity theorists Gruber and Wallace (1999, pp. 93–94) wrote, "Overtly or not, they [research methodologies] always call into play deeply held convictions about the nature of knowledge and truth. Just as form and content are inseparable, epistemic passions lurk everywhere." Those passions come with strengths, limits, and pitfalls. The empirical rigor that Wertheimer and his colleagues brought to holistic views was important to the justification of such views within the science of psychology. The Gestalt emphasis on perception as structure and Wertheimer's particular emphasis on both the structure of thought and the structure of problems put the organization of thinking front and center. That work helped lay the ground for constructivist developmental theories of creativity, building on Piaget and Vygotsky, which saw thinking as systemic and were still not well known in America in 1945.

At the same time, all methods are limited. For most of Wertheimer's career, his holistic views of thought came largely from experimental data, most of which were not designed to take the complexity of situations or long-term development into account. As a result, this approach tended to see thinking as a relatively short-term process. Yes, prior knowledge of a particular individual was sometimes taken into account, but the Gestalt focus was on moments of insight. In *Productive Thinking*, however, the method is case studies of both children and famous scientists. Experiments are designed to isolate variables and produce highly focused but generalizable findings. Case studies produce accounts of systemic complexity but are not designed to produce generalizable data (Stake, 1995). The shift in method fits the complex question at hand: the nature of thinking. Here, though, the mixing of psychological methods in service of philosophical aspirations becomes tricky. Just as Wertheimer had so successfully defined laws of perception through experiments, in tackling the larger question of productive thinking he was looking for general psychological principles covering all forms of thinking that generated new ideas. He was doing it, however, with a method designed to help understand particular and limited situations.

Beyond questions of methodological fit, Wertheimer's pronouncements about "real thinking" were on slippery ground. Holism and analytic reduction may be presented as a dichotomy, but they function as a continuum. In keeping with Wertheimer's own arguments, even the most holistic view must have structure, limiting boundaries. Toward the other end of the continuum, reductions can always be further reduced, *ad absurdum*. Within this tension, Wertheimer chose to mark the boundaries of his bold vision of real thinking by elevating it in relation to other ways of thinking. After all, prophets need an audience: people who have gone astray, blind to the prophetic truth. In *Productive Thinking* Wertheimer's vision includes both the prophecy and the audience.

At the end of *Productive Thinking* he posits a typology of three types of thinking: alpha being productive, gamma being reproductive and nongenerative, and beta being a mix of the two. Wertheimer presents the argument as explicitly philosophical, arguing for a view of humans as straightforwardly, sincerely, and courageously attacking problems. Such intellectual fervor is crucial to the dignity of humanity. Humans, in Wertheimer's view, inherently desire to get from their heart to the heart of the problems they confront. Yes, of course, learned facts and procedures become part of this quest, but the crucial point is that alpha thinking be the organizing principle.

Reading the combination of passion and analysis with which Wertheimer concludes brings two issues to mind. First, William James's (1890, p. 196) concept of "the psychologist's fallacy": the assumption that one's own experience is the same as the experience of an observed phenomenon. The description of "real thinking" (alpha thinking) was strikingly reminiscent of the approach and goals of the Gestalt theorists, a search for the underlying structure of problems. To contend that everyone must have similar goals whenever they are thinking was ironically reductive for a holistic thinker. Second, Wertheimer was writing in a time of war. The Nazi enemy was seen as mindlessly following a dictator, while Americans claimed to think for themselves. The emphasis on "real thinking" and devaluation of other ways of thinking may have reflected the context but is still problematic.

Even in America, most of most people's days—making breakfast, walking dogs, dressing children, paying bills—is blind reproduction of learned processes: gamma thinking. If that were not true, there would be little time or energy to focus on the hard problems, like what constitutes thinking. How, then, does vilifying reproductive thinking help? Universities, like the ones where Wertheimer taught and conducted research, thrive in part because of people doing groundbreaking work to understand the underlying structures of issues. They would not exist, however, without many more people doing much more mundane and routine work to maintain the institution. Yes, Wertheimer's view of "real thinking" is likely part of all of their work too, but not nearly so central as Wertheimer described his view of human nature. Is devaluing the necessary work of most people most of the time worth the glorification of the privileged ways some people want to and get to think? Would not focusing on the question of how received knowledge can relate to searches for unknown answers be more, well, *productive*? Would not thinking about the myriad possible relations of these different kinds of thinking within individual thought and within social dynamics be more holistic?

Finally, the case studies in *Productive Thinking* suggested a tension between the traditional Gestalt focus on the point of insight and the actual processes of thinking. The cases described relatively short- and long-term thought processes. On the longer side, Wertheimer organized the description of Einstein's thought in ten "acts," beginning when Einstein was 16 years old (1895) and ending in the theory of general relativity that was established in papers Einstein wrote between 1907 and 1915, in other words, a span of 20 years. Insights may be important whether learning basic math or revolutionizing physics. For the thinker, though, is it not likely that thinking is experienced more as a journey rather than just the achievement of a series of insights?

These questions, or at least the issues they raise, took form in the mind of another theorist after reading *Productive Thinking*. One of the editors of the first edition of the book was Wertheimer's former student, Solomon Asch. In the 1940s Asch was teaching psychology at Brooklyn College, and one of his students was a young, philosophically oriented student named Howard Gruber. Through his teacher Gruber read the then-unpublished manuscript of *Productive Thinking*. The book had a profound and lasting impact on a man who would become one of the leading researchers in creativity. Gruber heeded Wertheimer's call to holistic analysis but not the focus on insight. Instead the contradictions within Wertheimer's book gave Gruber the question that would drive much of the rest his career: How long does it take to think? (Grisanti, 1997).

Gruber would spend decades working closely with another groundbreaking holistic thinker, Jean Piaget, and writing the work for which Gruber (1981) would become famous: *Darwin on Man: A Psychological Study of Scientific Creativity*. This detailed analysis of Darwin's thinking, based on his extensive notebooks, showed the circuitous thought process that Darwin followed, including some extraordinary blind alleys in developing the theory of natural selection. Gruber found that, even after abandoning unsuccessful theories, key principles, factual observations, and heuristics from the failed theories remained part of Darwin's thinking going forward. Gruber called this circuitous path *by-productive thinking*, explicitly referencing Wertheimer and expanding his concept to include contributions of ideas developed over time that were not in and of themselves generative. This direct extension of Wertheimer, almost 30 years after Gruber read

Productive Thinking and rejected some of its conclusions, might itself be classified as a form of by-productive thinking.

Building on Wertheimer's exhortation to holism and Gruber's work, some of today's theorists go even further down the holistic road. These theorists have been inspired by the holistic approach and struck by the social and material systems at play in the case studies of Wertheimer and of Gruber and his associates. Participatory creativity theories (e.g., Clapp, 2016; Glăveanu, 2010, 2014; Hanchett Hanson, 2015) have added distributed cognition theory to the mix. Distributed cognition theory sees thought as socially, temporally, and materially distributed, not occurring entirely inside the head. This view aligns with Gruber's contention that the development of a new point of view occurs through creative *work*, the acts of painting, writing, researching, and so on. The social and temporal distribution was obvious in Wertheimer's 10 acts of Einstein's discovery of general relativity. Einstein was building on the work of other famous researchers, including Maxwell, Michelson, and Lorenz. The material distribution was apparent in the phenomena of physics and the books that conveyed that research to Einstein.

Just as Wertheimer's holistic views necessarily came with "epistemic passions" and their strengths, limitations, and affordances, so will today's emerging theories. Speaking within and to his own times, Wertheimer laid foundations on which the next generation built and on which another generation continues the work. Part of the relation of philosophy to psychology that informed Wertheimer's work is awareness of the sources and implications of ideas. Being aware of the aspirations, shortcomings, and opportunities within ongoing processes of change is key to taking the next step. These are among the processes that, today, we call creativity.

References

Arnheim, R. (1974). *Art and visual perception: A psychology of the creative eye* (2nd ed.). Berkeley: University of California Press.

Beghetto, R. A., & Kaufman, J. C. (Eds.) (2010). *Nurturing creativity in the classroom.* Cambridge, UK: Cambridge University Press.

Clapp, E. P. (2016). *Participatory creativity: Introducing access and equality to the creative classroom.* New York, NY: Routledge.

Craft, A. (2005). *Creativity in schools: Tensions and dilemmas.* London: Routledge.

Duncker, K. (1926). A qualitative (experimental and theoretical) study of productive thinking (solving of comprehensible problems). *Pedagogical Seminary and Journal of Genetic Psychology, 33*(4), 642–708.

Duncker, K. (1939). The influence of past experience upon perceptual properties. *American Journal of Psychology, 52*(2), 255–265.

Duncker, K. (1945). On problem solving I. S. Lees (Trans.) *Psychological Monographs, 58*(5). http://dx.doi.org/10.1037/h0093599.

Glăveanu, V. P. (2010). Creativity as cultural participation. *Journal for the Theory of Social Behaviour, 41*(1), 48–67.

Glăveanu, V. P. (2014). *Thinking through creativity and culture: Toward an integrated model.* New Brunswick, NJ: Transaction.

Goldstein, K. (1935/1995). *The organism: A holistic approach to biology derived from pathological data in man.* New York, NY: Zone Books. (Original work published in German; English translation first published 1939)

Grisanti, M. L. (1997). Interview with Howard E. Gruber. *International Journal of Group Tensions, 27*(4), 219–243.

Gruber, H. E. (1981). *Darwin on man: A psychological study of scientific creativity* (2nd ed.). Chicago: University of Chicago Press.

Gruber, H. E. (1989). The evolving systems approach to creative work. In D. B. Wallace & H. E. Gruber (Eds.), *Creative people at work* (pp. 3–24). Oxford: Oxford University Press.

Gruber, H. E., & Wallace, D. B. (1999). The case study method and evolving systems approach for understanding unique creative people at work. In R. J. Sternberg (Ed.), *Handbook of creativity* (pp. 93–115). Cambridge, UK: Cambridge University Press.

Guilford, J. P. (1950). Creativity. *American Psychologist, 5,* 444–454.

Hanchett Hanson, M. (2013). Creativity theory and educational practice: Why all the fuss? In J. B. Jones & L. J. Flint (Eds.), *The creative imperative: School librarians and teachers cultivating curiosity together* (pp. 19–37). Santa Barbara, CA: ABC-CLIO.

Hanchett Hanson, M. (2015). *Worldmaking: Psychology and the ideology of creativity.* London: Palgrave Macmillan.

James, W. (1890). *The principles of psychology.* Vol. 1. New York, NY: Henry Holt. Retrieved from https://books.google.com/books?id=JLcAAAAAMAAJ&pg=PA183&source=gbs_toc_r&cad=4#v=onepage&q&f=false.

King, B., & Wertheimer, M. (2005). *Max Wertheimer and Gestalt theory.* New Brunswick, NJ: Transaction.

Koffka, K. (1924/2002). *The growth of the mind.* R. M. Ogden (Trans.) New York, NY: Routledge.

Koffka, K. (1925). *Principles of Gestalt psychology.* London: Lund Humphries.

Köhler, W. (1920/1938). Physical Gestalten. In W. D. Ellis (Ed.), *A source book of Gestalt psychology* (pp. 17–54). London: Routledge & Kegan Paul. (Original work published in German)

Köhler, W. (1925). *The mentality of apes.* New York, NY: Harcourt Brace Jovanovich.

Maslow, A. H. (1943/2013). *A theory of human motivation.* Mansfield Centre, CT: Martino.

Maslow, A. H. (1954/1970). *Motivation and personality.* New York, NY: Harper & Row.

Rogers, C. R. (1961/1989). *On becoming a person: A therapist's view of psychotherapy.* New York, NY: Houghton Mifflin.

Rogers, C. R. (1969). *Freedom to learn.* Columbus, OH: Charles E. Merrill.

Runco, M. A. (2010). Divergent thinking, creativity, and ideation. In J. C. Kaufman & R. J. Sternberg (Eds.), *The Cambridge handbook of creativity* (pp. 413–446). Cambridge, UK: Cambridge University Press.

Sawyer, R. K. (Ed.). (2011). *Structure and improvisation in creative teaching.* Cambridge, UK: Cambridge University Press.

Scheerer, M. (1963). Problem-solving. *Scientific American, 208*(4), 118–128.

Simonton, D. K. (2003). Creative cultures, nations and civilizations: Strategies and results. In P. B. Paulus & B. A Nijstad (Eds.), *Group creativity: Innovation through collaboration* (pp. 304–325). Oxford: Oxford University Press.

Stahnisch, F., & Hoffmann, T. (2010). Kurt Goldstein and the neurology of movement during the interwar years: Physiological experimentation, clinical psychology and early rehabilitation. In C. Hoffstadt, F. Peschke, A. Schulz-Buchta, & M. Nagenborg (Eds.), *Was bewegt uns? Menschen im Spannungsfeld zwischen Mobilität und Beschleuningung* (pp. 283–312). Bochum, Germany: Projekt Verlag.

Stake, R. (1995). *The art of case study research.* London: Sage.

Weisberg, R. W. (2006). *Creativity: Understanding innovation in problem solving, science, invention and the arts.* Hoboken, NJ: John Wiley & Sons.

Wertheimer, M. (1945). *Productive thinking.* New York, NY: Harper & Brothers.

Wertheimer, M. (1923/2012). Investigations on Gestalt principles, II. (M. Wertheimer & K.W. Watkins, Trans.). In L. Spillmann (Ed.), *On perceived motion and figural organization* (pp. 127–182). Cambridge, MA: MIT Press. (Original work published in German.)

Functional Fixedness, Creativity, and Problem-Solving

Karl Duncker

Vlad P. Glăveanu

Summary

Karl Duncker was a Gestalt psychologist who made important contributions to the psychology of thinking, paving the way for the cognitive revolution. His work also informs contemporary approaches to creative problem-solving. For Duncker, the solution emerges from the problem situation through the reorganization of its elements and overcoming fixedness. In fact, his notion of functional fixedness has important consequences for creativity to this day. The text reproduced in this chapter is part of Duncker's seminal work *Zur Psychologie des Produktiven Denkens*, originally published in 1935 and translated into English as *On Problem-Solving* (1945). The final commentary will focus on the insights this text has to offer creative problem-solving researchers and also make connections to other relevant concepts (e.g., affordances).

Introduction

Karl Duncker (1903–1940) was a German Gestalt psychologist who made important contributions to the psychology of thinking—in particular problem-solving—and whose work paved the way for the cognitive revolution (Newell, 1985). He is well-known today for the problems he used to study thinking processes, experimentally, including the candles and box problem and the X-ray problem. Similar to his Gestaltist teachers, Duncker believed that solving such problems requires the person to reorganize the elements of the problem situation through "productive thinking," a process very close to what we refer to as creativity (see also Chapter 8, this volume). Against associationism, a productive thinking approach argues that the whole (the solution) is more than the sum of the parts (isolated ideas). Against behaviorism, it focuses on the experience and knowledge of the person rather than relying on simple stimulus-response schemas. Duncker was interested in how exactly people think and, for this purpose, used frequently think-aloud protocols (i.e., asking his participants to verbalize their thinking process while engaging in problem-solving).

For him, life was, "among other things, a sum total of solution-processes which refer to innumerable problems, great and small" (Duncker, 1945, p. 13). And yet, sadly, Duncker often found himself powerless when confronted with great challenges within his own life, something that led him to commit suicide at the age of 37 (Schnall, 1999). He was born in 1903 in Leipzig in a family of active Marxists, a family context that profoundly marked his career. Between 1923 and 1928 he studied at the Friedrich-Wilhelms-University in Berlin, where he worked with Köhler and Wertheimer and impressed them both—so much so that, when Köhler was appointed visiting professor for one year at Clark University, in 1925–1926, he asked Duncker to join him. During this period, Duncker (1926) received his master's degree from Clark University, with the thesis "An Experimental and Theoretical Study of Productive Thinking." When he returned to Berlin he became a university assistant and repeatedly attempted to obtain a permanent academic position. His hopes were crushed by the ascension to power of the Nazis. Duncker's habilitation thesis on problem-solving was rejected in 1935 due to his family's communist connections and the fact that he had been married to a Jewish woman. Deprived of the possibility of achieving his dream of building a life and academic career in Germany, Duncker left for England and worked for a while with Sir Frederic Bartlett at Cambridge. His health, however, began to deteriorate, and he began a treatment for depression. Concerned for him, Köhler, who had already emigrated to the United States, arranged for him to teach at his institution, Swarthmore College. Duncker spent only two years as an instructor there while his mental state continued to deteriorate, leading to a tragic ending in 1940.

Despite his rather short life and the fact that he was actively denied academic support in his home country, Duncker's early work left a definitive mark on cognitive psychology. While he worked on a variety of topics, including motion, pain, taste, ethics, and motivation, his legacy is first and foremost represented by his contributions to problem-solving. His master's thesis led to a 1935 book on this topic (*Psychology of Productive Thinking*), which was translated into English and published in 1945 under the title *On Problem-Solving*. Fragments from the chapter on functional fixedness in solving problems related to physical objects are reproduced here. Functional fixedness was defined by Duncker as a type of mental block that prevents the person from thinking about and consequently using an object in a new way, the way required to solve a difficult problem. In other words, Duncker dealt in this chapter with one of the main obstacles to creativity, especially when dealing with material objects (and beyond them). His concept of functional fixedness is important not only for cognitive psychology but also for creativity studies, in particular creative problem-solving. If fixedness is detrimental to creativity, how can we encourage mental flexibility? In Duncker's terms, how can we help the solution—or creative insight—arise from the demands of the problem situation itself?

Reading: *On Problem-Solving*

Source: Duncker, K. (1945). *On problem-solving*. (L. S. Lees, Trans.). *Psychological Monographs*, 58(5). Selections from Chapter 7, "On Functional Fixedness of Real Solution-Objects." Some references and footnotes from the original text have been deleted in the excerpt below. This work is in the public domain.

Setting the Problem: The Concept of Heterogeneous Functional Fixedness

In Chapter II, 6 and 7, . . . it was pointed out that the different parts of the situation, whose (appropriate) variations represent solutions of the problem, or which enter into solutions as "material," may display very different degrees of "disposability" (looseness). For the psychology of thinking, there hardly exist more fundamental differences among the various relevant elements of a problem-situation than those which determine how easily or with what difficulty they may be recognized as conflict-elements or as solution material. These differences are independent of possible "knowledge" by which *post festum*—the elements concerned could be evaluated with respect to their conflict-character or their suitability as material.

A few of the factors which determine disposability, specifically that of conflict elements, have already been worked out in Chapter II. Now we shall examine more closely the *disposability of solution material*, in the more specific form of "real solution-objects sought."

Whether a sought "object" is found more easily or with more difficulty depends, among other things, on the degree of "fixedness" of the object. A chimpanzee who stands in need of a stick (something long, firm . . .) sometimes has difficulties in recognizing the stick in a branch still growing on the tree, in seeing it as a percept apart. On the tree there is a "branch," a part of the visual unit "tree," and this part-character—more generally, this "fixedness" —is clearly responsible for the fact that [in] a search for something like a stick, the branch on a tree is less "within reach" than the branch on the ground.

What we just named "fixedness" may, however, be conditioned *functionally* as well as by such factors of visual organization. For instance, a stick that has just been used as a ruler is less likely to appear as a tool for other purposes than it would normally be. In the following, the discussion will be chiefly of such functional fixedness ("bias"), more particularly, of *heterogeneous* functional fixedness, i.e., fixedness as the result of a function *dissimilar* to that demanded. The question is: *What determines whether, and to what degree, heterogeneous functional fixedness of an object hinders the finding of this object?*

On this question I undertook a series of experiments.[1] The principle was as follows: For a particular purpose, a certain function, a suitable object is needed. *This object has already been used in the same problem-context, but in another way, in another function.* Question: what effect has this pre-utilization? When does it hinder the selection of the object or the new function, the "recentering" of the object?

Be it expressly noted that what, in the present chapter, is stated for thing-objects (specifically tools) is valid, in principle, for thought-material in general. . . .

Experimental Procedure, Method of Evaluation, and Problems

We experimented with all sorts of objects in daily use (e.g., boxes, pliers, etc.), which were first claimed in their usual function (F1) and then, within the same problem-situation, for a new, unusual function (F2). The crucial object was each time to be selected as the suitable tool out of a great number of objects which lay in confusion on a table.

In our problems, the pre-utilization of the crucial object was chosen in such a way as not to give it a special prominence in the problem situation. In other words, in F1 no new centering took place, but solely a freshening, an "actualization" of the usual centering of the object concerned. For F2, on the contrary, the object concerned was "unprepared," although by no means inappropriate.

In order to observe the effect of fixedness on recentering, each problem was given in two settings, once without and once after pre-utilization of the crucial object. The setting without pre-utilization we shall briefly designate *w.p.*, that after pre-utilization, *a.p.* The most important experiments were carried out on five different problems. One-half of the Ss received the problems in the settings (1) w.p.; (2) a.p.; (3) w.p.; (4) a.p.; (5) w.p.; the other half of the Ss, in the opposite settings. In this way, differences of results in the w.p. and the a.p. experiments were made independent of individual differences among the Ss and among the problems.

The following is a short description of the five problems and of the experimental technique.

> The *"gimlet problem"*: Three cords are to be hung side by side from a wooden ledge ("for experiments on space perception"). On the table lie, among many other objects, two short screw-hooks and the crucial object: a gimlet. *Solution*: for hanging the third cord, the gimlet is used. In the setting a.p., the holes for the screws had yet to be bored; in w.p., the holes were already there. Thus, F1: "gimlet"; F2: "thing from which to hang a cord."
>
> The *"box problem"*: On the door, at the height of the eyes, three small candles are to be put side by side ("for visual experiments"). On the table lie, among many other objects, a few tacks and the crucial objects: three little pasteboard boxes (about the size of an ordinary matchbox, differing somewhat in form and color and put in different places). *Solution*: with a tack apiece, the three boxes are fastened to the door, each to serve as platform for a candle. In the setting a.p., the three boxes were filled with experimental material: in one there were several thin little candles, tacks in another, and matches in the third. In w.p., the three boxes were empty. Thus F1: "container"; F2: "platform" (on which to set things).
>
> The *"pliers problem"*: A board (perhaps 8 inches broad) is to be made firm on two supports (as "flower stand or the like"). On the table lie, among other things, two iron joints (for fastening bars and the like on stands), a wooden bar perhaps 8 inches long (as the one "support") and the crucial object: the pliers. *Solution*: this pair of pliers is utilized as the second support of the board. In the setting a.p., the bar was nailed to the board and had to be freed with the help of the pliers; in w.p., it was only tied to the board. Thus F1: "pliers"; F2: "support."
>
> The *"weight problem"*: A pendulum, consisting of a cord and a weight, is to be hung from a nail ("for experiments on motion"). To this end, the nail must be driven

into the wall. On the table lies, among other things, the crucial object: a weight. *Solution*: with this weight (as "hammer"), the nail is driven into the wall. In the setting a.p., the weight is given expressly as pendulum-weight (with the string already tied to it); in w.p., a joint serves as pendulum-weight. Thus F1 "pendulum-weight"; F2: "hammer."

The "paperclip problem": A piece of white cardboard with four black squares fastened to it is to be hung on an eyelet screwed into the low ceiling ("for visual experiments"). On the table lie paperclips, among other things. *Solution*: a paperclip is unbent, one end is fastened to the eyelet and the other put through the cardboard. In the setting a.p., the four black squares must previously be attached to the cardboard with paper-clips; in w.p., on the other hand, they must be glued to it. Thus F1: "something for affixing"; F2: (unbent) "hook."

The differences among the five problems are to be discussed later. . . .

The general *instruction* for all the problems ran as follows: "You will receive several little technical tasks. For solution, certain objects are needed which you will find among the objects here on the table. Everything which lies on the table is completely at your disposal. You may use what you like in any fashion you wish. Please think aloud during the experiment, so that I may hear as many of your ideas as possible, including those which you take less seriously."

With each problem there lay on the table—aside from the objects already mentioned—all kinds of material, partly less suitable and partly completely unsuitable for the solution, such as paperclips, pieces of paper, string, pencils, tinfoil, old parts of apparatus, ashtrays, joints, pieces of wood, etc. Each problem had its own inventory. (No object was put at the subject's disposal which might be better suited to the solution than the object then crucial.) The objects lay in apparent confusion, but in definite places. The crucial object never occupied a prominent place.

The experiments were *evaluated* in two ways: (1) The solved and the unsolved problems were counted. Of course, a problem counted as "correctly" solved only when it was solved by use of the crucial object, which, as stated, was always the best and simplest of the possible solutions. A problem was broken off as unsolved if for two to three minutes the S produced no more proposals, and if at the same time his attitude had become so negative that no more sensible ideas seemed forthcoming. (2) The proposals preceding the solution and different from it, the "pre-solutions," were counted (but only with those experiments in which the correct solution was finally found, as otherwise measurements 1 and 2 would not have been independent of each other). As "pre-solutions" counted not only those actually carried out, but also proposals merely formulated, also such as the S rejected as unsuitable. If, however, an object was only "grazed," i.e., just touched or picked up quite briefly and silently laid aside again, the fact did not count as a pre-solution.

Of the two methods of evaluation just described, the first is naturally the more adequate and by far the more important, while the second is rather superficial and dependent on chance influences. We shall find, however, that both methods yield results which are essentially in agreement.

Principal Experiments and Principal Results

The principal result of the experiments is immediately evident from Table 9.3 (original number).

TABLE 9.3

		Problems	No. of Ss	No. of problems solved	No. of problems solved in %	Average no. of pre-solutions per problem
		Gimlet	10	10	100	0.3
		Box	7	7	100	1.3
w.p.		Pliers	15	15	100	1.9
		Weight	12	12	100	0.8
		Paperclip	7	6	85.7	0.8
Arith. Mean		—	—	97.1		1.0
		Gimlet	14*	10	71.4	1.6
		Box	7	3	42.9	2.3
a.p.		Pliers	9*	4	44.4	2.3
		Weight	12	9	75.0	0.8
		Paperclip	7	4	57.1	1.5
Arith. Mean		—	—	58.2		1.7

The inequalities in the number of Ss in w.p. and a.p. are due to the fact that certain Ss transformed the problem-setting intended for them into the opposite setting. In the gimlet problem, for instance, three Ss assigned to the w.p. group actually had to be counted in the a.p. group: one attempted, using the gimlet, to stuff the cords into the holes which were already there; the other two bored holes with it because they did not quite trust the holes which were there. On the other hand, one S assigned to the a.p. group immediately picked up the gimlet as "thing with which to hang up. . . ." Thus he did not use it in F1, and had therefore to be counted with the w.p. group.—In the pliers problem, three Ss did not utilize the pliers for freeing the bar which was nailed to the board, and therefore had to be counted in the w.p. group.

We see that the results of the a.p. experiments clearly deviate from those of the w.p, experiments in the expected direction. This holds in both measurements, which are independent of each other, and not only for the average of all five problems, but also within each single problem. Only in the weight problem are the two averages of pre-solutions equal.

Therefore we can say: *Under our experimental conditions, the object which is not fixed is almost twice as easily found as the object which is fixed.*

The quantitative results were supported and clarified through qualitative findings. When, at the close of an a.p. experiment, the S was asked "Why have you not used this object" (the crucial one) or, "Why have you used it only so late?," the answer was frequently: "But that is a tool," or, "Such a use would not be suited to the material," or, "I thought it was there simply for . . . (F1)."

The last observation might suggest the following objection: It is not the effect of a "bias" of the crucial object which is measured in the experiments but rather the effect of a bias of the subject. The S may be of the opinion that the experimenter has put the crucial object on the table especially as a tool for F1, that it does not belong to the actual experimental material. (Such false "self-instructions" are not infrequent in the relatively artificial situations of the laboratory.) This objection, however, hardly holds water. In the first place, little significance should be ascribed to statements after the fact, such as "I thought. . . ." They often express only "rationalizations." Secondly, there were many among our Ss for whom it was as if "the scales had fallen from their eyes" when the crucial object was afterwards pointed out. They did not have the feeling of having been victims of a false interpretation of the experimental conditions. In the third place, certain experiments to be cited later . . . also refute this objection. . . .

Analysis of the Factors Which Hinder Recentering

For an understanding of Table 9.6 [not reproduced here] an analysis of the ten hindering factors is required. We shall treat them in order.

1. "No signalling of the perceptual properties of the crucial object." In all six problems, an application or function of the object sought is originally anticipated, "something to. . . ." But for a search in the perceptual field—in our problems, the table is searched with the eyes—such a functional and topical signal is too vague, too *unprägnant*. . . . Visual search concerns visual properties. *The junctional and topical anticipation must therefore be transformed into an anticipation in terms of perceptual content, into a signalling of visual contents, in order to be prägnant, to "hit."*

Example: Something is sought "with which to drive a nail into the wall" (see the weight problem). This topical anticipation forthwith arouses the visual image of a "hammer" or of an object like a hammer, i.e., "hard and heavy" (transformation into signal in terms of content). And not until there is such a visual model is the visual search begun.

How promptly the original topical anticipation may lead to an (approximate) anticipation in terms of content follows from these remarks of Ss in the weight problem: "I am accustomed to use as a hammer whatever is at all solid and heavy," or: "Often enough I take a stone, if I have no hammer." It is generally true that, the more typical the function F2 is for the crucial object or its like, the more easily the original signal by function is transformed into a signal by content appropriate to the crucial object.

Analogously in the pliers problem, the functional and topical anticipation: "a support for the board," immediately calls forth the anticipation by content: "something long, solid. . . ." Just so, the anticipation "something from which to hang a cord" suggests something in the form of a hook or of an eyelet.

Two of our problems—the cork and the box problem—are in this respect worse off than the rest. Here, as a rule, the original functional and topical signal did not succeed in arousing an adequate model of search in terms of content. It could be seen quite clearly how in these two problems the visual search frequently took place under the original function-signal as such ("something to fix the bar which is a bit too short," or, "something to fasten the candles to the door"). But that means that here—*faute de mieux*—the search is with an *unprägnant* signal.

To such anticipations of function, not defined by content, quite different objects may correspond. The candles could simply be fastened to the door somehow or other with tacks or with the help of a cord or of a plug—solutions which were often actually tried. In other words, the anticipation was not specifically directed to something like boxes. It was interesting to see, both from reports and from observed behavior, that, with the box problem, two of the three successful Ss in the a.p. group arrived at the solution in this way: they started from tacks and looked for a "platform to be fastened to the door with tacks." To these Ss, therefore, the tacks suggested a signal already fairly concrete, which in turn could not fail to suggest immediately the visually represented properties: "light material," "supporting surface"—perhaps, as immediately as in the pliers problem the support-function suggests the visual properties: "something long, stable. . . ."

Now, if the general function alone is anticipated, there is a "gap" between signal and object. The filling in of this "gap" has to start from "below," from the object. *And it is really this emergence of the new centering (F2) from the object itself which is hindered by functional fixedness of this object.*

This statement will find corroboration in further experimental results to be cited below. There we shall see that a heterogeneous functional fixedness of the crucial object is unable to resist a sufficiently "pointed" (*prägnant*) property-signal. For the time being, the statement will suffice that the condition "no signalling of perceptual properties of the crucial object" radically hinders a recentering.

2. "F1 still quite real" means that at the time in which F2 becomes real the function F1 is still itself psychologically real, still "lives" as function. The boxes, e.g., persist in their ("static") function of containers. On the other hand, the ("dynamic") pliers-function of the pliers actually ceases along with its use as pliers. Here, therefore, no more than after-effects of the function F1 exist at the time when F2 becomes real. In a more general sense of the word (if we include after-effects in "reality"), F1 is of course in both cases "still real."

This general factor, the "overlapping of the spheres of reality of F1 and F2," will also be subjected to closer examination in the report on further experiments. Here its immediate plausibility may suffice: if something like functional fixedness exists at all, it must be the greater, the more real F1 still is.

A few examples from other experiments and observations: A child builds a tower. This collapses. A block remaining upright promptly becomes a "soldier," and when the "soldier" falls, it at once becomes a "sword."[2] This chain of recenterings is made possible, inter alia, through the fact that every time a structure is destroyed from without (cf. the collapse of the tower), the old function vanishes, so that the object becomes once more relatively *neutral.*— This same reduction of "reality" can be caused by "satiation." The recentering of play-things to be observed so often with children typically appears after they have played with a given object for some time and after satiation has therefore set in. According to Karsten, satiation finds its clearest expression in striving for variation. On the other hand, often it is indubitably the unfolding of the F2-situation which destroys the "reality" of the old situation and of the function F1 indigenous to it. In reference to this, an observation of my own: I lay the pencil as bookmark between two pages, while I read something at another place in the book. I wish to make a note on what I have read here, and unhesitatingly take for the writing (F2) the pencil, whose function as a bookmark then naturally becomes illusory. This is facilitated by the further fact that the function "for writing" is the habitual function of the pencil. . . .

3. "F1 habitual for the crucial object" means that the function Ft has really passed into the "flesh and blood" of the crucial object, and can now be called its "quasi-property." Now this is not the case with the weight problem. A weight is for weighing, but it is by no means familiar as pendulum weight. To be sure, a weight may originally have about as much affinity to a pendulum weight (F,) as to a hammer (F2). An object is of course especially easy to recenter when F2 represents its original function which is only temporarily supplanted by F1. (Example: a large log of firewood, still to be chopped, which has served as chopping block for its like, is itself eventually chopped up.)

4. "The crucial object not familiar as 'differently applicable.'" It is clear that a heterogeneous pre-utilization will "fix" the object the less, the more this object already has the character "variously applicable." A box, a pair of pliers, e.g., are probably less specialized in function than a paper clip or a gimlet. Thus, pliers are often used as substitute for a hammer, a box frequently as support.

A parallel from Köhler's experiments: "Besides, the blanket, is seen and used daily, and is thus unique and in a different category from other objects." . . . This is given as partial explanation of the fact that the blanket was relatively promptly used as substitute for a stick. The effect of the daily handling can hardly be conceived otherwise than in the sense of our factor of variable applicability—in connection with the factor of "contact."

5. "F2 not familiar as realizable by different objects." Some functions are "fixed" from the start to quite definite objects; other functions may be realized by rather heterogeneous objects. The statement of a subject . . . "I am accustomed to use anything suitable as a hammer," points directly to the fact that the hammer function does not tend to be very fastidious in the selection of its objects. In the same way, the function F2 in the box problem "something on which to put . . ." has, of course, countless possibilities of realization in objects. In the course of time one does put almost everything on about everything else.

6. "The crucial object must first be altered for F2." This factor is unambiguously present in the paperclip problem. A paper clip [that] is unbent and a proper paperclip have not much more in common than their material. To be sure, in the box problem, and similarly in the cork problem, the necessary alteration does not happen to the crucial objects *per se*; but it does happen to the visual whole of which the crucial object is a part. An empty box is visually something other than a filled one, an isolated stopper something other than one "sticking in" a bottle. An alteration (in our case, a rupture) of a whole alters the phenomenal character of the part.

7. "F1 given really" (not merely "in thought") means that F1 was or is an actual "fact," that it is not merely ideally ("merely psychologically") given—as is the function

of the weight as a pendulum-weight in the weight problem. (Despite the string fastened to it, the pendulum weight would be fully realized only if the pendulum were hung up.)

8. "The crucial object individually identical in F1 and F2." Only in the paperclip problem does F2 not take place with the identical object of F1, but merely with a representative of the same *genus proximum*. A whole genus may be functionally "fixed."

9. "The crucial object not very suitable for F2." This factor is related to Factor 1. The less adequate F2 is for the object, the more difficult is the recentering into F2. Pliers and cork were sometimes perceived as not especially suitable for F2, and once this happened with the weight.

10. "The crucial object not ready for F2 as a result of F1." This factor is just about the rule in our problems. Yet it happened in the gimlet problem that the gimlet used for boring (F1) obtruded itself as a thing on which to hang the cord because it was already sticking in place.

By this discussion, the ten hindering factors in Table 9.4 [not reproduced here] ought to have become concrete. Now if we look at Table 9.4, at least must strike us immediately the great difference between the first two problems and the sixth, in respect to the number and weight of the hindering factors. We have here all the correlation with our quantitative results which one can wish for. Also in respect to the difference between the first two and the last four problems, the correlation is fairly good—as good as one can expect with factors considered merely in a qualitative, not in a quantitative sense. . . .

The Dynamic Meaning of Heterogeneous Functional Fixedness

It is now time to raise the question *What sort of alteration does an object undergo through heterogeneous functional fixedness?*

As I see it, there are three kinds of alteration:

1. By means of F1, the crucial object is embedded in a particular context, in a functional whole, which is to some degree dynamically segregated. In this fashion the object is "*absorbed*," "*capsulated*." If this functional whole disintegrates—see the factor of "reality" . . .—its parts, the functions, certainly die with it, but naturally not in its elements, the objects. These it "releases from its grasp."

2. Through F1, *the relief of properties in the crucial object is altered*. The properties particularly claimed by the function Ft stand out, become dominant, "central" (hence the expression: "recentering"). Those claimed less or not at all recede, and sometimes drop out completely. The crucial object is so to speak specifically "polarized" by the forces of the functional "field."

3. In the degree to which F1 and F2 belong to the same comprehensive whole and are experienced as mutually required functions of this whole, a curious factor enters into play. The crucial object is expected to change over from one function into *another* function of the same comprehensive whole, i.e., into a function which is in active relation with the first. And this "shift of function within a system" frequently offers considerable difficulties to thinking.

As clarification of the concept of "shift of function within a system" I call two different functions of the same object "contrary." This is a generalization of the logical concept "contrary terms." For example, one calls long and short (or red and blue) contrary, because in a pure form they are mutually exclusive.

They belong to the same "dimension," concern the object in the same respect, have the same structural locus, and consequently are in specific and active relation to one another. Long and red, on the other hand, are not contrary terms; between them there is, in a way, a "dead interval."

Until now the concept "contrary" has been defined in logic only with reference to abstract or ideal wholes (namely, property dimensions). I apply it analogously in relation to "real wholes," i.e., to particular and sometimes unique real structures in which different functions demand each other in different places, such as, e.g., hammer and anvil, father and son, radius and tangent. Such functions may be called "really contrary." Now, if one and the same object is to take on in succession "really contrary" functions, we shall call this a "shift of function within a system."

All three factors probably play a role in heterogeneous functional fixedness as it appears in our experiments. The third factor is probably the least important, since our problem situations are not very "strong" (functional) *gestalten* (W. Köhler), and since consequently the intra-systemic functions F1 and F2 are in only weak "contrary" relation if in any.[3]

It is certainly probable that both factors 1 and 2 are here effective, yet it must be pointed out that in actual fact all our results could be explained by either of the factors alone. After all, we do not know their quantitative potency.

On the other hand, it may at first appear as though several arguments could be raised against an influence of factors 1 and 2 in our experiments. Against 1, one could object as follows: With homogeneous fixedness, which involves "capsulation" (factor 1) but no alteration of the relief of properties (factor 2), no inhibition, no hindering of the solution takes place, but on the contrary a facilitation. On this account, "capsulation" cannot decisively hinder the solution. This objection sounds very plausible at first. In reality, however, it is not valid. The "homogeneity" of the fixedness means (as was already observed) that when F1 has occurred just the function (or property) F2 of the object is actualised, brought into readiness, or even made a quasi-property of the crucial object. But through this the signal becomes *prägnant* in respect to the object. Now, we know that a *prägnant* signal may overcome fixedness. Thus that objection to the factor of capsulation becomes untenable. Homogeneous fixedness does mean capsulation; but it means at the same time that the signal becomes more precise, and this enables the search to penetrate all "capsule walls."

Against factor 2 as well an objection suggests itself at first. Suppose that in heterogeneous fixedness the relief of properties in the crucial object were really and essentially altered, so that the parts of the relief corresponding to the function F, became dominant, and those corresponding to the heterogeneous function F2 became in contrast recessive. Then, with heterogeneous fixedness, how could an F2-signal ever be *prägnant*? For, those properties of the crucial object which correspond to F2 would always be relatively recessive. To this I should like to answer: (1) With heterogeneous fixedness a maximally *prägnant* signal may not in fact be possible. (2) The heterogeneous deformation of the relief of properties is probably not so great that a search directed to certain properties could not find these properties despite the deformation.

---

1. For the conscientious carrying out of these experiments, I am greatly indebted to Miss Rosenbusch, cand, phi.
2. According to Muchow; see Scheerer (34), p. 232.
3. From the finding that the fixedness virtually disappears if F1 and F2 belong to expressly different problem situations, one could be tempted to infer that the third factor, too, has considerable influence. However, that finding can be fully explained by simple loss of "reality" (disintegration) of the functional whole to which F belongs, therefore by exclusive application of the factors 1 and 2.

Commentary

Creativity is intimately related to problem-solving. Indeed, as Torrance (1988, p. 57) noted, "when a person has no learned or practiced solution to a problem, some degree of creativity is required." One might argue that this is not always the case since, for example in art, the origin of creativity might be a personal experience or the need to express oneself. And yet, ultimately, there are many "problems," both conceptual and practical, that artists have to deal with in order to create their work. And in this process, artists and other creators reach several new insights about their situation, the problem at hand, and their own person. The connection between insight and creativity is also of long standing. Why else would we think of a lit light bulb as a symbol of creativity—what this societal representation of the phenomenon brings to the fore is the sudden reorganization of experience typical for many creative acts. The relationship between creativity, insight, and problem-solving has deep historical roots. It is in great part the legacy of the Enlightenment, a period that exalted reason, discoveries, and our problem-solving abilities (Glăveanu, 2017). Of course this is only one facet of creativity that should not be confused with the whole, or rather, it is a fundamental way of being creative, one that underpins a growing literature, from the 1980s onward, on creative problem-solving (e.g., Isaksen & Treffinger, 1985; Mumford, Whetzel, & Reiter-Palmon, 1997). This orientation counts Duncker as one of its forefathers (see also Lawrence & Dodds, 2007).

What did he propose exactly? As we can see from the text reproduced, for Duncker every problem presents the person with a number of elements, some of which will end up being part of the solution. These elements have different degrees of "disposability" when it comes to being recognized as "solution material" (1945, p. 85); the fundamental question for Duncker is how we can explain this and overcome the tendency to ignore available material that can help us solve a problem. His answer points us to the notion of functional fixedness. Referring specifically to objects in the section reproduced in this chapter, he writes, "Whether a sought 'object' is found more easily or with more difficulty depends, among other things, on the degree of 'fixedness' of the object" (p. 85). He gives as an example the chimpanzee who can't recognize the stick growing on a tree in the form of a branch as a stick because of the fixedness related to the perception of the tree as a whole. (In such cases, the object is "absorbed" or "capsulated" [p. 100]). There are many examples of this dynamic in human problem-solving.

Duncker called the phenomenon he studied "heterogeneous functional fixedness" in order to emphasize the fact that the function of the object demanded by the problem is different from its current function. To test his hypotheses, he organized a series of interesting experiments in which one and the same object is used in the context of the problem initially in one way (for instance, the conventional one) and then needs to be used in another way, in another function, in order to solve the problem. In other words, there is a pre-utilization of the object that hinders the person from "recentering"—discovering a new function of the object.

The experiments whose findings are (partially) reported in the excerpt present several of the problems used by Duncker and the objects they employed: a gimlet, a box (similar to a matchbox), pliers, a weight, and a paperclip. Important to note, these were presented to the person among several other objects, irrelevant for the problem at hand or at least leading to suboptimal solutions. In each case, the participants were asked to think aloud (i.e., verbalize their thinking process while solving the task). One of the best known problems in this series is the box problem, in which participants are asked to fix three small candles on the wall. They had at their disposal, among other things, tacks and three small pasteboard boxes. In different conditions the boxes were either empty or held the candles, tacks, or matches. The interest was to observe if participants could move from understanding the box functionally as a container only to seeing it as possible platforms for support—the function needed to solve the problem. The main finding was that the problem was twice as hard to solve when the object was "fixed," meaning that it was used according to its conventional function within the experiment.

What we can abstract for this summary is a dynamic model of creativity. First of all, Duncker (1945, p. 40) had a highly contextual way of theorizing creative problem-solving which started from "the problem situation as a whole unit of activity" involving, at the same time, "the situation, the person's solution and the productive thinking processes by which they are bound together." Second, Duncker thought about productive thinking— in many ways a synonym of creativity—as the interrelation between the development of the problem and the development of the solution (p. 43). The latter comes about from the former, and it involves reorganizing the elements of the problem and overcoming functional fixedness. While Duncker did not refer to creativity as such in his text (something that is not surprising given the fact that this notion entered the vocabulary of psychology more forcefully after 1950), his discussion of fixedness captures an essential feature of this phenomenon: in order to solve problems creatively, we often need to overcome preconceptions and conventional views and, in particular, develop a more flexible relation to the entities, material and symbolic, that surround us. This is not a call to "think outside of the box," commonly heard nowadays, but, on the contrary, one of paying more attention to what is "in" the box represented by the problem. In Duncker's own words, it is "meaningful to say that what is really done in any solution of problems consists in formulating the problem more productively" (p. 9).

The candles and box problem Duncker devised is particularly well-known and illustrates well the creative dynamic described above. It was the topic of several (largely successful) replications as well as extensions, both then and now (see Adamson, 1952; Frank & Ramscar, 2003; Higgins & Chaires, 1980), including using new samples such as children, demonstrating for instance that functional fixedness occurs from relatively early on, as soon as children acquire the conventional meaning of objects (for details see German & Defeyter, 2000). In the creativity literature there are several notable uses of this problem (e.g., Carnevale & Probst, 1998; Maddux, Adam & Galinsky, 2010; Ramm, Tjotta, & Torsvik, 2013). While these studies tested specific hypotheses related to creativity, one of the strongest focuses today, following Duncker's work, is represented by the phenomenon of "fixation," in particular "design fixation" (see, for example, the special issue organized by Cardoso & Badke-Schaub, 2011). Fixation is, in this context, defined as a process that interferes with creative reasoning by making the person become fixated on a certain way of solving a problem (Agogué, Poirel, Pineau, Houdé, & Cassotti, 2014) even when there is a shorter, simpler, or better approach (Crilly & Cardoso, 2017). In the case of design this can occur when previously successful solutions or sources of inspiration tend to be applied indiscriminately to solving new problems (for an extensive discussion see Youmans & Arciszewski, 2014). Being fixated on an old way of doing things deprives the designer from exploring alternatives and potentially reaching more creative outcomes. Developments within this literature include the study of collaborative fixation in brainstorming groups (Kohn & Smith, 2011) and overcoming fixation (Storm & Angello, 2010), including by focusing on obscure features of objects in problem-solving (McCaffrey, 2012).

Another highly promising line of research connected to Duncker's insights is represented by recent work done on affordances and creativity (see Costall, 2015; Glăveanu, 2012, 2016). This line of research bridges the Gestaltism of Duncker and the ecological psychology of Gibson. For the latter, "the affordances of the environment are what it offers the animal, what it provides or furnishes, either for good or ill" (Gibson, 1986, p. 127). In other words, affordances reflect a specific, action-based relation between a person and the objects or material entities within his or her environment. In fact, they can be conceptualized as action potentials and, understood in this way, can usefully reformulate Duncker's findings. Using an affordance lens, what the person gets fixated on is a certain affordance of the object, and in doing so, he or she does not perceive or act upon any other affordances which can in fact lead to a creative solution. Why do we get to focus so much on a specific affordance at the expense of all others? One way of understanding this is by using the notion of "canonical affordances," or what things are for, their conventional use (Costall & Richards, 2013). If a small box is "meant" to be a container, this canonical affordance obscures the fact that it has many other useful affordances within the problem situation, including being used as a support. Duncker (1945, p. 93) referred to canonical affordances in his text as the habitual function of the object, the one that "really passed into the 'flesh and blood' of the crucial object, and can now be called its 'quasi-property.'" He explained the process by which we go beyond this habitual (or canonical) function (or affordance) as "recentering." In a similar manner, I proposed recently a model of the creative process grounded in the notions of positioning and repositioning in order to develop new perspectives on a situation or a problem (Glăveanu, 2015). These new perspectives reveal hidden affordances and, in Duncker's terms, counter the rather natural tendency toward fixedness.

Where do we go from here? First of all I find it important to recover the insights provided by Duncker and his rich analysis of problem-solving. It is equally important to be critical of some of its limitations. For instance Duncker, for as much as he emphasized the problem as a "situation," remained firmly focused on the mental or intra-psychological processes of the person doing the (productive or creative) thinking. In this regard, the notion of affordance helps us transcend the dichotomy between person and situation by being co-constructed by both (see Costall, 2015). Second, and based on the observation above, we need to find new ways of discussing and studying thinking in the psychology of creativity, ways that bridge the gap between person and object, ideas and action, problem and solution. Following Duncker's inspiration, we need methodological innovations to study the dynamic unit that is the problem, the problem solver, and the solution. His use of both quantitative and qualitative methods and forms of analysis is notable in this regard. Creativity might not be all about problems and insights, or rather, it is not about problems and creative insights understood in a narrow, restrictive way. Duncker's work goes a long way when it comes to reframing our understanding of both.

References

Adamson, R. E. (1952). Functional fixedness as related to problem solving: A repetition of three experiments. *Journal of Experimental Psychology, 44,* 288–291.

Agogué, M., Poirel, N., Pineau, A., Houdé, O., & Cassotti, M. (2014). The impact of age and training on creativity: A design-theory approach to study fixation effects. *Thinking Skills and Creativity, 11,* 33–41.

Cardoso, C., & Badke-Schaub, P. (2011). Fixation or inspiration: Creative problem solving in design. *Journal of Creative Behavior, 45*(2), 77–82.

Carnevale, P. J., & Probst, T. M. (1998). Social values and social conflict in creative problem solving and categorization. *Journal of Personality and Social Psychology, 74*(5), 1300–1309.

Costall, A. (2015). Canonical affordances and creative agency. In V. P. Glăveanu, A. Gillespie, & J. Valsiner (Eds.), *Rethinking creativity: Contributions from social and cultural psychology* (pp. 45–57). New York, NY: Routledge.

Costall, A., & Richards, A. (2013). Canonical affordances: The psychology of everyday things. In P. Graves-Brown, R. Harrison, & A. Piccini (Eds.), *The Oxford handbook of the archaeology of the contemporary world* (pp. 82–93). Oxford: Oxford University Press.

Crilly, N., & Cardoso, C. (2017). Where next for research on fixation, inspiration and creativity in design? *Design Studies, 50,* 1–38.

Duncker, K. (1945). On Problem-Solving. (L. S. Lees, Trans.). *Psychological Monographs, 58*(5).

Frank, M. C., & Ramscar, M. (2003). How do presentation and context influence representation for functional fixedness tasks? *Proceedings of the 25th Annual Meeting of the Cognitive Science Society, 25*(25), 1345.

German, T. P., & Defeyter, M. A. (2000). Immunity to functional fixedness in young children. *Psychonomic Bulletin and Review, 7,* 707–12.

Gibson, J. J. (1986). *The ecological approach to visual perception.* Hillsdale, NJ: Erlbaum.

Glăveanu, V. P. (2012). What can be done with an egg? Creativity, material objects and the theory of affordances. *Journal of Creative Behavior, 46*(3), 192–208.

Glăveanu, V. P. (2015). Creativity as a sociocultural act. *Journal of Creative Behavior, 49*(3), 165–180.

Glăveanu, V. P. (2016). Affordance. In V. P. Glăveanu, L. Tanggaard, & C. Wegener (Eds.), *Creativity: A new vocabulary* (pp. 10–17). London: Palgrave.

Glăveanu, V. P. (2017). Creativity in perspective: A socio-cultural and critical account. *Journal of Constructivist Psychology, 31*(2), 118–129.

Higgins, E. T., & Chaires, W. M. (1980). Accessibility of interrelational constructs: Implications for stimulus encoding and creativity. *Journal of Experimental Social Psychology, 16*(4), 348–361.

Isaksen, S. G., & Treffinger, D. J. (1985). *Creative problem solving: The basic course.* New York, NY: Bearly Limited.

Kohn, N. W., & Smith, S. M. (2011). Collaborative fixation: Effects of others' ideas on brainstorming. *Applied Cognitive Psychology, 25*(3), 359–371.

Lawrence, J. A., & Dodds, A. E. (2007). Duncker's account of productive thinking: Exegesis and application of a problem-solving theory. In J. Valsiner (Ed.), *Thinking in psychological science: Ideas and their makers* (pp. 39–58). New Brunswick, NJ: Transaction.

Maddux, W. W., Adam, H., & Galinsky, A. D. (2010). When in Rome . . . learn why the Romans do what they do: How multicultural learning experiences facilitate creativity. *Personality and Social Psychology Bulletin, 36*(6), 731–741.

McCaffrey, T. (2012). Innovation relies on the obscure: A key to overcoming the classic problem of functional fixedness. *Psychological Science, 23*(3), 215–218.

Mumford, M. D., Whetzel, D. L., & Reiter-Palmon, R. (1997). Thinking creatively at work: Organization influences on creative problem solving. *Journal of Creative Behavior, 31*(1), 7–17.

Newell, A. (1985). Duncker on thinking: An inquiry into progress in cognition. In S. Koch & D. E. Leary (Eds.), *A century of psychology as science* (pp. 392–419). Washington, DC: American Psychological Association.

Ramm, J., Tjotta, S., & Torsvik, G. (2013). Incentives and creativity in groups. CESifo Working Paper No. 4374.

Schnall, S. (1999). Life as the problem: Karl Duncker's context. From Past to Future: Clark. *Papers on the History of Psychology, 1*(2), 13–28.

Storm, B. C., & Angello, G. (2010). Overcoming fixation: Creative problem solving and retrieval-induced forgetting. *Psychological Science, 21*(9), 1263–1265.

Torrance, E. P. (1988). The nature of creativity as manifest in its testing. In R. Sternberg (Ed.), *The nature of creativity: Contemporary psychological perspectives* (pp. 43–75). Cambridge, UK: Cambridge University Press.

Youmans, R. J., & Arciszewski, T. (2014). Design fixation: Classifications and modern methods of prevention. *AI EDAM, 28*(2), 129–137.

10

Abductive Reasoning and the Genesis of New Ideas

Charles S. Peirce

RONALD A. BEGHETTO

Summary

In this chapter I provide commentary on selections from Charles Sanders Peirce's *Collected Papers* as they pertain to creative reasoning. More specifically, I provide commentary on Peirce's concept of abductive reasoning and discuss how it comprises a larger process of creative inquiry. In order to support this effort, I introduce a model of creative reasoning that I hope can serve as a bridge between Peirce's ideas and concepts relevant to contemporary creativity theorists and researchers.

Introduction

Charles Sanders Peirce (1839–1914) was an influential yet sometimes overlooked contributor to many lines of thought, including pragmatism, semiotics, philosophy of science, mathematics, and logic—just to name a few. As I will argue, many of his ideas also presaged concepts and issues taken up by contemporary creativity researchers.

The challenge in connecting Peirce with contemporary work in creativity, however, is not simply that his oeuvre covers an abundance of topics (which it does), but that the ideas he expresses over the course of his writings are at turns suggestive, systematic, developmental, and ultimately unfinished (Anderson, 1987; Burks, 1946). Adding to this challenge is the fact that I am not a logician, semiotician, or Peircean scholar. As such, the danger of misrepresenting Peirce's ideas is ever present. One therefore must, as the

Peircean scholar Douglas Anderson (1987, p. 11) has said, "acknowledge such dangers and keep them in mind as one proceeds . . . but one must proceed."

The selection I have chosen for this commentary represents passages from the massive *Collected Papers of Charles Sanders Peirce* (CP). One of the editors of the papers has described them as "a disordered array of severed limbs" (Deely, 1994). Consequently the selection I have chosen to comment on is not a stand-alone document. Rather it represents excerpts, which I title "Abductive Reasoning as Part of a Larger Process of Creative Reasoning."

It is my hope that this selection will offer creativity researchers a window into a Peircean account of creative inquiry. Although the window may be clouded by the fragmentary nature of the selection and my particular vantage point as a creativity researcher, I believe there is still value in considering Peirce's ideas. Doing so can reveal several connections and insights relevant to contemporary perspectives on creative thought and action (as I hope to demonstrate in my commentary that follows the selection).

Reading: *Collected Papers of Charles Sanders Peirce*

Source: Peirce, C. S. *Collected Papers of Charles Sanders Peirce.* Vols. 5–8 (A. W. Burks, Ed.). Cambridge, MA: Belknap Press of Harvard University Press, 1958. Copyright © 1958 by the President and Fellows of Harvard College.

CP 5.171. Concerning the validity of Abductive inference, there is little to be said, although that little is pertinent to the problem we have in hand.

Abduction is the process of forming an explanatory hypothesis. It is the only logical operation which introduces any new idea, for induction does nothing but determine a value, and deduction merely evolves the necessary consequences of a pure hypothesis.

Deduction proves that something must be; Induction shows that something actually is operative; Abduction merely suggests that something may be.

Its only justification is that from its suggestion deduction can draw a prediction which can be tested by induction, and that, if we are ever to learn anything or to understand phenomena at all, it must be by abduction that this is to be brought about.

No reason whatsoever can be given for it, as far as I can discover; and it needs no reason, since it merely offers suggestions.

CP 5.172. A man must be downright crazy to deny that science has made many true discoveries. But every single item of scientific theory which stands established today has been due to Abduction.

But how is it that all this truth has ever been lit up by a process in which there is no compulsiveness nor tendency toward compulsiveness? Is it by chance? Consider the multitude of theories that might have been suggested. A physicist comes across some new phenomenon in his laboratory. How does he know but the conjunctions of the planets have something to do with it or that it is not perhaps because the dowager empress of China has at that same time a year ago chanced to pronounce some word of mystical power or some invisible jinnee may be present. Think of what trillions of trillions of hypotheses might be made of which one only is true; and yet after two or three or at the very most a dozen guesses, the physicist hits pretty nearly on the correct hypothesis. By chance he would not have been likely to do so in the whole time that has elapsed since the earth was solidified. You may tell me that astrological and magical hypotheses were resorted to at first and that it is only by degrees that we have learned certain general laws of nature in consequence of which the physicist seeks for the explanation of his phenomenon within the four walls of his laboratory. But when you look at the matter more narrowly, the matter is not to be accounted for in any considerable measure in that way. Take a broad view of the matter. Man has not been engaged upon scientific problems for over twenty thousand years or so. But put it at ten times that if you like. But that is not a hundred thousandth part of the time that he might have been expected to have been searching for his first scientific theory.

You may produce this or that excellent psychological account of the matter. But let me tell you that all the psychology in the world will leave the logical problem just where it was. I might occupy hours in developing that point. I must pass it by.

You may say that evolution accounts for the thing. I don't doubt it is evolution. But as for explaining evolution by chance, there has not been time enough.

CP 5.173. However man may have acquired his faculty of divining the ways of Nature, it has certainly not been by a self-controlled and critical logic. Even now he cannot give any exact reason for his best guesses. It appears to me that the clearest statement we can make of the logical situation—the freest from all questionable admixture—is to say that man has a certain Insight, not strong enough to be oftener right than wrong, but strong enough not to be overwhelmingly more often wrong than right, into the Thirdnesses, the general elements, of Nature. An Insight, I call it, because it is to be referred to the same general class of operations to which Perceptive Judgments belong. This Faculty is at the same time of the general nature of Instinct, resembling the instincts of the animals in its so far surpassing the general powers of our reason and for its directing us as if we were in possession of facts that are entirely beyond the reach of our senses. It resembles instinct too in its small liability to error; for though it goes wrong oftener than right, yet the relative frequency with which it is right is on the whole the most wonderful thing in our constitution.

CP 5.174. One little remark and I will drop this topic. If you ask an investigator why he does not try this or that wild theory, he will say, "It does not seem reasonable." It is curious that we seldom use this word where the strict logic of our procedure is clearly seen. We do [not] say that a mathematical error is not reasonable. We call that opinion reasonable whose only support is instinct. . . .

CP 5.181. The abductive suggestion comes to us like a flash. It is an act of *insight*, although of extremely fallible insight. It is true that the different elements of the hypothesis were in our minds before; but it is the idea of putting together what we had never before dreamed of putting together which flashes the new suggestion before our contemplation.

CP 5.189. Long before I first classed abduction as an inference it was recognized by logicians that the operation of adopting an explanatory hypothesis—which is just what abduction is—was subject to certain conditions. Namely, the hypothesis cannot be admitted, even as a hypothesis, unless it be supposed that it would account for the facts or some of them. . . .

CP 6.469. Every inquiry whatsoever takes its rise in the observation, in one or another of the three Universes,[1] of some surprising phenomenon, some experience which either disappoints an expectation or breaks in upon some habit of expectation of the *inquisiturus;* and each apparent exception to this rule only confirms it. There are obvious distinctions between the objects of surprise in different cases; but throughout this slight sketch of inquiry such details will be unnoticed, especially since it is upon such that the logic-books descant. The inquiry begins with pondering these phenomena in all their aspects, in the search of some point of view whence the wonder shall be resolved. At length a conjecture arises that furnishes a possible Explanation, by which I mean a syllogism exhibiting the surprising fact as necessarily consequent upon the circumstances of its occurrence together with the truth of the credible conjecture, as premises.

On account of this Explanation, the inquirer is led to regard his conjecture, or hypothesis, with favor. As I phrase it, he provisionally holds it to be "Plausible"; this acceptance ranges in different cases—and reasonably so—from a mere expression of it in the interrogative mood, as a question meriting attention and reply, up through all appraisals of Plausibility, to uncontrollable inclination to believe. The whole series of mental performances between the notice of the wonderful phenomenon and the acceptance of the hypothesis, during which the usually docile understanding seems to hold the bit between its teeth and to have us at its mercy, the search for pertinent circumstances and the laying hold of them, sometimes without our cognizance, the scrutiny of them, the dark laboring, the bursting out of the startling conjecture, the remarking of its smooth fitting to the anomaly, as it is turned back and forth like a key in a lock, and the final estimation of its Plausibility, I reckon as composing the First Stage of Inquiry. . . .

CP 7.202. Accepting the conclusion that an explanation is needed when facts contrary to what we should expect emerge, it follows that the explanation must be such a proposition as would lead to the prediction of the observed facts, either as necessary consequences or at least as very probable under the circumstances. A hypothesis then, has to be adopted, which is likely in itself, and renders the facts likely. This step of adopting a hypothesis as being suggested by the facts, is what I call *abduction.* I reckon it as a form of inference, however problematical the hypothesis may be held. What are to be the logical rules to which we are to conform in taking this step? There would be no logic in imposing rules, and saying that they *ought* to be followed, until it is made out that the purpose of hypothesis requires them.

Accordingly, it appears that the early scientists, Thales, Anaximander, and their brethren, seemed to think the work of science was done when a likely hypothesis was suggested. I applaud their sound logical instinct for that. Even Plato, in the Timaeus and elsewhere, does not hesitate roundly to assert the truth of anything, if it seems to render the world reasonable; and this same procedure, in a more refined modification, is the essence of modern historical criticism. It is all right as long as it is not found to interfere with the usefulness of the hypothesis. Aristotle departs a little from that method. His physical hypotheses are equally unfounded; but he always adds a "perhaps." That, I take it, was because Aristotle had been a great reader of other philosophers, and it had struck him that there are various inconsistent ways of explaining the same facts.

Ultimately, the circumstance that a hypothesis, although it may lead us to expect some facts to be as they are, may in the future lead us to erroneous expectations about other facts— this circumstance, which anybody must have admitted as soon as it was brought home to him, was brought home to scientific men so forcibly, first in astronomy, and then in other sciences, that it became axiomatical that a hypothesis adopted by abduction could only be adopted on probation, and must be tested.

CP 7.203. When this is duly recognized, the first thing that will be done, as soon as a hypothesis has been adopted, will be to trace out its necessary and probable experiential consequences. This step is *deduction*. . . .

CP 7.205. Deduction, of course, relates exclusively to an ideal state of things. A hypothesis presents such an ideal state of things, and asserts that it is the icon or analogue of an experience.

CP 7.206. Having, then, by means of deduction, drawn from a hypothesis predictions as to what the results of [an] experiment will be, we proceed to test the hypothesis by making the experiments and comparing those predictions with the actual results of the experiment. Experiment is very expensive business, in money, in time, and in thought; so that it will be a saving of expense, to begin with that positive prediction from the hypothesis which seems least likely to be verified. For a single experiment may absolutely refute the most valuable of hypotheses, while a hypothesis must be a trifling one indeed if a single experiment could establish it.

When, however, we find that prediction after prediction, notwithstanding a preference for putting the most unlikely ones to the test, is verified by experiment, whether without modification or with a merely quantitative modification, we begin to accord to the hypothesis a standing among scientific results. This sort of inference it is, from experiments testing predictions based on a hypothesis, that is alone properly entitled to be called *induction*. . . .

CP 7.218. Abduction, on the other hand, is merely preparatory. It is the first step of scientific reasoning, as induction is the concluding step. Nothing has so much contributed to present chaotic or erroneous ideas of the logic of science as failure to distinguish the essentially different characters of different elements of scientific reasoning; and one of the worst of these confusions, as well as one of the commonest, consists in regarding abduction and induction taken together (often mixed also with deduction) as a simple argument.

Abduction and induction have, to be sure, this common feature, that both lead to the acceptance of a hypothesis because observed facts are such as would necessarily or probably result as consequences of that hypothesis. But for all that, they are the opposite poles of reason, the one the most ineffective, the other the most effective of arguments. The method of either is the very reverse of the other's. Abduction makes its start from the facts, without, at the outset, having any particular theory in view, though it is motived by the feeling that a theory is needed to explain the surprising facts. Induction makes its start from a hypothesis which seems to recommend itself, without at the outset having any particular facts in view, though it feels the need of facts to support the theory.

Abduction seeks a theory. Induction seeks for facts. In abduction the consideration of the facts suggests the hypothesis. In induction the study of the hypothesis suggests the experiments which bring to light the very facts to which the hypothesis had pointed. . . .

CP 7.219. I now proceed to consider what principles should guide us in abduction, or the process of choosing a hypothesis. Underlying all such principles there is a fundamental and primary abduction, a hypothesis which we must embrace at the outset, however destitute of evidentiary support it may be. That hypothesis is that the facts in hand admit of rationalization, and of rationalization by us. That we must hope they do, for the same reason that a general who has to capture a position or see his country ruined must go on the hypothesis that there is some way in which he can and shall capture it. We must be animated by that hope concerning the problem we have in hand, whether we extend it to a general postulate covering all facts or not. Now, that the matter of no new truth can come from induction or from deduction, we have seen. It can only come from abduction, and abduction is, after all, nothing but guessing. We are therefore bound to hope that, although the possible explanations of our facts may be strictly innumerable, yet our mind will be able, in some finite number of guesses, to guess the sole true explanation of them. *That* we are bound to assume, independently of any evidence that it is true. Animated by that hope, we are to proceed to the construction of a hypothesis. . . .

CP 7.220. Now the only way to discover the principles upon which anything ought to be constructed is to consider what is to be done with the constructed thing after it is constructed. That which is to be done with the hypothesis is to trace out its consequences by deduction, to compare them with results of experiment by induction, and to discard the hypothesis, and try another, as soon as the first has been refuted; as it presumably will be. How long it will be before we light upon the hypothesis which shall resist all tests we cannot tell; but we hope we shall do so, at last.

In view of this prospect, it is plain that three considerations should determine our choice of a hypothesis. In the first place, it must be capable of being subjected to experimental testing. It must consist of experiential consequences with only so much logical cement as is needed to render them rational. In the second place, the hypothesis must be such that it will explain the surprising facts we have before us which it is the whole motive of our inquiry to rationalize. This explanation may consist in making the observed facts natural chance results, as the kinetical theory of gases explains facts; or it may render the facts necessary, and in the latter case as implicitly asserting them or as the ground for a mathematical demonstration of their truth. In the third place, quite as necessary a consideration as either of those I have mentioned, in view of the fact that the true hypothesis is only one out of innumerable possible false ones, in view, too, of the enormous expensiveness of experimentation in money, time, energy, and thought, is the consideration of economy.

Now economy, in general, depends upon three kinds of factors: cost; the value of the thing proposed, in itself; and its effect upon other projects. Under the head of cost, if a hypothesis can be put to the test of experiment with very little expense of any kind, that should be regarded as a recommendation for giving it precedence in the inductive procedure. For even if it be barely admissible for other reasons, still it may clear the ground to have disposed of it. . . .

Under the head of value, we must place those considerations which tend toward an expectation that a given hypothesis may be true. These are of two kinds, the purely instinctive and the reasoned. In regard to instinctive considerations, I have already pointed out that it is a primary hypothesis underlying all abduction that the human mind is akin to the truth in the sense that in a finite number of guesses it will light upon the correct hypothesis. Now inductive experience supports that hypothesis in a remarkable measure. For if there were no tendency of that kind, if when a surprising phenomenon presented itself in our laboratory, we had to make random shots at the determining conditions, trying such hypotheses as that the aspect of the planets had something to do with it, or what the dowager empress had been doing just five hours previously, if such hypotheses had as good a chance of being true as those which seem marked by good sense, then we never could have made any progress in science at all. . . .

From the instinctive, we pass to reasoned, marks of truth in the hypothesis. Of course, if we know any positive facts which render a given hypothesis objectively probable, they recommend it for inductive testing. When this is not the case, but the hypothesis seems to us likely, or unlikely, this likelihood is an indication that the hypothesis accords or discords with our preconceived ideas; and since those ideas are presumably based upon some experience, it follows that, other things being equal, there will be, in the long run, some economy in giving the hypothesis a place in the order of precedence in accordance with this indication. But experience must be our chart in economical navigation; and experience shows that likelihoods are treacherous guides. Nothing has caused so much waste of time and means, in all sorts of researches, as inquirers' becoming so wedded to certain likelihoods as to forget all the other factors of the economy of research; so that, unless it be very solidly grounded, likelihood is far better disregarded, or nearly so; and even when it seems solidly grounded, it should be proceeded upon with a cautious tread, with an eye to other considerations, and a recollection of the disasters it has caused.

The third category of factors of economy, those arising from the relation of what is proposed to other projects, is especially important in abduction, because very rarely can we positively expect a given hypothesis to prove entirely satisfactory; and we must always consider what will happen when the hypothesis proposed breaks down. . . .

CP 8.209. Abduction having suggested a theory, we employ *de*duction to deduce from that ideal theory a promiscuous variety of consequences to the effect that if we perform certain acts, we shall find ourselves confronted with certain experiences. We then proceed to try these experiments, and if the predictions of the theory are verified, we have a proportionate confidence that the experiments that remain to be tried will confirm the theory.

I say that these three are the only elementary modes of reasoning there are. . . . Abduction furnishes all our ideas concerning real things, beyond what are given in perception, but is mere conjecture, without probative force. Deduction is certain but relates only to ideal objects. Induction gives us the only approach to certainty concerning the real that we can have. In forty years diligent study of arguments, I have never found one which did not consist of those elements.

---

1. The following is how Peirce expanded on the three universes: [CP 6.455.] Of the three Universes of Experience familiar to us all, the first comprises all mere Ideas, those airy nothings to which the mind of poet, pure mathematician, or another **might** give local habitation and a name within that mind. Their very airy-nothingness, the fact that their Being consists in mere capability of getting thought, not in anybody's Actually thinking them, saves their Reality. The second Universe is that of the Brute Actuality of things and facts. I am confident that their Being consists in reactions against Brute forces, notwithstanding objections redoubtable until they are closely and fairly examined. The third Universe comprises everything whose being consists in active power to establish connections between different objects, especially between objects in different Universes. Such is everything which is essentially a Sign—not the mere body of the Sign, which is not essentially such, but, so to speak, the Sign's Soul, which has its Being in its power of serving as intermediary between its Object and a Mind. Such, too, is a living consciousness, and such the life, the power of growth, of a plant. Such is a living constitution—a daily newspaper, a great fortune, a social "movement."

Commentary

How do Peirce's ideas as represented in this selection have relevance for contemporary creativity researchers? I would argue that the relevance is most directly found in his concept of abductive reasoning and how it comprises a larger process of creative inquiry. In what follows, I offer a model that I hope can serve as a bridge between Peirce's ideas and concepts relevant to contemporary creativity theorists and researchers.

Figure 10.1 depicts my attempt to illustrate and provide a Peircean account of how three modes of reasoning (i.e., abduction, deduction, and induction) represent a more general process of creative inquiry. In the sections that follow, I will discuss each of the components of this Peircean-inspired model.

I also discuss how the ideas represented in the model align with several key concepts of contemporary creativity theory and research: understanding the conditions and process from which creativity emerges, the dynamic features of the phenomenon of creativity, and even the definition of creativity itself.

A CATALYST FOR NEW IDEAS

> Disruptive
> Experience

Peirce offers a "logic of discovery" (Burks, 1946, p. 302), which describes the conditions from which new ideas are introduced, developed, and tested. Specifically, a Peircean account asserts that "some surprising phenomenon, some experience which either disappoints an expectation, or breaks in upon some habit of expectation" (CP 6.469), creates a rupture in our experience, which serves as a catalyst for creative inquiry.

This assertion aligns with how some creativity researchers have described the onset of the creative process. Specifically, when we face an ill-defined problem or surprising situation, we find ourselves uncertain how to proceed (Mumford & McIntosh, 2017; Pretz, Naples, & Sternberg, 2003; but see Glăveanu, 2012). In other words, we experience a state of genuine doubt, which we are motivated to resolve (Beghetto & Schreiber, 2016; Burks, 1946).

Peirce explains that these ruptures in our routines and habits can occur at three levels of experience: the world of Ideas, "those airy-nothings"; the world of "Brute Actuality— of things and facts"; and the world of Signs or "connections between different objects, especially between objects in different Universes" (CP 6.455). In this way, disruptions that spark creative inquiry can be *encountered* (e.g., we find ourselves confronted with

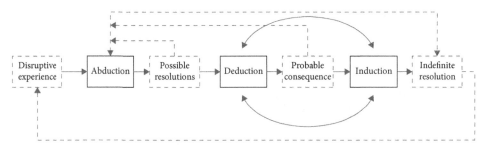

FIGURE 10.1 **A Peircean Inspired Model of Creative Reasoning.**

the anomalous phenomenon) or *encouraged* (e.g., we invite the unexpected into our experience through free play of ideas and actions).

Such assertions align with my own work. I have, for example, described how unexpected moments, experiences of doubt and surprise, and ruptures in our experiences can serve as opportunities for creative thought and action (Beghetto, 2016a, 2016b). More specifically, in Beghetto (2016b) I have asserted how new ways of thought and action can emerge from *internal ruptures* (e.g., resulting from one's own inner dialogues), *social external ruptures* (e.g., resulting from surprising interactions among people), and *social-material ruptures* (e.g., resulting from noticing disruptive sociomaterial features of the environment).

Whatever its origin, the process of creative inquiry (at least according to this account) is sparked by a disruptive experience, which moves us into an active effort to resolve it.

THE INTRODUCTION OF NEW IDEAS

> Abduction

When we find ourselves in a state of wonder, doubt, surprise, or unease, we engage in abductive reasoning to resolve the disruption we are experiencing. In this way the process of creative inquiry has the goal of moving us from an unsettled to a settled state. Peirce puts it this way: "The inquiry begins with pondering these phenomena in all their aspects, in the search of some point of view whence the wonder shall be resolved. At length a conjecture arises that furnishes a possible Explanation" (CP 6.469).

Peirce describes the resulting insight as coming "to us like a flash. . . . It is the idea of putting together what we had never before dreamed of putting together which flashes the new suggestion before our contemplation" (CP 5.181). Peirce's description of how new ideas and insights are generated is strikingly similar to what contemporary creativity researchers have described as the creative insights resulting from the combination of different (even opposite) stimuli (Rothenberg, 2014; Sawyer, 2012; Ward & Kolomyts, 2010).

Although Peirce does not provide a description of the psychological mechanisms at work during abductive reasoning, he does make clear that the resulting insights do not come out of thin air: "It is true that the different elements of the hypothesis were in our minds before" (CP 5.181). In other words, our efforts to resolve disruptive phenomena takes place in medias res (Anderson, 1987), that is, in the midst of prior action, knowledge, and understanding of the situation or domain at hand.

In this way there is an implicit recognition in Peirce's system that "creativity of any kind cannot begin without a certain amount of funded experience" (Anderson, 1987, p. 148). Put simply, we need to have some experiential or conceptual context in order to recognize the disruption in the first place. Again, such assertions square with claims made by creativity researchers regarding the important role that prior knowledge and experiences play in creative thought. Guilford (1950, p. 448), for instance, asserted, "No creative person can get along without previous experiences or facts."

Moreover the role of prior knowledge in understanding and working through ill-defined problems and situations also aligns with how creativity researchers have described the preparation and problem definition work necessary for resolving complex challenges and nonroutine problems (Kozbelt, Beghetto, & Runco, 2010; Sawyer, 2012).

Finally, abductive reasoning is also involved in learning anything new. As Peirce explained, "If we are ever to learn anything or to understand phenomena at all, it must be by abduction that this is to be brought about" (CP 5.171). In this way a Peircean account of creative reasoning also predates similar arguments made by creativity researchers who have asserted links between creativity and learning (see Beghetto, 2016c; Guilford, 1967).

EVALUATING THE REASONABLENESS OF ABDUCTIVE INSIGHTS

> Possible
> resolutions

Abductive insights are aimed at explaining or resolving a surprising phenomenon. Abductive insights are evaluated in light of their ability to *reasonably*—albeit *provisionally*—resolve the disruptive experience at hand. As Peirce explained, an abductive insight "cannot be admitted, even as a hypothesis, unless it be supposed that it would account for the facts or some of them" (CP 5.189).

The idea that novel (abductive) insights must also be reasonable aligns with the two-criteria (e.g., novelty and usefulness) definitions of creativity espoused by many creativity researchers (e.g., Kaufman, 2016; Plucker, Beghetto, & Dow, 2004; Runco & Jaeger, 2012; but see Corazza, 2016, and Smith & Smith, 2017, for variations on this definition).

Peirce offered additional guidelines for evaluating the acceptability of abductive insights: "capable of being subjected to experimental testing"; "[explaining] the surprising facts we have before us"; and taking into consideration "economy" [i.e., "cost, the value of the thing proposed, in itself, and its effects upon other projects]" (CP 7.220). Again, these additional criteria are similar to how creativity researchers have described the role of convergent thinking used to evaluate the merit of candidate ideas, insights, and actions when creatively solving complex challenges and ill-defined problems (Beghetto, 2016a; Mumford & McIntosh, 2017; Sawyer, 2012).

Peirce also recognized that what we "provisionally" accept to be "plausible . . . ranges in different cases" (CP 6.469). An abductive insight deemed as acceptable in one domain (e.g., physics) will be different from what is deemed acceptable in other domains (e.g., painting). Even with these variations, reasonableness still serves as a core criterion across situations and cases, as Anderson (1987, p. 60) has explained: "Whereas scientific reasoning ends with reasonable ideas, art ends with reasonable feelings." This recognition that there is variability across different cases also aligns with contemporary perspectives on the domain-specific nature of creativity (e.g., Baer & Garrett, 2010).

REFINING OF IDEAS AND OUTLINING PROBABLE CONSEQUENCES

> Deduction

Once abductive insights have been deemed acceptable, they then get tested and refined through deductive reasoning. More specifically, in a Peircean account of creative reasoning, we use deduction to determine the necessary and experiential consequences of pursuing our abductive insights.

As Peirce explained, once we have adopted an abductive insight "we employ deduction to deduce from that ideal theory a promiscuous variety of consequences to the effect that if we perform certain acts, we shall find ourselves confronted with certain experiences" (CP 8.209).

Deductive reasoning refines abductive insights into probable consequences (CP 7.202) by pruning away abductive possibilities in an effort to arrive at more viable options. Again, this refining of ideas aligns with the convergent and evaluative processes described by contemporary creativity researchers (e.g., Beghetto, 2016a, Mumford & McIntosh, 2017; Sawyer, 2012).

PREDICTED OUTCOMES

```
┌ ─ ─ ─ ─ ─ ─ ┐
│   Probable   │
│ consequence  │
└ ─ ─ ─ ─ ─ ─ ┘
```

The probable consequences—which have been deductively rendered out of abductive possibilities—have a logical necessity to them (i.e., they demonstrate that "something *must be*" [CP 5.171]). The insights that result from abductive reasoning move from a more tentative or possible state of "something may be" to a more probable state through deduction and then ultimately tested, through induction, to determine whether "something actually is operative" (CP 5.171).

Again the specific features vary by discipline. In domains like the sciences, for instance, abductive insights that have been deductively rendered into logically coherent consequences will eventually be put to the test through experimentation. In domains where the constraints on logical necessity and experimental testing are not as strict, such as the arts, deductive reasoning is used to narrow possibilities in an effort to start moving a creative work toward resolution.

Anderson (1987) provides an example in his discussion of artistic creative deduction. Anderson explains that when Cezanne placed an initial broad brushstroke in the middle of one of his paintings, the stroke limited the future trajectory of the work. And with each successive stroke, the indefinite beginning transformed into a more definite telos, moving back and forth as necessary (between induction and deduction), and ultimately coming to rest in a resolution (i.e., a finished painting).

These claims also align with descriptions of the creative process put forth by creativity researchers (e.g., Sawyer, 2012). Once possibilities have been generated, they are then evaluated, refined, and prepared for experiential testing (e.g., testing whether they resolve the ill-defined problem or complex situation at hand). The process can have starts and stops, cycle back and forth between deductive and inductive phases, and, if not abandoned, continue until a viable resolution has been achieved.

EXPERIENTIAL TESTING OF REFINED, ABDUCTIVE INSIGHTS

```
┌ ─ ─ ─ ─ ─ ─ ┐
│             │
│  Induction  │
│             │
└ ─ ─ ─ ─ ─ ─ ┘
```

Once an abductive insight has moved through deductive reasoning to "produce conditional predictions concerning our future experience" (CP 7.115), we then, according to Peirce, use inductive reasoning to "bring these predictions to the test, and thus to form our final estimate of the value of the [abductive insight]" (CP 7.115).

Induction, in a Peircean account of creative reasoning, is the experiential testing ground for our creative insights. In the case of the sciences, for instance, this might involve determining whether abductive hypotheses can be refuted through experimental testing. In the arts, this testing takes on a different flavor. As Anderson (1987) explains, the creative artist tests the resulting work against his or her aesthetic judgment to determine whether it resolves the unsettled or disruptive experience that prompted the creative effort in the first place.

Put simply, induction works to test whether a deductively refined abductive insight is operative in resolving some surprising phenomenon, unsettling feeling, or disruptive experience. Each of the three types of creative reasoning plays a different but related role in the process of creative inquiry.

ACCEPTANCE OF OUTCOMES

> Indefinite
> resolution

Taken together, a Peircean account of creative reasoning describes a process that commences with a disruptive experience, which is then followed by an attempt to generate possible resolutions of that disruption through abductive reasoning. Candidate possibilities are selected based on their reasonableness, explanatory power, value, and economic feasibility.

These possibilities are then narrowed and refined through deductive reasoning, which renders out probable consequences that can be tested experientially. This process can move through multiple iterations before coming to rest in a state of indefinite resolution (which can be reanimated by subsequent disruptions). As Peirce explained,

> When . . . we find that prediction after prediction, notwithstanding a preference for putting the most unlikely ones to the test, is verified by experiment, whether without modification or with a merely quantitative modification, we begin to accord to the hypothesis a standing among scientific results. (CP 7.206)

Hypotheses that have been accorded scientific standing can, of course, be refuted or further refined at some later date. Even in cases where a creative work is finished and the creator never again alters it, we can still assert with Anderson (1988, p. 145) that "whereas a hypothesis can grow to adapt to new facts, a work of art may grow to adapt to new interpretations." A finished painting, for instance, is still open to new and different interpretations by audiences, critics, and connoisseurs.

A Peircean account of creativity therefore recognizes that the work is never entirely resolved. The process of creative reasoning is dynamic, open, and ultimately unfinished. This assertion also aligns with arguments put forth by contemporary creativity researchers (e.g., Beghetto & Corazza, 2019) and empirical work aimed at exploring the more dynamic features of creativity. Gadja et al. (2017), for instance, have demonstrated how a student's novel idea, which has been accepted, dismissed, or ignored by the teacher, can later become reanimated and built upon by other students engaged in that discussion.

INSPIRING FUTURE DIRECTIONS

Once you get through the density of Peirce's prose, there is an underlying precision and elegance to his ideas. He offers a perspective that situates creative insights in the context of a broader process of creative inquiry. As discussed, abductive (or creative) reasoning is a special form of reasoning that emerges out of states of surprise or doubt, which eventually can lead to new ways of thought and action through deductive refinement and inductive testing. Importantly, this is a dynamic and ultimately unfinished process.

Creative reasoning from a Peircean perspective is always tentative. It is represented by signs—such as hunches, symptoms, and clues (see Shank & Cunningham, 1996). But it is not capricious. Rather it is funded by prior experiences and knowledge. In this way it is part of a dynamic sense-making or, more precisely, semiotic process. This more dynamic, meaning-making view of creativity challenges creativity researchers to move beyond static conceptions and static measures of the process.

A Peircean account of creative inquiry can offer contemporary researchers complementary and differing perspectives on how they conceptualize and study creative thought. Still, there is much left unsaid and unresolved in a Peircean account of creative reasoning. Part of this has to do with the fact that I have provided only small slices of Peirce's oeuvre and that those slices have been limited by the narrow scope of this commentary as well as my own particular interpretations, biases, and perspectives. Part of this also has to do with the particular Peircean account being presented, which is narrowly focused on the role abductive reasoning plays in a more general process of creative reasoning.

Consequently we do not have an adequate account of how the process of reasoning presented herein fits within Peirce's broader system of semiotics. Moreover we do not have an adequate exploration of the more micropsychological processes that might explain how abductive insights occur, nor do we have an adequate accounting of the role played by of the sociocultural-historical context.

Fortunately there are examples of very promising and compelling efforts aimed at more directly addressing some of these limitations, such as Anderson's (1988) account of creativity and the philosophy of Peirce; Ohlsson's (2011) account of creative insight; and Glăveanu, Gillespie, and Valsiner's (2015) volume providing social and cultural perspectives on creativity. These efforts provide a good starting point for those interested in rounding out the very rough and incomplete sketch of a Peircean perspective I have offered herein.

A more complete connection between Peircean and contemporary perspectives on creativity can result in promising new directions for how creativity researchers conceptualize, study, and understand creative phenomenon. Doing so will require making the much needed step toward more integrated, dynamic, and multidisciplinary accounts of creative thought and action.

References

Anderson, D. R. (1987). *Creativity and the philosophy of C. S. Peirce*. Hingham, MA: Kluwer.

Baer, J., & Garrett, T. (2010). Teaching for creativity in an era of content standards and accountability. In R. A. Beghetto & J. C. Kaufman (Eds.), *Nurturing creativity in the classroom* (pp. 6–23). New York: Cambridge University Press.

Beghetto, R. A. (2016a). *Big wins, Small steps: How to lead for and with creativity*. Thousand Oaks, CA: Corwin Press.

Beghetto, R. A. (2016b). Creative openings in the social interactions of teaching. *Creativity: Theories-Research-Applications, 3*, 261–273.

Beghetto, R. A. (2016c). Creative learning: A fresh look. *Journal of Cognitive Education and Psychology, 15*, 6–23.

Beghetto, R. A., & Corazza, G. (Eds.). (2019). *Dynamic perspectives on creativity*. Cham, Switzerland: Springer.

Beghetto, R. A., & Schreiber, J. B. (2016). Creativity in doubt: Toward understanding what drives creativity in learning. In R. Leikin & B. Sriraman (Eds.), *Creativity and giftedness: Interdisciplinary perspectives from mathematics and beyond*. Dordrecht, Netherlands: Springer Science and Business.

Burks, A. W. (1946). Peirce's theory of abduction. *Philosophy of Science, 13*, 301–306.

Corazza, G. (2016). Potential originality and effectiveness: The dynamic definition of creativity. *Creativity Research Journal, 28*, 258–267.

Deely, J. (1994). (Ed.). The collected papers of Charles Sanders Peirce. Vols. 1–5. Charlottesville, VA: Intelex.

Gajda, A., Beghetto, R. A., & Karwowski, M. (2017). Exploring creative learning in the classroom: A multi-method approach. *Thinking Skills and Creativity, 24*, 250 – 267.

Glăveanu, V. P. (2012). Habitual creativity: Revising habit, reconceptualizing creativity. *Review of General Psychology, 16*, 78.

Glăveanu, V. P., Gillespie, A., & Valsiner, J. (Eds.) (2015). *Rethinking creativity: Perspectives from cultural psychology*. London: Routledge.

Guilford, J. P. (1950). Creativity. *American Psychologist, 5*, 444–454.

Guilford, J. P. (1967). Creativity and learning. In D. B. Lindsley & A. A. Lumsdaine (Eds.), *Brain function*, vol. 4: *Brain function and learning*. Los Angeles: University of California Press.

Kaufman, J. C. (2016). Creativity 101 (2nd ed.). New York, NY: Springer.

Kozbelt, A., Beghetto, R. A., & Runco, M. A. (2010). Theories of creativity. In J. C. Kaufman & R. J. Sternberg (Eds.), *The Cambridge handbook of creativity* (pp. 20–47). New York, NY: Cambridge University Press.

Mumford, M., McIntosh, T. (2017). Creative thinking processes: The past and the future. *Journal of Creative Behavior, 51*, 317–322.

Ohlsson, S. (2011). *Deep learning: How the mind overrides experience*. New York, NY: Cambridge University Press.

Peirce, C. S. (1958). *Collected Papers of Charles Sanders Peirce*. Vols. 5–8 (A. W. Burks, Ed.). Cambridge, MA: Belknap Press of Harvard University Press.

Plucker, J., Beghetto, R. A., & Dow, G. (2004). Why isn't creativity more important to educational psychologists? Potential, pitfalls, and future directions in creativity research. *Educational Psychologist, 39*, 83–96.

Pretz, J. E., Naples, A. J., & Sternberg, R. J. (2003). Recognizing, defining, and representing problems. In J. E. Davidson & R. J. Sternberg (Eds.), *The psychology of problem solving* (pp. 3–30). New York, NY: Cambridge University Press.

Rothenberg, A. (2014). *Flight from wonder: An investigation of scientific creativity*. New York, NY: Oxford University Press.

Runco, M. A., & Jaeger, G. J. (2012). The standard definition of creativity. *Creativity Research Journal, 24*, 92–96.

Sawyer, R. K. (2012). *Explaining creativity: The science of human innovation* (2nd ed.). New York, NY: Oxford University Press.

Shank, G., & Cunningham, D. J. (1996, October). Modeling the six modes of Peircean abduction for educational purposes. Paper presented at annual meeting of the Midwest AI and Cognitive Science Conference, Bloomington, IN.

Smith, J. K., & Smith, L. F. (2017). The 1.5 criterion model of creativity: Where less is more, more or less. *Journal of Creative Behavior, 51*, 281–284.

Ward, T. B., & Kolomyts, Y. (2010). Cognition and creativity. In J. C. Kaufman & R. J. Sternberg (Eds.), *The Cambridge handbook of creativity* (pp. 93–112). New York, NY: Cambridge University Press.

PART FOUR

Beyond Creative Thinking

11

Imitation and Creativity
Gabriel Tarde and James Mark Baldwin

Vlad P. Glăveanu

Summary

Gabriel Tarde and James Mark Baldwin developed, at the turn of the twentieth century, complex theories of imitation that place it at the heart of human development and the development of society. In both cases, these theories aimed to account for the dynamic interplay between continuity and change, sameness and difference, the old and the new. Their thinking on this topic is thus as important for creativity as it is for imitation, and both Tarde and Baldwin, in their own right, addressed the issue of novelty, invention, and innovation in their work. This chapter includes selections from Tarde's seminal book *The Laws of Imitation* and one of Baldwin's essays on imitation. Taken together, they reshape the way we understand creativity, its importance, and its underlining processes, a topic I return to in the final commentary.

Introduction

What do Gabriel Tarde (1843–1904), a French sociologist and criminologist, and James Mark Baldwin (1861–1934), an American philosopher and developmental psychologist, have in common? Interestingly enough, the link between the two is not represented only by the fact that they built theoretical models of imitation and habit, but that their legacy seemed, for different reasons, to have been forgotten within their disciplines for at least half a century. In Tarde's case, this was due to the fact that his intellectual rival, Émile Durkheim, was recognized early on as the father of sociology. In Baldwin's case, it had to do with a scandal—being arrested by police at a brothel in Baltimore—that ended his academic career in America. And yet, again in both cases, there is a strong resurgence of their thought within the social sciences, a movement that began a few decades ago and is still gathering pace. For example, Tarde's work has been both praised and built upon by renowned scholars from different disciplines, including the philosopher Gilles Deleuze and the sociologist Bruno Latour. Baldwin's thought and its significance were recovered by psychologists such as Robert Wozniak and Jaan Valsiner.

What is the legacy of Gabriel Tarde? To place it in context, it is important to note a few life circumstances. He was born in 1843 near Bordeaux in France, the son of a military officer and judge who died when Tarde was seven years old. He was enrolled in the local Jesuit school, then went on to study law in Toulouse and Paris. Tarde was made director of criminal statistics at the Ministry of Justice in Paris, lectured at different institutions, and, toward the end of his life, became chair of modern philosophy at the Collège de France. Despite having achieved considerable fame during his lifetime, Tarde had been criticized for promoting a radically different vision of society than the one advocated by Durkheim. If the latter saw it as a collective entity, Tarde regarded society as a collection of individuals. This focus on persons and the microprocesses of social life—such as imitation—makes his work particularly valuable, then and now, for both sociologists and social psychologists who continue to find great inspiration in his seminal books: *The Laws of Imitation* (*Les lois de l'imitation*, 1890) and *The Social Logic* (*La logique sociale*, 1895).

James Mark Baldwin, born almost two decades after Tarde, in 1816 in Columbia, South Carolina, was one of the psychologists marked by his legacy. Baldwin started his education at Princeton and, like many Americans interested in psychology at the time, studied in Germany for a few semesters. During his European trip, he visited Wilhelm Wundt's laboratory in Leipzig as well as Friedrich Paulsen in Berlin and Carl Stumpf in Freiburg. When Baldwin returned to the United States he worked first as an instructor at Princeton and then received an appointment at Lake Forest University in Illinois in both philosophy and psychology. Despite his early visit to Germany, some of Baldwin's most prominent intellectual partners were French philosophers and developmentalists, and he built extensively on the works of not only Tarde but also Janet, Binet, and Bergson. This legacy and the observations he made of his own children led him to theorize imitation as the foundation for the development of both the species and the person. Baldwin's major works include the *Handbook of Psychology* (1890) and *Mental Development in the Child and the Race* (1896). After the incident that marked the end of his career and cost him his position at Johns Hopkins University, Baldwin spent the last years of his life in France, where he remained intellectually and socially active until his death in 1934.

This chapter focuses on Tarde's and Baldwin's work on imitation as a fundamental process for creativity and invention. This association, seemingly counterintuitive, is highlighted in the selections below from Tarde's *The Laws of Imitation* (1903) and Baldwin's "Imitation: A Chapter in the Natural History of Consciousness" (1894). In the commentary, I discuss at length the importance of imitation and habit for how we understand and study creativity and the ways in which this importance has been recognized (or not) by more recent scholarship.

Reading 1: *The Laws of Imitation*

Source: Tarde, G. (1903). *The laws of imitation* (E. C. Parsons, Trans., from the 2nd French edition). New York, NY: Henry Holt. Selections from Chapter 8, "Remarks and Corollaries" (pp. 366–393). The original footnotes have been excluded from the text. Work in the public domain.

After having studied the principal laws of imitation we have still to make their general meaning clear, to complete them by certain observations, and to point out several important consequences which proceed from them.

The supreme law of imitation seems to be its tendency towards indefinite progression. This immanent and immense kind of ambition is the soul of the universe. It expresses itself, physically, in the conquest of space by light, vitally, in the claim of even the humblest species to cover the entire globe with its kind. It seems to impel every discovery or innovation, however futile, including the most insignificant individual innovations, to scatter itself through the whole of the indefinitely broadened social field. But unless this tendency be backed up by the coming together of inventions which are logically and ideologically auxiliary, or by the help of the prestige which belongs to alleged superiorities, it is checked by the different obstacles which it has successively to overcome or to turn aside. These obstacles are the logical and teleological contradictions which are opposed to it by other inventions, or the barriers which have been raised up by a thousand causes, by racial pride and prejudice, for the most part, between different families and tribes and peoples and, within each people or tribe, between different classes. Consequently, if a good idea is introduced in one of these groups, it propagates itself without any difficulty until it finds itself stopped short by the group's frontiers. Fortunately, this arrest is only a slowing up. It is true that, at first, in the case of class barriers, a happy innovation which has happened to originate and make its way in a lower class, does not, during periods of hereditary aristocracy and of physiological inequality, so to speak, spread further, unless the advantage of adopting it appear plain to the higher classes; but, on the other hand, innovations which have been made or accepted by the latter classes easily reach down, as I have shown already, to those lower levels which are accustomed to feel their prestige. And it happens that, as a result of this prolonged descent, the lower strata gradually mount up, step by step, to swell the highest ranks with their successive increments. Thus, through assimilating themselves with their models, the copies come to equal them, that is, they become capable of becoming models in their turn, while assuming a superiority which is no longer hereditary, which is no longer centred in the whole person, but which is individual and vicarious. The march of imitation from top to bottom still goes on, but the inequality which it implies has changed in character. Instead of an aristocratic, intrinsically organic inequality, we have a democratic inequality, of an entirely social origin, which we may call inequality if we wish, but which is really a reciprocity of invariably impersonal prestiges, alternating from individual to individual and from profession to profession. In this way, the field of imitation has been constantly growing and freeing itself from heredity.

In the second place, in regard to barriers between families, tribes, or peoples, it is equally true that while the knowledge or institutions or beliefs or industries which belong to any group while it is powerful and triumphant, spread without difficulty to neighbouring groups that have been conquered and brought low; on the other hand, the examples of the weak and vanquished, if we except the case of those whose civilisation is obviously superior, are practically non-existent for their conquerors. Hence it follows, parenthetically, that war is much more of a civiliser for the conquered than for the conqueror, for the latter does not deign to learn from the former, whereas the former submits himself to the ascendency of victory and borrows from his enemy a number of fruitful ideas to add to his national store. The Egyptians took nothing from the books of the captive Hebrews. They made a great mistake.

Whereas the Jews gained much inspiration from the hieroglyphics of their masters. But, as I have said, when a people dominates others through its brilliancy, others, who heretofore had imitated none but their forefathers, imitate it. Now, this extra-national propagation of imitation, to which I have given the name of fashion, is, at bottom, merely the application to the relations between states of the law which governs the relations between classes. Thanks to the invasion of fashion, imitation always descends from the state which is for the time being superior to those which are for the time inferior, just as it descends from the highest to the lowest rungs of the social ladder. Consequently, we shall not be surprised to see the rule of fashion producing effects in the former case similar to those produced by it in the matter. In effect, just as the radiation of the examples of the higher classes results in preparing the way for their enlargement, where imitation is facile and reciprocal, through the absorption of the lower classes by them, so the contagious prestige of preponderating states results in preparing the way for their extension, for the extension of states which were originally families, then tribes, and, later, cities and nations, and which have been constantly enlarged through the assimilation of neighbours whom they have annexed, or through the annexation of neighbours whom they have assimilated.

Another analogy. Just as the play of imitation from top to bottom leads, in its continuation, to so-called democratic equality, that is to say, to the fusion of all classes into one, in which reciprocal imitation is admirably practised through the acceptance of one another's respective superiorities, so a prolonged process of fashion-imitation ends by putting pupil-peoples upon the same level, both in their armaments and in their arts and sciences, with their master-people. It creates a kind of federation between them like that which is called in modern times, for example, the European balance of power. By this is meant the reciprocity of every kind of service or exchange which goes on incessantly between the different great centres which divide up European civilisation. In this way, in international relations, the free and unimpeded domain of imitation has been enlarged with scarcely an interruption.

But, at the same time, Tradition and Custom, the conservative forms of imitation, have been fixing and perpetuating its new acquisitions and consolidating its increments in the heart of every class of people that has been raised up through the example of higher classes or of more civilised neighbours. At the same time, too, every germ of imitation which may have been secreted in the brain of any imitator in the form of a new belief or aspiration, of a new idea or faculty, has been steadily developing in out-ward signs, in words and acts which, according to the law of the march from within to without, have penetrated into his entire nervous and muscular systems.

Here then we have the laws of the preceding chapters in focus from the same point of view. Through them, the tendency of imitation, set free from generation, towards geometric progression, expresses and fulfils itself more and more. Every act of imitation, therefore, results in the preparation of conditions that will make possible and that will facilitate new acts of imitation of an increasingly free and rational and, at the same time, precise and definite character. These conditions are the gradual suppression of caste, class, and nationality barriers and, I may add, the lessening of distances through more rapid means of locomotion, as well as through greater density of population. This last condition is realised in the degree that fruitful, that is to say, widely imitated, agricultural or industrial inventions, and the equally fruitful discovery of new lands promote the world-wide circulation of the most inventive and, at the same time, the most imitative races. Let us suppose that all these conditions are combined and that they are fulfilled in the highest degree. Then, wherever a happy initiative might show itself in the whole mass of humanity, its transmission by imitation would be almost instantaneous, like the propagation of a wave in a perfectly elastic medium. We are approaching this strange ideal. Already, in certain special phases, where the most essential of the conditions which I have indicated happen to be combined, social life reveals the reality of the aforesaid tendency. We see it, for example, in the world of scholars, who, although they are widely scattered, are in constant touch with one another through multiple international communications. We see it, too, in the perpetual and universal contact of merchants. Haeckel said in an address delivered in 1882 on the success of Darwin's theories: "The prodigious influence which the decisive victory of the evolutionary idea exercises over all the sciences, an influence which *grows in geometric progression* year by year, opens out to us the most consoling perspectives." In fact, the success of Darwin and Spencer has been amazingly swift. As for the rapidity of commercial imitation as soon as it is given free scope, it has been a matter for observation in every period, not merely in our own. Read in Ranke the description of the progress of Antwerp from 1550 to 1566. During those sixteen years the commerce of that city with Spain doubled; with Portugal, Germany, and France it was more than tripled; with England, it increased twenty-fold! Unfortunately, war put an end to this prosperity. But in such intermittent flights we see the steady force which pushes on to indefinite commercial expansion. . . .

I hasten to add that, on one of its important sides, historical reversibility or irreversibility cannot be explained by the laws of imitation alone. Successive inventions and discoveries, which imitation lays hold of in order to spread them abroad, do not follow one another accidentally. A rational tie which we do not need to dwell upon here, but which has been clearly pointed out by Auguste Comte in his conception of the development of the sciences and which has been definitely traced out by Cournot, in his masterly treatise upon *L'Enchainement des idées fondamentales*, binds them to one another; and we cannot but admit that to a large extent their order, the order, for example, of mathematical discoveries from Pythagoras to us, might have been inverted. Here, irreversibility is based upon the laws of inventive logic, and not upon those of imitation.

Let us stop for a moment to justify, in passing, the distinction that I have just drawn. The order of successive inventions is distinct from the order of successive imitations, although imitation does mean imitation of invention. The laws, in fact, which govern the first of these two series should not be confused with those, even the logical ones, which govern the second. It is not necessary for *all* imitations of inventions to pass through the terms of the irreversible series which inventions, whether they be imitated or not, must necessarily traverse one by one. We could, if put to it, conceive of a succession of inventions, which were logically antecedent to the final consummate one, unfolding in one and the same master mind; and, as a matter of fact, it is seldom that an inventor does not climb up several obscure rungs in such a ladder before reaching the illustrious step. The laws of invention belong essentially to individual logic; the laws of imitation belong in part to social logic. Moreover, just as imitation does not fall exclusively within social logic, but depends upon extra-logical influence as well, is it not obvious that invention itself is produced mentally, through conditions which are not alone the apparition of premises in the mind of which it is the logical conclusion, but which are also other associations of ideas, called inspiration, intuition, genius?

Meanwhile, let us not forget that every invention and every discovery consists in the inter- ference in somebody's mind of certain old pieces of information that have generally been handed down by others. What did Darwin's thesis about natural selection amount to? To having proclaimed the fact of competition among living things? No, but in having for the first time combined this idea with the ideas of *variability* and *heredity*. The former idea, as it was proclaimed by Aristotle, remained sterile until it was associated with the two latter ideas. From that as a starting point, we may say that the generic term, of which invention is but a species, is the fruitful interference of repetitions. If this be true, I may perhaps be allowed to set forth, without emphasis, an hypo- thesis which occurs to me at this point. However numerous may be the different kinds of things which are repeated, if we suppose that the centres of these repetitive radiations, otherwise known as inventions or the biological or physical analogues of inventions, be regularly placed, their interferences may be foreseen; and these interferences or new centres will themselves present as much regularity in their disposition as did the primary centres. In such a universe, everything, however complex it might be, would be regular; nothing would either be or seem accidental. If, on the contrary, we assume that the primitive centres are irregular in position, the position of the secondary centres will also be unordered and their irregularity will equal that of the primary centres. Thus, there will never be in the world anything but *the same quantity of irregularity*, so to speak, only it will appear under the most changing forms. Let me add that, in spite of all, these changing forms must have a certain indefinable likeness. The original irregularity is reflected in its enlarged copies, the derived irregularities. From this I conclude that, although the idea of Repetition dominates the whole universe, it does not constitute it. For the bottom of it, I think, is a certain sum of innate, eternal, and indestructible diversity without which the world would be as monotonous as it is vast. Stuart Mill was led by his reflections to a similar postulate. . . .

It has often been remarked that civilisation has the effect of raising the level of the masses from an intellectual and moral, from an aesthetic and economic point of view, rather than of rearing still higher in these different respects the higher peaks of society. But this vague, indefinite formula has been not unjustly the subject of refutation because of failure to point out the cause of the phenomenon in view. This cause we know. Since every inven- tion which has once been launched clear of the mass of those that are already established in the social environment, must spread out and establish itself in turn by winning a place for itself in one class after another until it reaches the very lowest, it follows that the final result to which the indefinite continuation of all these outspreadings from centres which appear at distant points and in high places, must be a general and uniform illumination. It is in this way, by virtue of the law of vibratory radiation, that the sources of heat as they appear one after another tend to produce, according to a famous deduction of physicists, a great universal equilibrium of temperature which is higher than the actual temperature of inter-stellar space, but lower than that of suns. It is in this way, too, that the dissemination of species according to the law of their geometric progression, or, in other terms, of their prolific radiation, tends to cover the entire earth, which is still very unequally peopled, with a uniform stratum of living beings which will be denser throughout its whole extent than the average density of its present population. Obviously, the terms of our comparisons correspond exactly. The surface of the earth is the domain that is open to the radiation of light, just as space is the domain that is open to that of heat and light and as the human species, inasmuch as it is a living species, is the domain that is open to the spread of inventive genius. After this statement, we can understand how cosmopolitan and democratic assimilation is an inevitable tendency of history for the same reason that the complete and uniform peopling of the globe and the complete and uniform calorification of space are the objects of the vital and of the physical universe. It is so of necessity, for of the two chief forces, invention and imitation, which help us to interpret the whole of history, the former, the source of privileges, monopolies, and aristocratic inequalities, is intermittent, rare, and eruptive only at certain infrequent periods, whereas the latter, which is so democratic and levelling, is continuous and incessant like the stream deposition of the Nile or Euphrates. But we can understand also that it may well happen that at periods when works of genius crowd upon and stimulate one another, in feverish and inventive ages like ours, the progress of civilisation is accompanied by a momentary increase of every kind of inequality, or, if the imaginative fever has centred in one place, of a special kind. In our day, when the creative spirit has turned primarily towards the sciences, the distance between our most distinguished scholars and the most uncultivated dregs of our population is much greater from the point of view of the sum and substance of learning than it was in the Middle Ages or antiquity. In the innovating periods of which I speak the whole question consists of knowing whether the precipitate eruption of inventions has been faster than their current of example. Now, this is a question of fact which statistics alone can solve.

Believing that the transition from an aristocratic to a democratic order is irreversible, Tocqueville refuses to think that any aristocracy can be formed in a democratic environment. But I must be clear on this point. If, in consequence of the cause of which we know, societies hasten toward an increasing assimilation and an incessant accumulation of similarities, it does not follow that they are also progressing towards a greater and greater development of democracy. For imitative assimilation is only the stuff out of which societies are made; this stuff is cut out and put into use by social logic, which tends to the most solid kind of unification through the specialisation and co-operation of aptitudes, and through the specialisation and mutual confirmation of minds. It is therefore quite possible and even probable that a very strong hierarchy may be the destined goal of any civilisation, although every consummate civilisation which has reached its ultimate fruition is marked by the diffusion of the same wants and ideas, if not by the same powers and wealth, throughout the mass of its citizens. This much, however, may be granted to Tocqueville— after an aristocracy which is based upon the hereditary prestige of birth has been destroyed in a country, it can never come to life again. We know, in fact, that the social form of Repetition, imitation, tends to free itself more and more from its vital form, from heredity.

Reading 2: "IL—Imitation: A Chapter in the Natural History of Consciousness"

Source: Baldwin, J. M. (1894). IL—Imitation: A chapter in the natural history of consciousness. *Mind, 3*(9), 26–55. Published by Oxford University Press on behalf of the Mind Association. Selection reproduced, with permission, from Prof. J. Mark Baldwin. The original footnotes have been excluded from the text.

Imitation is a matter of such familiarity to us all that it goes usually unattended to: so much so that professed psychologists have left it largely undiscussed. Whether it be one of the more ultimate facts or not, suppose we assume it to be so; let us then see what we can explain by it, and where we may be able to trace its influence in the developed mind.

1. We may make it a part of our assumption—what I have endeavoured to prove elsewhere—that an imitation is an ordinary sensori-motor reaction which finds its differentia in the single fact that it imitates: that is, its peculiarity is found in the locus of its muscular discharge. It is what I have called a "circular activity" on the bodily side—brain-state due to stimulus, muscular reaction which reproduces the stimulus, same brain-state again due to same stimulus, and so on. The questions to be asked now are: Where in our psychophysical theory do we find [a] place for this peculiar "circular" order of reaction; what is its value in consciousness and in mental development, and how does it itself arise and come to occupy the place it does?

If the only peculiarity about imitation is that it imitates, it would follow that we might find imitations wherever there is any degree of interaction between the nervous organism and the external world. The effect of imitation, it is clear, is to make the brain a "repeating organ"; and the muscular system is, as far as this function goes, the expression and evidence of this fact. The place of imitation in life development is theoretically solvable in two ways, therefore: (1) by an exploration of Nature and mind for actual imitations, and (2) by the deduction of this function from the theory of repetition in neurology and psychology—this latter provided we find that Nature does not herself present enough *de-facto* repetitions to supply the demands of neurology and psychology. If this last condition be unfulfilled—that is, if Nature does actually repeat herself through her stimulating agencies, light, sound and so forth, sufficiently often and with sufficient regularity to secure nervous and mental development—then imitation is probably a side phenomenon, an incident merely.

Without taking either of these questions in the broadest sense, I wish, while citing incidentally cases of the occurrence of imitation, to show the importance of repetitions and of the imitative way of securing repetitions, in the progress of mind.

2. If it be true, at the outset, that organic development proceeds by reactions, and if there be the two kinds of reaction usually distinguished, *i.e.*, those which involve consciousness as a necessary factor and those which do not, then the first question becomes: In which of these categories do imitative reactions fall? Evidently in large measure in the category of consciousness. If we further distinguish this category in as far as it marks the area of conscious life which is "plum up," so to speak, against the environment—directly amenable to external stimulation—by the word "suggestion," we have thus marked off the most evident surface features of imitation. Imitation is then, so far, an instance of suggestive reaction.

3. Now let us look more closely at the kind of consciousness, and find its analogies. A mocking bird imitates a sparrow, a beaver imitates an architect, a child imitates his nurse, a man imitates his rector. Calling the idea of the result, as we look at the result (not as the imitator may or may not look at it), the "copy," we find that we are forced to consider the psychological elements involved very different in these four cases. This copy as defined in our minds, we are forced to think, is also clearly defined in the mind of the man, it is rudely defined in the mind of the child, it is not defined at all in the mind of the mocking bird, and

in the mind of the beaver it is something else which is defined, and rudely. These cases are ordinarily distinguished by mutually exclusive words, *i.e.*, in order: volition, suggestion, reflex reaction, instinct. Yet this one thing they do have in common, a constructive idea which we see objectively, and which each, in its result, repeats. It will be profitable to inquire into the origin and significance of this "copy" in each of these cases.

4. In the case of simple imitative suggestion we find what seems to be the most evident and schematic type. Here we have a simple visual or auditory copy shedding its influence out into the world in a reaction which repeats the copy. But we find other reactions side by side with it which do nothing of the kind. Psychologists classify these reactions under the heads of instincts, impulses, reflexes, volitions. Now it is not making [a] very great assumption in view of current theories to hold that imitations repeated become reflexes (reflex speech, the walking reflex, for example), nor to hold, that reflexes when repeated, consolidated, and inherited, become instincts; nor yet again to hold that instincts when snubbed, contradicted, and disused, are broken up into impulses. Then impulses consciously indulged, ratified, and repeated, in opposition to snubbing, evidently become volitions. If we did find it possible, at present, to admit these assumptions, and to give names to the two processes involved, calling the "repeating" process the law of habit, and the "snubbing" process the *law of accommodation*, we would have a suggestive line of thought based upon what is actually the state of things in the most advanced neurology. Yet we must not forget that both these principles are in operation at once, and we have a possible twofold derivation of each term in the series. For example, looked at from the point of view of accommodation, or phylogenetically, as Ziehen points out, impulsive actions are due to the breaking up of instincts; but on the side of habit, or ontogenesis, they come by volition. The dispute as to the origin of instinct may be settled from this twofold point of view.

Now let us see how in these several cases we can account for the copy. In the case of simple suggestive imitation, it is there in consciousness for reproduction, and is reproduced. How does this come about?

5. Suppose at first an organism giving random reactions, some of which are useful; now for development the useful reactions must be repeated, and thus made to outweigh the reactions which are damaging or useless. Evidently if there are any among the useful reactions which result in an immediate duplication of their own stimulus, these must persist, and on them must rest the development of the organism. These are the imitative reactions. Thus it is that a thing in nature once endowed with the reacting property might so select its stimulations as to make its relations to its environment [the] means to its own progress: imitative reactions, as now defined, being the only means to such selection.

This, it is plain, assumes consciousness in such an organism: for it is difficult to see how a reaction which reproduces its own stimulus in an exact material way could ever begin, or ever stop when begun; that is, how it would differ from a self-perpetuating whirlwind, or from an elastic ball for ever rebounding between two equal resistances. This last we do find even in consciousness in certain cases, but in as much as they are self-repeating, they do not present any law of development, and so approximate to a state of things in which consciousness might be conceived to be absent. At any rate, I find it more philosophical to make consciousness as original as anything else, and to hold with Lewes that reactive tissue is always conscious.

6. Development begun on this basis could proceed only if two requisites were fulfilled: first, the reaction which sustains the copy must persist, and second, there must be a constant creation of new copies. The first means consolidation of tissues, a law of increasing fixedness in nerve processes, tending to give rise to great functional habits, which at any stage of progress represent the acquired copies of the ôrganism and its degree of adaptation to the environment. But, how is this persistence possible in the absence of the objective stimulus? Evidently it is not possible, unless there be some way whereby the energies of the reaction in question may be started by something equivalent to the working of the original external stimulus. This is accomplished in the organism by an arrangement whereby a variety of copies conspire, so to speak, to "ring up" one another. When an external stimulus starts one of them, that starts up many others in a series, and all the reactions which wait upon these copies tend to realise themselves. Thus the great practised habits of the organism get confirmed by stimulation again and again, while the increasing variety of the conspiring copies—constantly recruited from the new experiences of the world—make up a large and ever larger mass of elements, or centres, which vibrate in delicate counterpoise together.

7. Of course it is evident that the arrangement thus sketched is the physical basis of memory. A memory is a copy for imitation taken over from the world into consciousness. Memory is a device to nullify distance in space and time. It remedies lack of immediate connexion with the accidental occurrences of the world. Every act I set myself to do is either to imitate something which I find now before me, or to reproduce, by making objective to myself, something whose elements I remember—something whose copy I get set within me by a "ring up" from elements which are in immediate connexion with what is now before me.

8. The theory so far advanced, with extreme brevity, is in accord with that first announced (obscurely I think) by Tarde. Tarde's theory is improved, in quotation, and endorsed by Sighele. It may be analysed into two moments, *i.e.*, (a), the securing of repetitions by imitation, and (b), the theory of memory considered as a means of perpetuating and increasing the effects of repetition, in mental development, by the formation of habits. This latter moment I find only vaguely and inadequately stated by Tarde. It is readily seen that this assumes the fact of imitation, makes of it an original endowment or instinct, and is, in so far, open to the objections which may be urged (cf. Bain, *Senses and Intellect*, 3rd ed., pp. 413 ff. . . .) against such a view. The theory which I am now proposing supplies this lack: it gives a derivation of imitation based upon an analysis of the imitative reaction itself. This analysis—the outcome of which I have expressed by calling imitation a "circular reaction," *i.e.*, one which repeats its own stimulus—gives us a means of defining imitation and fixing the limits of the concept. . . . The third and fundamental moment, therefore, which the development stated above endeavours to supply, is the rise of imitation from simple contractility under two concurrent agencies; (1) the occurrence, among the "spontaneous variations" of discharge, of movements which secure at once the repetition of the first stimulus, and (2), the continuance of such of these self-repeating re-actions as are useful (pleasurable). Those which are damaging (painful) or useless, by that very fact, lower the vitality of the organism and so hinder their own recurrence. This derivation of imitation secured, we are able to develop independently the two principles urged by Tarde and Sighele, as follows in this paper. . . .

11. Reflexion convinces us that we have now reached a principle of wide-reaching application in mental development. We see how it is possible for reactions which were originally

simple imitative suggestions to lose all appearance of their true origin. Copy-links at first distinctly present as external things, and afterwards present with almost equal distinctness as internal memories, may become quite lost in the rapid progress of consciousness. New connexions get established in the network of association, and motor discharges get stimulated thus which were possible at first only by imitation and owed their formation to it. A musician plays by reading printed notes, and forgets that in learning the meaning of the notes he imitated the movements and sounds which his instructor made: but the intermediate copies have so fallen away that his performance seems to offer no surface imitation at all. His sound copy system, of course, persists to the end to guide his muscular reactions. But a musician of the visual type goes farther. He may play from memory of the printed notes; that is, he may play from a transplanted visual copy of notes which themselves are but shorthand or substitute expressions of earlier sound and muscular copies, and finally the name only of a familiar selection may be sufficient to start a performance guided only by a subconscious muscular copy series. If this principle should be proved to be of universal application we would then be able to say that every intelligent action is stimulated by copies whose presence the action in question tends to reproduce. . . .

13. Accommodation, then, is the principle by the action of which, in the constant exercise of imitation, new adaptations are acquired, and the system of copies to which it is the end of our actions to conform, is indefinitely recruited.

14. Continued accommodation is possible only because the other principle, *habit*, all the time conserves the past and gives *points d'appui* in solidified structure for new accommodations. Inasmuch, further, as the copy by transference from the world to the mind, in memory, becomes capable of internal revival, accommodation takes on a new character—a conscious subjective character—in *volition*. Volition arises as a phenomenon of "persistent imitative suggestion," as I have argued in a more severe way elsewhere. That is, volition arises when a copy remembered vibrates with other copies remembered or presented, and when all the connexions, in thought and action, of all of them are together set in motion incipiently. The residue of motive is connected with what we call attention, and the final co-ordination of all the motor elements involved is volition, or choice. The physical basis of memory, association, thought, is also that of will—the cerebrum—and pathological cases show clearly that aboulia is fundamentally a defect of synthesis in perception and memory, arising from one or more breaks in the copy system whose rise I have sketched in what precedes. . . .

29. The place of imitation has now been made out in a tentative way throughout the development of the active life. It seems to be everywhere. But it is, of course, a matter of natural history that this type of action is of such extraordinary and unlooked-for importance. If we grant a phylogenetic development of mind, imitation, as defined above, may be considered the law and the only law of the progressive interaction of the organism and its environment. The further philosophical questions as to the nature of mind, its worth and its dignity, remain under adjudication. We have learned too much in modern philosophy to argue from the natural history of a thing to its ultimate constitution and meaning—and we commend this consideration to the biologists. As far as there is a more general lesson to be learned from the considerations advanced, it is that we should avoid just this danger, *i.e.*, of interpreting one kind of existence for itself, in an isolated way, without due regard to other kinds of existence with which its manifestations are mixed up. The antithesis, for example, between the self and

the world is not a valid antithesis psychologically considered. The self is realised by taking in "copies" from the world, and the world is enabled to set higher copies only through the constant reactions of the individual self upon it. Morally I am as much a part of society as physically I am a part of the world's fauna; and as my body gets its best explanation from the point of view of its place in a zoological scale, so morally I occupy a place in the social order; and an important factor in the understanding of me is the understanding of it.

The great question is—when put in the phraseology of imitation—What is the final World-copy, and how did it get itself set?

Commentary

What does creativity have to do with imitation? Perhaps there is a reverse relationship at play: the more one imitates, the less creative the outcomes. This either/or type of connection between the two can be found equally in science and commonsense understandings of creativity. For instance, Davis (1999, p. 166) noted that imitation is "the most obvious barrier to creative thinking and innovation," and he is not the only one. In fact, the pragmatists were among the first to postulate a negative correlation between creativity and repetition or habits. William James (1890) famously referred, in this context, to habits as virtually automatic sequences of behavior, useful to a great extent but largely unconscious—in other words, the antithesis of voluntary, creative forms of action. This conception was challenged, however, at the turn of the century. It was precisely the work of Tarde and, later on, Baldwin that gave imitation another meaning and a much greater role in the developmental history of the species, of society, and of the person. Both of them, as reflected in the texts reproduced here, firmly believed in the impossibility of extricating creativity (or invention) from imitation. For Tarde, invention was the birthplace of imitation and its direct outcome. For Baldwin, most acts of imitation lead to the emergence of novelty. In other words, Tarde and Baldwin postulated not only that we actually get to create *while* imitating, but that we become creative *because* of imitating others.

In this commentary, I will explain why and how this is the case by drawing on the work of these two scholars and considering its resonance in past and present literature on creativity. I will start with Tarde not only because he developed his ideas before Baldwin, but mainly because his work makes the link between societal and individual processes of imitation and invention. I will then analyze Baldwin's view of development as an interplay between habit and accommodation in which "persistent" forms of imitation occupy a key position. The commentary ends with a few reflections on what a study of the imitative basis of creativity can offer the field.

Tarde is largely recognized today as the father of micro- or molecular sociology and as one of the first sociologists to have taken small-scale social interactions as his unit of analysis and used these observations to reflect on macrosocial systems. This preference placed him and his work in antithesis with Durkheim (1985), who was striving to look at the general and normative within society rather than the interpersonal and its heterogeneity (Tonkonoff, 2013). For Durkheim, society is an entity, characterized by collective forms of thinking, feeling, and acting, and thus distinct from any particular individual. For Tarde, society is made up of individuals and their relations. And these relations are marked by individual inventions and their social transmission through imitation. Within these particularities, Tarde saw the universal. As he mentions in the text reproduced in this chapter, imitation is the "supreme law," the "tendency toward indefinite progression" that makes itself manifest within the natural and social world (1903, p. 366). At the same time, imitation could not be understood outside of or separated from invention—by which he mostly means individual creativity. In fact, as he notes later on in the same text, if repetition "dominates the whole universe, it does not constitute it" (p. 383); at the heart of it, instead, Tarde places diversity. How does diversity come about?

In order to answer this question we must first understand what Tarde meant by "imitation" and "invention" as he deliberately used these terms differently than their dictionary definition. Elsewhere in the book from which fragments have been reproduced here, he notes that imitation is "action at a distance of one mind upon another" (1903, p. xiv) or, more plainly, "when a man unconsciously and involuntarily reflects the opinion of others, or allows an action of others to be suggested to him, he imitates this idea or act" (p. xiii). With the term "invention" Tarde refers to "individual initiatives," whether conscious or not, revolutionary or mundane (p. xiv). The relation he postulates between imitation and invention is straightforward. Inventions come out of imitation, and what people imitate is always an invention of sorts. In his words, "All inventions and discoveries are composed of prior imitations . . . and these composites are themselves imitated and are destined to become, in turn, elements of still more complex combinations" (p. 45). While this combinatorial view of creativity is commonly accepted today (see Simonton, 2010), Tarde contributed with his account to challenging old beliefs about geniuses as creating ex nihilo, or out of thin air (Glăveanu, 2010).

How does the creative process take place, then? Tarde (1903, p. 382) explicitly points to the association of different strands of imitation, as expressed in the selection reproduced in the present chapter:

> Let us not forget that every invention and every discovery consists in the interference in somebody's mind of certain old pieces of information that have generally been handed down by others. What did Darwin's thesis about natural selection amount to? To having proclaimed the fact of competition among living things? No, but in having for the first time combined this idea with the ideas of variability and heredity. The former idea, as it was proclaimed by Aristotle, remained sterile until it was associated with the two latter ideas. From that as a starting point, we may say that the generic term, of which invention is but a species, is the fruitful interference of repetitions.

Tarde thus managed to make imitation the main process of creativity, something that seems rather counterintuitive. How can imitating something be creative? The answer, for Tarde, is that we always imitate not one but *many things at once* (see also Tarde, 1902). Moreover he thought this was the basis of true originality:

> Let us be sure, however, that we understand one another about this progressive resemblance of individuals. Far from smothering their true originality, it fosters and favors it. What is contrary to personal pre-eminence is the imitation of a single man whom people copy in everything. But when, instead of patterning one's self after one person or after a few, we borrow from a hundred, a thousand, or ten thousand persons, each of whom is considered under a particular aspect, the elements of thought or action which we subsequently combine, the very nature and choice of these elementary copies, as well as their combination, expresses and accentuates our original personality. And this is, perhaps, the chief benefit that results from the prolonged action of imitation. (1903, p. xxiv)

As a sociologist, Tarde was mostly concerned with the regularity or the pattern of invention and imitation, and, in this regard, he proposed several universal laws (see Djellal & Gallouj, 2014), many of which continue to inform the literature on the diffusion of innovation (Kinnunen, 1996). These laws were divided by him into physical and social, and the latter divided further into logical causes (based on a rational assessment of what is good and useful) and nonlogical causes (sensible to other criteria such as reputation, group membership, etc.). Despite the fact that all these factors make it hard to predict exactly which invention will be transmitted and how, Tarde did postulate some general trajectories of imitation that are interesting and yet rather strangely linear: we imitate internal models (e.g., ideas or goals) before external models (e.g., forms of expression); the inferior, in terms of social class, always imitates the superior. The latter point is particularly problematic as it would imply, on the surface, the dominance of higher classes when it comes to innovation and creativity. And yet, Tarde's vision of society was much more democratic then that. Indeed, he claimed that such acts of imitation end up making the social world more equal and encourage mutual acts of imitation. Whether this reflects a certain degree of naiveté on Tarde's part is debatable. What is clear, though, is his optimism for the power of imitation to make us more "free and rational," to lead "the gradual suppression of caste, class, and nationality barriers and (. . .) the lessening of distances through more rapid means of locomotion, as well as through greater density of population" (1903, pp. 369–370). The second part of this prediction came true; the first is, sadly, far from reality.

James Mark Baldwin continued, in many ways, the work of Tarde, but he did so within the framework of developmental science. He is rightfully acknowledged today at a key contributor to the "sociogenetic perspective in the social sciences" (Valsiner & Van der Veer, 2000, p. 138), a perspective that considers the intertwined development of individuals and society. The key to understanding this intertwinement for Baldwin is, once more, imitation. In the fragments of the paper on this topic reproduced in this chapter, Baldwin starts from the observation that imitation is rarely discussed by psychologists and often goes unnoticed due to its pervasive nature. After all, human beings are creatures of habit and the brain is a "repeating organ" (1894, p. 26). But, and this is very important for our discussion here, repetition is never perfect, nor is it intended to be so. We always imitate with a difference, and this difference represents the engine of novelty, creativity, and development. This is why the aim of Baldwin was "to show the importance of repetitions and of the imitative way of securing repetitions, in the progress of mind" (p. 27; also Baldwin, 1903).

What is imitation for Baldwin? He largely defined it as a circular activity, a reaction that reproduces its own stimulus. In other words, there is a certain circularity or repetition involved in any act of imitation. And yet, importantly, Baldwin distinguished between two types of imitation: simple and persistent. "Simple imitation" is the basic form, and it is mostly what is understood by this phenomenon in lay terms. However, the notion of "persistent imitation" is specific for Baldwin and makes the natural connection between imitation and creativity. Elsewhere in the text of the article reproduced here, he notes that persistent imitation is "the 'try-try-again' experience of early volition" (1894, p. 50). In other words, imitation requires effort and volition and can result in creativity, especially since, when imitating, children as well as adults rarely engage in acts of simple imitation. Rather, they experiment with the model and go beyond it, "producing imitated versions that deliberately modify the model" (Valsiner & Van der Veer, 2000, p. 153). Persistent imitation is thus a form of creative reconstruction, oriented toward novelty and the future (see Valsiner, 2000).

Baldwin further formalized his conception by discussing two basic principles that govern human behavior: the principle of habit and the principle of accommodation.

Persistent forms of imitation make the link between habits and accommodation, where the latter is defined as:

> the principle by the action of which, in the constant exercise of imitation, new adaptations are acquired, and the system of copies to which it is the end of our actions to conform, is indefinitely recruited. Continued accommodation is possible only because the other principle, habit, all the time conserves the past and gives *points d'appui* in solidified structure for new accommodation. (1894, p. 35)

What we have here is a view of creativity and the creative process highly compatible with that of Tarde: we act creatively by mobilizing different strands of imitation and various habits, even if we forget they are imitations and habits (see the example of the musician playing in Baldwin's text). And yet, where Baldwin goes even further with his psychological analysis is the idea—captured in the notion of persistent imitation—that we create *while* imitating. To accommodate means, for him, consciously changing and deconstructing habits, leading to new thoughts and actions; at the same time, "accommodation is in each case simply the result and fruit of the habit itself which is exercised" (Baldwin, 1903, p. 217). This is, for Baldwin, the creative nature of developmental processes: the fact that they build on habits in ways that expand, refine, and adapt them to new conditions. In the end, "invention is as natural as imitation. Indeed normal imitation is rarely free from invention!" (Baldwin, 1911, pp. 149–150).

This dynamic was very clear for Baldwin in the case of children and children's play. After all, play is at once highly imitative (i.e., the child adopts and plays out different social roles and activities associated with them) and highly original (due to the unique combination of these roles and their imitation). Interestingly from a creativity perspective, the child is often original without necessarily wanting to be so. As Baldwin (1906, p. 114) writes elsewhere:

> We may say that each of the situations which arises from his effort to reproduce the copy is an invention of the child's. It is so because he works it out; no one else in the world knows it nor can reproduce it. He aims, it is true, not at doing anything new; he aims at the thing the copy sets for him to imitate. But what he does differs both from this and from anything he has ever done before.

In order to capture such forms of mini and little-c creativity (see Kaufman & Beghetto, 2009), one would need to be sensitive to micro changes and the fact that no "copy" made by a human being is ever perfect and the processes that led to it are never mechanical. Imagine you are setting yourself the task of reproducing, perfectly, a water bottle. The final outcome might resemble it more or less, and it will be judged probably as not creative since its aim is to copy something that already exists. And yet, from Baldwin's perspective, and I fundamentally agree with it, a lot of ingenuity and perseverance would be involved in the act of making a new water bottle in the absence of any specialized tools or mechanical reproduction. In fact the more closely the bottle looks like the "original," the greater the creativity. (Think also about the reproductive current that dominated art for centuries; was Vermeer less creative than Picasso for trying—and succeeding—to capture a scene before any photographic means were available?)

Persistent forms of imitation are more common than we expect in our daily lives, and, as Baldwin argued, they underpin the development of the human self and of human forms of society. Imitation and habit are not to be looked down upon but celebrated for the part they play in this process. In the end, "every new thing is an adaptation, and every adaptation arises right out of the bosom of old processes and is filled with old matter" (Baldwin, 1903, p. 218).

Have these fundamental ideas from Tarde and Baldwin been "imitated" (persistently) in the creativity literature? While the notion that the association of existing elements is central for the creative process is dominant today, the value of imitation and habit for creativity is largely ignored or minimized. Some recent empirical research tries to counter this tendency (see Gabora & Tseng, in press; Mecca & Mumford, 2014), but most of these studies impose a rather strict separation between imitation and creativity and rarely get to see the intertwined nature of the two as postulated by the two thinkers discussed here. It is also rare that the work of Tarde and Baldwin is directly used to theorize creativity (with some exceptions, see Johansson, 2010; Valsiner, 2018), and this means that, unfortunately, their particular understanding is rarely reflected or built upon. Another exception is represented by my own work on creativity in craft, a domain in which tradition, imitation, and habit are at the core of creative activity. This line of research led me to recover the scholarship of Baldwin regarding habits (along with that of Dewey, Joas, and Bourdieu) and postulate the notion of "habitual creativity." In my view, habitual creativity "defines the ways in which novelties form an intrinsic part of habitual action by constantly adjusting it to dynamic contexts, allowing for transitions between and combination of different 'routines,' and finally perfecting practices, thus resulting in mastery" (Glăveanu, 2012, p. 84). In other, more recent work, I argue for the creative value of translation (see Glăveanu, 2016) and the fact that it involves, at all times, the creative transformation of the original.

What is the future of Tarde and Baldwin in creativity studies? My hope, in proposing this chapter, is that I managed to reintroduce these two scholars and their seminal work to a community interested exactly in what they wanted to understand most: the emergence of novelty and of "inventions" in mind and society. Adopting their view of imitation as a central creative process, literally the engine of creativity, would have significant consequences for future theory and practice. In the end, I outline three of them:

1. Advancing our understanding of imitation and creativity without creating a clear-cut separation between the two. While it is tempting, for research purposes, to ask what is being imitated and what is being created in a certain activity, more meaningful questions, in line with Tarde's and Baldwin's views, would be: What is creative within this imitative act? How does it lead to novelty, and how is this novelty imitated further?
2. If the process of creativity is to be looked at in a new way, then so are its outcomes. It would be interesting to see what it would mean to consider creative products as "copies." What would it mean to trace back (and forward!) the imitative features of a new creation? Could the act of copying be seen, itself, as creative? The last question is answered in the affirmative by Ingold and Hallam (2007), who persuasively argue that copying and imitation are built on improvisation and their outcome is never given in advance.
3. Last but not least, how can we rethink the relation between tradition and creativity? If creativity grows out of tradition, then isn't it the case that tradition itself is always the past transformed? Seen from the perspective of traditions and habits, creativity is never a break with the past but a continuation of it with new means. It is, essentially, not about the "new," but most of all about "renewal" achieved through effort, exercise, and persistent imitation.

References

Baldwin, J. M. (1894). IL—Imitation: A chapter in the natural history of consciousness. *Mind, 3*(9), 26–55.

Baldwin, J. M. (1903). *Mental development in the child and the race: Methods and processes* (2nd ed.). London: Macmillan.

Baldwin, J. M. (1906). *Social and ethical interpretations in mental development.* London: Macmillan.

Baldwin, J. M. (1911). *The individual and society or psychology and sociology.* Boston: Richard G. Badger.

Davis, G. A. (1999). Barriers to creativity and creative attitudes. In M. A. Runco & S. R. Pritzker (Eds.), *Encyclopedia of creativity* (Vol. 1, pp. 165–174). San Diego, CA: Academic Press.

Djellal, F., & Gallouj, F. (2014). The laws of imitation and invention: Gabriel Tarde and the evolutionary economics of innovation. Retrieved from: https://halshs.archives-ouvertes.fr/halshs-00960607/.

Durkheim, É. (1985). *The rules of sociological method and selected texts on sociology and its method* (S. Lukes, Ed.; W. D. Halls, Trans.). New York, NY: Free Press.

Gabora, L., & Tseng, S. (in press). The social benefits of balancing creators and imitators: Evidence from an agent-based model. *Psychology of Aesthetics, Creativity, and the Arts.* Retrieved from: https://people.ok.ubc.ca/lgabora/papers/Gabora-Tseng-PACA2017.pdf.

Glăveanu, V. P. (2010). Paradigms in the study of creativity: Introducing the perspective of cultural psychology. *New Ideas in Psychology, 28*(1), 79–93.

Glăveanu, V. P. (2012). Habitual creativity: Revisiting habit, reconceptualising creativity. *Review of General Psychology, 16*(1), 78–92.

Glăveanu, V. P. (2016). Translation. In V. P. Glăveanu, L. Tanggaard, & C. Wegener (Eds.), *Creativity: A new vocabulary* (pp. 172–180). London: Palgrave.

Ingold, T., & Hallam, E. (2007). Creativity and cultural improvisation: An introduction. In E. Hallam & T. Ingold (Eds.), *Creativity and cultural improvisation* (pp. 1–24). Oxford: Berg.

James, W. (1890). *The principles of psychology.* Vol. 1. New York, NY: Dover.

Johansson, A. W. (2010). Innovation, creativity and imitation. In F. Bill, B. Bjerke, & A. W. Johansson (Eds.), *(De)Mobilizing the entrepreneurship discourse: Exploring entrepreneurial thinking and action* (pp. 123–139). Cheltenham, UK: Edward Elgar.

Kaufman, J. C., & Beghetto, R. A. (2009). Beyond big and little: The four c model of creativity. *Review of General Psychology, 13*(1), 1–12.

Kinnunen, J. (1996). Gabriel Tarde as a founding father of innovation diffusion research. *Acta sociologica, 39*(4), 431–442.

Mecca, J. T., & Mumford, M. D. (2014). Imitation and creativity: Beneficial effects of propulsion strategies and specificity. *Journal of Creative Behavior, 48*(3), 209–236.

Simonton, D. K. (2010). Creative thought as blind-variation and selective-retention: Combinatorial models of exceptional creativity. *Physics of Life Reviews, 7*(2), 156–179.

Tarde G. (1895). *La logique sociale.* Paris: Félix Alcan.

Tarde, G. (1902). L'invention, moteur de l'évolution sociale. *Revue internationale de sociologie, 10*(7), 562–574.

Tarde, G. (1903). *The laws of imitation* (E. C. Parsons, Trans., from the 2nd French edition). New York, NY: Henry Holt.

Tonkonoff, S. (2013). A new social physic: The sociology of Gabriel Tarde and its legacy. *Current Sociology, 61*(3), 267–282.

Valsiner, J. (2000). *Culture and human development: An introduction.* London: Sage.

Valsiner, J. (2018). Roots of creativity: Variability amplification through persistent imitation. In T. Zittoun & V. P. Glăveanu (Eds.), *Handbook of imagination and culture* (pp. 47–60). New York, NY: Oxford University Press.

Valsiner, J., & Van der Veer, R. (2000). *The social mind: Construction of the idea.* Cambridge, UK: Cambridge University Press.

12

Abraham Maslow

Tragedies of Actualization

Michael Hanchett Hanson

Summary

In "A Theory of Human Motivation," Abraham Maslow (1943) posited self-actualization as the pinnacle of a hierarchy of human motivations, laying a cornerstone for much of the rest of his work. The theory is, however, problematic. Subsequent empirical work has generally not supported it. Internal contradictions between Maslow's bold assertions and many exceptions make the theory impossible to validate and ultimately bring into question its usefulness. The extreme individualistic assumptions of the theory undermine its face validity. Most important, the goal of self-actualization contributed to a view of human development and potential with problematic dichotomies between person and world, actualized and nonactualized. The dangers of these dichotomies can be seen in Maslow's idealization of those he considered strong and biologically superior and his contempt for the weak: everyone else. The logic of self-actualization also contributed to subtler forms of these dichotomies in the work of Maslow's colleague, Carl Rogers. Ultimately the popular influence of theories of self-actualization without evidence of validity, due in large part to Maslow's passion, aspirations, and determination, brings to mind ancient Greek tragedy: counsel against hubris and an appreciation of pervasive human frailties.

Introduction

The idea of self-actualization has so permeated American social discourse that today the imperative to self-actualize is more often assumption than assertion. The same is increasingly true of globalized views of the meaning and goals of life, and creativity theories have been one means of spreading the idea (Hanchett Hanson, 2015). Today's concept of self-actualization originated in the writings of Kurt Goldstein, a groundbreaking neuropsychologist who worked in Germany with patients who had suffered brain injuries during and after World War I (Stahnisch & Hoffmann, 2010). Influenced by the holism of Gestalt psychology, Goldstein conducted extensive research into how people with brain injuries could be helped. He did this at a time when the standard of practice was simply to study and arrange for adequate care—not treat—these patients (Harrington, 1998). After fleeing the Nazis in the 1930s, Goldstein (1935/1995) wrote *The Organism: A Holistic Approach to Biology Derived from Pathological Data in Man,* in which he posited his theory of self-actualization as the single drive for all living organisms. This view was proposed in contrast to Freud's theories of multiple drives, particularly the dueling drives of life (Eros) and death (Thanatos) within each person.

Goldstein's work, though recognized by experts (Sacks, 1995), is not widely known. The idea of self-actualization, however, was widely popularized by humanistic psychologists who made it central to their work. Of those theorists, the most successful were Carl Rogers and Abraham Maslow. Rogers, like Goldstein, was a clinician trying to find ways to treat patients. Maslow, in contrast, was primarily an academic trying to lay the intellectual foundation for humanistic theories.

"A Theory of Human Motivation," featured below, was an early articulation of his theory, published in 1943. This essay was the cornerstone for much of the rest of his work. It presented self-actualization within the context of a broader theory of motivation, a hierarchy of needs going from basic physiological needs to emotional needs to the pinnacle of self-actualization. The schema was presented as a rational argument, based on clinical insights, rather than an empirical conclusion. In some fields Maslow's hierarchy continues to be influential in large part because it is a compelling common-sense argument. It corresponds to firsthand experience of feeling distracted when hungry or at times of heartbreak (loss of love). In addition, the pinnacle of the motivational hierarchy—self-actualization—can be inspiring. That one is naturally destined to ever greater achievement and success can have a dizzying effect when contrasted to the actual limitations and frustrations of everyday life.

Maslow's motivational hierarchy gained popularity as part of a wave of humanistic psychology that spread beyond academic walls and clinical offices over the next 30 years. During that time the work of Maslow and his colleagues, especially Carl Rogers and Rollo May, became best-sellers, advising Americans on how to fulfill their lives during the heady postwar, frightening Cold War, and turbulent antiwar periods of the 1950s, 1960s and 1970s. In other words, "A Theory of Human Motivation" was an initial ripple of what would become a wave of popular humanistic psychology that has had lasting impact.

Reading: "A Theory of Human Motivation"

Source: Maslow, A. H. (1943). A theory of human motivation. *Psychological Review,* 50(4), 370–396. This article is in the public domain. References have been included as notes. Original notes have been kept as such.

Introduction

In a previous paper[1] various propositions were presented which would have to be included in any theory of human motivation that could lay claim to being definitive. These conclusions may be briefly summarized as follows:

1. The integrated wholeness of the organism must be one of the foundation stones of motivation theory.

2. The hunger drive (or any other physiological drive) was rejected as a centering point or model for a definitive theory of motivation. Any drive that is somatically based and localizable was shown to be atypical rather than typical in human motivation.

3. Such a theory should stress and center itself upon ultimate or basic goals rather than partial or superficial ones, upon ends rather than means to these ends. Such a stress would imply a more central place for unconscious than for conscious motivations.

4. There are usually available various cultural paths to the same goal. Therefore conscious, specific, local-cultural desires are not as fundamental in motivation theory as the more basic, unconscious goals.

5. Any motivated behavior, either preparatory or consummatory, must be understood to be a channel through which many basic needs may be simultaneously expressed or satisfied. Typically an act has *more* than one motivation.

6. Practically all organismic states are to be understood as motivated and as motivating.

7. Human needs arrange themselves in hierarchies of prepotency. That is to say, the appearance of one need usually rests on the prior satisfaction of another, more pre-potent need. Man is a perpetually wanting animal. Also no need or drive can be treated as if it were isolated or discrete; every drive is related to the state of satisfaction or dissatisfaction of other drives.

8. *Lists* of drives will get us nowhere for various theoretical and practical reasons. Furthermore any classification of motivations must deal with the problem of levels of specificity or generalization of the motives to be classified.

9. Classifications of motivations must be based upon goals rather than upon instigating drives or motivated behavior.

10. Motivation theory should be human-centered rather than animal-centered.

11. The situation or the field in which the organism reacts must be taken into account but the field alone can rarely serve as an exclusive explanation for behavior. Furthermore the field itself must be interpreted in terms of the organism. Field theory cannot be a substitute for motivation theory.

12. Not only the integration of the organism must be taken into account, but also the possibility of isolated, specific, partial or segmental reactions.

    It has since become necessary to add to these another affirmation.

13. Motivation theory is not synonymous with behavior theory. The motivations are only one class of determinants of behavior. While behavior is almost always motivated, it is also almost always biologically, culturally and situationally determined as well.

The present paper is an attempt to formulate a positive theory of motivation which will satisfy these theoretical demands and at the same time conform to the known facts, clinical and observational as well as experimental. It derives most directly, however, from clinical experience. This theory is, I think, in the functionalist tradition of James and Dewey, and is fused with the holism of Wertheimer,[2] Goldstein,[3] and Gestalt Psychology, and with the dynamicism of Freud[4] and Adler.[5] This fusion or synthesis may arbitrarily be called a "general-dynamic" theory.

It is far easier to perceive and to criticize the aspects in motivation theory than to remedy them. Mostly this is because of the very serious lack of sound data in this area. I conceive this lack of sound facts to be due primarily to the absence of a valid theory of motivation. The present theory then must be considered to be a suggested program or framework for future research and must stand or fall, not so much on facts available or evidence presented, as upon researches yet to be done, researches suggested perhaps, by the questions raised in this paper.

The Basic Needs

THE "PHYSIOLOGICAL" NEEDS

The needs that are usually taken as the starting point for motivation theory are the so-called physiological drives. Two recent lines of research make it necessary to revise our customary notions about these needs, first, the development of the concept of homeostasis, and second, the finding that appetites (preferential choices among foods) are a fairly efficient indication of actual needs or lacks in the body.

Homeostasis refers to the body's automatic efforts to maintain a constant, normal state of the blood stream. Cannon[6] has described this process for (1) the water content of the blood, (2) salt content, (3) sugar content, (4) protein content, (5) fat content, (6) calcium content, (7) oxygen content, (8) constant hydrogen-ion level (acid-base balance) and (9) constant temperature of the blood. Obviously this list can be extended to include other minerals, the hormones, vitamins, etc.

Young in a recent article[7] has summarized the work on appetite in its relation to body needs. If the body lacks some chemical, the individual will tend to develop a specific appetite or partial hunger for that food element.

Thus it seems impossible as well as useless to make any list of fundamental physiological needs for they can come to almost any number one might wish, depending on the degree of specificity of description. We can not identify all physiological needs as homeostatic. That sexual desire, sleepiness, sheer activity and maternal behavior in animals, are homeostatic, has not yet been demonstrated. Furthermore, this list would not include the various sensory pleasures (tastes, smells, tickling, stroking) which are probably physiological and which may become the goals of motivated behavior.

In a previous paper[8] it has been pointed out that these physiological drives or needs are to be considered unusual rather than typical because they are isolable, and because they are localizable somatically. That is to say, they are relatively independent of each other, of other motivations and of the organism as a whole, and secondly, in many cases, it is possible to demonstrate a localized, underlying somatic base for the drive. This is true less generally than has been thought (exceptions are fatigue, sleepiness, maternal responses) but it is still true in the classic instances of hunger, sex, and thirst.

It should be pointed out again that any of the physiological needs and the consummatory behavior involved with them serve as channels for all sorts of other needs as well. That is to say, the person who thinks he is hungry may actually be seeking more for comfort, or dependence, than for vitamins or proteins. Conversely, it is possible to satisfy the hunger need in part by other activities such as drinking water or smoking cigarettes. In other words, relatively isolable as these physiological needs are, they are not completely so.

Undoubtedly these physiological needs are the most prepotent of all needs. What this means specifically is, that in the human being who is missing everything in life in an extreme fashion, it is most likely that the major motivation would be the physiological needs rather than any others. A person who is lacking food, safety, love, and esteem would most probably hunger for food more strongly than for anything else.

If all the needs are unsatisfied, and the organism is then dominated by the physiological needs, all other needs may become simply non-existent or be pushed into the background. It is then fair to characterize the whole organism by saying simply that it is hungry, for consciousness is almost completely preempted by hunger. All capacities are put into the service of hunger-satisfaction, and the organization of these capacities is almost entirely determined by the one purpose of satisfying hunger. The receptors and effectors, the intelligence, memory, habits, all may now be defined simply as hunger-gratifying tools. Capacities that are not useful for this purpose lie dormant, or are pushed into the background.

The urge to write poetry, the desire to acquire an automobile, the interest in American history, the desire for a new pair of shoes are, in the extreme case, forgotten or become of secondary importance. For the man who is extremely and dangerously hungry, no other interests exist but food. He dreams food, he remembers food, he thinks about food, he emotes only about food, he perceives only food and he wants only food. The more subtle determinants that ordinarily fuse with the physiological drives in organizing even feeding, drinking or sexual behavior, may now be so completely overwhelmed as to allow us to speak at this time (but only at this time) of pure hunger drive and behavior, with the one unqualified aim of relief.

Another peculiar characteristic of the human organism when it is dominated by a certain need is that the whole philosophy of the future tends also to change. For our chronically and extremely hungry man, Utopia can be defined very simply as a place where there is plenty of food. He tends to think that, if only he is guaranteed food for the rest of his life, he will be perfectly happy and will never want anything more. Life itself tends to be defined in terms of eating. Anything else will be defined as unimportant. Freedom, love, community feeling, respect, philosophy, may all be waved aside as fripperies which are useless since they fail to fill the stomach. Such a man may fairly be said to live by bread alone.

It cannot possibly be denied that such things are true but their *generality* can be denied. Emergency conditions are, almost by definition, rare in the normally functioning peaceful society. That this truism can be forgotten is due mainly to two reasons. First, rats have few motivations other than physiological ones, and since so much of the research upon motivation has been made with these animals, it is easy to carry the rat-picture over to the human being. Secondly, it is too often not realized that culture itself is an adaptive tool, one of whose main functions is to make the physiological emergencies come less and less often. In most of the known societies, chronic extreme hunger of the emergency type is rare, rather than common. In any case, this is still true in the United States. The average American citizen is experiencing appetite rather than hunger when he says "I am hungry." He is apt to experience sheer life-and-death hunger only by accident and then only a few times through his entire life.

Obviously a good way to obscure the "higher" motivations, and to get a lopsided view of human capacities and human nature, is to make the organism extremely and chronically hungry or thirsty. Anyone who attempts to make an emergency picture into a typical one, and who will measure all of man's goals and desires by his behavior during extreme physiological deprivation is certainly being blind to many things. It is quite true that man lives by bread alone—when there is no bread. But what happens to man's desires when there is plenty of bread and when his belly is chronically filled?

At once other (and "higher") needs emerge, and these, rather than physiological hungers, dominate the organism. And when these in turn are satisfied, again new (and still "higher") needs emerge, and so on. This is what we mean by saying that the basic human needs are organized into a hierarchy of relative prepotency.

One main implication of this phrasing is that gratification becomes as important a concept as deprivation in motivation theory, for it releases the organism from the domination of a relatively more physiological need, permitting thereby the emergence of other more social goals. The physiological needs, along with their partial goals, when chronically gratified cease to exist as active determinants or organizers of behavior. They now exist only in a potential fashion in the sense that they may emerge again to dominate the organism if they are thwarted. But a want that is satisfied is no longer a want. The organism is dominated and its behavior organized only by unsatisfied needs. If hunger is satisfied, it becomes unimportant in the current dynamics of the individual.

This statement is somewhat qualified by a hypothesis to be discussed more fully later, namely that it is precisely those individuals in whom a certain need has always been satisfied who are best equipped to tolerate deprivation of that need in the future, and that furthermore, those who have been deprived in the past will react differently to current satisfactions than the one who has never been deprived.

THE SAFETY NEEDS

If the physiological needs are relatively well gratified, there then emerges a new set of needs, which we may categorize roughly as the safety needs. All that has been said of the physiological needs is equally true, although in lesser degree, of these desires. The organism may equally well be wholly dominated by them. They may serve as the almost exclusive organizers of behavior, recruiting all the capacities of the organism in their service, and we may then fairly describe the whole organism as a safety-seeking mechanism. Again we may say of the receptors, the effectors, of the intellect and the other capacities that they are primarily safety-seeking tools. Again, as in the hungry man, we find that the dominating goal is a strong determinant not only of his current world-outlook and philosophy but also of his philosophy of the future. Practically everything looks less important than safety (even sometimes the physiological needs which, being satisfied, are now underestimated). A man, in this state, if it is extreme enough and chronic enough, may be characterized as living almost for safety alone.

Although in this paper we are interested primarily in the needs of the adult, we can approach an understanding of his safety needs perhaps more efficiently by observation of infants and children, in whom these needs are much more simple and obvious. One reason for the clearer appearance of the threat or danger reaction in infants, is that they do not inhibit this reaction at all, whereas adults in our society have been taught to inhibit it at all costs. Thus even when adults do feel their safety to be threatened we may not be able to see this on the surface. Infants will react in a total fashion and as if they were endangered, if they are disturbed or dropped suddenly, startled by loud noises, flashing light, or other unusual sensory stimulation, by rough handling, by general loss of support in the mother's arms, or by inadequate support.[9]

In infants we can also see a much more direct reaction to bodily illnesses of various kinds. Sometimes these illnesses seem to be immediately and *per se* threatening and seem to make the child feel unsafe. For instance, vomiting, colic or other sharp pains seem to make the child look at the whole world in a different way. At such a moment of pain, it may be postulated that, for the child, the appearance of the whole world suddenly changes from sunniness to darkness, so to speak, and becomes a place in which anything at all might happen, in which previously stable things have suddenly become unstable. Thus a child who because of some bad food is taken ill may, for a day or two, develop fear, nightmares, and a need for protection and reassurance never seen in him before his illness.

Another indication of the child's need for safety is his preference for some kind of undisrupted routine or rhythm. He seems to want a predictable, orderly world. For instance, injustice, unfairness, or inconsistency in the parents seems to make a child feel anxious and unsafe. This attitude may be not so much because of the injustice *per se* or any particular pains involved, but rather because this treatment threatens to make the world look unreliable, or unsafe, or unpredictable. Young children seem to thrive better under a system which has at least a skeletal outline of rigidity, in which there is a schedule of a kind, some sort of routine, something that can be counted upon, not only for the present but also far into the future. Perhaps one could express this more accurately by saying that the child needs an organized world rather than an unorganized or unstructured one.

The central role of the parents and the normal family setup are indisputable. Quarreling, physical assault, separation, divorce or death within the family may be particularly terrifying. Also parental outbursts of rage or threats of punishment directed to the child, calling him names, speaking to him harshly, shaking him, handling him roughly, or actual physical punishment sometimes elicit such total panic and terror in the child that we must assume more is involved than the physical pain alone. While it is true that in some children this terror may represent also a fear of loss of parental love, it can also occur in completely rejected children, who seem to cling to the hating parents more for sheer safety and protection than because of hope of love.

Confronting the average child with new, unfamiliar, strange, unmanageable stimuli or situations will too frequently elicit the danger or terror reaction, as for example, getting lost or even being separated from the parents for a short time, being confronted with new faces, new situations or new tasks, the sight of strange, unfamiliar or uncontrollable objects, illness or death. Particularly at such times, the child's frantic clinging to his parents is eloquent testimony to their role as protectors (quite apart from their roles as food-givers and love-givers).

From these and similar observations, we may generalize and say that the average child in our society generally prefers a safe, orderly, predictable, organized world, which he can count on, and in which unexpected, unmanageable or other dangerous things do not happen, and in which, in any case, he has all-powerful parents who protect and shield him from harm.

That these reactions may so easily be observed in children is in a way a proof of the fact that children in our society, feel too unsafe (or, in a word, are badly brought up). Children who are reared in an unthreatening, loving family do *not* ordinarily react as we have described above.[10] In such children the danger reactions are apt to come mostly to objects or situations that adults too would consider dangerous.[11]

The healthy, normal, fortunate adult in our culture is largely satisfied in his safety needs. The peaceful, smoothly running, "good" society ordinarily makes its members feel safe enough from wild animals, extremes of temperature, criminals, assault and murder, tyranny, etc. Therefore, in a very real sense, he no longer has any safety needs as active motivators. Just as a sated man no longer feels hungry, a safe man no longer feels endangered. If we wish to see these needs directly and clearly we must turn to neurotic or near-neurotic individuals, and to the economic and social underdogs. In between these extremes, we can perceive the expressions of safety needs only in such phenomena as, for instance, the common preference for a job with tenure and protection, the desire for a savings account, and for insurance of various kinds (medical, dental, unemployment, disability, old age).

Other broader aspects of the attempt to seek safety and stability in the world are seen in the very common preference for familiar rather than unfamiliar things, or for the known rather than the unknown. The tendency to have some religion or world-philosophy that organizes the universe and the men in it into some sort of satisfactorily coherent, meaningful whole is also in part motivated by safety-seeking. Here too we may list science and philosophy in general as partially motivated by the safety needs (we shall see later that there are also other motivations to scientific, philosophical or religious endeavor).

Otherwise the need for safety is seen as an active and dominant mobilizer of the organism's resources only in emergencies, *e.g.*, war, disease, natural catastrophes, crime waves, societal disorganization, neurosis, brain injury, chronically bad situation.

Some neurotic adults in our society are, in many ways, like the unsafe child in their desire for safety, although in the former it takes on a somewhat special appearance. Their reaction is often to unknown, psychological dangers in a world that is perceived to be hostile, overwhelming and threatening. Such a person behaves as if a great catastrophe were almost always impending, *i.e.*, he is usually responding as if to an emergency. His safety needs often find specific expression in a search for a protector, or a stronger person on whom he may depend, or perhaps, a Fuehrer.

The neurotic individual may be described in a slightly different way with some usefulness as a grown-up person who retains his childish attitudes toward the world. That is to say, a neurotic adult may be said to behave "as if" he were actually afraid of a spanking, or of his mother's disapproval, or of being abandoned by his parents, or having his food taken away from him. It is as if his childish attitudes of fear and threat reaction to a dangerous world had gone underground, and untouched by the growing up and learning processes, were now ready to be called out by any stimulus that would make a child feel endangered and threatened.[12]

The neurosis in which the search for safety takes its clearest form is in the compulsive-obsessive neurosis. Compulsive-obsessives try frantically to order and stabilize the world so that no unmanageable, unexpected or unfamiliar dangers will ever appear.[13] They hedge themselves about with all sorts of ceremonials, rules, and formulas so that every possible contingency may be provided for and so that no new contingencies may appear. They are much like the brain injured cases, described by Goldstein,[14] who manage to maintain their equilibrium by avoiding everything unfamiliar and strange and by ordering their restricted world in such a neat, disciplined, orderly fashion that everything in the world can be counted upon. They try to arrange the world so that anything unexpected (dangers) cannot possibly occur. If, through no fault of their own, something unexpected does occur, they go into a panic reaction as if this unexpected occurrence constituted a grave danger. What we can see only as a none-too-strong preference in the healthy person, e.g., preference for the familiar, becomes a life-and-death necessity in abnormal cases.

THE LOVE NEEDS

If both the physiological and the safety needs are fairly well gratified, then there will emerge the love and affection and belongingness needs, and the whole cycle already described will repeat itself with this new center. Now the person will feel keenly, as never before, the absence of friends, or a sweetheart, or a wife, or children. He will hunger for affectionate relations with people in general, namely, for a place in his group, and he will strive with great intensity to achieve this goal. He will want to attain such a place more than anything else in the world and may even forget that once, when he was hungry, he sneered at love.

In our society the thwarting of these needs is the most commonly found core in cases of maladjustment and more severe psychopathology. Love and affection, as well as their possible expression in sexuality, are generally looked upon with ambivalence and are customarily hedged about with many restrictions and inhibitions. Practically all theorists of psychopathology have stressed thwarting of the love needs as basic in the picture of maladjustment. Many clinical studies have therefore been made of this need and we know more about it perhaps than any of the other needs except the physiological ones.[15]

One thing that must be stressed at this point is that love is not synonymous with sex. Sex may be studied as a purely physiological need. Ordinarily sexual behavior is multi-determined, that is to say, determined not only by sexual but also by other needs, chief among which are the love and affection needs. Also not to be overlooked is the fact that the love needs involve both giving *and* receiving love.[16]

THE ESTEEM NEEDS

All people in our society (with a few pathological exceptions) have a need or desire for a stable, firmly based, (usually) high evaluation of themselves, for self-respect, or self-esteem, and for the esteem of others. By firmly based self-esteem, we mean that which is soundly based upon real capacity, achievement and respect from others. These needs may be classified into two subsidiary sets. These are, first, the desire for strength, for achievement, for adequacy, for confidence in the face of the world, and for independence and freedom.[17] Secondly, we have what we may call the desire for reputation or prestige (defining it as respect or esteem from other people), recognition, attention, importance or appreciation.[18] These needs have been relatively stressed by Alfred Adler and his followers, and have been relatively neglected by Freud and the psychoanalysts. More and more today however there is appearing wide-spread appreciation of their central importance.

Satisfaction of the self-esteem need leads to feelings of self-confidence, worth, strength, capability and adequacy of being useful and necessary in the world. But thwarting of these needs produces feelings of inferiority, of weakness and of helplessness. These feelings in turn give rise to either basic discouragement or else compensatory or neurotic trends. An appreciation of the necessity of basic self-confidence and an understanding of how helpless people are without it, can be easily gained from a study of severe traumatic neurosis.[19, 20]

THE NEED FOR SELF-ACTUALIZATION

Even if all these needs are satisfied, we may still often (if not always) expect that a new discontent and restlessness will soon develop, unless the individual is doing what he is fitted for. A musician must make music, an artist must paint, a poet must write, if he is to be ultimately happy. What a man *can* be, he *must* be. This need we may call self-actualization.

This term, first coined by Kurt Goldstein, is being used in this paper in a much more specific and limited fashion. It refers to the desire for self-fulfillment, namely, to the tendency for him to become actualized in what he is potentially. This tendency might be phrased as the desire to become more and more what one is, to become everything that one is capable of becoming.

The specific form that these needs will take will of course vary greatly from person to person. In one individual it may take the form of the desire to be an ideal mother, in another it may be expressed athletically, and in still another it may be expressed in painting pictures or in inventions. It is not necessarily a creative urge although in people who have any capacities for creation it will take this form.

The clear emergence of these needs rests upon prior satisfaction of the physiological, safety, love and esteem needs. We shall call people who are satisfied in these needs, basically satisfied people, and it is from these that we may expect the fullest (and healthiest) creativeness.[21] Since, in our society, basically satisfied people are the exception, we do not know much about self-actualization, either experimentally or clinically. It remains a challenging problem for research.

THE PRECONDITIONS FOR THE BASIC
NEED SATISFACTIONS

There are certain conditions which are immediate prerequisites for the basic need satisfactions. Danger to these is reacted to almost as if it were a direct danger to the basic needs themselves. Such conditions as freedom to speak, freedom to do what one wishes so long as no harm is done to others, freedom to express one's self, freedom to investigate and seek for information, freedom to defend one's self, justice, fairness, honesty, orderliness in the group are examples of such preconditions for basic need satisfactions. Thwarting in these freedoms will be reacted to with a threat or emergency response. These conditions are not ends in themselves but they are *almost* so since they are so closely related to the basic needs, which are apparently the only ends in themselves. These conditions are defended because without them the basic satisfactions are quite impossible, or at least, very severely endangered.

If we remember that the cognitive capacities (perceptual, intellectual, learning) are a set of adjustive tools, which have, among other functions, that of satisfaction of our basic needs, then it is clear that any danger to them, any deprivation or blocking of their free use, must also be indirectly threatening to the basic needs themselves. Such a statement is a partial solution of the general problems of curiosity, the search for knowledge, truth and wisdom, and the ever-persistent urge to solve the cosmic mysteries.

We must therefore introduce another hypothesis and speak of degrees of closeness to the basic needs, for we have already pointed out that *any* conscious desires (partial goals) are more or less important as they are more or less close to the basic needs. The same statement may be made for various behavior acts. An act is psychologically important if it contributes directly to satisfaction of basic needs. The less directly it so contributes, or the weaker this contribution is, the less important this act must be conceived to be from the point of view of dynamic psychology. A similar statement may be made for the various defense or coping mechanisms. Some are very directly related to the protection or attainment of the basic needs, others are only weakly and distantly related. Indeed if we wished, we could speak of more basic and less basic defense mechanisms, and then affirm that danger to, the more basic defenses is more threatening than danger to less basic defenses (always remembering that this is so only because of their relationship to the basic needs).

THE DESIRES TO KNOW AND TO UNDERSTAND

So far, we have mentioned the cognitive needs only in passing. Acquiring knowledge and systematizing the universe have been considered as, in part, techniques for the achievement of basic safety in the world, or, for the intelligent man, expressions of self-actualization. Also freedom of inquiry and expression have been discussed as preconditions of satisfactions of the basic needs. True though these formulations may be, they do not constitute definitive answers to the question as to the motivation role of curiosity, learning, philosophizing, experimenting, etc. They are, at best, no more than partial answers.

This question is especially difficult because we know so little about the facts. Curiosity, exploration, desire for the facts, desire to know may certainly be observed easily enough. The fact that they often are pursued even at great cost to the individual's safety is an earnest of the partial character of our previous discussion. In addition, the writer must admit that, though he has sufficient clinical evidence to postulate the desire to know as a very strong drive in intelligent people, no data are available for unintelligent people. It may then be largely a function of relatively high intelligence. Rather tentatively, then, and largely in the hope of stimulating discussion and research, we shall postulate a basic desire to know, to be aware of reality, to get the facts, to satisfy curiosity, or as Wertheimer phrases it, to see rather than to be blind.

This postulation, however, is not enough. Even after we know, we are impelled to know more and more minutely and microscopically on the one hand, and on the other, more and more extensively in the direction of a world philosophy, religion, etc. The facts that we acquire, if they are isolated or atomistic, inevitably get theorized about, and either analyzed or organized or both. This process has been phrased by some as the search for "meaning." We shall then postulate a desire to understand, to systematize, to organize, to analyze, to look for relations and meanings.

Once these desires are accepted for discussion, we see that they too form themselves into a small hierarchy in which the desire to know is prepotent over the desire to understand. All the characteristics of a hierarchy of prepotency that we have described above, seem to hold for this one as well.

We must guard ourselves against the too easy tendency to separate these desires from the basic needs we have discussed above, *i.e.*, to make a sharp dichotomy between "cognitive" and "conative" needs. The desire to know and to understand are themselves conative, *i.e.*, have a striving character, and are as much personality needs as the "basic needs" we have already discussed.[22]

Further Characteristics of the Basic Needs

THE DEGREE OF FIXITY OF THE HIERARCHY OF BASIC NEEDS

We have spoken so far as if this hierarchy were a fixed order, but actually it is not nearly as rigid as we may have implied. It is true that most of the people with whom we have worked have seemed to have these basic needs in about the order that has been indicated. However, there have been a number of exceptions.

1. There are some people in whom, for instance, self-esteem seems to be more important than love. This most common reversal in the hierarchy is usually due to the development of the notion that the person who is most likely to be loved is a strong or powerful person, one who inspires respect or fear, and who is self confident or aggressive. Therefore such people who lack love and seek it, may try hard to put on a front of aggressive, confident behavior. But essentially they seek high self-esteem and its behavior expressions more as a means-to-an-end than for its own sake; they seek self-assertion for the sake of love rather than for self-esteem itself.

2. There are other, apparently innately creative people in whom the drive to creativeness seems to be more important than any other counter-determinant. Their creativeness might appear not as self-actualization released by basic satisfaction, but in spite of lack of basic satisfaction.

3. In certain people the level of aspiration may be permanently deadened or lowered. That is to say, the less prepotent goals may simply be lost, and may disappear forever, so that the person who has experienced life at a very low level, *i.e.*, chronic unemployment, may continue to be satisfied for the rest of his life if only he can get enough food.

4. The so-called psychopathic personality is another example of permanent loss of the love needs. These are people who, according to the best data available,[23] have been starved for love in the earliest months of their lives and have simply lost forever the desire and the ability to give and to receive affection (as animals lose sucking or pecking reflexes that are not exercised soon enough after birth).

5. Another cause of reversal of the hierarchy is that when a need has been satisfied for a long time, this need may be underevaluated. People who have never

experienced chronic hunger are apt to underestimate its effects and to look upon food as a rather unimportant thing. If they are dominated by a higher need, this higher need will seem to be the most important of all. It then becomes possible, and indeed does actually happen, that they may, for the sake of this higher need, put themselves into the position of being deprived in a more basic need. We may expect that after a long-time deprivation of the more basic need there will be a tendency to reevaluate both needs so that the more pre-potent need will actually become consciously prepotent for the individual who may have given it up very lightly. Thus, a man who has given up his job rather than lose his self-respect, and who then starves for six months or so, may be willing to take his job back even at the price of losing his self-respect.

6. Another partial explanation of *apparent* reversals is seen in the fact that we have been talking about the hierarchy of prepotency in terms of consciously felt wants or desires rather than of behavior. Looking at behavior itself may give us the wrong impression. What we have claimed is that the person will *want* the more basic of two needs when deprived in both. There is no necessary implication here that he will act upon his desires. Let us say again that there are many determinants of behavior other than the needs and desires.

7. Perhaps more important than all these exceptions are the ones that involve ideals, high social standards, high values and the like. With such values people become martyrs; they will give up everything for the sake of a particular ideal, or value. These people may be understood, at least in part, by reference to one basic concept (or hypothesis) which may be called "increased frustration-tolerance through early gratification." People who have been satisfied in their basic needs throughout their lives, particularly in their earlier years, seem to develop exceptional power to withstand present or future thwarting of these needs simply because they have strong, healthy character structure as a result of basic satisfaction. They are the "strong" people who can easily weather disagreement or opposition, who can swim against the stream of public opinion and who can stand up for the truth at great personal cost. It is just the ones who have loved and been well loved, and who have had many deep friendships who can hold out against hatred, rejection or persecution.

I say all this in spite of the fact that there is a certain amount of sheer habituation which is also involved in any full discussion of frustration tolerance. For instance, it is likely that those persons who have been accustomed to relative starvation for a long time, are partially enabled thereby to withstand food deprivation. What sort of balance must be made between these two tendencies, of habituation on the one hand, and of past satisfaction breeding present frustration tolerance on the other hand, remains to be worked out by further research. Meanwhile we may assume that they are both operative, side by side, since they do not contradict each other. In respect to this phenomenon of increased frustration tolerance, it seems probable that the most important gratifications come in the first two years of life. That is to say, people who have been made secure and strong in the earliest years, tend to remain secure and strong thereafter in the face of whatever threatens.

DEGREES OF RELATIVE SATISFACTION

So far, our theoretical discussion may have given the impression that these five sets of needs are somehow in a step-wise, all-or-none relationships to each other. We have spoken in such terms as the following: "If one need is satisfied, then another emerges." This statement might give the false impression that a need must be satisfied 100 per cent before the next need emerges. In actual fact, most members of our society who are normal, are partially satisfied in all their basic needs and partially unsatisfied in all their basic needs at the same time. A more realistic description of the hierarchy would be in terms of decreasing percentages of satisfaction as we go up the hierarchy of prepotency. For instance, if I may assign arbitrary figures for the sake of illustration, it is as if the average citizen is satisfied perhaps 85 per cent in his physiological needs, 70 per cent in his safety needs, 50 per cent in his love needs, 40 per cent in his self-esteem needs, and 10 per cent in his self-actualization needs.

As for the concept of emergence of a new need after satisfaction of the prepotent need, this emergence is not a sudden, saltatory phenomenon but rather a gradual emergence by slow degrees from nothingness. For instance, if prepotent need A is satisfied only 10 per cent then need B may not be visible at all. However, as this need A becomes satisfied 25 per cent, need B may emerge 5 per cent, as need A becomes satisfied 75 per cent need B may emerge 90 per cent, and so on.

UNCONSCIOUS CHARACTER OF NEEDS

These needs are neither necessarily conscious nor unconscious. On the whole, however, in the average person, they are more often unconscious rather than conscious. It is not necessary at this point to overhaul the tremendous mass of evidence which indicates the crucial importance of unconscious motivation. It would by now be expected, on a priori grounds alone, that unconscious motivations would on the whole be rather more important than the conscious motivations. What we have called the basic needs are very often largely unconscious, although they may, with suitable techniques, and with sophisticated people become conscious.

CULTURAL SPECIFICITY AND
GENERALITY OF NEEDS

This classification of basic needs makes some attempt to take account of the relative unity behind the superficial differences in specific desires from one culture to another. Certainly in any particular culture an individual's conscious motivational content will usually be extremely different from the conscious motivational content of an individual in another society. However, it is the common experience of anthropologists that people, even in different societies, are much more alike than we would think from our first contact with them, and that as we know them better we seem to find more and more of this commonness. We then recognize the most startling differences to be superficial rather than basic, e.g., differences in style of hair dress, clothes, tastes in food, etc. Our classification of basic needs is in part an attempt to account for this unity behind the apparent diversity from culture to culture. No claim is made that it is ultimate or universal for all cultures. The claim

is made only that it is relatively *more* ultimate, more universal, more basic, than the superficial conscious desires from culture to culture, and makes a somewhat closer approach to
common-human characteristics. Basic needs are *more* common-human than superficial
desires or behaviors.

MULTIPLE MOTIVATIONS OF BEHAVIOR

These needs must be understood not to be exclusive or single determiners of certain kinds
of behavior. An example may be found in any behavior that seems to be physiologically
motivated, such as eating, or sexual play or the like. The clinical psychologists have long
since found that any behavior may be a channel through which flow various determinants.
Or to say it in another way, most behavior is multi-motivated. Within the sphere of motivational determinants any behavior tends to be determined by several or *all* of the basic needs
simultaneously rather than by only one of them. The latter would be more an exception
than the former. Eating may be partially for the sake of filling the stomach, and partially for
the sake of comfort and amelioration of other needs. One may make love not only for pure
sexual release, but also to convince one's self of one's masculinity, or to make a conquest, to
feel powerful, or to win more basic affection. As an illustration, I may point out that it would
be possible (theoretically if not practically) to analyze a single act of an individual and see in
it the expression of his physiological needs, his safety needs, his love needs, his esteem needs
and self-actualization. This contrasts sharply with the more naive brand of trait psychology
in which one trait or one motive accounts for a certain kind of act, *i.e.*, an aggressive act is
traced solely to a trait of aggressiveness.

MULTIPLE DETERMINANTS OF BEHAVIOR

Not all behavior is determined by the basic needs. We might even say that not all behavior
is motivated. There are many determinants of behavior other than motives.[24] For instance,
one other important class of determinants is the so-called field determinants. Theoretically,
at least, behavior may be determined completely by the field, or even by specific isolated external stimuli, as in association of ideas or certain conditioned reflexes. If in response to the
stimulus word "table," I immediately perceive a memory image of a table, this response certainly has nothing to do with my basic needs.

Secondly, we may call attention again to the concept of "degree of closeness to the basic
needs" or "degree of motivation." Some behavior is highly motivated, other behavior is only
weakly motivated. Some is not motivated at all (but all behavior is determined).

Another important point[25] is that there is a basic difference between expressive behavior and coping behavior (functional striving, purposive goal seeking). An expressive behavior does not try to do anything; it is simply a reflection of the personality. A stupid man
behaves stupidly, not because he wants to, or tries to, or is motivated to, but simply because
he *is* what he is. The same is true when I speak in a bass voice rather than tenor or soprano.
The random movements of a healthy child, the smile on the face of a happy man even when
he is alone, the springiness of the healthy man's walk, and the erectness of his carriage are

other examples of expressive, non-functional behavior. Also the *style* in which a man carries out almost all his behavior, motivated as well as unmotivated, is often expressive.

We may then ask, is *all* behavior expressive or reflective of the character structure? The answer is "No." Rote, habitual, automatized, or conventional behavior may or may not be expressive. The same is true for most "stimulus-bound" behaviors.

It is finally necessary to stress that expressiveness of behavior, and goal-directedness of behavior are not mutually exclusive categories. Average behavior is usually both.

GOALS AS [A] CENTERING PRINCIPLE IN MOTIVATION THEORY

It will be observed that the basic principle in our classification has been neither the instigation nor the motivated behavior but rather the functions, effects, purposes, or goals of the behavior. It has been proven sufficiently by various people that this is the most suitable point for centering in any motivation theory.[26]

ANIMAL- AND HUMAN-CENTERING

This theory starts with the human being rather than any lower and presumably "simpler" animal. Too many of the findings that have been made in animals have been proven to be true for animals but not for the human being. There is no reason whatsoever why we should start with animals in order to study human motivation. The logic or rather illogic behind this general fallacy of "pseudo-simplicity" has been exposed often enough by philosophers and logicians as well as by scientists in each of the various fields. It is no more necessary to study animals before one can study man than it is to study mathematics before one can study geology or psychology or biology.

We may also reject the old, naive behaviorism which assumed that it was somehow necessary, or at least more "scientific" to judge human beings by animal standards. One consequence of this belief was that the whole notion of purpose and goal was excluded from motivational psychology simply because one could not ask a white rat about his purposes. Tolman[27] has long since proven in animal studies themselves that this exclusion was not necessary.

MOTIVATION AND THE THEORY OF PSYCHOPATHOGENESIS

The conscious motivational content of everyday life has, according to the foregoing, been conceived to be relatively important or unimportant accordingly as it is more or less closely related to the basic goals. A desire for an ice-cream cone might actually be an indirect expression of a desire for love. If it is, then this desire for the ice-cream cone becomes [an] extremely important motivation. If however the ice cream is simply something to cool the mouth with or a casual appetitive reaction, then the desire is relatively unimportant. Everyday conscious desires are to be regarded as symptoms, as *surface indicators of more basic needs*. If we were to take these superficial desires at their face value we would find ourselves in a state of complete confusion which could never be resolved, since we would be dealing seriously with symptoms rather than with what lay behind the symptoms.

Thwarting of unimportant desires produces no psychopathological results; thwarting of a basically important need does produce such results. Any theory of psychopathogenesis must then be based on a sound theory of motivation. A conflict or a frustration is not necessarily pathogenic. It becomes so only when it threatens or thwarts the basic needs or partial needs that are closely related to the basic needs.[28]

THE ROLE OF GRATIFIED NEEDS

It has been pointed out above several times that our needs usually emerge only when more prepotent needs have been gratified. Thus gratification has an important role in motivation theory. Apart from this, however, needs cease to play an active determining or organizing role as soon as they are gratified.

What this means is that, *e.g.*, a basically satisfied person no longer has the needs for esteem, love, safety, etc. The only sense in which he might be said to have them is in the almost metaphysical sense that a sated man has hunger, or a filled bottle has emptiness. If we are interested in what *actually* motivates us, and not in what has, will, or might motivate us, then a satisfied need is not a motivator. It must be considered for all practical purposes simply not to exist, to have disappeared. This point should be emphasized because it has been either overlooked or contradicted in every theory of motivation I know.[29] The perfectly healthy, normal, fortunate man has no sex needs or hunger needs, or needs for safety, or for love, or for prestige, or self-esteem, except in stray moments of quickly passing threat. If we were to say otherwise, we should also have to aver that every man had all the pathological reflexes, e.g., Babinski, etc., because if his nervous system were damaged, these would appear.

It is such considerations as these that suggest the bold postulation that a man who is thwarted in any of his basic needs may fairly be envisaged simply as a sick man. This is a fair parallel to our designation as "sick" of the man who lacks vitamins or minerals. Who is to say that a lack of love is less important than a lack of vitamins? Since we know the pathogenic effects of love starvation, who is to say that we are invoking value-questions in an unscientific or illegitimate way, any more than the physician does who diagnoses and treats pellagra or scurvy? If I were permitted this usage, I should then say simply that a healthy man is primarily motivated by his needs to develop and actualize his fullest potentialities and capacities. If a man has any other basic needs in any active, chronic sense, then he is simply an unhealthy man. He is as surely sick as if he had suddenly developed a strong salt-hunger or calcium hunger.[30]

If this statement seems unusual or paradoxical the reader may be assured that this is only one among many such paradoxes that will appear as we revise our ways of looking at man's deeper motivations. When we ask what man wants of life, we deal with his very essence.

Summary

1. There are at least five sets of goals, which we may call basic needs. These are briefly physiological, safety, love, esteem, and self-actualization. In addition, we are motivated by the desire to achieve or maintain the various conditions upon which these basic satisfactions rest and by certain more intellectual desires.

2. These basic goals are related to each other, being arranged in a hierarchy of prepotency. This means that the most prepotent goal will monopolize consciousness and will tend of itself to organize the recruitment of the various capacities of the organism. The less prepotent needs are minimized, even forgotten or denied. But when a need is fairly well satisfied, the next prepotent ("higher") need emerges, in turn to dominate the conscious life and to serve as the center of organization of behavior, since gratified needs are not active motivators.

    Thus man is a perpetually wanting animal. Ordinarily the satisfaction of these wants is not altogether mutually exclusive, but only tends to be. The average member of our society is most often partially satisfied and partially unsatisfied in all of his wants. The hierarchy principle is usually empirically observed in terms of increasing percentages of non-satisfaction as we go up the hierarchy. Reversals of the average order of the hierarchy are sometimes observed. Also it has been observed that an individual may permanently lose the higher wants in the hierarchy under special conditions. There are not only ordinarily multiple motivations for usual behavior, but in addition many determinants other than motives.

3. Any thwarting or possibility of thwarting of these basic human goals, or danger to the defenses which protect them, or to the conditions upon which they rest, is considered to be a psychological threat. With a few exceptions, all psychopathology may be partially traced to such threats. A basically thwarted man may actually be defined as a "sick" man, if we wish.

4. It is such basic threats which bring about the general emergency reactions.

5. Certain other basic problems have not been dealt with because of limitations of space. Among these are (a) the problem of values in any definitive motivation theory, (b) the relation between appetites, desires, needs and what is "good" for the organism, (c) the etiology of the basic needs and their possible derivation in early childhood, (d) redefinition of motivational concepts, i.e., drive, desire, wish, need, goal, (e) implication of our theory for hedonistic theory, (f) the nature of the uncompleted act, of success and failure, and of aspiration-level, (g) the role of association, habit, and conditioning, (h) relation to the theory of inter-personal relations, (i) implications for psychotherapy, (j) implication for theory of society, (k) the theory of selfishness, (l) the relation between needs and cultural patterns, (m) the relation between this theory and Allport's theory of functional autonomy. These as well as certain other less important questions must be considered as motivation theory attempts to become definitive.

1. Maslow, A. H. A preface to motivation theory. *Psychosomatic Med.*, 1943, 5, 85–92.
2. Wertheimer, M. Unpublished lectures at the New School for Social Research.
3. Goldstein, K. *The organism.* New York: American Book Co., 1939.
4. Freud, S. *New introductory lectures on psychoanalysis.* New York: Norton, 1933.
5. Adler, A. *Social interest.* London: Faber & Faber, 1938.
6. Cannon, W. B. *Wisdom of the body.* New York: Norton, 1932.
7. Young, P. T. The experimental analysis of appetite. *Psychol. Bull*, 1941, 38, 129–164.
8. Maslow, A. H. A preface to motivation theory. *Psychosomatic Med.*, 1943, 5, 85–92.
9. As the child grows up, sheer knowledge and familiarity as well as better motor development make these "dangers" less and less dangerous and more and more manageable. Throughout life it may be said that one of the main conative functions of education is this neutralizing of apparent dangers through knowledge, e.g., I am not afraid of thunder because I know something about it.

10. Shirley, M. Children's adjustments to a strange situation. *J. Abnorm. (soc.) Psychol.*, 1942, 37, 201–217.

11. A "test battery" for safety might be confronting the child with a small exploding firecracker or with a bewhiskered face, having the mother leave the room, putting him upon a high ladder, a hypodermic injection, having a mouse crawl up to him, etc. Of course I cannot seriously recommend the deliberate use of such "tests" for they might very well harm the child being tested. But these and similar situations come up by the score in the child's ordinary day-to-day living and may be observed. There is no reason why these stimuli should not be used with, for example, young chimpanzees.

12. Not all neurotic individuals feel unsafe. Neurosis may have at its core a thwarting of the affection and esteem needs in a person who is generally safe.

13. Maslow, A. H. & Mittelmann, B. *Principles of abnormal psychology*. New York: Harper & Bros., 1941.

14. Goldstein, K. *The organism*. New York: American Book Co., 1939.

15. Maslow, A. H. & Mittelmann, B. *Principles of abnormal psychology*. New York: Harper & Bros., 1941.

16. For further details see Maslow, A. H. The dynamics of psychological security-insecurity. *Character & Pers.*, 1942, 10, 331–344 and Plant, J. *Personality and the cultural pattern*. New York: Commonwealth Fund, 1937, Chapter 5.

17. Whether or not this particular desire is universal we do not know. The crucial question, especially important today, is "Will men who are enslaved and dominated inevitably feel dissatisfied and rebellious?" We may assume on the basis of commonly known clinical data that a man who has known true freedom (not paid for by giving up safety and security but rather built on the basis of adequate safety and security) will not willingly or easily allow his freedom to be taken away from him. But we do not know that this is true for the person born into slavery. The events of the next decade should give us our answer. See discussion of this problem in Fromm, E. *Escape from freedom*. New York: Farrar and Rinehart, 1941.

18. Perhaps the desire for prestige and respect from others is subsidiary to the desire for self-esteem or confidence in oneself. Observation of children seems to indicate that this is so, but clinical data give no clear support for such a conclusion.

19. For more extensive discussion of normal self-esteem, as well as for reports of various researches, see Maslow, A. H. Dominance, personality and social behavior in women. *J. Soc. Psychol.*, 1939, 10, 3–39.

20. Kardiner, A. *The traumatic neurosis of war*. New York: Hoeber, 1941.

21. Clearly creative behavior, like painting, is like any other behavior in having multiple determinants. It may be seen in "innately creative" people whether they are satisfied or not, happy or unhappy, hungry or sated. Also it is clear that creative activity may be compensatory, ameliorative or purely economic. It is my impression (as yet unconfirmed) that it is possible to distinguish the artistic and intellectual products of basically satisfied people from those of basically unsatisfied people by inspection alone. In any case, here too we must distinguish, in a dynamic fashion, the overt behavior itself from its various motivations or purposes.

22. Wertheimer, M. Unpublished lectures at the New School for Social Research.

23. Levy, D. M. Primary affect hunger. *Amer. J. Psychiat.*, 1937, 94, 643–652.

24. I am aware that many psychologists and psychoanalysts use the term "motivated" and "determined" synonymously, *e.g.*, Freud. But I consider this an obfuscating usage. Sharp distinctions are necessary for clarity of thought and precision in experimentation.

25. To be discussed fully in a subsequent publication.

26. The interested reader is referred to the very excellent discussion of this point in Murray's *Explorations in Personality* (Murray, H. A., et al. *Explorations in personality*. New York: Oxford University Press, 1938).

27. Tolman, E. C. *Purposive behavior in animals and men*. New York: Century, 1932.

28. Maslow, A. H. Conflict, frustration, and the theory of threat. *J. Abnorm. (Soc.) Psychol.*, 1943, 38, 81–86.

29. Note that acceptance of this theory necessitates basic revision of the Freudian theory.

30. If we were to use the word "sick" in this way, we should then also have to face squarely the relations of man to his society. One clear implication of our definition would be that (1) since a man is to be called sick who is basically thwarted, and (2) since such basic thwarting is made possible ultimately only by forces outside the individual, then (3) sickness in the individual must come ultimately from a sickness in the society. The "good" or healthy society would then be defined as one that permitted man's highest purposes to emerge by satisfying all his prepotent basic needs.

Commentary

This essay and the subsequent works that elaborated on it made Abraham Maslow a famous figure in American psychology. He was also a tragic figure at a scale worthy of ancient

Greek drama. Like his humanistic colleagues Maslow was simultaneously a product and a leader of his times. These theorists were passionate in advocating their visions of humanity during the post–World War II and Cold War years. Maslow was distinguished, however, by the intellectual lengths to which he was willing to go in promoting his vision of humanity, as well as the depths of his disappointments and bitterness when the world did not fulfill his ideals.

A MAN OF AND FOR HIS TIMES
INTERPLAY OF BIOGRAPHY AND HISTORY

Maslow had a difficult childhood (Hoffman, 1988). He was the son of Russian Jewish immigrants and experienced anti-Semitism growing up in Brooklyn in the 1910s and 1920s. He was often bullied as a child, and, by his account, his parents were emotionally abusive. His father was distant and often absent. The mother kept a lock on the refrigerator so that Abraham could eat only at her whim. At one point she killed in front of him kittens he had rescued. As a child Maslow withdrew. He had few friends but loved books and was an exceptional student. We do not have to revert to the psychoanalytic theories, which Maslow himself was revising, to see the deeply personal roots of his vision: the first-generation American's paean to freedom and the bullied and unloved child's quest to escape the past and embrace an idealized potential.

In the 1930s Maslow was completing postdoctorate work in psychology at Columbia University. At that time many German intellectuals, fleeing Nazi repression, were taking positions in New York City. Maslow made connections with some of these leading minds in psychology, including Kurt Goldstein, from whom he took the idea of self-actualization; Alfred Adler, who mentored Maslow and whose individualistic ideas of self-creation influenced Maslow's work; and the Gestalt psychologist Max Wertheimer, whose views of "real thinking" were also reflected in Maslow's work. (See Chapter 8 on Wertheimer in this volume.)

FOCUS ON CREATIVITY

In the economic growth of postwar America, the idea of creativity was also becoming increasingly important (Hanchett Hanson, 2015; Weiner, 2000). Here again Maslow reflected and led his times. In the 1943 essay, he was already discussing creativity, but mostly as exceptions to the motivational norms he was proposing. Later he elaborated considerably, particularly on the relationship between self-actualization and creativity. In a preliminary "study" of self-actualized individuals (see discussion below), Maslow defined self-actualization as broadly fitting the concept as used in everyday speech. These were people who were both achievement-oriented and lacked neuroses (Maslow, 1954/1970). Acknowledging that many creative people might not fit this definition because of neuroses, Maslow distinguished the concepts of self-actualization and creativity. All self-actualized people were creative, but not all creative people were self-actualized. Furthermore Maslow saw creative thinking in everyday actions, not just extraordinary achievements. In all contexts, though, creative thinking was elevated above other ways of thinking. Creative thinking was *real thinking* (Maslow, 1954/1970). It was bold, courageous, and always adaptive, as opposed to "habit, expectation, learning, custom and convention" (p. 222).

Later still, Maslow (1962/2011) proposed a typology of creativity with three types: *primary creativity* defined as a tendency toward creative ideation in any activity; *secondary creativity* describing the hard work of consolidation and application of preexisting ideas; and *integrated creativity,* including both the primary and secondary types. Although in theory all three types were important, Maslow argued that primary creativity should be the focus of research. In spite of humanistic concerns with the development of meaningful lives and claims of holism, then, Maslow put research back to almost the exact same place that Guilford (1950) had proposed with the idea of divergent thinking. For practical purposes, creativity was treated as a kind of trait that was at once reductive and abstract, an ability to come up with lots of unusual ideas about anything without meaningful regard for context, experience, goals, or development.

Here Maslow added emphasis on child-like innocence, again building on themes from the 1943 essay on motivation. Child-like immersion in the moment defined primary creativity, which involved uninhibited "giving up" (Maslow, 1971/1993, p. 61) of senses of past and future. Yes, adults demonstrating secondary or integrated creativity would have to develop more sophisticated perspectives, but the focus of psychology should be on this child-like innocence for people of any age. This kind of rhetoric, promoted by Maslow and others, has become so common that it may not even seem peculiar today. It is easy to forget that developmental theorists, like Piaget and Vygotsky, did not support this kind of artificial splitting off and idealization of children's ideation. For Piaget, uninhibited ideational combinations were treated as part of the developmental path toward abstract thought. For Vygotsky (1930/2004), imagination was crucial to life and creativity across the lifespan, but the innocent imagination of childhood was inherently inferior to the sophisticated versions of adults. Maslow's odd splitting off of one aspect of child development as a heroic ideal for the "real thinking" of everyone devalued social awareness, perspective taking, contextual sensitivity, learning, and planning—achievements of development. It also devalued many children. Although he did not cite the then still nascent attachment theories, Maslow was aware that not all children were boldly imaginative. Great artists were like bold children but explicitly *not* like those who clung to their mothers (Maslow, 1954/1970). His air of contempt for vulnerabilities, even those of children, would be a consistent theme throughout Maslow's work.

TRAGEDIES

THE BIG PICTURE: NOT SCIENCE, NOT CLEAR, AND PROBABLY NOT TRUE

THE MOTIVATIONAL HIERARCHY

Maslow's hierarchy of motivation was an impressive synthesis, a hypothesis that integrated fragments from very different types of research, themselves grounded in different theoretical frameworks. The hierarchy hypothesis was not itself based on research, however. Yes, the idea made sense, but psychological questions often turn out to be more complex than general impressions. Of course, Maslow tried to account for complexities with many possible exceptions—so many that the exceptions themselves become problematic. Let us begin, though, with subsequent research on the basic assumptions of the hierarchy.

After Maslow published this theory, a number of researchers tried to validate it. Mahmoud A. Wahba and Lawrence G. Bridwell (1976) analyzed the data from many of these studies, including factor analyses, cross-sectional studies, and longitudinal studies. One of the questions that would have to be validated is whether or not Maslow chose the right needs for his five levels. Wahba and Bridwell analyzed 10 studies using factor analyses of questionnaires designed to validate the five levels of motivation. None supported all five of Maslow's categories as independent factors. One found four distinct factors that corresponded to Maslow's theory, but two did not find support for any of the five factors as independent categories. Some studies found that some deficiency factors (e.g., esteem) and growth factors (e.g., self-actualization) clustered independently. Self-actualization was an independent factor in some studies, and in others it was not. Concerning the factor analyses, the authors concluded, "Overall, the results . . . are clearly not supportive of Maslow's need classification scheme" (p. 220). Other factor analyses studied human need classifications without reference to Maslow or other specific theories. These did not support the five categories that Maslow proposed or the hierarchy.

Another key aspect of Maslow's hierarchy is the relationship between deprivation and domination (importance of the need). The higher the deprivation, the more important the need. Reviewing 10 studies, Wahba and Bridwell (1976) found support for the deprivation-domination thesis in autonomy and self-actualization but not for security, social, and esteem needs.

The other side of the deprivation question is gratification-activation: Does some degree of gratification at one level of the hierarchy trigger movement toward the next? Wahba and Bridwell (1976) reviewed four cross-sectional studies designed specifically to test this aspect of Maslow's theory. Two of the studies showed no support for Maslow's theory, and two showed limited support. One did show that people tend to regress to the lowest level of Maslow's hierarchy in a deprived environment. According to Wahba & Bridwell, these findings suggested that deprivation-domination might function only for physiological needs.

All of the experimental and quasi-experimental studies suffered from being able to test only small portions of a sweeping theory that was supposed to apply to the entire lifespan. The best way to analyze Maslow's hierarchy would be with longitudinal studies. Wahba and Bridwell (1976) analyzed two such studies that were specifically designed to test Maslow's theory, using cross-lagged and static correlational analyses. Neither study found substantial support for the theory. One did show that managers' concerns moved from safety to growth as they advanced in position, but the authors concluded that this was a function of career stage rather than need hierarchy. Yet in spite of little evidence in its favor and considerable evidence against it, Wahba and Bridwell concluded that Maslow's theory was still hard to categorically disprove in part because the theory was not designed to be tested.

Just reading the 1943 essay confirms their contention. This was not a theory of behavior, in part, because there were multiple determinants for behavior, beyond motivation. In addition, although the motivations were structured as a hierarchy, multiple motivations contributed to behaviors as simple as eating ice cream. Although Maslow's descriptions of the levels were almost entirely of conscious desires, he asserted that most functions of the motivations would be unconscious. (That itself invalidates self-report methods used in many studies of motivation.) Maslow cited developmental impacts in some situations. For example, early, consistent gratification or prolonged deprivation could lead to increased frustration tolerance. Those arguments, however, contradicted the bold assertion that once a need is satisfied, it can no longer motivate: satisfied needs "must be considered for all practical purposes simply not to exist, to have disappeared" (Maslow, 1943, p. 393).

As Maslow (1943, p. 394) stated at the end of the essay, he was attempting to analyze the "very essence" of humanity. Even if one accepts the concept of such an essence, how can it be studied if it is not consciously accessible, is not discernable through behavior, and has no developmental impact in most situations? Indeed apart from the question of how to study such a theory, why study it?

If psychological research does not support but cannot quite invalidate the theory, it rests on its face validity. Even on the basis of everyday logic, though, the theory has problems. Some critics (e.g., Geller, 1982; Rutledge, 2011) have noted the lack of consideration of social and interpersonal contexts in Maslow's hierarchy. In Maslow's hierarchy people *gratify* their needs for love and esteem, which affect the extent of development but not the course of the individual's development. Instead the impact of social relations on the individual is primarily to get the person to the next level of motivation. For Maslow's (1943, p. 395) "perpetually wanting animal," love is important because it allows the person to advance to acquiring the esteem of others, which allows the person to advance to self-actualization. Remember that this instrumental view of love and esteem are not just aspects of these experiences in certain circumstances but the "very essence" of the human.

A young psychologist publishes a theory without sufficient evidence but supporting the individualism of the ideologies of his nation in a time of war. The essay synthesizes ideas from different quarters of psychology and juxtaposes strong, confident, healthy, freedom-loving people to "some neurotic adults" at home and those "who search for a protector, or a stronger person on whom he may depend, or perhaps, a Fuehrer" (Maslow, 1943, p. 380) abroad. Such work might be considered historically interesting and scientifically questionable, but not exceptional. Can it be called tragic? As the basis of a life's work by an intelligent man who would put so much of his considerable energy and passion into elaborating it, this was tragedy. Furthermore there is a tragic dimension to the continued use of this theory in some circles even today, apparently based mostly on its logic and individualistic ideology.

On the other hand, as is evident at the end of the essay as well as in Maslow's subsequent work, the most important feature of his theory is the pinnacle of the hierarchy: self-actualization. If that proposition is true, the details of the specific levels of motivation and how they work might just be nuances to repair. Unfortunately Maslow's concept of self-actualization leads to even murkier territory.

THE SELF-ACTUALIZATION STUDY

By his own account, a cornerstone of Maslow's (1954/1970) vision of the self-actualized person came from a "study" he conducted of people he considered to be self-actualized. Although Maslow acknowledged that this research had methodological weaknesses, he treated the data more seriously than was justified. The analysis came down to his personal opinions concerning partial biographies of people he admired. The criteria for inclusion were vague: (1) the subjects had to lack neurotic symptoms, and (2) they had to fit the definition of self-actualization as used in ordinary language. In the end 23 individuals were analyzed: nine historical figures (Jane Addams, Albert Einstein, Aldous Huxley, William James, Thomas Jefferson, Abraham Lincoln in his later years, Eleanor Roosevelt, Albert Schweitzer, Baruch Spinoza), nine living contemporaries whom Maslow knew, and five partial cases of contemporaries Maslow himself did not think fully fit his criteria but could be useful to the study. There was an obvious lack of cultural and historical diversity in this investigation of a phenomenon that, according to the 1943 essay, approached the "common-human." That is just one among many problems, however. Many of the living people refused to participate, and even for most of the historical figures Maslow himself did not believe he had complete data. The "findings" were not presented as individual case studies, which would have required justification of interpretations of specific behaviors. Instead Maslow presented an overall profile of what these "self-actualized people" were like.

He found 18 groups of characteristics, most of which—by design—fit the ideas of self-actualization that Maslow and other humanistic psychologists were promoting. (Remember: fitting the common concept of self-actualization was a criterion for including them in the study. The term "self-actualization" had just been coined by Goldstein and then picked up and promoted by humanistic psychologists, including Maslow.) For example, Maslow found his subjects to be spontaneous and unconventional with a child-like enthusiasm for the world but not antagonistic to authority.

There were more disconcerting findings, though. The people Maslow studied tended to be aloof. They simultaneously felt deeply about humanity and alienated. They spent a great deal of time alone and were at times vain, hot-tempered, and ruthless. When they broke off close relationships, they might not show ambivalence or regret, and some did not grieve when loved ones died. Maslow admitted these points, but his analysis revealed the bias of the entire project. These antisocial attributes were not even potentially problematic. He did not consider that these behaviors might be linked to his subjects' extreme sense of autonomy or to their sense of alienation. He did not consider that lack of guilt, regret, or grief might indicate an overall avoidance of or compensation for negative emotions. Instead Maslow concluded that these attitudes were signs of the extraordinary strength of self-actualized people, strengths that ordinary people could not appreciate. The weak simply could not understand the strong.

INTERPLAY OF IDEALS AND CONTEMPT

This interplay between idealistic optimism and contempt for weakness was already evident in the 1943 essay. There the environment of freedom was the central requirement for actualization. Those who did not self-actualize were not described as unfortunate, however. They were *sick*, akin to someone suffering from malnutrition. Over time this initial hint of contempt would grow considerably as Maslow's optimism faded.

An aspect of Maslow's thinking that would remain constant during this shift was patriotism. In 1943 "the Fuehrer" was mentioned only once, even though the overall description of the kind of society that facilitated self-actualization unquestionably fit American ideals and implicitly condemned images of Nazi conformity. During the Cold War Maslow was even more explicit. He argued that American freedom and diversity would encourage more countries to become allies with the US against the Soviet Union (Maslow, 1971/1993). (The striking exception to the argument for diversity was Maslow's view of homosexuals, whom he grouped with "sadists . . . neurotics, psychotics, suicidals" [p. 12].)

THE IDEALS

As the freedom argument became more explicitly patriotic, so did seemingly incompatible ideals of social engineering. The Cold War arguments concerning freedom and diversity, cited above, were presented as part of a call for development of a "Heraclitan" human, one who was strong and almost infinitely adaptable (Maslow, 1971/1993). This social engineering argument accompanied the awareness that few people were self-actualized, even given the freedom of living in America. Meanwhile, in his journals, Maslow (1982) was thinking more as a social Darwinist. Since the early 1960s he had written in his journals about "aggridants" (e.g., pp. 22–24, 231, 340), people who would self-actualize, not because of social privilege but because of biological superiority. This line of thinking was reflected in the evolution of his theory of motivation. Over time the lower needs were seen as dependent on one's environment, as described in the 1943 essay. External factors determined whether or not needs for food and security could be satisfied. The higher, growth needs, like self-actualization, depended on the person. Not self-actualizing once lower needs were met was due to flaws in the person.

THE CONTEMPT

With this enthusiasm for apparent strength came increasingly explicit contempt for people whom Maslow considered weak. His study of self-actualized people led him to see people who did not determine their own destinies as "profoundly sick, abnormal or weak," "flabby whiners" (Maslow, 1954/1970, p. 161). To support his social-engineering vision, he proposed that the Heraclitan person was crucial to democratic societies, which needed their self-starting strength. Democracies specifically did not need the "whiners." As the importance of biological superiority of "aggridants" grew in Maslow's thinking, the solutions for the weak became darker. In his journals he wrote about neglecting inferior humans so that they would die off or commit suicide (Maslow, 1982).

In the later 1960s Maslow no longer felt sympathy for many of his students, who were using their freedom to protest the Vietnam War, or for fellow academics who were taking more critical stances toward American policies (Hoffman, 1988; Maslow, 1982). Always the Cold Warrior, Maslow supported the Vietnam war and, characteristically, felt contempt for his students' views. He died in 1970 at the age of 62. Reading his journals from the last few years of his life reveals a man who was becoming increasingly isolated from the world where he had worked most of his life and alienated from the sociopolitical climate of the country he so loved. In those entries he described himself as a lone voice, speaking the truth before others could see it. Rather than question any of his own views, he took refuge in his rugged individualist identity. The last entry in his published journal is from May 7, 1970, one month before he died. After describing his isolation, he ended the entry, "So *again* I must stay to myself: to work!" (Maslow, 1982, p. 355).

Maslow's story is complex. He was not an intellectual thinking about human potential with scientific remove. He was passionate and intensely personal, building his ideas around deep contempt for some and idealization of others. The traumas of his childhood may have contributed. The historical context also played a role. In addition, the idea of self-actualization itself carries tragic potential. For without childhood traumas or his confrontational temperament or judgmental style or the Cold War, the course of Maslow's thinking still makes sense. He was extending the assumptions of self-actualization.

THE LOGIC OF SELF-ACTUALIZATION

Maslow came to Goldstein's idea of self-actualization with a concern for achieving human ideals. Another, very different psychologist, Carl Rogers (1951, 1961/1989), came to the same idea as a clinician, concerned with helping people who were in distress. In spite of the differences between Rogers and Maslow, in some ways the logic of self-actualization laid the same traps for both.

Rogers saw the self as developing within a perceptual field. The obstacles to self-actualization were primarily the internalization of others' expectations. Everyone made a choice: to follow one's own honest reactions to the perceptual field or to try to please others. The first led to more adaptive and spontaneous people who were following the drive to self-actualize. These people would always react rationally to their environment, given the available information. In contrast, trying to please others led to tension, rigidity, and neuroses. Honesty within the perceptual field did not make everything "sweetness and light" (Rogers, 1951, p. 521) but more real, comfortable, and adaptive.

That view allows for complexity in life and difficulties, but still emphasizes the individual's actions *on* the world more than *within* it. Relational aspects of development are important but secondary to the individual's perceptions. The more difficult twist came with actualization as the single drive and goal of development. As in Maslow, the logic of self-actualization led Rogers to an idealized split between people as they are and as they *should be*, even though Rogers's more conventional, psychological view of the "unhealthy" was less shocking than Maslow's open contempt for the weak. In clinical work, Rogers (1951, 1961/1989) advocated that the therapist take a position of *unconditional positive regard* for the patient. He also advocated *unconditional positive regard* in education to nurture creativity (Rogers, 1954). This approach may have been a needed corrective in respecting patients' and students' points of view. As Rogers recognized, however, authentic positive regard is often difficult. Patients were often in "pretty sad shape" (Rogers in Kirschenbaum & Henderson, 1989, p. 61). In that case, he said that the therapist had to maintain positive regard for the patient's *potential,* not for the patient as he or she presented (Kirschenbaum & Henderson, 1989). A similar argument was made for nurturing creativity: the positive regard was for *potential* (Rogers, 1954). The idea of such a potential being more than a construction of the therapist's or teacher's own imagination makes sense only within the view of self-actualization as singular, unidirectional, and always good. In Rogers's (1951, 1961/1989) view, achievement and success as a murderer, thief, demagogue, fascist, or terrorist was not self-actualization, but a perversion of the person's innate rationality. If people were just honest about their perceptions, they would be reasonable, constructive, and *creative*.

If, however, life is more complex than that, and people contain the potential to be both good or bad, there is a problem. If, even when honest about perceptions, people are not necessarily rational, there is a problem. If "good" is inherently a matter of perspective and open to interpretation, rather than simply a rational reaction to one's environment, there is also a problem. These possibilities undermine both Maslow's Heraclitan heroes and Rogers's idealized concept of potential.

Critics of self-actualization have taken just such positions. Two well-known exchanges challenged Rogers's view of self-actualization as overly simplistic. In one, the philosopher Martin Buber argued that people have the potential for both what people would generally call good and what they would call bad in their given context (Kirschenbaum & Henderson, 1989). The direction a person's development takes depends on relationships in the person's life, and true positive regard for the person's potential had to accept the person's current and the potential "good" and the "bad." Similarly, the existential psychologist Rollo May (1982/1989) argued that the reason creativity is important is because human nature always holds the potential for good and evil. Therefore creativity was not a form of child-like play but an anxiety-filled, existential encounter between the self and the world, one in which the complexity of human nature always make the stakes high and outcomes uncertain (see also May, 1974). Furthermore, in holding to a view of the individual self as innately good and rational, Rogers was simply projecting people's evil onto the world. Far from achieving the rationalism on which Rogers built his views (in line with the ideals to which Maslow aspired), Rogers had set up false dichotomies in order to maintain a narcissistic view of the individual as pure, according to May. The cost of this view was high since the creation of self and culture were intrinsically intertwined.

Richard Evans (1975) asserted that the individualism of self-actualization set up unrealistic expectations of personal achievement and happiness, without consideration of human relations and context in general. When such expectations were not met, ironically the individuals felt like failures instead of self-actualized. From a philosophical perspective, Leonard Geller (1982) analyzed the logical incoherence of theories of self-actualization and concluded that the imperative to self-actualize actually made the human interactions needed for growth more difficult. He noted the "bitter irony" that Maslow and Rogers, who were deeply concerned about the human condition, developed theories that "strengthened the very dehumanization against which they were reacting" (p. 72).

MASLOW AS TRAGEDY

Much of the self-actualization rhetoric brings Nietzsche to mind: individualism, the idealization of the superman, "become what thou art" (Nietzsche, 1882/1910, p. 209), contempt for "herd morality" (1886/1966). As I have written elsewhere in this volume, Nietzsche continues to provide important, thought-provoking challenges to our concepts of creativity. At the same time, the problems encountered in applying the idea of self-actualization are those of the extreme individualism often associated with Nietzsche's philosophy. A key difference is that Nietzsche (1872/1967) embraced tragedy as an aesthetic that the ancient Greeks knew but modernity had lost. His key imperative was accepting life fully and enthusiastically, a good in and of itself as it presents, not as an imagined potential or idealized self. He specifically argued against instrumental views of the joy of life, like the promise of political or economic success that the humanistic Cold Warriors promised (Nietzsche, 1882/1910).

Indeed the ancient Greek sense of tragedy comes to mind in contemplating Maslow's work. In the path from antifascist advocate of freedom to a fascist-like vision of the rule of the biologically superior, each step made some sense—as long as self-actualization was always the ultimate, singular, and positive goal. As in the case of Oedipus, it is the circular conclusion that is tragic. Maslow's life and work can be seen as a cautionary tale: reminders of the need for questioning our own assumptions, using the tools of scientific investigation to avoid unwarranted conclusions, trying to take into account the complexities of our own perspectives and contexts. The dimensions of his passion, aspirations, and determination as simultaneous virtues and self-defeating flaws outstrip any idea of mere caution, however. The nearly "common-human" may well be the always present potential for tragedy in the human experience as expressed through his work and life, rather than the promised fruits of self-actualization. For, today, we can no more ensure achievement of ideals or the goodness of our perspectives than could those who championed self-actualization. In the end, Maslow's story evokes an appreciation of pervasive human frailties in ways that he probably would have hated.

References

Evans, R. I. (1975). *Carl Rogers: The man and his ideas*. New York, NY: E. P. Dutton.

Geller, L. (1982). The failure of self-actualization theory: A critique of Carl Rogers and Abraham Maslow. *Journal of Humanistic Psychology, 22*(2), 56–73.

Goldstein, K. (1935/1995). *The organism: A holistic approach to biology derived from pathological data in man*. New York, NY: Zone Books. (Original work published in German; English translation first published 1939)

Guilford, J. P. (1950). Creativity. *American Psychologist, 5*, 444–454.

Hanchett Hanson, M. (2015). *Worldmaking: Psychology and the ideology of creativity*. London: Palgrave Macmillan.

Harrington, A. (1998). Kurt Goldstein's neurology of healing and wholeness: A Weimar story. In C. Lawrence & G. Weisz (Eds.), *Greater than the parts: Wholeness in biomedicine 1920–1950* (pp. 25–45). Oxford: Oxford University Press.

Hoffman, E. (1988). *The right to be human: A biography of Abraham Maslow* (rev. ed.). New York, NY: Tarcher.

Kirschenbaum, H., & Henderson, V. L. (Eds.). (1989). *Carl Rogers: Dialogues*. Boston: Houghton Mifflin.

Maslow, A. H. (1943). A theory of human motivation. *Psychological Review, 50*(4), 370–396.

Maslow, A. H. (1954/1970). *Motivation and personality*. New York, NY: Harper & Row.

Maslow, A. H. (1962/2011). *Toward a psychology of being*. Mansfield Centre, CT: Martino.

Maslow, A. H. (1971/1993). *The farther reaches of human nature*. New York, NY: Penguin Books.

Maslow, A. H. (1982). *The journals of Abraham Maslow* (abridged ed.) (R. J. Lowry & J. Freedman, Eds.). Lexington, MA: Lewis.

May, R. (1974). *The courage to create*. New York, NY: Norton.

May, R. (1982/1989). The problem of evil: An open letter to Carl Rogers. In H. Kirschenbaum & V. L. Henderson (Eds.), *Carl Rogers: Dialogues* (pp. 239–51). Boston: Houghton Mifflin.

Nietzsche, F. (1872/1967). *The birth of tragedy and the case of Wagner* (W. Kaufmann, Trans.). New York: Random House.

Nietzsche, F. (1882/1910) *The joyful wisdom* (La gaya scienza) (T. Common, Trans.). In O. Levy (Ed.), *The complete works of Friedrich Nietzsche*. Vol. 10. London: T. N. Foulis. (Original published in German as *Die fröhliche Wissenschaft*)

Nietzsche, F. (1886/1966). *Beyond good and evil* (W. Kaufmann, Trans.). New York, NY: Vintage Books.

Rogers, C. R. (1951). *Client-centered therapy*. New York, NY: Houghton Mifflin.

Rogers, C. R. (1954). Toward a theory of creativity. *Review of General Semantics, 11*(4), 249–260.

Rogers, C. R. (1961/1989). *On becoming a person: A therapist's view of psychotherapy*. New York, NY: Houghton Mifflin.

Rutledge, P. B. (2011). Social networks: What Maslow misses. *Psychology Today*. Retrieved from: https://www.psychologytoday.com/blog/positively-media/201111/social-networks-what-maslow-misses-0.

Sacks, O. (1995). Foreword. In K. Goldstein, *The organism: A holistic approach to biology derived from pathological data in man* (pp. 7–14). New York, NY: Zone Books.

Stahnisch, F., & Hoffmann, T. (2010). Kurt Goldstein and the neurology of movement during the interwar years: Physiological experimentation, clinical psychology and early rehabilitation. In C. Hoffstadt, F. Peschke, A. Schulz-Buchta, & M. Nagenborg (Eds.), *Was bewegt uns? Menschen im Spannungsfeld zwischen Mobilität und Beschleuningung* (pp. 283–312). Bochum, Germany: Projekt Verlag.

Vygotsky, L. S. (1930/2004). Imagination and creativity in childhood. *Journal of Russian and East European Psychology, 42*(1), 7–97. Retrieved from: http://lchc.ucsd.edu/mca/Mail/xmcamail.2008_03.dir/att-0189/Vygotsky__Imag___Creat_in_Childhood.pdf.

Wahba, M. A., & Bridwell, L. G. (1976). Maslow reconsidered: A review of research on the need hierarchy theory. *Organizational Behavior and Human Performance, 15*, 212–240. Retrieved from: http://larrybridwell.com/Maslo.pdf.

Weiner, R. P. (2000). *Creativity and beyond: Cultures, values and change*. Albany: State University of New York Press.

13

Do We Make Our Own Luck?

Reflections on Ernst Mach's Analysis of Invention and Discovery

DAVID H. CROPLEY

Summary

In 1896 Ernst Mach began his tenure as a professor at the University of Vienna by reflecting on the role that accident might play in the process of discovery and invention. In this chapter, his paper is dissected with the benefit of a modern view of creativity. Notwithstanding a mistranslation of the central concept of his discussion, Mach's analysis of the intersection of elements of the person, the process, and the environment is a surprisingly current, psychological view of creativity and innovation.

Introduction

Ernst Mach (1838–1916) is renowned for his contributions in physics, especially in relation to the physics of sound and fluid mechanics. Both the *Mach number*, the ratio of the relative velocity of a body and fluid to the local velocity of sound in the fluid, and the *Mach angle*, relating to the supersonic movement of a body in a fluid, are named after him. He was also known for his contributions to the philosophy of science, in particular, to logical positivism.

The present work (Mach, 1896) is the text of the inaugural lecture given by Mach on taking up the professorship of history and theory of inductive science at the University of Vienna, on October 20, 1895, and was published in *The Monist*[1] in January 1896.

---

1. *The Monist* is a quarterly, peer-reviewed journal, first established in 1890 and addressing topics in philosophy. The journal ceased publication in 1936 but resumed publication in 1962 and is now published by Oxford University Press.

Mach's lecture/paper begins, in keeping with the nature of his appointment, by examining the interrelationship between *philosophy* and *science*. Careful examination suggests that he was differentiating between *induction* (that is, theory generation) and *deduction* (namely, theory testing). Mach's purpose here—and a reason it is relevant to creativity research—is to set the scene for an interdisciplinary view of the scientific world. More specifically, he seeks to shed light on "the relations between physics, psychology, and theory of knowledge," using "the part which accidental circumstances play in the development of inventions and discoveries" (1896, p. 163). Mach, in other words, saw key aspects of creativity, problem-solving, and innovation as an exemplar of an interdisciplinary application of the scientific method.

Mach's paper ranges across topics central to creativity, touching on elements of the process of problem-solving, the value of inventions, the role of memory and experience in creativity, attention, and many other concepts that nowadays influence creativity research. His paper has been moderately influential, having been cited, for example, by Teresa Amabile (1983) in her enormously successful "The Social Psychology of Creativity: A Componential Conceptualization." However, Mach's greatest tangible impact in creativity research has been as a catalyst for the concept of blind variation and selective retention, first mooted by Campbell (1960) and expanded by Simonton (e.g., 2003).

Notwithstanding this impact, it may be argued that the true value of Mach's work on invention and discovery is to remind us that creativity (and innovation) bring together key concepts from psychology (e.g., cognition, personality, motivation) and blend these with application domains (e.g., engineering, teaching) to help explain how novel and useful solutions to problems are generated and exploited.

Reading: "On the Part Played by Accident in Invention and Discovery"

Source: Mach, E. (1896). On the part played by accident in invention and discovery. *The Monist, 6(2)*, 161–175. Reproduced in full. Work in the public domain.

It is characteristic of the naive and sanguine beginnings of thought in youthful men and nations, that all problems are held to be soluble and fundamentally intelligible on the first appearance of success. The sage of Miletus, on seeing the plant take its rise from moisture, believed he had comprehended the whole of nature, and he of Samos, on discovering that definite numbers corresponded to the lengths of harmonical strings, imagined he could exhaust the nature of the world by means of numbers. Philosophy and science in such periods are blended. Wider experience, however, speedily discloses the error of this course, gives rise to criticism, and leads to the division and ramification of the sciences.

At the same time, the necessity of a broad and general view of the world remains; and to meet this need philosophy parts company with special inquiry. It is true, the two are often found united in gigantic personalities. But as a rule their ways diverge more and more widely from each other. And if the estrangement of philosophy from science can reach a point where data unworthy of the nursery are deemed none too scanty as foundations of the world, on the other hand the thorough-paced specialist may go to the extreme of rejecting point-blank the possibility of a broader view, or at least of deeming it superfluous, forgetful of Voltaire's apothegm, nowhere more applicable than here, *Le superflu—chose très nécessaire.*

It is true, the history of philosophy, owing to the insufficiency of its constructive data, is and must be largely a history of error. But it would be the height of ingratitude on our part to forget that the seeds of thoughts which still fructify the soil of special research, such as the theory of irrationals, the conceptions of conservation, the doctrine of evolution, the idea of the specific energies, and so forth, may be traced back in distant ages to philosophical sources. Furthermore, to have deferred or abandoned the attempt at a broad philosophical view of the world from a full knowledge of the insufficiency of our materials, is quite a different thing from never having undertaken it at all. The revenge of its neglect, moreover, is constantly visited upon the specialist by his committal of the very errors which philosophy long ago disclosed. As a fact, in physics and physiology, particularly during the first half of this century, are to be met intellectual productions which for naive simplicity yield not an iota to those of the Ionian school, or to the Platonic ideas, or to that much reviled ontological proof.

Latterly, there has been evidence of a gradual change in this state of affairs. Recent philosophy has set itself more modest and more attainable ends; she is no longer inimical to special inquiry; in fact, she is zealously taking a part in that inquiry. On the other hand, the special sciences, mathematics and physics, no less than philology, have become eminently philosophical. The material presented is no longer accepted uncritically. The glance of the inquirer is bent to the neighboring fields, whence that material has been derived. The different special departments are striving for closer union, and gradually the conviction is gaining ground that philosophy can consist only of mutual, complemental criticism, interpenetration, and union of the special sciences into a consolidated whole. As the blood in nourishing the body separates into countless capillaries, only to be collected again and to meet in the heart, so in the science of the future all the rills of knowledge will be gathered more and more into a common and undivided stream.

It is this view—not an unfamiliar one to the present generation—that I purpose to advocate. Cherish no hope, or rather have no fear, that I shall erect systems for you. I shall remain a natural inquirer. Nor expect that it is my intention to skirt all the fields of natural inquiry. I can attempt to be your guide only in that branch which is familiar to me, and even there I can assist in the furtherment of only a small portion of the allotted task. If I shall succeed in rendering plain to you the relations of physics, psychology, and the theory of knowledge, so that you may draw from each of them profit and light, redounding to each, I shall regard my work as not having been in vain.

Therefore, to illustrate by an example how, consonantly with my powers and views, I conceive such inquiries should be conducted, I shall treat to-day, in the form of a brief sketch, of the following special and limited subject—of *the part which accidental circumstances play in the development of inventions and discoveries.*

When we Germans say of a man that he was not the inventor of gunpowder,[1] we impliedly cast a grave suspicion on his abilities. But the expression is not a felicitous one, as there is probably no invention in which deliberate thought had a smaller, and pure luck a larger, share than in this. It is well to ask, Are we justified in placing a low estimate on the achievement of an inventor because accident has assisted him in his work? Huygens, whose discoveries and inventions are justly sufficient to entitle him to an opinion in such matters, lays great emphasis on this factor. He asserts that a man capable of inventing the telescope without the concurrence of accident must have been gifted with superhuman genius.[2]

A man living in the midst of civilisation finds himself surrounded by a host of marvellous inventions, considering none other than the means of satisfying the needs of every-day life. Picture such a man transported to the epoch preceding the invention of these ingenious appliances, and imagine him undertaking in a serious manner to comprehend their origin. At first the intellectual power of the men capable of producing such marvels will strike him as incredible, or, if we adopt the ancient view, as divine. But his astonishment is considerably allayed by the disenchanting yet elucidative revelations of the history of primitive culture, which to a large extent prove that these inventions took their rise very slowly and by imperceptible degrees.

A small hole in the ground with fire kindled in it constituted the primitive stove. The flesh of the quarry, wrapped with water in its skin, was boiled by contact with heated stones. Cooking by stones was also performed in wooden vessels. Hollow gourds were protected from the fire by coats of clay. Thus, from the burned clay accidentally originated the enveloping pot, which rendered the gourd superfluous, although for a long time thereafter the clay was still spread over the gourd, or pressed into woven wicker-work, before the potter's art assumed its final independence. Even then the wicker-work ornament was retained, as a sort of attest of its origin.

We see, thus, it is by accidental circumstances, that is, by such as lie without his purpose, foresight, and power, that man is gradually led to the acquaintance of improved means of satisfying his wants. Let the reader picture to himself the genius of a man who could have foreseen without the help of accident that clay handled in the ordinary manner would produce a useful cooking utensil! The majority of the inventions made in the early stages of civilisation, including language, writing, money, and the rest, could not have been the product of deliberate methodical reflexion for the simple reason that no idea of their value and significance could have been had except from their practical use. The invention of the bridge may have been suggested by the trunk of a tree which had fallen athwart a mountain-torrent; that of the tool by the use of a stone accidentally taken into the hand to crack nuts. The use of fire probably started in and was disseminated from regions where volcanic eruptions, hot springs, and burning jets of natural gas afforded opportunity for quietly observing and turning to practical account the properties of fire.

Only after that had been done could the significance of the fire drill be appreciated, an instrument which was probably discovered by boring a hole through a piece of wood. The suggestion of a distinguished inquirer that the invention of the fire drill originated on the occasion of a religious ceremony is both fantastic and incredible. And as to the use of fire, we should no more attempt to derive that from the invention of the fire drill than we should from the invention of sulphur matches. Unquestionably the opposite course was the real one.[3]

Similar phenomena, though still largely veiled in obscurity, mark the initial transition of nations from a hunting to a nomadic life and to agriculture.[4] We shall not multiply examples, but content ourselves with the remark that the same phenomena recur in historical times, in the ages of great technical inventions, and, further, that regarding them the most whimsical notions have been circulated—notions which ascribe to accident an unduly exaggerated part, and one which in a psychological respect is absolutely impossible. The observation of steam escaping from a teakettle and of the clattering of the lid is supposed to have led to the invention of the steam engine. Just think of the gap between this spectacle and the conception of the performance of a large amount of work by steam, for a man totally ignorant of the steam engine! Let us suppose, however, that an engineer, versed in the practical construction of pumps, should accidentally dip into water an inverted bottle that had been filled with steam for drying and still retained its steam. He would see the water rush violently into the bottle, and the idea would very naturally suggest itself of founding on this experience a convenient and useful atmospheric steam-pump, which by imperceptible degrees, both psychologically possible and immediate, would then undergo a natural and gradual transformation into Watt's steam-engine.

But granting that the most important inventions are brought to man's notice accidentally and in ways that are beyond his foresight, yet it does not follow that accident alone is sufficient to produce an invention. The part which man plays is by no means a passive one. Even the first potter in the primeval forest must have felt some stirrings of a genius within him. In all such cases, the inventor is obliged *to take note* of the new fact, he must discover and grasp its advantageous feature, and must have the power to turn that feature to account in the realisation of his purpose. He must *distinguish* the new feature, impress it upon his memory, unite and interweave it with the rest of his thought; in short, he must possess the capacity *to profit by experience.*

The capacity to profit by experience might well be set up as a test of intelligence. That power varies considerably in men of the same race, and increases enormously as we advance from the lower animals to man. The former are limited almost entirely to the reflex actions which they have inherited with their organism, they are almost totally incapable of individual experience, and considering their simple wants are scarcely in need of it. The ivory snail (*Eburna spirata*) never learns to avoid the carnivorous Actinia, no matter how often it may wince under the latter's shower of needles, having apparently no memory whatever for pain.[5] A spider can be lured forth repeatedly from its hole by touching its web with a tuning fork. The moth plunges again and again into the flame which has burnt it. The humming-bird hawk moth[6] dashes repeatedly against the painted roses of the wallpaper, like the unhappy and desperate thinker who never wearies of attacking in the same way the same insoluble chimerical problem. As aimlessly almost as Maxwell's gaseous molecules and in the same unreasoning manner common flies in their search for light and air stream against the glass pane of a half-opened window and remain there from sheer inability to find their way around the narrow frame. But a pike separated from the minnows of his aquarium by a glass partition, learns after the lapse of a few months, though only after having butted himself half to death, that he cannot attack these fishes with impunity. What is more, he leaves them in peace even after the removal of the partition, though he will bolt at once a strange fish. Considerable memory must be attributed to birds of passage, a memory which, probably owing to the absence of disturbing thoughts, acts with the precision of that of some idiots. Finally, the susceptibility to training evinced by the higher vertebrates is indisputable proof of the ability of these animals to profit by experience.

A powerfully developed *mechanical* memory, which recalls vividly and faithfully old situations, is sufficient for avoiding definite particular dangers, or for taking advantage of definite particular opportunities. But more is required for the development of *inventions*. More extensive chains of images are necessary here, the excitation by mutual contact of widely different trains of ideas, a more powerful, more manifold, and richer connexion of the contents of memory, a more powerful and impressionable psychical life, heightened by use. A man stands on the bank of a mountain-torrent, which is a serious obstacle to him. He remembers that he has crossed just such a torrent before on the trunk of a fallen tree. Hard by trees are growing. He has often moved the trunks of fallen trees. He has also felled trees before, and then moved them. To fell trees he has used sharp stones. He goes in search of such a stone, and as the old situations that crowd into his memory and are held there in living reality by the definite powerful interest which he has in crossing just this torrent—as these impressions are made to pass before his mind in the *inverse order* in which they were here evoked, he invents the bridge.

There can be no doubt but the higher vertebrates adapt their actions in some moderate degree to circumstances. The fact that they give no appreciable evidence of advance by the accumulation of inventions, is satisfactorily explained by a difference of degree or intensity of intelligence as compared with man; the assumption of a difference of kind is not necessary. A person who saves a little every day, be it ever so little, has an incalculable advantage over him who daily loses that amount, or is unable to keep what he has accumulated. A slight quantitative difference in such things explains enormous differences of advancement.

The rules which hold good in prehistoric times also hold good in historical times, and the remarks made on invention may be applied almost without modification to discovery; for the two are distinguished solely by the use to which the new knowledge is put. In both cases the investigator is concerned with some *newly observed* relation of new or old properties, abstract or concrete. It is observed, for example, that a substance which gives a chemical reaction *A* is also the cause of a chemical reaction *B*. If this observation fulfills no purpose but that of furthering the scientist's insight, or of removing a source of intellectual discomfort, we have a discovery; but an invention, if in using the substance giving the reaction *A* to produce the desired reaction *B*, we have a practical end in view, and seek to remove a cause of material discomfort. The phrase, *disclosure of the connexion of reactions,* is broad enough to cover discoveries and inventions in all departments. It embraces the Pythagorean proposition, which is a combination of a geometrical and an arithmetical reaction, Newton's discovery of the connexion of Kepler's motions with the law of the inverse squares, as perfectly as it does the detection of a small appropriate alteration in the construction of a tool, or of an appropriate change in the methods of work of a dyeing establishment.

The disclosure of new provinces of facts before unknown can only be brought about by accidental circumstances, under which are *remarked* facts that commonly go unnoticed. The achievement of the discoverer here consists in his *sharpened attention,* which detects the uncommon features of an occurrence and their determining conditions from their most evanescent marks,[7] and discovers means of submitting them to exact and full observation. Under this head belong the first disclosures of electrical and magnetic phenomena, Grimaldi's observation of interference, Arago's discovery of the increased check suffered by a magnetic needle vibrating in a copper envelope as compared with that observed in a bandbox, Foucault's observation of the stability of the plane of vibration of a rod accidentally struck while rotating in a turning-lathe, Mayer's observation of the increased redness of venous blood in the tropics, Kirchhoff's observation of the augmentation of the D-line in the solar spectrum by the interposition of a sodium lamp, Schonbein's discovery of ozone from the phosphoric smell emitted on the disruption of air by electric sparks, and a host of others. All these facts, of which unquestionably many were *seen* numbers of times before they were *noticed,* are examples of the inauguration of momentous discoveries by accidental circumstances, and place the importance of strained attention in a brilliant light.

But not only is a significant part played in the beginning of an inquiry by co-operative circumstances beyond the foresight of the investigator; their influence is also active in its prosecution. Dufay, thus, whilst following up the behavior of *one* electrical state which he had assumed, discovers the existence of *two.* Fresnel learns by accident that the interference-bands received on ground glass are seen to better advantage in the open air. The diffraction-phenomenon of two slits proved to be considerably different from what Fraunhofer had anticipated, and in following up this circumstance he was led to the important discovery of grating-spectra. Faraday's induction-phenomenon departed widely from the initial conception which occasioned his experiments, and it is precisely this deviation that constitutes his real discovery.

Every man has pondered on some subject. Every one of us can multiply the examples cited, by less illustrious ones from his own experience. I shall cite but one. On rounding a railway curve once, I accidentally remarked a striking apparent inclination of the houses and trees. I discovered from this that the direction of the total physical acceleration of a mass carries with it as its physiological reaction the perception of the vertical. Afterwards, in attempting to inquire more carefully into this phenomenon, and this only, in a large whirling machine, the collateral phenomena conducted me to the sensation of the angular acceleration, vertigo, Flouren's experiments on the section of the circular canals, and so on, from which gradually resulted views relating to the sensations of direction which are also held by Breuer and Brown, which were at first contested on all hands, but are now regarded on many sides as correct, and which have been recently enriched by the interesting inquiries of Breuer concerning the *macula acustica,* and Kreidel's experiments with magnetically orientable crustacea. Not disregard of accident but a direct and purposeful employment of it advances research.

The more powerful the psychical connexion of the memory pictures is, —and it varies according to the individual and the mood, —the more apt is the same accidental observation to be productive of results. Galileo knows that the air has weight; he also knows of the "resistance to a vacuum," expressed both in weight and in the height of a column of water. But the two ideas dwelt asunder in his mind. It remained for Torricelli to vary the specific gravity of the liquid measuring the pressure, and not till then was the air included in the list of pressure-exerting fluids. The reversal of the lines of the spectrum was seen repeatedly before Kirchhoff, and had been mechanically explained. But it was left for his penetrating vision to discern the evidence of the connexion of this phenomenon with questions of heat, and to him alone through persistent labor was revealed the sweeping significance of the fact for the mobile equilibrium of heat. Supposing, then, that such a rich organic connexion of the elements of memory exists, and is the prime distinguishing mark of the inquirer, next in importance certainly is that *intense interest* in a definite object, in a definite idea, which fashions advantageous combinations of thought from elements before disconnected, and obtrudes that idea into every observation made, and into every thought formed, making it enter into relationship with all things. Thus Bradley, deeply engrossed with the subject of aberration, is led to its solution by an exceedingly unobtrusive experience in crossing the Thames. It is permissible, therefore, to ask whether accident leads the discoverer, or the discoverer accident, to a successful outcome in scientific quests.

No man should dream of solving a great problem unless he is so thoroughly saturated with his subject that everything else sinks into comparative insignificance. During a hurried meeting with Mayer in Heidelberg once, Jolly remarked, with a rather dubious implication, that if Mayer's theory were correct water could be warmed by shaking. Mayer went away without a word of reply. Several weeks later, and now unrecognised by Jolly, he rushed into the latter's presence exclaiming: "Es ischt aso!" (It is so, it is so!). It was only after considerable explanation that Jolly found out what Mayer wanted to say. The incident needs no comment.[8] A person deadened to sensory impressions and given up solely to the pursuit of his thoughts, also can light on an idea that will divert his mental activity into totally new channels. In such cases it is a psychical accident, an intellectual experience, as distinguished from a physical accident, to which the person owes his discovery—a discovery which is here made "deductively" by means of mental copies of the world, instead of experimentally. *Purely* experimental inquiry, moreover, does not exist, for, as Gauss says, virtually we always experiment with our thoughts. And it is precisely that constant, corrective interchange or intimate union of experiment and deduction, as it was cultivated by Galileo in his *Dialogues* and by Newton in his *Optics,* that is the foundation of the benign fruitfulness of modern scientific inquiry as contrasted with that of antiquity, where observation and reflexion ofttimes pursued their several courses like two strangers.

We have to wait for the appearance of a favorable physical accident. The movement of our thoughts obeys the law of association. In the case of meagre experience the result of this law is simply the mechanical reproduction of definite sensory experiences. On the other hand, if the psychical life is subjected to the incessant influences of a powerful and rich experience, then every representative element in the mind is connected with so many others that the actual and natural course of the thoughts is easily influenced and determined by insignificant circumstances, which accidentally are decisive. Hereupon, the process termed imagination produces its protean and infinitely diversified forms. Now what can we do to guide this process, seeing that the combinatory law of the images is without our reach? Rather let us ask, what influence can a powerful and constantly recurring idea exert on the movement of our thoughts? According to what has preceded, the answer is involved in the question itself. The *idea* dominates the thought of the inquirer, not the latter the former.

Let us see, now, if we can acquire a profounder insight into the process of discovery. The condition of the discoverer is, as James has aptly remarked, not unlike the situation of a person who is trying to remember something that he has forgotten. Both are sensible of a gap, and have only a remote presentiment of what is missing. Suppose I meet in company a well-known and affable gentleman whose name I have forgotten, and who to my horror asks to be introduced to someone. I set to work according to Lichtenberg's rule, and run down the alphabet in search of the initial letter of his name. A vague sympathy holds me at the letter *G.* Tentatively I add the second letter and am arrested at *e,* and long before I have tried the third letter *r,* the name "Gerson" breaks sonorously upon my ear, and my anguish is gone. While taking a walk I meet a gentleman from whom I receive a communication. On returning home, and in attending to weightier affairs, the matter slips my mind. Moodily, but in vain, I ransack my memory. Finally I observe that I am going over my walk in thought. On the street corner in question the gentleman again stands before me and repeats his communication. In this process are recalled successively to consciousness all the percepts which were connected with the percept that was lost, and with them, finally, that, too, is brought to light. In the first case—where the experience had already been made and is permanently impressed on our thought—a *systematic* procedure is both possible and easy, for we know that a name must be composed of a limited number of sounds. But at the same time it should be observed that the labor involved in such a combinatorial task would be enormous if the name were long and the responsiveness of the mind weaker.

It is often said, and not wholly without justification, that the scientist has solved a riddle. Every problem in geometry may be clothed in the garb of a riddle. Thus: "What thing is that thing M which has the properties A, B, C?" "What circle is that which touches the straight lines A, B, touching B in the point C?" The first two conditions marshal before the imagination the group of circles whose centres lie in the line of symmetry of A, B. The third condition reminds us of all the circles having centres in the straight line which stands at right angles to B in C. The common term, or common terms, of these groups of images solve the riddle—satisfy the problem. Puzzles dealing with things or words induce similar processes, but the memory in such cases is exerted in many directions and more varied and less clearly ordered provinces of ideas have to be surveyed. The difference between the situation of a geometer who has a construction to make, and that of an engineer, or a scientist, confronted with a problem, is simply this, that the first moves in a field with which he is thoroughly acquainted, whereas the two latter are obliged to familiarise themselves with this field subsequently, and in a measure far transcending what is commonly required. In this process the mechanical engineer has at least always a definite goal before him and definite means to accomplish his aim, whilst in the case of the scientist that aim is in many instances presented only in vague and general outlines. Often the very formulation of the riddle devolves on him. Frequently it is not until the aim has been reached that the broader outlook requisite for systematic procedure is obtained. By far the larger portion of his success, therefore, is contingent on luck and instinct. It is immaterial, so far as its character is concerned, whether the process in question is brought rapidly to a conclusion in the brain of one man, or whether it is spun out for centuries in the minds of a long succession of thinkers. The same relation that a word solving a riddle bears to that riddle is borne by the modern conception of light to the facts discovered by Grimaldi, Romer, Huygens, Newton, Young, Malus, and Fresnel, and only by the help of this slowly developed conception is our mental vision enabled to embrace the broad domain of facts in question.

A welcome complement to the discoveries which the history of civilisation and comparative psychology have furnished, is to be found in the confessions of great scientists and artists. Scientists *and* artists, we might say, for Liebig courageously declared there was no essential difference between the labors of the two. Are we to regard Leonardo da Vinci as a scientist or as an artist? If it is the business of the artist to build up his work from a few motives, it is the task of the scientist to discover the motives which permeate reality. If scientists like Lagrange or Fourier are in a certain measure artists in the presentation of their results, on the other hand, artists like Shakespeare or Ruysdael are scientists in the insight which must have preceded their creations.

Newton, when questioned about his methods of work, could give no other answer but that he was wont to ponder again and again on a subject; and similar utterances are accredited to D'Alembert and Helmholtz. Scientists and artists both recommend persistent labor. After the repeated survey of a field has afforded opportunity for the interposition of advantageous accidents, has rendered all the traits that suit with the mood or the dominant thought more vivid, and has gradually relegated to the background all things that are inappropriate, making their future appearance impossible; then from the teeming, swelling host of fancies which a free and high-flown imagination calls forth, suddenly that particular form arises to the light which harmonises perfectly with the ruling idea, mood, or design. Then it is that that which has resulted slowly as the result of a gradual selection, appears as if it were the outcome of a deliberate act of creation. Thus are to be explained the statements of Newton, Mozart, Richard Wagner, and others, when they say that thoughts, melodies, and harmonies had poured in upon them, and that they had simply retained the right ones. Undoubtedly, the man of genius, too, consciously or instinctively, pursues systematic methods, wherever it is possible; but in his delicate presentiment he will omit many a task or abandon it after a hasty trial on which a less endowed man would squander in vain his energies. Thus, the genius accomplishes[9] in a brief space of time undertakings for which the life of an ordinary man would far from suffice. We shall hardly go astray if we regard genius as only a slight deviation from the average mental endowment—as possessing simply a greater sensitiveness of cerebral reaction and a greater swiftness of reaction. The men who, obeying their inner impulses, make sacrifices for an idea instead of advancing their material welfare, may appear to the full-blooded Philistine as fools; yet we shall scarcely adopt Lombroso's view, that genius is to be regarded as a disease, although it is unfortunately true that a more sensitive brain, a more fragile constitution, succumbs far more readily to sickness.

The remark of C. G. J. Jacobi that mathematics is slow of growth and only reaches the truth by long and devious paths, that the way to its discovery must be prepared for long beforehand, and that then the truth will make its long-deferred appearance as if impelled by some divine necessity[10]—all this holds true of every science. We are astounded often to note that it required the combined labors of many eminent thinkers for a full century to reach a truth which it takes us only a few hours to master and which once acquired seems extremely easy to reach under the right sort of circumstances. To our humiliation we learn that even the greatest men are born more for life than for science. The extent to which even they are indebted to accident—to that singular conflux of the physical and the psychical life in which the continuous but yet imperfect and never-ending adaptation of the latter to the former finds its distinct expression—that has been the subject of our remarks today. Jacobi's poetical thought of a divine necessity acting in science will lose none of its loftiness for us if we discover in this necessity the same power that destroys the unfit and fosters the fit. For loftier, nobler, and more romantic than poetry is the truth and the reality.

Inaugural lecture delivered on assuming the Professorship of the History and Theory of Inductive Science in the University of Vienna, October 20, 1895 (Unpublished). Translated by Thomas J. McCormack (1865–1932).

1. The phrase is, *Er hat das Pulver nicht erfunden.*

2. "Quod si quis tanta industria exstitisset, ut ex naturae principiis et geometria hanc rem eruere potuisset, eum ego supra mortalium sortem ingenio valuisse dicendum crederem. Sed hoe tantum abest, ut fortuito reperti artificii rationem non adhuc satis explicari potuerint viri doctissimi." Hugenii Dioptrica (de telescopiis).
3. I must not be understood as saying that the fire drill has played no part in the worship of fire or of the sun.
4. Compare on this point he extremely interesting remarks of Dr. Paul Carus in his *Philosophy of the Tool* Chicago, 1893.
5. Mobius, *Naturwissenschaftlicher Verein fur Schleswig-Holstein*, Kiel, 1893, p. 113 et seq.
6. I am indebted for this observation to Professor Hatscheck.
7. Cf. Hoppe, *Entdecken und Finden*, 1870.
8. This story was related to me by Jolly, and subsequently repeated in a letter from him.
9. I do not know whether Swift's academy of schemers in Lagado, in which great discoveries and inventions were made by a sort of verbal game of dice, was intended as a satire on Francis Bacon's method of making discoveries by means of huge synoptic tables constructed by scribes. It certainly would not have been ill placed.
10. The original passage in Latin is quoted by Simony, *In ein ringförmiges Band einen Knoten zu machen*, Vienna, 1881, p. 41.

Commentary

Mach begins with, to the modern ear, a somewhat obtuse discussion of the interrelationship, or otherwise, of *philosophy* and *science*. His purpose in this is to argue for a closer relationship between the two, in a manner that is entirely reminiscent of the scientific method in its true, broad sense. Thus theories emerge from an inductive process—think of the story of Newton and the apple—and are then tested (Do oranges also obey this rule?) through a deductive process. While this may seem to have nothing to do with creativity research, in fact the field can, perhaps, congratulate itself that both induction and deduction retain a place in creativity research.

Notwithstanding Mach's (1896, p. 162) observation that "the history of philosophy [theory generation] . . . is and must be largely a history of error," creativity research in the modern, post-*Sputnik* era has not been afraid to propose theories of how, where, and why individuals are creative, even if those theories have proven imperfect in the light of empirical evidence. Put another way, it is refreshing that in creativity research there remains room for new theories to be developed—is creativity only a force for good, for example (Cropley, Kaufman, & Cropley, 2008)—even as deductive methods test existing theories of creative cognition, personality, and place.

Mach's (1896, p. 162) intent was also to argue that a closer relationship between philosophy and science, must, by necessity, involve a more interdisciplinary mix of the special sciences—mathematics and physics (in his view)—with disciplines such as psychology, such that "the glance of the inquirer" might be "bent to the neighboring fields" in a manner that might speed up the move to a more enlightened and "consolidated whole." Modern creativity research can make a strong claim to have fulfilled Mach's interdisciplinary goal, building on his exploration of "the part which accidental circumstances play in the development of inventions and discoveries" (p. 163), through such broad and diverse investigations of creativity in education, creativity as an enabler of business innovation, neuroscientific elements of idea generation, and many more.

The main body of Mach's paper addresses a question that is absolutely fundamental to creativity, creative problem-solving, and innovation. In essence, he asks, Is luck a necessity in discovery and invention? We can preempt Mach's discussion by noting that if invention is entirely dependent on luck, then creativity researchers, engineers, and many more may be out of a job!

Mach's position, in fact, seems more moderate. In contrast to Huygens (the 17th-century mathematician and physicist), whom Mach (1896, p. 163) quotes as asserting that "a man capable of inventing the telescope without the concurrence of accident must have been gifted with superhuman genius," Mach asks only if and how luck might have assisted the inventor. Huygens's more extreme position with respect to luck and invention was likely also influenced by his interest in probability and his pioneering work on games of chance.

Mach begins his exploration of the role of accident (or luck) in discovery and invention by asking the reader to consider what the invention of modern conveniences would look like to someone considering them in advance of their invention. In modern terms, how would we, in the 21st century, view the origin of some future technological marvel if we were shown it now? Would we assume that this item could have emerged, suddenly and miraculously, only through some incredible intellectual ability or divine intervention? Alternatively, would we see it merely as the conclusion of a long, slow process of incremental change?

Mach, it seems, explains examples like this through a combination of two things. First, they are the result of gradual, *incremental* improvements to existing needs and artifacts. Second, that "accidental circumstances," by which he means circumstances "that lie [outside of the inventor's] purpose, foresight, and power" (1896, p. 164), lead the inventor to the solution. While this may be true for some, and possibly many inventions, Mach's argument seems to exclude the possibility of radical, or disruptive, solutions that emerge as deliberate responses to problems or needs. As evidence of the incremental or accidental pathway, Mach asks us to consider that "the majority of the inventions made in the early stages of civilization . . . could not have been the product of deliberate methodical reflection for the simple reason that no idea of their value and significance could have been had except from their practical use" (p. 164). What this seems to suggest is that these inventions were, in fact, not inventions at all, but lucky discoveries—that is, solutions that were waiting for a problem (and therefore a use).

Having led the reader to imagine that, at least in early civilization, invention was largely a gradual process of lucky discoveries applied to some useful purpose—blind variation and selective retentions, perhaps—Mach then moderates his account by suggesting not only that the role of accident in this process is exaggerated but that such a reliance on accident leaves no room for psychology. Here we begin to see both a more nuanced description of invention and discovery and also one in which the psychology of creativity has an important role. In Mach's example of the engineer perceiving the possibilities of steam we also see an echo of Pasteur's dictum *Chance favors only the prepared mind* (in Peterson, 1954, p. 493). The importance of knowledge, and preparation, in the inventive (creative) process therefore render accident less a probabilistic phenomenon and more a deterministic feature of a structured and rigorous process. Perhaps what began as accident is simply a convenient label for the divergent thinking and incubation that we now accept as central to creative problem-solving?

Mach (1896, p. 166) grapples with the interplay between accident and deliberation in the process of invention, ultimately by acknowledging a key role for the inventor's ability "to take note" of new facts and phenomena, to appreciate their significance and value, and to make use of this knowledge. Mach's account here becomes more and more cognitive in nature, linking perception, memory, and association as key elements of invention—something he sums up as "the capacity *to profit by experience*" (p. 166).

At this point in his paper, Mach begins the process of constructing a rather modern framework of creative problem-solving. Invention is *not* a process of accidental, fortuitous discovery. It is not, even in ancient times, a process of slavish (blind) trial and error, with the path to successful, useful inventions littered with wasteful, impractical solutions. The modern engineer employs a variety of convergent strategies to move, quickly and efficiently, from the large set of possible solutions that result from divergent thinking to a single best solution, profiting from his or her experience to do so. Mach understood that invention draws on psychological elements of cognition and personality and follows a process in which accident is a naive term for a combination of experience, memory, perception, and other psychological elements, employed to satisfy a need.

Beginning with memory, Mach notes that this is manifest in different ways, and with different levels of sophistication, in animals and humans. He notes that mere "mechanical" memory—the ability to recall old situations—is a useful element of survival; however, he is clear that memory, as a component of invention, requires much more. Two elements emerge in his discussion of memory that are instantly recognizable to the modern creativity researcher. Mach (1896, p. 167) refers to "extensive chains of images" and "the excitation by mutual contact of widely different trains of ideas" or "richer connection of the contents of memory." These suggest both remote associates in the sense made familiar to creativity research by Mednick (1962) but also components of divergent thinking tests (e.g., Guilford, 1967; Torrance, 1966)—especially flexibility (the ability to produce many different categories of ideas) and elaboration (the ability to build on or develop those ideas).

Here Mach addresses a distinction that, up to this point, has been glossed over: the differences, if any, between invention and discovery. His explanation, which also sheds some light on the earlier discussion of accident, is that both involve new knowledge and new relationships, but that while discovery is limited to satisfying an intellectual need (e.g., curiosity), invention is concerned with satisfying practical, material needs. Even in his discussion of discovery, Mach draws the same conclusion as he formed regarding invention. Accident is again something that results from a combination of knowledge, preparation, memory, and need, but is far more deliberate and deterministic than it is random and probabilistic.

Even as he seeks to cite examples of a more probabilistic kind of *accident* in discovery, Mach, perhaps unwittingly, reinforces the case that accident is far from accidental! Each example—Grimaldi (interference), Arago (electromagnetism), Foucault (vibration), Mayer (blood), Kirchhoff (solar spectra), Schoenbein (ozone), Dufay (electricity), Fresnel (optics), Fraunhofer (diffraction), Faraday (electromagnetic induction)—is noteworthy for the fact that the discovery was made by an expert, well versed in the broad area of study in which the *accident* occurred. Preparation, knowledge, and memory—Mach's ability to profit by experience—again emerge as critical enablers of the process.

In some ways, therefore, Mach's paper seems rather self-contradictory. There is no doubt that he appreciates the psychological elements of what we now think of as creativity and creative problem-solving. At the same time, he continues to argue for accident as an important element of the process of discovery and invention. While this may be a deliberate exposition of both sides of the discussion, it may also reflect differences in what we mean by accident in modern parlance. Mach (1896, p. 169) himself gives some clarity to this issue when, deep into his article, he uses the term "cooperative circumstances" to describe that which is "beyond the foresight of the investigator" but, by implication, entirely within the means of the investigator to perceive, utilize, and profit from. He gives a further clue both to the real meaning of *accident* and to his view of its role when he states, "Not disregard of accident but a direct and purposeful employment of it advances research" (p. 170). It is worth noting that Mach's original title, in German, was "Die Rolle des *Zufalls* bei Erfindungen und Entdeckungen," and that *Zufall* translates more accurately as "coincidence" (whereas *Unfall* is the term for "accident"). The former seems far more in keeping with the notion of cooperative circumstances, and perhaps some of Mach's intended meaning has been clouded simply by a slightly inaccurate translation. Nevertheless this is where we see Mach's influence on modern creativity research most clearly.

Mach begins to assemble the critical elements that he has identified in the process of discovery and invention into a structure and order. Of primary importance, in his view, is memory—not only memory, but also the interaction between an observation, memory, the mood of the individual, and the value of associations that result. Mach then argues that attention and interest are critical to how the connections between memory and observation are used. He believes, unequivocally, in these interrelationships when stating, "No man should dream of solving a great problem unless he is so thoroughly saturated with his subject that everything else sinks into comparative insignificance" (1896, pp. 170–171)—we know where Mach stands on the role of knowledge, and preparation, in creativity and invention.

An example, not given by Mach, serves to illustrate his points on invention, discovery, and cooperative circumstances very clearly. In 1870 the German pathologist Eugen Semmer published an account of his attempts to find a cure for infections, working with horses. Unfortunately his experiments were hampered by the contaminating presence of mold spores in his lab. These *penicillium notatum* spores were causing his horses to recover from their infections, thus interfering with his attempts to find a means of curing them. Once Semmer had identified this contaminant, he was able to clean his lab, and continue with his (unsuccessful) research. Alexander Fleming, working some sixty years later, was investigating the antibacterial properties of nasal mucus. Much like Semmer, Fleming's experimental apparatus became contaminated with mold spores. Unlike Semmer, however, Fleming immediately realized the significance of what had happened, and his discovery of the antibacterial properties of *penicillium notatum* was a major medical breakthrough. There is, however, one more piece to this story. While Fleming may be said to have *discovered* penicillin, profiting from the cooperative circumstances that occurred in his lab, not least because he possessed the knowledge, preparation, attention, and curiosity necessary to profit by his experience, we might nevertheless argue that the need that was satisfied was largely intellectual. It took another team of scientists, the Australian Howard Florey and his German-born colleague Ernest Chain, to turn penicillin into a useful and effective drug, even after earlier attempts to do so had been abandoned. In other words, Florey and Chain drew on the same qualities as Fleming to *invent* a life-saving drug and solve a practical, material need. All three—Fleming, Florey, and Chain—shared the 1945 Nobel Prize for Medicine.

What is even more striking about this example is that Semmer—who failed to discover penicillin and failed to invent antibiotics—was no fool. He possessed relevant expertise and knowledge, and his curiosity enabled him to identify correctly the cause of his horses' unexpected recovery. He seems to have possessed the same qualities, identified by Mach, as critical to profiting from experience. Perhaps the single, missing element of the puzzle, which prevented circumstances from cooperating fully, was that Semmer was attempting to solve the wrong problem. Put differently, Semmer was asking the wrong question, or lacked just enough flexibility and openness to redefine his problem to align with what he had, in effect, discovered.

As Mach leans more and more toward a recognizable psychological model of invention and discovery—creativity, in other words—he further refines his meaning of accident. Psychical accidents are now identified as distinct from physical accidents, and are simply the psychological and cognitive cooperative circumstances (or coincidences) that drive the interaction of memory, attention, preparation, and knowledge in the pursuit of solutions to practical, material needs. Mach also, at this point, notes that psychical life—the psychological experience of the individual, in other words—is far more fertile ground for invention than a world in which cooperative circumstances emerge only in the form of physical accidents (e.g., literally being in the right place at the right time). He introduces the concept of imagination and begins to explore another question that is critical in modern creativity research. That is, to what extent is invention, or discovery—that is, creativity—something that can be controlled or guided or deliberately applied in some way? We might say, therefore, to what extent can these psychical accidents be deliberately fostered for the purpose of satisfying material needs? Mach describes two examples of process—deliberate and systematic—intended to push discovery along its natural path.

As Mach's discussion begins to draw to a conclusion, he presents two further ideas, each of which resonates with the modern view of creativity. The first of these is *problem definition*. Modern creativity (and innovation) researchers have noted the critical importance of understanding the nature of the problem to be solved, as a factor in the success of the subsequent problem-solving activity—the missing element in Semmer's story (see, e.g., Reiter-Palmon and Robinson, 2009, or a broader discussion of the stages of creative problem-solving in Cropley, 2015).

The second idea that has occupied the attention of some modern creativity researchers is the process employed by eminent—or Big C—creatives (see Kaufman, 2016, for a discussion). How do famous creative individuals go about the process of generating new and effective solutions to the problems they address? Mach (1896, p. 174) anticipates the research of Simonton (e.g., 2010), recognizing that the answer "is to be found in the confessions of great scientists and artists." Mach concluded that one characteristic of the Big-C creative is that "the man of genius, too, consciously or instinctively, pursues systematic methods . . . but . . . will omit many a task or abandon it after a hasty trial" (p. 174) and does this far more efficiently than less gifted individuals do.

Conclusions

What can we conclude from the work of Ernst Mach in relation to creativity, innovation, and creative problem-solving? Although Mach seems, at times, to lure the reader into some unsophisticated models of problem-solving—that, especially in early civilizations, mankind's progress was driven by lucky discoveries that happened to have utility—he seems to do this simply to lay the groundwork for a surprisingly modern concept of creativity. Accident, insofar as it plays a role in discovery and invention, is not the random appearance of otherwise hidden solutions, but instead is a term used to explain the intersection of knowledge, expertise, preparation, attention, memory, and imagination in "cooperative circumstances" and for the purpose of finding solutions to practical, material needs. The elements that Mach describes are not out of place in a modern creativity or innovation framework spanning person, process, and product, and Mach's ideas continue to exert influence on the field more than 100 years after they were expounded.

References

Amabile, T. M. (1983). The social psychology of creativity: A componential conceptualization. *Journal of Personality and Social Psychology, 45*(2), 357–376.

Campbell, D. T. (1960). Blind variation and selective survival as a general strategy in knowledge processes. In M. C. Yovits & S. Cameron (Eds.), *Self-organizing systems* (pp. 205–231). New York, NY: Pergamon Press.

Cropley, D. H. (2015). *Creativity in engineering: Novel solutions to complex problems.* San Diego, CA: Academic Press.

Cropley, D. H., Kaufman, J. C., & Cropley, A. J. (2008). Malevolent creativity: A functional model of creativity in terrorism and crime. *Creativity Research Journal, 20*(2), 105–115.

Guilford, J. P. (1967). *The nature of human intelligence.* New York, NY: McGraw-Hill.

Kaufman, J. C. (2016). *Creativity 101* (2nd ed.). New York, NY: Springer.

Mach, E. (1896). On the part played by accident in invention and discovery. *The Monist, 6*(2), 161–175.

Mednick, S. A. (1962). The associative basis of creativity. *Psychological Review, 69,* 220–232.

Peterson, H. (Ed.) (1954). *A treasury of the world's great speeches.* Danbury, CT: Grolier.

Reiter-Palmon, R., & Robinson, E. J. (2009). Problem identification and construction: What do we know, what is the future? *Psychology of Aesthetics, Creativity, and the Arts, 3*(1), 43–47.

Simonton, D. K. (2003). Scientific creativity as constrained stochastic behavior: the integration of product, person, and process perspectives. *Psychological Bulletin, 129*(4), 475–494.

Simonton, D. K. (2010). Creativity in highly eminent individuals. In J. C. Kaufman & R. J. Sternberg (Eds.), *The Cambridge handbook of creativity* (pp. 174–188). New York, NY: Cambridge University Press.

Torrance, E. P. (1966). *Torrance tests of creative thinking: Technical norms manual.* Lexington, MA: Personnel Press.

PART FIVE

Creativity Development and Education

14

Imagination and Creativity in Childhood

L. S. Vygotsky

SEANA MORAN AND VERA JOHN-STEINER

Summary

In this chapter, we convey how a Vygotskian approach to creativity is gaining momentum as creativity scholars extend his ideas related to symbol use, meaning-making, social interaction, and play. Using chapters 3 and 4 from Vygotsky's *Imagination and Creativity in Childhood*, we explore the fundamental role of imagination in the ongoing creation and re-creation of reality over time. Vygotsky's contributions to creativity research emphasized how common and pervasive it is in human life and culture. Although Vygotsky's work during the early 20th century only emerged in Western scholarship in the 1960s, it foreshadowed several leaps in our understanding of creativity since then—not only related to children's play but also to adult worldmaking and broader cultural development.

Introduction

During his lifetime, Vygotsky's scholarly career in psychology started and ended with works related to creativity: his dissertation on the psychology of art (1965/1971) and a short paper on acting (1936/1999; see Moran & John-Steiner, 2003). Although his formal education was in education and law, not in psychology, he was aware of the work of other psychology scholars in the international arena at the time (especially French psychologist Theodule Ribot, whom Vygotsky copiously quoted, but also French psychotherapist Pierre Janet, and German experimentalist Wilhelm Wundt and gestaltist Karl Buhler). He also drew considerably from literary authors like Tolstoy, Pushkin, and Goethe. Yet, he synthesized their ideas into a *new* framework that became cultural-historical psychology.

With his earlier work in literary criticism starting in 1916, some might say Vygotsky exemplified his ideas (Kozulin, 1990; Leontiev, 1979). He took a creative perspective on human development through his ideas of mediation and social interaction. He proposed that, by using symbols and other psychological tools, and by learning from or collaborating with others, both individuals' subjective experiences as well as cultural objects and shared understandings could be transformed. We create the culture we live in by devising signs and tools to help us understand, communicate, master oneself and the world, and contribute to our communities. We can create meaningful stimuli for our own and for each other's development. Imagination is a key part of how we stretch ourselves, others, and our cultures to higher forms of development.

The excerpt below, chapters 3 and 4 from *Imagination and Creativity in Childhood*, was written by Vygotsky in 1930, midway through his academic psychology career (1924–1934), which was cut short by tuberculosis at age 37 (Lev Vygotsky Archive, n.d.). *Imagination and Creativity in Childhood* could be viewed as part of a larger turning point in his work, which up to then focused primarily on a *one*-way educational view of development from more knowledgeable cultural members to less knowledgeable through social interaction. Afterward, he became more focused on the multiple ways that cultural members learn from each other, not only through everyday interactions but also artifacts, play, tools, signs, and speech, by which persons can contribute their own subjective sense of the world to a shared reality (see Veresov, 1999). We are not just receivers of prior culture from more knowledgeable others, we are all cultural producers. Thus, although this paper by Vygotsky focuses on children, it has influenced the general literature on creativity across the lifespan (Moran & John-Steiner, 2003).

His life's (1896–1934) historical context during the Russian Revolution, and his use and quoting of Trotsky's work (Kozulin, 1990), led to his work being banned during the Stalin era (Cole & Scribner, 1978). Luckily, his work experienced a rebirth in both Russia and the West in the 1960s (when *Thought and Language* was published) and 1970s (when *Psychology of Art* and the especially influential *Mind in Society* were published). Some might say that Vygotsky's career really took off after his death, as many of his writings were published posthumously (Kozulin, 1990). Vygotsky's influence on creativity research was slow to take hold, and researchers often only realized after the fact how Vygotsky's work presaged their own. In 2017, on the 100th anniversary of the year Vygotsky started his dissertation on the psychology of art, a Vygotskian approach to creativity continues to gain momentum with a variety of new extensions of his ideas (e.g., Blunden, 2010; Connery, John-Steiner, & Marjanovic-Shane, 2010; Moran, Cropley, & Kaufman, 2014; Smagorinsky, 2016; Stetsenko, 2016).

Reading: "Imagination and Creativity in Childhood"

Source: Vygotsky, L.S. (1930/2004). Imagination and creativity in childhood (M. E. Sharpe, Inc., Trans.). *Journal of Russian and East European Psychology, 42*(1), 7–97. (From *Voobrazhenie i tvorchestvo v detskom vozraste*, Moscow: Prosveshchenie, 1967; Original work published as *Voobrazhenie i tvorchestvo v shkol'nom voraste*, Moscow-Leningrad: GIZ). Used with permission from Taylor & Francis. Deleted sections are primarily long quotes from other scholars' work, especially Ribot. We also cut a long section associated with a confusing diagram in chapter 4. We cut these sections to focus the excerpt on Vygotsky's contributions to the conceptualization of imagination rather than his reiteration of others' ideas.

Chapter 3. The Mechanism of Creative Imagination

As everything we have said above demonstrates, imagination is an extremely complex process. It is this complexity that is primarily responsible for how difficult it is to study the process of creation and that often leads to incorrect ideas about this process being something extraordinary and completely exceptional. It is not our task here to provide a full description of the components of this process. That would require a very long psychological analysis that would not interest us here. However, in order to give readers some picture of the complexity of this activity we will touch very briefly on certain process components. Every act of the imagination has a very long history. What we call the act of creation is typically only the climactic moment of a birth that occurs as a result of a very long internal process of gestation and fetal development.

At the very start of this process, as we already know, there is always a perception of the external and internal, which is the basis of our experience. What the child sees and hears thus provides the first points of support for his future creation. He accumulates materials out of which he will subsequently construct his fantasies. Next comes a very complex process of reworking this material. The most important components of this process are dissociation and association of the impressions acquired through perception. Every impression is a complex whole consisting of a number of separate parts. Dissociation is the breakup of a complex whole into a set of individual parts. Certain individual parts are isolated from the background of the others; some are retained and others are forgotten. Dissociation is thus a necessary condition for further operation of the imagination.

In order to subsequently join together the various elements, a person must first break the natural association of elements in which they were initially perceived. Before generating the image of Natasha in *War and Peace*, Tolstoy had to separate out the individual traits of two of his female relatives. If he had not done this, he would not have been able to combine them, "to grind them up together," to create the image of Natasha. It is this isolation of individual traits and neglect of others that we call dissociation. This process is extremely important in all human mental development; it is the foundation of abstract thinking, the basis of concept formation.

This ability to isolate the individual traits of a complex whole is significant in absolutely all human creative reworking of impressions. The process of dissociation is followed by a process of change to which these dissociated elements are subjected. This process of change or distortion is based on the dynamic nature of our internal neural stimulation and the images that correspond to them. The traces of external impressions are not laid down inalterably in our brain like objects in the bottom of a basket. These traces are actually processes, they move, change, live, and die, and this dynamism guarantees that they will change under the influence of imagination. We may cite as an example of such internal change the processes of exaggeration and minimization of individual elements of experience, which have enormous significance for imagination in general and for children's imagination in particular.

The impressions supplied by reality are transformed through these processes, increasing or decreasing their natural size. Children's passion for exaggeration, like the passion of adults for exaggeration, has a very profound internal basis—the influence of our internal feelings on external impressions. We exaggerate because we want to see things in an exaggerated form, because this exaggeration corresponds to our needs, to our internal state. Children's passion for exaggeration is well reflected in fairy tale images. . . .

Karl Buhler, with complete justification, suggests that this process of alteration, and especially exaggeration, provides the child with practice dealing with quantities of which he has no direct experience. . . .

Similar play with exaggerated numbers proves to be extremely important for humans. We can see the proof of this in astronomy and other natural sciences, which have to operate not with smaller, but with vastly greater numbers. . . .

We see that exaggeration, like imagination in general, is essential in art and science alike. If this capacity, which is so amusingly expressed in the story made up by the five-and-a-half-year-old girl, did not exist, humanity would not have been able to create astronomy, geology, or physics.

The next component of the processes of imagination is association, that is, unification of the dissociated and altered elements. As was shown above, this association can be based on various qualities and take various forms, from the purely subjective association of images to objective, scientific association corresponding, for example, to geographical concepts. And, finally, the last aspect of the preliminary work of the imagination is the combination of individual images, their unification into a system, the construction of a complex picture. But creative imagination does not stop here. As we have already noted, the full cycle of this process will be completed only when imagination is embodied or crystallized in external images.

However, we will discuss separately the process of crystallization, or the transformation of imagination into reality. Here, as we are speaking only of the internal aspect of imagination, we should mention the basic psychological factors on which the operation of these individual processes depend. The first such factor is always, as psychological analysis has established, the human need to adapt to the environment. If life surrounding him does not present challenges to an individual, if his usual and inherent reactions are in complete equilibrium with the world around him, then there will be no basis for him to exercise creativity. A creature that is perfectly adapted to its environment would not want anything, would not have anything to strive for, and, of course, would not be able to create anything. Thus, creation is always based on lack of adaptation, which gives rise to needs, motives, and desires. . . .

The presence of needs or drives thus triggers the working of the imagination. Activation of traces of neural stimulation provides material for the imagination to operate on. These two conditions are necessary and sufficient for understanding the operation of the imagination and all the processes it comprises.

There is still the question of the factors that imagination depends on. We have listed the psychological factors above, although not all together.

We have already said that the operation of the imagination depends on experience, on needs, and the interests in which these needs are expressed. It is also easy to understand that this process depends on combinatorial abilities and practice in exercising them, that is, embodying constructs of the imagination in material form; it also depends on the individual's technical abilities and on traditions, that is, on those creative models that influence a person. All these factors are enormously important, but so obvious and simple, that we will not speak of them in detail here. Much less obvious, and thus much more important, is the effect of another factor, the environment. Typically, imagination is portrayed as an exclusively internal activity, one that does not depend on external conditions, or, in the best case, depends on these conditions only to the extent that they determine the material on which the imagination must operate. The process of imagination per se, its direction, at first glance, appears to be guided only from within, by the feelings and needs of the individual, and thus to be wholly subjective and not based on objective factors. In actuality this is not true. Psychology long ago established a law according to which the drive to create is always inversely proportional to the simplicity of the environment. . . .

Every inventor, even a genius, is also a product of his time and his environment. His creations arise from needs that were created before him and rest on capacities that also exist outside of him. This is why we emphasize that there is a strict sequence in the historical development of science and technology. No invention or scientific discovery can occur before the material and psychological conditions necessary for it to occur have appeared. Creation is a historical, cumulative process where every succeeding manifestation was determined by the preceding one.

This explains the disproportionate distribution of innovators and creators among different classes. The privileged classes supply an incomparably greater percent of scientific, technical, and artistic creators, because it is in these classes that all the conditions needed for creation are present. . . .

Chapter 4. Imagination in Children and Adolescents

The functioning of creative imagination proves to be very complex and depends on a whole series of extremely diverse factors. It is quite obvious that this activity cannot be the same in children as it is in adults because these factors take different forms in the different stages of childhood. This is why, during every developmental stage of childhood, creative imagination operates in a particular way, one that is characteristic of that particular stage of the child's development. We have seen that imagination depends on experience, and a child's experience forms and grows gradually, and, in its profound individuality, is different from that of an adult. The child's relationship to his environment, which, through its complexity or simplicity, traditions, and influences stimulates and directs the process of creation, is very different from the adult's. The interests of the child and the adult also differ, and it is thus easy to understand why a child's imagination functions differently from an adult's.

How then does the child's imagination differ from that of an adult? The opinion still persists that a child's imagination is richer than that of the adult. Childhood is considered the time when fantasy is most highly developed, and, according to this belief, as the child develops, his imagination and the strength of his fantasy diminishes. This opinion is based on a whole series of observations of the working of the imagination.

[Johann Wolfgang von] Goethe said that children make anything out of anything, and this undemanding, very tolerant quality of children's fantasy, which becomes more fastidious in adulthood, is frequently mistaken for freedom or richness of imagination. What is more, the products of children's fantasy diverge sharply and obviously from adult reality and this is taken as support for the conclusion that children live in a world of their imagination more than in the real world. Other factors are the inaccuracies and distortions of actual experience and exaggeration that are characteristic of children's fantasy and children's propensity for fairy tales and other fantastic stories.

All this, taken together, has caused people to assert that fantasy is richer and more diverse in childhood than in adulthood. However, this opinion is not confirmed when it is considered scientifically. We know that a child's experience is vastly poorer than an adult's. We further know that children's interests are simpler, more elementary, and thus also poorer; finally, their relationship to the environment does not have the complexity, subtlety, and diversity that characterizes the behavior of adults, and these are the most important factors that determine the workings of the imagination. A child's imagination, as this analysis shows, is not richer, but poorer than that of an adult. In the process of development, the imagination develops like everything else and is fully mature only in the adult.

This is why products of true creative imagination in all areas of creativity belong only to those who have achieved maturity. As maturity is approached, the imagination also matures, and in the transitional period between childhood and adulthood—in adolescence, starting at the time of puberty—we observe a powerful enhancement of the imagination combined with the rudiments of mature fantasy. Authors who write about the imagination have pointed out that there is a close relationship between puberty and the development of the imagination. We can understand this relationship when we consider that, at this time, a great deal of experience has been accrued and assimilated; the so-called permanent interests develop, childish interests are curtailed, and, as a result of general maturation, the working of the imagination begins to assume its final form. . . .

The development of imagination and that of reason are very different in childhood and this relative independence of children's imagination from the operation of reason is the expression not of the richness but of the poverty of children's fantasy.

The child can imagine vastly less than the adult, but he has greater faith in the products of his imagination and controls them less, and thus imagination, in the everyday, vulgar sense of this word, that is, what is unreal and made up, is of course greater in the child than in the adult. However, not only is the material that the imagination operates on to create its constructs poorer in a child than in an adult, but the nature of the combinations that this material enters into—their quality and variety—is significantly more impoverished than that of adults. Of all the types of relationship to reality we listed above, a child's imagination is equal to that of the adult only with regard to the first, that is, the reality of the elements it uses for its constructions. In addition, the actual emotional roots of the child's imagination are as strong as those of the adult. As for all the other types of association, it should be noted that these develop only over the years, very slowly and very gradually. . . .

"Both of these intellectual forms," writes Ribot, "now confront each other as rival forces." The imagination "continues to operate, but, undergoes a preliminary transformation involving adaptation to rational requirements. It is no longer pure imagination, but a combined form." However this does not occur in everyone. In many people development takes another path . . . indicating a decrease or curtailment of the imagination. "Creative imagination diminishes—this is the most common instance. Only the particularly richly endowed imagination constitutes an exception, the majority of people gradually get lost in the prose of everyday life, bury the dreams of their youth, consider love an illusion, and so forth. This, however, is only regression, but not annihilation, because the creative imagination does not disappear completely in anyone, it merely becomes incidental." . . .

If we understand the unique crossroads that the curve of the imagination now passes through, we will have the key to the correct understanding of the entire process of creativity at this age. During this period the imagination undergoes a profound transformation: it changes from subjective to objective. . . .

We know that adolescence is marked by a whole series of antithetical attitudes, contradictions, and polarizations. This is responsible for the fact that this age is critical or transitional; this is the age where childhood's physiological equilibrium is disturbed and the equilibrium of the adult has not yet been achieved. Thus, during this period imagination undergoes a revolution, destruction of the previous equilibrium, and a search for a new equilibrium. The fact that the work of the imagination in the form it took during childhood declines in adolescents is clearly demonstrated by the fact that children of this age generally lose their bent for drawing. Only a few continue to draw, mainly those who are particularly talented in this area or who are encouraged to do so by external conditions such as special drawing lessons. The child begins to have a critical attitude toward his own drawing, his childish schema cease to satisfy him, they seem too subjective, and he comes to the conclusion that he cannot draw, and, for this reason, he stops. We also see this curtailment of childish fantasy in the fact that the child loses interest in the naive games of earlier childhood and in fairy tales and fantastic stories. The duality of the new form of imagination that is born now can be readily deduced from the fact that the most widespread and common form of creative work during this period is literary creation. It is stimulated by a strong increase in subjective experiences and a growth and deepening of the interior life of the adolescent, who, during this period, develops his own internal world. However, this subjective aspect seeks to find embodiment in an objective form—in poems, stories, or whatever creative forms the adolescent perceives in the adult literature surrounding him. The development of this contradictory imagination runs parallel to the further diminishment of his subjective qualities and the growth and strengthening of objective qualities. Typically, the majority of adolescents also lose interest in literary creativity very soon. The adolescent begins to adopt the same sort of critical attitude he previously took to his drawing. He begins to be dissatisfied with the objective quality of his writing and stops doing it. Thus, an increase in imagination and its profound transformation are characteristic of this critical phase.

At the same time, the two major types of imagination are exhibited very clearly at this stage. These are plastic and emotional, or external and internal imagination. These two major types are primarily distinguished by the materials from which fantasy constructs its products and by the rules of this construction. Plastic imagination primarily utilizes the data provided by external impressions, it builds using elements borrowed from without; emotional imagination, on the other hand, builds with elements taken from within. The first of these types can thus be called objective and the second, subjective. The manifestations of both types of imagination and their gradual differentiation is characteristic of the adolescent period. . . .

It is frequently asked whether the operation of the imagination depends on talent. There is a very widespread opinion that creativity is the province of the select few and that only those who are gifted with some special talent should develop it in themselves and have the right to consider themselves to have a vocation for creation. This is not true, as we have attempted to explain above. If we understand creativity in its true psychological sense as the creation of something new, then this implies that creation is the province of everyone to one degree or another; that it is a normal and constant companion in childhood. . . .

Commentary

In Vygotsky's view, imagination is a culturally dependent higher mental function that provides the ability to combine mental phenomena—images, signs, psychological tools, concepts, emotions, memories, features of artifacts encountered, and basically anything that a person can experience—into new configurations. These configurations, in turn, may bring about new capabilities, possibilities, opportunities, or resources for the individual and, if shared, sometimes for everyone in the culture. Imagination is not just "make believe"; it makes reality.

In Chapter 1 of *Imagination and Creativity in Childhood*, not part of the excerpt here, Vygotsky reiterates the conventional wisdom of his time, counterposing imagination with memory. Whereas memory is a reproductive function of already mastered behaviors from previous experiences to support habits, imagination is a productive function to address the need to adapt to change or to unexpected events. Memory helps humans succeed in familiar situations and stable environments. But it is imagination that helps humans drive their lives forward into an unknown future.

However, in Chapter 2, also a preface to the excerpt here, Vygotsky (1960/1987) realizes that memory is not the opposite of imagination; being stuck in the present moment is. Individuals with no imagination can sense what is going on only in the immediate time and place they are in (Vygotsky, 1931/1998). The extent of their reality is the here and now. Individuals free themselves from the immediate environment by setting up intermediaries to expand what they can think about to incorporate others' experiences and potential experiences (Moran & John-Steiner, 2003). Imagination gives birth to that freedom, which may be particularly profound for individuals or groups who are oppressed by or marginalized from the mainstream culture (Jovchelovitch, 2015).

Thus the first key insight of Vygotsky is that imagination is not the absence of reality but rather the foundation of human reality that extends beyond right now (see also Zittoun & Gillespie, 2016). Imagination is not a "flight of fancy" within minds that have no purpose (Smolucha, 1992a). Imagination's purpose is to create reality: it is the mother of culture, providing tools to plan, share, build on each other's perspectives, devise tools and signs, consider the future, and create artifacts that can communicate with future generations.

Vygotsky (1978) is best known for the idea that human psychology is based on mediation: individuals use language, other symbol systems, artifacts, and relationships to help them navigate their world. One question, though: Where do the mediators come from? Many originate from someone's imagination. Words, concepts, material things, institutions, and other cultural elements were all invented at some point in the past. Thus Vygotsky's second key insight is that culture develops, in part, through imagination. Instead of conceiving of individuals as separate, from a cultural-historical perspective, it may be helpful to consider an individual mind as a factory of cultural possibilities that, when shared and evaluated, become cultural actuality—what is more commonly called "creativity" (Glăveanu, 2010).

Vygotsky was interested in origins and turning points (Moran & John-Steiner, 2003). Most of psychology has emphasized the individual as the unit of analysis. An individual's body and psychology must mature sufficiently for him or her to be "grown up" enough to join the culture or enter into "society" properly. But Vygotsky turned that individualistic argument on its head and suggested that culture, not the individual, is the origin of development. As a social species, humans are born into a culture, which nurtures how they think about and operate within the world. But because all human communication capacities are limited, imagination is needed to bridge gaps in current understanding or across individual and group differences so that knowledge may be appropriated (Pelaprat & Cole, 2011; Zittoun & de Saint Laurent, 2014). Thus Vygotsky's third key insight is that culture promotes and requires imagination from its members, and that imagination develops socially, starting at a very young age and continuing throughout life.

PRESCIENT

These insights put Vygotsky ahead of his time. He was a visionary, anticipating creativity research decades later, especially regarding how imagination functions through the plasticity of the human mind's functioning, how imagination is prevalent in most cultures, and how imagination plays with and through experience. Each of these impacts of Vygotsky's work on current and emerging scholarship in creativity is discussed below.

Vygotsky was not so much directly *influential* on Western creativity research because his work was in Russian and quashed by Stalin for much of the 20th century. He was introduced to English-language scholars midcentury (Vygotsky, 1934/1962). But his writings were dense, so it took another 16 years for a more accessible introduction to become available (Vygotsky, 1978). His *Collected Works* were not translated and published until around the turn of the 21st century. In the mean time, scholars had arrived at similar ideas independently of Vygotsky's work.

But it would be accurate to say that Vygotsky's ideas were *prescient* of later psychologists' work. Vygotsky's ideas are forerunners of recent conceptions of imagination as a common human faculty (e.g., Feldman's "transformational imperative," in Ambrose, 2014); imagination as related to play, emotion, and education in children (e.g., Russ, Robins, & Christiano, 1999; Smolucha, 1992b); imagination as a social and collaborative process (e.g., John-Steiner, 2000; Sawyer & DeZutter, 2009); imagination as part of a system of individual and cultural creativity (e.g., Csikszentmihalyi, 1996; Moran, 2014); and imagination requiring time and effort to manifest creativity (e.g., Gruber & Davis's [1988] "networks of enterprises" and "evolving systems"; Wallace & Gruber, 1989).

Vygotsky also foresaw several key findings in 20th-century creativity research, such as the "fourth grade slump," when many children turn away from creative endeavors (Torrance, 1968); crystallizing experiences and misalignments with the environment that trigger emotions and cognitive reframings signaling a need for a new approach (Moran, 2014; Walters & Gardner, 1986); and the role of others besides the creator in evaluating imaginative productions (Csikszentmihalyi, 1996; Moran, 2014).

Looking forward into the 21st century, given the growing interest in dynamic and collaborative frameworks for understanding creativity (e.g., Moran, 2009) and in samples of ordinary individuals in everyday situations (e.g., Jovchelovitch, 2015), as well as the growing capabilities to collect more detailed data regarding how individual minds build on each other's contributions (see Wikipedia example in Moran, 2014), it will be interesting to see how Vygotsky's prescient ideas may become more directly—and perhaps even experimentally—examined.

PLASTIC

Imagination is the avant-garde of reality. Reality, in part, depends on how individuals and groups represent experiences to themselves and to each other through symbols. News, fiction, movies, songs, and humor are made real through emotional involvement created by imagination. Individuals can step outside the flow of experience to abstractly parse and remix elements of their experiences, then to reinject the remix back into concrete situations with the possibility of redirecting the flow of their lives. Not only can imagination help humans adapt to environmental changes; it can change the environment. Imagination thus expands experience beyond what one person actually senses (Zittoun & Cerchia, 2013).

When a problem arises, switching from a habitual response to an imaginative approach is purposeful. This switch makes sense when past meaning is lost or does not work: *What now?* But imagination does not pull random or crazy ideas out of thin air. Rather the process resembles recycling. An object—say, a bottle—used for the purpose of drinking soda when a person is thirsty also can be used as a candleholder for an impromptu romantic dinner. Or a concept—say, sweetness—describing a flavor in cooking also can refer to kindness in social relations. What is important to notice is that the properties of the object or concept must be perceived and capitalized on. Vygotsky called this "dissociation." One role imagination plays is figuring out how to disentangle the properties in a useful way for the new purpose (i.e., a framework). Another role is deciding which properties are most useful for the new purpose (i.e., selection). And yet another role is connecting the parts for the new purpose (i.e., building). Through this process, imagination remixes what came before.

Although children have conceptual mix-ups all the time, and those mix-ups can be charming, Vygotsky warned us not to confuse these mix-ups with the experiential remixes of imagination. He anticipated later work relating imagination to perspective-taking, self-regulation, and shared understanding (e.g., Harris, 2000). Because imagination operates on experience, and most children have fewer and less nuanced experiences than most adults, they have less psychological material for their imaginations to work with. Plus, they don't know what they don't know. So children are more likely to be confident in their wacky ideas even as the products of their imagination are less likely to be workable.

Still, also because they have a paucity of real experience, children *need* imagination. Their everyday lives may be so constrained that imagination is a powerful tool for them to extend their experiential options. Without many opportunities to practice such extension beyond "what is," children just repeat the same options presented to them, overlearn the culture's "right answers," and potentially lose the ability to get outside their own limited perspectives. Thus the cultivation of the imagination is just as important—and in some ways, more so—than the cultivation of knowledge.

Indeed it is important for one's mind to first break from knowledge—what Vygotsky called the "natural association" that a culture most strongly teaches to its young. Otherwise a person may not consider the other associations possible. Unfortunately it may be that technology today is making it more difficult for children to move beyond the "answers" that are so easily supplied to them through search engines, social media, or apps (Carr, 2011; Moran, 2016; cf. Gardner & Davis, 2013). Children are sheltered from seeing the gaps in their own understandings and in cultural understandings. These gaps are important to perceive so they stimulate imagination (Pelaprat & Cole, 2011). The struggle to make sense of a situation and devise helpful symbolic mediation to move forward is important for human development, and imagination plays a key role in that process (Clarà, 2016).

In the extreme, this derailment of imagination can lead to xenophobia, bigotry, anxiety of things unfamiliar or "other" (Glăveanu & de Saint Laurent, 2015). With the internet, the famed "echo chamber" of surrounding oneself only with people and ideas one already knows can further cripple imagination. But imagining opposites or other alternatives can help overcome these social biases (Lord, Lepper, & Preston, 1984). Without at least some imagination, connecting with others who are different becomes difficult. These individuals become adults who cannot step outside their current circumstances to learn from others, reflect on their own experiences, and build new possibilities for themselves (Smolucha, 1992a; Zittoun & de Saint Laurent, 2014). By not dissociating fantasy and concepts, emotion and representation, subjectivity of oneself from objectivity on the world, they lose the flexibility to think beyond their own perspectives and current circumstances.

What makes Vygotsky's view of the functioning of imagination so relevant to today's scholarship is that he emphasized how imagination not only associates and combines (e.g., James, 1890; Ward, Smith, & Vaid, 1997). The imagination also distinguishes. No matter how many different ways ideas or elements might be put together (e.g., Sternberg, Kaufman, & Pretz, 2001), imagination is more than a connector. People are more flexible if they can also perceive properties of objects, concepts, environments—then work with those more abstract aspects or dimensions to foster novel relationships. That is, the imagination is more powerful and adept at manipulation of signs and tools if it can first pull apart entities to find new "threads" for connection. Imagination makes distinctions as well as connections, which helps it bend reality into new forms.

Into the 21st century, Vygotsky's work challenges both scholars and practitioners of creativity to maintain the reciprocity of connection and distinction of our individual or group contributions via their integration into a greater good. For example, in 2017 there was a surge of separate venues in which individuals could express their imaginative viewpoints, especially via the internet. The concern was that these "echo chambers" and "fake facts" might create difficulties for individuals trying to connect their new ideas to history and to other minds because the shared meaning by which they could bridge their different viewpoints had become scarcer. How can new uses of Vygotsky's ideas build stronger frameworks for interdependence?

PLAYFUL

Although Vygotsky originally focused on how imagination helps individuals escape the here and now, some of his followers extend his argument to suggest that imagination is also required to experience the present (Pelaprat & Cole, 2011). Imagination bends sensory data into perceptions that connect oneself to one's world within and across moments. Imagination is a worldmaker (Goodman, 1978; Hanchett Hanson, 2015).

Worldmaking starts early in life. In accord with his general theory that development first occurs socially, then is internalized, Vygotsky proposed that pretend play was how imagination first develops. Although play is usually enjoyable, it is not frivolous, but rather is serious developmental business. Play emphasizes effort, activity, and leaps in development. (The word "play" comes from Old English for "leaps of joy.") Play is the primary means by which children can expand their experiential repertoire despite environmental or social constraints. Instead, ideally, children create their own constraints in collaboration with other players: make-believe is a team sport (Moran & John-Steiner, 2003; Smolucha, 1992b).

Through play, children tinker with objects' various properties, humans' various roles, and symbols' possible meanings. Eventually they don't need toys or objects. Instead they manipulate options through fantasy (Vygotsky, 1978). Games, sports, and improvisational theater of made-up rules create situations through which children master their own bodies and behavior. Eventually they can even conjure an ideal future self to help themselves develop—creating a zone of proximal development within oneself (Zittoun & de Saint-Laurent, 2014).

Play is probably the aspect of Vygotsky's thinking on imagination that has been most studied in contemporary research. The research ranges from explorations of mother-child play to understand an object can represent more than one thing (Smolucha, 1992b) to how play results in children behaving more maturely than their years (Smolucha & Smolucha, 2012) and developing agency (Marjanovic-Shane & White, 2014). It also emphasizes social and emotional dimensions, such as understanding emotions and building intersubjectivity (Göncü & Gaskins, 2011), creating "playworlds" in which imaginations across generations can come together in equality (Nilsson & Ferholt, 2014).

More recent research extends play's important role in development to youth and adults. Heath and Seop's (1998) work on youth graffiti, Smagorinsky's (2016) work with autistic youth, and Hanchett Hanson's (2012) social justice youth theater exemplify ways that youth can "play" at making important contributions to communities and, in the process, gather important feedback about the consequences of their actions in the real world.

Sawyer's (2000) work on improvisation in various artistic and linguistic domains, "playworlds" to enrich adult emotional experience (Ferholt, 2009), and the growing maker movement (Halverson & Sheridan, 2014) democratize play across age stages. Pretend play starts children on the path to adult creativity (Russ & Wallace, 2013). Into the 21st century, how might Vygotsky's ideas be used to explore how and why an increasing number of tasks and domains are becoming viewed as play? What would he say about workplaces' and societies' "gamification" of all experience?

PERVASIVE

Even though Vygotsky posited that imagination was not a special mental function limited to creative geniuses but rather was common to all, imagination has become even more pervasive today. American culture, in particular, seems to long for ever more imagination and innovation through maker spaces, innovation labs, and hacker garages in which "normal" rules don't apply (Moran, 2014). Significant research, following Vygotsky's lead, shows that imagination thrives on cross-generational participation, apprenticeship, and collaboration (Glăveanu, 2010; Greenfield, 2007; John-Steiner, 2000; St. John, 2010).

Perhaps it is time to extend the notion of "thought communities" to "imagination communities." Imagination both emerges from and supports conversation, social understanding, and cooperation. Without imagination to bridge the gap between individuals and make mutuality possible, humans would not be able to build on each other's ideas and products. Imagination is distributed across individuals (Sawyer & DeZutter, 2009) so that shared meaning can emerge. Imagination is foundational for societies to function because understanding each other requires each person to take a "leap" beyond the actual words said or actions taken, and that interpretation is aided by imagination (Glăveanu & de Saint Laurent, 2015). Humans' greatest inventions are their own development and life path (Zittoun & de Saint Laurent, 2014), culture itself (Wagner, 2016) and how the two are intertwined (Moran, 2016; Moran & John-Steiner, 2003, 2004; Valsiner, 2000).

Imagination starts with children trying to extend their limited experiences with caregivers who go along with their "what if" and "let's pretend" games. Then imagination becomes increasingly intentional and mastered as children learn to talk to themselves and control their own behaviors with less external support. In school they learn to encapsulate their thoughts within concepts, and they learn the norms of their culture. If these norms are learned too rigidly, such that they become understood as the "one and only right way" to do something, then children may reduce their imaginative capacity (Torrance, 1968). Finally, imagination can create tools, signs, and artifacts novel not only in the person's experience but also in the culture's evolution. These imaginative outputs can become part of the cultural canon passed on to later generations. Whereas, at first, a person learns to imagine from others, eventually for some, a person can help others imagine even beyond current cultural boundaries.

As imagination further democratizes, especially with social media, one question arises: Are digital communities sufficient to provide the rich experiences needed for imagination to grow? There is growing concern that technology may thwart imagination because the "virtual" presents everything to children on demand and reduces emotional communication (Turkle, 2012, 2016). There is no gap to trigger the need for imagination. Although increasingly sophisticated and ubiquitous as learning environments, computer games design in—and thus limit—the features of experience. They do not allow children themselves to surmise and experiment with a variety of features (Barab, Thomas, Dodge, Carteaux & Tuzun, 2005). Could Vygotsky's work on imagination be used as a foundation to explore the emotional or aesthetic impacts of such developments as well as the moral impacts of technology on the development of imagination (Moran, 2016)? Or perhaps a more hopeful way to phrase this possibility is this: How might Vygotsky's perspective effectively be used to both understand and develop better venues for cultivating and sustaining imagination?

References

Ambrose, D. (2014). Transformational imperative for the field: An interview with David Henry Feldman. *Roeper Review, 36*, 207–209.

Barab, S., Thomas, M., Dodge, T., Carteaux, R., & Tuzun, H. (2005). Making learning fun: Quest Atlantis, a game without guns. *Educational Technology Research & Design, 53*(1), 86–107.

Blunden, A. (2010). *An interdisciplinary theory of activity.* Boston, MA: Brill.

Carr, N. (2011). *The shallows: What the internet is doing to our brains.* New York, NY: Norton.

Clarà, M. (2016). Vygotsky and Vasilyuk on perezhivanie: Two notions and one word. *Mind, Culture, and Activity, 23*(4), 284–293. doi: 10.1080/10749039.2016.1186194.

Cole, M., & Scribner, S. (1978). Introduction. In L. S. Vygotsky, *Mind in society: The development of higher psychological processes* (M. Cole, V. John-Steiner, S. Scribner, & E. Souberman, Eds.; pp. 1–14). Cambridge, MA: Harvard University Press.

Connery, M. C., John-Steiner, V. P., & Marjanovic-Shane, A. (Eds.). (2010). *Vygotsky and creativity: A cultural-historical approach to play, meaning making, and the arts.* New York, NY: Peter Lang.

Csikszentmihalyi, M. (1996). *Creativity.* New York: Harper Collins.

Ferholt, B. (2009). *The development of cognition, emotion, imagination, and creativity as made visible through adult-child joint play: Perezhivanie through playworlds* (Unpublished doctoral dissertation). University of California, San Diego.

Gardner, H., & Davis, K. (2013). *The app generation: How today's youth navigate identity, intimacy, and imagination in a digital world.* New Haven, CT: Yale University Press.

Glăveanu, V. P. (2010). Creativity as cultural participation. *Journal for the Theory of Social Behavior, 41*(1), 48–67.

Glăveanu, V. P., & de Saint Laurent, C. (2015). Editorial: Political imagination, otherness and the European crisis. *Europe's Journal of Psychology, 11*(4), 557–564.

Göncü, A., & Gaskins, S. (2011). Comparing and extending Piaget's and Vygotsky's understandings of play: Symbolic play as individual, sociocultural, and educational interpretation. In A. Pellegrini (Ed.), *The Oxford handbook of the development of play* (pp. 48–57). New York, NY: Oxford University Press.

Goodman, N. (1978). *Ways of worldmaking.* Indianapolis, IN: Hackett.

Greenfield, P. M. (2007). Culture and learning. In C. Casey & R. B. Edgerton (Eds.), *A companion to psychological anthropology: Modernity and psychocultural change* (pp. 72–89). Malden, MA: Blackwell.

Gruber, H. E., & Davis, S. N. (1988). Inching our way up Mount Olympus: The evolving-systems approach to creative thinking. In R. J. Sternberg (Ed.), *The nature of creativity* (pp. 243–270). New York, NY: Cambridge University Press.

Halverson, E. R., & Sheridan, K. M. (2014). The maker movement in education. *Harvard Educational Review, 84*(4), 495–504.

Hanchett Hanson, M. (2012). Creating self and world: Youth development in The Possibility Project. *Knowledge Quest*, online edition.

Hanchett Hanson, M. (2015). *Worldmaking: Psychology and ideology of creativity*. London: Palgrave Macmillan.

Harris, P. L. (2000). *The work of the imagination*. Malden, MA: Wiley-Blackwell.

Heath, S. B., & Soep, E. (1998). Youth development and the arts in non-school hours. *Grantmakers in the Arts, 9*(1), 9–16, 32.

James, W. (1890). Imagination. In *The principles of psychology* (pp. 44–75). New York, NY: Henry Holt.

John-Steiner, V. (2000). *Creative collaboration*. New York, NY: Oxford University Press.

Jovchelovitch, S. (2015). The creativity of the social: Imagination, development and social change in Rio de Janeiro's favelas. In V. P. Glǎveanu, A. Gillespie, & J. Valsiner (Eds.), *Rethinking creativity: Contributions from social and cultural psychology* (pp. 76–92). Hove, UK: Routledge.

Kozulin, A. (1990). *Vygotsky's psychology: A biography of ideas*. Cambridge, MA: Harvard University Press.

Leontiev, A. N. (1979). On Vygotsky's creative development. Retrieved from www.marxists.org/archive/leontev/works/1979/vygotsky.htm.

Lev Vygotsky Archive. (n.d.). Retrieved from www.marxists.org/archive/vygotsky.

Lord, C. G., Lepper, M. R., & Preston, E. (1984). Considering the opposite: A corrective strategy for social judgment. *Journal of Personality and Social Psychology, 47*(6), 1231–1243.

Marjanovic-Shane, A., & White, E. J. (2014). When the footlights are off: A Bakhtinian interrogation of play as postupok. *International Journal of Play, 3*(2), 119–135.

Moran, S. (2009). Creativity: A systems perspective. In T. Richards, M. Runco, & S. Moger (Eds.), *The Routledge companion to creativity* (pp. 292–301). London: Routledge.

Moran, S. (2014). An ethics of possibility. In S. Moran, D. H. Cropley, & J. C. Kaufman (Eds.), *The ethics of creativity* (pp. 281–298). Basingstoke, UK: Palgrave Macmillan.

Moran, S. (2016). *Ethical ripples of creativity and innovation*. Basingstoke, UK: Palgrave Macmillan.

Moran, S., Cropley, D., & Kaufman, J. (Eds.). (2014). *The ethics of creativity*. Basingstoke, UK: Palgrave Macmillan.

Moran, S., & John-Steiner, V. (2003). Creativity in the making: Vygotsky's contribution to the dialectic of creativity and development. In K. Sawyer et al. (Eds.), *Creativity and development* (pp. 61–90). New York, NY: Oxford University Press.

Moran, S., & John-Steiner, V. (2004). How collaboration in creative work impacts identity and motivation. In D. Miell & K. Littleton (Eds.), *Collaborative creativity: Contemporary perspectives* (pp. 11–25). London: Free Association Books.

Nilsson, M., & Ferholt, B. (2014). Vygotsky's theories of play, imagination, and creativity in current practice: Gunilla Lindqvist's "creative pedagogy of play" in U.S. kindergartens and Swedish Reggio-Emilia inspired preschools. *Perspectiva, 32*(3), 919–950.

Pelaprat, E., & Cole, M. (2011). "Minding the gap": Imagination, creativity and human cognition. *Integrative Psychological and Behavioral Science, 45*, 397–418.

Russ, S. W., Robins, A. L., &. Christiano, B. A. (1999). Pretend play: Longitudinal prediction of creativity and affect in fantasy in children. *Creativity Research Journal, 12*, 129–139.

Russ, S. W., & Wallace, C. E. (2013). Pretend play and creative processes. *American Journal of Play, 6*(1), 136–148.

Sawyer, R. K. (2000). Improvisation and the creative process: Dewey, Collingwood, and the aesthetics of spontaneity. *Journal of Aesthetics and Art Criticism, 58*(2), 149–161.

Sawyer, R. K., & DeZutter, S. (2009). Distributed creativity: How collective creations emerge from collaboration. *Psychology of Aesthetics, Creativity, and the Arts, 3*(2), 81–92.

Smagorinsky, P. (2016). *Creativity and community among autism-spectrum youth: Creating positive social updrafts through play and performance*. Basingstoke, UK: Palgrave Macmillan.

Smolucha, F. (1992a). A reconstruction of Vygotsky's theory of creativity. *Creativity Research Journal, 5*(1), 49–67.

Smolucha, F. (1992b). The relevance of Vygotsky's theory of creative imagination for contemporary research on play. *Creativity Research Journal, 5*(1), 69–76.

Smolucha, L., & Smolucha, F. (2012). Vygotsky's theory of creativity: On figurative and literal thinking. In O. Sarach (Ed.), *Contemporary perspectives on research in creativity in early childhood education* (pp. 63–88). Charlotte, NC: Information Age.

St. John, P. (2010). Crossing scripts and swapping riffs: Preschoolers make musical meaning. In C. Connery, V. John-Steiner, & A. Marjanovic-Shane (Eds.), *Vygotsky and creativity: A cultural-historical approach to meaning-making, play, and the arts* (pp. 63–82). New York, NY: Peter Lang.

Sternberg, R. J., Kaufman, J. C., & Pretz, J. E. (2001). The propulsion model of creative contributions applied to the arts and letters. *Journal of Creative Behavior, 35*(2), 75–101.

Stetsenko, A. (2016). *The transformative mind: Expanding Vygotsky's approach to development and education.* New York, NY: Cambridge University Press.

Torrance, E. P. (1968). A longitudinal examination of the fourth grade slump in creativity. *Gifted Child Quarterly, 12*(4), 195–199.

Turkle, S. (2012). *Alone together: Why we expect more from technology and less from each other.* New York, NY: Basic Books.

Turkle, S. (2016). *Reclaiming conversation: The power of talk in a digital age.* New York, NY: Penguin.

Valsiner, J. (2000). *Culture and human development.* Thousand Oaks, CA: Sage.

Veresov, N. (1999) *Undiscovered Vygotsky: Etudes on the pre-history of cultural-historical psychology.* New York, NY: Peter Lang.

Vygotsky, L. S. (1930/1998). Imagination and creativity in childhood. *Soviet Psychology, 28*(10), 84–96. (Original work published as *Voobrazhenie i tvorchestvo v shkol'nom voraste,* Moscow-Leningrad: GIZ)

Vygotsky, L. S. (1930/2004). Imagination and creativity in childhood (M. E. Sharpe, Inc., Trans.). *Journal of Russian and East European Psychology, 42*(1), 7–97.

Vygotsky, L. S. (1931/1998). Imagination and creativity in the adolescent. In R. W. Rieber (Ed.), *The collected works of L. S. Vygotsky* (Vol., 5, M. J. Hall, Trans., pp. 151–166). New York, NY: Plenum Press. (Original work published in *Pedologija podrostka,* Moscow: Izd-vo BZO pri Pedfake 2-go MGU)

Vygotsky, L. S. (1934/1962). *Thought and language* (E. Hanfmann & G. Vakar, Trans.). Cambridge, MA: MIT Press. (Original work published as *Myshlenie I rech',* Moscow-Leningrad: Sotsekgiz)

Vygotsky, L. S. (1936/1999). On the problem of the psychology of the actor's creative work. In R. W. Rieber (Ed.), *The collected works of L. S. Vygotsky* (Vol., 6, M. J. Hall, Trans., pp. 237–244). New York, NY: Kluwer Academic/Plenum. (Original work written 1932; published in P. M. Yakobson, *Psikhologija stsenicheskikh chuvst aktera,* pp. 197–211, Moscow)

Vygotsky, L. S. (1960/1987). Imagination and its development in childhood. In R. W. Rieber & A. S. Carton (Eds.), *The collected works of L. S. Vygotsky* (Vol., 1, N. Minick, Trans., pp. 339–350). New York: Plenum Press. (Original work written 1932; published in *Razvitie vysshikh psikhicheskikh funktsii,* Moscow: Izd-vo APN, RSFSR)

Vygotsky, L. S. (1965/1971). *The psychology of art* (Scripta Technica, Inc., Trans.). Cambridge, MA: MIT Press. (Original work published as *Psikhologiia iskusstva;* first written as dissertation, 1917, accepted 1925)

Vygotsky, L. S. (1978). *Mind in society: The development of higher psychological processes* (M. Cole, V. John-Steiner, S. Scribner, & E. Souberman, Eds.). Cambridge, MA: Harvard University Press.

Wagner, R. (2016). *The invention of culture.* Chicago, IL: University of Chicago Press.

Wallace, D. B., & Gruber, H. E. (Eds.). (1989). *Creative people at work.* New York, NY: Oxford University Press.

Walters, J., & Gardner, H. (1986). The crystallizing experience: Discovering an intellectual gift. In R. J. Sternberg & J. E. Davidson (Eds.), *Conceptions of giftedness* (pp. 306–331). New York, NY: Cambridge University Press.

Ward, T. B., Smith, S. M., & Vaid, T. (1997). *Creative thought: An investigation of conceptual structures and processes.* Washington, DC: American Psychological Association.

Zittoun, T., & Cerchia, F. (2013). Imagination as expansion of experience. *Integrative Psychological and Behavioral Science, 47,* 305–324.

Zittoun, T., & de Saint-Laurent, C. (2014). Life-creativity: Imagining one's life. In V. P. Glăveanu, A. Gillespie, & J. Valsiner (Eds.), *Rethinking creativity: Contributions from social and cultural psychology* (pp. 58–75). Hove, UK: Routledge.

Zittoun, T., & Gillespie, A. (2016). *Imagination in human and cultural development.* New York, NY: Routledge.

15

The Meaning of Play
Erik H. Erikson

JESSICA D. HOFFMANN AND ROSE H. MILLER

Summary

Primarily known for his psychosocial stages of development, Erik Homburger Erikson was also keenly interested in childhood play and studied it in varying degrees throughout his career. In these two early texts, "The Meaning of Play" (1948) and "Clinical Studies in Childhood Play" (1943), Erikson provides a rich account of the intricacies and implications of children's play as it relates to larger societal notions of creativity and productivity. His detailed clinical notes provide a fascinating and useful background for the modern scholar, despite being largely unreferenced in the public debate about the utility of children's play. Even though Erikson's notes could today be regarded as dated and overly psychoanalytic, much of their content still proves to be informative to the modern reader. His argument that children's play is equal to much more than the sum of its functional parts is one that has been expanded upon greatly by more recent researchers, such that much of the conversation regarding play today accepts the broader significance of childhood play. That this notion might be, at least in part, attributable to some of Erikson's work is an idea that has not been explored before but that ought to be given appropriate weight given the insight that these two excerpts have to offer.

Introduction

Two years before he published his most famous work, *Childhood and Society*, in which he first originated the psychosocial stages of development, Erik Erikson (1948, 1950) wrote a brief essay, "The Meaning of Play," in which he explored the nuances of children's play as it related to psychological and physical aspects of development. Erikson's long-standing interest in children's play went largely unnoticed, perennially overshadowed by his famous work on development throughout the lifespan. Grounded mainly in the realm of psychoanalytic thought, Erikson's writings on play explore the symbolic significance of play, both in and of itself and as an indicator of childhood developmental and psychological processes.

As a clinician at the Institute of Child Welfare in Berkeley, California, Erikson had ample opportunity to observe how children interacted with the world around them and was fascinated by play as a functional tool for understanding children's thoughts and emotions. Trained as a psychoanalyst at the Vienna Psychoanalytic Institute, Erikson wrote about play as a tool that could be thought of as functionally parallel to dream analysis as it was used in adult psychoanalysis. Thus he regarded play not only as symbolic and meaningful but also as diagnostically useful and revealing of inner desires and character. Play was a window into the childhood psyche that surpassed in functionality the use of language, because children were naturally inclined to play as a way to develop mastery of the world around them. Play also lacked the element of untruthfulness that words so often contained.

Public opinion commonly vacillates between regarding children's play as highly important and relevant to childhood development and as frivolous and indulgent. That Erikson was so keenly interested in play suggests that his contributions to the field reach farther than the psychosocial stages for which he is most often cited, and perhaps even influenced the popular conversation regarding the importance or utility of play for understanding childhood development. Furthermore, his writings on play themselves indicate that play is steeped in value not only for psychoanalysts but for society as a whole, as it both reflects the inner desires of children and the societies from which they emerge and provides a meaningful outlet for creativity and exploration that sadly might otherwise be lost. Erikson's serious and substantial approach to play indicates its utility beyond just the scope of analysis and psychological inquiry. Given the ongoing debate regarding the utility and importance of play and, accordingly, creativity, such a respectful approach to what some regard as an insubstantial subject by one of the field's most well-regarded scholars allows for entry into a topic that might otherwise be ignored or written off as peripheral.

The selections below are the article "The Meaning of Play" in its entirety and selected pages (411–414 and 418–420) from a chapter of *Child Behavior and Development: A Course of Representative Studies* titled "Clinical Studies in Childhood Play."

Reading 1: "The Meaning of Play"

Source: Erikson, E. H. (1948). The meaning of play. *Bulletin of the National Association for Nursery Education, 3*, 37–38. Copyright © 1948 NAEYC®. Reprinted with permission.

The Meaning of Play

The title suggests three questions:

1. What has the <u>word</u> "play" come to mean to adults?
2. What is the meaning of play as a <u>function</u> in adulthood?
3. What is the <u>symbolic</u> meaning of play acts?

Mark Twain defined play thus: "Play consists of whatever a body is not obliged to do." With tongue in cheek he thus went along with those theorists who define play by what it is not, namely, work. And, indeed, on the adult level play is a periodical stepping out of physical and economic confinement into a sphere of imaginary freedom. Free play means latitude, elbow room. Play affords a feeling independence from the pressure of time (dallying, idling), gravity (juggling, dancing), fate (games of chance), and personal identity (play acting).

In other words, play is extra-economic. The adult forgets his defined role in goods-producing, commodity-exchanging life, to do something which is not necessary, but re-creative.

Adult playfulness breaks down where goalmindedness becomes too strong. Sex play ends where sex act begins. Game ends where gambling begins. Play-acting ends where the player "means it."

A child's play, by comparison, is pre-economic. It does not produce commodities. But it is the creative activity of a growing organism which is orienting itself in physical and social reality. Yet in much of the literature in the nursery school field, play is still treated with condescending tolerance or apologetic rationalizations such as that, after all, play helps motor and memory development, or can be utilized for more rapid socialization, or is good for "mental hygiene." These are truths, but partial ones.

A child's play dramatization is an activity of make-believe in which mutually exclusive categories are reconciled. For example Tom Sawyer's friend Ben, when he is "boat and captain and engine bells combined," enjoys imaginary mastery over complicated machinery. It probably makes him forget his own dangling body and his pre-adolescent mind and their as yet conflicting wills. Similarly, a smaller child, when building a tower and delightedly seeing it collapse, enjoys causing to an inanimate object that experience which a short while ago has been so painful to himself: falling.

Psychologists are right when they establish the fact that children of the same developmental level tend to do the same thing in play. But they often fail to recognize that a child uses the medium of these play acts in order to relieve and overcome his failures, disappointments, and repressed drives. This Freud first demonstrated in the analysis of a play act which consisted of a small child's throwing an object attached to a string behind a couch and pulling it back again. Certain details suggested that the child was dramatizing his mother's departure and return, which in real life was beyond his control.

Typical play acts have a common meaning for all children of a certain developmental level; they have a special meaning for certain sub-groups; and they have at the same time (as only detailed observation can show) unique meaning for individual children.

The child's play is the infantile form of the universal human capacity to deal with changing reality by dramatizations: in dream and thought, on the stage and on the drawing board. Man creates model-situations which help him (all at once) to relive past failures, to release leftover affects, to satisfy urgent drives, to exercise developing skills, and to be the wiser in anticipating the future.

In learning to play in childhood, man learns to learn and plan as an adult. As William Blake put it: "The child's toys and the old man's reasons are the fruit of the two seasons."

Reading 2: *Clinical Studies in Childhood Play*

Source: Erikson, E. H. (1943). Clinical studies in childhood play. In R. G. Barker, J. S. Kounin, & H. F. Wright (Eds.), *Child Behavior and Development: A Course of Representative Studies* (pp. 411–428). New York, NY: McGraw-Hill. Selections from "Introduction" (pp. 411–414) and "Building a House with Blocks" (pp. 418–420). Reproduced with permission.

Introduction

Psychoanalysis not only assumes, with others, a vague self-teaching, self-healing function in childhood play, it also detects a detailed correspondence between central personality problems and both the content and the form of individual play creations. However, the clinical psychoanalysis of play has shared the methodological limits of other psychoanalytic mediums with which Freud did not concern himself in details (as he did with dreams, slips, witticisms, etc.). The discernible phantasy content of play is welcome as a substitution for dreams and other mediums which are not plentiful in contacts with a small child; its specific variables, however (such as the variables of extension in actual space), have not been considered worth any special consideration.

How much or how little scientific ore may be contained in the clinical experience comes to light only through the therapist's constant efforts at making explicit some of the implicit (preconscious) steps of selecting, associating, and reasoning which constitute his clinical "intuition" at a given time and in a given technique. In this way, he delivers new problems to the doorsteps of more exact investigation. More he cannot claim to do, for his observation, if genuinely clinical, cannot avoid or measure powerful personal equations: beyond the fact that he observes with the naked eye and ear, he has the dutiful intention to influence the very material under observation, and this influence underlies the constant change of the therapist's function in science and society.

Let us, therefore, view only two short play episodes, and these as if they were contained in a moving picture which we can turn to slow motion or arrest completely in order to keep selected items before our eyes until we have finished saying what we have to say about them.

Two Play Episodes

THE INITIAL SITUATION

Our patient is Mary. She is just three years old. She is described as not robust, rather a little pale, even timid; but she looks (and is) intelligent, pretty, and quite girlish. She is said to be dramatic: lovable, outgoing, playful, and coquettish if master of the situation; stubborn, babyish, and shut-in when disturbed. Recently she has enriched her inventory of expression by violent anxiety attacks which bring her to me: after being seemingly adjusted quite well to a play group (it is her first one and she has had extremely little contact with children), she began to scream uncontrollably until her mother came to take her home. This is paralleled by nightmares during which she strikes about wildly. Her mother, on picking her up (in order "to hold her tightly") notices that her breath is "foul" and attributes the tension to bad tonsils. The nursery school contributes the observation that Mary has a queer way of lifting things and has a rigid posture; her tension seems to increase in connection with the routines of resting and going to the toilet.

With this information at hand we invite Mary to our office in order to see in what direction her play will point.

Every psychotherapist has certain vague expectations in regard to what a disturbed child entering his room for the first time may be expecting of him and may do. Against this generalized picture the behavior of a single child stands out in its dramatic individuality.

Our young patient usually arrives hand in hand with his mother. He can be expected to have made a mental note of the fact that our office is in a "hospital-like" institution. On entering the waiting room he finds a friendly secretary and is then invited into an inner room, about half of which (signified by "adult furniture") is set aside for the therapist's plainly nonmedical business, the other half (signified by the floor space and an array of ordinary toys) for a child's play. He is told sooner or later that he is expected to let his mother withdraw to the waiting room and to allow the connecting door to be closed; the therapist and the toys are then to be at his disposal.

This situation confronts the young patient with a maze of conflicting possibilities. We should like to describe it as consisting of several overlapping fields of ambiguity which are created by the child's relation to mother, therapist, toys, and inner conflict.

There is first of all his *mother*. He may hold on to her hand or body, insist on staying with her in the waiting room, demand that the door remain open, or stubbornly remain near the door which has closed between her and him. If he does this, the situation is for him still related mainly to one goal, his mother, and through her the way home from a vague danger. This idea, however, is rarely unequivocally pleasant. Our small patient usually has reached a deadlock with his mother, who cannot understand why he does not "simply drop" his problem; while the home atmosphere, in which he has been subjected to varying educational methods, has become charged with unsolved conflicts. Thus, frightened as he may be, he feels attracted by the *doctor possibilities,* the second field, and one from which offers possible escape from the unbearable pressures of the domestic situation. Something which the mother or somebody else has said usually has created a slight hope in the child that the therapist may be a person who understands the conditions and the tempo in which a symptom of fear can be gradually abandoned without giving place to chaos within or more trouble without. Many a child has learned also to expect that he will be able to play for time by repeating to this new therapist what has satisfied the old ones. On the other hand the therapist has been called a "doctor" and the medical implications of the surroundings add to the mere strangeness of the situation and create the expectation in the child that some kind of surprise attack is to be made on his physical or moral inviolacy. The mother, with the best intentions, often transfers the negative aspects of the mother field into the field of doctor possibilities; she insists, for example, on reporting in the child's presence latest developments, on admonishing or even threatening him or on trying to secure the therapist's promise of diagnosis or advice. Literally and psychologically, therefore, the mother has to be referred to the waiting room; the child must feel that time has another quality in the doctor sphere, in which, paradoxically, there is no hurry about getting well.

In the meantime, a third ambiguous field has competed with mother and therapist in dominating the child's expectancies, *viz.*, the *toys*. For the child they open another haven, in which space too has another quality, and the therapist usually is quite glad to resign for a while in favor of this quasi-free sphere. Indeed, "what would we do without toys," has become a common exclamation now that we have relaxed our efforts to ignore this most natural tool. The toys evoke in the child that remainder of playful explorativeness which his neurosis and the present doctor situation has not been able to submerge; and, once he has started to select and manipulate we can be sure that the temptation to play and to be the unquestioned and in-violable master in a microcosmic sphere will be great. However, we again see the child man-ifest hesitation. He has experienced too often the fact that the imagined omnipotence in the toy world only makes him feel his importance more keenly when he is suddenly interrupted by his worldly superiors. Playfulness does not rule until (and then only as long as) pressing purposes and fears have lost their compelling power. Thus the child often begins to play with hesitation, with selection, with one eye on the therapist or the door—but he begins to play.

Peace seems to reign. The mother is comfortably seated in the waiting room and has promised "not to go away"; the doctor has been diagnosed as a person who will not make surprise attacks on one's bodily or moral reserve; the toys, sure not to question or to ad-monish, promise a time of "unpurposeful" play.

However, it is at this point that the most dangerous field of ambiguity, *viz.*, the child's re-luctance to confess and his need to communicate his *conflict*, takes possession of the peaceful situation. Whatever it is that drives the child—an urge to get rid of some past or to prepare himself for some future or both—the ever present Gestalt of the life task which has proved too much for him appears in the metaphoric representation of the microsphere. It is here that our "sign reading" sets in and that the tools which Freud gave us become indispensable; for they make us realize that, in the playful arrangement which the child is driven to super-impose on the inventory of toys we offer him, he offers us an outline of the small inner maze in which he is caught. Our small patients either show an anxious care in excluding this or that toy from their play or they work themselves toward a border line where they themselves suddenly find their own doings unsafe, not permissible, unworkable, or unsatisfactory to the point of extreme discomfort. They cannot go on playing in peace—a phenomenon which we shall call "play disruption."

If we temporarily neglect social connotations such as "play," "serious deed," "habit," "symptoms," etc., and instead concentrate on the configurations which often form the diverse symptomatic activities of a child, we find it useful to differentiate three spheres in which symptomatic behavior presents itself:

A child playing by himself may find amusement in the play world of his own body—his fingers, his toes, his voice, constituting the periphery of a world which is self-sufficient in the mutual enchantment of its parts. Let us call this most primitive area of play *autosphere*. Gradually objects which are close at hand are included, and their laws taken into account.

If, at another stage, the child weaves phantasies around the reality of objects, he may construct a small toy world. Blocks may serve as the building stones for a miniature world in which an ever-increasing number of bodily, mental, and social experiences are externalized and dramatized. This area of manifestation we may call *microsphere*. Wherever it is clear that an isolated object is used as a means to extend or intensify the mode of expression of an organ or an organ system and does not become a part of an extrabodily microcosmic arrangement we call it an extension of the autosphere. Let us say a block if rhythmically banged against another block is a part of an autocosmic extension; while it would become a part of a microcosmic arrangement when, with consideration for its physical laws and its usual connotation, it is placed on another block so that together they may form a building. This building, a product of the manipulative-constructive faculty, may "represent" a body, but it is not any more a tool of any part of the autosphere.

We can term *macrosphere* that area of play in which the child moves as in a kind of trance among life-sized objects, pretending that they are whatever background he needs for his imagination. Thus he manifests his need of omnipotence in a material which all too often is rudely claimed by adults because it has other, "grownup" purposes.

Thus sections of the body, toys, and the body as a whole in its spatial relationships to the whole room or to the whole house may serve displaced impulses in various degrees of compulsive, naughty, or playful acts.

We shall readily see that, especially for the disturbed child from three to six years old (the age range in our study), acting in the autosphere leads back easily into the sphere of regressive habits, while play in the macrosphere makes the child try out the environment in a manner both surprising and displeasing to attending adults. There remains then, by force of age preference and expediency, the microsphere as a haven for overhauling the boats before taking further trips into the unknown. Our disturbed children approach this sphere, break down or hesitate before they reach it, experience a disruption in it, or suffer a belated disruption after having overestimated the omnipotence provided by it. The "sign magic" used during such behavior seems to us to outline where in the child's life the sphere of relative tolerance borders on the danger sphere of unbearable pressures.

BUILDING A HOUSE WITH BLOCKS

Mary goes to the corner where the blocks are on the floor. She selects two blocks and arranges them in such a way that she can stand on them each time she comes to the corner to pick up the other blocks. She carries blocks to the middle of the room and builds a small house for a toy cow. For about 15 min. she is completely absorbed in the task of arranging the house so that it is strictly rectangular and at the same time fits tightly about the cow. She then adds five blocks to one long side of the house and experiments with a sixth block until the position marked X satisfies her (see Figure 15.1). Then with a radiant smile and a mischievous twinkle in her eyes she gets up.

A. Though the mother is present, Mary does not seem moved by impulses of adherence. She builds freely in the middle of the room, moving to the corner and back without hesitation.

As in the first contact, play begins with an autosphere extension, *viz.,* creating a base for the feet, and then concentrates on the microsphere.

The emotional note is peaceful concentration on small-scale play with a certain maternal quality of care and order. There is no climax of excitement, and the play ends on a note of satiation.

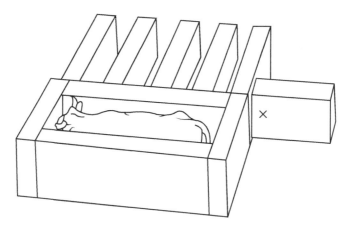

FIGURE 15.1. **Block construction by Mary.**

Her play has as content the building of a close-fitting stable for a toy cow and the adorning of the stable building with six wings (five plus one).

B. The mother has remained in the room. Mary has concentrated quickly and so deeply on her play that it seems better to let her finish it.

Mary, with all her rigidity, balances well standing on the two blocks bending down. The fact that she has to create a foot extension (protection? Overcompensation?) for herself before picking up blocks reminds us of the fact that during the previous contact she had to add an extension (the doll) to another extremity, her hand, before she pushed the objects in the room. We now associate such extensions with the ideas of "scar" and "operation."

The house is built with a special expression of maternal "care." The five wings, to which (after some doubt as to where to put it) a sixth is added, again remind one of the amputation of her sixth finger.

But this time, although again beginning with the representation of the extension of the extremity, Mary's play does not lead into an aggressive outbreak (and the subsequent representation of a catastrophe). It finds satiation in the building of a female protective configuration. There is a pervading femininity about today's behavior which serves to underscore in retrospect and by contrast the danger dramatized during the first contact, *viz.,* the loss from the genital region of an object for an aggressive pushing. The combination of a handlike configuration with a female-protective one is accompanied by play concentration and play satiation and concerns positive ideas of restoration and safety—and this concerning the same organ systems (hand, genital region) which in play disruption appeared endangered.

C. Interpretation: The blocks serve Mary: (1) as additions to her feet (extension? protection?); (2) for the building of a house (female-protective configuration) around an animal: safe body content; (3) for the addition of extensions to the building: six fingers to a hand.

Maternal herself and master of the microsphere, Mary restores her body's inviolability by representing as restituted the losses alluded to during the first contact: her feet are extended (protected?); the content of her female body (tonsils? penis? baby?) is well protected; the sixth finger is returned to the hand. The play ends on a note of satiety.

The configurations of Mary's house seemed to us to be a condensed expression of (a) her concern over certain parts of her body, (b) the feminine protective mode governing her psychosexual stage. She thus not only employs the house body metaphor which Freud found in dreams[1] . . . which poets use when they please ("this mortal house," as Shakespeare puts it) and which primitives seem to have in mind in certain rituals[2] . . . she also expresses in the architecture of her playhouse certain emphases and corrections of her subjective body build. In a longitudinal study of children now older than Mary we are finding that this clinical observation admits of fruitful generalizations.[3]

---

1. Freud, Sigmund. *Introductory lectures on psychoanalysis.* London: Allen & Unwin, 1922.
2. Observations on the Yurok: World image and childhood tradition. *University of California Publications in American Archaeology and Anthropology, 35,* No. 10. In press.
3. Most of the play acts observed and interpreted by clinicians are common to all children. Nevertheless, clinical investigation remains within its legitimate sphere when treating these acts as unique and trying to understand their meaning within the psychologic of an individual's system of meanings. Under what conditions, then, the same acts—here produced by Mary—can be said to have a common meaning in all cases, or a special one in some, is best investigated in longitudinal studies; here the normative relevance and the common as well as unique meaning of typical configurations can be studied with equal care.

   Adapting a previous exploration with college students to the realities of a Guidance Study. . . , the writer for the last three years has confronted nearly 200 children within a few days of their tenth, eleventh, twelfth, and thirteenth birthdays with a square table, blocks, and a selection of ordinary toys. They were asked to arrange on the table an exciting scene of an imaginary moving picture. The themes and configurations produced are now being analyzed in regard both to unique elements (and their relation to unique life data) and to elements common to ages, stages, and types. It is already generally apparent that differences in house configurations promise to present reliable relations to psychosexual, maturational, and health status. Also, the relative dominance of organ modes during periods of rapid maturation is receiving quantitative substantiation.

   The observation of an individual's ideational and affective play behavior and of utilization of the available play space promises to reveal (a) what part of his life subjectively presents a potential "heel of Achilles," (b) the relation of this part to his subjective life space determined as it is by his *psychosexual* status and by his particular *creative* and *defensive* ways of synthesizing past and anticipating future.

Commentary

For most, the name Erik Erikson is synonymous with the psychosocial stages of development and the term "identity crisis." He is best known as an originator of ego psychology and is listed as the 12th most eminent psychologist of the 20th century for his psychosocial stages (Haggbloom et al., 2002). Erikson was fond of observing similarities and differences in cultures, environments, and biological factors, often credited with building on and expanding the theories of those who came before him. In this vein, Erikson wrote about children's play, its clinical interpretation, and the importance of play for healthy development, impacting the fields of play therapy and creativity research. While his influence on the field of play is dwarfed when compared with his notoriety for the eight-stage model, his ideas about play are in fact quite astute, and his writing continues to have relevance today.

In the two excerpts shared here, we witness Erikson's early writing about the value of play and get a glimpse into what can be learned about a child by observing her play. It was later that Erikson more succinctly pulled together the powerful line about the importance of free play, quoted in his obituary: "You see a child play, and it is so close to seeing an artist paint, for in play a child says things without uttering a word. You can see how he solves his problems. You can see what's wrong. Young children, especially, have enormous creativity, and whatever is in them rises to the surface in free play" (*New York Times*, 1994). From a creativity perspective, Erikson's early writing on play, which we examine here, can be viewed as his raw data—rich with meaning but still unrefined. The excerpts are teeming with budding ideas. By returning now to his detailed clinical notes, we find truths about play and creativity that are still applicable today and which could inform modern conversations about the importance of childhood play.

THE PURPOSE OF PLAY

The purpose of play has been an age-old question. Theories of the 19th century, deemed classical theories, included that play occurs because children have too much energy (e.g., Spencer, 1873), that play helps children rest or relax (Lazarus, 1883), and that play is a product of human evolution that either helps children develop adaptive skills for life (Groos, 1901) or weakens their primitive instincts to differentiate humans from animals (Hall, 1920). In the mid-20th century, Erikson built upon the psychoanalytic scholars, his experiences tutoring and teaching art to children at the Hietzing School in Vienna, receiving mentorship and training in psychoanalysis from Anna Freud, and conducting groundbreaking research into childhood and child rearing among the Lakota and Yurok tribes while at the University of California, Berkeley. Erikson's theory of play expanded on that of Sigmund Freud: that play has a role in the emotional development of children, and that through it children can act out wish fulfillment and master traumatic events in their lives. However, while Freud believed that childhood play was the equivalent of adult fantasy (a way to escape reality), Erikson believed that play acts held more value than simple escapism. As an ego psychologist, he focused on the adaptive and creative characteristics of the ego, maintaining that children use play not only to express themselves or for superfluous enjoyment but also to begin working through conflicts and finding potential solutions.

Where the importance of play lives most clearly in the works of Erikson today is within the third and fourth stages of his psychosocial model of development. Stage 3, initiative versus guilt, occurs between ages 3 and 5, during which children begin to interact more with their peers, engaging in pretend play and social play and making up games together. Play is therefore one mechanism through which preschool-age children can learn about themselves and others. Stage 4, when children are in elementary school, approximately ages 6 to 12, is the industry versus inferiority stage, in which children's success and sense of competence helps them to develop confidence. The world of pretend continues to be a safe place in which to try out new skills and experiment with uncomfortable emotional themes. Children this age often act out stories from their lives, such as playing school or house, and thus begin to feel mastery over the social scripts that they will need to navigate similar situations in "real life."

Closely after Erikson, the cognitive developmental theories of Piaget (1962) and Vygotsky (1966) emerged, emphasizing that play is a cognitive, voluntary activity that contributes to child development in cognition, problem-solving, and creative thought. Among even more modern theories of play, some harken back to Erikson more than others. There are those with clear connections to the work of Erikson, such as those examining the role of emotion-laden play and imagination in childhood for adaptive functioning and adult creativity (Russ, 2004, 2014), and those who view play as a therapeutic path for mastering emotional conflict, such as Sue Knell's *Cognitive Behavioral Play Therapy* (1993), in which she begins with a comprehensive review of the historical underpinnings of both psychoanalytic and more structured play therapies. Berk, Mann, and Ogan (2006) outline the role of play in the development of self-regulation, referencing both Erikson and Vygotsky—Erikson for maintaining that the role of play helps children to explore social roles and "gain a sense of their future," and Vygotsky for expanding this notion by stating boldly that pretense itself is a unique zone of proximal development.

THE ROLE OF ADULTS IN CHILDREN'S PLAY

Erikson's writing also contributes to the role of the adult caregivers in children's play. He believed that children's play must be supported and acknowledged by the adults in their lives. In the second excerpt, Erikson writes, "Literally and psychologically, therefore, the mother has to be referred to the waiting room; the child must feel that time has another quality in the doctor sphere, in which, paradoxically, there is no hurry about getting well." This simple idea, that play requires some freedom of choice, has since been validated by scientific research (Johnson, Christie, & Wardle, 2005; King, 1979). Especially for young children, the same task (e.g., washing dishes, cleaning up) can be perceived as either play or work depending not only on the amount of pleasure derived but also whether the task was chosen or assigned. Second, it is the adult's job to create the safe space and time for play, and the fewer parameters (time limits, rules about aggressive themes in play), the better. Finally, Erikson both implicitly and explicitly makes the case that the benefits of play come naturally, and that, by definition, any attempt to artificially create the healing or learning that play can produce will not work, for it will no longer be the child's play.

The role of adults has been explored further in recent research through play-based interventions for preschool and elementary school children. In a process analysis study in which each child's behavior was analyzed in relation to the adult behavior that had come before it during a 30-minute play training session, Hoffmann (2016) found that active watching was the adults' most powerful tool, while prompting, questioning, and praising (all done in an attempt to help the child play better) ended up being interruptions and distractions that pulled children out of their flow. In two play interventions with preschoolers, one including parent play sessions at home between intervention sessions, and another working with preschoolers individually with no parent component, significant improvements in children's play were found only for the study including parents (Christian, Fehr, & Russ, 2011; Fehr & Russ, 2016). Another study with preschool children playing in groups of same-age children, gently facilitated by two adults, has also shown significant improvement in children's imagination, plot organization, and comfort playing (Fehr, Hoffmann, Ramasami, & Hadler, 2017).

Erikson's work in this area is also strongly reflected today in the play therapy community, where the knowledge that allowing a child safe space to play functions as a therapeutic strategy. Erikson (1940, p. 561) asserts, "The child uses play to make up for defeats, sufferings and frustrations, especially those resulting from a technically and culturally limited use of the language." For instance, at the Austen Riggs Center (2017), which houses the Erikson Institute for Education and Research, the activities program started by Erikson's wife, Joan, is based on the principal that "art, crafts, drama, intellectual pursuits, involvement in the nursery school or greenhouse program are productive for personal growth and development in any individual." The activities program focuses on creativity and exploration, encouraging patients to learn in an "interpretation-free zone," inspired by Eriksonian notions of play (Dewey, 2013). Recently a senior consultant at the center published a book entitled *A Spirit That Impels: Play, Creativity, and Psychoanalysis*, in which he explores famous creative works through a psychoanalytic lens, arguing that the two processes inform and enrich each other's products (Gerard Fromm, 2013). Far from being irrelevant to modern psychoanalytic treatment, Erikson's conception of play lives on, providing indispensable enrichment for patients and clinicians alike.

The role of adults in providing children with time for play is relevant far beyond the therapy room. In Eriksonian terms, children who are not given real opportunities for play and creative production risk developing a sense of guilt instead of initiative, which will hinder future social interactions and creativity. We see this in many of the supposedly creative toys given to children, which do not support the development of imagination and fantasy (e.g., Legos with instructions for building a single, correct object; paint-by-number coloring books). While the language has changed, the sentiment of those who fight for imaginative playtime remains the same. One primary example is the toy company Creativity for Kids, acquired by Faber-Castell in 1999, whose philosophy is based on a commitment to provide children with toys and activities that promote uniqueness, individuality, and self-expression (Faber-Castell, n.d.).

The role of adults is also key for providing free play time during the school day. This is an area in which knowledge and policy about play appears to be changing for the better. A Gallup Poll sponsored by the Robert Wood Johnson Foundation (2010), the National Association of Elementary School Principals (NAESP), and Playworks found that parents, teachers, and principals all believe play is important for children, and as of 2013 Connecticut state law dictates that recess may not be taken away from students as a form of discipline (An Act concerning Childhood Obesity and Physical Exercise in Schools, 2013).

OBSERVATION AND MEASUREMENT OF PLAY

Erikson saw great value in observing the play of a single child. He demonstrated in his clinical notes that by observing a child's play we can learn about the cognitive, affective, and interpersonal processes of the child, a point more recently articulated and carried forward by Sandra Russ (2004, 2014). The modern view of children's play is that in addition to being fun and a path to mastery, information is communicated to those who observe carefully. Even for preschool children, many of whose words expressed during play may be unintelligible, a careful observer can ascertain pleasant or unpleasant affect and a sense of an organized or disorganized storyline, and observe whether or not the child is enjoying the play, whether or not the child has the ability for pretense, and how long he or she can pay attention, among countless other variables.

The notes we see in the second excerpt are a precursor to the play construction assessment, which Erikson (1951) would later use to report on the sex differences in children's play. Erikson conducted an experiment with 140 preadolescent children who were instructed, "Choose any of the things you see here and construct on this table an exciting scene out of an imaginary moving picture." Erikson concluded that boys and girls built different types of structures that paralleled their anatomical makeup; compared to girls, boys build more and higher towers, more elaborate structures, and structures that include more movement and fewer enclosures. We see that in his notes of the girl playing, written almost 10 years earlier, he has already begun to make notes about the enclosed, lower structure built by the girl during her play session.

Although Erikson's writings on sex differences in play construction came under much scrutiny, they also led to important follow-up studies and a continued emphasis on exploring individual differences through play observation, clearly remaining valuable despite certain limitations inherent in such a highly gendered analysis, and the importance of developing measures of play and creativity that do not discriminate by gender or culture. In a reevaluation of Erikson's concept of "inner space," Caplan (1979) argues that since Erikson gave both girls and boys blocks and dolls and furniture to play with, the children likely picked the gender-correct toy for their sex, with girls picking dolls and furniture (which cannot be built into a tower) and boys picking blocks. In an attempted replication of Erikson's study with preschool children, Caplan found little evidence for sex differences in how the children played.

That observing children's play can reveal much about their development has led to the use of play assessments in other fields as well. For example, the Ounce Scale (Meisels, Dombro, Marsden, Weston, & Jewkes, 2003) is an infant and toddler assessment developed by Samuel Meisels, president of the Erikson Institute from 2002 to 2013; it uses observation of children's everyday activities in their normal environment to document their knowledge, skills, dispositions, and social and emotional development. Another measure of play used in occupational therapy also stemmed from Erikson's work, as well as that of Piaget. Play History (Takata, 1974), a semistructured interview for a parent or caregiver of a child between the ages of 0 and 16 years, asks about past and present play experiences in terms of epochs of play, encompassing sensorimotor and simple symbolic and constructive play, dramatic and complex play, games, and recreational play.

While Erikson observed play primarily in a clinical context for diagnostic purposes, this basic point about the utility of observing play is the basis for current instruments that measure children's play. One such measure is the Affect in Play Scale (Russ, 1993, 2004), which measures both affective and cognitive processes in play using two puppets (one male, one female), and three blocks. The Affect in Play Scale in particular has been used in building the case that childhood pretend play is the foundation of adult creativity (Russ, 2014). Children's play has been found repeatedly to relate to their divergent thinking ability (Hoffmann & Russ, 2012; Kaugars & Russ, 2009; Russ & Grossman-McKee, 1990; Russ, Robins, & Christiano, 1999) and their storytelling ability (Hoffmann & Russ, 2012, 2016) and to predict their creativity and positive affect over time (Fiorelli & Russ, 2012). This too stems from the lifespan approach of Erikson (1948, p. 38), who stated, "In learning to play in childhood, man learns to learn and plan as an adult."

NEW DIRECTIONS

Establishing scientifically the benefits of play for child development is an ongoing process (Lillard et al., 2013), Erikson being one of the first major psychologists to consider the social and emotional benefits of play for children. Why Erikson is not cited more often for these ideas may be partially due to the fact that his psychosocial stages overshadowed his earlier work on play. Another potential issue is the era in which he wrote about play: one in which play behaviors were often interpreted in the context of Freud's sexual stages and stereotyped, gender-normative writing was more accepted. These psychoanalytic overtones may make Erikson's work unpalatable to some in the present day, but we argue that the knowledge contained in his work is nevertheless worth the re-exploration.

Play disruption, introduced by Erikson, is another concept with continued relevance to play and creativity research. Erikson describes two processes, both worthy of further exploration. One regards the basic urge to play, which Erikson so vividly describes in his clinical notes, as Mary sees the toys but is unsure about the safety of a new space and the examiner. This hunger to engage in play has more recently been explored by Russ and Dillon (2011), who found that despite increasingly limited time and resources to engage in fantasy play, children have actually shown no decrease in their play abilities and in fact display increased organization and imagination when given the opportunity and space to play. Further research is needed to understand these dynamics. Under what circumstances does play deprivation lead to decreased play and imagination, what Erikson would term "guilt" or a lack of confidence, and when does restriction of time to play instead create a hunger to play and increased play behaviors when given the chance?

The second point Erikson makes addresses what exactly makes play fun. He notes that children can often not help but begin to work through their issues in play—the content of a child's play rarely remains benign for long, as if children can't help but move toward emotionally challenging territory. In the play research with typically developing children, this point too has been carried forward: what makes play fun, exciting, a thrill is that it exists on the edge between pretense and reality. Play wrestling is fun because there is real competition and real physical threat; pretend play with dolls, animals, cars, or blocks is fun when it also contains an element of emotional or physical danger. If play is too real, it is not play; if play is too pretend, it is not fun.

Erikson's writing represents the kind of detailed process notes emblematic of psycho-analytic and psychodynamic play therapists of his time. Yet in an attempt to quantify the science of creativity, play research has moved away from anecdotal evidence, case studies, and nuanced qualitative notes toward self-report scales, divergent thinking tasks, and con-sensus scoring of creative products. Many gains have come from this; however, there is a lesson to be relearned and revived from Erikson's writing: that a deep exploration of a single individual's play can teach us much about the role of play in development, the clinical benefits of play, and the creative process. Technology can be harnessed to track every bit of detail as a person composes, edits, deletes, pauses, and proofreads a piece of creative writing. Smartphones can help us use experience-sampling methods to track artists over weeks. Process analysis coding systems allow us to analyze exchanges between multiple people in real time, such as between a parent and child (e.g., the Interact system; Dumas, 1987) or a play facilitator and child player (Hoffmann, 2016). Analyzing sequences of beha-vior in detail has grown in sophistication due to advances in technology (see Bakeman & Quera, 2011); these techniques can also be applied to play interventions and studying the creative process more broadly to answer questions such as *What happens in between a creative idea and the final product? What happens between creative potential and creative achievement?* The field of creativity research is ready to answer hard questions. We must boldly follow in Erikson's path to fearlessly collect overwhelmingly rich data on individuals and synthesize from across domains.

References

An Act concerning Childhood Obesity and Physical Exercise in Schools. (2013). Substitute House Bill No. 6525. Public Act No. 13-173. Retrieved from Connecticut General Assembly database: https://www.cga.ct.gov/2013/ACT/pa/pdf/2013PA-00173-R00HB-06525-PA.pdf.

Austen Riggs Center. (2017). Our treatment. Retrieved from: http://www.austenriggs.org/activities-program.

Bakeman, R., & Quera, V. (2011). *Sequential analysis and observational methods for the behavioral sciences.* New York, NY: Cambridge University Press.

Berk, L. E., Mann, T. D., & Ogan, A. T. (2006). Make-believe play: Wellspring for development of self-regulation. In D. G. Singer, R. M. Golinkoff, & K. Hirsh-Pasek (Eds.), *Play = learning: How play motivates and enhances children's cognitive and social-emotional growth* (pp. 74–100). New York, NY: Oxford University Press.

Caplan, P. J. (1979). Erikson's concept of inner space: A data-based reevaluation. *American Journal of Orthopsychiatry, 49,* 100–108. doi:10.1111/j.1939-0025.1979.tb02590.x.

Christian, K., Fehr, K., & Russ, S. (2011, August). *Effects of a play intervention on play skills in pre-school children: A pilot study.* Poster presented at the annual meeting of the American Psychological Association, Washington, DC.

Dewey, S. R. (2013, December 9). Finding purpose through play. *Riggs Blog.* Retrieved from http://www.austenriggs.org/blog-post/finding-purpose-through-play.

Dumas, J. E. (1987). INTERACT: A computer-based coding and data management system to assess family interactions. In R. J. Prinz (Ed.), *Advances in Behavioral Assessment of Children and Families, 3,* 177–203.

Erikson, E. H. (1940). Studies in the interpretation of play: Clinical observation of play disruption in young children. *Genetic Psychology Monographs, 22,* 557–671.

Erikson, E. H. (1943). Clinical studies in childhood play. In R. G. Barker, J. S. Kounin, & H. F. Wright (Eds.), *Child behavior and development: A course of representative studies* (pp. 411–428). New York, NY: McGraw-Hill.

Erikson, E. H. (1948). The meaning of play. *Bulletin of the National Association for Nursery Education, 3,* 37–38.

Erikson, E. H. (1950). *Childhood and society.* New York, NY: Norton.

Erikson, E. H. (1951). Sex differences in the play configurations of preadolescents. *American Journal of Orthopsychiatry, 21,* 667–692. doi:10.1111/j.1939-0025.1951.tb00021.x.

Faber-Castell. (n.d.). About us. Retrieved from http://www.fabercastell.com/company/about-us.

Fehr, K., Hoffmann, J. D., Ramasami, J, & Hadler, D. (2017). Fostering the pretend play of young children through group intervention: Implications for creativity and socioemotional functioning. Manuscript submitted for publication.

Fehr, K., & Russ, S. W. (2016). Pretend play and creativity in preschool-aged children: Associations and brief intervention. *Psychology of Aesthetics, Creativity, and the Arts, 10*(3), 296–308. https://doi.org/10.1037/aca0000054.

Fiorelli, J. A., & Russ, S. W. (2012). Pretend play, coping, and subjective well-being in children: A follow-up study. *American Journal of Play, 5,* 81–103. https://doi.org/10.1037/e700772011-001.

Fromm, M. G. (Ed.). (2013). *A spirit that impels: Play, creativity, and psychoanalysis.* London, UK: Karnac.

Groos, K. (1901). *The play of man.* New York, NY: D. Appleton.

Haggbloom, S. J., Warnick, R., Warnick, J. E., Jones, V. K., Yarbrough, G. L., Russell, T. M., . . . & Monte, E. (2002). The 100 most eminent psychologists of the 20th century. *Review of General Psychology, 6,* 139–152. https://doi.org/10.1037//1089-2680.6.2.139.

Hall, G. S. (1920). *Educational problems.* Vol. 2. New York, NY: D. Appleton.

Hoffmann, J. D. (2016). Intervening without interfering: Supporting the imaginative play of elementary school girls. *International Journal of Creativity and Problem Solving, 26,* 85–105.

Hoffmann, J., & Russ, S. (2012). Pretend play, creativity, and emotion regulation in children. *Psychology of Aesthetics, Creativity, and the Arts, 6,* 175–184. doi:10.1037/a0026299.

Hoffmann, J. D., & Russ, S. W. (2016). Fostering pretend play skills and creativity in elementary school girls: A group play intervention. *Psychology of Aesthetics, Creativity, and the Arts, 10,* 114–125. doi:10.1037/aca0000039.

Johnson, J., Christie, J., & Wardle, F. (2005). *Play, development, and early education.* New York, NY: Allyn & Bacon.

Kaugars, A. S. & Russ, S. W. (2009). Assessing preschool children's pretend play: Preliminary validation of the Affect in Play Scale—Preschool Version. *Early Education and Development, 20,* 733–755. https://doi.org/10.1080/10409280802545388.

King, N. R. (1979). Play: The kindergartners' perspective. *Elementary School Journal, 80,* 80–87. http://dx.doi.org/10.1086/461176.

Knell, S. M. (1993). *Cognitive-behavioral play therapy.* Northvale, NJ: Aronson.

Lazarus, M. (1883). *Concerning the fascination of play.* Berlin: Dummler.

Lillard, A. S., Lerner, M. D., Hopkins, E. J., Dore, R. A., Smith, E. D., & Palmquist, C. M. (2013). The impact of pretend play on children's development: A review of the evidence. *Psychological Bulletin, 139,* 1–34. https://doi.org/10.1037/a0029321.

Meisels, S. J., Dombro, A. L., Marsden, D. B., Weston, D. R., & Jewkes, A. M. (2003).The Ounce Scale. New York, NY: Pearson Early Learning.

New York Times. (1994, May 13). Erik Erikson, 91, psychoanalyst who reshapes view of human growth, dies. Retrieved from http://www.nytimes.com/learning/general/onthisday/bday/0615.html.

Piaget, J. (1962). *Play, dreams and imitation in childhood.* London: Routledge & Kegan Paul.

Robert Wood Johnson Foundation. (2010, February). The state of play: Gallup Survey of Principals on School Recess. Retrieved from: http://d6test.naesp.org/resources/1/Gallup_Poll/StateOfPlayFeb2010.pdf.

Russ, S. W. (1993). *Affect and creativity: The role of affect and play in the creative process.* Hillsdale, NJ: Lawrence Erlbaum.

Russ, S. W. (2004). *Play in child development and psychotherapy: Toward empirically supported practice.* Mahwah, NJ: Erlbaum.

Russ, S. W. (2014). *Pretend play in childhood: Foundation of adult creativity.* Washington, DC: American Psychological Association.

Russ, S., & Dillon, J. (2011). Changes in children's play over a 23-year period: A cross-temporal meta-analysis. *Creativity Research Journal, 23,* 330–338. https://doi.org/10.1080/10400419.2011.621824.

Russ, S. W. & Grossman-McKee, A. (1990). Affective expression in children's fantasy play, primary process thinking on the Rorschach and divergent thinking. *Journal of Personality Assessment, 54,* 756–771. https://doi.org/10.1080/00223891.1990.9674036.

Russ, S. W., Robins, A., & Christiano, B. (1999). Pretend play: Longitudinal prediction of creativity and affect in fantasy in children. *Creativity Research Journal, 12,* 129–139. https://doi.org/10.1207/s15326934crj1202_5.

Spencer, H. (1873). *Principles of psychology.* New York, NY: Appleton.

Takata, N. (1974). Play as a prescription. In M. Reilly (Ed.), *Play as exploratory learning: Studies in curiosity behavior* (pp. 209–246). Beverley Hills, CA: Sage.

Vygotsky, L. (1966). The role of play in child development. In M. Cole V. John-Steiner, S. Scribner, & E. Souberman (Eds.), *Mind in Society: The Development of Higher Psychological Processes* (pp. 92–104). Cambridge, MA: Harvard University Press.

16

Creativity in the Classroom
John Dewey

Beth A. Hennessey

Summary

The widely held view of creativity as an ephemeral and entirely mysterious gift bestowed on only a chosen few has generally prevented the promotion of student creativity from being seen as a viable, or even an especially important or desirable, educational aim. At present, prevailing educational policies and practices in the US and many other nations around the world are further from a creativity-friendly, open-ended, student-centered model than at almost any other time in history. Recently, however, a growing number of educators and business leaders have cautioned that today's students are finishing high school and college without the creativity and innovative thinking skills they'll need to succeed in the 21st-century workplace. This essay argues that a careful reading of John Dewey's 1938 treatise *Education and Experience* can enable would-be reformers to break away from many of the 21st-century assumptions that have long prevented them from envisioning a clear and viable path for educational change. Dewey's philosophy and educational prescriptions fit nicely with contemporary social psychology scholarship and empirical findings on creativity in the classroom and offer a blueprint for enacting impactful and lasting pedagogical change.

Introduction

With the exception of a relatively small number of short-lived curricular attempts to "teach" creativity (e.g., brainstorming techniques and lateral thinking; de Bono, 1985), American school policies and pedagogies have generally failed to incorporate the concept of creativity. The majority of American classrooms now follow a "back to basics" approach driven by a one-size-fits-all philosophy and dominated by high-stakes testing (see Hennessey,

2015). Overall, while some other nations have been doing more to promote the open-ended and innovative thinking of students, the exclusion of creativity from the academic agenda has been the norm rather than the exception.

Recently, however, a growing number of educators and policymakers worldwide have pushed for a reexamination of educational priorities. In the US, business leaders and employers have begun to call for a revamping of the educational system. They caution that today's students are finishing high school and college without the skills they'll need to succeed in the workplace (American Association of Colleges and Universities, 2015). The modern workforce needs persons who show individuality, are flexible, confident in their abilities, and able to collaborate and communicate to come up with creative solutions to problems. Scholars like Tony Wagner at Harvard's Innovation Lab agree that if students are to graduate with the capacity to "think big," schools must make the development of creativity and innovation a primary objective (see Wagner, 2012). The school reform vision must shift from the current goal of making the system incrementally "better" to a complete overhaul and reimagining of what it means to be in school in the first place. Students must be helped to develop intrinsic motivation and the conviction that they really do have what it takes to be creative problem-solvers.

If the development of creative potential is to be taken seriously, classrooms must be entirely reconfigured so as to become crucibles for deep and meaningful learning, places where students of all ages are helped to develop a sense of agency, individuality, and freedom. Classrooms must offer students the gift of time, ample time, to deeply immerse themselves in projects and problems. They must be given the license to take risks and make mistakes and collaborate with one another. They must learn to trust their intuition, to persevere, to pick themselves up and try again in the face of failure (see Hennessey, 2015). This is a tall order by any measure—but not an impossible one. My own thinking, research, and scholarship in this area has recently been bolstered by a careful rereading of the works of John Dewey. How fitting that it would take the philosophizing and wisdom of this great scholar who wrote during the late 19th and early 20th centuries to allow me to break away from many of the 21st-century assumptions that have long prevented me (and most others) from envisioning a clear and viable path for educational reform.

John Dewey (1859–1952) was an eminent American psychologist and philosopher. A founding member, along with William James and Charles Sanders Peirce, of the pragmatist school, Dewey subscribed to the idea that students of all ages learn by putting thoughts into action. His progressive approach emphasized the importance of meaningful activity for learning and held that students must be invested in what they are learning. Ideas were to be used as tools and instruments of prediction, problem-solving and action rather than as mere descriptors of reality (Gutek, 2014). Dewey felt strongly that early educational environments should offer children concrete experiences in areas that interest them; then, over time, students could be helped to build on their basic understandings to connect with more formal subject matter. Dewey is probably best known for his work in logic, scientific inquiry, and the philosophy of education. However, his writings also came to significantly influence the study of aesthetics and the philosophy of art. His book *Art as Experience* (1934/2005) is viewed as one of the most influential 20th-century contributions to this area of inquiry. Unlike the majority of his contemporaries, who conceived of art in terms of language and other symbol systems, Dewey saw art in terms of experience. For Dewey, art and science were similar in many ways. The doing (and appreciation) of art he likened to the solving of a puzzle; in his writings and philosophizing, he effectively replaced the question "What is art?" with "When is art?" (Leddy, 2006).

This same emphasis on experience and scientific method is echoed in Dewey's 1938 book *Experience and Education*. Here Dewey draws a number of parallels between the experience of the scientist and the student. Throughout this book he underscores the importance of purposeful learning, freedom, and experimentation. For Dewey, the quality of the educational experience is key. Emphasis is placed on the student's interactions with the environment—both physical interactions with objects and, equally important, social interactions with teachers and other students, what Dewey's philosophical anthropology sees as the community or culture of the classroom.

Given the time period in which he was writing, it is not at all surprising that Dewey never once uses the terms "creativity," "creation," or "create" as he outlines his vision for a new, progressive education. Nelson's (2015) documentation of the history of these concepts reveals that, prior to the mid-19th century and the introduction of the Darwinian model, the words "creative" and "creativity" were not used at all; it was not until the middle of the next century, during the Cold War, that these terms came to be employed with any frequency. But it is clear that, in Dewey's view, the development of creativity must be at the core of the mission of any school. For Dewey, the student is far more than just an empty vessel waiting to have knowledge delivered or "poured in." The purpose of education is not just to transmit customs, beliefs, and occupations to the young, but to help create fully functioning, generative members of society. In Dewey's view, schools must be institutions of creation rather than simply instruments of transmission (Simpson, 2001). Education must be seen as development from within rather than formation from without, and this development can be realized only via the provision of purposeful classroom experiences based on the principles of continuity and interaction. The following text is excerpted from Dewey's *Experience and Education*, Chapter 3.

Reading: *Criteria of Experience*

Source: Dewey, J. (1938). "Criteria of Experience." Chapter 3 in *Experience and education*. New York, NY: Kappa Delta Pi. Copyright © 1988 by the Board of Trustees, Southern Illinois University, reprinted with permission of the publisher.

If there is any truth in what has been said about the need of forming a theory of experience in order that education may be intelligently conducted upon the basis of experience, it is clear that the next thing in order in this discussion is to present the principles that are most significant in framing this theory. I shall not, therefore, apologize for engaging in a certain amount of philosophical analysis, which otherwise might be out of place. I may, however, reassure you to some degree by saying that this analysis is not an end in itself but is engaged in for the sake of obtaining criteria to be applied later in discussion of a number of concrete and, to most persons, more interesting issues.

I have already mentioned what I called the category of continuity, or the experiential continuum. This principle is involved, as I pointed out, in every attempt to discriminate between experiences that are worthwhile educationally and those that are not. It may seem superfluous to argue that this discrimination is necessary not only in criticizing the traditional type of education but also in initiating and conducting a different type. Nevertheless, it is advisable to pursue for a little while the idea that it is necessary. One may safely assume,

I suppose, that one thing which has recommended the progressive movement is that it seems more in accord with the democratic ideal to which our people is committed than do the procedures of the traditional school, since the latter have so much of the autocratic about them. Another thing which has contributed to its favorable reception is that its methods are humane in comparison with the harshness so often attending the policies of the traditional school.

The question I would raise concerns why we prefer democratic and humane arrangements to those which are autocratic and harsh. And by "why," I mean the reason for preferring them, not just the causes which lead us to the preference. One cause may be that we have been taught not only in the schools but by the press, the pulpit, the platform, and our laws and law-making bodies that democracy is the best of all social institutions. We may have so assimilated this idea from our surroundings that it has become an habitual part of our mental and moral make-up. But similar causes have led other persons in different surroundings to widely varying conclusions—to prefer fascism, for example. The cause for our preference is not the same thing as the reason why we should prefer it.

It is not my purpose here to go in detail into the reason. But I would ask a single question: Can we find any reason that does not ultimately come down to the belief that democratic social arrangements promote a better quality of human experience, one which is more widely accessible and enjoyed, than do non-democratic and anti-democratic forms of social life? Does not the principle of regard for individual freedom and for decency and kindliness of human relations come back in the end to the conviction that these things are tributary to a higher quality of experience on the part of a greater number than are methods of repression and coercion or force? Is it not the reason for our preference that we believe that mutual consultation and convictions reached through persuasion, make possible a better quality of experience than can otherwise be provided on any wide scale?

If the answer to these questions is in the affirmative (and personally I do not see how we can justify our preference for democracy and humanity on any other ground), the ultimate reason for hospitality to progressive education, because of its reliance upon and use of humane methods and its kinship to democracy, goes back to the fact that discrimination is made between the inherent values of different experiences. So I come back to the principle of continuity of experience as a criterion of discrimination.

At bottom, this principle rests upon the fact of habit, when habit is interpreted biologically. The basic characteristic of habit is that every experience enacted and undergone modifies the one who acts and undergoes, while this modification affects, whether we wish it or not, the quality of subsequent experiences. For it is a somewhat different person who enters into them. The principle of habit so understood obviously goes deeper than the ordinary conception of a habit as a more or less fixed way of doing things, although it includes the latter as one of its special cases. It covers the formation of attitudes, attitudes that are emotional and intellectual; it covers our basic sensitivities and ways of meeting and responding to all the conditions which we meet in living. From this point of view, the principle of continuity of experience means that every experience both takes up something from those which have gone before and modifies in some way the quality of those which come after. As the poet states it,

all experience is an arch wherethro'
Gleams that untraveled world, whose margin fades
For ever and for ever when I move.

So far, however, we have no ground for discrimination among experiences. For the principle is of universal application. There is some kind of continuity in every case. It is when we note the different forms in which continuity of experience operates that we get the basis of discriminating among experiences. I may illustrate what is meant by an objection, which has been brought against an idea which I once put forth—namely, that the educative process can be identified with growth when that is understood in terms of the active participle, *growing*.

Growth, or growing as developing, not only physically but intellectually and morally, is one exemplification of the principle of continuity. The objection made is that growth might take many different directions: a man, for example, who starts out on a career of burglary may grow in that direction, and by practice may grow into a highly expert burglar. Hence it is argued that "growth" is not enough; we must also specify the direction in which growth takes place, the end towards which it tends. Before, however, we decide that the objection is conclusive we must analyze the case a little further.

That a man may grow in efficiency as a burglar, as a gangster, or as a corrupt politician, cannot be doubted. But from the standpoint of growth as education and education as growth the question is whether growth in this direction promotes or retards growth in general. Does this form of growth create conditions for further growth, or does it set up conditions that shut off the person who has grown in this particular direction from the occasions, stimuli, and opportunities for continuing growth in new directions? What is the effect of growth in a special direction upon the attitudes and habits which alone open up avenues for development in other lines? I shall leave you to answer these questions, saying simply that when and only when development in a particular line conduces to continuing growth does it answer to the criterion of education as growing. For the conception is one that must find universal and not specialized limited application.

I return now to the question of continuity as a criterion by which to discriminate between experiences which are educative and those which are mis-educative. As we have seen, there is some kind of continuity in any case since every experience affects for better or worse the attitudes which help decide the quality of further experiences, by setting up certain preference and aversion, and making it easier or harder to act for this or that end. Moreover, every experience influences in some degree the objective conditions under which further experiences are had. For example, a child who learns to speak has a new facility and new desire. But he has also widened the external conditions of subsequent learning. When he learns to read, he similarly opens up a new environment. If a person decides to become a teacher, lawyer, physician, or stock-broker, when he executes his intention he thereby necessarily determines to some extent the environment in which he will act in the future. He has rendered himself more sensitive and responsive to certain conditions, and relatively immune to those things about him that would have been stimuli if he had made another choice.

But, while the principle of continuity applies in some way in every case, the quality of the present experience influences the *way* in which the principle applies. We speak of spoiling a child and of the spoilt child. The effect of over-indulging a child is a continuing one. It sets up an attitude, which operates as an automatic demand that persons and objects cater to his desires and caprices in the future. It makes him seek the kind of situation that will enable him to do what he feels like doing at the time. It renders him averse to and comparatively incompetent in situations, which require effort and perseverance in overcoming obstacles. There is no paradox in the fact that the principle of the continuity of experience may operate so as to leave a person arrested on a low plane of development, in a way which limits later capacity for growth.

On the other hand, if an experience arouses curiosity, strengthens initiative, and sets up desires and purposes that are sufficiently intense to carry a person over dead places in the future, continuity works in a very different way. Every experience is a moving force. Its value can be judged only on the ground of what it moves toward and into. The greater maturity of experience which should belong to the adult as educator puts him in a position to evaluate each experience of the young in a way in which the one having the less mature experience cannot do. It is then the business of the educator to see in what direction an experience is heading. There is no point in his being more mature if, instead of using his greater insight to help organize the conditions of the experience of the immature, he throws away his insight. Failure to take the moving force of an experience into account so as to judge and direct it on the ground of what it is moving into means disloyalty to the principle of experience itself. The disloyalty operates in two directions. The educator is false to the understanding that he should have obtained from his own past experience. He is also unfaithful to the fact that all human experience is ultimately social: that it involves contact and communication. The mature person, to put it in moral terms, has no right to withhold from the young on given occasions whatever capacity for sympathetic understanding his own experience has given him.

No sooner, however, are such things said than there is a tendency to react to the other extreme and take what has been said as a plea for some sort of disguised imposition from outside. It is worth while, accordingly, to say something about the way in which the adult can exercise the wisdom his own wider experience gives him without imposing a merely external control. On one side, it is his business to be on the alert to see what attitudes and habitual tendencies are being created. In this direction he must, if he is an educator, be able to judge what attitudes are actually conducive to continued growth and what are detrimental. He must, in addition, have that sympathetic understanding ~ individuals as individuals which gives him an idea of what is actually going on in the minds of those who are learning. It is, among other things, the need for these abilities on the part of the parent and teacher which makes a system of education based upon living experience a more difficult affair to conduct successfully than it is to follow the patterns of traditional education.

But there is another aspect of the matter. Experience does not go on simply inside a person. It does go on there, for it influences the formation of attitudes of desire and purpose. But this is not the whole of the story. Every genuine experience has an active side which changes in some degree the objective conditions under which experiences are had. The difference between civilization and savagery, to take an example on a large scale, is found in the degree in which previous experiences have changed the objective conditions under which subsequent experiences take place. The existence of roads, of means of rapid movement and transportation, tools, implements, furniture, electric light and power, are illustrations. Destroy the external conditions of present civilized experience, and for a time our experience would relapse into that of barbaric peoples.

In a word, we live from birth to death in a world of persons and things which in large measure is what it is because of what has been done and transmitted from previous human activities. When this fact is ignored, experience is treated as if it were something which goes on exclusively inside an individual's body and mind. It ought not to be necessary to say that experience does not occur in a vacuum. There are sources outside an individual which give rise to experience. It is constantly fed from these springs. No one would question that a child in a slum tenement has a different experience from that of a child in a cultured home; that the country lad has a different kind of experience from the city boy, or a boy on the sea-shore one different from the lad who is brought up on inland prairies. Ordinarily we take such facts for granted as too commonplace to record. But when their educational import is recognized, they indicate the second way in which the educator can direct the experience of the young without engaging in imposition. A primary responsibility of educators is that they not only be aware of the general principle of the shaping of actual experience by environing conditions, but that they also recognize in the concrete what surroundings are conducive to having experiences that lead to growth. Above all, they should know how to utilize the surroundings, physical and social, that exist so as to extract from them all that they have to contribute to building up experiences that are worth while.

Traditional education did not have to face this problem; it could systematically dodge this responsibility. The school environment of desks, blackboards, a small schoolyard, was supposed to suffice. There was no demand that the teacher should become intimately acquainted with the conditions of the local community, physical, historical, economic, oc-cupational, etc., in order to utilize them as educational resources. A system of education based upon the necessary connection of education with experience must, on the contrary, if faithful to its principle, take these things constantly into account. This tax upon the educator is another reason why progressive education is more difficult to carry on than was ever the traditional system.

It is possible to frame schemes of education that pretty systematically subordinate ob-jective conditions to those which reside in the individuals being educated. This happens whenever the place and function of the teacher, of books, of apparatus and equipment, of everything which represents the products of the more mature experience of elders, is system-atically subordinated to the immediate inclinations and feelings of the young. Every theory which assumes that importance can be attached to these objective factors only at the expense of imposing external control and of limiting the freedom of individuals rests finally upon the notion that experience is truly experience only when objective conditions are subordinated to what goes on within the individuals having the experience.

I do not mean that it is supposed that objective conditions can be shut out. It is recognized that they must enter in: so much concession is made to the inescapable fact that we live in a world of things and persons. But I think that observation of what goes on in some families and some schools would disclose that some parents and some teachers are acting upon the idea of *subordinating* objective conditions to internal ones. In that case, it is assumed not only that the latter are primary, which in one sense they are, but that just as they temporarily exist they fix the whole educational process.

Let me illustrate from the case of an infant. The needs of a baby for food, rest, and activity are certainly primary and decisive in one respect. Nourishment must be provided; provision must be made for comfortable sleep, and so on. But these facts do not mean that a parent shall feed the baby at any time when the baby is cross or irritable, that there shall not be a program of regular hours of feeding and sleeping, etc. The wise mother takes account of the needs of the infant but not in a way which dispenses with her own responsibility for regulating the objective conditions under which the needs are satisfied. And if she is a wise mother in this respect, she draws upon past experiences of experts as well as her own for the light that these shed upon what experiences are in general most conducive to the normal development of infants. Instead of these conditions being subordinated to the immediate internal condition of the baby, they are definitely ordered so that a particular kind of *interaction* with these immediate internal states may be brought about.

The word "interaction," which has just been used, expresses the second chief principle for interpreting an experience in its educational function and force. It assigns equal rights to both factors in experience-objective and internal conditions. Any normal experience is an interplay of these two sets of conditions. Taken together, or in their interaction, they form what we call a *situation*. The trouble with traditional education was not that it emphasized the external conditions that enter into the control of the experiences but that it paid so little attention to the internal factors which also decide what kind of experience is had. It violated the principle of interaction from one side. But this violation is no reason why the new education should violate the principle from the other side—except upon the basis of the extreme *Either-Or* educational philosophy which has been mentioned.

The illustration drawn from the need for regulation of the objective conditions of a baby's development indicates, first, that the parent has responsibility for arranging the conditions under which an infant's experience of food, sleep, etc., occurs, and, secondly, that the responsibility is fulfilled by utilizing the funded experience of the past, as this is represented, say, by the advice of competent physicians and others who have made a special study of normal physical growth. Does it limit the freedom of the mother when she uses the body of knowledge thus provided to regulate the objective conditions of nourishment and sleep? Or does the enlargement of her intelligence in fulfilling her parental function widen her freedom? Doubtless if a fetish were made of the advice and directions so that they came to be inflexible dictates to be followed under every possible condition, then restriction of freedom of both parent and child would occur. But this restriction would also be a limitation of the intelligence that is exercised in personal judgment.

In what respect does regulation of objective conditions limit the freedom of the baby? Some limitation is certainly placed upon its immediate movements and inclinations when it is put in its crib, at a time when it wants to continue playing, or does not get food at the moment it would like it, or when it isn't picked up and dandled when it cries for attention. Restriction also occurs when mother or nurse snatches a child away from an open fire into which it is about to fall. I shall have more to say later about freedom. Here it is enough to ask whether freedom is to be thought of and adjudged on the basis of relatively momentary incidents or whether its meaning is found in the continuity of developing experience.

The statement that individuals live in a world means, in the concrete, that they live in a series of situations. And when it is said that they live in these situations, the meaning of the word "in" is different from its meaning when it is said that pennies are "in" a pocket or paint is "in" a can. It means, once more, that interaction is going on between an individual and objects and other persons. The conceptions of *situation* and of *interaction* are inseparable from each other. An experience is always what it is because of a transaction taking place between an individual and what, at the time, constitutes his environment, whether the latter consists of persons with whom he is talking about some topic or event, the subject talked about being also a part of the situation; or the toys with which he is playing; the book he is reading (in which his environing conditions at the time may be England or ancient Greece or an imaginary region); or the materials of an experiment he is performing. The environment, in other words, is whatever conditions interact with personal needs, desires, purposes, and capacities to create the experience which is had. Even when a person builds a castle in the air he is interacting with the objects which he constructs in fancy.

The two principles of continuity and interaction are not separate from each other. They intercept and unite. They are, so to speak, the longitudinal and lateral aspects of experience. Different situations succeed one another. But because of the principle of continuity something is carried over from the earlier to the later ones. As an individual passes from one situation to another, his world, his environment, expands or contracts. He does not find himself living in another world but in a different part or aspect of one and the same world. What he has learned in the way of knowledge and skill in one situation becomes an instrument of understanding and dealing effectively with the situations which follow. The process goes on as long as life and learning continue. Otherwise the course of experience is disorderly, since the individual factor that enters into making an experience is split. A divided world, a world whose parts and aspects do not hang together, is at once a sign and a cause of a divided personality. When the splitting-up reaches a certain point we call the person insane. A fully integrated personality, on the other hand, exists only when successive experiences are integrated with one another. It can be built up only as a world of related objects is constructed.

Continuity and interaction in their active union with each other provide the measure of the educative significance and value of an experience. The immediate and direct concern of an educator is then with the situations in which interaction takes place. The individual, who enters as a factor into it, is what he is at a given time. It is the other factor, that of objective conditions, which lies to some extent within the possibility of regulation by the educator. As has already been noted, the phrase "objective conditions" covers a wide range. It includes what is done by the educator and the way in which it is done, not only words spoken but the tone of voice in which they are spoken. It includes equipment, books, apparatus, toys, games played. It includes the materials with which an individual interacts, and, most important of all, the total social set-up of the situations in which a person is engaged.

When it is said that the objective conditions are those which are within the power of the educator to regulate, it is meant, of course, that his ability to influence directly the experience of others and thereby the education they obtain places upon him the duty of determining that environment which will interact with the existing capacities and needs of those taught to create a worth-while experience. The trouble with traditional education was not that educators took upon themselves the responsibility for providing an environment. The trouble was that they did not consider the other factor in creating an experience; namely, the powers and purposes of those taught. It was assumed that a certain set of conditions was intrinsically desirable, apart from its ability to evoke a certain quality of response in individuals. This lack of mutual adaptation made the process of teaching and learning accidental. Those to whom the provided conditions were suitable managed to learn. Others got on as best they could. Responsibility for selecting objective conditions carries with it, then, the responsibility for understanding the needs and capacities of the individuals who are learning at a given time. It is not enough that certain materials and methods have proved effective with other individuals at other times. There must be a reason for thinking that they will function in generating an experience that has educative quality with particular individuals at a particular time.

It is no reflection upon the nutritive quality of beefsteak that it is not fed to infants. It is not an invidious reflection upon trigonometry that we do not teach it in the first or fifth grade of school. It is not the subject per se that is educative or that is conducive to growth. There is no subject that is in and of itself, or without regard to the stage of growth attained by the learner, such that inherent educational value can be attributed to it. Failure to take into account adaptation to the needs and capacities of individuals was the source of the idea that certain subjects and certain methods are intrinsically cultural or intrinsically good for mental discipline. There is no such thing as educational value in the abstract. The notion that some subjects and methods and that acquaintance with certain facts and truths possess educational value in and of themselves is the reason why traditional education reduced the material of education so largely to a diet of predigested materials. According to this notion, it was enough to regulate the quantity and difficulty of the material provided, in a scheme of quantitative grading, from month to month and from year to year. Otherwise a pupil was expected to take it in doses that were prescribed from without. If the pupil left it instead of taking it, if he engaged in physical truancy, or in the mental truancy of mind-wandering and finally built up an emotional revulsion against the subject, he was held to be at fault. No question was raised as to whether the trouble might not lie in the subject-matter or in the way in which it was offered. The principle of interaction makes it clear that failure of adaptation of material to needs and capacities of individuals may cause an experience to be non-educative quite as much as failure of an individual to adapt himself to the material.

The principle of continuity in its educational application means, nevertheless, that the future has to be taken into account at every stage of the educational process. This idea is easily misunderstood and is badly distorted in traditional education. Its assumption is, that by acquiring certain skills and by learning certain subjects which would be needed later (perhaps in college or perhaps in adult life) pupils are as a matter of course made ready for the needs and circumstances of the future. Now "preparation" is a treacherous idea. In a certain sense every experience should do something to prepare a person for later experiences of a deeper and more expansive quality. That is the very meaning of growth, continuity, reconstruction of experience. But it is a mistake to suppose that the mere acquisition of a certain amount of arithmetic, geography, history, etc., which is taught and studied because it may be useful at some time in the future, has this effect, and it is a mistake to suppose that acquisition of skills in reading and figuring will automatically constitute preparation for their right and effective use under conditions very unlike those in which they were acquired.

Almost everyone has had occasion to look back upon his school days and wonder what has become of the knowledge he was supposed to have amassed during his years of schooling, and why it is that the technical skills he acquired have to be learned over again in changed form in order to stand him in good stead. Indeed, he is lucky who does not find that in order to make progress, in order to go ahead intellectually, he does not have to unlearn much of what he learned in school. These questions cannot be disposed of by saying that the subjects were not actually learned for they were learned at least sufficiently to enable a pupil to pass examinations in them. One trouble is that the subject-matter in question was learned in isolation; it was put, as it were, in a water-tight compartment. When the question is asked, then, what has become of it, where has it gone to, the right answer is that it is still there in the special compartment in which it was originally stowed away. If exactly the same conditions recurred as those under which it was acquired, it would also recur and be available. But it was segregated when it was acquired and hence is so disconnected from the rest of experience that it is not available under the actual conditions of life. It is contrary to the laws of experience that learning of this kind, no matter how thoroughly engrained at the time, should give genuine preparation.

Nor does failure in preparation end at this point. Perhaps the greatest of all pedagogical fallacies is the notion that a person learns only the particular thing he is studying at the time. Collateral learning in the way of formation of enduring attitudes, of likes and dislikes, may be and often is much more important than the spelling lesson or lesson in geography or history that is learned. For these attitudes are fundamentally what count in the future. The most important attitude that can be formed is that of desire to go on learning. If impetus in this direction is weakened instead of being intensified, something much more than mere lack of preparation takes place. The pupil is actually robbed of native capacities which otherwise would enable him to cope with the circumstances that he meets in the course of his life. We often see persons who have had little schooling and in whose case the absence of set schooling proves to be a positive asset. They have at least retained their native common sense and power of judgment, and its exercise in the actual conditions of living has given them the precious gift of ability to learn from the experiences they have. What avail is it to win prescribed amounts of information about geography and history, to win ability to read and write, if in the process the individual loses his own soul: loses his appreciation of things worth while, of the values to which these things are relative; if he loses desire to apply what he has learned and, above all, loses the ability to extract meaning from his future experiences as they occur?

What, then, is the true meaning of preparation in the educational scheme? In the first place, it means that a person, young or old, gets out of his present experience all that there is in it for him at the time in which he has it. When preparation is made the controlling end, then the potentialities of the present are sacrificed to a suppositious future. When this happens, the actual preparation for the future is missed or distorted. The ideal of using the present simply to get ready for the future contradicts itself. It omits, and even shuts out, the very conditions by which a person can be prepared for his future. We always live at the time we live and not at some other time, and only by extracting at each present time the full meaning of each present experience are we prepared for doing the same thing in the future. This is the only preparation which in the long run amounts to anything.

All this means that attentive care must be devoted to the conditions which give each present experience a worth while meaning. Instead of inferring that it doesn't make much difference what the present experience is as long as it is enjoyed, the conclusion is the exact opposite. Here is another matter where it is easy to react from one extreme to the other. Because traditional schools tended to sacrifice the present to a remote and more or less unknown future, therefore it comes to be believed that the educator has little responsibility for the kind of present experiences the young undergo. But the relation of the present and the future is not an *Either-Or* affair. The present affects the future anyway. The persons who should have some idea of the connection between the two are those who have achieved maturity. Accordingly, upon them devolves the responsibility for instituting the conditions for the kind of present experience which has a favorable effect upon the future. Education as growth or maturity should be an ever-present process.

Commentary

Dewey wrote *Experience and Education* in an attempt to correct many of the misunderstandings and controversies that his earlier books and essays had provoked (Waks, 2013). While this and every chapter from this 1938 volume may be among the simplest of Dewey's later writings, the ideas presented here have been criticized for being overly philosophical and dense, and they too have frequently been misinterpreted (Ravitch, 2000; Waks, 2013). At the core of this publication is an attempt to construct a pedagogical theory that both honors the principle of learning through personal experience and ensures that the experiences had by all students are worthwhile and conducive to continued growth. In Dewey's view, every experience moves us forward, and it is the job of educators to be vigilant in their assessment of exactly what it is that students are moving toward. In answer to the question of how best to meet these pedagogical goals, Dewey calls here for educational environments predicated on democratic social principles and an overarching regard for students' individual freedoms.

As explained previously, Dewey never formulated an explicit theory of creativity perhaps because, as some have speculated (see Hallman, 1964), he did not believe that separate theorizing was necessary. He regarded creative behavior as he did any natural act arising out of the continuity of nature and human experience. It was his view that just like any other thought process or behavior, creativity results from the interaction of person and environment; in the case of creativity, however, mental operations combine past and present experiences into new and unprecedented combinations (Hallman, 1964).

At the core of Dewey's philosophy is the message that children's own instincts must structure the material that is presented to them. These instincts form the foundation of their knowledge and all the eventual understandings that will build from it. Student motivation, "the power and purposes of those taught," holds the key. And it is this emphasis on motivation that aligns Dewey's philosophizing so closely with more recent work on what has come to be termed the "social psychology of creativity." In Dewey's (1938, p. 42) words, "The trouble with traditional education was . . . that it paid so little attention to the internal factors which also decide what kind of experience is had." In the contemporary literature, these internal deciding factors are most often framed in terms of a distinction between intrinsic and extrinsic motivation. Intrinsic motivation is operationalized as the motivation to approach a task or problem out of sheer interest in the activity itself. An intrinsic motivational orientation carries with it an excitement about the challenges that lay ahead. The solution to a problem or the eventual outcome of a project may not be at all obvious, but somewhere deep inside, the student believes that he or she has the requisite skills necessary for a successful outcome. Extrinsic motivation, on the other hand, is the motivation to do something for some external goal, some incentive outside of the task itself that is driving task engagement, such as an impending grade or the promise of a reward. A large segment of the theorizing and research being done in this area asks the question of how we can best set up educational environments so that they are optimally conducive to students' intrinsic motivation and creativity (see Hennessey, 2003, 2010, 2013). Dewey too focused on the impact of classroom environment on educational experience. In fact, in the chapter excerpted here he wrote, "A primary responsibility of educators is that they not only be aware of the general principle of the shaping of actual experience by environing conditions, but that they also recognize in the concrete what surroundings are conducive to having experiences that lead to growth" (1938, p. 40).

Dozens of empirical investigations have demonstrated an inextricable link between motivation and creativity of performance. And it is features of the classroom environment that in large part shape that motivational orientation. Students of all ages have been randomly assigned to constraint or no-constraint conditions and then asked to produce tangible products and make self-reports of task interest and enjoyment. Across age groups and situations, the results are clear: when working in a competitive classroom environment or under the expectation of reward or evaluation, task enjoyment and interest is likely to be undermined and creativity also suffers (see Hennessey, 2003, 2010, 2013). Motivational orientation marks the boundary between what students are capable of doing and what they actually will do in any given situation. Without the right kind of motivation, they are unlikely to take risks, play with ideas, or accept the possibility that they might fail. Without the right kind of motivation, creativity is nearly impossible (see Hennessey, 2013).

Expected reward, expected evaluation, competition, time limits, and surveillance have all been demonstrated to undermine student intrinsic motivation and creativity (see Hennessey, 2003, 2010, 2013). Importantly, this list of creativity killers is composed of exactly the kinds of pedagogical elements Dewey referred to as "objective conditions" or "situations." Dewey (1938, p. 45) cautions educators to pay attention both to what they are setting out to accomplish and the ways in which they attempt to meet their goals—"not only words spoken but the tone of voice in which they are spoken," "the total social setup of the situation" in which the student is engaged. Dewey clearly understood that some classroom surroundings are far more conducive than others to providing experiences that lead to growth. He clearly understood that intrinsic motivation is an especially delicate and fleeting state. Student intrinsic task motivation cannot be taken for granted.

In the classroom, intrinsic motivation is almost always preferable to an extrinsic motivational orientation. Extrinsic motivation is likely to lead to better performance only on tasks requiring rote recitation, precise performance under strong time pressure, and the completion of familiar, repetitive procedures. An intrinsically motivated state, characterized by deeply focused attention, enhanced cognitive functioning, and increased and persistent activity (Alexander & Murphy, 1994; Maehr & Meyer, 1997), leads to deeper, more long-lasting learning and better problem-solving on open-ended tasks (McGraw, 1978; McGraw & McCullers, 1979). Dewey was way ahead of his time when he identified the link between student interest and curiosity and effort expended in the classroom. He instructed teachers to take responsibility for understanding the needs, interests, and capacities of the particular students who are learning at a given time and cautioned that it is not enough that certain materials and methods may have been shown to be effective with other students at other times. Dewey's (1938, p. 47) principle of interaction makes it clear that a failure to adapt materials and curriculum to the needs and capacities of individual learners may "cause an experience to be non-educative."

Researchers like Simon (1967) would later empirically demonstrate that learners driven by intrinsic motivation and curiosity try harder and exert more consistent effort to reach their learning goals. In fact a large number of related investigations have demonstrated that when students approach new concepts with high levels of curiosity and interest, information is better learned and remembered (e.g., Flink, Boggiano, & Main, 1992; Hidi, 1990; Lepper & Cordova, 1992; Tobias, 1994). Importantly, in fact, intrinsic motivation promotes far more than memory and persistence. Students' motivational orientation also helps to determine the kinds of activities they will choose to pursue in the first place. When given a choice of open-ended tasks requiring a creative solution, extrinsically motivated students tend to opt for the easiest possible problems (Condry & Chambers, 1978; Pittman, Emery, & Boggiano, 1982). Intrinsically motivated learners are more likely to perceive that they are playing rather than working; as a result, they take risks and explore solutions to questions or activities that represent for them an appropriate level of difficulty and challenge.

In addition to emphasizing the importance of student motivation and interest, Dewey also admonishes educators to remember that "experience does not occur in a vacuum" (a phrase that many contemporary creativity researchers have applied to creative behavior and even adopted as their own). All human experience is ultimately social. Lessons learned in the classroom involve far more than the academic content being delivered. Dewey uses the term "collateral learning" to refer to the formation of enduring attitudes, likes, and dislikes and makes the case that such attitudes can have a far more enduring and important impact on students than any spelling or geography lesson. According to Dewey (1938, p. 48):

> The most important attitude that can be formed is that of desire to go on learning. If impetus in this direction is weakened instead of being intensified, something much more than mere lack of preparation takes place. The pupil is actually robbed of native capacities which otherwise would enable him to cope with the circumstances that he meets in the course of his life.

Here again Dewey's philosophizing is nothing short of visionary. Important and influential work carried out by Jackson (1968) and colleagues in the 1960s revealed the power of the so-called hidden curriculum—the unspoken and usually unintended lessons that students learn while in school. Dewey's concept of collateral learning also captures perfectly the more recent work being done in the areas of locus of control, academic self-concept, self-esteem, and the development of' "noncognitive skills" such as self-control as well as the formation of students' implicit theories about intelligence and views of their own ability (e.g., West et al., 2016; Yeager & Dweck, 2012). When students believe that no amount of hard work or perseverance will compensate for what they perceive as a lack of personal ability, creativity (and all learning) is bound to suffer. As the title of a recent paper by Dweck (2010) puts it, "even geniuses work hard."

Taken together, the insights offered by Dewey in this 1938 volume as well as his other works nicely parallel empirical findings in the social psychology of creativity literature and related research areas with applications to educational practice. Empirical work reported by Rathunde and Csikszentmihalyi (2005a, 2005b) quantifies just how different the learning experience (and the potential for creativity) can be in a traditional versus a more "open," progressive environment like that prescribed by Dewey. These investigators compared the experience of middle schoolers in Montessori classrooms with the experiences of same-age peers in more typical mainstream school environments. In today's American educational landscape, Montessori schools, with their emphasis on intrinsically motivated concentration and learning by doing, offer one of the few contemporary pedagogical approximations to the Dewey-based "progressive" classroom.[1] Montessori and traditional classroom students matched for potentially important family and school variables, including parental education and teacher-student ratios, wore electronic watches and were instructed to fill out response forms about what they were doing and experiencing whenever they were a prompted by a beep. More specifically, these prompts were delivered at random intervals throughout the school day and students provided information about affect/mood, potency (energy level), salience (feelings that an activity was important), intrinsic motivation, and flow.

Experience sampling (ESM) results pointed to the profound effect that the class-room context can have on students' motivation, creativity, and overall quality of experience. In the Montessori schools, students were given several hours each day to choose how they would spend their time. The Montessori teachers saw themselves as mentors and worked to create a cognitively rich environment and a flexible curriculum that balanced freedom of choice with clear rules. The traditional schools put far less emphasis on student intrinsic motivation and generally did not offer opportunities for free choice. Instead seatwork was required and a lecture format was used to deliver information in rigid, blocked periods of 45 to 50 minutes each. Multivariate analysis of covariance of the approximately 4,000 ESM signals collected from the two groups revealed that Montessori students reported a richer, more positive quality of experience while doing academic work. In particular, Montessori students reported a significantly higher per-centage of flow experience than did traditional students, as well as more positive affect, energy, and intrinsic motivation while engaged in academic work. There were, however, no between-group differences in experience when students were hanging out in the halls, eating lunch or talking with friends.

Of particular importance was the fact that Montessori students reported feeling high motivation and high salience at the same time at a significantly higher rate than did tra-ditional students. In fact the most common experience for the traditional students was what Dewey (1913) referred to as drudgery, or the feeling that one is doing something important, but enjoyment is lacking. This relatively high frequency of drudgery reported by the traditional students was, as Rathunde and Csikszentmihalyi (2005a, 2005b) point out, consistent with the frequently observed drop in students' intrinsic motivation after entering middle school (Eccles et al., 1993).

Why, then, do we not see more classrooms modeled after Dewey's philosophy? Why, in fact, are current, mainstream educational practices with their one-size-fits-all mentality virtually the antithesis of what Dewey would recommend? What would Dewey have to say about the highly restrictive and regimented Common Core curriculum being implemented in the US, not to mention America's virtually single-minded focus on high-stakes testing? What would he say about the emphasis placed on the accumulation of "facts," often to the detriment and even the elimination of the arts? The answer to these questions is that he

---

1. During the Great Depression, the Progressive Education Association conducted an eight-year study designed to evaluate the effects of progressive programs. More than 1,500 students over four years were compared to an equal number of matched students attending more "traditional," conventional schools. At college age, the students who had experienced progressive teaching methods were found to be equal to or had surpassed traditional students in terms of grades, extracurricular participation, dropout rates, intellectual curiosity, and resourcefulness. In addition, the data showed that the more a school departed from the traditional college preparatory program, the better was the record of their graduates (Kohn, 1999).

would, and did, have a great deal to say. In Chapter 3 of *Experience and Education* Dewey (1938, p. 49) wrote:

> What avail is it to win prescribed amounts of information about geography and history, to win ability to read and write, if in the process the individual loses his own soul: loses his appreciation of things worthwhile, of the values to which these things are relative; if he loses desire to apply what he has learned and, above all, loses the ability to extract meaning from his future experiences as they occur?
>
> What, then, is the true meaning of preparation in the educational scheme? In the first place, it means that a person, young or old, gets out of his present experience all that there is in it for him at the time in which he has it. When preparation is made the controlling end, then the potentialities of the present are sacrificed to a suppositious future. When this happens, the actual preparation for the future is missed or distorted. The ideal of using the present simply to get ready for the future contradicts itself. It omits, and even shuts out, the very conditions by which a person can be prepared for his future.

At the turn of the 20th century, Dewey's blueprint for educational reform in the US was seen to be fueled by a host of radical ideas. But over time, his philosophy of education came to influence many thousands of teachers and classrooms. His was a philosophy of possibility (Greene, 1997), and for a few decades it really did seem as though American educators might succeed in realizing those possibilities. By the middle of the 20th century, a great number of students had been schooled according to the so-called progressive approach. But eventually there came a major change in educational priorities. Concerns about Russia's launching of *Sputnik* and related pressures during the Cold War prompted policymakers to revert to more "trusted," conventional teaching methods in an effort to boost US students' test scores and international standing. Dewey's use of the term "progressive" refers to the progressive impact of experience in learning and not to left-wing or liberal political doctrine. But this is not to say that politics haven't played an important role in the evolution of how American policymakers have viewed his learning-by-doing educational model. In fact pedagogical approaches fall in and out of favor in large part because the public schools are seen as a vehicle for curing the ills of society (Cuban, 2004). When progressive methods failed to be the panacea that society was hoping for, the educational pendulum swung toward a far more traditional, top-down instructional approach.

Yet this "move to the right" of the pedagogical continuum also failed to yield the large numbers of students policymakers had hoped would enter the engineering and science fields, and inequities in educational outcomes for students of different races also continued to loom large. In response, the educational pendulum again swung toward a second wave of the "learning by doing" approach, fueled by the hope that this change in pedagogy would promote student creativity (Cuban, 2004). The "open classroom" movement of the 1960s and early 1970s, while not directly based on Dewey's teachings, bore a great similarity to the progressive classrooms of the 1930s and 1940s. Working individually or in small groups, students learned at their own pace as they interacted with materials organized around "learning centers" (Cuban, 2004). Under this system, teachers at both the elementary and secondary levels resembled coaches or mentors more than they did "bosses" at the top of a classroom hierarchy. Over time this "active learning" or "discovery learning" model became increasingly popular until, once again, societal concerns (this time centered on a faltering economy and the Vietnam War) prompted the conclusion that "open" schools had failed to make their mark. By the early

1980s, open classrooms were virtually extinct (Cuban, 2004) and soon were replaced with what would eventually become perhaps the most restrictive American educational framework yet, as dictated by the Common Core (see National Governors Association for Best Practices, 2010).

Perhaps not surprisingly, eight years after its implementation, public and professional support for Common Core has also begun to wane. Business leaders, scholars, and practicing teachers argue that schools must once again be reimagined so as to make the promotion of students' creative thinking and innovation a top priority (see Wagner, 2012). Concerned groups of teachers, administrators, parents, and students have come to question and fight against what many professionals now believe is the abuse of standardized testing (and children). National organizations like FairTest have called for a broad reexamination of state and federal educational policies. Organizers in Seattle, Chicago, Toledo, New York City, Long Island, New Mexico, and beyond have staged massive boycotts of high-stakes tests, and a growing number of teachers across the country have refused to administer particularly flawed and punitive exams. Critics of Common Core argue that the gulf between what students are interested in and the ways they best learn and what their teachers are told they must teach and how they must teach is growing ever wider and must be bridged. Once again Dewey's call for classrooms to be restructured to better serve students, rather than bureaucrats and politicians, is being heard. But why should this latest swing of the pedagogical pendulum back toward Dewey's educational ideals and emphasis on what is now often termed problem-based or inquiry-based learning be any different than previous short-lived, and sometimes even failed, progressive education attempts? In answer to this question, Dewey would undoubtedly caution educators and policymakers on three important counts. First, he would urge them to remember that their focus must never be just on the physical trappings of the school environment or even the content of the curriculum. A classroom filled with learning stations or a "school without walls" says nothing about the *way* teaching is done or how learning is progressing. Even a commitment to individualized instruction tells us little about whether students' motivational orientation, whether they perceive that they are in charge of their own learning, or whether they are actively engaged in an integration of experiences is taking place. It is these and related internal factors that determine student success. Dewey would also most likely point out, as did their predecessors, that many contemporary educators attempting to take a "progressive" approach wrongly assume that a rejection of the ideas, principles, and goals driving more "traditional" educational models means that they must opt for educational practices at the opposite extreme of the continuum: schools devoid of any philosophical base or concrete educational expectations where pretty much anything goes and children are free to learn (or not) as they see fit.

While Dewey had great confidence in children's natural instincts, curiosity, and ability, he also understood that students' educational needs are not always aligned with their interests. He would admonish educators never to infer that just because an experience is enjoyed, it is necessarily educative. A student-driven, process-based curriculum is especially vulnerable to failure because it may not always provide sufficient structure for meaningful and valuable learning to take place. Teachers in a progressive classroom environment must constantly balance the humanistic goals of fueling students' passions and allowing them to be in control of their own learning with the equally necessary goal of assuring that each educational experience being had, each attitude being formed, is conducive to continued growth and learning that is worthwhile. In fact it was Dewey's expectation that students would adapt to the curriculum in the same way that their teachers would adapt material to their students.

In the opinion of some scholars, it was fundamental misunderstandings about the importance of setting limits and sometimes even making choices for students that led to the demise of open classrooms and once lauded experimental schools such as A. S. Neill's Summerhill (Kytle, 2012). Educators even in the most progressive educational environments must maintain control and rely on their maturity and experience to decide what is best, most educative for their students. Dewey never recommended that children of any age be allowed to do anything they wish. Yet as he points out, this responsibility for setting limits is so much more complex when the role of the teacher is framed not as a traditional all-powerful task master but as a mentor to equals. This lack of strict student and teacher roles is just one of a host of complexities of the progressive classroom described by Dewey (1938, p. 40) as a "tax upon the educator"—one of many reasons he believed that teaching in a progressive environment is far more difficult than teaching in a more traditional system. When traditional sources of external control and coercion are removed from the classroom environment, a whole new set of challenges arises. Educators are left to rely on students' own mechanisms of internal control. In other words, they must cultivate students' own internal motivation and find ways to promote and channel that motivation in appropriate and meaningful directions.

The third cautionary message that Dewey would deliver would most likely focus on what he termed the principle of "continuity" and its educational policy applications. His emphasis on continuity means that the future must be taken into account at every stage of the educational process. While this premise seems simple enough, Dewey warns that, in actuality, this idea has too often been misunderstood. Educators must never assume that the mastery of a certain set of skills or the acquisition of a particular body of knowledge will adequately prepare students for the future. At issue here, of course, is the fundamental problem with educational initiatives like Common Core and its concomitant overemphasis on standardized assessments. As Dewey (1938, p. 49) observes:

> When preparation is made the controlling end, then the potentialities of the present are sacrificed to a suppositious future. . . . The ideal of using the present simply to get ready for the future contradicts itself. It omits, and even shuts out, the very conditions by which a person can be prepared for his future.

In recent years many employers have learned firsthand this important lesson. They have come to understand that the acquisition of "testable" facts and figures is not enough. If students are truly to be made ready to join the workforce of the 21st century, they must be helped to develop the confidence and intrinsic motivation to tackle difficult problems. Educational reformers hoping to return to a progressive educational approach where student intrinsic motivation and creativity are allowed to grow and flourish must carefully study and internalize the sometimes complex and often misunderstood principles guiding Dewey's vision. For far too long, much of the educational policymaking in the US and around the world has been devoid of theory, driven instead by politicians and business leaders who concentrate on the financial bottom line and make their decisions based on unfounded assumptions rather than empirical research findings or any kind of overarching philosophy. But if educational reforms are to be successful and long-lasting, they must be directly tied to theory. Without this theoretical base, classroom practice will continue to be predicated on short-sighted, one-dimensional "quick fixes" like Common Core. As Dewey cautions, attention must be paid to both our educational means (methods) and ends (learning outcomes). We must move our sights beyond an emphasis on narrowly defined concepts of accountability and testing standards toward the provision of classroom environments designed to nurture young learners so that they are ready, willing, and able to persevere, take chances, make connections, and apply their insights to new situations.

References

Alexander, P. A., & Murphy, P. K. (1994, April). *The research base for APA's learner-centered principles.* Paper presented at the annual meeting of the American Educational Research Association, New Orleans, LA.

American Association of Colleges and Universities (2015, January). *Falling short? College earning and career success.* Washington DC: Hart Research Associates. Retrieved from: Association of American Colleges and Universities website, https://aacu.org/leap/public-opinion-research/2015-survey-results.

Condry, J., & Chambers, J. (1978). Intrinsic motivation and the process of learning. In M. R. Lepper and D. Greene (Eds.), *The hidden costs of reward* (pp. 61–84). Hillsdale, NJ: Lawrence Erlbaum.

Cuban, L. (2004). The open classroom: Were schools without walls just another fad? *Education Next, 4*(2), 68–71.

de Bono, E. (1985). *Six thinking hats: An essential approach to business management.* Boston: Little, Brown.

Dewey, J. (1913). *Interest and effort in education.* Cambridge, MA: Riverside.

Dewey, J. (1934/2005). *Art as experience.* New York, NY: Perigee.

Dewey, J. (1938). *Experience and education.* New York, NY: Kappa Delta Pi.

Dweck, C. S. (2010). Even geniuses work hard. *Educational Leadership, 68*(1), 16–20.

Eccles, J., Midgley, C., Wigfield, A., Buchanan, C. M., Reuman, D., Flanagan, C., & Mac Iver, D. (1993). Development during adolescence: The impact of stage-environment fit on young adolescents' experience in schools and families. *American Psychologist, 48*(2), 90–101.

Flink, C., Boggiano, A. K., & Main, D. S. (1992). Children's achievement-related behaviors: The role of extrinsic and intrinsic motivational orientations. In A. K. Boggiano & T. S. Pittman (Eds.), *Achievement and motivation: A social-developmental perspective* (pp. 189–214). New York, NY: Cambridge University Press.

Greene, M. (1997, Spring). Teaching as possibility: A light in dark times. *Journal of Pedagogy, Pluralism & Practice, 1.* http://www.lesley.edu/journal-pedagogy-pluralism-practice/maxine-greene/teaching-as-possibility/.

Gutek, G. (2014). *Philosophical, ideological, and theoretical perspectives on education.* Saddle River, NJ: Pearson.

Hallman, R. J. (1964). The concept of creativity in Dewey's educational philosophy. *Educational Theory, 14*(4), 270–285.

Hennessey, B. A. (2003). The social psychology of creativity. *Scandinavian Journal of Educational Psychology, 47*(3), 253–271.

Hennessey, B. A. (2010). The creativity-motivation connection. In J. C. Kaufman and R. J. Sternberg (Eds.), *The Cambridge handbook of creativity* (pp. 342–365). New York, NY: Cambridge University Press.

Hennessey, B. A. (2013). Motivation is everything. In J. Jones & L. Flint (Eds.), *The creative imperative: School librarians and teachers cultivating curiosity together* (pp. 85–95). Santa Barbara, CA: Libraries Unlimited.

Hennessey, B. A. (2015). If I were secretary of education: A focus on intrinsic motivation and creativity in the classroom. *Psychology of Aesthetics, Creativity and the Arts, 9*(2), 187–192.

Hidi, S. (1990). Interest and its contribution as a mental resource for learning. *Review of Educational Research, 60*(4), 549–571.

Jackson, P. W. (1968). *Life in classrooms.* New York, NY: Holt, Rinehart and Winston.

Kohn, A. (1999). *The schools our children deserve.* New York, NY: Houghton Mifflin.

Kytle, J. (2012). *To want to learn: Insights and provocations for engaged learning* (2nd ed.). New York, NY: Palgrave Macmillan.

Leddy, T. (2006). Dewey's aesthetics. In *Stanford encyclopedia of philosophy.* Retrieved from: https://plato.stanford.edu/entries/dewey-aesthetics/.

Lepper, M. R., & Cordova, D. I. (1992). A desire to be taught: Instructional consequences of intrinsic motivation. *Motivation and Emotion, 16*(3), 187–208.

Maehr, M. L., & Meyer, H. A. (1997). Understanding motivation and schooling: Where we've been, where we are, and where we need to go. *Educational Psychology Review, 9*(4), 371–409.

McGraw, K. O. (1978). The detrimental effects of reward on performance: A literature review and a pre-diction model. In M. Lepper & D. Greene (Eds.), *The hidden costs of reward* (pp. 33–60). Hillsdale, NJ: Erlbaum.

McGraw, K. O., & McCullers, J. (1979). Evidence of a detrimental effect of extrinsic incentives on breaking a mental set. *Journal of Experimental Social Psychology, 15*(3), 285–294.

National Governors Association Center for Best Practices, Council of Chief State School Officers. (2010). *Common core state standards.* Washington, DC: National Governors Association for Best Practices Council of Chief State School Officers. Retrieved from: http://www.corestandards.org/.

Nelson, C. (2015). Discourses of creativity. In R. H. Jones (Ed.), *Handbook of language and creativity* (pp. 170–189). New York, NY: Routledge.

Pittman, T. S., Emery, J., & Boggiano, A. K. (1982). Intrinsic and extrinsic motivational orientations: Reward-induced changes in preference for complexity. *Journal of Personality and Social Psychology, 42*(5), 789–797.

Rathunde, K., & Csikszentmihalyi, M. (2005a). Middle school students' motivation and quality of ex-perience: A comparison of Montessori and traditional school environments. *American Journal of Education, 111*(3), 341–371.

Rathunde, K., & Csikszentmihalyi, M. (2005b). The social context of middle school: Teachers, friends, and activities in Montessori and traditional school environments. *Elementary School Journal, 106*(1), 59–79.

Ravitch, D. (2000). *Left back: A century of failed school reforms.* New York, NY: Touchstone.

Simon, H. A. (1967). Motivational and emotional controls of cognition. *Psychological Review, 74*(1), 29–39.

Simpson, D. J. (2001). John Dewey's concept of the student. *Canadian Journal of Education, 26*(2), 183–200.

Tobias, S. (1994). Interest, prior knowledge and learning. *Review of Educational Research, 64*(1), 37–54.

Wagner, T. (2012). *Creating innovators: The making of young people who will change the world.* New York, NY: Scribner's.

Waks, L. J. (2013). *John Dewey's experience and education: A reader's guide.* Retrieved from: https://www.amazon.com/John-Deweys-Experience-Education-Readers-ebook/dp/B00HAOO0EU.

West, M. R., Kraft, M. A., Finn, A. S., Martin, R., Duckworth, A. L., Gabrieli, C. F. O., & Gabrieli, J. D. E. (2016). Promise and paradox: Measuring students' non-cognitive skills and the impact of schooling. *Educational Evaluation and Policy Analysis, 38*(1), 148–170.

Yeager, D. S., & Dweck, C. S. (2012). Mindsets that promote resilience: When students believe that personal characteristics can be developed. *Educational Psychologist, 47*(4), 302–314.

PART SIX

Genius and Creativity

17

The Nature and Nurture of Creative Genius

Francis Galton

DEAN KEITH SIMONTON

Summary

Francis Galton's research on the inheritance of individual differences was inspired by reading Charles Darwin's *The Origin of Species*. At first, Galton introduced the family pedigree method to study the inheritance of natural ability in a large sample of geniuses, including eminent creators. However, in response to criticism, he devised the first self-questionnaire to investigate the possible role of environmental factors in the development of eminent scientists. The result was his 1874 *English Men of Science*. Besides representing the first direct study of notable creators and examining such factors as family background and education, this survey was the very first to explicitly define the nature-nurture issue that has become a mainstay of developmental research. Although Galton's later work looked at other individual difference variables, his emphasis on nature over nurture intensified until he introduced the concept of eugenics and advocated its practice. Nonetheless his 1874 work exerted a continued influence on later approaches to the study of creativity, including the use of samples of eminent creators and the attempt to tease out genetic and environmental influences. These influences suggest several options for future research.

Introduction

Francis Galton (1822–1911) was an English polymath who made major contributions to psychology, psychometrics, statistics, genetics, criminology, geography, meteorology, and anthropology. He first attained fame as an African explorer, even writing a best-selling book on the nuts and bolts of traveling abroad under rugged conditions. As the younger cousin of Charles Darwin, he avidly read the very first edition of the latter's 1859 *The Origin of Species*. Darwin's discussion of natural variability and individual differences inspired Galton to study the inheritance of variation in human abilities. The first major manifestation of this research was his 1869 *Hereditary Genius: An Inquiry into Its Laws and Consequences* (Simonton, 2003). After studying the family pedigrees of eminent creators and leaders, Galton argued that "natural ability" was totally inherited. This unqualified genetic determinism was immediately criticized. Among those critics was Alphonse de Candolle (1873), who conducted an investigation pinpointing the importance of environmental influences. In response, Galton carried out the survey that provides the reading for the current chapter.

Three special features of this empirical inquiry deserve special emphasis. First, Galton introduced an entirely new technique for studying highly creative people, namely the self-report questionnaire. In contrast, his 1869 book had used already published biographical data. Second, Galton explicitly defined a crucial debate in understanding creative development: the nature-nurture issue. Although the alliterative contrast between "nature" and "nurture" had been used before—including in Shakespeare's *The Tempest*—it was Galton who made these two terms endure in later developmental research (cf. Teigen, 1984). Third, he was the first to identify some of the key variables associated with nurture rather than nature—most notably the importance of birth order.

Despite the fact that Galton had initiated the empirical study of environmental influences on creative development, his research after 1874 gravitated back to nature rather than nurture. Besides introducing methods and statistics that would become foundational for modern behavior genetics, he also attempted to develop techniques for directly assessing individual differences in natural ability, namely, his anthropometric tests. He also scrutinized human variation in many other variables, such as visual imagery, the perception of high pitches, and fingerprint patterns, the last providing the scientific basis for identifying criminals. However, a later innovation was his coining the term "eugenics" and becoming a major advocate of eugenic policies (Galton, 1883). He clearly believed that nature was far more important than nurture. It is worth pointing out that Galton's position here was far more extreme than Darwin's, and he waited until after his cousin's death before making his extremism more explicit. He even endowed in his will the Galton Chair of Eugenics at University College London, a position first occupied by Karl Pearson. Eugenics having become largely discredited by some rather ugly applications that occurred in the first half of the 20th century, this position has been renamed the Galton Chair of Genetics.

The selections below come from the first chapter, "Antecedents," in which Galton presents his substantive questions, methodology, and some empirical findings regarding the family origins of eminent scientists.

Reading: *English Men of Science: Their Nature and Nurture*

Source: Galton, F. (1874). *English men of science: Their nature and nurture.* London: Macmillan. Selections from Chapter 1. Work in the public domain.

The intent of the book is to supply what may be termed a Natural History of the English Men of Science of the present day. It will describe their earliest antecedents, including the hereditary influences, the inborn qualities of their mind and body, the causes that first induced them to pursue science, the education they received and their opinions on its merits. The advantages are great of confining the investigation to men of our own period and nation. Our knowledge of them is more complete, and where deficient, it may be supplemented by further inquiry. They are subject to a moderate range of those influences which have the largest disturbing power, and are therefore well fitted for statistical investigation; lastly, the results we may obtain are of direct practical interest. The inquiry is a complicated one at the best; it is advantageous not to complicate it further by dealing with notabilities whose histories are seldom autobiographical, never complete and not always very accurate; and who lived under the varied and imperfectly appreciated conditions of European life, in several countries, at numerous periods during many different centuries.

Definition of "Man of Science."—I do not attempt to define a "scientific man," because no frontier line or *definition* exists, which separates any group of individuals from the rest of their species. Natural groups have nuclei but no outlines; they blend on every side with other systems whose nuclei have alien characters. A naturalist must construct his picture of nature on the same principle that an engraver in mezzotint proceeds on his plate, beginning with the principal lights as so many different points of departure, and working outwards from each of them until the intervening spaces are covered. Some definition of an ideal scientific man might possibly be given and accepted, but who is to decide in each case whether particular individuals fall within the definition? It seems to me the best way to take the verdict of the scientific world as expressed in definite language. It may be over lenient in some cases, in others it may never have been uttered, but on the whole it appears more satisfactory than any other verdict which exists or is attainable. To have been elected a Fellow of the Royal Society . . . is a real assay of scientific merit. Owing to various reasons, many excellent men of science of mature ages, may not be Fellows, but those who bear that title cannot but be considered in some degree as entitled to the epithet of "scientific." I therefore look upon this fellowship as a "pass examination," so to speak, and from among the Fellows of the Royal Society I select those who have yet further qualifications. One of these is the fact of having earned a medal for scientific work; another, of having presided over a learned Society, or a section of the British Association; another, of having been elected on the council of the Royal Society; another, of being professor at some important college or university. These and a few other similar signs of being appreciated by contemporary men of science, are the qualifications for which I have looked in selecting my list of typical scientific men. I have only deviated from these technical rules in two or three cases, where there appeared good reason for their relaxation and where the returns appeared likely to be of peculiar interest. On these principles I drew up a list of 180 men; most of them were qualified on more than one count, and many on several counts. Also, the list appeared nearly exhaustive in respect to those men of mature age who live in or near London, since other private tests suggested few additions. As two of these tests have been proposed by several correspondents, it may be well to describe them. The one is the election of individuals, on account of their scientific eminence, to a certain well-known literary and scientific club, the name of which it is unnecessary to mention. The committee of this club have the power of electing annually, out of their regular turn, nine persons eminent for science, literature, art, or public services. The two or three men who have in each year received this coveted privilege on the ground of science now amount to a considerable number, and they are all on my list. Again, there are certain dining clubs in connection with the Royal Society, the one meeting on the afternoon of every evening that it meets, and the other more rarely, and there are about fifty members to each of these clubs, the same persons being in many instances members of both. The election to either of the clubs is a testimony of some value to the estimation of the scientific status of a man by his contemporaries; almost all the members are on my list. No doubt, many persons of considerable position living in Edinburgh, Dublin, and elsewhere at a distance from London, are not among those with whose experiences I am about to deal. But that is no objection; I do not profess or care to be exhaustive in my data, only desiring to have a sufficiency of material, and to be satisfied that it is good so far as it goes, and a perfectly fair sample. I do not particularly want a list that shall include every man of science in England, but seek for one that is sufficiently extended for my purposes, and that contains none but truly scientific men, in the usual acceptation of that word.

However, I have made some further estimates, and conclude that an exhaustive list of men of the British Isles, of the same mature ages and general scientific status as those of whom I have been speaking, would amount to 300, but not to more.

Some of my readers may feel surprise that so many as 300 persons are to be found in the United Kingdom who deserve the title of scientific men; probably they have been accustomed to concentrate their attention upon a few notabilities, and to ignore their colleagues. It must, however, be recollected that all biographies, even of the greatest men, reveal numerous associates and competitors whose merit and influence were far greater than had been suspected by the outside world. Great discoveries have often been made simultaneously by workers ignorant of each other's labours. This shows that they had derived their inspiration from a common but hidden source, as no mere chance could account for simultaneous discovery. In illustration of this view it will suffice to mention a few of the great discoveries in this generation. That of photography is most intimately associated with the names of Niépce, Daguerre and Talbot, who were successful in 1839 along different lines of research, but Thomas Wedgewood was a photographer in 1802, though he could not fix his pictures. As to the origin of species, Wallace is well known to have had an independent share in its discovery, side by side with the far more comprehensive investigations of Darwin. In spectrum analysis the remarks of Stokes were anterior to and independent of the works of Kirchhoff and Bunsen. Electric telegraphy has numerous parents, German, English and American. The idea of conservation of energy has unnumbered roots. The simultaneous discovery of the planet Neptune on theoretical grounds by Leverrier and Adams is a very curious instance of what we are considering. In patent inventions the fact of simultaneous discovery is notoriously frequent. It would therefore appear that few discoveries are wholly due to a single man, but rather that vague and imperfect ideas, which float in conversation and literature, must grow, gather, and develop, until some more perspicacious and prompt mind than the rest clearly sees them. Thus, Laplace is understood to have seized on Kant's nebular hypothesis and Bentham on Priestley's phrase, "the greatest happiness of the greatest number," and each of them elaborated the idea he had so seized, into a system.

The first discoverers beat their contemporaries in point of time and by doing so they become leaders of thought. They direct the intellectual energy of the day into the channels they opened; it would have run in other channels but for their labour. It is therefore due to them, not that science progresses, but that her progress is as rapid as it is, and in the direction towards which they themselves have striven. We must neither underrate nor overrate their achievements. I would compare the small band of men who have achieved a conspicuous scientific position, to islands, which are not the detached objects they appear to the vulgar eye, but only the uppermost portions of hills, whose bulk is unseen. To pursue this metaphor; the range of my inquiry dips a few fathoms below the level at which popular reputation begins.

It is of interest to know the ratio which the numbers of the leading scientific men bear to the population of England generally. I obtain it in this way. Although 180 persons only were on my list, I reckon, as already mentioned, that it would have been possible to have included 300 of the same ages, without descending in the scale of scientific position; also it appears that the ages of half of the number on my list lie between 50 and 65, and that about three-quarters of these may be considered, for census comparisons, as English. I combine these numbers, and compare them with that of the male population of England and Wales, between the same limits of age, and find the required ratio to be about one in 10,000. What then are the conditions of nature, and the various circumstances and conditions of life,—which I include under the general name of nurture,—which have selected that one and left the remainder? The object of this book is to answer this question.

Data

My data are the autobiographical replies to a very long series of printed questions addressed severally to the 180 men whose names were in the list I have described, and they fill two large portfolios. I cannot sufficiently thank my correspondents for the courteousness with which they replied to my very troublesome queries, the great pains they have taken to be precise and truthful in their statements, and the confidence reposed in my discretion. Those of the answers which are selected for statistical treatment somewhat exceed 100 in number. In addition to these, I have utilized several others which were too incomplete for statistical purposes, or which arrived late, but these also have been of real service to me; sometimes in corroborating, at others in questioning previous provisional conclusions. I wish emphatically to add that the foremost members of the scientific world have contributed in full proportion to their numbers. It must not for a moment be supposed that mediocrity is unduly represented in my data.

Natural history is an impersonal result; I am therefore able to treat my subject anonymously, with the exception of one chapter in which the pedigrees of certain families are given.

Nature and Nurture

The phrase "nature and nurture" is a convenient jingle of words, for it separates under two distinct heads the innumerable elements of which personality is composed. Nature is all that man brings with himself into the world; nurture is every influence from without that affects him after his birth. The distinction is clear: the one produces the infant such as it actually is, including its latent faculties of growth of body and mind; the other affords the environment amid which the growth takes place, by which natural tendencies may be strengthened or thwarted, or wholly new ones implanted. Neither of the terms implies any theory; natural gifts may or may not be hereditary; nurture does not especially consist of food, clothing, education or tradition, but it includes all these and similar influences whether known or unknown.

When nature and nurture compete for supremacy on equal terms in the sense to be explained, the former proves the stronger. It is needless to insist that neither is self-sufficient; the highest natural endowments may be starved by defective nurture, while no carefulness of nurture can overcome the evil tendencies of an intrinsically bad physique, weak brain, or brutal disposition. Differences of nurture stamp unmistakable marks on the disposition of the soldier, clergyman, or scholar, but are wholly insufficient to efface the deeper marks of individual character. The impress of class distinctions is superficial, and may be compared to those which give a general resemblance to a family of daughters at a provincial ball, all dressed alike, and so similar in voice and address as to puzzle a recently-introduced partner in his endeavors to recollect with which of them he is engaged to dance; but an intimate friend forgets their general resemblance in the presence of the far greater dissimilarity which he has learned to appreciate. There are twins of the same sex so alike in body and mind that not even their own mothers can distinguish them. Their features, voice, and expressions are similar; they see things in the same light, and their ideas follow the same laws of association. This close resemblance necessarily gives way under gradually accumulated influences of difference of nurture, but it often lasts till manhood. I have been told of a case in which two twin brothers, both married, the one a medical man, the other a clergyman, were staying at the same house. One morning, for a joke, they changed their neckties, and each personated the other, sitting by his wife through the whole of the breakfast without discovery. Shakespeare was a close observer of nature; it is, therefore, worth recollecting that he recognizes in his thirty-six plays three pairs of family likeness so deceptive as to create absurd confusion. Two of these pairs are in the *Comedy of Errors*, and the other in *Twelfth Night*. I heard of a case not many years back in which a young Englishman had travelled to St. Petersburg, then much less accessible than now, with no letters of introduction, and who lost his pocket-book, and was penniless. He was walking along the quay in some despair at his prospects, when he was startled by the cheery voice of a stranger who accosted him, saying he required no introduction because his family likeness proclaimed him to be the son of an old friend. The Englishman did not conceal his difficulties, and the stranger actually lent him the sum he needed on the guarantee of his family likeness, confirmed, no doubt, by some conversation. In this and similar instances how small has been the influence of nurture; the child had developed into manhood, along a predestined course laid out in his nature. It would be impossible to find a converse instance in which two persons, unlike at birth, had been moulded by similarity of nurture into so close a resemblance that their nearest relations failed to distinguish them. Let us quote Shakespeare again as an illustration; in *A Midsummer-Night's Dream* . . . Helena and Hermia, who had been inseparable in childhood and girlhood, and had identical nurture . . . were physically quite unlike: the one was short and dark, the other tall and fair; therefore, the similarity of their nurture did not affect their features. The moral likeness was superficial, because a sore trial of temper, which produced a violent quarrel between them, brought out great dissimilarity of character. In the competition between nature and nurture, when the differences in either case do not exceed those which distinguish individuals of the same race living in the same country under no very exceptional conditions, nature certainly proves the stronger of the two. . . .

Occupation of Parents and Position in Life

My list contains men who have been born in every social grade, from the highest order in the peerage down to the factory hand and simple peasant, but the returns which I shall discuss do not range quite so widely. These are 96 in number, and may be classified as follows—but the same name appears in two classes on eleven occasions [*sic*], so that the total entries are raised to 107:

Noblemen and private gentlemen	9
Army and navy, 6; civil service, 9; subordinate officers, 3	18
Law, 11; medical, 9; clergy and ministers, 6; teachers, 6; architect, 1; Secretary to an insurance office, 1	34
Bankers, 7; merchants, 21; manufacturers, 15	43
Farmers	2
Others	1
	107

The terms used in the third and fourth groups must be understood in a very general sense; thus, there are some "merchants" on a very small scale indeed, and others on a very large one.

It is by no means the case that those who have raised themselves by their abilities are found to be abler than their contemporaries who began their careers with advantages of fortune and social position. They are not more distinguished as original investigators, neither are they more discerning in those numerous questions, not strictly scientific, which happen to be brought before the councils of scientific societies. There can be no doubt but that the upper classes of a nation like our own, which are largely and continually recruited by selections from below, are by far the most productive of natural ability. . . .

It is . . . a fact, that in proportion to the pains bestowed on their education generally, the sons of clergymen rarely take a lead in science. The pursuit of science is uncongenial to the priestly character. It has fallen to my lot to serve for many years on the councils of many scientific societies, and, excepting a very few astronomers and mathematicians . . . I can only recall 3 colleagues who were clergymen. . . . The reason for the abstinence of clergymen from scientific work cannot be that they are too busy, too much home-tied, or cramped in pecuniary means, because other professional men, more busy, more at the call of others, and having less assured revenues, are abundantly represented on all the council lists. . . .

Primogeniture, &C.

The following statement shows, in percentages, the position of the scientific men in respect to age among their brothers and sisters:

Only sons, 22 cases; eldest sons, 26 cases; youngest sons, 15 cases. Of those who are neither eldest nor youngest, 13 come in the elder half of the family; 12 in the younger half; and 11 are exactly in the middle. Total, 99.

It further appears that, at the time of the birth of the scientific men, the ages of their fathers average 36 years, and those of their mothers 30. . . .

Putting these facts together, viz. (1) that elder sons appear nearly twice as often as younger sons; (2) that, as regards intermediate children, the elder and younger halves of the family contribute equally; and (3) that only sons are as common as eldest sons, we must conclude that the age of the parents, within the limits with which we chiefly have to deal, has little influence on the nature of the child; secondly, that the elder sons have, on the whole, decided advantages of nurture over the younger sons. They are more likely to become possessed of independent means, and therefore able to follow the pursuits that have most attraction to their tastes; they are treated more as companions by their parents, and have earlier responsibility, both of which would develop independence of character; probably, also, the first-born child of families not well-to-do in the world would generally have more attention in his infancy, more breathing space, and better nourishment, than his younger brothers and sisters in their several turns.

Commentary

I will examine some of the later influences that might be directly or indirectly attributed to Galton's 1874 survey, and then turn to some new research directions that might also ensue from the same inspiration.

LATER INFLUENCES

The introduction noted three special features found in Galton's (1874) work excerpted above. Each of these can be seen in subsequent creativity research.

Directly investigating eminent creators. The first contribution was methodological: the direct study of highly creative people by having them fill out self-report questionnaires. To appreciate the importance of this innovation, it may help to name some members of the sample: Arthur Cayley, Charles Darwin, T. H. Huxley, W. S. Jevons, William Lassell, James Clerk Maxwell, Richard Owen, and Herbert Spencer (Hilts, 1975). All of these respondents made sufficient contributions to their respective domains that they remain subjects of extensive encyclopedia entries—such as Wikipedia biographies—even today.

Naturally, given the extreme effort involved in procuring willing samples of eminently creative respondents, this approach is very rare, albeit notable examples do exist in the literature (Feist, 2014). The sampling criteria might include expert nominations, receipt of a major award, such as the Nobel Prize, or some other high standard (e.g., Csikszentmihalyi, 1997; Zuckerman, 1977). For instance, Anne Roe (1953) used expert nominations to obtain her sample of 64 eminent physical, biological, and social scientists. Of course, the survey questionnaire can be accompanied or replaced by direct face-to-face interviews and psychometric assessments (Feist, 2014; Nakamura & Fajans, 2014). Thus Roe administered both projective and psychometric tests to her scientists (see also Cattell & Drevdahl, 1955).

Another enhancement to this technique is to obtain a sample of creative individuals who vary appreciably in eminence. That way the researcher can directly examine how biographical and individual-difference variables correlate with variation in achieved eminence (e.g., Feist, 1993; Grosul & Feist, 2014). This approach was standard practice in the classic research carried out at the Institute for Personality Assessment and Research (e.g., Barron, 1969; Helson & Crutchfield, 1970; MacKinnon, 1962). Thus, rather than compare, say, eminent architects with the general population, those architects could be compared with their far less eminent colleagues. Most of what we know about the highly creative personality has adopted this method.

Nature and nurture in creative development. It hardly need be said that Galton's introduction of the nature-nurture question reverberates not just through creativity research but also through all scientific inquiries into human development. Moreover he didn't just define the issue but also introduced major methods for addressing the issue. Earlier I mentioned that his 1869 book used the family pedigree method to examine the inheritance of natural ability. There he actually calculated mathematically how inheritance fades with decreased degree of relatedness. In the 1874 book, Galton added the self-report questionnaire to the methodological repertoire, a technique that enabled him to obtain retrospective records of environmental experiences.

Nor did he stop there. Already in his 1874 book Galton had pioneered the statistical analysis of the correlation of two variables (not included in the excerpt). This led him in later work to formulate the general principle of the bivariate correlation as described in scatterplots (Galton, 1889). Along with this principle was his concept of regression: the less strongly one variable correlates with another, the more the prediction of one from the other would regress toward the mean. If no relationship exists whatsoever, then you would just predict the mean. One of his students, Karl Pearson, provided a mathematical formula for calculating the correlation coefficient, a statistic that is represented by r, which stands for "regression."

This is the "Pearson product-moment correlation coefficient" that is taught in statistics classes—and that can be seen in almost all creativity research that uses correlational rather than experimental designs. It is also the primary statistic used for measuring inheritance (e.g., the correlation between parents' heights and their child's height). Although originally used to study inheritance, this same coefficient later became the mainstay of all correlational research, including that on nurture rather than nature. The coefficient itself is not committed to either side of the question. Even so, the correlation proved especially useful for calculating the degree of heritability for any individual-difference variable. This utility is most conspicuous in twin studies. Which brings me to the last point on Galton's influence regarding this matter.

It was Galton (1883) himself who first suggested that twins might be ideally suited for investigating genetic inheritance. Particularly crucial is the contrast between monozygotic (identical) twins, who are genetically identical, and dizygotic (fraternal) twins, who are no more similar genetically than any two siblings from the same parents. Later researchers realized the importance of comparing not just monozygotic and dizygotic twins, but also twins reared together and those who were reared apart (Bouchard, Lykken, McGue, Segal, & Tellegen, 1990). In conjunction with advanced correlational techniques (especially structural equation models), researchers were thus able to tease out more precise heritability estimates. These heritabilities were calculated for every intellectual and dispositional trait having any relevance for understanding creativity (Bouchard, 2004). Suffice it to say that almost all individual differences are inheritable to some degree, especially such variables as intelligence and openness to experience. Yet the heritability coefficients are not so large as to rule out a significant involvement of environmental influences. So creativity has to be the function of both nature and nurture. Neither alone suffices to produce a creative person. If anything, the views that Galton expressed in the excerpt probably understate the overall importance of nurture.

Familial influences. The modern discipline that emerged from Galton's original forays into the nature-nurture question is known as behavior genetics (Plomin, DeFries, Knopik, & Neiderhiser, 2016). One critical feature of behavior genetic research is its attempt to separate out two distinct kinds of nurture influences within a given family: shared environment and nonshared environment. The first consists of all environmental factors that are shared by all children growing up in the same family, whereas the second is defined by all environmental factors that tend to be unique to each child. This distinction is extremely important. Once adjustment is made for any genetic similarities and contrasts, the nonshared environment explains why siblings differ even when they grow up in the same family, whereas the shared environment explains why siblings in the same family differ from siblings from a different family.

Although Galton was not aware of this modern distinction, he actually provides illustrations in the selection. On the one hand, birth order constitutes a clear-cut instance of nonshared environmental influences. First-born, last-born, and middle-born children do not grow up in the same family environment because the first-born has younger siblings, the last-born older siblings, and the middle child both younger and older siblings. On the other hand, parental occupation is most often considered a case of shared family environment. If father is a doctor and mother a lawyer, that will usually hold for all of their children, unless there's some dramatic disruption, such as parental loss or divorce.

In any event, subsequent creativity researchers continued Galton's (1874) inquiries into familial influences on creative development, with a special fascination with birth order effects (e.g., Feist, 1993; Roe, 1953; Simonton, 2008). His particular finding of a primogeniture effect has been replicated many times, albeit with some qualifications (e.g., Roe, 1953; Simonton, 2008; Terry, 1989; cf. Clark & Rice, 1982; Feist, 1993). First-borns are more likely to become scientists, for example, but scientific revolutionaries may be more prone to be later-borns (Sulloway, 2014). While classical composers are more inclined to be first-borns (Schubert, Wagner, & Schubert, 1977), creative writers are more disposed to have been later-borns (Bliss, 1970). The apparent reason for these contrasts is that first-borns are more likely to gravitate to creative domains that are well established and highly constrained, whereas the later-borns are more likely to be attracted to domains that are more unconventional and open to innovation. In rough terms, the former require less creativity than the latter.

More recent research has gone a step further, finding that birth order is just one of many developmental influences that help determine a creator's choice of creative domain (Simonton, 2009). In fact birth order can be subsumed under a set of what have been called *diversifying experiences* (Damian & Simonton, 2014). These are events in childhood and adolescence "that help weaken the constraints imposed by conventional socialization" (Simonton, 2000, p. 153). These events can include early parental death or divorce, cognitive or physical disability, poverty or economic instability, and immigrant or minority background. Vulnerabilities with respect to subclinical psychopathology can also count (Carson, 2014). Accordingly artists display more psychopathology than scientists (Simonton, 2014a), and revolutionary scientists exhibit more psychopathology than do mainstream scientists (Ko & Kim, 2008). Yet each creative domain favors a specific optimal level of diversifying experiences to attain eminence, a sweet spot that is determined by the aggregate of those experiences. That means that a trade-off relation holds between the various diversifying experiences. More of this one mandates less than that one.

A fascinating illustration of this developmental trade-off was demonstrated in the lives of eminent African Americans (Damian & Simonton, 2015). In some respects, this sample shows the same pattern seen in the majority culture; artists exhibit higher levels of psychopathology than do scientists, for example. Yet because of the inordinate adversity African Americans must normally face in their lives, they start off with a high level of diversifying experiences, which means that psychopathological symptoms should be less prominent—and that is in fact the case. It is telling, for example, that not one of the artistic creators in the sample committed suicide even though suicide is relatively commonplace among majority-culture creative artists, especially poets (Ludwig, 1992). Enough is enough.

NEW DIRECTIONS

How can the research inspired by Galton (1874) over 150 years ago best be carried forward? I have three suggestions. These concern behavior genetics, laboratory experiments, and significant samples.

Behavior genetics. Scientific treatment of the nature-nurture issue has made major advances since Galton's day and continues to progress at an amazing pace. Although major questions remain to be resolved, the current state of the field has already shed considerable light on the origins of creative genius (see Johnson & Bouchard, 2014, for review). For example, we now know that many supposed environmental factors are actually largely genetic. This is why the shared environment seldom emerges as a component of most individual differences. It is also becoming apparent that genes can operate in far more complex ways than Galton could ever imagine. For instance, creative genius may operate according to emergenesis, meaning that various genetic components are integrated in a multiplicative rather than additive manner (Lykken, 1998). Emergenic inheritance makes creative genius even more exceptional (Simonton, 1999b), and the phenomenon actually undermines the degree of familial influence that Galton (1869) originally hypothesized (Waller, Bouchard, Lykken, Tellegen, & Blacker, 1993). Finally, behavior geneticists are now making headway deciphering the human genome, thereby identifying genes and sets of genes underlying outstanding creativity.

Laboratory experiments. Although Galton did conduct laboratory experiments, his research on creative genius tended to employ correlational methods. However, it is certainly possible to introduce manipulations that simulate specific environmental factors. An excellent illustration is a laboratory experiment that used virtual reality to provide simulations of diversifying experiences and thus found increases in cognitive flexibility on divergent thinking tasks (Ritter et al., 2012; see also Vohs, Redden, & Rahinel, 2013). Although these effects are obviously more transient than the developmental impact of, say, early orphanhood, the results can still contribute to the overall theoretical account of how nurture can operate (Damian & Simonton, 2014). That potential contribution is especially valuable insofar as experiments are far better at teasing out causal direction.

Significant samples. After just arguing that more laboratory experiments are needed, I am now going to argue for a seeming opposite: creativity researchers should also devote more effort to conducting studies of what has been called "significant samples" (Simonton, 1999a). These are samples that are highly representative of the population of interest, and even in some cases are equivalent to the population (e.g., all Nobel laureates in the sciences or all Oscar-winning film composers). I already mentioned that Galton's 1874 survey constitutes the first direct examination of exceptional creativity using the questionnaire method. I also noted that earlier he had introduced an alternative approach, namely the historiometric (Galton, 1869). The use of significant samples differs strikingly from what has become the norm in much creativity research: the use of college student participants. There's no denying that such use allows the rapid generation of publishable research. University laboratories become efficient factories for generating journal articles.

But the practice has a downside as well, most notably the replication problem (Makel, 2014). Statistical significance may not be what it seems. Yet with significant samples, significance can be judged by effect sizes sans *p* values (Simonton, 2014b). Indeed, if the study's sample consists of Nobel laureates, significance tests become meaningless. To what general population would the researcher be generalizing the results? To all scientists?

Consequently I argue that the old should become the new. We need more inquiries like Galton's, but using much more modern psychometric and interview methods.

References

Barron, F. X. (1969). *Creative person and creative process.* New York: Holt, Rinehart & Winston.

Bliss, W. D. (1970). Birth order of creative writers. *Journal of Individual Psychology, 26,* 200–202.

Bouchard, T. J., Jr. (2004). Genetic influence on human psychological traits: A survey. *Current Directions in Psychological Science, 13,* 148–151.

Bouchard, T. J., Jr., Lykken, D. T., McGue, M., Segal, N. L., & Tellegen, A. (1990). Sources of human psychological differences: The Minnesota study of twins reared apart. *Science, 250,* 223–228.

Candolle, A. de (1873). *Histoire des sciences et des savants depuis deux siècles.* Geneva: Georg.

Carson, S. H. (2014). Cognitive disinhibition, creativity, and psychopathology. In D. K. Simonton (Ed.), *The Wiley handbook of genius* (pp. 198–221). Oxford: Wiley.

Cattell, R. B., & Drevdahl, J. E. (1955). A comparison of the personality profile (16 P.F.) of eminent researchers with that of eminent teachers and administrators, and of the general population. *British Journal of Psychology, 46,* 248–261.

Clark, R. D., & Rice, G. A. (1982). Family constellations and eminence: The birth orders of Nobel Prize winners. *Journal of Psychology, 110,* 281–287.

Csikszentmihalyi, M. (1997). *Creativity: Flow and the psychology of discovery and invention.* New York, NY: HarperCollins.

Damian, R. I., & Simonton, D. K. (2014). Diversifying experiences in the development of genius and their impact on creative cognition. In D. K. Simonton (Ed.), *The Wiley handbook of genius* (pp. 375–393). Oxford: Wiley.

Damian, R. I., & Simonton, D. K. (2015). Psychopathology, adversity, and creativity: Diversifying experiences in the development of eminent African Americans. *Journal of Personality and Social Psychology, 108,* 623–636.

Feist, G. J. (1993). A structural model of scientific eminence. *Psychological Science, 4,* 366–371.

Feist, G. J. (2014). Psychometric studies of scientific talent and eminence. In D. K. Simonton (Ed.), *The Wiley handbook of genius* (pp. 62–86). Oxford: Wiley.

Galton, F. (1869). *Hereditary genius: An inquiry into its laws and consequences.* London: Macmillan.

Galton, F. (1874). *English men of science: Their nature and nurture.* London: Macmillan.

Galton, F. (1883). *Inquiries into human faculty and its development.* London: Macmillan.

Galton, F. (1889). *Natural inheritance.* London: Macmillan.

Grosul, M., & Feist, G. J. (2014). The creative person in science. *Psychology of Aesthetics, Creativity, and the Arts, 8,* 30–43.

Helson, R., & Crutchfield, R. S. (1970). Mathematicians: The creative researcher and the average Ph.D. *Journal of Consulting and Clinical Psychology, 34,* 250–257.

Hilts, V. L. (1975). *A guide to Francis Galton's English Men of Science.* Philadelphia, PA: American Philosophical Society.

Johnson, W., & Bouchard, T. J., Jr. (2014). Genetics of intellectual and personality traits associated with creative genius: Could geniuses be Cosmobian Dragon Kings? In D. K. Simonton (Ed.), *The Wiley handbook of genius* (pp. 269–296). Oxford: Wiley.

Ko, Y., & Kim, J. (2008). Scientific geniuses' psychopathology as a moderator in the relation between creative contribution types and eminence. *Creativity Research Journal, 20,* 251–261.

Ludwig, A. M. (1992). Creative achievement and psychopathology: Comparison among professions. *American Journal of Psychotherapy, 46,* 330–356.

Lykken, D. T. (1998). The genetics of genius. In A. Steptoe (Ed.), *Genius and the mind: Studies of creativity and temperament in the historical record* (pp. 15–37). New York, NY: Oxford University Press.

MacKinnon, D. W. (1962). The nature and nurture of creative talent. *American Psychologist, 17,* 484–495.

Makel, M. C. (2014). The empirical march: Making science better at self-correction. *Psychology of Aesthetics, Creativity, and the Arts, 8,* 2–7.

Nakamura, J., & Fajans, J. (2014). Interviewing highly eminent creators. In D. K. Simonton (Ed.), *The Wiley handbook of genius* (pp. 33–61). Oxford: Wiley.

Plomin, R., DeFries, J. C., Knopik, V. S., & Neiderhiser, J. M. (2016). Top 10 replicated findings from behavioral genetics. *Perspectives on Psychological Science, 11,* 3–23.

Ritter, S. M., Damian, R. I., Simonton, D. K., van Baaren, R. B., Strick, M., Derks, J. & Dijksterhuis, A. (2012). Diversifying experiences enhance cognitive flexibility. *Journal of Experimental Social Psychology, 48,* 961–964.

Roe, A. (1953). *The making of a scientist.* New York: Dodd, Mead.

Schubert, D. S. P., Wagner, M. E., & Schubert, H. J. P. (1977). Family constellation and creativity: Firstborn predominance among classical music composers. *Journal of Psychology, 95,* 147–149.

Simonton, D. K. (1999a). Significant samples: The psychological study of eminent individuals. *Psychological Methods, 4,* 425–451.

Simonton, D. K. (1999b). Talent and its development: An emergenic and epigenetic model. *Psychological Review, 106,* 435–457.

Simonton, D. K. (2000). Creativity: Cognitive, developmental, personal, and social aspects. *American Psychologist, 55,* 151–158.

Simonton, D. K. (2003). Francis Galton's *Hereditary Genius*: Its place in the history and psychology of science. In R. J. Sternberg (Ed.), *The anatomy of impact: What has made the great works of psychology great* (pp. 3–18). Washington, DC: American Psychological Association.

Simonton, D. K. (2008). Gender differences in birth order and family size among 186 eminent psychologists. *Journal of Psychology of Science and Technology, 1,* 15–22.

Simonton, D. K. (2009). Varieties of (scientific) creativity: A hierarchical model of disposition, development, and achievement. *Perspectives on Psychological Science, 4,* 441–452.

Simonton, D. K. (2014a). More method in the mad-genius controversy: A historiometric study of 204 historic creators. *Psychology of Aesthetics, Creativity, and the Arts, 8,* 53–61.

Simonton, D. K. (2014b). Significant samples—not significance tests! The often overlooked solution to the replication problem. *Psychology of Aesthetics, Creativity, and the Arts, 8,* 11–12.

Sulloway, F. J. (2014). Openness to scientific innovation. In D. K. Simonton (Ed.), *The Wiley handbook of genius* (pp. 546–563). Oxford: Wiley.

Teigen, K. H. (1984). A note on the origin of the term "nature and nurture": Not Shakespeare and Galton, but Mulcaster. *Journal of the History of the Behavioral Sciences, 20,* 363–364.

Terry, W. S. (1989). Birth order and prominence in the history of psychology. *Psychological Record, 39,* 333–337.

Vohs, K., Redden, J., & Rahinel, R. (2013). Physical order produces healthy choices, generosity, conventionality, whereas disorder produces creativity. *Psychological Science, 24,* 1860–1867.

Waller, N. G., Bouchard, T. J., Jr., Lykken, D. T., Tellegen, A., & Blacker, D. M. (1993). Creativity, heritability, familiality: Which word does not belong? *Psychological Inquiry, 4,* 235–237.

Zuckerman, H. (1977). *Scientific elite.* New York: Free Press.

18

On Great Thoughts

William James

DEAN KEITH SIMONTON

Summary

William James was a pioneer in the early history of American psychology. A decade before writing his influential introductory textbook on the subject, he wrote an essay on whether individuals can exert an impact on the course of history. The key concept was that the genius represents a spontaneous variation analogous to the variations in Charles Darwin's theory of evolution by natural selection. The individual provides the variations—the potentially "great thoughts"—that are then selected or rejected by the sociocultural environment. James's argument was diametrically opposed to the ideas of Herbert Spencer, who argued that history was totally determined by forces in which individuals, even creative geniuses, had no causal relevance. James's Darwinian position eventually merged with other theories of social innovation and evolution to support the emergence of the blind-variation and selective-attention theory of creativity. Although subsequent work on this theory somewhat qualifies James's conception of how great ideas are created, the core position remains this: individual psychology must underlie the advent of sociocultural change; future research must continue to elaborate this basic affirmation.

Introduction

William James (1842–1910) is often called the "father of American psychology." In fact his 1890 textbook, *The Principles of Psychology*, has become a classic in the field. The volume contains erudite and articulate treatment of almost every psychological subject under the sun. James was also considered one of the progenitors of the functionalist school of psychology, a school that was strongly influenced by Darwin's theory of evolution by natural selection. This Darwinian influence is immediately apparent in James's 1880 article, which was chosen for this chapter's selection. Here James argues that the place of the "great man" in social evolution is closely analogous to that of the "spontaneous variation" in biological evolution. The creator or leader spontaneously generates "great thoughts" at the individual level that are then either selected or rejected by the larger sociocultural environment. Accordingly the single person can constitute an actual causal agent in historical change. More specifically, the creator can and does create history. This causal agency bears a connection with his somewhat later essay on free will (James, 1884), a phenomenon that has been shown to have an intimate relation with creativity (Simonton, 2013b).

Significantly, James's position here is explicitly opposed to a then-prevailing evolutionary theory of a very different kind: the strict sociocultural determinism advocated by the English philosopher Herbert Spencer (McGranahan, 2011). According to Spencer, the individual genius, creator, or leader is nothing more than an epiphenomenon that features no causal significance whatsoever. The history of world civilization would have taken precisely the same course even if every so-called genius had died in the crib. At most, all of the great figures in the arts and sciences, politics and war, would just have contrasting proper names. In particular, Isaac Newton's great *Principia* would have been written by anyone in the same time and place who was exposed to the same deterministic causes. Just the title page would specify a different author.

James ignored the subject of "great men" in his 1890 text but returned to it much later, in his 1902 *The Varieties of Religious Experience*. There he treats the possible relation between genius and psychopathology. The mental disorder associated with the latter may provide the means for the former to devise the most creative ideas. Yet he did not develop these connections further. His interests had shifted from psychology to philosophy, with special focus on developing his own version of pragmatism.

Because James sometimes ventures into somewhat esoteric territory, his article appears here in an edited version that has been substantially shortened.

Reading: *Great Men, Great Thoughts, and the Environment*

Source: James, W. (1880). Great men, great thoughts, and the environment. *Atlantic Monthly, 46*, 441–459. Selections. Work in the public domain.

A remarkable parallel, which I think has never been noticed, obtains between the facts of social evolution on the one hand, and of zoölogical evolution as expounded by Mr. Darwin on the other.

It will be best to prepare the ground for my thesis by a few very general remarks on the method of getting at scientific truth. It is a common platitude that a *complete* acquaintance with any one thing, however small, would require a knowledge of the entire universe. Not a sparrow falls to the ground but *some* of the remote conditions of his fall are to be found in the milky way, in our federal constitution, or in the early history of Europe. That is to say, alter the milky way, alter our federal constitution, alter the facts of our barbarian ancestry, and the universe would be . . . a different universe from what it is. One fact involved in the difference might be that the particular little street-boy who threw the stone which brought down the sparrow might not find himself opposite the sparrow at that particular moment; or, finding himself there, he might not be in that particular serene and disengaged mood of mind which expressed itself in throwing the stone. But, true as all this is, it would be very foolish for any one who was inquiring the cause of the sparrow's fall to overlook the boy as too personal, proximate, and so to speak anthropomorphic an agent, and to say that the true cause is the federal constitution, the westward migration of the Celtic race, or the structure of the milky way. If we proceeded on that method, we might say with perfect legitimacy that a friend of ours, who had slipped on the ice upon his door-step and cracked his skull, some months after dining with thirteen at the table, died *because* of that ominous feast. I know, in fact, one such instance; and I might, if I chose, contend with perfect logical propriety that the slip on the ice was no real accident. "There *are* no accidents," I might say, "for science. The whole history of the world converged to produce that slip. If anything had been left out, the slip would not have occurred just there and then. To say it would is to deny the relations of cause and effect throughout the universe. The real cause of the death was not the slip, *but the conditions which engendered the slip*, and among them his having sat at a table, six months previous, one among thirteen. *That* is truly the reason why he died within the year." It will soon be seen whose arguments I am, in form, reproducing here. I would fain lay down the truth without polemics or recrimination. But unfortunately we never fully grasp the import of any true statement until we have a clear notion of what the opposite untrue statement would be. The error is needed to set off the truth, much as a dark background is required for exhibiting the brightness of a picture.

Now the error which I am going to use as a foil to set off what seems to me the truth of my own statements is contained in the statements of the so-called evolutionary philosophy of Mr. Herbert Spencer and his disciples. Our problem is, What are the causes that make communities change from generation to generation,— that make the England of Queen Anne so different from the England of Elizabeth, the Harvard College of to-day so different from that of thirty years ago?

I shall reply to this problem, The difference is due to the accumulated influences of individuals, of their examples, their initiatives, and their decisions. The Spencerian school replies, The changes are irrespective of persons, and independent of individual control. They are due to the environment, to the circumstances, the physical geography, the ancestral conditions, the increasing experience of outer relations. . . .

Now, I say that these theorizers are guilty of precisely the same fallacy as he who should ascribe the death of his friend to the dinner with thirteen, or the fall of the sparrow to the milky way. Like the dog in the fable, who drops his real bone to snatch at its image, they drop the real causes to snatch at others, which from no possible human point of view are available or attainable. Their fallacy is a practical one. Let us see where it lies. Although I believe in free-will myself, I will waive that belief in this discussion, and assume with the Spencerians the predestination of all human actions. On that assumption I gladly allow that *were the intelligence* investigating the man's or the sparrow's death *omniscient* and *omnipresent*, able to take in the whole of time and space at a single glance, there would not be the slightest objection to the milky way or the fatal feast being invoked among the sought-for causes. Such a divine intelligence would see instantaneously all the infinite lines of convergence towards a given result, and it would, moreover, see *impartially*: it would see the fatal feast to be as much a condition of the sparrow's death as of the man's; it would see the boy with the stone to be as much a condition of the man's fall as of the sparrow's.

The human mind, however, is constituted on an entirely different plan. It has no such power of universal intuition. Its finiteness obliges it to see but two or three things at a time. If it wishes to take wider sweeps it has to use "general ideas," as they are called, and in so doing to drop all concrete truths. Thus, in the present case, if we as men wish to feel the connection between the milky way and the boy and the dinner and the sparrow and the man's death, we can do so only by falling back on the enormous emptiness of what is called an abstract proposition. We must say, All things in the world are fatally predetermined, and hang together in the adamantine fixity of a system of natural law. But in the vagueness of this vast proposition we have lost all the concrete facts and links. And in all practical matters the concrete links are the only things of importance. The human mind is *essentially* partial. It can be efficient at all only by *picking out* what to attend to, and ignoring everything else,—by narrowing its point of view. Otherwise, what little strength it has is dispersed, and it loses its way altogether. Man always wants his curiosity gratified for a particular purpose. If, in the case of the sparrow, the purpose is punishment, it would be idiotic to wander off from the cats, boys, and other possible agencies close by in the street, to survey the early Celts and the milky way: the boy would meanwhile escape. And if, in the case of the unfortunate man, we lose ourselves in contemplation of the thirteen-at-table mystery, and fail to notice the ice on the step and cover it with ashes, some other poor fellow, who never dined out in his life, may slip on it in coming to the door, and fall and break his head, too.

It is, then, a necessity laid upon us as human beings to limit our view. In mathematics we know how this method of ignoring and neglecting quantities lying outside a certain range has been adopted in the differential calculus. The calculator throws out all the "infinitesimals" of the quantities he is considering. He treats them (under certain rules) as if they did not exist. In themselves they exist perfectly all the while; but they are as if they did not exist for the purposes of his calculation. Just so an astronomer, in dealing with the tidal movements of the ocean, takes no account of the waves made by the wind, or by the pressure of all the steamers which day upon night are moving their thousands of tons upon its surface. . . . Just so a businessman's punctuality may overlook an error of five minutes, while a physicist, measuring the velocity of light, must count each thousandth of a second.

There are, in short, *different cycles of operation* in nature; different departments, so to speak, relatively independent of one another, so that what goes on at any moment in one may be *compatible* with almost any condition of things at the same moment in the next. The mold on the biscuit in the store-room of a man-of-war vegetates in absolute indifference to the nationality of the flag, the direction of the voyage, the weather, and the human dramas that may go on board; and a mycologist may study it in complete abstraction from all these larger details. Only by so studying it, in fact, is there any chance of the mental concentration by which alone he may hope to learn something of its nature. And conversely, the captain who, in manœvring the vessel through a naval battle, should think it necessary to bring the moldy biscuit into his calculations would very likely lose the battle by reason of the excessive "thoroughness" of his mental nature.

The causes which operate in these incommensurable cycles are connected with one another only *if we take the whole universe into account*. For all lesser points of view it is lawful—nay, more; it is for human wisdom necessary—to regard them as disconnected and irrelevant to one another.

And now this brings us nearer to our special topic. If we look at an animal or a human being distinguished from the rest of his kind by the possession of some extraordinary peculiarity, good or bad, we shall be able to discriminate between the causes which originally *produced* the peculiarity in him and the causes which *maintain* it after it is produced. And we shall see, if the peculiarity be one that he was born with, that these two sets of causes belong to two such irrelevant cycles. It was the triumphant originality of Darwin to see this, and to act accordingly. Separating the causes of production under the title of "tendencies to spontaneous variation," and relegating them to a physiological cycle which he forthwith agreed to ignore altogether . . . he confined his attention to the causes of preservation, and under the names of natural selection and sexual selection studied them exclusively as functions of the cycle of the environment.

Pre-Darwinian philosophers had also tried to establish the doctrine of descent with modification. But they all committed the blunder of clumping the two cycles of causation into one. What preserves an animal with his peculiarity, if it be a useful one, they saw to be the nature of the environment to which the peculiarity was adjusted. The giraffe with his peculiar neck is preserved by the fact that there are in his environment tall trees whose leaves he can digest. But these philosophers went further, and said that the presence of the trees not only maintained an animal with a long neck to browse upon their branches, but also produced him. They *made* his neck long by the constant striving they aroused in him to reach up to them. The environment, in short, was supposed by these writers to mold the animal by a kind of direct pressure, very much as a seal presses the wax into harmony with itself. Numerous instances were given of the way in which this goes on under our eyes. The exercise of the forge makes the right arm strong, the palm grows callous to the oar, the mountain air distends the chest, the chased fox grows cunning and the chased bird shy, the arctic cold stimulates the animal combustion, and so forth. Now these changes, of which many more examples might be adduced, are at present distinguished by the special name of *adaptive* changes. Their peculiarity is that that very feature in the environment to which the animal's nature grows adjusted, itself *produces* the adjustment. The "inner relation," to use Mr. Spencer's phrase, "corresponds" with its own efficient cause.

Darwin's first achievement was to show the utter insignificance in amount of these changes produced by direct adaptation, the immensely greater mass of changes being produced by internal molecular accidents, of which we know nothing. His next achievement was to define the true problem with which we have to deal when we study the effects of the visible environment on the animal. That problem is simply this: Is the environment more likely to *preserve or to destroy him,* on account of this or that peculiarity with which he may be born? In calling those peculiarities with which an animal is born with "spontaneous" variations, Darwin does not for a moment mean to suggest that they are not the fixed outcome of natural law. If the total system of the universe be taken into account, the causes of these variations and the visible environment which preserves or destroys them undoubtedly do, in some remote and roundabout way, hang together. What Darwin means is that, since the environment is a perfectly known thing, and its relations to the organism in the way of destruction or preservation are tangible and distinct, it would utterly confuse our finite understandings and frustrate our hopes of science to mix in with it facts from such a disparate and incommensurable cycle as that in which the variations are produced. This last cycle is that of occurrences before the animal is born. It is the cycle of influences upon ova and embryos; in which lie the causes that tip them and tilt them towards masculinity or femininity, towards strength or weakness, towards health or disease, and towards divergence from the parent type. What are the causes there?

In the first place, they are molecular and invisible; inaccessible, therefore, to direct observation of any kind. Secondly, their operations are *compatible* with any social, political and physical conditions of the environment. The same parents, living in the same environing conditions, may at one birth produce a genius, at the next an idiot or a monster. The visible external conditions are therefore not direct determinants of this cycle; and the more we consider the matter, the more we are forced to believe that two children of the same parents are made to differ from each other by causes as disproportionate to their ultimate effects as is that famous pebble on the Rocky Mountain crest, which separates two rain-drops, to the Gulf of St. Lawrence and the Pacific Ocean towards which it makes them severally flow.

The great mechanical distinction between transitive forces and discharging forces is nowhere illustrated on such a scale as in physiology. Almost all causes there are forces of *detent,* which operate by simply unlocking energy already stored up. They are upsetters of unstable equilibria, and the resultant effect depends infinitely more on the nature of the materials upset than on that of the particular stimulus which joggles them down. Galvanic work, equal to unity, done on a frog's nerve will discharge from the muscle to which the nerve belongs mechanical work equal to seventy thousand; and exactly the same muscular effect will emerge if other irritants than galvanism are employed. The irritant has merely started or provoked something which then went on of itself,—as a match may start a fire which consumes a whole town. And qualitatively as well as quantitatively the effect may be absolutely incommensurable with the cause. We find this condition of things in all organic matter. Chemists are distracted by the difficulties which the instability of albuminoid compounds opposes to their study. Two specimens, treated in what outwardly seem scrupulously identical conditions, behave in quite different ways. We all know about the invisible factors of fermentation, and how the fate of a jar of milk—whether it turn into a sour clot or a mass of koumiss—depends on whether the lactic acid ferment or the alcoholic is introduced first, and gets ahead of the other in starting the process. Now, when the result is the tendency of an ovum, itself invisible to the naked eye, to tip towards this direction or that in its further evolution,—to bring forth a genius or a dunce, even as the rain-drop passes east or west of the pebble,—is it not obvious that the deflecting cause must lie in a region so recondite and minute, must be such a ferment of a ferment, an infinitesimal of so high an order, that surmise itself may never succeed even in attempting to frame an image of it? . . .

Such being the case, was not Darwin right to turn his back upon that region altogether, and to keep his own problem carefully free from all entanglement with matters such as these? The success of his work is a sufficient affirmative reply.

And this brings us at last to the heart of our subject. The causes of production of great men lie in a sphere wholly inaccessible to the social philosopher. He must simply accept geniuses as data, just as Darwin accepts his spontaneous variations. For him, as for Darwin, the only problem is, these data being given, How does the environment affect them, and how do they affect the environment? Now, I affirm that the relation of the visible environment to the great man is in the main exactly what it is to the "variation" in the Darwinian philosophy. It chiefly adopts or rejects, preserves or destroys, in short *selects* him. And whenever it adopts and preserves the great man, it becomes modified by his influence in an entirely original and peculiar way. He acts as a ferment, and changes its constitution, just as the advent of a new zoölogical species changes the faunal and floral equilibrium of the region in which it appears.

We all recollect Mr. Darwin's famous statement of the influence of cats on the growth of clover in their neighborhood. . . . Just so the great man . . . brings about a rearrangement, on a large or a small scale, of the pre-existing social relations.

The mutations of societies, then, from generation to generation, are in the main due directly or indirectly to the acts or the examples of individuals whose genius was so adapted to the receptivities of the moment, or whose accidental position of authority was so critical, that they became ferments, initiators of movement, setters of precedent or fashion, centers of corruption, or destroyers of other persons, whose gifts, had they had free play, would have led society in another direction.

We see this power of individual initiative exemplified on a small scale all about us, and on a large scale in the case of the leaders of history. It is only following the common-sense method of a Lyell, a Darwin and a Whitney to interpret the unknown by the known, and reckon up cumulatively the only causes of social change we can directly observe. Societies of men are just like individuals, in that both at any given moment offer ambiguous potentialities of development. Whether a young man enters business or the ministry may depend on a decision which has to be made before a certain day. He takes the place offered in the counting-house, and is *committed*. Little by little, the habits, the knowledges, of the other career, which once lay so near, cease to be reckoned even among his possibilities. At first, he may sometimes doubt whether the self he murdered in that decisive hour might not have been the better of the two; but with the years such questions themselves expire, and the old alternative *ego,* once so vivid, fades into something less substantial than a dream. It is no otherwise with nations. They may be committed by kings and ministers to peace or war, by generals to victory or defeat, by prophets to this religion or that, by various geniuses to fame in art, science or industry. A war is a true point of bifurcation of future possibilities. Whether it fail or succeed, its declaration must be the starting-point of new policies. Just so does a revolution, or any great civic precedent, become a deflecting influence, whose operations widen with the course of time. Communities obey their ideals; and an accidental success fixes an ideal, as an accidental failure blights it. . . .

The fermentative influence of geniuses *must* be admitted as, at any rate, one factor in the changes that constitute social evolution. The community *may* evolve in many ways. The accidental presence of this or that ferment decides in which way it *shall* evolve. . . . Rembrandt must teach us to enjoy the struggle of light with darkness, Wagner to enjoy peculiar musical effects; Dickens gives a twist to our sentimentality . . . Emerson kindles a new moral light within us. . . . But if this be true of individuals in the community, how can it be false of the community as a whole? If shown a certain way, a community may take it; if not, it will never find it. And the ways are to a large extent indeterminate in advance. A nation may obey either of many alternative impulses given by different men of genius, and still live and be prosperous, just as a man may enter either of many businesses. Only, the prosperities may differ in their type.

But the indeterminism is not absolute. Not every "man" fits every "hour." Some incompatabilites there are. A given genius may come either too early or too late. Peter the Hermit would now be sent to an insane asylum. John Mill in the tenth century would have lived and died unknown. . . . What could a Watt have effected in a tribe which no precursive genius had taught to smelt iron or to turn a lathe?

Now, the important thing to notice is that what makes a certain genius now incompatible with his surroundings is usually the fact that some previous genius of a different strain has warped the community away from the sphere of his possible effectiveness. After Voltaire, no Peter the hermit. . . . Each bifurcation cuts off certain sides of the field altogether, and limits the future possible angles of deflection. . . .

Every painter can tell us how each added line deflects his picture in a certain sense. Whatever lines follow must be built on those first laid down. . . . Just so the social surroundings of the past and present hour exclude the possibility of accepting certain contributions from individuals. But they do not positively define what contributions shall be accepted, for in themselves they are powerless to fix what the nature of the individual offerings shall be. . . .

Thus social evolution is a resultant of the interaction of two wholly distinct factors: the individual, deriving his peculiar gifts from the play of physiological and infra-social forces, but bearing all the power of initiative and origination in his hands; and, second, the social environment, with its power of adopting or rejecting both him and his gifts. Both factors are essential to change. The community stagnates without the impulse of the individual. The impulse dies away without the sympathy of the community.

All this seems nothing more than common-sense. . . . But there are never wanting minds to whom such views seem personal and contracted, and allied to an anthropomorphism long exploded in other fields of knowledge. . . . We all know, too, how the controversy has been kept up between the partisans of a "science of history" and those who deny the existence of anything like necessary "laws" where human societies are concerned. Mr. Spencer, at the opening of his *Study of Sociology,* makes an onslaught on the "great-man theory" of history, from which a few passages may be quoted:

The genesis of societies by the action of great men may be comfortably believed so long as, resting in general notions, you do not ask for particulars. But now, if, dissatisfied with vagueness, we demand that our ideas shall be brought into focus and exactly defined, we discover the hypothesis to be utterly incoherent. If, not stopping at the explanation of social progress as due to the great man, we go back a step and ask, Whence comes the great man? we find that the theory breaks down completely. The question has two conceivable answers: his origin is supernatural, or it is natural. Is his origin supernatural? Then he is a deputy god, and we have theocracy once removed,—or, rather, not removed at all. . . . Is this an unacceptable solution? Then the origin of the great man is natural; and immediately this is recognized, he must be classed with all other phenomena in the society that gave him birth as a product of its antecedents. Along with the whole generation of which he forms a minute part, along with its institutions, language, knowledge, manners, and its multitudinous arts and appliances, he is a *resultant*. . . . You must admit that the genesis of the great man depends on the long series of complex influences which has produced the race in which he appears, and the social state into which that race has slowly grown. . . . Before he can remake his society, his society must make him. All those changes of which he is the proximate initiator have their chief causes in the generations he descended from. If there is to be anything like a real explanation of those changes, it must be sought in that aggregate of conditions out of which both he and they have arisen.

Now, it seems to me that there is something which one might almost call impudent in the attempt which Mr. Spencer makes, in the first sentence of this extract, to pin the reproach of vagueness upon those who believe in the power of initiative of the great man.

Suppose I say that the singular moderation which now distinguishes social, political and religious discussion in England, and contrasts so strongly with the bigotry and dogmatism of sixty years ago, is largely due to J. S. Mill's example. I may possibly be wrong about the facts; but I am, at any rate, "asking for particulars," and not "resting in general notions." And if Mr. Spencer should tell me it started from no personal influence whatever, but from the "aggregate of conditions," the "generations," Mill and all his contemporaries "descended from," the whole past order of nature in short, surely he, not I, would be the person "satisfied with vagueness."

The fact is that Mr. Spencer's sociological method is identical with that of one who would invoke the zodiac to account for the fall of the sparrow, and the thirteen at table to explain the gentleman's death. . . .

To believe that the cause of everything is to be found in its antecedents is the starting-point, the initial postulate, not the goal and consummation, of science. If she is simply to lead us out of the labyrinth by the same hole we went in by three or four thousand years ago, it seems hardly worth while to have followed her through the darkness at all. If anything is humanly certain it is that the great man's society, properly so called, does *not* make him before he can remake it. Physiological forces, with which the social, political, geographical, and to a great extent anthropological conditions have just as much and just as little do as conditions of the crater of Vesuvius has to do with the flickering of this gas by which I write, are what make him. Surely Mr. Spencer does not hold that the convergence of sociological pressures so impinged on Stratford-upon-Avon about the 26th of April, 1564, that a W. Shakespeare, with all his mental peculiarities, had to be born there,—as the pressure of water outside a certain boat will cause a stream of a certain form to ooze into a particular leak? And does he mean to say that if the aforesaid W. Shakespeare had died of cholera infantum, another mother at Stratford-upon-Avon would needs have engendered a duplicate copy of him, to restore the sociologic equilibrium? . . . Here, as elsewhere, it is very hard, in the midst of Mr. Spencer's vagueness, to tell what he does mean at all. . . .

Sporadic great men come everywhere. But for a community to get vibrating through and through with intensely active life, many geniuses coming together and in rapid succession are required. This is why great epochs are so rare,—why the sudden bloom of a Greece, an early Rome, a Renaissance, is such a mystery. Blow must follow blow so fast that no cooling can occur in the intervals. Then the mass of the nation glows incandescent, and may continue to glow by pure inertia long after the originators of its internal movement have passed away. We often hear surprise expressed that in these high tides of human affairs not only the people should be filled with stronger life, but that individual geniuses should seem so exceptionally abundant. This mystery is just about as deep as the time-honored conundrum as to why great rivers flow by great towns. It is true that great public fermentations awaken and adopt many geniuses, who in more torpid times would have had no chance to work. But over and above this there must be an exceptional concourse of genius about a time, to make the fermentation begin at all. The unlikeliness of the *concourse* is far greater than the unlikeliness of any particular genius; hence the rarity of these periods and the exceptional aspect which they always wear. . . .

It is folly, then, to speak of the "laws of history" as of something inevitable, which science has only to discover, and whose consequences any one can then foretell but do nothing to alter or avert. Why, the very laws of physics are conditional, and deal with *ifs*. The physicist does not say, "The water *will* boil anyhow"; he only says it will boil if a fire is kindled beneath it. And so the utmost the student of sociology can ever predict is that *if* a genius of a certain sort show the way, society will be sure to follow.

To conclude: The evolutionary view of history, when it denies the vital importance of individual initiative, is, then, an utterly vague and unscientific conception, a lapse from modern scientific determinism into the most ancient oriental fatalism. The lesson of the analysis that we have made . . . forms an appeal of the most stimulating sort to the energy of the individual. . . .

I now pass to the last division of my subject, the function of the environment in *mental* evolution. After what I have already said, I may be quite concise. Here, if anywhere, it would seem at first sight as if that school must be right which makes the mind passively plastic, and the environment actively productive of the form and order of its conceptions; which, in a word, thinks that all mental progress must result from a series of adaptive changes, in the sense already defined of that word. We know what a vast part of our mental furniture consists of purely remembered, not reasoned, experience. The entire field of our habits and associations by contiguity belongs here. The entire field of those abstract conceptions which were taught us with the language into which we were born belongs here also. And, more than this, there is reason to think that the order of "outer relations" experienced by the individual may itself determine the order in which the general characters imbedded therein shall be noticed and extracted by his mind. . . . The pleasures and benefits, moreover, which certain parts of the environment yield, and the pains and hurts which other parts inflict, determine the direction of our interest and our attention, and so decide at which points the accumulation of mental experiences shall begin. It might, accordingly, seem as if there were no room for any agency other than this; as if the distinction we have found so useful between "spontaneous variation," as the producer of changed forms, and the environment, as their preserver and destroyer, did not hold in the case of mental progress; as if, in a word, the parallel with Darwinism might no longer obtain, and Spencer might be quite right with his fundamental law of intelligence, which says, "The cohesion between psychical states is proportionate to the frequency with which the relation between the answering external phenomena has been repeated in experience." . . .

But, in spite of all these facts, I have no hesitation whatever in holding firm to the Darwinian distinction even here. I maintain that the facts in question are all drawn from the lower strata of the mind, so to speak,—from the sphere of its least evolved functions, from the region of intelligence which man possesses in common with the brutes. And I can easily show that throughout the whole extent of those mental departments which are highest, which are most characteristically human, Spencer's law is violated at every step; and that as a matter of fact the new conceptions, emotions, and active tendencies which evolve are originally *produced* in the shape of random images, fancies, accidental out-births of spontaneous variation in the functional activity of the excessively instable human brain, which the outer environment simply confirms or refutes, adopts or rejects, preserves or destroys,—*selects*, in short, just as it selects morphological and social variations due to molecular accidents of an analogous sort.

It is one of the tritest of truisms that human intelligences of a simple order are very literal. They are slaves of habit, doing what they have been taught without variation; dry, prosaic, and matter-of-fact in their remarks; devoid of humor, except of the coarse physical kind which rejoices in a practical joke; taking the world for granted; and possessing in their faithfulness and honesty the single gift by which they are sometimes able to warm us into admiration. But even this faithfulness seems to have a sort of inorganic ring, and to remind us more of the immutable properties of a piece of inanimate matter than of the steadfastness of a human will capable of alternative choice. . . .

But turn to the highest order of minds, and what a change! Instead of thoughts of concrete things patiently following one another in a beaten track of habitual suggestion, we have the most abrupt cross-cuts and transitions from one idea to another, the most rarefied abstractions and discriminations, the most unheard-of combinations of elements, the subtlest associations of analogy; in a word, we seem suddenly introduced into a seething caldron of ideas, where everything is fizzling and bobbing about in a state of bewildering activity, where partnerships can be joined or loosened in an instant, treadmill routine is unknown, and the unexpected seems the only law. According to the idiosyncrasy of the individual, the scintillations will have one character or another. They will be sallies of wit and humor; they will be flashes of poetry and eloquence; they will be constructions of dramatic fiction or of mechanical devices, logical or philosophic abstractions, business projects, or scientific hypotheses, with trains of experimental consequences based thereon; they will be musical sounds, or images of plastic beauty or picturesqueness, or visions of moral harmony. But, whatever their differences may be, they will all agree in this,—that their genesis is sudden and, as it were, spontaneous. That is to say, the same premises would not, in the mind of another individual, have engendered just that conclusion; although, when the conclusion is offered to the other individual, he may thoroughly accept and enjoy it, and envy the brilliancy of him to whom it first occurred.

To Professor Jevons is due the great credit of having emphatically pointed out . . . how the genius of discovery depends altogether on the number of these random notions and guesses which visit the investigator's mind. To be fertile in hypotheses is the first requisite, and to be willing to throw them away the moment experience contradicts them is the next. The Baconian method of collating tables of instance may be a useful aid at certain times. But one might as well expect a chemist's note-book to write down the name of the body analyzed, or a weather table to sum itself up into a prediction of probabilities of its own accord, as to hope that the mere fact of mental confrontation with a certain series of facts will be sufficient to make *any* brain conceive their law. The conceiving of the law is a spontaneous variation in the strictest sense of the term. It flashes out of one brain, and no other, because the instability of that brain is such as to tip and upset itself in just that particular direction. But the important thing to notice is that the good flashes and the bad flashes, the triumphant hypotheses and the absurd conceits, are on an exact equality in respect of their origin. Aristotle's absurd Physics and his immortal Logic flow from one source: the forces that produce the one produce the other.

Commentary

We will first treat the subsequent influence of James's 1880 article on creativity research, and then turn to new directions.

SUBSEQUENT INFLUENCE

James's arguments must be placed in a larger context about what prior thinkers believed about the origins of "great thoughts." At the time that he published the essay, psychology barely existed as a scientific discipline, Wilhelm Wundt having founded the first laboratory for conducting psychological experiments just a year before. Moreover the subject matter of those experiments was entirely devoted to basic mental processes rather than to a phenomenon as complex as creativity. Accordingly, in James's day all thinking relevant to the topic was produced by either philosophers or by scientists who engaged in philosophical thinking. Earlier thinkers like Francis Bacon and René Descartes argued that great thoughts would emerge from totally logical reasoning (inductive and deductive, respectively). Although some philosophers, such as Immanuel Kant, held that rational thinking could apply only to the sciences, not the arts, this separation was not considered relevant to understanding the origin of great ideas, for the arts were focused more on the emotions.

The first philosopher and proto-psychologist to offer an alternative position was Alexander Bain (1855/1977) in his book *The Senses and the Intellect*. Here he argued that new ideas could not be obtained by straightforward induction or deduction but rather depended on laborious experimentation that required the intrusion of chance. As he put it, "The greatest practical inventions being so much dependent upon chance, the only hope of success is to multiply the chances by multiplying the experiments" (p. 597). Or, as the Nobel laureate Linus Pauling advised one of his graduate students, "Have lots of ideas and throw away the bad ones" (in Bynum & Porter, 2006, p. 485). Bain's concept sounds similar to Darwin's theory of evolution by natural selection: variations are first generated, and then the fittest are selected. In point of fact, Darwin was working on his evolutionary theory during the time that Bain's book was published. Curiously, a friend of Darwin's suggested to him that he might read Bain's book. Darwin actually purchased the volume, shelved it in his library, and never read it! If Darwin had read Bain, he certainly would have cited it, but he didn't.

Nor did James read Bain, as evident in the selection. However, James did cite Jevons (1877/1900, p. 577), an economist and logician, who espoused very similar ideas in 1877, shortly before the 1880 essay:

> It would be an error to suppose that the great discoverer seizes at once upon the truth, or has any unerring method of divining it. In all probability the errors of the great mind exceed in number those of the less vigorous one. Fertility of imagination and abundance of guesses at truth are among the first requisites of discovery; but the erroneous guesses must be many times as numerous as those that prove well founded. The weakest analogies, the most whimsical notions, the most apparently absurd theories, may pass through the teeming brain, and no record remain of more than a hundredth part. The truest theories involve suppositions which are inconceivable, and no limit can really be placed to the freedom of hypotheses.

Jevons's description of the discovery process has obvious echoes in James's essay. Indeed the passage quoted above is virtually paraphrased (with much Jamesian elaboration) in the paragraph that begins "But turn to the highest order of minds, and what a change!" (James, 1880, p. 456). In any event, because James had read Darwin rather than Bain, he conceived the process as Darwinian rather than Bainian.

The foregoing ideas of Bain, James, and Jevons are amply illustrated in the introspective reports that the mathematician Henri Poincaré provided regarding his own creative process (Martindale, 2009). In one of the most frequently quoted passages, Poincaré (1921, p. 387) wrote, "Ideas rose in crowds; I felt them collide until pairs interlocked, so to speak, making a stable combination." He compared these colliding ideas to "the hooked atoms of Epicurus" that buzz around "like the molecules of gas in the kinematic theory of gases," with the result that "their mutual impacts may produce new combinations" (p. 393). Poincaré clearly presented a combinatorial model in which many combinations were generated until a useful combination appeared. Interestingly, he argued that this combinatorial process largely took place in the unconscious mind: "Among the great numbers of combinations blindly formed by the subliminal self, almost all are without interest and without utility; but just for that reason they are also without effect upon the esthetic sensibility. Consciousness will never know them; only certain ones are harmonious, and, consequently, at once useful and beautiful" (p. 392). These views were later picked up and developed by fellow mathematician Jacques Hadamard (1945), who reported Albert Einstein's own introspections about the critical place that "combinatory play" had in his own creativity.

Poincaré's use of the adverb "blindly" is telling. It shows up again as an adjective in the seminal article "Blind Variation and Selective Retention in Creative Thought as in Other Knowledge Processes," by Donald T. Campbell (1960), the eminent social psychologist and methodologist. Here Campbell put forward what is often called the BVSR theory of creativity (cf. BV+SR in Nickles, 2003). The creative person generates "blind" variations and then selects and retains those that work. In describing BVSR, Campbell quotes Bain, Poincaré, and Hadamard at length, making it evident that it is a combinatorial model. Even so, he completely ignores James's ideas. Apparently Campbell was very concerned that BVSR would be identified as "Darwinian." He never cites any of Darwin's works, and refers to Darwin only twice in passing, the first time simply to emphasize that Darwin had been anticipated by Bain anyway. As Martindale (2009) has noted, the priority of Bain means that BVSR is not contingent on Darwinian ideas.

Perhaps because of Campbell's (1960) choice to underplay Darwin, BVSR had more initial impact on philosophy than on psychology, particularly when transformed into his evolutionary epistemology, a system that had close connections with Karl Popper's philosophy of science (see Campbell, 1974). It was not until the mid-1980s and early 1990s that BVSR began to receive more attention from psychologists who study creativity and related topics. For example, Staw (1990) used BVSR to provide an evolutionary account of creativity and innovation in the workplace. The same year Martindale (1990) incorporated BVSR in his evolutionary theory of stylistic change in the arts, thus indicating its applicability beyond science and technology. Particularly notable was his connecting primordial (or primary process) imagery with blind variation, enabling him to operationalize the latter concept using his famous Regressive Imagery Dictionary.

Yet in terms of sheer number of articles and books devoted to developing BVSR, Simonton's research program clearly stands out. Starting in 1985, he developed the theory in dozens of empirical inquiries, mathematical models, Monte Carlo simulations, and research integrations (see, especially, Simonton, 1997, 1999, 2003). Unlike Campbell (1960), Simonton explicitly incorporated James (1880), placing special emphasis on the thought processes that James believed necessary for great thoughts. Although these BVSR developments attracted some criticism, Simonton's latest work has responded to those criticisms (e.g., Simonton, 2010, 2011, 2013a). Ironically the major problem with his formulation of BVSR was that he departed too far from Campbell's (1960) original version. To give two examples, Simonton errored in calling BVSR "Darwinian" (rather than just "selectionist") and in defining the creative product as the unit of variation-selection rather than the "thought trial." After correcting these and other mistakes, Simonton then decided that BVSR had to be placed on a more formal basis.

Given the latter decision, Simonton recognized a fundamental flaw in all creativity research: researchers had never reached consensus on a scientifically valid definition of what it means for an idea or response to be creative! Instead they disagreed on the specific criteria, the number of criteria, how the criteria were scaled, the manner in which the criteria were combined, and who actually assessed an idea or response on those criteria. You can't even talk about the best way to measure or study creativity if you don't even know what you're measuring or studying. In response, Simonton (2013a, 2016, 2018b) advocated a three-criterion multiplicative definition (all criteria on a 0–1 decimal scale) in which the criteria are assessed at two levels, the personal and the consensual, where the former involves solely the creator's final subjective judgment at the time a creative product is complete and the latter the judgments of rather numerous others in the position to make their own assessments.

The specific definition for personal or "little-c" creativity is $c = (1 - p)u(1 - v)$, where p is the initial probability, u its final utility (usefulness, value, meaningfulness, appropriateness, truth, beauty, etc.), and v the creator's prior knowledge of the utility (e.g., as determined by domain-specific expertise). The factor $(1 - p)$ then signifies originality, while the factor $(1 - v)$ represents the increment added to the creator's knowledge, an increment often called "surprisingness" or "nonobviousness" in other three-criterion definitions, such as that used by the US Patent Office (e.g., Boden, 2004).

Consensual or "Big-C" creativity applies these same criteria, but the criteria are judged by very numerous others besides the creator, such as professional peers, consumers, connoisseurs, patrons, critics, editors, compilers, museum curators, festival jurors, scholars, and historians—depending on the domain and the time perspective of the evaluation. In terms of the James (1880) reading, these people collectively constitute the "environment" that ultimately determines whether the "thoughts" of the "great man" are actually great or not. This environmental selection process goes well beyond any pure psychology of creativity because it can incorporate additional interpersonal, sociocultural, economic, political, and historical processes (Simonton, 2018a).

Because these formal developments are so recent, they naturally lead to new directions in research.

NEW DIRECTIONS

One immediate implication of the new formal definition of creativity is that highly creative ideas are necessarily rare even at the personal level. After all, the most creative ideas or responses (where $c \to 1$) have very low probabilities ($p \to 0$), very high utilities ($u \to 1$), and very low prior knowledge values ($v \to 0$). Any idea with a high probability or a low utility or a high prior knowledge value cannot possibly be very creative because of the multiplicative nature of the definition. That does not mean that other kinds of ideas or responses do not make some indirect contribution to creativity. For instance, in problem-finding (where $p \to 1$, $u \to 0$, and $v \to 0$), the creator first learns that a high probability response doesn't work. An example would be when a theoretical prediction is disconfirmed by the data (Simonton, 2016, 2018b). Such disconfirmations often lead to creative discoveries.

Another crucial implication of the new definition is that BVSR becomes absolutely required to produce highly creative ideas (Simonton, 2013a). To see why, it helps to first establish that highly "sighted" ideas or responses cannot possibly be creative. Here sightedness is defined as $s = puv$, which approaches unity as $p \to 1$, $u \to 1$, and $v \to 1$. The latter values describe habitual or routine responses, not creative ones. Indeed as $s \to 1$, it necessarily follows that $c \to 0$. The obvious next question is what happens when $s \to 0$, which is equivalent to asking what occurs when the ideas or responses become more blind (i.e., $b = 1 - s$). At this point we encounter a paradox: although highly creative ideas are necessarily high in blindness (because both p and v approach zero), not all highly blind ideas are creative. On the contrary, most will not be. As said earlier, highly creative ideas or responses are very rare. Hence the creator has no other option but to generate and test "blind" ideational or behavioral combinations to determine their actual utility values, rejecting combinations where $u \to 0$.

If you reread James's (1880) depiction of the creative process as well as the Jevon (1877) passage on which it was seemingly based, both authors are indubitably advocating BVSR. Ideas or responses require the "trial and error" first suggested by Bain (1855/1977). Many experiments are needed before success can be secured, if it is attained at all. As Campbell (1960) established, too, Poincaré's (1921) introspections quite vividly illustrate BVSR in action (Martindale, 2009). In fact these descriptions may all be consolidated into ideas or responses with the parameter values $p \to 0$ and $v \to 0$ (i.e., these are low probability events that have unknown utilities). These are often the kinds of thoughts or behaviors generated in fantasy, daydreaming, tinkering, exploration, and play (Simonton, 2016, 2018b). Even if most of the outcomes will yield $u \to 0$, with sufficient time something may emerge where $u \to 1$, and the creator has a Eureka experience! Note that such low probability events most likely emerge when the creator is in a low arousal state, a psychological condition that has often been associated with creative illuminations (Boden, 2004). The very first literal Eureka experience took place when Archimedes was taking a bath.

That said, it must be emphasized that BVSR embodies a set of very diverse processes and procedures that share one and only one characteristic: they all generate ideas or responses whose utilities are unknown in advance. BVSR makes no assumptions about how those variations are actually generated. This point was emphatically made by Campbell (1960) when he pointed out that any systematic search also represents BVSR. Excellent examples can be found in the trial-and-error methods that Thomas Edison used to search for optimal incandescent lamp filaments or storage battery electrodes and electrolytes (Simonton, 2015). The inventor would go through huge inventories of possibilities, checking them off one by one, until he found something that passed muster. The trials would run into the thousands! That indicates that the probability of any one trial would be far less than one-thousandth. And because v was equivalently low, successful results were often extremely surprising. Who would have predicted that the first commercially viable filament would be a particular kind of carbonized bamboo fiber?

Briefly put, there's no such thing as *the* creative process or procedure. Creativity researchers have wasted much effort trying to identify a distinctive mechanism that underlies all creative acts. There is none. Any one candidate may work some of the time, but no candidate will work all of the time. Even ordinary thinking can come up with genius-grade insights (Weisberg, 2014). Because there's no guaranteed method, there's "no free lunch" (Nickles, 2003). Each creator just has to display sufficient determination and flexibility to keep at it. With enough effort and variability, something might work—or not. Edison devoted a considerable amount of time to inventing a practical fuel cell, even blowing out his laboratory's windows during one experiment, but he never managed to do so. Consequently the best creativity researchers can hope for is to construct an ample inventory of processes and procedures that work at least some of the time. Shortcuts or sure bets just aren't available—at least not for anything creative.

References

Bain, A. (1855/1977). *The senses and the intellect* (D. N. Robinson, Ed.). Washington, DC: University Publications of America.

Boden, M. A. (2004). *The creative mind: Myths and mechanisms* (2nd ed.). New York, NY: Routledge.

Bynum, W. F., & Porter, R. (Eds.). (2006). *The Oxford dictionary of scientific quotations.* Oxford: Oxford University Press.

Campbell, D. T. (1960). Blind variation and selective retention in creative thought as in other knowledge processes. *Psychological Review, 67*, 380–400.

Campbell, D. T. (1974). Evolutionary epistemology. In P. A. Schlipp (Ed.), *The philosophy of Karl Popper* (pp. 413–463). La Salle, IL: Open Court.

Hadamard, J. (1945). *The psychology of invention in the mathematical field.* Princeton, NJ: Princeton University Press.

James, W. (1880, October). Great men, great thoughts, and the environment. *Atlantic Monthly, 46*, 441–459.

James, W. (1884). The dilemma of determinism. *Unitarian Review and Religious Magazine, 22*, 193–224.

James, W. (1890). *The principles of psychology.* New York: Holt.

James, W. (1902). *The varieties of religious experience: A study in human nature.* London: Longmans, Green.

Jevons, W. S. (1877/1900). *The principles of science: A treatise on logic and scientific method* (2nd ed.). London: Macmillan.

Martindale, C. (1990). *The clockwork muse: The predictability of artistic styles.* New York, NY: Basic Books.

Martindale, C. (2009). Evolutionary models of innovation and creativity. In T. Rickards, M. Runco, & S. Moger (Eds.), *Routledge companion to creativity* (pp. 109–118). London: Taylor & Francis.

McGranahan, L. (2011). William James's social evolutionism in focus. *The Pluralist, 6*, 80–92.

Nickles, T. (2003). Evolutionary models of innovation and the Meno problem. In L. V. Shavinina (Ed.), *The international handbook on innovation* (pp. 54–78). New York, NY: Elsevier Science.

Poincaré, H. (1921). *The foundations of science: Science and hypothesis, the value of science, science and method* (G. B. Halstead, Trans.). New York, NY: Science Press.

Simonton, D. K. (1997). Creative productivity: A predictive and explanatory model of career trajectories and landmarks. *Psychological Review, 104*, 66–89.

Simonton, D. K. (1999). Creativity as blind variation and selective retention: Is the creative process Darwinian? *Psychological Inquiry, 10*, 309–328.

Simonton, D. K. (2003). Scientific creativity as constrained stochastic behavior: The integration of product, process, and person perspectives. *Psychological Bulletin, 129*, 475–494.

Simonton, D. K. (2010). Creativity as blind-variation and selective-retention: Constrained combinatorial models of exceptional creativity. *Physics of Life Reviews, 7*, 156–179.

Simonton, D. K. (2011). Creativity and discovery as blind variation: Campbell's (1960) BVSR model after the half-century mark. *Review of General Psychology, 15*, 158–174.

Simonton, D. K. (2013a). Creative thought as blind variation and selective retention: Why sightedness is inversely related to creativity. *Journal of Theoretical and Philosophical Psychology, 33*, 253–266.

Simonton, D. K. (2013b). Creative thoughts as acts of free will: A two-stage formal integration. *Review of General Psychology, 17*, 374–383.

Simonton, D. K. (2015). Thomas Alva Edison's creative career: The multilayered trajectory of trials, errors, failures, and triumphs. *Psychology of Aesthetics, Creativity, and the Arts, 9*, 2–14.

Simonton, D. K. (2016). Creativity, automaticity, irrationality, fortuity, fantasy, and other contingencies: An eightfold response typology. *Review of General Psychology, 20*, 194–204.

Simonton, D. K. (2018a). Creative genius as causal agent in history: James's 1880 theory revisited and revitalized. *Review of General Psychology, 22*, 406–420.

Simonton, D. K. (2018b). Defining creativity: Don't we also need to define what is *not* creative? *Journal of Creative Behavior, 52*, 80–90.

Staw, B. M. (1990). An evolutionary approach to creativity and innovations. In M. A. West & J. L. Farr (Eds.), *Innovation and creativity at work: Psychological and organizational strategies* (pp. 287–308). New York, NY: Wiley.

Weisberg, R. W. (2014). Case studies of genius: Ordinary thinking, extraordinary outcomes. In D. K. Simonton (Ed.), *The Wiley-Blackwell handbook of genius* (pp. 139–165). Oxford: Wiley-Blackwell.

19

Genius and Eminence
Catharine M. Cox

DEAN KEITH SIMONTON

Summary

Although Catharine Cox's (1926) study of 301 geniuses was published as the second volume of Lewis Terman's (1925–1959) five-volume *Genetic Studies of Genius*, it adopts a completely different approach to addressing the relation between early intellectual giftedness and later adulthood achievement. Rather than a psychometric prospective study of high-IQ children, Cox conducted a historiometric retrospective study of eminent creators and leaders, estimating early IQs from biographical data. For a subset of 100 geniuses, she also augmented the IQ scores with measures on 67 character traits, and thereby established the key role played by personality factors, most notably drive and persistence. The net result is a monograph that represents the greatest single historiometric investigation ever conducted, providing a model for subsequent research on the relation between IQ and achieved eminence in both creativity and leadership. Later inquiries also reinforced the supreme importance of motivational factors in attaining success. Future research should update the list of eminent creators and leaders for whom we have comparable IQ estimates. In addition, the inventory of personality variables should expand to include several omitted factors, including traits associated with subclinical psychopathology.

Introduction

In 1921 Lewis M. Terman launched an ambitious longitudinal study: the five-volume *Genetic Studies of Genius*. Having just recently standardized the Stanford-Binet intelligence test, he decided to administer that test to a large sample of young boys and girls, identify those who were the most intellectually gifted, and then follow their progress all the way to maturity to see if the brightest also become the best. Amazingly, the investigation is still going on, albeit largely as a gerontological inquiry (Duggan & Friedman, 2014). However, because the typical child started out only 11 years old, Terman would have a long wait before he would discover the outcome. In fact, Terman died before the fifth volume was published (Terman & Oden, 1959). Fortunately, he acquired a new and highly capable graduate student, Catharine Cox (1890–1984), who wanted to do her doctoral dissertation on the same basic question, but using an entirely different approach. She would start with world-famous creators and leaders, estimate their childhood and adolescent IQs from biographical data, and then determine whether such high achievers would have qualified for her mentor's sample had they been able to take the same test decades, even centuries earlier. This bold thesis idea might seem a nonstarter, except that Terman (1917) had already shown how IQ might be estimated from historical data. More specifically, her mentor had inferred that Francis Galton must have had an IQ very close to 200. She just applied a much more sophisticated version of his novel technique to a sample of 301 geniuses—and did much, much more besides!

Terman was obviously very pleased with Cox's completed dissertation. She not only earned her Ph.D. but also had her thesis published as the second volume of *Genetic Studies of Genius*. This publication was remarkable given that this is the only volume out of the five that does not include Terman as author or coauthor (Terman, 1925–1959). Unhappily, Cox did not use her thesis as a springboard for future research. The only other time she returned to these geniuses was in a small, qualitative study of their mental and physical health, published a decade later (Miles & Wolfe, 1936; cf. Simonton & Song, 2009). Otherwise her research went off into entirely different directions. For example, she collaborated with Terman on the development of a masculinity-femininity scale and the study of sex differences and started independent work on how mental speed changes with age. Just as critical was the fact that the year following her dissertation's publication, Cox married Walter Miles, one of Terman's colleagues, and thus became Catharine Cox Miles (or C. C. Miles) on all of her subsequent books and articles, thereby losing the explicit authorship connection with her 1926 monumental effort. In addition, because her new husband was a widower with three teenage children, she became an instant stepmother, and then added two children of their own (albeit one died at birth). Because Walter was an accomplished research psychologist—who soon became president of the American Psychological Association—the two collaborated together on some projects, submerging all the more her own independent research efforts. When he was called to a professorship at Yale University, Catharine followed, but obtained a position as a clinical psychologist, diverting her even more from original research (Robinson & Simonton, 2014). Her single best work was thus her very first, the source of this chapter's reading.

The selections are taken from Chapter 1 ("Introduction") and Chapter 13 ("Conclusions").

Reading: *The Early Mental Traits of Three Hundred Geniuses*

Source: Cox, C. (1926). *The early mental traits of three hundred geniuses.* Vol. 2 in *Genetic Studies of Genius* (L. M. Terman, Ed.). Stanford, CA: Stanford University Press. Selections from Chapter 1, "Introduction" (pp. 3–9), and Chapter 13, "Conclusions" (pp. 215–219). Copyright © 1926 by the Board of Trustees of the Leland Stanford Jr. University, renewed 1954. All rights reserved. Used with the permission of Stanford University Press, www.sup.org.

Chapter 1. Introduction

The factors which determine the appearance and development of geniuses have presented a persistent problem ever since man, in his earliest study of man, began to take account of individual differences. Like our earliest psychologically inquisitive ancestors, we are concerned to know what weight is to be attached to various circumstances, such as birth, endowment, and education, in the character of a man of genius, whose appearance among his fellows has long been recognized as due not to a single cause, but rather to "the happy result of many concomitant circumstances." It was known to the author of the greatest ideal republic that the ablest citizens in the state are the sons and daughters of the ablest parents. Plato was further aware that the transmission of physical and mental characteristics by heredity would not insure the full realization of their possibilities in the individual. Hence, as a preliminary to an adequate education for the choicest spirits, he provided that a selection should take place in childhood by simple intelligence tests, which he believed would suffice to determine the more gifted. The abilities of the superior youths were then to be developed by a special course of training devised to afford adequate stimulus and appropriate opportunity.

The whole problem of the origin, selection, and education of the gifted is one of profound concern, now as in Plato's day; for upon an adequate solution of it depend the appropriate and sufficient training of children of ability, the conservation of talent, and a possible increase in the production of significant and creative work. The study of the heredity, native gifts, and kinds of education that have most contributed to advance those who in the past became the ablest citizens of our world has long been recognized as a means of throwing considerable light upon the conditions which may be expected to produce and foster genius in our time and hereafter.

Galton and others have investigated the part played by the circumstances of birth, the first of the three important factors which condition the appearance and the development of geniuses. Our concern is now with the second factor: for an investigation of the native endowment of the most able individuals follows logically upon the investigation of their heredity and must precede any attempt to analyze the third element—the contribution of education.

In the study summarized in the following pages an attempt has been made to find in historical accounts of the early years of great men an answer to the question: What degree of mental endowment characterizes individuals of genius in their childhood and youth? We are primarily concerned with an examination and an evaluation of the general native ability of which the early behavior of geniuses gives evidence. Ultimately this problem must be solved by experimental methods; they alone can render a decisive and unequivocal answer. It is possible, however, that the true solution may be roughly indicated by historical research, even though the methods of such an investigation are less exact and the results obtained are correspondingly less absolute.

The purpose of this study is to characterize a group of young geniuses with respect to certain mental traits. The subjects described are 301 of the most eminent men and women of history. The data discussed are the historical records of their heredity, their childhood, and their youth. The method employed is that of historiometry. The criteria used in measuring the traits concerned are recognized psychological indices.

The group of subjects whose early behavior forms the basis of the present study includes great men and women who lived between the years 1450 and 1850. It is a representative group, and results obtained from an investigation of the childhood of its members may be expected to hold true for eminent men and women in general. In so far as interest obtains in these particular geniuses, a characterization of their early development has unique value; research into the early lives of less eminent individuals can scarcely equal a study of this group in intrinsic interest; and subjects who in individual significance would approach the level of the subjects in this study could not readily be obtained for a laboratory experiment, even if it were extended over the next four hundred years.

The present investigation, in dealing with the problem of the degree of native mental endowment characterizing those who achieve eminence, scrutinizes one aspect of the question of the relation between endowment and achievement. The correlative aspect of the larger problem is the degree of eminence attained by children possessing a given degree of native mental endowment. Stated in its simplest terms, this question is concerned, on the one hand, with the level of native endowment which produces the most superior men, and, on the other, with the level of attainment or the degree of eminence attained by the most superior children. Its final solution in both aspects requires a complete natural history of the most highly endowed individuals. . . .

A study based on the documentary evidence of history, where research is devoted to historical instead of to living subjects, offers a practical substitute for an experimental research. Historical data are available for a vast number of subjects; and a study of any group of them offers interesting and distinctly suggestive results, indicating the nature of the answer to the question which concerns us, even if our conclusions must await ultimate verification from a study which is based directly on living subjects. . . .

Records pertaining to the childhood and youth of 301 eminent individuals, including artists, musicians, soldiers, statesmen, and writers, offer the facts to be carefully collected and examined for the present inquiry. They furnish a basis for answering the questions involved in our problem.

The first of these concerns the "brightness," measured by intelligence test standards, of men and women of the greatest achievement. How would these young geniuses of the past have tested on an intelligence scale? . . . And, secondly, if the youthful intelligence does not sufficiently account for the later achievement, what other recorded traits of character may explain it? Do great energy and passionate ardor compensate for less intellectual power? Are any two of these three, health, interest, and ability, equal to any other two, as Galton has asserted, in making a mark that the world can and must see and recognize? . . . Are there *characteristics of genius*—traits that mark all of those who will one day attain eminence? And if there are, to what extent is *intelligence* one of them?

How shall we approach these problems? Do historical reports afford a basis for ratings of intelligence, of character traits, or of interests? The answer lies in the results of the study. For if the records are true—and of this verisimilitude is the best evidence—and if from these records reliable and valid results are obtained by the same methods we should apply in rating individuals today, then they may be accepted as comparable to results based on living subjects. Either the historical or the experimental method is valid and reliable for the purpose to which it is put. The judgments reported here are those of two or more qualified judges. The agreement of their estimates has been measured, and from the measures of agreement the probable accuracy of the obtained values has been computed. . . .

The results obtained will contribute to the solution of the problem of the native endowment of genius in proportion to the degree of accuracy of the original records, the care with which they have been assembled, the ability and insight of the investigators and of the judges, and the validity and the reliability of their standards of measurement.

The investigator has been acutely sensible of the temerity of the present undertaking and almost painfully aware of a persistent hesitancy in facing its peculiar problems. The attitude of one venturing upon a task of this kind has been well expressed by Galton: "I have been conscious of no slight misgiving that I was committing a kind of sacrilege whenever . . . I had occasion to take the measurement of modern intellects vastly superior to my own, or to criticize the genius of the most magnificent historical specimens to our race. It was a process that constantly recalled to me a once familiar sentiment in by-gone days of African travel, when I used to take altitudes of the huge cliffs that domineered above me as I traveled along their bases, or to map the mountainous landmarks of unvisited tribes, that loomed in faint grandeur beyond my actual horizon."

The records which the heroes of the past have left of their remarkable achievement in childhood and youth offer a mine of psychological material. It is believed that conclusions derived from an evaluation of certain items may prove suggestive in connection with a comparative study of gifted children today, and that the original case studies will be found to contain information of unusual significance and wide general interest even in the abbreviated from in which they have been presented here. . . .

Chapter 13. Conclusions

The questions proposed at the outset of this study may now be answered, at least tentatively, as a result of a detailed examination of historical records and the evidence of the numerous historiometric measurements. . . . The primary concern of the investigation as a whole was this: What degree of *mental endowment* characterizes individuals of genius in their childhood and youth? Secondary in the present study, although otherwise of no less importance, was the question of the presence even in childhood of *traits of character other than "brightness"* which contribute to later high achievement. These two questions were the starting point for the discussions of the preceding pages. Each has been considered in detail. During the progress of this investigation it became evident that consideration of the main problem involved an additional question: What was the *hereditary background* of a group of young persons who later achieved very great distinction and what contribution was made by early *environment* to their development? The answer to this third question has been given a place because of the light it throws upon the problem as a whole.

Stated briefly in their logical order the three conclusions are as follows:

1. *Youths who achieve eminence have, in general, (a) a heredity above the average and (b) superior advantages in early environment.* It is evident that the forebears of young geniuses have made a definite contribution both physically and socially to the extraordinary

progress of their offspring. . . . The inheritance of a child of able parents is undoubtedly
superior, yet it is not sufficient in itself to account for genius. . . . Indeed . . . there were
other children of the same parents, the brothers and sisters of our young geniuses, who
did not achieve eminence equal to that of the peculiarly gifted member of the family.
The individual is the inheritor of ability, but he is unique with respect to the physiological and psychological organization of his inherited qualities. A favorable ancestral
background is a definite asset; yet the peculiar combination of inherited traits which
makes up a genius—the most favorable chance combination among many only less favorable ones—is an equally significant factor. . . .

The average opportunity of our young geniuses for superior education and for
elevating and inspiring social contacts was unusually high. Instruction by leading
scholars of the day and friendly association with contemporary notables were not exceptional experiences. . . . But again there were exceptions. . . . Thus it appears that while
individual chances for eminence are usually dependent upon a favorable opportunity,
eminence is not a function either of heredity or of environment alone.

2.   *Youths who achieve eminence are distinguished in childhood by behavior which indicates
an unusually high IQ.* . . . Accounts of the early years of our subjects are full of examples
of early mental maturity. In their reported interests, in their school standing and progress, and in their early production and achievement, the members of the group were, in
general, phenomenal. Later achievement was foreshadowed in youthful behavior, and
it is probable that early manifestations of superior intelligence would have been found
in every case had the records of all been faithfully kept.

Since there is a constant relation between the sufficiently of the account and the
estimated IQ of the subject (the IQ increasing with the reliability of the data), it appears
that the true IQ's of the subjects of the present study are even higher than the obtained
estimates. A corrected estimate indicates that the true mean IQ for the group is not
below 155 and probably at least as high as 165. . . . We are probably warranted in
expecting superior adult achievement whenever in childhood the IQ is above 150. But
we may not be warranted in expecting a world genius even if the 200 IQ level is reached;
for there are other factors involved in achieving greatness besides an essential degree
of intellectual capacity. The tests—and it is in comparison with test performances that
the IQ's of our cases have been reckoned—cannot measure spontaneity of intellectual
activity; perhaps, too, they do not sufficiently differentiate between high ability and
unique ability, between the able individual and the extraordinary genius. The significant conclusion in the present study is derived from the evidence it presents that *the extraordinary genius who achieves the highest eminence is also the gifted individual whom
intelligence tests may discover in childhood.* The converse of this proposition is yet to be
proved.

3.   That all equally intelligent children do not as adults achieve equal eminence is in part
accounted for by our last conclusion: *youths who achieve eminence are characterized not
only by high intellectual traits, but also by persistence of motive and effort, confidence in
their abilities, and great strength or force of character.* The average score of all the good
traits of the young geniuses is distinctly above the average score of the same traits in un-
selected individuals. The superior youths considered in the present study pursued high

ideals, developed significant interests, and created new expressions of scientific and philosophical thought before they had reached the age of manhood. . . . Achievements like these are not the accidents of a day. They are the natural growth of persistent interest and great zeal combined with rare special talents.

These conclusions summarize the facts concerning a special group of geniuses, but the group concerned is representative of all those whose later achievements reach the highest level, and so conclusions true for its members are probably true for other similar, or approximately similar, individuals. Appearing usually in superior families (and the more usually so when educational and other early environmental inequality persists) young geniuses are found to display in childhood superior intelligence, superior talents, and superior traits of character. The converse has not been definitely demonstrated, but the appearance in childhood of a combination of the highest degree of general ability, special talent, seriousness of purpose, and indomitable persistence may well be greeted as indicating a capacity for adult achievement of the highest rank. The child is father of the man: the gifted youth will be the leader of the future.

Commentary

These selections do not include any actual IQ scores. That omission stems from the fact that the tables reporting the scores are big and complex: the main table reporting all of the scores is more than a dozen pages long! Even when they can fit on a single page, the scores are most often accompanied by various statistics that most readers would find very esoteric. Part of the difficulty stems from the fact that Cox calculated IQs for two separate groups: main group A, consisting of 282 geniuses, and a subsidiary group B, containing only 19 creators and leaders that was used to calibrate the calculations. Even more complicating is the fact that for every genius in each group she provides *four* alternative estimates. In the first place, she estimated each IQ for two separate periods, the first from birth to age 17, and the second for the next decade to age 27—in essence, from childhood to adolescence, and then from adolescence to early adulthood. Yet she calculated scores corrected for data reliability (discussed later), a correction introduced for both the early and the later estimates.

For example, the philosopher John Stewart Mill received raw IQ estimates of 190 and 170, for early and later periods, respectively, with corresponding data reliabilities of .82 and .82 (which are in the same league as standard psychometric instruments, like IQ tests). Using the latter, he obtained corrected IQs of 200 and 190, again respectively. Because Cox was using the old definition of IQ as a literal intelligence quotient (viz., mental age divided by chronological age times 100), these estimates mean that in childhood and adolescence his mental age was about twice his chronological age. To put this intellectual precocity in more concrete terms, consider the following passage taken from Mill's dossier:

He began to learn Greek at 3; and from then to his 9th year he studied Greek classics, making daily reports of his reading. At the same time . . . he read innumerable historical works. At 7 he read Plato; at 8 he began the study of Latin. Before the end of the year he was busily reading the classical Latin writers. He did not neglect mathematics: at 8 his course included geometry and algebra; at 9 conic sections, spherics, and Newton's arithmetic were added. . . . At 10 and 11 both mathematical

TABLE 19.1 **Cox's (1926) Estimated IQs for Select Creative Geniuses**

Name	Dates	Age 0–17		Age 17–27	
		Raw IQ	Corrected IQ	Raw IQ	Corrected IQ
Beethoven	1770–1827	135	150	140	165
Cervantes	1547–1616	105	145	110	155
C. Darwin	1809–1882	135	155	140	165
Descartes	1596–1650	150	170	160	180
Dickens	1812–1870	145	160	155	180
Galileo	1564–1642	145	160	165	185
Leibnitz	1646–1716	185	195	190	205
Michelangelo	1475–1564	145	160	160	180
Montaigne	1533–1592	140	155	140	165
Mozart	1756–1791	150	160	155	165
Newton	1642–1727	130	150	170	190
Pascal	1623–1662	180	190	180	195
Rembrandt	1606–1669	110	130	135	155

and classical studies were continued; astronomy and mechanical philosophy were also included. In fluxions [calculus], begun at 11, Mill was largely self-taught. (Cox, 1926, p. 707)

Nor was Mill's precocity confined to passive learning: "At the age of 5 Mill discussed the comparative merits of Marlborough and Wellington [two great British generals] with Lady Spencer, the wife of the First Lord of the Admiralty" (Cox, 1926, p. 709), and at age 6½ he wrote his own history of Rome. One does not need an actual IQ score to infer that Mill was very, very bright.

Table 19.1 provides some additional examples where this same estimation technique was applied to some of the greatest creative geniuses in Western civilization. The names themselves should be famous enough to require no introduction.

Subsequent Influence

Let me begin by noting that Cox's IQ estimates have left an enduring impact on popular culture. If you google "IQ" plus the name of a famous creator or leader who happens to have been included among the 301, you'll most often obtain one of her IQ estimates for that genius. Sometimes you'll even get the complete list. Like any internet meme, these IQ scores often are bandied about without proper credit to the source. Too often, as well, her scores are cited without proper attention to which of her four IQ estimates are actually being used, and sometimes her four estimates are just averaged into a single estimate.

In any event, I will now discuss the methodological and substantive influences of Cox's classic doctoral dissertation, as represented in the selections.

Methodological influences. Cox explicitly identified her method as "historiometry" and her IQ measures as "historiometric." She adopted these terms directly from Frederick Woods (1909, 1911), who introduced historiometry as a new name for an exact science. Unfortunately Woods's own definition of historiometry was not very exact. It was defined simply as the technique whereby "the facts of history of a personal nature have been subjected to statistical analysis by some more or less objective method" (Woods, 1909,

p. 703). Many decades later a more precise definition was published: "Historiometrics is a scientific discipline in which nomothetic hypotheses about human behavior are tested by applying quantitative analyses concerning historical individuals" (Simonton, 1990, p. 3). A hypothesis is "nomothetic" if it concerns some general law or at least statistical regularity. For example, Cox had hypothesized that (a) highly eminent creators and leaders would exhibit stellar IQs and (b) the degree of eminence would correlate positively with the genius's IQ—both of which hypotheses were confirmed.

Although Woods (1911, p. 568) thought that historiometry was ideally suited for developing the "psychology of genius," his own applications of the methodology concerned European royal families and monarchs rather than creators, in the former case actually assessing kings, queens, and their close relatives on both intellect and virtue (Woods, 1906, 1913). Yet Woods (1909) also provided an inventory of past investigations that could be said to apply historiometry even though the term had not been invented yet. His best examples include Francis Galton's (1869) *Hereditary Genius*, which used the biographical record to study family pedigrees, and James McKeen Cattell's (1903) statistical analysis of eminent creators and leaders. The latter had used standard references, such as biographical dictionaries and encyclopedias, to measure the relative achieved eminence of 1,000 creators and leaders. The more space devoted to a particular historical figure in multiple sources, the higher that person's rank. Such "space measures" of eminence have been widely used in research on exceptional creativity and leadership (e.g., Murray, 2003; Simonton, 1998a, 2014). The assumption is that those creators or leaders who have the biggest impact on history will see more space devoted to them in reference works—space largely dedicated to narrating their accomplishments.

In support of this last assumption, space measures have been shown to correlate highly with alternative ways of assessing achieved eminence, such as citation measures in the sciences and performance frequencies in the arts (Simonton, 1990). Indeed all alternative assessments can be explained by a single latent variable that has been called "Galton's G" (Simonton, 1991b). That is, the diverse ways of assessing eminence can all be taken as mere "fallible" indicators of an underlying "true score" representing historical reputation. This underlying factor is also highly stable across time; those who attain eminence in one century have a high probability of retaining their eminence in following centuries (Ginsburgh & Weyers, 2014). That same transhistorical stability applies to single creative products, such as operas (Simonton, 1998b). The success of an opera during its first run predicts performance and recording frequencies decades, even centuries later.

From the perspective of the current selection, the more important point is that Cox (1926) used Cattell's (1903) scores in her own study. She used them in two ways. First, she largely restricted her sample to those historical figures who scored in the upper half of the rank ordering. It was for this reason that her study included such obvious great creators as Ludwig van Beethoven, René Descartes, Johann Wolfgang von Goethe, Michelangelo Buonarroti, and Isaac Newton, but also excluded Giacomo Casanova, Antonio da Correggio, Pierre de Fermat, John Keats, and Christopher Wren, to name a few omitted creative geniuses of note. Hence Cattell's ordered list provided a sampling criterion. Second, among those 301 who made it into the final sample—after deleting 199 according to other criteria (such as needing to be born since 1450)—she used Cattell's ranked eminence measure as a variable to determine whether eminence correlated positively with estimated IQ. As already noted, that expected correlation was in fact found.

Of course, the validity of that IQ-eminence correlation depends very much on the validity of her IQ estimates. This dependence brings us to another influential methodological contribution: the use of multiple raters or judges in at-a-distance assessment of individual-difference variables. After first compiling the raw biographical data on intellectual development, she did not rely on just her own judgment in estimating IQ. Instead she enlisted independent raters, including her mentor Terman and one of Terman's collaborators, Florence Goodenough, who invented the Goodenough Draw-a-Man Test, a nonverbal measure of children's intelligence (Rogers, 1999). Given these multiple expert assessments, she was then able to calculate not just an overall composite estimate but also calculate the reliability of the resulting IQ scores. She again used independent raters when she assessed a subset of 100 geniuses on 67 character traits, a major contribution to at-a-distance personality assessment (cf. Song & Simonton, 2007). She calculated reliabilities here too. In contrast, earlier historiometric studies relied on the lone investigator to execute the judgments (viz. Ellis, 1904; Woods, 1906, 1913). Interjudge reliability could not then be calculated.

All told, Cox's 1926 historiometric inquiry was clearly the state of the art. We might even say that her methodological improvements were too good: her thesis was certainly a hard act to follow. Subsequent historiometric inquiries were far less sophisticated, often returning to the practice of the researchers doing their own ratings (e.g., R. B. Cattell, 1963; Raskin, 1936; Thorndike, 1936, 1950). It took exactly a half century before historiometric research began to improve beyond her methodical innovations. Significantly, those enhancements began with a reanalysis of her own raw data and IQ estimates (Simonton, 1976).

Substantive influences. In her conclusion, Cox provided a convenient summary of what she considered her three central results. So I'll just return to these statements, and then update them based on more recent research. For all statements the original italics have been removed and very minor editing was inserted for the third conclusion. Here we go.

1. "Youths who achieve eminence have, in general, (a) a heredity above the average and (b) superior advantages in early environment" (Cox, 1926, p. 215). Right from the start Cox asserts that both nature and nurture participate in the development of high achievers (cf. Galton, 1874). However, it is fair to say that the case for nurture (environment) was far better than that for nature (heredity). After all, she did not conduct an actual behavioral genetic analysis, but merely observed that her geniuses tended to come from distinguished family pedigrees (as in Galton, 1869). In contrast, the early environmental influences were obviously superior with respect to both family background and educational opportunities. Hence it is difficult to separate out the influences. Certainly John Stuart Mill inherited some pretty decent genes from his father, James, who was himself a distinguished philosopher. But James also homeschooled his son to enable him to accelerate his training. Accordingly there can be no doubt that the youth's environmental advantages were superb. It is very probable that nurture exerted far more impact than nature in this instance.

   Speaking in more general terms, although highly eminent creators are more prone to come from superior socioeconomic backgrounds, that tendency does not necessarily mandate a positive correlation between creative achievement and those environmental variables (Simonton, 2002). Indeed the lack of correspondence was demonstrated by a secondary analysis of Cox's own data (Simonton, 1976). Achieved eminence exhibited no correlation whatsoever with father's occupational status. Although father's status was correlated positively with both IQ and educational level, it exerted no direct effect on eminence. So it seems that superior environmental advantages merely provide the opportunities for achievement, but other factors determine the degree of eminence actually attained. More eminent creators come from the professional classes than from the working classes, but the former are not necessarily more eminent than the latter (see also Feist, 1993; Wispé, 1965; cf. Chambers, 1964; Raskin, 1936). One of those more direct effects is described next.

2. "Youths who achieve eminence are distinguished in childhood by behavior which indicates an unusually high IQ" (Cox, 1926, p. 216). This conclusion affirms retrospectively what Terman hoped to confirm prospectively once his sample of intellectually gifted children grew up to become mature adults (but see Terman & Oden, 1959). Although she didn't calculate the averages across all 301, a later analysis showed that the uncorrected IQs averaged 153 for the earlier estimates and 164 for the later estimates (Simonton, 1976). The earlier average corresponds nicely with the mean IQ of Terman's (1925) 1,528 11-year-olds, namely IQ 151. She also calculated the correlation coefficient between the later average (17–27 years old) and Cattell's (1903) eminence measure, obtaining .25. If this correlation is calculated across all 301 geniuses, it shrinks to .23, a still respectable figure (Simonton, 1976). Indeed the moderate positive correlation between estimated general intelligence and achieved eminence has been replicated many times (Simonton, 2009). The association holds not just for general samples of notable creators and leaders (Simonton, 1991b; Walberg, Rasher, & Hase, 1978) but also for more specialized samples, such as presidents of the United States (Simonton, 2006), European absolute monarchs (Simonton, 1983), and illustrious African Americans (Simonton, 2008). What renders this consistent pattern remarkable is that these studies all deal with samples with extreme range restriction on both intelligence and eminence (see also Kell & Lubinski, 2014).

   That said, Cox's results also show that the expected IQs vary across domains. These domain contrasts have been replicated in subsequent research as well. As a first cut, eminent creators tend to have higher IQs than eminent leaders, a difference of about half a standard deviation (i.e., 6–7 points; Simonton, 1976). In addition, IQ contrasts are seen within creative and leadership domains as well (Simonton & Song, 2009). For instance, among creative domains, eminent philosophers enjoy IQs about a standard deviation above the mean, whereas eminent artists and composers have IQs about a half standard deviation below the mean. In part, these differences may reflect the extent to which a domain depends on verbal intelligence rather than visual or musical intelligence (cf. Gardner, 1993).

   These complications aside, the fact remains that Cox was the very first investigator to estimate the correlation between IQ and achieved eminence. But she was also the very first researcher to empirically establish that a high IQ was not sufficient, which brings us to the third point.

3. "Youths who achieve eminence are characterized not only by high intellectual traits, but also by persistence of motive and effort, confidence in their abilities, and great strength or force of character" (Cox, 1926, p. 218). Using the scores on the personality traits, Cox concluded that "high but not the highest intelligence, combined with the greatest degree of persistence, will achieve greater eminence than the highest degree of intelligence with somewhat less persistence" (p. 187). Cox's conclusions on this point were later cited by Angela Duckworth and her colleagues in developing the Grit Scale, a measure of perseverance and passion for lifelong goals (Duckworth, Peterson, Matthews, & Kelly, 2007). Furthermore, it has since become apparent why this motivational aspect of genius proves so important. In the first place, considerable effort is required to acquire the domain-specific expertise needed before a person can make world-class contributions. This developmental requirement has been called the

"10-year rule," meaning that the individual must devote a decade to intense study and practice (Ericsson, 2014). Second, exceptional achievement as an adult requires a long and highly productive career (Kozbelt, 2014; McKay & Kaufman, 2014). Although "one-hit wonders" certainly exist, their long-term impact seldom rivals that of true genius. Extraordinary productivity is especially required given that not everything produced will be a success (Simonton, 1997). On the contrary, hits will be vastly outnumbered by misses. For instance, Thomas Edison may have more than a 1,000 patents, but most of those patents were for inventions that totally failed to make money, and some failures cost him millions of dollars (Simonton, 2015). But he persevered, continuing to invent from ages 21 to 84, the last year of his life.

NEW DIRECTIONS

Although Amazon.com lists Cox's magnum opus as out of print, it includes a reader re-view that gave it five stars, but also added that the book needed updating given that none of the geniuses was born after 1850. But that's not the only reason. The treatment of personality could be vastly improved. Obviously her original inventory of 67 fails to meet modern standards. Most notably, it fails to capture openness to experience, a Big-Five Factor that has been shown to correlate with both creativity and leadership (McCrae & Greenberg, 2014; Simonton, 2006). Because openness often exhibits a positive corre-lation with general intelligence, we then must ask which of the two variables correlates most highly with achieved eminence. Perhaps the dispositional trait is more crucial than the cognitive ability.

Interestingly openness to experience is positively correlated with cognitive disinhibition—the tendency *not* to filter out extraneous stimuli and associations—which in turn is positively linked with psychopathology (Carson, 2014). These connections naturally must bring up the mad-genius controversy: Are geniuses, especially creative geniuses, more prone to at least subclinical symptoms? Even though this issue has been around for centuries, it is not surprising that Cox avoided empirical treatment of the question. After all, it was her mentor's purpose to demonstrate that the intellectually gifted were above average in both physical and mental health. The same expectation would hold for her 301 geniuses as well. Yet a decade later she returned to this question, directly assessing 282 of these creators and leaders on both mental and physical health (Miles & Wolfe, 1936). Even so, as mentioned before, she conducted only a qualitative investigation, sans any direct quantitative test of any association (Simonton, 2010). Happily, her raw data were deposited in an archive where they could be retrieved to be used in a more complete statistical analysis (Simonton & Song, 2009). Among the interesting results was that the imagina-tive writers—poets, novelists, and dramatists—were more prone to exhibit inferior mental health. This result replicates what has been found for other samples as well (Kaufman, 2001; Ludwig, 1998; Simonton, 2014).

Nonetheless more empirical work needs to be done on this question. And that work should include historiometric studies like Cox's. Only when samples include uni-versally recognized geniuses can the mad-genius hypothesis receive direct scrutiny (cf. Simonton, 2016). At the same time, the issue is too important and interesting to simply ignore. In the future, perhaps, another ambitious and able graduate student will de-cide to attempt an updated version of Cox's original 842-page doctoral thesis! That updated investigation could then take full advantage of all that creativity researchers have learned since 1926, suggesting many new hypotheses that she could not even dream of.

References

Carson, S. H. (2014). Cognitive disinhibition, creativity, and psychopathology. In D. K. Simonton (Ed.), *The Wiley handbook of genius* (pp. 198–221). Oxford: Wiley.

Cattell, J. M. (1903). A statistical study of eminent men. *Popular Science Monthly, 62*, 359–377.

Cattell, R. B. (1963). The personality and motivation of the researcher from measurements of contemporaries and from biography. In C. W. Taylor & F. Barron (Eds.), *Scientific creativity: Its recognition and development* (pp. 119–131). New York, NY: Wiley.

Chambers, J. A. (1964). Relating personality and biographical factors to scientific creativity. *Psychological Monographs: General and Applied, 78*(7, Whole No. 584).

Cox, C. (1926). *The early mental traits of three hundred geniuses.* Stanford, CA: Stanford University Press.

Duckworth, A. L., Peterson, C., Matthews, M. D., & Kelly, D. R. (2007). GRIT: Perseverance and passion for long-term goals. *Journal of Personality and Social Psychology, 92*, 1087–1101.

Duggan, K. A., & Friedman, H. S. (2014). Lifetime biopsychosocial trajectories of the Terman gifted children: Health, well-being, and longevity. In D. K. Simonton (Ed.), *The Wiley handbook of genius* (pp. 488–507). Oxford: Wiley.

Ellis, H. (1904). *A study of British genius.* London: Hurst & Blackett.

Ericsson, K. A. (2014). Creative genius: A view from the expert-performance approach. In D. K. Simonton (Ed.), *The Wiley handbook of genius* (pp. 321–349). Oxford: Wiley.

Feist, G. J. (1993). A structural model of scientific eminence. *Psychological Science, 4*, 366–371.

Galton, F. (1869). *Hereditary genius: An inquiry into its laws and consequences.* London: Macmillan.

Galton, F. (1874). *English men of science: Their nature and nurture.* London: Macmillan.

Gardner, H. (1993). *Creating minds: An anatomy of creativity seen through the lives of Freud, Einstein, Picasso, Stravinsky, Eliot, Graham, and Gandhi.* New York, NY: Basic Books.

Ginsburgh, V., & Weyers, S. (2014). Evaluating excellence in the arts. In D. K. Simonton (Ed.), *The Wiley handbook of genius* (pp. 511–532). Oxford: Wiley.

Kaufman, J. C. (2001). The Sylvia Plath effect: Mental illness in eminent creative writers. *Journal of Creative Behavior, 35*, 37–50.

Kell, H. J., & Lubinski, D. (2014). The Study of Mathematically Precocious Youth at maturity: Insights into elements of genius. In D. K. Simonton (Ed.), *The Wiley handbook of genius* (pp. 397–421). Oxford: Wiley.

Kozbelt, A. (2014). Musical creativity over the lifespan. In D. K. Simonton (Ed.), *The Wiley handbook of genius* (pp. 451–472). Oxford: Wiley.

Ludwig, A. M. (1998). Method and madness in the arts and sciences. *Creativity Research Journal, 11*, 93–101.

McCrae, R. R., & Greenberg, D. M. (2014). Openness to experience. In D. K. Simonton (Ed.), *The Wiley handbook of genius* (pp. 222–243). Oxford: Wiley.

McKay, A. S., & Kaufman, J. C. (2014). Literary geniuses: Their life, work, and death. In D. K. Simonton (Ed.), *The Wiley handbook of genius* (pp. 473–487). Oxford: Wiley.

Miles, C. C., & Wolfe, L. S. (1936). Childhood physical and mental health records of historical geniuses. *Psychological Monographs, 47*, 390–400.

Murray, C. (2003). *Human accomplishment: The pursuit of excellence in the arts and sciences, 800 B.C. to 1950.* New York, NY: HarperCollins.

Raskin, E. A. (1936). Comparison of scientific and literary ability: A biographical study of eminent scientists and men of letters of the nineteenth century. *Journal of Abnormal and Social Psychology, 31*, 20–35.

Robinson, A., & Simonton, D. K. (2014). Catharine Morris Cox Miles and the lives of others (1890–1984). In A. Robinson & J. L. Jolly (Eds.), *A century of contributions to gifted education: Illuminating lives* (pp. 101–114). London: Routledge.

Rogers, K. B. (1999). The lifelong productivity of the female researchers in Terman's *Genetic Studies of Genius* longitudinal study. *Gifted Child Quarterly, 43*, 150–169.

Simonton, D. K. (1976). Biographical determinants of achieved eminence: A multivariate approach to the Cox data. *Journal of Personality and Social Psychology, 33*, 218–226.

Simonton, D. K. (1983). Intergenerational transfer of individual differences in hereditary monarchs: Genetic, role-modeling, cohort, or sociocultural effects? *Journal of Personality and Social Psychology, 44*, 354–364.

Simonton, D. K. (1990). *Psychology, science, and history: An introduction to historiometry.* New Haven, CT: Yale University Press.

Simonton, D. K. (1991a). Latent-variable models of posthumous reputation: A quest for Galton's G. *Journal of Personality and Social Psychology, 60,* 607–619.

Simonton, D. K. (1991b). Personality correlates of exceptional personal influence: A note on Thorndike's (1950) creators and leaders. *Creativity Research Journal, 4,* 67–78.

Simonton, D. K. (1997). Creative productivity: A predictive and explanatory model of career trajectories and landmarks. *Psychological Review, 104,* 66–89.

Simonton, D. K. (1998a). Achieved eminence in minority and majority cultures: Convergence versus divergence in the assessments of 294 African Americans. *Journal of Personality and Social Psychology, 74,* 804–817.

Simonton, D. K. (1998b). Fickle fashion versus immortal fame: Transhistorical assessments of creative products in the opera house. *Journal of Personality and Social Psychology, 75,* 198–210.

Simonton, D. K. (2002). *Great psychologists and their times: Scientific insights into psychology's history.* Washington, DC: American Psychological Association.

Simonton, D. K. (2006). Presidential IQ, openness, intellectual brilliance, and leadership: Estimates and correlations for 42 US chief executives. *Political Psychology, 27,* 511–639.

Simonton, D. K. (2008). Childhood giftedness and adulthood genius: A historiometric analysis of 291 eminent African Americans. *Gifted Child Quarterly, 52,* 243–255.

Simonton, D. K. (2009). The "other IQ": Historiometric assessments of intelligence and related constructs. *Review of General Psychology, 13,* 315–326.

Simonton, D. K. (2010). The curious case of Catharine Cox: The 1926 dissertation and her Miles-Wolfe 1936 follow-up. *History of Psychology, 13,* 205–206.

Simonton, D. K. (2014). More method in the mad-genius controversy: A historiometric study of 204 historic creators. *Psychology of Aesthetics, Creativity, and the Arts, 8,* 53–61.

Simonton, D. K. (2015). Thomas Alva Edison's creative career: The multilayered trajectory of trials, errors, failures, and triumphs. *Psychology of Aesthetics, Creativity, and the Arts, 9,* 2–14.

Simonton, D. K. (2016). Reverse engineering genius: Historiometric studies of exceptional talent. *Annals of the New York Academy of Sciences, 1377,* 3–9.

Simonton, D. K., & Song, A. V. (2009). Eminence, IQ, physical and mental health, and achievement domain: Cox's 282 geniuses revisited. *Psychological Science, 20,* 429–434.

Song, A. V., & Simonton, D. K. (2007). Personality assessment at a distance: Quantitative methods. In R. W. Robins, R. C. Fraley, & R. F. Krueger (Eds.), *Handbook of research methods in personality psychology* (pp. 308–321). New York, NY: Guilford Press.

Terman, L. M. (1917). The intelligence quotient of Francis Galton in childhood. *American Journal of Psychology, 28,* 209–215.

Terman, L. M. (1925). *Mental and physical traits of a thousand gifted children.* Stanford, CA: Stanford University Press.

Terman, L. M. (1925–1959). *Genetic studies of genius* (5 vols.). Stanford, CA: Stanford University Press.

Terman, L. M., & Oden, M. H. (1959). *The gifted group at mid-life.* Stanford, CA: Stanford University Press.

Thorndike, E. L. (1936). The relation between intellect and morality in rulers. *American Journal of Sociology, 42,* 321–334.

Thorndike, E. L. (1950). Traits of personality and their intercorrelations as shown in biographies. *Journal of Educational Psychology, 41,* 193–216.

Walberg, H. J., Rasher, S. P., & Hase, K. (1978). IQ correlates with high eminence. *Gifted Child Quarterly, 22,* 196–200.

Wispé, L. G. (1965). Some social and psychological correlates of eminence in psychology. *Journal of the History of the Behavioral Sciences, 7,* 88–98.

Woods, F. A. (1906). *Mental and moral heredity in royalty.* New York, NY: Holt.

Woods, F. A. (1909, November 19). A new name for a new science. *Science, 30,* 703–704.

Woods, F. A. (1911, April 14). Historiometry as an exact science. *Science, 33,* 568–574.

Woods, F. A. (1913). *The influence of monarchs: Steps in a new science of history.* New York, NY: Macmillan.

PART SEVEN

Creativity, Imagination, and Daydreaming

20

On "Creative Writers and Day-Dreaming" by Sigmund Freud (1908)

Tania Zittoun

Summary

Relatively early in his career, Freud wrote a short text on creativity, arguing that, far from being the privilege of a few artists, it was part of a process naturally developing as a continuation of children's play. After presenting that text, this chapter discusses it in the light of past and recent developments, focusing on the idea that creativity is a process. British psychoanalysis has examined that idea, with an emphasis on what may hinder creativity and its variations. In Russia, however, Vygotsky's work, without quoting them explicitly, has largely drawn on Freud's intuitions, yet including them in a more socioculturally aware psychology. Three ideas need further theoretical and empirical investigation: the continuum between child and adult creativity; the nuances between daydream, imagination, and creativity; and the role of emotions and personal motives in any creative endeavor.

Introduction

"Creative Writers and Day-Dreaming" (1908/2001) is a short text written by Sigmund Freund (1856–1939), a medical doctor and neurologist known as the founder of psychoanalysis.

Freud (1910/1957) defined psychoanalysis as a theory, a method of investigation, and a therapy. One of the breakthroughs of his approach to illnesses otherwise unexplainable in the late 19th century was to listen to hysterical or depressed patients and believe that their pain had a meaning to be reconstructed. He progressively made the hypothesis of the existence of powerful unconscious dynamics in people. The basic argument, roughly summarized, is that desires (sexual, ambitious, narcissistic, etc.) surge, and that for various reasons—mainly linked to internalized sociocultural rules and conventions—these need to be repressed, or disguised and transformed into acceptable forms. These transformations occur at a semiotic level and follow various processes, as identified in the dreamwork, or are sublimated. Eventually these substitutive forms appear in embodied symptoms, dreams, lapsus linguae—as well as in authentic scientific and artistic work. These dynamics thus require a certain model of the psyche, presented in the early 1900s as a layered apparatus, with deeper and more embodied zones (unconscious dynamics) and more superficial ones, accessible through dreams or analysis (preconscious dynamics); human consciousness is thus a very small portion of our psychic life.[1] On this basis, psychoanalysis as therapy develops techniques aimed at turning unconscious motives into conscious ones.

Besides his work as a doctor, Freud was extremely well informed about archaeology, poetry, sculpture, music, and painting. Arts had an important status in his work, providing inspiration (as did the figure of Goethe [Zittoun, 2017]), cases to be analyzed, and, in the text presented here, problems to be explained.

"Creative Writers and Day-Dreaming" was initially written as a conference paper given by Freud in 1907 at the publisher and bookseller Hugo Heller's place in Vienna.[2] In this address to a literary audience, Freud questions the origin of creativity in the poet: Is it unique and specific—genius—or is it present in each of us? His provocative argument is that creativity in the artist is actually a dynamic present in everyone, and even more, a continuation of child's play. The core argument unfolds as follows: children can freely externalize their inner lives and desires in the symbolic world of play, expressing their needs and finding resolutions to tensions; becoming young adults and adults, people learn to hide these inner lives and desires and, in most cases, engage in fantasizing; poets, those who create art, actually translate such fantasies into an artistic form. Creativity is hence triggered by current events that reactivate infantile experiences, from which a desire oriented toward the future will find a new accomplishment. Creative artifacts thus result from the synthesis of the artist's earlier and current experiences, transformed through unique aesthetic work. These allow everyone to enjoy now transformed fantasies.

Reading: "Creative Writers and Day-Dreaming"

Source: Freud, S. (1908/2001). "Creative writers and day-dreaming." In J. Strachey and A. Freud (Eds.), Jensen's "Gradiva" and other works. Vol. 9 of The Standard Edition of the Complete Psychological Works of Sigmund Freud (pp. 141–153). London: Vintage. Translated from the German under the general editorship of James Strachey, in collaboration with Anna Freud, assisted by Alix Strachey and Alan Tyson. (Original English edition 1959 by Hogarth Press). Reproduced with permission from the Institute of Psychoanalysis, London. All notes to Freud's text are from the 1959 Hogarth edition, reproduced in the 2001 Vintage edition.

---

1. This early formulation of Freud's model was revised and enriched many times.
2. According to the introduction to the Standard Edition.

We laymen have always been intensely curious to know—like the Cardinal who put a similar question to Ariosto[1]—from what sources that strange being, the creative writer, draws his material, and how he manages to make such an impression on us with it and to arouse in us emotions of which, perhaps, we had not even thought ourselves capable. Our interest is only heightened the more by the fact that, if we ask him, the writer himself gives us no explanation, or none that is satisfactory; and it is not at all weakened by our knowledge that not even the clearest insight into the determinants of his choice of material and into the nature of the art of creating imaginative form will ever help to make creative writers of *us*.

If we could at least discover in ourselves or in people like ourselves an activity which was in some way akin to creative writing! An examination of it would then give us a hope of obtaining the beginnings of an explanation of the creative work of writers. And, indeed, there is some prospect of this being possible. After all, creative writers themselves like to lessen the distance between their kind and the common run of humanity; they so often assure us that every man is a poet at heart and that the last poet will not perish till the last man does.

Should we not look for the first traces of imaginative activity as early as in childhood? The child's best-loved and most intense occupation is with his play or games. Might we not say that every child at play behaves like a creative writer, in that he creates a world of his own, or rather, re-arranges the things of his world in a new way which pleases him? It would be wrong to think he does not take that world seriously; on the contrary, he takes his play very seriously and he expends large amounts of emotion on it. The opposite of play is not what is serious but what is real. In spite of all the emotion with which he cathects his world of play, the child distinguishes it quite well from reality; and he likes to link his imagined objects and situations to the tangible and visible things in the real world. This linking is all that differentiates the child's "play" from "phantasying."

The creative writer does the same as the child at play. He creates a world of phantasy which he takes very seriously—that is, which he invests with large amounts of emotion— while separating it sharply from reality. Language has preserved this relationship between children's play and poetic creation. It gives [in German] the name of *Spiel* [play] to those forms of imaginative writing which require to be linked to tangible objects and which are capable of representation. It speaks of a *Lustspiel* or *Trauerspiel* [comedy or tragedy: literally, "pleasure play" or "mourning play"] and describes those who carry out the representation as *Schauspieler* [players: literally "show-players"]. The unreality of the writer's imaginative world, however, has very important consequences for the technique of his art; for many things which, if they were real, could give no enjoyment, can do so in the play of phantasy, and many excitements which, in themselves, are actually distressing, can become a source of pleasure for the hearers and spectators at the performance of a writer's work.

There is another consideration for the sake of which we will dwell a moment longer on this contrast between reality and play. When the child has grown up and has ceased to play, and after he has been labouring for decades to envisage the realities of life with proper seriousness, he may one day find himself in a mental situation which once more undoes the contrast between play and reality. As an adult he can look back on the intense seriousness with which he once carried on his games in childhood; and, by equating his ostensibly se- rious occupations of today with his childhood games, he can throw off the too heavy burden imposed on him by life and win the high yield of pleasure afforded by *humour*.[2]

As people grow up, then, they cease to play, and they seem to give up the yield of pleasure which they gained from playing. But whoever understands the human mind knows that hardly anything is harder for a man than to give up a pleasure which he has once experienced. Actually, we can never give anything up; we only exchange one thing for another. What appears to be a renunciation is really the formation of a substitute or surrogate. In the same way, the growing child, when he stops playing, gives up nothing but the link with real objects; instead of *playing,* he now *phantasies.* He builds castles in the air and creates what are called *day-dreams.* I believe that most people construct phantasies at times in their lives. This is a fact which has long been overlooked and whose importance has therefore not been sufficiently appreciated.

People's phantasies are less easy to observe than the play of children. The child, it is true, plays by himself or forms a closed psychical system with other children for the purposes of a game; but even though he may not play his game in front of the grownups, he does not, on the other hand, conceal it from them. The adult, on the contrary, is ashamed of his phantasies and hides them from other people. He cherishes his phantasies as his most intimate possessions, and as a rule he would rather confess his misdeeds than tell anyone his phantasies. It may come about that for that reason he believes he is the only person who invents such phantasies and has no idea that creations of this kind are widespread among other people. This difference in the behaviour of a person who plays and a person who phantasies is accounted for by the motives of these two activities, which are nevertheless adjuncts to each other.

A child's play is determined by wishes: in point of fact by a single wish—one that helps in his upbringing—the wish to be big and grown up. He is always playing at being "grown up," and in his games he imitates what he knows about the lives of his elders. He has no reason to conceal this wish. With the adult, the case is different. On the one hand, he knows that he is expected not to go on playing or phantasying any longer, but to act in the real world; on the other hand, some of the wishes which give rise to his phantasies are of a kind which it is essential to conceal. Thus he is ashamed of his phantasies as being childish and as being unpermissible.

But, you will ask, if people make such a mystery of their phantasying, how is it that we know such a lot about it? Well, there is a class of human beings upon whom, not a god, indeed, but a stern goddess—Necessity—has allotted the task of telling what they suffer and what things give them happiness.[3] These are the victims of nervous illness, who are obliged to tell their phantasies, among other things, to the doctor by whom they expect to be cured by mental treatment. This is our best source of knowledge, and we have since found good reason to suppose that our patients tell us nothing that we might not also hear from healthy people.

Let us now make ourselves acquainted with a few of the characteristics of phantasying. We may lay it down that a happy person never phantasies, only an unsatisfied one. The motive forces of phantasies are unsatisfied wishes, and every single phantasy is the fulfilment of a wish, a correlation of unsatisfying reality. These motivating wishes vary according to the sex, character and circumstances of the person who is having the phantasy; but they fall naturally into two main groups. They are either ambitious wishes, which serve to elevate the subject's personality; or they are erotic ones. In young women the erotic wishes predominate almost exclusively, for their ambition is as a rule absorbed by erotic trends. In young men egoistic and ambitious wishes come to the fore clearly enough alongside of erotic ones. But we will not lay stress on the opposition between the two trends; we would rather emphasize the fact that they are often united. Just as, in many altarpieces, the portrait of the donor is to be seen in a corner of the picture, so, in the majority of ambitious phantasies, we can discover in some corner or other the lady for whom the creator of the phantasy performs all his heroic deeds and at whose feet all his triumphs are laid. Here, as you see, there are strong enough motives for concealment; the well-brought-up young woman is only allowed a minimum of erotic desire, and the young man has to learn to suppress the excess of self-regard which he brings with him from the spoilt days of his childhood, so that he may find his place in a society which is full of other individuals making equally strong demands.

We must not suppose that the products of this imaginative activity—the various phantasies, castles in the air and day-dreams—are stereotyped or unalterable. On the contrary, they fit themselves in to the subject's shifting impressions of life, change with every change in his situation, and receive from every fresh active impression what might be called a "date-mark." The relation of a phantasy to time is in general very important. We may say that it hovers, as it were, between three times—the three moments of time which our ideation involves. Mental work is linked to some current impression, some provoking occasion in the present which has been able to arouse one of the subject's major wishes. From there it harks back to a memory of an earlier experience (usually an infantile one) in which this wish was fulfilled; and it now creates a situation relating to the future which represents a fulfilment of the wish. What it thus creates is a day-dream or phantasy, which carries about it traces of its origin from the occasion which provoked it and from the memory. Thus past, present and future are strung together, as it were, on the thread of the wish that runs through them.

A very ordinary example may serve to make what I have said clear. Let us take the case of a poor orphan boy to whom you have given the address of some employer where he may perhaps find a job. On his way there he may indulge in a day-dream appropriate to the situation from which it arises. The content of his phantasy will perhaps be something like this. He is given a job, finds favour with his new employer, makes himself indispensable in the business, is taken into his employer's family, marries the charming young daughter of the house, and then himself becomes a director of the business, first as his employer's partner and then as his successor. In this phantasy, the dreamer has regained what he possessed in his happy childhood—the protecting house, the loving parents and the first objects of his affectionate feelings. You will see from this example the way in which the wish makes use of an occasion in the present to construct, on the pattern of the past, a picture of the future.

There is a great deal more that could be said about phantasies; but I will only allude as briefly as possible to certain points. If phantasies become over-luxuriant and over-powerful, the conditions are laid for an onset of neurosis or psychosis. Phantasies, moreover, are the immediate mental precursors of the distressing symptoms complained of by our patients. Here a broad by-path branches off into pathology.

I cannot pass over the relation of phantasies to dreams. Our dreams at night are nothing else than phantasies like these, as we can demonstrate from the interpretation of dreams.[4] Language, in its unrivalled wisdom, long ago decided the question of the essential nature of dreams by giving the name of "day-dreams" to the airy creations of phantasy. If the meaning of our dreams usually remains obscure to us in spite of this pointer, it is because of the circumstance that at night there also arise in us wishes of which we are ashamed; these we must conceal from ourselves, and they have consequently been repressed, pushed into the unconscious. Repressed wishes of this sort and their derivatives are only allowed to come to expression in a very distorted form. When scientific work had succeeded in elucidating this factor of *dream-distortion,* it was no longer difficult to recognize that night-dreams are wish-fulfilments in just the same way as day-dreams—the phantasies which we all know so well.

So much for phantasies. And now for the creative writer. May we really attempt to compare the imaginative writer with the "dreamer in broad daylight,"[5] and his creations with day-dreams? Here we must begin by making an initial distinction. We must separate writers who, like the ancient authors of epics and tragedies, take over their material readymade, from writers who seem to originate their own material. We will keep to the latter kind, and, for the purposes of our comparison, we will choose not the writers most highly esteemed by the critics, but the less pretentious authors of novels, romances and short stories, who nevertheless have the widest and most eager circle of readers of both sexes. One feature above all cannot fail to strike us about the creations of these storywriters: each of them has a hero who is the centre of interest, for whom the writer tries to win our sympathy by every possible means and whom he seems to place under the protection of a special Providence. If, at the end of one chapter of my story, I leave the hero unconscious and bleeding from severe wounds, I am sure to find him at the beginning of the next being carefully nursed and on the way to recovery; and if the first volume closes with the ship he is in going down in a storm at sea, I am certain, at the opening of the second volume, to read of his miraculous rescue—a rescue without which the story could not proceed. The feeling of security with which I follow the hero through his perilous adventures is the same as the feeling with which a hero in real life throws himself into the water to save a drowning man or exposes himself to the enemy's fire in order to storm a battery. It is the true heroic feeling, which one of our best writers has expressed in an inimitable phrase: "Nothing can happen to *me!*"[6] It seems to me, however, that through this revealing characteristic of invulnerability we can immediately recognize His Majesty the Ego, the hero alike of every day-dream and of every story.[7]

Other typical features of these egocentric stories point to the same kinship. The fact that all the women in the novel invariably fall in love with the hero can hardly be looked on as a portrayal of reality, but it is easily understood as a necessary constituent of a day-dream. The same is true of the fact that the other characters in the story are sharply divided into good and bad, in defiance of the variety of human characters that are to be observed in real life. The "good" ones are the helpers, while the "bad" ones are the enemies and rivals, of the ego which has become the hero of the story.

We are perfectly aware that very many imaginative writings are far removed from the model of the naïve day-dream; and yet I cannot suppress the suspicion that even the most extreme deviations from that model could be linked with it through an uninterrupted series of transitional cases. It has struck me that in many of what are known as "psychological" novels only one person—once again the hero—is described from within. The author sits inside his mind, as it were, and looks at the other characters from outside. The psychological novel in general no doubt owes its special nature to the inclination of the modern writer to split up his ego, by self-observation, into many part-egos, and, in consequence, to personify the conflicting currents of his own mental life in several heroes. Certain novels, which might be described as "eccentric," seem to stand in quite special contrast to the type of the day-dream.

In these, the person who is introduced as the hero plays only a very small active part; he sees the actions and sufferings of other people pass before him like a spectator. Many of Zola's later works belong to this category. But I must point out that the psychological analysis of individuals who are not creative writers, and who diverge in some respects from the so-called norm, has shown us analogous variations of the day-dream, in which the ego contents itself with the role of spectator.

If our comparison of the imaginative writer with the day-dreamer, and of poetical creation with the day-dream, is to be of any value, it must, above all, show itself in some way or other fruitful. Let us, for instance, try to apply to these authors' works the thesis we laid down earlier concerning the relation between phantasy and the three periods of time and the wish which runs through them; and, with its help, let us try to study the connections that exist between the life of the writer and his works. No one has known, as a rule, what expectations to frame in approaching this problem; and often the connection has been thought of in much too simple terms. In the light of the insight we have gained from phantasies, we ought to expect the following state of affairs. A strong experience in the present awakens in the creative writer a memory of an earlier experience (usually belonging [to] his childhood) from which there now proceeds a wish which finds its fulfillment in the creative work. The work itself exhibits elements of the recent provoking occasion as well as of the old memory.[8]

Do not be alarmed at the complexity of this formula. I suspect that in fact it will prove to be too exiguous a pattern. Nevertheless, it may contain a first approach to the true state of affairs; and, from some experiments I have made, I am inclined to think that this way of looking at creative writings may turn out not unfruitful. You will not forget that the stress it lays on childhood memories in the writer's life—a stress which may perhaps seem puzzling— is ultimately derived from the assumption that a piece of creative writing, like a day-dream, is a continuation of, and a substitute for, what was once the play of childhood.

We must not neglect, however, to go back to the kind of imaginative works which we have to recognize, not as original creations, but as the refashioning of readymade and familiar material. Even here, the writer keeps a certain amount of independence, which can express itself in the choice of material and in changes in it which are often quite extensive. In so far as the material is already at hand, however, it is derived from the popular treasure-house of myths, legends and fairy tales. The study of constructions of folk-psychology such as these is far from being complete, but it is extremely probable that myths, for instance, are distorted vestiges of the wishful phantasies of whole nations, the *secular dreams* of youthful humanity.

You will say that, although I have put the creative writer first in the title of my paper, I have told you far less about him than about phantasies. I am aware of that, and I must try to excuse it by pointing to the present state of our knowledge. All I have been able to do is to throw out some encouragements and suggestions which, starting from a study of phantasies, lead on to the problem of the writer's choice of his literary material. As for the other problem by what means the creative writer achieves the emotional effects in us that are aroused by his creations—we have as yet not touched on it at all. But I should like at least to point out to you the path that leads from our discussion of phantasies to the problems of poetical effects.

You will remember how I have said that the day-dreamer carefully conceals his phantasies from other people because he feels he has reasons for being ashamed of them.

I should now add that even if he were to communicate them to us he could give us no pleasure by his disclosures. Such phantasies, when we learn them, repel us or at least leave us cold. But when a creative writer presents his plays to us or tells us what we are inclined to take to be his personal daydreams, we experience a great pleasure, and one which probably arises from the confluence of many sources. How the writer accomplishes this is his innermost secret; the essential *ars poetica* lies in the technique of overcoming the feeling of repulsion in us which is undoubtedly connected with the barriers that rise between each single ego and the others. We can guess two of the methods used by this technique. The writer softens the character of his egoistic day-dreams by altering and disguising it, and he bribes us by the purely formal—that is, aesthetic —yield of pleasure which he offers us in the presentation of his phantasies. We give the name of an *incentive bonus*, or a *fore-pleasure*, to a yield of pleasure such as this, which is offered to us so as to make possible the release of still greater pleasure arising from deeper psychical sources.[9] In my opinion, all the aesthetic pleasure which a creative writer affords us has the character of a fore-pleasure of this kind, and our actual enjoyment of an imaginative work proceeds from a liberation of tensions in our minds. It may even be that not a little of this effect is due to the writer's enabling us thenceforward to enjoy our own day-dreams without self-reproach or shame. This brings us to the threshold of new, interesting, and complicated enquiries; but also, at least for the moment, to the end of our discussion.

1. Cardinal Ippolito d'Este was Ariosto's first patron, to whom he dedicated the *Orlando Furioso*. The poet's only reward was the question "Where did you find so many stories, Lodovico?"
2. See section 7 of Chapter 7 of Freud's book on jokes (1905).
3. This is an allusion to some well-known lines spoken by the poet-hero in the final scene of Goethe's *Torquato Tasso:*

    Und wenn der Mensch in seiner Qua! verstummt,
    Gab mir ein Gott, zu sagen, wie ich leide.
    And when mankind is dumb in its torment, a god granted me to tell how I suffer.

4. Cf. Freud, *The Interpretation of Dreams* (1900).
5. "Der Traumer am hellichten Tag."
6. "Es kann dir nix g'schehen!" This phrase from Anzengruber, the Viennese dramatist, was a favorite one of Freud's. Cf. "Thoughts on War and Death" (1915), *Standard Ed.*, 14, 296.
7. Cf. "On Narcissism" (1914), *Standard Ed.*, 14, 91.
8. A similar view had already been suggested by Freud in a letter to Fliess of July 7, 1898, on the subject of one of C. F. Meyer's short stories (Freud, 1950, Letter 92).
9. This theory of "fore-pleasure" and the "incentive bonus" had been applied by Freud to jokes in the last paragraph of Chapter 6 of his book on the subject (1905). The nature of "fore-pleasure" was also discussed in the *Three Essays* (1950). See especially *Standard Ed.*, 7, 208ff.

Commentary

TRACING THE INFLUENCE OF FREUD'S IDEAS IN CREATIVITY RESEARCH

When Freud presented "Creative Writers and Day-Dreaming" as a conference paper, it was positively received—more so than his earlier *Interpretation of Dreams*—and reviewed in the daily newspapers. Not mentioning explicitly sexuality and the unconscious, the paper has thus been considered by commentators to be Freud's position on the "applied" uses of psychoanalysis (Hillenaar, 2007, p. 145).

The main point of "Creative Writers and Day-Dreaming" is the continuity between children's play and adult fantasy and the common dynamics at work between laymen and artists. Regarding the actual work of the artist, Freud is more implicit; he mainly gives the example of "easy" literature that simply plays with common desires (narcissistic, ambitious, or erotic). An author who constantly revised his model in the light of new cases and theoretical elaboration (Zittoun, 2015), Freud will come back to his earlier formulation in his later work. (The topic occurs in almost every one of his publications up until the late 1930s [Delrieu, 2008, pp. 89–96]).

In his *Introductory Lectures*, Freud (1915–1916/1999, p. 478) thus writes that the "true artist" knows how to elaborate his own fantasies in such a way that they lose their too personal features, to "model" certain material until they reproduce his imaginary ideas and attach to it such pleasure that it may pass over the usual (sociocultural) repressions. Hence his implicit theory of creativity takes shape: it implies working with invested material and personal experiences, yet giving to them a semiotic form (in whatever mode, e.g., literary, visual), distancing them enough from their source so that they acquire some generality, and giving them a form that is "pleasurable" to the self and the audience. This is where aesthetic mastery intervenes, as the "pleasurability" may imply at least three aspects: that the creation satisfies a shared cultural aesthetic of conventions and norms, both in content and form; that the art form creates tensions and their possible resolution; yet that they also play enough with conventions to bring an extra quality to it: that of overcoming codes and rules.

As with any production by Freud, this paper received abundantly comments in the psychoanalytical community (e.g., Anargyros-Klinger, Reiss-Schimmel, & Wainrib, 1998; Spector Person, Fonagy, & Figueira, 1995/2013). According to Trosman (1995/2013, pp. 33–34), the psychoanalytical study of creativity took three directions: the study of artistic creation as an indirect way to analyze their authors; the study of literary or artistic work; and the analysis of the sources of creativity—Freud's 1908 paper belonging to the third type. In what follows, I will ignore the references to Freud's paper made by literary criticism, psychoanalysis, or cultural studies interested in the first two directions and will turn to two lines of work interested in creativity as a process.

A first important line of studies clearly inspired by Freud's "Creative Writers and Day-Dreaming" stems from British psychoanalysis. At the end of his life Freud moved to London, where his daughter, Anna Freud, became one of the leading figures in the psychoanalytical community, the other one being Melanie Klein, developing her object-relations approach. These ideas are systematically discussed by authors interested in artistic creativity and especially therapists treating people impeded in their creativity (see, e.g., Milner's [1950/2010] *On Not Being Able to Paint*). Some of the criticism of Freud's text focuses on the superficial needs it addresses (i.e., fame and women), its ignorance of the actual creative process (aesthetic transformation), and the fact that it considers the creator in isolation (Segal, 1991; Wright, 2002).

An important British psychoanalyst, Donald W. Winnicott, developed a core concern in the 1950–1970s for the conditions under which life can be creative. Winnicott did not mention explicitly Freud's text (as he often did not quote his sources), yet one of his main arguments has a comparable continuity hypothesis: it follows the development of the child's capacity to be alone within his relation to the mother figure, allowing also for his creative capacity—coming from the experience of omnipotence of being able to "create" the mother—and progressively expanded to transitional phenomena, children's play, adult daily creativity, and cultural creation in science and the arts (Winnicott, 1988, 1989, 2001). Winnicott thus maintains Freud's idea of a continuum, yet brings in the fact that creativity is enabled by fundamental relational dynamics.

The same argument is developed in Hanna Segal's (1991) *Dream, Phantasy and Art*; she closely discusses Freud's 1908 paper and a series of criticisms it has raised, before expanding Freud's argument along a more Kleinian line. Her proposition is that the need to create, or the creative impulse, is rooted in infantile experiences of the loss of an initial harmony, and is thus an attempt to "rediscover and recreate this lost world" (Segal, 1991, p. 94). The creative process itself is a way of "working through" experience, that is, engaging in psychic work, turning emotional or rough experience into a semiotic form; the authentic work or aesthetic process demands balance between the "ugly" and beautiful aspects of one's experience within the chosen artistic language. Hence artistic creativity is both an internal work and a work addressed to an external audience.

The same group of scholars also discussed Freud's apparent hypothesis of an equivalence between daydream and artistic creativity. Based on his work with young children and adults impeded in their creativity, Winnicott (2001) distinguished a sterile rumination, or fantasy, from imagination that actually participates in the elaboration and transformation of experience.[3] This intuition is followed by Segal (1991, pp. 106–109), who distinguishes daydreaming as an "as-if" phenomena, which can remain purely private, from imagination, which he sees as a "what-if" dynamic and which takes into account the demands of reality, where it can lead to actual creativity; imagination demands the work of creation, artistic (or scientific) command, and faces various internal and external obstacles. Wright (2002) similarly brings Freud's (1908/2001) proposition together with Winnicott's.

A second line of study was developed in total independence, in Russia. First interested in literature and the arts, then emerging as a key developmental psychologist, Lev S. Vygotsky (1971, pp. 73–75) explicitly summarizes Freud's 1908 text in his *Psychology of Art*, the result of his work in the USSR in 1915–1922 (Leontiev, 1971). He however follows this summary with a wide-ranging review of different, more or less psychoanalytical accounts of artwork or artists' lives, which according to him present a quite inconsistent picture. Vygotsky (1971, p. 80; quoting Marx) criticizes these accounts, then rejects the proposition that creativity is anchored in unconscious motives, as it finally excludes consciousness and mainly ignores social dynamics that may play a role in the choice of topics to be addressed by art or the diversity of artistic forms. Vygotsky thus seems to radically reject Freud's 1908 propositions, yet these reappear in his work. First, in the second part of the *Psychology of Art* Vygotsky develops a model of *catharsis* through art, which is actually a model of working through emotions through the art form, compatible with a processual understanding of Freud's work. Second, Freud's 1908 argument is still present, without the critical tone, in Vygotsky's (1931/1994, p. 275) "Imagination and Creativity of the Adolescent," where the argument of continuity between the child's fantasy and the adult's art is mentioned in reference to "a psychologist" without explicitly naming Freud.[4] Vygotsky further discusses children's play development in adolescence, where he sees two developmental lines: one where the adolescent continues fantasizing to elaborate emotional frustrations and needs (still quoting Freud's 1908 text without naming him; Vygotsky, 1931/1994, pp. 283–284),[5] and the other where imagination becomes coupled with the

---

3. In addition, the Kleinians will distinguish between "fantasy" as conscious daydreaming and "phantasy" as unconscious scenarios (Isaacs, 1948), which leads to the question: In which is creativity grounded?
4. The editors put a note to an unattributed quote, saying the author could not be found; it was likely Freud.
5. The editors refer to the previous note.

development of intelligence, abstraction, and the mastery of more complex cultural knowledge, and where it can become creativity in the arts or science. Vygotsky's work on art and imagination starts to be abundantly quoted in developmental and cultural psychology, yet Freud is rarely acknowledged in that field.[6]

In psychology of creativity more broadly defined, Freud and the 1908 text is usually mentioned as one point in the study of creativity (Albert & Runco, 1999) and reduced either to the "psychodynamic" hypothesis of the origin of creativity (Sternberg & Lubart, 1999, p. 6) or to being a case of a creative author himself (Gardner, 1993). Even Jack Martin's (2016) recent sociocultural approach to creativity using perspective exchange theory mentions Freud's 1908 paper only as an example of Freud's creative work, not for its content (but for a rare exception, see Glăveanu, 2011). However, there are elements of its content to be further examined.

NEW DIRECTIONS FOR RESEARCH BASED ON THESE HISTORICAL INSIGHTS

There is a series of ideas in Freud's essays that deserve further exploration in psychology, and especially in its sociocultural branch, and that have been identified by the two lines of studies highlighted earlier; I will mention three.

First, the hypothesis of a developmental continuum from children's play to adult creativity needs closer attention. Are their functions, their processes, and their outcomes equivalent or comparable? What is it that develops, and how much is that continuum dependent on other developmental dynamics—maturation, cultural learning, personal and social experience, and so on? In the literature we have recently distinguished a "continuum hypothesis" in the development of imagination (and creativity) similar to Freud's proposition from a "parallel hypothesis," for instance in the cognitive work of Bogdan (2013), who suggests that children's relation to objects develops in a route parallel to people's relation to others. To these we have opposed a third, "recursive hypothesis": the mutual dependency and equal importance of people's relation to others and objects in the development of imagination and creativity (Zittoun & Gillespie, 2016, pp. 94–97). But this still needs careful empirical investigation, for instance through much needed, careful longitudinal studies.

Second, the similarities or specificities of the processes involved in daydreaming, playing, imagining, and creating have to be further explored. As suggested earlier, psychoanalytical authors have tried to disentangle this knot by suggesting that some processes have a different hypothetical quality than others, are more or less conscious, or have outcomes in the real world and are not only beneficial for the self. This needs to be further examined in a more unified theory of mind and psychological elaboration, taking into account both the sociocultural dynamics at stake as well as the psychic work involved. Recent progress in semiotic cultural psychology may allow us to go in that direction (Gillespie & Zittoun, 2013; Salvatore, 2016; Salvatore & Zittoun, 2011; Valsiner, 2017), but further theoretical integration is required.

---

6. A PsycINFO search with keywords "Freud, Vygotsky, and creativity" (May 28, 2017) lists five occurrences, two being scholarly discussions on Vygotsky, one a psychodynamic paper, one an encyclopedia, and the third Vygotsky's work. Developmental work on imagination, even when sharing the hypothesis of continuity between childhood play and adult imagination and creativity, does not mention Freud's (1908/2001) paper either (e.g., Singer & Singer, 1992).

Third, current research on creativity, especially in cultural approaches, has not looked at the inner emotional work of engaging in a creative process, or its consequences for the self in a constitutive sense. Whether or not one subscribes to Freud's assumption of the existence of unconscious dynamics, one cannot ignore that inspiration, creative block, energy, flow, or whatever lay or scientific terms are used to describe the creative process refer to emotional, embodied dynamics. Even Vygotsky, with all his insistence on sociocultural dynamics, would not deny these internal aspects. Seen as dynamics as well, these can be shared, mediated, culturally transformed; they do not need to be reduced to personality traits or characteristics. The suggestion is thus to examine, in daily creativity as much as in scientific or artistic creation, what supports engagements, allows overcoming obstacles, or what "drives" people, and which may be, on the one hand, socially supported, and on the other, as suggested by Freud, related to different layers of personal experience. Conversely, Winnicott's intuition that it is creativity that makes life worth living probably refers to some fundamental dynamics at the core of what makes us human; it may be worth examining this perspective on creativity to understand life in extreme or challenging situations. Here, I believe, theory needs to avoid the sociocultural trap that loses the subject and the personalist trap that reduces dynamics to a measurable "motivation." Theoretical work may thus also be needed to bind intuitions developed by psychoanalysis with other domains of psychology currently examining these sociocultural and psychic dynamics of living (e.g., Brown & Reavey, 2015; Dreier, 2007; Hviid, 2015; Stenner, 2015).

As a whole, with all its limitations—its time and context of production, its relatively early formulation in Freud's overall work, its superficiality on some aspects—"Creative Writers and Day-Dreaming" remains a rich and inspirational text for creativity research. Although I have addressed only some of the issues it raises, I believe it can still root important explorations as it invites us to consider the hybrid, temporal, and synthetic nature of the creative process, referring to various layers of emotionally invested experience, yet turned toward the social world and drawing from the past into the future.

References

Albert, R. S., & Runco, M. A. (1999). The concept of creativity: Prospects and paradigms. In R. J. Sternberg (Ed.), *Handbook of creativity* (pp. 15–31). Cambridge, UK: Cambridge University Press.

Anargyros-Klinger, A., Reiss-Schimmel, I., & Wainrib, S. (1998). *Créations, psychanalyse*. Paris: Presses Universitaires de France.

Bogdan, R. J. (2013). *Mindvaults: Sociocultural grounds for pretending and imagining*. Cambridge, MA: MIT Press.

Brown, S., & Reavey, P. (2015). *Vital memory and affect: Living with a difficult past*. London: Routledge.

Delrieu, A. (2008). *Sigmund Freud: Index thématique* (3rd ed., revised and updated). Paris: Economica Anthropos.

Dreier, O. (2007). *Psychotherapy in everyday life*. New York, NY: Cambridge University Press.

Freud, S. (1908/2001). "Creative writers and day-dreaming." In J. Strachey and A. Freud (Eds.), *Jensen's "Gradiva" and other works*. Vol. 9 of *The Standard Edition of the Complete Psychological Works of Sigmund Freud* (pp. 141–153). London: Vintage. Freud, S. (1910/1957). Five lectures on psychoanalysis. In J. Strachey & A. Freud (Eds.), *Five lectures on psycho-analysis, Leonardo da Vinci and other works*, vol. 11 of *The standard edition of the complete psychological works of Sigmund Freud* (pp. 1–56). London: Hogarth Press and Institute of Psycho-analysis.

Freud, S. (1915–1916/1999). *Conférences d'introduction à la psychanalyse* (J.-B. Pontalis, Ed., F. Cambon, Trans.). Paris: Editions Gallimard/Folio.

Gardner, H. (1993). *Creating minds: An anatomy of creativity seen through the lives of Freud, Einstein, Picasso, Stravinsky, Eliot, Graham, and Gandhi* (Vol. 16). New York, NY: Basic Books.

Gillespie, A., & Zittoun, T. (2013). Meaning making in motion: Bodies and minds moving through in-stitutional and semiotic structures. *Culture & Psychology, 19*(4), 518–532. https://doi.org/10.1177/1354067X13500325.

Glăveanu, V. P. (2011). Children and creativity: A most (un)likely pair? *Thinking Skills and Creativity, 6*(2), 122–131. https://doi.org/10.1016/j.tsc.2011.03.002

Hillenaar, H. (2007). Le créateur littéraire et la fantaisie. *Gradiva, 2*(10), 145–159.

Hviid, P. (2015). Borders in education and living: A case of trench warfare. *Integrative Psychological and Behavioral Science, 50*(1), 44–61. https://doi.org/10.1007/s12124-015-9319-1.

Isaacs, S. (1948). The nature and function of phantasy. *International Journal of Psycho-Analysis, 29*, 73–97.

Leontiev, A. N. (1971). Introduction. In L. S. Vygotsky, *The psychology of art* (pp. 3–6). Cambridge, MA: MIT press.

Martin, J. (2016). Position exchange, life positioning, and creativity. In V. P. Glăveanu (Ed.), *The Palgrave handbook of creativity and culture research* (pp. 243–261). London: Palgrave.

Milner, M. (1950/2010). *On not being able to paint* (E. Letley, Ed.). (2nd revised ed.). London: Routledge.

Salvatore, S. (2016). *Psychology in black and white: The project of a theory driven science*. Charlotte, NC: Information Age.

Salvatore, S., & Zittoun, T. (2011). Outlines of a psychoanalytically informed cultural psychology. In S. Salvatore & T. Zittoun (Eds.), *Cultural psychology and psychoanalysis: Pathways to synthesis* (pp. 3–46). Charlotte, NC: Information Age.

Segal, H. (1991). *Dream, phantasy and art*. London: Routledge.

Singer, D. G., & Singer, J. L. (1992). *The house of make-believe: Children's play and the developing imagination*. Cambridge, MA: Harvard University Press.

Spector Person, E., Fonagy, P., & Figueira, S. A. (Eds.). (1995/2013). *On Freud's "Creative writers and day-dreaming."* London: International Psychanalytical Association/Karnac.

Stenner, P. (2015). Emotion: Being moved beyond the mainstream. In I. Parker (Ed.), *Handbook of critical psychology* (pp. 43–51). Hove, UK: Routledge.

Sternberg, R. J., & Lubart, T. I. (1999). The concept of creativity: Prospects and paradigms. In R. J. Sternberg (Ed.), *Handbook of creativity* (pp. 3–14). Cambridge, UK: Cambridge University Press.

Trosman, H. (1995/2013). A modern view of Freud's "Creative writers and day-dreaming." In E. Spector Person, P. Fonagy, & S. A. Figueira (Eds.), *On Freud's "Creative writers and day-dreaming"* (pp. 33–38). London: International Psychanalytical Association/Karnac.

Valsiner, J. (2017, April). *Unity of the human mind at the age of globalization*. 4th Hans Kilian Preis Lecture presented at the Kilian Price Ceremony, Bochum.

Vygotsky, L. S. (1931/1994). Imagination and creativity of the adolescent. In R. Van der Veer & J. Valsiner (Eds.), *The Vygotsky reader* (pp. 266–288). Oxford: Blackwell.

Vygotsky, L. S. (1971). *The psychology of art*. Cambridge, MA: MIT press.

Winnicott, D. W. (1988). *Human nature*. London: Free Association Books.

Winnicott, D. W. (1989). *Psychoanalytic explorations* (C. Winnicott, R. Shepherd, & M. Davis, Eds.). London: Karnac Books.

Winnicott, D. W. (2001). *Playing and reality*. Philadelphia, PA: Routledge.

Wright, K. (2002). To make experience sing. In L. Caldwell (Ed.), *Art, creativity, living* (pp. 75–96). London: Karnac Books.

Zittoun, T. (2015). Compatibility between early psychoanalysis and pragmatism. In P. J. Rosenbaum (Ed.), *Making our ideas clear: Pragmatism in psychoanalysis* (pp. 23–42). Charlotte, NC: Information Age.

Zittoun, T. (2017). Fantasy and imagination—from psychoanalysis to cultural psychology. In B. Wagoner, I. Bresco de Luna, & S. H. Awad (Eds.), *The psychology of imagination: History, theory and new research horizons* (pp. 137–150). Charlotte, N.C.: Information Age.

Zittoun, T., & Gillespie, A. (2016). *Imagination in human and cultural development*. London: Routledge.

21

Théodule Ribot's *Essay on the Creative Imagination*

A Plea for the Study of Multiple Creativities

CHRISTOPHE MOUCHIROUD AND TODD LUBART

Summary

Théodule Ribot's (1900/1906) *Essay on the Creative Imagination* can be considered the first major work in the field of psychology of creativity in France. Ahead of most of his fellow scientists, Ribot shared with Binet a desire to study "higher" mental processes and to go beyond associationism and its focus on elementary mental processes. In this essay, Ribot considers creativity in ways that can inspire today's scientists. First, creativity is considered as the interaction between intellectual, emotional, and subconscious processes. Second, Ribot emphasizes that creativity can exist beyond the domains of the arts and sciences and proposes a taxonomy of creativity domains, including commercial and moral creativity.

Introduction

Ribot contributed significantly to the birth of psychology as a scientific discipline in France, independent from philosophy. In 1873 he became the first recipient of a French doctorate degree in psychology (Braunstein & Pewzner, 1999; Nicolas, 2002) and in 1885 was the first to teach experimental psychology at the Sorbonne. Ribot not only exposed French psychologists to foreign research, such as the British associationists (Ribot, 1875) and German experimentalists (Ribot, 1879), but he also developed his own psychopathological approach to the study of the mind (see Mouchiroud & Lubart, 2006). He contributed to the field of creativity research late in his career and authored in 1900 *Essay on the*

Creative Imagination, which was translated into English and prefaced in 1906 by Baron. In this chapter, we provide and comment on excerpts from this essay.

Ribot shares essential traits with another French author, Alfred Binet (see Chapters 7 and 24 in this volume), characteristics that place both of them in the French differential psychology school. First, they do not limit experimental psychology to the study of elementary processes like perceptions and sensations, as they explore more complex mental processes (Binet & Henri, 1895), including intelligence and imagination. In this respect, they go further than associationism, which was the dominant trend in psychology at the turn of the 19th century. Another common feature shared by Binet and Ribot is their use of the multivariate approach to model human behavior in general and creativity in particular. They consider that a creative behavior is the result of interacting mental processes (both conscious and subconscious) and that different domains of creative expression should be associated with different combinations of processes, thus the importance of studying the many fields of creative endeavors. Indeed in the introduction of his essay, Ribot stresses the imbalance in studies between fields of creativity, with scientific and artistic domains having been the almost exclusive object of investigations. One of his goals was therefore to demonstrate that many more fields of creative expression exist and that these deserve further scrutiny.

Ribot announces the structure of the book in his introduction, together with a very detailed table of contents: first the analytical section, concerned with the multiple origins of creativity and the creative process (with distinct parts on the intellectual, emotional, and subconscious dimensions, concluding on the need to add a synthetic dimension concerning the interrelations of the previous three), a genetic section, dealing with the development of creativity in its various forms, and a "concrete" section, presenting types of creators and fields of expression.

The richness of Ribot's essay makes it extremely difficult to select the best and most interesting parts. Other enlightening excerpts could have been selected for the present chapter. We decided to illustrate through our choices the diversity of his vision of the creative process, as well as the diversity of the fields in which, according to him, creativity can occur. We offer three excerpts that describe the creative process in its relation to the three dimensions: intellectual, emotional, and subconscious. And we select two presentations of creativity domains that were (and remain today) largely unexplored: the commercial and the moral domain.

Reading: *Essay on the Creative Imagination*

Source: Ribot, T. (1900/1906). *Essay on the creative imagination* (A. H. N. Baron, Trans.). Chicago: Open Court. Selections. Work in the public domain.

Chapter 1: The Intellectual Factor (pp. 25–29)

Association by resemblance presupposes a joint labor of association and dissociation—it is an active form. Consequently it is the principal source of the material of the creative imagination, as the sequel of this work will sufficiently show.

After this rather long but necessary preface, we come to the intellectual factor rightly so termed, which we have been little by little approaching. The essential, fundamental element of the creative imagination in the intellectual sphere is the capacity of thinking by analogy;

that is, by partial and often accidental resemblance. By analogy we mean an imperfect kind of resemblance: like is a genus of which analogue is a species.

Let us examine in some detail the mechanism of this mode of thought in order that we may understand how analogy is, by its very nature, an almost inexhaustible instrument of creation.

1. Analogy may be based solely on the *number of attributes compared*. Let *a b c d e f* and *r s t u d v* be two beings or objects, each letter representing symbolically one of the constitutive attributes. It is evident that the analogy between the two is very weak, since there is only one common element, *d*. If the number of the elements common to both increases, the analogy will grow in the same proportion. But the agreement represented above is not infrequent among minds unused to a somewhat severe discipline. A child sees in the moon and stars a mother surrounded by her daughters. The aborigines of Australia called a book a "mussel," merely because it opens and shuts like the valves of a shellfish.
2. Analogy may have for its basis the *quality* or *value* of the compound attributes. It rests on a variable element, which oscillates from the essential to the accidental, from the reality to the appearance. To the layman, the likeness between cetacians and fishes are great; to the scientist, slight. Here, again, numerous agreements are possible, provided one take no account either of their solidity or their frailty.
3. Lastly, in minds without power, there occurs a semi-unconscious operation that we may call a transfer through the omission of the middle term. There is analogy between *a b c d e* and *g h a i f* through the common letter *a*; between *g h a i f* and *x y f z q* through the common letter *f*; and finally an analogy becomes established between *a b c d e* and *x y f z q* for no other reason than that of their common analogy with *g h a i f*. In the realm of the affective states, transfers of this sort are not at all rare.

Analogy, an unstable process, undulating and multiform, gives rise to the most unforeseen and novel groupings. Through its pliability, which is almost unlimited, it produces in equal measure absurd comparisons and very original inventions.

After these remarks on the mechanism of thinking by analogy, let us glance at the processes it employs in its creative work. The problem is, apparently, inextricable. Analogies are so numerous, so various, so arbitrary, that we may despair of finding any regularity whatever in creative work. Despite this, it seems, however, reducible to two principal types or processes, which are personification, and transformation or metamorphosis.

Personification is the earlier process. It is radical, always identical with itself, but transitory. It goes out from ourselves toward other things. It consists in attributing life to everything, in supposing in everything that shows signs of life—and even in inanimate objects—desires, passions, and acts of will analogous to ours, acting like ourselves in view of definite ends. This state of mind is incomprehensible to an adult civilized man; but it must be admitted, since there are facts without number that show its existence. We do not need to cite them—they are too well known. They fill the works of ethnologists, of travelers in savage lands, of books of mythology. Besides, all of us, at the commencement of our lives, during our earliest childhood, have passed through this inevitable stage of universal animism. Works on child-psychology abound in observations that leave no possible room for doubt on this point. The child endows everything with life, and he does so the more in proportion as he is more imaginative. But this stage, which among civilized people lasts only a brief period, remains in the primitive man a permanent disposition and one that is always active. This process of personification is the perennial fount whence have gushed the greater number of myths, an enormous mass of superstitions, and a large number of aesthetic productions. To sum up in a word, all things that have been invented *ex analogia hominis*.

Transformation or metamorphosis is a general, permanent process under many forms, proceeding not from the thinking subject toward objects, but from one object to another, from one thing to another. It consists of a transfer through partial resemblance. This operation rests on two fundamental bases—depending at one time on vague resemblances (a cloud becomes a mountain, or a mountain a fantastic animal; the sound of the wind a plaintive cry, etc.), or again, on a resemblance with a predominating emotional element: A perception provokes a feeling, and becomes the mark, sign, or plastic form thereof (the lion represents courage; the cat, artifice; the cypress, sorrow; and so on). All this, doubtless, is erroneous or arbitrary; but the function of the imagination is to invent, not to perceive. All know that this process creates metaphors, allegories, symbols; it should not, however, be believed on that account that it remains restricted to the realm of art or of the development of language. We meet it every moment in practical life, in mechanical, industrial, commercial, and scientific invention, and we shall, later, give a large number of examples in support of this statement.

Chapter 2: The Emotional Factor (pp. 37–38)

Whatever the truth may be in this matter, the emotional factor brings about new combinations by several processes. There are the ordinary, simple cases, with a natural, emotional foundation, depending on momentary dispositions. They exist because of the fact that representations that have been accompanied by the same emotional state tend later to become associated: the emotional resemblance reunites and links disparate images. This differs from association by contiguity, which is a repetition of experience, and from association by resemblance in the intellectual sense. The states of consciousness become combined, not because they have been previously given together, not because we perceive the agreement of resemblance between them, but because they have a common emotional note. Joy, sorrow, love, hatred, admiration, ennui, pride, fatigue, etc., may become a center of attraction that groups images or events having otherwise no rational relations between them, but having the same emotional stamp, joyous, melancholy, erotic, etc. This form of association is very frequent in dreams and reveries, i.e., in a state of mind in which the imagination enjoys complete freedom and works haphazard. We easily see that this influence, active or latent, of the emotional factor, must cause entirely unexpected groupings to arise, and offers an almost unlimited field for novel combinations, the number of images having a common emotional factor being very great.

Chapter 3: The Subconscious Factor (pp. 59–62)

These momentary dispositions in latent form can excite novel relations in two ways—through mediate association and through a special mode of grouping which has recently received the name "constellation."

I. Mediate association has been well known since the time of Hamilton, who was the first to determine its nature and to give a personal example that has become classic. Loch Lomond recalled to him the Prussian system of education because, when visiting the lake, he had met a Prussian officer who conversed with him on the subject. His general formula is this: A recalls C, although there is between them neither contiguity nor resemblance, but because a middle term, B, which does not enter consciousness, serves as a transition between A and C. . . .

It is clear that by its very nature mediate association can give rise to novel combinations. Contiguity itself, which is usually only repetition, becomes the source of unforeseen relations, thanks to the elimination of the middle term. Nothing, moreover, proves that there may not sometimes be several latent intermediate terms. It is possible that *A* should call up *D* through the medium of *b* and *c*, which remain below the threshold of consciousness. It seems even impossible not to admit this in the hypothesis of the subconscious, where we see only the two end links of the chain, without being able to allow a break of continuity between them.

II. In his determination of the regulating causes of association of ideas, Ziehen designates one of these under the name of "constellation," which has been adopted by some writers. This may be enunciated thus: The recall of an image, or of a group of images, is in some cases the result of a sum of predominant tendencies.

An idea may become the starting point of a host of associations. The word "Rome" can call up a hundred. Why is one called up rather than another, and at such a moment rather than at another? There are some associations based on contiguity and on resemblance which one may foresee, but how about the rest? Here is an idea *A*; it is the center of a network; it can radiate in all directions—*B, C, D, E, F*, etc. Why does it call up now *B*, later *F*?

It is because every image is comparable to a force, which may pass from the latent to the active condition, and in this process may be reinforced or checked by other images. There are simultaneous and inhibitory tendencies. B is in a state of tension and C is not; or it may be that D exerts an arresting influence on C. Consequently, C cannot prevail. But an hour later conditions have changed and victory rests with C. This phenomenon rests on a physiological basis: the existence of several currents diffusing themselves through the brain and the possibility of receiving simultaneous excitations.

THIRD PART: THE PRINCIPAL TYPES OF IMAGINATION

PRELIMINARY (PP. 179–180)

The expression "creative imagination," like all general terms, is an abbreviation and an abstraction. There is no "imagination in general," but only *men who imagine*, and who do so in different ways; the reality is in them. The diversities in creation, however numerous, should be reducible to types that are *varieties* of imagination, and the determination of these varieties is analogous to that of character as related to will. Indeed, when we have settled upon the physiological and psychological conditions of voluntary activity we have only done a work in *general* psychology. Men being variously constituted, their modes of action bear the stamp of their individuality; in each one there is a personal factor that, whatever its ultimate nature, puts its mark on the will and makes it energetic or weak, rapid or slow, stable or unstable, continuous or intermittent. The same is true of the creative imagination. We cannot know it completely without a study of its varieties, without a special psychology, toward which the following chapters are an attempt.

Chapter 6: The Commercial Imagination (pp. 281–298)

Taking the word "commercial" in its broadest signification, I understand by this expression all those forms of the constructive imagination that have for their chief aim the production and distribution of wealth, all inventions making for individual or collective enrichment. Even less studied than the form preceding, this imaginative manifestation reveals as much ingenuity as any other. The human mind is largely busied in that way. There are inventors of all kinds; the great among these equal those whom general opinion ranks as highest. Here, as elsewhere, the great body invent nothing, live according to tradition, in routine and imitation.

Invention in the commercial or financial field is subject to various conditions with which we are not concerned:

(1) External conditions: Geographical, political, economic, social, etc., varying according to time, place, and people. Such is its external determinism—human and social—here in place of cosmic, physical, as in mechanical invention.

(2) Internal, psychological conditions, most of which are foreign to the primary and essential inventive act: on one hand, foresight, calculation, strength of reasoning; in a word, capacity for reflection; on the other hand, assurance, recklessness, soaring into the unknown—in a word, strong capacity for action. Whence arise, if we leave out the mixed forms, two principal types—the calculating, the venturesome. In the former the rational element is first. They are cautious, calculating, selfish exploiters, with no great moral or social preoccupations. In the latter, the active and emotional element predominates. They have a broader sweep. Of this sort were the merchant-sailors of Tyre, Carthage, and Greece; the merchant-travelers of the Middle Ages, the mercantile and gain-hungry explorers of the fifteenth, sixteenth, and seventeenth centuries; later, in a changed form, the organizers of great companies, the inventors of monopolies, American "trusts," etc. These are the great imaginative minds.

Eliminating, then, from our subject, what is not the purely imaginative element in order to study it alone, I see only two points for us to treat, if we would avoid repetition—at the initial moment of invention, the intuitive act that is its germ; during the period of development and organization, the necessary and exclusive role of schematic images.

By "intuition," we generally understand a practical, immediate judgment that goes straight to the goal. Tact, wisdom, scent, divination, are synonymous or equivalent expressions. First let us note that intuition does not belong exclusively to this part of our subject, for it is found *in parvo* throughout; but in commercial invention it is preponderating on account of the necessity of perceiving quickly and surely, and of grasping chances. "Genius for business," someone has said, "consists in making exact hypotheses regarding the fluctuations of values"; to characterize the mental state is easy, if it is a matter merely of giving examples; very difficult, if one attempts to discover its mechanism.

The physician who in a trice diagnoses a disease, who, on a higher level, groups symptoms in order to deduce a new disease from them, like Duchenne de Boulogne; the politician who knows human nature, the merchant who scents a good venture, etc., furnish examples of intuition. It does not depend on the degree of culture; not to mention women, whose insight into practical matters is well known, there are ignorant people, peasants, even savages who, in their limited sphere, are the equals of fine diplomats.

But all these facts teach us nothing, concerning its psychological nature. Intuition presupposes acquired experience of a special nature that gives the judgment its validity and turns it in a particular direction. Nevertheless, this accumulated knowledge of itself gives no evidence as to the future. Now, every intuition is an anticipation of the future, resulting from only two processes: inductive or deductive reasoning, e.g., the chemist foreseeing a reaction; imagination, i.e., a representative construction. Which is the chief process here? Evidently the former, because it is not a matter of fancied hypothesis, but of adaptation of former experience to a new case. Intuition resembles logical operations much more than it does imaginative combinations. We may liken it to unconscious reasoning, if we are not afraid of the seeming contradiction of this expression which supposes a logical operation without consciousness of the middle term. Although questionable, it is perhaps to be preferred to other proposed explanations such as automatism, habit, "instinct"; "nervous connections"; Carpenter, who as promoter of "unconscious cerebration" deserves to be consulted, likens this state to reflection. In ending, he reprints a letter that John Stuart Mill wrote to him on the subject, in which he says in substance that this capacity is found in persons who have experience and lean toward practical things, but attach little importance to theory.[1]

Every intuition, then, becomes concrete as a judgment, equivalent to a conclusion. But what seems obscure and even mysterious in it is the fact that, from among many possible solutions, it finds at the first shot the proper one. In my opinion this difficulty arises largely from a partial comprehension of the problem. By "intuition" people mean only cases in which the divination is correct; they forget the other, far more numerous, cases that are failures.

The act by which one reaches a conclusion is a special case of it. What constitutes the originality of the operation is not its accuracy, but its *rapidity*—the latter is the essential character, the former accessory. . . .

Besides that initial intuition that shows opportune business and moments, commercial imagination presupposes a well-studied, detailed campaign for attack and defence, a rapid and reliable glance at every moment of execution in order to incessantly modify this plan— *it is a kind of war*.[2] All this totality of special conditions results from a general condition, namely, competition, strife. We shall come back to this point at the end of the chapter.

Let us follow to the end the working of this creative imagination. Like the other forms, this kind of invention arises from a need, a desire—that of the spreading of "self-feeling," of the expansion of the individual under the form of enrichment. But this tendency, and with it the resulting imaginative creation, can undergo changes.

It is a well-known law of the emotional life that what is at first sought as a means may become an end and be desired for itself. Every sensual passion may at length undergo a sort of idealization; people study a science at first because it is useful, and later because of its fascination; and we may desire money in order to spend it, and later in order to hoard it. Here it is the same: the financial inventor is often possessed with a kind of intoxication—he no longer labors for lucre, but for art; he becomes, in his own way, an author of romance. His imagination, set at the beginning toward gain, now seeks only its complete expansion, the assertion and eruption of its creative power, the pleasure of inventing for invention s sake,[3] daring the extraordinary, the unheard-of—it is the victory of pure construction. The natural equilibrium between the three necessary elements of creation—mobility, combination of images, calculation—is destroyed. The rational element gives way, is obliterated, and the speculator is launched into adventure with the possibility of a dazzling success or astounding catastrophe. But let us note well that the primary and sole cause of this change is in the affective and motor element, in an hypertrophy of the lust for power, in an unmeasured and morbid want of expansion of self. Here, as everywhere, the source of invention is the emotional nature of the inventor. . . .

In closing, let us note that financial imagination does not always have as its goal the enriching of an individual or of a closely limited group of associates: it can aim higher, act on greater masses, address itself strenuously to a problem as complex as the reformation of the finances of a powerful state.

All the civilized nations count in their history men who imagined a financial system and succeeded, with various fortunes, in making it prevail. The word "system," consecrated by usage, makes unnecessary any comment, and relates this form of imagination to that of scientists and philosophers. Every system rests on a master-conception, on an ideal, a center about which there is assembled the mental construction made up of imagination and calculation which, if circumstances permit, must take shape, must show that it can live. . . .

We said above that commerce, in its higher manifestations, is a kind of war.[4] Here, then, would be the place to study the military imagination. The subject cannot be treated save by a man of the profession, so I shall limit myself to a few brief remarks based on personal information, or gleaned from authorities. Between the various types of imagination hitherto studied we have shown great differences as regards their external conditions. While the so-called forms of pure imagination, whence esthetic, mythic, religious, mystic creations arise, can realize themselves by submitting to material conditions that are simple and not very exacting, the others can become embodied only when they satisfy an *ensemble* of numerous, inevitable, rigorously determined conditions; the goal is fixed, the materials are rigid, there is little choice of the appropriate means. If there be added to the inflexible laws of nature unforeseen human passions and determinations, as in political or social invention, or the offensive combination of opponents, as in commerce and war; then the imaginative construction is confronted with problems of constantly growing complexity. The most ingenious inventor cannot invent an object as a whole, letting his work develop through an immanent logic: the early plan must be continually modified and readapted; and the difficulty arises not merely from the multiple elements of the problem to be solved, but from ceaseless changes in their positions. So one can advance only step by step, and go forward by calculations and strict examination of possibilities. Hence it results that underneath this thick covering of material and intellectual conditions (calculation, reasoning), spontaneity (the aptness for finding new combinations, "that art of inventing without which we hardly advance"[5] reveals itself to few clear-sighted persons; but, in spite of everything, this creative power is everywhere, flowing like subterranean streams, a vivifying agency. These general remarks, although not applicable exclusively to the military imagination, find their justification in it, because of its extreme complexity. Let us rapidly enumerate, proceeding from without inwards, the enormous mass of representations that it has to move and combine in order to make its construction adequate to reality, able at a precise moment to cease being a dream: (1) Arms, engines, instruments of destruction and supply, varying according to time, place, richness of the country, etc. (2) The equally variable human element—mercenaries, a national army; strong, tried troops or weak and new. (3) The general principles of war, acquired by the study of the masters. (4) More personal is the power of reflection, the habitual solving of tactical and strategic problems. "Battles," said Napoleon, "are thought out at length, and in order to be successful it is necessary that we think several months in regard to what may happen." All the foregoing should be headed "science." Advancing more and more within the secret psychology of the individual, we come to art, the characteristic work of pure imagination. (5) Let us note the exact, rapid intuition at the commencement of the opportune moments. (6) Lastly, the creative element, the conception, a natural gift bearing the hall mark of each inventor. Thus "the Napoleonic esthetics was always derived from a single concept, based on a principle that may be summed up thus: Strict economy wherever it can be done; expenditure without limit on the decisive point. This principle inspires the strategy of the master; it directs everything, especially his battle-tactics, in which it is synthetized and summed up."[6]

Such, in analytical terms, appears the hidden spring that makes everything move, and it is to be attributed neither to experience nor to reasoning, nor to wise combinations, for it arises from the innermost depths of the inventor. "The principle exists in him in a latent state, i.e., in the depths of the unconscious, and unconsciously it is that he applies it, when the shock of the circumstances, of goal and means, causes to flash from his brain the spark stimulating the artistic solution *par excellence*, one that reaches the limits of human perfection."[7]

Chapter 7: The Utopian Imagination (pp. 299–310)

When[8] the human mind creates, it can use only two classes of ideas as materials to embody its idea:

(1) Natural phenomena, the forces of the organic and inorganic worlds. In its scientific form, seeking to explain, to know, it ends in the hypothesis, a disinterested creation. In its industrial aspect, aiming towards application and utilization, it ends in practical, interested inventions.
(2) Human, i.e., psychic elements—instincts, passions, feelings, ideas, and actions. Esthetic creation is the disinterested form, social invention is the utilitarian form.

Consequently, we may say that invention in science resembles invention in the fine arts, both being speculative; and that mechanical and industrial invention approaches social invention through a common tendency toward the practical. I shall not insist on this distinction, which, to be definite, rests only on partial characters; I merely wish to mention that invention, whose role in social, political and moral evolution is large, must, in order to be a success, adopt certain processes while neglecting others. This the Utopians do not do. The development of human societies depends on a multitude of factors, such as race, geographic and economic conditions, war, etc., which we need neither enumerate nor study. One only belongs to our topic—the successive appearance of idealistic conceptions that, like all other creations of mind, tend to realize themselves, the moral ideal consisting of new combinations arising from the predominance of one feeling, or from an unconscious elaboration (inspiration), or from analogy.

At the beginning of civilizations we meet semi-historic, semi-legendary persons Manu, Zoroaster, Moses, Confucius, etc., who were inventors or reformers in the social and moral spheres. That a part of the inventions attributed to them must be credited to predecessors or successors is probable; but the invention, no matter who is its author, remains none the less invention. We have said elsewhere, and may repeat, that the expression *inventor* in morals may seem strange to some, because we are imbued with the notion of a knowledge of good and evil that is innate, universal, bestowed on all men and in all times. If we admit, on the other hand, as observation compels us to do, not a ready-made morality, but a morality in the making, it must be, indeed, the *creation* of an individual or of a group. Everybody recognizes inventors in geometry, in music, in the plastic and mechanic arts; but there have also been men who, in their moral dispositions, were very superior to their contemporaries, and were promoters, initiators.[9] For reasons of which we are ignorant, analogous to those that produce a great poet or a great painter, there arise moral geniuses who feel strongly what others do not feel at all, just as does a great poet, in comparison with the crowd. But it is not enough that they feel: they must create, they must realize their ideal in a belief and in rules of conduct accepted by other men. All the founders of great religions were inventors of this kind. Whether the invention comes from themselves alone, or from a collectivity of which they are the sum and incarnation, matters little. In them moral invention has found its complete form; like all invention, it is organic. The legend relates that Buddha, possessed with the desire of finding the perfect road of salvation for himself and all other men, gives himself up, at first, to an extravagant asceticism. He perceives the uselessness of this and renounces it. For seven years he meditates, then he beholds the light. He comes into possession of knowledge of the means that give freedom from *Karma* (the chain of causes and effects), and from the necessity of being born again. Soon he renounces the life of contemplation, and during fifty years of ceaseless wanderings preaches, makes converts, organizes his followers. Whether true or false historically, this tale is psychologically exact. A fixed and besetting idea, trial followed by failure, the decisive moment of *Eureka!* Then the inner revelation manifests itself outwardly, and through the labors of the master and his disciples becomes complete, imposes itself on millions of men. In what respect does this mode of creation differ from others, at least in the practical order?

Thus, from the viewpoint of our present study, we may divide ethics into living and dead. Living ethics arise from needs and desires, stimulate an imaginative construction that becomes fixed in actions, habits and laws; they offer to men a concrete, positive ideal which, under various and often contrary aspects, is always happiness. The lifeless ethics, from which invention has withdrawn, arise from reflection upon, and the rational codification of, living ethics. Stored away in the writings of philosophers, they remain theoretical, speculative, without appreciable influence on the masses, mere material for dissertation and commentary.

In proportion as we recede from distant origins the light grows, and invention in the social and moral order becomes manifest as the work of two principal categories of minds—the fantastic, the positive. The former, purely imaginative beings, visionaries, Utopians, are closely related to poets and artists. The latter, practical creators or reformers, capable of organizing, belong to the family of inventors in the industrial-commercial-mechanical order.

The chimerical form of imagination, applied to the social sciences, is the one that, taking account neither of the external determinism nor of practical requirements, spreads out freely. Such are the creators of ideal republics, seeking for a lost or to-be-discovered-in-the-future golden age, constructing, as their fancy pleases, human societies in their large outlines and in their details. They are social novelists, who bear the same relation to sociologists that poets do to critics. Their dreams, subjected merely to the conditions of an inner logic, have lived only within themselves, an ideal life, without ever passing through the test of application. It is the creative imagination in its unconscious form, restrained to its first phase. Nothing is better known than their names and their works: the *Republic* of Plato, Thomas More's *Utopia*, Campanula's *City of the Sun*, Harrington's *Oceana*, Fenelon's *Salente*, etc. However idealistic they may be, one could easily show that all the materials of their ideal are taken from the surrounding reality, they bear the stamp of the *milieu*, be it Greek, English, Christian, etc., in which they lived, and it should not be forgotten that in the Utopians everything is not chimerical—some have been revealers, others have acted as stimuli or ferments. True to its mission, which is to make innovations, the constructive imagination is a spur that arouses; it hinders social routine and prevents stagnation. . . .

With practical inventors and reformers the ideal falls—not that they sacrifice it for their personal interests, but because they have a comprehension of possibilities. The imaginative construction must be corrected, narrowed, mutilated, if it is to enter into the narrow frame of the conditions of existence, until it becomes adapted and determined. This process has been described several times, and it is needless to repeat it here in other terms. Nevertheless, the ideal—understanding by this term the unifying principle that excites creative work and supports it in its development—undergoes metamorphosis and must be not only individual but collective; the creation does not realize itself save through a "communion of minds," by a co-operation of feelings and of wills; the work of one conscious individual must become the work of a social consciousness. That form of imagination, creating and organizing social groups, manifests itself in various degrees according to the tendency and power of creators. There are the founders of small societies, religious in form—the Essenes, the earliest Christian communities, the monastic orders of the Orient and Occident, the great Catholic or Mohammedan congregations, the semi-lay, semi-religious sects like the Moravian Brotherhood, the Shakers, Mormons, etc. Less complete because it does not cover the individual altogether in all the acts of life is the creation of secret associations, professional unions, learned societies, etc. The founder conceives an ideal of complete living or one limited to a given end, and puts it into practice, having for material men grouped of their free choice, or by co-optation.

There is invention operating on great masses—social or political invention strictly so called—ordinarily not proposed but imposed, which, however, despite its coercive power, is subject to requirements even more numerous than mechanical, industrial, or commercial invention. It has to struggle against natural forces, but most of all against human forces—inherited habits, customs, traditions. It must make terms with dominant passions and ideas, finding its justification, like all other creation, only in success.

Without entering into the details of this inevitable determination, which would require useless repetition, we may sum up the role of the constructive imagination in social matters by saying that it has undergone a regression—i.e., that its area of development has been little by little narrowed; not that inventive genius, reduced to pure construction in images, has suffered an eclipse, but on its part it has had to make increasingly greater room for experiment, rational elements, calculation, inductions and deductions that permit foresight—for practical necessities. If we omit the spontaneous, instinctive, semiconscious invention of the earliest ages, that was sufficient for primitive societies, and keep to creations that were the result of reflection and of great pretension, we can roughly distinguish three successive periods:

(I)   A very long idealistic phase (Antiquity, Renaissance) when triumphed the pure imagination, and the play of the free fancy that spends itself in social novels. Between the creation of the mind and the life of contemporary society there was no relation; they were worlds apart, strangers to one another. The true Utopians scarcely troubled themselves to make applications. Plato and More—would they have wished to realize their dreams?

(II)   An intermediate phase, when an attempt is made to pass from the ideal to the practical, from pure speculation to social facts. Already, in the eighteenth century, some philosophers (Locke, Rousseau) drew up constitutions, at the request of interested persons. During this period, when the work of the imagination, instead of merely becoming fixed in books, tends to become objectified in acts, we find many failures and some successes. Let us recall the fruitless attempts of the "phalansteries" in France, in Algeria, Brazil, and in the United States. Robert Owen was more fortunate;[10] in four years he reformed New Larnak, after his ideal, and with varying fortune founded short-lived colonies. Saint-Simonism has not entirely died out; the primitive civilization after his ideal rapidly disappeared, but some of his theories have filtered into or have become incorporated with other doctrines.

(III) A phase in which imaginative creation becomes subordinated to practical life: The conception of society ceases to be purely idealistic or constructed a priori by deduction from a single principle; it recognizes the conditions of its environment, adapts itself to the necessities of its development. It is the passage from the absolutely autonomous state of the imagination to a period when it submits to the laws of a rational imperative. In other words, the transition from the esthetic to the scientific, and especially the practical, form. Socialism is a well-known and excellent example of this. Compare its former Utopias, down to about the middle of the last century, with its contemporary forms, and without difficulty we can appreciate the amount of imaginative elements lost in favor of an at least equivalent quantity of rational elements and positive calculations.

1. Carpenter, *Mental Physiology*, chapter XI (end).
2. "C'est une forme de la guerre" (Italics in the original French version. We propose an alternative translation: "it is one form war can have.")
3. This condition has been well-described by various novelists, among them Zola, in *Money*.
4. A general, a former professor in the War College, told me that when he heard a great merchant tell of the quick and sure service of his commercial information, the conception of the whole, and the care in all the details of his operations, he could not keep from exclaiming, "Why, that is war!"
5. Leibniz.
6. Bonnal (1899). *Les maîtres de la guerre* [The war masters]. Paris: Montgredien (p. 137).
7. [Bonnal (1899)], p. 6.
8. [The] title, as will be seen later, corresponds only in part to the contents of this chapter.
9. In support, see the Psychology of Emotions (Ribot, 1896), Second Part, chapter VIII, p. 300.
10. For an excellent account of the principles of these movements, see Rae, *Contemporary Socialism*; for Owen's ideals, his *Autobiography*; and for an account of some of the trials, Bushee's "Communistic Societies in the United States," *Political Science Quarterly*, vol. XX, pp. 625 ff.—*Trans.*

Commentary

When explaining the title of his essay, Ribot defines imagination as the ability to image, to form representations. There is a progression, he writes, a continuum between reproduction and production of representations, the first only representing reality, whereas the other is based on mental images. Thus the usefulness to differentiate creative (or productive) and reproductive forms of imaging. Later, the Gestalt psychologist Wertheimer (1945) distinguished also reproductive from "productive thinking" in his description of the creative process. For Ribot, not enough attention had been devoted to creative imagination, whereas reproductive imagination was largely explored by his fellow psychologists.

There are several theses in Ribot's essay that are still useful for today's creativity scientists. First is the idea of studying creativity as a combination of mental processes and resources, constrained by external (environmental) forces—later referred to as, for instance, the multivariate approach to creativity (Lubart, Mouchiroud, Tordjman & Zenasni, 2015). He calls specifically for the birth of a "special psychology" (1900/1906, p. 180) that would take into account the individual differences in the creative process.

The study of creative processes should be pursued along three paths: *intellectual*, *emotional*, and *subconscious*. Concerning the intellectual dimension, Ribot, along with Claparède (1903), remarks that previous studies have overly emphasized associative processes to the detriment of dissociative processes, such as the ability to sort out sensory information, an ability later named *selective encoding*.[1] He states that dissociative processes have two origins: internal, such as the practical usefulness of the information, and external, relating to the individual's experience. Conversely, a key associative feature is the ability to form analogies, defined by Ribot as "an imperfect form of similarity." Analogies are produced by two means: (1) through "personification," as when we assume that objects and beings around us have desires, passions, and wills similar to ours (invention *ex analogia hominis* that can be traced to the child's universal animism, which some adults are still able to utilize), and (2) through transformation and metamorphosis, from one object to another, with links based on partial similarities as well as through mediated associations. At times relations are established via emotions, whose influence on the creative process is also discussed (see excerpt pp. 37–38). Indeed Ribot acknowledged fully the importance

---

1. Gestalt psychologists will later devote a great deal of attention to dissociation processes.

of affect in the creative process (stating repeatedly that emotions are the primary factors in creativity), together with the interplay between intellect and affect. More specifically, he recognized that both positive and negative emotions could influence creative performance. He developed also the idea of emotions as mediators for creative associations, a proposition later modeled by Lubart and Getz (1997).

The third factor worth investigating is the role of the unconscious. Ribot saw the unconscious as responsible for the occurrence of mediated associations, themselves key sources of creative behaviors. In his view, this unconscious work concerns mainly the part of the process later called the illumination phase (Wallas, 1926). The "reality" of this unconscious work could be evidenced, he says, because among other aspects it could be altered experimentally with psychotropics. However, Ribot is well aware that invoking unconscious processes will make it difficult to expose them scientifically. Later, as he presents intuition (1900/1906, p. 283), he defines it as "unconscious reasoning," underlying the puzzling usage of an oxymoron. The role of chance is also discussed, but only with relation to conscious work; in the same vein as the French scientist Pasteur, Ribot wrote, "Chance luck happens only to those who deserve it" (p. 137).[2]

A second thesis in Ribot's essay is that we must take into account the plural nature of creative expression. First, creativity should not be considered an exclusive ability, given only to the rare "gifted" or geniuses. Ribot is a clear advocate of the "little-c big-C continuum" ("Every normal person creates little or much," he writes, and "Invention is . . . unduly limited when we attribute it to great inventors only" [1900/1906, p. 156]). One of the reasons why we must consider minor forms of creativity is that they are numerous in some domains, such as the practical/mechanical domain in his taxonomy.

For Ribot, creativity should not be considered a general ability, applicable to any domain of expression. Rather, one should explore creative abilities and specificities in each domain. But how to define those domains of creativity? One separation is proposed between two general forms, aesthetic inventions versus "practical inventions" (1900/1906, p. 37). This may relate to the importance given to adaptation, one of the main components of creativity. Indeed Ribot sees more constraints in creative expressions in practical domains than in artistic ones.[3]

RIBOT'S TYPOLOGY OF FORMS OF CREATIVE IMAGINATION

First Ribot noted that genius appears at different ages depending on the domain. Musicians are generally more precocious (12–13 years old) than poets (16 years) or scientists (20 years). Later, Simonton (1997) will successfully test this idea of specific trends in creativity paths depending on the domain. Ribot interpreted this form of variation in terms of the "psychological conditions" necessary for the development of each form of imagination. For example, he argued that the acquisition of musical sounds is anterior to speech—a hypothesis that is still considered in developmental linguistics (see, e.g., Brandt, Slevc, & Gebrian, 2012)—so this could explain the earlier burst of creativity in music. Let us consider the typology proposed by Ribot.

---

2. "Le hasard heureux n'arrive qu'à ceux qui le méritent."
3. Yet Ribot notes that even art springs from a need. We could actually see art as a very practical invention, to fight our melancholia or fear of death (cf. terror management theory, derived from Becker's [1973] work). As Le Clezio stated, "One day we will find out that there was no art, but only medicine" (our translation, cited in Deleuze & Guattari, 1991, p 163).

The first two forms of imagination are artistic: *plastic imagination*, based on images ("It is the imagination that materializes" [1900/1906, p. 184]), thus on perceptions and (spatial) sensations more than affects, is opposed to *diffuse* ("diffluente") *imagination*, a form that uses images between perceptions and concepts—coined emotional abstracts. Examples of plastic imagination can be found in painters, sculptors, but also poets or writers such as Victor Hugo, who, Ribot says, writes almost exclusively about visions and motions. Examples of diffuse imagination are impressionists in painting or symbolists in music.

Next, Ribot argued for the existence of three additional subtypes of diffuse imagination. First, he proposes *numerical imagination*, supported by the symbolic uses of numerals as well as large numbers in religions and myths. A second type of diffuse form is *musical imagination*, a form that is very much dependent on culture. Last he proposed *mystical imagination*. Here perceptions and sensations are considered useless and reasoning fallacious, which led Ribot to consider this type as a pure form of diffuse imagination.

Scientific imagination is presented next. It includes different subtypes, such as geometry, chemistry, and physics. All proceed from three basic steps: to observe, to hypothesize, and to verify. Ribot underlined the need for more studies on each of the subtypes.

The seventh form is *practical* or *mechanical imagination*, broadly defined as "inventive capacity as applied to practical life" (1900/1906, p. 258). This form is conceived as depending in large part on flexibility. Ribot cites an anonymous engineer who proposed four steps in this creative domain, a sequential model that closely matched Wallas's (1926; see also Chapter 2 in this volume): problem-finding, incubation, birth of the solution, and finalization. Ribot insisted that the last step was not the least, but rather the most difficult part, because one needs an unusual degree of perseverance in adjusting every detail of the solution. Practical imagination leads both to little-c and big-C creativity, Ribot says, and is the largest domain of creativity in terms of quantity of productions (1900/1906, p. 275).

We reproduced large excerpts of the last two domains, *commercial* and *utopian imagination*s. *Commercial imagination* is described in military terms ("a well-studied, detailed campaign for attack and defense" [1900/1906, p. 289]), and this resemblance gives Ribot the opportunity to discuss *military imagination*. Just like warfare, commercial imagination is characterized both by intuition and the ability to draw precise hypotheses on the fluctuation of market values. Contrary to previous types, Ribot argued, commercial imagination leads to a protean form of creation, as the initial plan must be constantly readjusted. When it comes to explaining the motivational aspects of this form of creativity, Ribot puts first the nonrational aspect ("a hypertrophy of the lust for power, in an unmeasured and morbid want of expansion of self" [p. 241]). His moral position toward commercial imagination is similar to that of Aristotle, who coined the word *chrematistics* to describe and criticize the accumulation of wealth for its own sake instead of as a medium for trade exchanges.

Yet commercial imagination can have a social goal, when an individual or a group is able to design and convince a community to use a new financial system. The example of John Law, the Scottish economist and financial inventor, creator of the first central bank in 1716 in France, is then presented.

The last type is *utopian imagination* and specifically concerns the social and moral domains. Like commercial imagination, it is heavily constrained by external forces. According to Ribot, this form of imagination stems from the fact that moral judgment is not innate, but socially constructed. Simply stated, morality is a social invention. Examples illustrate this form, as the individuals who in some ancient cultures were forerunners in opposing human sacrifice, or in the personal story of prophets and philosophers like Buddha, who took years of solitary reflection to devise a novel philosophical system and devoted the rest of his life to its practice and transmission. Even though this form of creativity relates to more recent constructs, such as collective creativity (Family, 2003), moral creativity (Gruber, 1993; Runco & Nemiro, 2003), and social and societal creativity (Glăveanu, 2015; Mouchiroud & Lubart, 2002; Mouchiroud & Zenasni, 2013), the amount of research in this domain remains scarce in psychology, even though its social significance is clear.

Ribot was a precursor in acknowledging both the interplay between cognitive and affective processes in creativity and the interaction between abilities and fields of expression. Accordingly, creative expression depends on an individual profile of creative abilities and resources, that will meet (or not) a creative domain that matches (or not) the individual profile. This conception of the creative process provides a coherent and heuristic framework for today's research in creativity, in the same vein as the multivariate approach (Lubart et al., 2015). Finally, Ribot's comment on the imbalance between the amount of studies devoted to creativity in arts and sciences compared to other domains remains a valid observation and a call for today's scientists to explore those fields.

References

Becker, E. (1973). *The denial of death*. New York, NY: Simon & Schuster.

Binet, A., & Henri, V. (1895). La psychologie individuelle [Individual psychology]. *L'Année Psychologique*, 2, 415–465.

Brandt, A. K., Slevc, R., & Gebrian, M. (2012). Music and early language acquisition. *Frontiers in Psychology*, 3, ArtID 327, 1–17, doi: 10.3389/fpsyg.2012.00327.

Braunstein, J.-F., & Pewzner, E. (1999). *Histoire de la psychologie* [History of psychology]. Paris: Colin.

Claparède, E. (1903). *L'association des idées* [The association of ideas]. Paris: Doin.

Deleuze, G., & Guattari, F. (1991). *Qu'est-ce que la philosophie?* [What is philosophy?]. Paris: Editions de Minuit.

Family, G. (2003). Collective creativity: A complex solution for the complex problem of the state of our planet. *Creativity Research Journal*, 15(1), 83–90.

Glăveanu, V. P. (2015). Developing society: Reflections on the notion of societal creativity. In A.-G. Tan & C. Perleth (Eds.), *Creativity, culture, and development* (pp. 183–200). Singapore: Springer.

Gruber, H. E. (1993). Creativity in the moral domain: Ought implies can implies create. *Creativity Research Journal*, 6(1–2), 3–15.

Lubart, T. I., & Getz, I. (1997). Emotion, metaphor, and the creative process. *Creativity Research Journal*, 10, 285–301.

Lubart, T. I., Mouchiroud, C., Tordjman, S., & Zenasni, F. (2015). *La psychologie de la créativité* [Psychology of creativity]. Paris: Armand Colin.

Mouchiroud, C., & Lubart, T. I. (2002). Social creativity: A cross-sectional study of 6- to 11-year-old children. *International Journal of Behavioral Development*, 26(1), 60–69.

Mouchiroud, C., & Lubart, T. I. (2006). Past, present, and future perspectives on creativity in France and French-speaking Switzerland. In R. J. Sternberg & J. C. Kaufman (Eds.), *International handbook of creativity* (pp. 96–123). Cambridge, UK: Cambridge University Press.

Mouchiroud, C, & Zenasni, F. (2013). Individual differences in the development of social creativity. In M. Taylor (Ed.), *The Oxford handbook of the development of imagination* (pp. 387–402). New York, NY: Oxford University Press.

Nicolas, S. (2002). *Histoire de la psychology française: Naissance d'une nouvelle science* [History of French psychology: Birth of a new science]. Paris: In Press Editions.

Ribot, T. (1875). *La psychologie anglaise contemporaine (Ecole expérimentale)* [Contemporary English psychology (experimental school)]. Paris: Ladrange.

Ribot, T. (1879). *La psychologie allemande contemporaine (Ecole expérimentale)* [Contemporary German psychology (experimental school)]. Paris: Germer Baillière.

Ribot, T. (1896). *La psychologie des sentiments* [The psychology of emotions]. Paris: Alcan.

Ribot, T. (1900/1906). *Essay on the creative imagination* (A. H. N. Baron, Trans.). Chicago: Open Court.

Runco, M. A., & Nemiro, J. (2003). Creativity in the moral domain: Integration and implications. *Creativity Research Journal, 15*, 91–105.

Simonton, D. K. (1997). Creative productivity: A predictive and explanatory model of career trajectories and landmarks. *Psychological Review, 104*, 66–89.

Wallas, G. (1926). *The art of thought*. New York, NY: Harcourt, Brace.

Wertheimer, M. (1945). *Productive thinking*. New York, NY: Harper.

22

On Bartlett's (1928)
"Types of Imagination"

Tania Zittoun

Summary

Known for his work on memory, Sir Frederick C. Bartlett also repeatedly wrote about imagination as part of his attempt to understand the dynamics of mind. Bartlett's 1928 text explores autobiographical and literary material so as to identify three types of imagination (assimilative, creative, and constructive) on a continuum, depending on how passive or intentional these are. This chapter discusses how three of Bartlett's propositions have been taken on by research: processes of imagination, typology of people, and methodological choices. Finally, it is proposed that researchers pursue the exploration of variations of processes involved in imagination as proposed by Bartlett, as well as his original methodologies.

Introduction

Sir Frederick C. Bartlett (1896–1969) was a psychologist known mostly for his work on memory. Trained in philosophy, sociology, and ethics, he worked all his life at the University of Cambridge, where he directed the Psychological Laboratory from 1922 on, and remained in constant dialogue with the scholars (anthropologists, philosophers) of his time (Rosa, 1996; Wagoner, 2017b). His core contribution is the idea that mind is constructive, that is, that remembering or imagining is based on a multitude of experiences transformed, following specific processes, according to the person's past trajectories as well as social and cultural norms (Wagoner, 2017a, 2017b). Imagination was a subject of interest for Bartlett since his first experimental studies published in 1916, where he exposed people to inkblots—among other tests—and documented their associations. Variations of these studies appear in 1921 and 1925 and are summarized in Bartlett's (1932/1995, Chapter 2) seminal book.[1] There his analysis is based on the variety of associations "projected" and reflecting people's interests and occupation. He proposes to distinguish two types of respondents, the first one citing specific images, either emotionally charged or simply lively detailed, from a second group, who propose generalizing and distanced answers (Bartlett, 1932/1995, pp. 39–43).

Bartlett was in search of general theoretical explanations that could account for the variations he observed. It is thus that we can read his 1928 paper "Types of imagination," which examines dominances in people's ways of imagining. In this paper, Bartlett refers not to experiments but exclusively to autobiographical material from writers and scientists. The paper's core argument is a distinction between three types of imagination: an "assimilative imagination," mainly based on emotional resonance and associations triggered by external events; a "creative interpretation," which demands resonance but is also an active re-creation of someone else's proposition; and a "constructive imagination," in which it is a person's intentionality that guides and organizes the process of imagining.

Reading: "Types of Imagination"

Source: Bartlett, F. C. (1928). Types of imagination. *Journal of Philosophical Studies*, 3(9), 78–85. © Royal Institute of Philosophy, published by Cambridge University Press, reproduced with permission.

At first sight it may seem as if Imagination can easily be characterized as a continuous process of having images; but this is very soon found to be inadequate and misleading. On the one hand we have a great number of good witnesses who insist that in their best imaginative work they have made use of no images, or of very few; and on the other, everybody makes [a] distinction between flights of fancy, for example, which certainly involve successions of images, and true imagination. Perhaps a better method of approach is found when we examine how the material dealt with in the imaginative process is built together. In the flight of fancy image follows image, and the transition from one to the next seems to be determined by something in the nature of each individual step of the whole chain, or by each individual act of imaging. Thus the train as a whole is very apt, to the outsider, to appear jerky, ill-connected, having little internal consistency, though from each step to the next the connexion may be more or less evident. The sequence presents the characteristics of what is now generally called free association. In imagination the bond is to be found in the whole imaginative structure considered in its completeness. A plan or programme is at work which cannot be found by any amount of analysis of any separate bit of the material dealt with. It is both interesting and important to try to understand the kind of links that may build together the material used by imaginative processes, whether this material consist of images or not. Such a quest may help to define significant differences between types of imagination, and may thus help to throw light upon the parts played by imaginative effort in the mental life of man.

---

1. In these studies, Bartlett presents people with 36 inkblot cards, face down. He asks them to turn one card at a time and say whatever comes to mind: "Here are a number of ink-blots. They represent nothing in particular, but might recall almost anything. See what you can make of them, as you sometimes find shapes for clouds, or see faces in a fire" (Bartlett, 1932/1995, p. 34). He describes how the subjects hold these cards at arm's length and try to make sense of them.

First, then, we may take a relatively simple and fundamental form which may be called assimilative imagination.

This is best characterized by illustration. At the beginning of his profoundly interesting book, *Long Ago and Far Away*,[1] W. H. Hudson tells how he came to write an autobiography:

> I was feeling weak and depressed when I came down from London one November evening to the south coast: the sea, the clear sky, the light colours of the afterglow kept me too long on the front in an east wind in that low condition, with the result that I was laid up for six weeks with a very serious illness.

This was the beginning of a remarkable and protracted imaginative state of mind.

> On the second day of my illness, during an interval of comparative ease, I fell into recollections of my childhood, and at once I had that far, forgotten past with me again as I had never previously had it. It was not like that mental condition, known to most persons, when some sight or sound or, more frequently, the perfume of some flower associated with our early life restores the past suddenly and so vividly that it is almost an illusion. That is an intensely emotional condition, and vanishes as quickly as it comes. This was different. It was as if the cloud shadows and haze had passed away and the entire wide prospect beneath me made clearly visible. Over it all my eyes could range at will, choosing this or that point to dwell upon, to examine it in all its details; or in the case of some person known to me as a child to follow his life till it ended or passed from sight; then to return to the same point again to repeat the process with other lives and resume my rambles in the old familiar haunts.

The vision stayed, and Hudson decided

> to try to save it from the oblivion which would presently cover it again. Propped up with pillows, I began with pencil and writing-pad to put it down in some sort of order, and went on with it at intervals during the whole six weeks of my confinement, and in this way produced the first rough draft of my book.

In this case the materials for the imaginative reconstruction of the artist came from the treasury of his own early experiences. He took them as they came and shaped them afresh. But the material may just as well come from other sources. In *Years of Childhood*[2] Aksakoff records how, as a very young boy, he went with his mother to visit some friends, and there made his first acquaintance with *The Arabian Nights*. No other book, he says, had ever aroused in him such sympathy and interest. He read the stories whenever he could, and was always completely absorbed by them. Once his mother, having searched for him everywhere, at length found him in his bedroom, so carried away by what he read that he had neither eyes nor ears for anything else. He did not notice that she had come into the room. She went out and fetched somebody else, and still the young Aksakoff remained entirely unaware of their presence. He was, as he says, "lost in a world of dreams."

This kind of rare imaginative sympathy is sometimes produced by material of a very different order, as in the famous story of how Malebranche found a copy of Descartes's *De*

Homine on a second-hand stall. He read, and as he read his breath came fast, and his heart beat so furiously that for awhile he found that he must put the book aside.

There is indeed no limit to the kind of object upon which the assimilative imagination may foster. A picture, a poem, a stage-play, a work in marble, a building, religious belief, intellectual constructions, the human form or person, a scene of natural beauty—anything, given only the necessary conditions, may set the process going. And what are these necessary conditions?

First there is something that seems most fitly called "a resonance of feeling." A stretched string has its natural period, so that anything near by which is vibrating with that period can set it readily into sympathetic movement. Everybody knows how Helmholtz used this principle in the building of his famous theory of auditory perception. In the inner ear, he pointed out, we have an immensely complicated mechanism, the elements of which all have their natural periods and vibrate in sympathy with the movements of the external air, so giving us the world of sound in which we live. I think it not wholly fanciful to hold that we have with us larger systems of feeling, of memories, of ideas, of aspiration which move when the fit objects appear; and then we capture these objects complete by the assimilative imagination.

There is, however, no process of imagination which is not in some part intellectual, cognitive. In the assimilative imagination there is a cognitive attitude, a direction upon objects or material. This is not, as Hudson points out, arrested and held by particular outstanding detail only. It is directed, without effort of analysis upon a whole situation. It may indeed stay for a time with an item and then move to another, ranging over the whole, now rapidly and now at leisure. But there is no search to find out how the whole is built. There is no instructed picking out of this and rejection of that. The situation stands before the dreamer and he takes it all in. This is a type of cognitive attitude which psychology shows to be extremely fundamental, extremely primitive.

Further, in assimilative imagination there is a complete absence of criticism. The dreamer does not weigh and value the material with which he deals. He and it are for the time being in a kind of functional unity, so that there is no question of its doing one thing and his doing another. There is no part of him withheld from his material. He is, as we say, for the time "rapt," "carried away," and has no reserves. But this does not mean that the situation which awakens his dream is merely assimilated without change. There is nothing in human imagination, at whatsoever level, that is dead and changeless. It is altered, but the person who alters it is as surprised as anybody else to know what he has done. His *criticism* has not produced the change, but those deep-lying tendencies which are at the basis of his psychological life, and which work always, though he may not know what they are doing. This is beautifully illustrated by Aksakoff.

When the little Russian returned from his visit he continued to read the tales, with exactly the same immediate effect. But now he began to repeat them to his sister and his aunt:

> With such burning animation and what may be called such self-forgetfulness that, without being aware of it, I filled out the narratives of Scheherazade with many details of my own invention; I spoke of all I had read, exactly as if I had been on the spot and seen it with my own eyes. When I had excited the attention and curiosity of my two hearers, I began, complying with their wishes, to read the book to them aloud; and then my own additions were detected and pointed out by my aunt, whose objections were confirmed by my sister. Again and again my aunt stopped me by saying: "What

you told us is not there. How's that? You must have made it up out of your own head. What a story-teller you are! It's impossible to believe you." I was much taken aback by such an accusation and forced to reflect. . . . I was much surprised myself not to find in the book what I believed I had read there and what was firmly fixed in my head. I became more cautious and kept myself in hand until I got excited; when once excited, I forgot all precautions and my heated imagination usurped absolute power.

At this point assimilative imagination comes very near another and, as I would believe, a higher kind, and we get *creative interpretation.*

The singer, the musician playing the works of another, the conductor of a choir or an orchestra, the actor, the poet as he reads poetry, sometimes even the philosopher as he expounds another's thought, may all show a creative effort of interpretation. Here also is that resonance of feeling in which the interpreter and the interpreted are at one. The cognitive attitude is once again directed primarily upon the whole complex construction in which the interpreter is interested. The good actor, for instance, never merely says the single brilliant sentence, or does the single significant action. All his words and actions have the colour and weight of his whole part in all its intricacy of interweaving with other parts. The creative interpreter of another's music is not merely playing a sequence of notes, but is making alive the passion and meaning of the whole. It is the whole that he absorbs and in absorbing reshapes. And he does reshape. The lack of criticism has gone. He, the interpreter, is an integral and leading part of the whole imaginative effort. He now does not quite lose himself. He may even make of his material something greater than it ever was before he came upon it and gave it his stamp.

It is a difficult thing to state the nature of the criticism which is actively present in all creative interpretation. It may perhaps be said that such criticism has no reference to any supposed objective purpose or centre of the work which is being interpreted, but only to the personal experience of the interpreter. He alters, adds, omits, and if he is charged with these things he will say: "Yes, I did all this, though at the time I generally did not know." But if you ask him for his reasons he is dumb, or merely invents. In a way he has no reasons. They are buried in his life.

Perhaps all that type of imagination which we are apt to call "visionary," as, for example, in the work of Plato, the writer of the Book of Job, Vaughan, Blake, Coleridge, Shelley,[3] is really creative interpretation of material, the stuff of which comes in the main from the life and experience of the interpreter himself. The things made by the visionary are like dreams, sometimes are dreams. He is an artist for the moment, and then often drops to the ordinary again like an actor when his play is done. His work is often fragmentary, episodical, the fire of his creation like a leaping flame. He resonates to what is in him, knows it all at once, reshapes it without guessing how, and very soon passes on, a perfectly ordinary being again.

Some, however, are not so. Their vision is not of the moment but of the years. They have the intellectual imagination. "To preserve Romance," says Meredith, "we must be in the heads of our people as well as in the hearts."

This is a very different psychological realm from that of assimilative imagination or creative interpretation. Resonance of feeling now plays but a small part, if any. Lack of analysis and of criticism have gone. We have, in fact, what I would like to call genuine *constructive imagination.* Plan, purpose, some kind of formulated objective aim, now comes to the front. An idea, an aspiration, an interest towards an end achieves articulation, and thereupon ensues a period of hard and conscious endeavour, often long drawn out and alternating with periods in which little or no conscious effort is involved. The material to be dealt with is collected, analysed, evaluated, criticized, set together into its new forms. At this level of imaginative effort an actual sketch of proposed work is often set down by the author long before the final product is complete. Milton in 1643 entered in his notebooks drafts which show that already his plans for a great imaginative poem had set in the direction of *Paradise Lost*. Publication came twenty years later. Darwin began to keep notebooks on the general phenomena of evolution in 1832. Ten years later he made his first rough sketch of what was to become *The Origin of Species*. In 1844 this sketch was considerably expanded. Then for fourteen years he read widely, experimented and observed laboriously, and in 1859 the book was published. He was excessively critical throughout, spoke of his style as "incredibly bad and most difficult to clear," and so heavily corrected his proofs as, according to his own statement, almost to rewrite the book. In 1841 Adams, then an undergraduate at St. John's College, Cambridge, made a memorandum that he would investigate the explanation of the perturbations of the planet Uranus. In 1843 he graduated and began to put his plans into active operation. Two years later he had completed his calculations, which he sent to the Astronomer Royal, and which would, if they had been followed up, have resulted in the earlier discovery of the planet Neptune.

On the other hand, the gap between the articulation of a plan and its full achievement may be very small, as, for instance, in the case of Anthony Trollope. Some of his novels have all the marks of conscious, critical, intellectual imaginative effort. As is well known, he constructed a preliminary "lay out" for most of them, but having completed this, generally set to work on the story immediately and produced it at considerable speed.

The points of importance are: the adumbration of a scheme; the articulation of a plan; the collection of material, not only from past personal experience but notably from all kinds of sources through contemporary observation; the sorting and criticism of the material, and its relating to the central plan. The plan, preformed, shapes all that follows, though at the same time the plan itself grows, changes, may even become very different from what it was at the beginning. It is never in abeyance, however, and all that follows its articulation is significant in relation to it. This fact and the mode of collection of the material give to constructive imagination a cognitive, an objective, intellectual character which is only partially achieved by the other types. The criticism involved is not now that more than half-blind selective stressing, omission, changing of time, colour, balance of form and emotion of creative interpretation. It is dominated by the assignment of more or less definite values to the details of the collected material in relation to the general aim of the work.

In any long-continued effort of constructive imagination there are almost always moments, or stretches, of assimilative imagination and, it may be, of creative interpretation. Very often, indeed, the whole work takes its rise in just such a moment. These vital points can always be easily detected. They carry about them an excitement, an enthusiasm, an emotional quality, often an unexpectedness amounting almost to irrelevance, that are less marked in the main work. "Two things," says Kant, "fill the soul with ever new and increasing admiration and reverence: the starry sky above me and the moral law within me." Many sentences come from Kant with a sudden burst, as if they are warm with a life that is for the most part kept in hiding. All masters of constructive imagination have these bursts. We say of them: "Here is insight," as if their makers are responding to something from within.

In general, however, the constructive imagination is awake to the outside world, collecting details from everywhere and constantly preoccupied, not so much with their character as detail for descriptive purposes as with their interrelations. Thus its scope is wider, its products as a rule vaster, and the architecture of its products generally to the forefront. It depends not upon the single presented datum, or upon the single completed work, but it utilizes a mass of material which it finds as detail and leaves as a completed structure.

What is it that determines to which of these types of imaginative work a man is bent? Very little systematic attempt has been made to answer this important psychological problem. I will hazard a few remarks, stating them with a dogmatism that is far from adequately representing my actual attitude.

The determination of type of imagination is far more a matter of temperament than of training. The assimilative type presupposes predominantly (a) a capacity for wonder and (b) a certain attitude of submissiveness. It is on the whole characteristic of childhood and of somewhat relaxed states of mind. It is of all imaginative work probably the most partial and specialized. Thus it raises in an acute form the vexed question of specialized inherited abilities and interests. It appears most probable that psychologists will have to admit a far more complete furniture of specialized interests operating or ready to operate at very early phases of individual mental life than they have been wont to do. These, combined with a certain readiness to be impressed and a marked degree of submissiveness, give us the temperamental setting of assimilative imagination.

Given the specialized interest, the capacity for wonder, and, instead of submissiveness, a certain active attitude of sympathetic co-operation, and for assimilative imagination we get creative interpretation. The first type produces the acceptor, the second the executor. The kind of "comradeship" attitude of the interpreter towards the material with which he has to deal is difficult to characterize, but it is undeniably of genuine psychological importance. It is an attitude by virtue of which a man is peculiarly reactive to hints, half-formulated or half-articulated desires and statements, filling them out, carrying them farther, putting into them what they mean, and not merely accepting as already in them what they actually say. There is in it neither arrogation of superiority nor acceptance of inferiority. Some people constantly display this attitude in their relationships towards their environment, both social and material. This class contributes the great executants of life in all realms. From it come the creative interpreters.

The third class has a far wider mental range. The capacity for wonder remains as fundamental as ever, but because it has a different temperamental setting it produces exceedingly different results. Submissiveness has gone, and there is less of an attitude of sympathetic fellowship with whatever is the source of the wonder than of mastery. The material dealt with is not simply accepted or interpreted, but is taken as a problem and a challenge; and thus it is used and changed. Dominance is the essential temperamental characteristic of the genuine constructive imagination. It gathers its own material wherever it can, often searching wide fields; and what it gathers it shapes. Sometimes the dominance is confined within its own somewhat specialized field, but more often it bursts out into expression in every part of a man's life, so that its owner is spoken of as "a man to be reckoned with." Thus of all types of imagination, this is the one whose products arouse most opposition, not merely because they are the most original, but because they breathe a certain uncompromising aggressiveness.

---

1. London, 1918.
2. English translation by J. M. Duff. London. 1916.
3. Cf. Walter de la Mare: *Rupert Brooke and the Intellectual Imagination*, London, 1919, p. 13.

Commentary

TRACING BARTLETT'S IDEAS AND THEIR INFLUENCE ON CREATIVITY RESEARCH

Bartlett's text is interesting for various reasons. With reference to existing debates on imagination, he first proposes that imagination is not only visual (it is not only about "images"), and second, he goes beyond the idea that imagination can be either creative or reproductive, an idea durably present in psychology (James, 1890; Ribot, 1900/2007). Third, rather than judging types of imagination mainly based on their social newness of a creative process (e.g., as in later small-c and big-C) or product, Bartlett distinguishes them according to the prevalence in people's conduct, of inner motives, or the demands of social and cultural reality.

Bartlett thus proposes a threefold typology of an imagination which can be visual, musical, sensory, or abstract, and that is organized on a continuum. For Bartlett, imagination always demands some form of thinking or cognition and some anchoring in personal and emotional experience; what varies is only the predominance of one over the other, and the assimilative versus a more active, accommodative, or intentional process, and on the inclusion of the demands of the world. "Assimilative imagination" is all absorbed in a person's experience and is mainly governed by emotional resonance between a situation and a person's life. "Creative imagination," where the idea of being creative rather than relatively passive appears, demands a new synthesis of given material with inner resonance and emotions, yet with some active engagement. Finally, "constructive imagination," which is probably the closest to what others would have called "creative imagination," is active, intentional, distanced from emotions; if it still draws on personal motives, it is now submitted to a larger plan.

It is thus worth highlighting the processes identified here by Bartlett: there is (a) an "idea, an aspiration, an interest toward an end" or "adumbration of a scheme"; this provides (b) "a plan for articulation"; then (c) material is collected from personal experience as well as from "contemporary observation," and criticized, reflected upon, organized according to the plan; (d) the plan is brought to completion, yet it may grow and change or be substantially transformed. As a whole, there might be a very long or shorter gap from the initial intuition to completion, extending to years, and the process may involve phases of the two other types of imagination. For Bartlett, it is first the "mode of collection" of the material which is specific in this type of imagination and which has a "cognitive, an objective, an intellectual character": we could say that this type of thinking process precisely creates distance from the initial personal experience predominant in the two other types. This distance is increased by two other components; first, as mentioned, it is "open to the outside world"; second, it is preoccupied with the "interrelations" between things—it is through these synthetic and creative acts that it gets a "wider scope."

Bartlett concludes the text with three paragraphs distinguishing types of people, following the statement "The determination of type of imagination is far more a matter of temperament than of training." Assimilative imagination thus demands a "capacity to wonder" and submissiveness; when submissiveness is replaced by "sympathetic cooperation" people engage in creative imagination; they may become creative interpreters, a type of "great executants." Constructive imagination demands the capacity to wonder, but neither submissiveness nor sympathetic cooperation, rather "dominance" and its related "uncompromising aggressiveness." Of course one can question this division between leaders and executants and this bossy and lonely model of the misunderstood and focused creator. Although this type of temperament may be taken for granted at this time (Bordogna, 2001)—William James (1907/1975) himself explained different philosophical works based on temperament—it is quickly stated and little supported in Bartlett's paper. It may even appear contradictory with Bartlett's later emphasis on human experience in constructive thinking processes. It is thus not really a surprise that already in *Remembering*, published four years later, Bartlett (1932/1995, p. 39) had a more nuanced hypothesis on this typology of people, writing:

> The relatively set ways of reacting which are illustrated by a given "type" have for the most part, been acquired gradually. We have no right to regard them as psychologically innate, or as absolute psychological starting points, unless we have better reasons for this than mere classification itself.

Bartlett has mainly been remembered as a memory researcher (Van der Veer, 2001); it is only relatively recently that other parts of his work have come to researchers' attention, especially his work of thinking in general, which is now seen as displaying a cultural psychological sensitivity (Rosa, 1996; Wagoner, 2017a). However, his work on imagination and creativity is little discussed. Others after him have, however, proposed analyses that may be inspired by his work on creativity, or more likely, that reflect some part of his propositions.

A first group of studies could reflect Bartlett's interest for the processes involved in the three types of imagination. For instance Wolff (1947) tries to distinguish types of imagination, more or less based on subjective experience, drawing on different cultural material, more or less open to the social world; although he focuses on images, he attempts to identify the processes involved, yet only Bartlett's (1932/1995) *Remembering* book is quoted. Regarding the various types, in later work, the idea of "assimilative imagination" will be reduced to the idea of "absorption" in fiction and the arts (Nell, 1988) and usually dismissed for its passivity, with no idea of a continuum with other forms of imagination or creativity; recent studies in that field look for brain correlates (e.g., Calarco, Fong, Rain, & Mar, 2017). "Creative interpretation" has been examined, for instance, in the domain of music, where it has been argued that both listening and playing require creativity and imagination (Hargreaves, Hargreaves, & North, 2012; Hargreaves, MacDonald, & Miell, 2012; Hargreaves, Miell, & MacDonald, 2012), but it does not seem that these studies refer to Bartlett's work either. "Constructive imagination" is probably what has been recently most explored by creativity research, where current studies propose relatively similar understanding of the creative process: emphasis on an overall view, cultivation and critical examination of material, time for the process, openness to the world and subjective involvement, evolution of the project, etc. (Sternberg, 2016; Tanggaard, 2014). Here again it is hard to find any mention of Bartlett's work on imagination.

A second group of studies explores not the process but the typology of people imagining, or personality components. A rare mention of Bartlett's 1928 paper can be found in a study on mental economy in imagination (Havelka, 1968). More frequently, types of imagination are further distinguished (Hunter, 2013) or personality types are examined in links to creative performances (Barron & Harrington, 1981), yet without reference to Bartlett. However, the role of personality in creativity has become less important in research (Runco, 2004), with, of course, exceptions (e.g. Liang & Lin, 2015).

A third potential development of Bartlett's work regards his methodological choices. As head of an experimental laboratory, Bartlett gave quite a bit of attention to methodological techniques; he himself devised a wide range of methods, some of them, such as the guided reproduction, are currently revalorized in cultural psychology (Wagoner, 2009; Wagoner & Gillespie, 2014; Wagoner & Jensen, 2015). Bartlett (1950) seemed to have privileged experimental studies later in his life, as a programmatic paper for the study of intelligence suggests. The original demonstration made in 1928, that is, the use of autobiographic novels, letters, and diaries, has, however, not been explicitly highlighted. It is therefore interesting to note that Bartlett first engaged in experiments to trigger people's imagination (inkblots), identified interesting variations, and only then expanded his first intuitions and exemplified them through autobiographical and literary material used as qualitative data. The fragmented aspects identified in local experiments thus become part of a more meaningful whole through these richer, case-study-based materials. To my knowledge, this specific methodological move, and its implicit abductive quality, has not been highlighted sufficiently. Even more, it may be that even authors who have analyzed the creativity of specific artists and scientists through their work (Gardner, 1993) or through interviews with creative people (Csikszentmihalyi, 1997) have first undertaken case studies, then turned their analysis into dimensions to be more systematically tested. Other studies made the more explicit choice to focus on autobiographical material to access processes of thinking and imagination (Gillespie & Zittoun, 2010; Valsiner, 2014; Zittoun & Gillespie, 2012, 2016; Zittoun et al., 2013)—yet here also, with no explicit mention of Bartlett.

NEW DIRECTIONS OF RESEARCH BASED ON THESE HISTORICAL INSIGHTS

Bartlett's work has been largely discussed, his work on memory and thinking valorized (Wagoner, 2017a), and his theory of schemes criticized (Van der Veer, 2001). Little has so far been said on his explorations of imagination and the creative process (see, e.g., Wagoner & Glăveanu, 2016). It might be that this was a side issue for the author, or that his treatment of the question was anecdotal. Based on the reading proposed here, however, two lines of reflection are worth pursuing.

The first concerns the continuum that allows articulating what Bartlett calls types of imagination. Instead of considering as different or specific phenomena absorption in fiction, creative interpretation, and actual creation, it may be much more productive to see these as variations of the same processes or variations in configuration along various dimensions, such as emotional commitment, distantiation through critical analysis, openness to the social and material reality, etc. This would allow researchers, as proposed elsewhere, to pursue the project of more integrative understanding of the human mind and the role of imagination and creativity within (Zittoun & Gillespie, 2016). It might also give further means to support people's creative commitment (see also Sternberg, 2016) and thus counter the idea that modalities of creativity depend on genetic or personality predispositions.

Second, as mentioned earlier, interesting methodological choices were made by Bartlett throughout his work on imagination—experimentation preceding more complete analysis of richer data, itself allowing expanding and enriching a theoretical sketch. This move itself might be worth analyzing and may inspire variations of ideographic or case studies, allowing generalization at the level of the processes (Marková, 2016; Molenaar & Valsiner, 2008; Zittoun, 2016, 2017)—obviously a more constructive move than attempts to generalize typologies of people.

References

Barron, F., & Harrington, D. M. (1981). Creativity, intelligence, and personality. *Annual Review of Psychology, 32*(1), 439–476. https://doi.org/10.1146/annurev.ps.32.020181.002255.

Bartlett, F. C. (1916). An experimental study of some problems of perceiving and imagining. *British Journal of Psychology*, (8), 222–266.

Bartlett, F. C. (1928). Types of imagination. *Journal of Philosophical Studies, 3*(9), 78–85.

Bartlett, F. C. (1932/1995). *Remembering: A study in experimental and social psychology.* Cambridge, UK: Cambridge University Press.

Bartlett, F. C. (1950). Programme for experiments on thinking. *Quarterly Journal of Experimental Psychology, 2*(4), 145–152. https://doi.org/10.1080/17470215008416591.

Bordogna, F. (2001). The psychology and physiology of temperament: Pragmatism in context. *Journal of the History of the Behavioral Sciences, 37*(1), 3–25. https://doi.org/10.1002/1520-6696(200124)37:1<3::AID-JHBS2>3.0.CO;2-J.

Calarco, N., Fong, K., Rain, M., & Mar, R. (2017). Absorption in narrative fiction and its possible impact on social abilities. In F. Hakelmuder, M. M. Kuijpers, E. S. Tan, K. Bálint, & M. M. Doicaru (Eds.), *Narrative absorbtion* (pp. 295–317). Amsterdam: John Benjamins.

Csikszentmihalyi, M. (1997). *Creativity: Flow and the psychology of discovery and invention.* London: Harper & Row.

Gardner, H. (1993). *Creating minds: An anatomy of creativity seen through the lives of Freud, Einstein, Picasso, Stravinsky, Eliot, Graham, and Gandhi* (Vol. 16). New York, NY: Basic Books.

Gillespie, A., & Zittoun, T. (2010). Studying the movement of thought. In A. Toomela & J. Valsiner (Eds.), *Methodological thinking in psychology: 60 years gone astray?* (pp. 69–88). Charlotte, NC: Information Age.

Hargreaves, D. J., Hargreaves, J. J., & North, A. C. (2012). Imagination and creativity in music listening. In D. J. Hargreaves, D. Miell, & R. A. R. MacDonald (Eds.), *Musical imaginations: Multidisciplinary perspectives on creativity, performance, and perception* (pp. 156–172). Oxford: Oxford University Press.

Hargreaves, D. J., MacDonald, R. A. R., & Miell, D. (2012). Explaining musical imaginations: Creativity, performance, and perception. In D. J. Hargreaves, D. Miell, & R. A. R. MacDonald (Eds.), *Musical imaginations: Multidisciplinary perspectives on creativity, performance, and perception* (pp. 1–14). Oxford: Oxford University Press.

Hargreaves, D. J., Miell, D., & MacDonald, R. A. R. (Eds.). (2012). *Musical imaginations: Multidisciplinary perspectives on creativity, performance, and perception.* Oxford: Oxford University Press.

Havelka, J. (1968). The theory of modes I: The structure of creative intention and its relation to various aspects of mental economy. In *The nature of the creative process in art* (pp. 137–188). Dordrecht: Springer.

Hunter, M. (2013). Imagination may be more important than knowledge: The eight types of imagination we use. *Review of Contemporary Philosophy*, (12), 113–120.

James, W. (1890). Imagination. In *The principles of psychology* (Vol. 2, Chapter 18). New York, NY: Dover.

James, W. (1907/1975). *Pragmatism: A new name for some old ways of thinking.* Cambridge, MA: Harvard University Press.

Liang, C., & Lin, W.-S. (2015). The interplay of creativity, imagination, personality traits, and academic performance. *Imagination, Cognition and Personality, 34*(3), 270–290. https://doi.org/10.1177/0276236614568638.

Marková, I. (2016). *The dialogical mind: Common sense and ethics.* Cambridge, UK: Cambridge University Press.

Molenaar, P. C. M., & Valsiner, J. (2008). How generalization works through the single case: A simple idiographic process analysis of an individual psychotherapy. In S. Salvatore, J. Valsiner,

S. Strout-Yagodzynski, & J. Clegg (Eds.), *YIS: Yearbook of ideographic science* (pp. 23–38). Rome: Firera.

Nell, V. (1988). *Lost in a book: The psychology of reading for pleasure*. New Haven, CT: Yale University Press.

Ribot, T. (1900/2007). *Essai sur l'imagination créatrice*. Paris: L'Harmattan.

Rosa, A. (1996). Bartlett's psycho-anthropological project. *Culture & Psychology, 2*(4), 355–378.

Runco, M. A. (2004). Creativity. *Annual Review of Psychology, 55*(1), 657–687. https://doi.org/10.1146/annurev.psych.55.090902.141502.

Sternberg, R. J. (2016). Creativity, intelligence, and culture. In V. P. Glăveanu (Ed.), *The Palgrave handbook of creativity and culture research* (pp. 77–99). London: Palgrave.

Tanggaard, L. (2014). *Fooling around: Creative learning pathways*. Charlotte, NC: Information Age.

Valsiner, J. (2014). *An invitation to cultural psychology*. London: Sage.

Van der Veer, R. (2001). Remembering Bartlett. *Culture & Psychology, 7*(2), 223–229.

Wagoner, B. (2009). The experimental methodology of constructive microgenesis. In J. Valsiner, P. C. M. Molenaar, M. C. D. Lyra, & N. Chaudhary (Eds.), *Dynamic process methodology in the social and developmental sciences* (pp. 99–121). New York, NY: Springer.

Wagoner, B. (2017a). *The constructive mind: Bartlett's psychology in reconstruction*. Cambridge, UK: Cambridge University Press.

Wagoner, B. (2017b). Frederic Bartlett. In S. Bernecker & K. Michaelian (Eds.), *Routledge handbook of the philosophy of memory* (pp. 537–545). London: Routledge.

Wagoner, B., & Gillespie, A. (2014). Sociocultural mediators of remembering: An extension of Bartlett's method of repeated reproduction. *British Journal of Social Psychology, 53*(4), 622–639. https://doi.org/10.1111/bjso.12059.

Wagoner, B., & Glăveanu, V. P. (2016). *Memory*. In V. P. Glăveanu, L. T. Pedersen, & C. Wegener (Eds.), *Creativity—A New Vocabulary* (pp. 69–77). Springer.

Wagoner, B., & Jensen, E. (2015). Microgenetic evaluation: Studying learning in motion. In G. Marsico, R. A. Ruggieri, & S. Salvatore (Eds.), *Reflexivity and psychology* (Vol. 6, pp. 293–310). Charlotte, NC: Information Age.

Wolff, W. (1947). Imagination. In *What is psychology: A basic survey* (pp. 152–176). New York, NY: Grune & Stratton.

Zittoun, T. (2016). Studying "higher mental functions": The example of imagination. In J. Valsiner, G. Marsico, N. Chaudhary, T. Sato, & Dazzani (Eds.), *Psychology as a science of human being: The Yokohama manifesto* (Vol. 13, pp. 129–147). Dordrecht: Springer.

Zittoun, T. (2017). Modalities of generalization through single case studies. *Integrative Psychological and Behavioral Science, 51*(2), 171–194. https://doi.org/10.1007/s12124-016-9367-1.

Zittoun, T., & Gillespie, A. (2012). Using diaries and self-writings as data in psychological research. In E. Abbey & S. E. Surgan (Eds.), *Emerging methods in psychology* (pp. 1–26). New Brunswick, NJ: Transaction.

Zittoun, T., & Gillespie, A. (2016). *Imagination in human and cultural development*. London: Routledge.

Zittoun, T., Valsiner, J., Vedeler, D., Salgado, J., Gonçalves, M., & Ferring, D. (2013). *Human development in the lifecourse: Melodies of living*. Cambridge, UK: Cambridge University Press.

PART EIGHT

Creativity in Art and Design

23

Creativity as a Process
John Dewey's *Art as Experience*

KEITH SAWYER

Summary

John Dewey was perhaps the most influential American philosopher between the two world wars. He is primarily known for his progressive theories of education, which remain influential today. Less well known are his writings on creativity and art. In this chapter, I provide some of my favorite excerpts from Dewey's 1934 book, *Art as Experience*. This book contains extended discussions that echo many themes of contemporary creativity research. Dewey argues that creativity doesn't come from a sudden moment of insight; that the creative process is a problem-finding process; that the creative process should be the object of study, not the physical object generated; and that all artistic activity, in fact all human experience, demonstrates and engages with creativity. Creativity is a central aspect of being human, not an isolated moment that happens to only a few geniuses.

Introduction

John Dewey (1859–1952) was one of the most influential of the American philosophers known as *pragmatists*. He is best known for his theories and activities in education. For example, in 1896 he founded the Laboratory School at the University of Chicago, based on his progressive theories of problem-based learning. Dewey's philosophical theory of experience was an ambitious attempt to explain all of human experience—including science and nature, and also art. Perhaps his most effective theoretical description of experience appears in his one book about art, *Art as Experience* (1934/1980). The book is based on a series of lectures that Dewey delivered at Harvard in 1931, the first in the annual series of the William James Lectures that continue today. The aesthetician Monroe Beardsley (1966, p. 332) called this book "by widespread agreement, the most valuable work on aesthetics written in English (and perhaps in any language) so far in our century" (also see Jackson, 1998). So perhaps it is surprising that Dewey has had no impact on contemporary creativity research. His name does not appear in the indexes of the leading overviews of the field (including Kaufman & Sternberg, 2010; Runco, 2014; Sawyer, 2012; Weisberg, 2006). I chose the excerpts below to introduce Dewey to contemporary creativity research.

Dewey's writings on art came rather late in his career; he was 72 when he delivered his Harvard lectures in 1931. His views on art were developed partly in connection with Albert C. Barnes, the legendary art collector whose collection became the Barnes Foundation museum in Philadelphia (e.g., Hein, 2011). Dewey had a long and close relationship with Barnes; he was named the director of the foundation in 1925. In the introduction to *Art as Experience*, Dewey (1934/1980, p. viii) writes, "My greatest indebtedness is to Dr. A. C. Barnes. The chapters have been gone over one by one with him," and the book is dedicated to Barnes "in Gratitude." Rather than empirical research, Dewey's views on art were based on his direct experience with art, particularly with the modern art in Barnes's collection. At the time, it was still controversial whether or not modern art "belonged in the mainstream of aesthetics and art history" (Hein, 2011, p. 135). In responding to this issue, Dewey's position was that all art, whether contemporary or classic, elite or popular, is subject to the same theoretical and psychological frameworks.

Dewey's book contains extended discussions that echo many themes of contemporary creativity research. I've chosen extended excerpts that align with current themes in contemporary creativity research, and I've grouped them into these themes:

- Creativity does not come from a moment of insight but rather a process through time.
- Art is a communication between creator and perceiver; it is not the physical work.
- The generation of art is a problem-finding process.
- What is created is a process, not the physical object.
- There is no substantial difference between the classic "high" arts and the popular "low" arts.

Each of these five themes corresponds roughly to one of the book's 14 chapters. For each heading, I begin with the chapter title, followed by the corresponding theme in contemporary creativity research.

Dewey's book is difficult to read, in part because of redundancies across chapters, and also in part because the various themes appear in multiple chapters. To help make each theme more clear, in some cases I insert into an excerpt paragraphs from earlier or later chapters.

Reading: *Art as Experience*

Source: Dewey, J. (1934/1980). *Art as experience.* New York, NY: Perigee Books. Originally published in Dewey, J., *The Later Works*, vol. 10: *1934* (J. A. Boydston, Ed.). Copyright © 1987 by the Board of Trustees, Southern Illinois University; reprinted by permission of the publisher. To indicate page numbers from the original text, I have used square brackets. I have also used these when text crosses to a new page. Paragraph breaks in the excerpts correspond to paragraph breaks in the original text. In some cases, my excerpt transitions to an earlier page, when the paragraphs are related to the same theme, and the narrative flow reads better out of sequence from the original book. I have indicated this with italic text.

Chapter 4. "The Act of Expression": Creativity Is Not a Moment of Insight

[70] Works of art often present to us an air of spontaneity, a lyric quality, as if they were the unpremeditated song of a bird. But man . . . is not a bird. His most spontaneous outbursts, if expressive, are not overflows of momentary internal pressures. . . .

[72] In one of his letters to his brother Van Gogh says that "emotions are sometimes so strong that one works without knowing that one works, and the strokes come with a sequence and coherence like that of words in a speech or letter." Such fullness of emotion and spontaneity of utterance come, however, only to those who have steeped themselves in experiences of objective situations; to those who have long been absorbed in observation of related material and whose imaginations have long been occupied with reconstructing what they see and hear. Otherwise the state is more like one of frenzy in which the sense of orderly production is subjective and hallucinatory. Even the volcano's outburst presupposes a long period of prior compression, and, if the eruption sends forth molten lava and not merely separate rocks and ashes, it implies a transformation of original raw materials. "Spontaneity" is the result of long periods of activity, or else it is so empty as not to be an act of expression. . . .

New ideas come leisurely yet promptly to consciousness only when work has pre- [73] viously been done in forming the right doors by which they may gain entrance. Subconscious maturation precedes creative production in every line of human endeavor. The direct effort of "wit and will" of itself never gave birth to anything that is not mechanical; their function is necessary, but it is to let loose allies that exist outside their scope. . . . When patience has done its perfect work, the man is taken possession of by the appropriate muse and speaks and sings as some god dictates.

Persons who are conventionally set off from artists, "thinkers," scientists, do not operate by conscious wit and will to anything like the extent popularly supposed. They, too, press forward toward some end dimly and imprecisely figured, groping their way as they are lured on by the identity of an aura in which their observations and reflections swim. Only the psychology that has separated things which in reality belong together holds that scientists and philosophers think while poets and painters follow their feelings. In both, and to the same extent in the degree in which they are of comparable rank, there is emotionalized thinking, and there are feelings whose substance consists of appreciating meanings or ideas. As I have already said, the only significant distinction concerns the kind of material to which emotionalized imagination adheres. Those who are called artists have for their subject-matter the qualities of things of direct experience; "intellectual" inquirers deal with these qualities at one remove, through the medium of symbols that stand for qualities but are not significant in their immediate presence. . . . There is no difference as far as dependence on emotionalized ideas and subconscious maturing are concerned. [74] . . . But only superstition will hold that, because the meaning of paintings and symphonies cannot be translated into words, or that of poetry into prose, therefore thought is monopolized by the latter. If all meanings could be adequately expressed by words, the arts of painting and music would not exist. There are values and meanings that can be expressed only by immediately visible and audible qualities, and to ask what they mean in the sense of something that can be put into words is to deny their distinctive existence.

[Break to an earlier page]

[46] Any idea that ignores the necessary role of intelligence in production of works of art is based upon identification of thinking with use of one special kind of material, verbal signs and words. . . . the production of a work of genuine art probably demands more intelligence than does most of the so-called thinking that goes on among those who pride themselves on being "intellectuals."

Chapter 6. "Substance and Form": Art Is a Communication between Creator and Perceiver

[106] Objects of art . . . are a language. Rather they are many languages. For each art has its own medium and that medium is especially fitted for one kind of communication. Each medium says something that cannot be uttered as well or as completely in any other tongue. . . .

Language only exists when it is listened to as well as spoken. The hearer is an indispensable partner. The work of art is complete only as it works in the experience of others than the one who created it. Thus language involves what logicians call a triadic relation. There is the speaker, the thing said, and the one spoken to. The external object, the product of art, is the connecting link between artist and audience. Even when the artist works in solitude all three terms are present. The work is there in progress, and the artist has to become vicariously the receiving audience. He can speak only as his work appeals to him as one spoken to through what he perceives. He observes and understands as a third person might note and interpret. . . .

[107] If an art product is taken to be one of *self*-expression and the self is regarded as something complete and self-contained in isolation, then of course substance and form fall apart. That in which a self-revelation is clothed is, by the underlying assumption, external to the things expressed. The externality persists no matter which of the two is regarded as form and which as substance. It is also clear that if there be *no* self-expression, no free play of individuality, the product will of necessity be but an instance of a species; it will lack the freshness and originality found only in things that are individual on their own account. . . .

[108] What is true of the producer is true of the perceiver. He may perceive academically, looking for identities with which he already is familiar; or learnedly, pedantically, looking for materials to fit into a history or article he wishes to write, or sentimentally for illustrations of some theme emotionally dear. But if he perceives esthetically, he will create an experience of which the intrinsic subject matter, the substance, is new. . . . no two readers hav[e] exactly the same experience [of a poem]. . . . A new poem is created by every one who reads poetically.

A work of art no matter how old and classic is actually, not just potentially, a work of art only when it lives in some individualized experience. . . . As a work of art, it is recreated every time it is esthetically experienced. . . . It is absurd to ask what an artist "really" meant by his product; he himself would find different meanings in it at [109] different days and hours and in different stages of his own development. If he could be articulate, he would say "I meant . . . whatever you or any one can . . . in virtue of your own vital experience, get out of it." Any other idea makes the boasted "universality" of the work of art a synonym for monotonous identity.

[Break to earlier pages for the next two paragraphs]

[104] Because objects of art are expressive, they communicate. I do not say that communication to others is the intent of an artist. But it is the consequence of his work. . . . Indifference to response of the immediate audience is a necessary trait of all artists that have something new to say. . . .

[105] The artist works to create an audience to which he does communicate. In the end, works of art are the only media of complete and unhindered communication between man and man that can occur in a world full of gulfs and walls that limit community of experience.

[Break to earlier pages for the following two paragraphs]

[51] Even the composition conceived in the head and, therefore, physically private, is public in its significant content, since it is conceived with reference to execution in a product that is perceptible and hence belongs to the common world. Otherwise it would be an aberration or a passing dream.

[81] Works of art that are not remote from common life, that are widely enjoyed in a community, are signs of a unified collective life. But they are also marvelous aids in the creation of such a life. The remaking of the material of experience in the act of expression is not an isolated event confined to the artist and to a person here and there who happens to enjoy the work. In the degree in which art exercises its office, it is also a remaking of the experience of the community in the direction of greater order and unity.

Chapter 7. "The Natural History of Form": Art Is a Problem-Finding Process

[138] A rigid predetermination of an end-product whether by artist or beholder leads to the turning out of a mechanical or academic product. . . . The latter is rather of the nature of a stencil, even though the copy from which the stencil is made exists in mind and not as a physical thing. A statement that an artist does not care how his work eventuates would not be literally true. But it is true that he cares about the end-result as a completion of what goes before and not because of its conformity or lack of conformity with a ready-made antecedent scheme. He is willing to leave the outcome to the adequacy of the means from which it issues and which it sums up. Like the scientific inquirer, he permits the subject-matter of his perception in connection with the problems it presents to deter- [139] mine the issue, instead of insisting upon its agreement with a conclusion decided upon in advance. . . .

The unexpected turn, something which the artist himself does not definitely foresee, is a condition of the felicitous quality of a work of art; it saves it from being mechanical. It gives the spontaneity of the unpremeditated to what would otherwise be a fruit of calculation. The painter and poet like the scientific inquirer know the delights of discovery. Those who carry on their work as a demonstration of a preconceived thesis may have the joys of egotistic success but not that of fulfillment of an experience for its own sake. In the latter they learn by their work, as they proceed, to see and feel what had not been part of the original plan and purpose.

The consummatory phase is recurrent throughout a work of art, and in the experience of a great work of art the points of its incidence shift in successive observations of it. This fact sets the insuperable barrier between mechanical production and use and esthetic creation and perception. In the former there are no ends until the final end is reached. Then work tends to be labor and production to be drudgery. But there is no final term in appreciation of a work of art. It carries on and is, therefore, instrumental as well as final. Those who deny this fact confine the significance of "instrumental" to the process of contributing to some narrow, if not base, office of efficacy. . . . We are carried to a refreshed attitude toward the circumstances of exigencies of ordinary experience. The work, in the sense of working, of an object of art does not cease when the direct act of perception stops. It continues to operate in indirect channels. Indeed, persons who draw back at the mention of "instrumental" in connection with art often glorify art for precisely the enduring serenity, refreshment, or re-education of vision that are induced by it. The [140] real trouble is verbal. Such persons are accustomed to associate the work with instrumentalities for narrow ends—as an umbrella is instrumental to protection from rain or a mowing machine to cutting grain. . . .

Skill is then admired not as part of the external equipment of the artist, but as an enhanced expression belonging to the object. For it facilitates the carrying on a continuous process to its own precise and definite conclusion. It belongs to the product and not merely to the producer, because it is a constituent of form; just as the grace of a greyhound marks the movements he performs rather than is a trait possessed by the animal as something outside the movements. . . .

Some of the traits mentioned are more often referred to technique than to form. The attribution is correct whenever the qualities in question are referred to the artist rather than to his work. There is a technique that obtrudes, like the flourishes of a writing master. If skill and economy suggest their author, they take as away from the work itself. The traits of the work which [141] suggest the skill of its producer are then *in* the work but they are not *of* it. And the reason they are not of it is precisely the negative side of the point which I am emphasizing. They do not take us anywhere in the institution of unified developing experience; they do not act as inherent forces to carry the object of which they are a professed part to consummation. Such traits are like any other superfluous or excrescent element. . . . Technique is neither identical with form nor yet wholly independent of it. It is, properly, the skill with which the elements constituting form are managed. Otherwise it is show-off or a virtuosity separated from expression. . . .

[144] There is . . . a tendency among lay critics to confine experimentation to scientists in the laboratory. Yet one of the essential traits of the artist is that he is born an experimenter. Without this trait he becomes a poor or a good academician. The artist is compelled to be an experimenter because he has to express an intensely individualized experience through means and materials that belong to the common and public world. This problem cannot be solved once for all. It is met in every new work undertaken. Otherwise an artist repeats himself and becomes esthetically dead. Only because the artist operates experimentally does he

open new fields of experience and disclose new aspects and qualities in familiar scenes and objects. . . .

The "classic" when it was produced bore the marks of adventure. This fact is ignored by classicists in their protests against romantics who undertake the development of new values. . . . That which is now classic is so because of completion of adventure, not because of its absence.

Chapter 8. "The Organization of Energies": Creativity Is a Process, Not the Product

[162] There is a difference between the art product (statue, painting, or whatever), and the *work* of art. The first is physical and potential; the latter is active and experienced. It is what the product does, its working. For nothing enters experience bald and unaccompanied, whether it be a seemingly formless happening, a theme intellectually systematized, or an object elaborated with every loving care of united thought and emotion. Its very entrance is the beginning of a complex interaction; upon the nature of this interaction depends the character of the thing as finally experienced. When the structure of the object is such that its force interacts happily (but not easily) with the energies that issue from the experience itself; when their mutual affinities and antagonisms work together to bring about a substance that develops cumulatively and surely (but not too steadily) toward a fulfilling of impulsions and tensions, then indeed there is a work of art. . . .

An esthetic experience, the work of art in its actuality, is *perception*. Only as these rhythms, even if embodied in an outer object that is itself a product of art, become a rhythm in experience itself are they esthetic. . . .

[Shift ahead to Chapter 10 only for this paragraph, then back to Chapter 8]

[214] Art is a quality of doing and of what is done. Only outwardly, then, can it be designated by a noun substantive. The *product* of art—temple, painting, statue, poem—is not the *work* of art.

[Shift back to Chapter 8]

[163] The order of the elements of spatial objects *as* spatial and physical, that is apart from their entrance into that interaction which causes an experience, is, comparatively at least, fixed. Aside from a slow process of weathering, the lines and planes of a statue stay the same, and so do the configurations and intervals of a building. From this fact is derived the [erroneous] conclusion that there are two kinds of fine arts, the spatial and the temporal, and that only the latter are marked by rhythm: the counterpart of this error being that only buildings and statues possess symmetry. The mistake would be serious if it affected only theory. In fact denial of rhythm to pictures and buildings obstructs perception of qualities that are absolutely indispensable in their esthetic effect. . . .

[175] What has been said may seem to exaggerate the temporal aspect of perception. I have, without doubt, stretched out elements that are usually more or less telescoped. But in no case can there be *perception of an object* except in a process developing in time. . . .

The denial of rhythm to pictures, edifices, and statues, or the assertion that it is found in them only metaphorically, rests upon ignorance of the inherent nature of every perception. . . .

[176] It is precisely when we get from an art product the feeling of dealing with a *career*, a history, perceived at a particular point of its development, that we have the impression of life. That which is dead does not extend into the past nor arouse any interest in what is to come.

The common element in all the arts, technological and useful, is organization of energy as means for producing a result. . . .

[177] We do not need to feel, therefore, that we are speaking metaphorically nor apologize for animism when we speak of a painting as alive, and its figures, as well as architectural and sculptural forms, as manifesting movement. . . .

[182] In seeing a picture or an edifice, there is the same compression from accumulation in time that there is in hearing music, reading a poem or novel, and seeing a drama enacted. No work of art can be instantaneously perceived because there is then no opportunity for conservation and increase of tension, and hence none for that release and unfolding which give volume to a work of art. In most intellectual work, in all save those flashes that are distinctly esthetic, we have to go backwards; we have consciously to retrace previous steps and to recall distinctly particular facts and ideas. Getting ahead in thought is dependent upon these conscious excursions of memory into the past. But only when esthetic perception is interrupted (whether by lapse on the part of artist or perceiver) are we compelled to turn back, say in seeing a play on the stage, to ask ourselves what went before in order to get the thread of movement. What is retained from the past is embedded within what is now perceived and so embedded that, by its compression there, it forces the mind to stretch forward to what is coming. The more there is compressed from the continuous series of prior perceptions, the richer the present perception and the more intense the forward impulsion. . . .

[183] It follows that the separation of rhythm and symmetry from each other and the division of the arts into temporal and spatial is more than a misapplied ingenuity. It is based on a principle that is destructive, so far as it is heeded, of esthetic understanding. . . .

[184] Nevertheless, though the distinction between spatial and temporal arts is wrongly drawn, since all objects of art are matters of perception and perception is not instantaneous, music in its evident temporal emphasis illustrates perhaps better than any other art the sense in which form is the moving integration of an experience. In music, form, for which even the musical have to find spatial language and which even the musical often see as a structure, the form develops with the hearing of the music. Any point in the musical development, that is to say, any tone, is what it is in that musical object—or perception—by virtue of what has gone before and what is musically impinging or prophesied. A melody is set by the tonic note, to which an expectancy of return is set up as a tension of attention. The "form" of the music becomes form in the career of the listening. Moreover, any section of the music and any cross-section of it has precisely the balance and symmetry, in chords and harmonies, as a painting, statue, or building. A melody is a chord deployed in time.

Chapter 9. "The Common Substance of the Arts": Elite versus Popular Art

[187] I had occasion in another connection to refer to the difference between the popular arts of a period and the official arts. Even when favored arts came out from under patronage and control of priest and ruler, the distinction of kinds remained even though the name "official" is no longer a fitting designation. Philosophic theory concerned itself only with those arts that had the stamp and seal of recognition by the class having social standing and authority. Popular arts must have flourished, but they obtained no literary attention. They were not worthy of mention in theoretical discussion. Probably they were not even thought of as arts. . . .

[188] In literature the dominant tradition in theory was similar. It was constantly asserted that Aristotle had once for all delimited the scope of tragedy, the highest literary mode, by declaring that the misfortunes of the noble and those in high place were its proper material, while those of the common people were intrinsically fit for the lesser mode of comedy. Diderot virtually announced a historic revolution in theory when he said there was need for bourgeois tragedies, and that, instead of putting on the stage only kings and princes, private persons are subject to terrible reverses which inspire pity and terror. . . .

[189] The novel has been the great instrument of effecting change in prose literature. It shifted the center of attention from the court to the bourgeoisie, then to the "poor" and the laborer, and then to the common person irrespective of station. . . . The part played by folk-music . . . in the expansion and renewal of music is too well known to require more than notice. Even architecture, the most conservative of all the arts, has felt the influence of a transformation similar to that the other arts have undergone. . . . The art of established "orders" has been influenced as much by revolt against fixation in social classes as by technological developments in cement and steel.

This brief sketch has only one purpose: to indicate that, in spite of formal theory and canons of criticism, there has taken place one of those revolutions that do not go backward. . . . It belongs to the very character of the creative mind to reach out and seize any material that stirs it so that the value of that material may be pressed out and become the matter of a new experience.

Commentary

Many aspects of Dewey's theory are aligned with findings that have emerged from contemporary creativity research. In the following, I interpret each of the five themes above in light of creativity research.

CHAPTER 4: CREATIVITY IS NOT A MOMENT OF INSIGHT

Dewey argued that creativity does not reside in a moment of insight. Spontaneity in art is a myth. Of course, ideas are important in creativity, but no single idea is responsible for the created work. Instead works emerge over time, with small ideas occurring throughout the process. Any given creative process is preceded by years of investment in mastering a creative language. Once the creative process begins, it takes hard work, conscious effort, and extended time to generate the final work. Dewey argued that art involves the same degree of conscious effort and expertise as the sciences, and that art and science have no differences in the nature of their creative process.

Dewey's argument that creativity cannot be explained by appeal to a moment of insight is consistent with contemporary psychology. Cognitive psychologists have found no evidence to support the Gestaltist notion that creative ideas are associated with a sudden transformation of thought and mental structures (Sawyer, 2012, pp. 107–114). Instead psychologists have documented the mental processes involved when the mind creates rather small associations between ideas, concepts, and memories. This contemporary view is grounded in cognitive psychology, which explains creative thoughts using the same mental processes and structures as other thought processes that we do not view as creative.

CHAPTER 6: ART IS A SOCIAL EXCHANGE

Dewey argued that creativity is not found in the physical work itself; instead art resides in the communication between the creator and the perceiver. It is the communication itself—both the experience of the creator when creating the work, and the perceiver while experiencing the work, that constitutes "art." The physical artifact that we think of as the artwork merely mediates this communication. Art is what the work does, not the work itself.

In a related claim, Dewey argued that artwork is never a matter of self-expression. Each work is an expression of an entire community of individuals. This view challenges conceptions of creativity that associate it with internal struggles of the creator; with the unique insights and worldviews of a creator, that may be thought to be very different from the general public; that the artist is a visionary who sees things that others cannot see; that the artist is ahead of his time, to be recognized only years later. Contemporary creativity research has largely dismissed these conceptions of creativity as myths associated with a Western conception of creativity as individual expression.

CHAPTER 7: PROBLEM-FINDING

The creative process is not based in a single flash of insight. Instead artworks emerge from a process that is wandering, unpredictable, and improvisational. This process allows an opportunity for new thoughts, ideas, and problems to emerge during the process, so that the original motivation for beginning the process may be left behind as the creative path shifts in direction. Sawyer (2012, p. 87) calls this the *action theory* of creativity, that "the execution of the creative work is essential to the creative process." He observed that creativity research has demonstrated that this theory is more accurate than an "idealist" theory that appeals to a moment of insight:

> Only an action theory can explain creativity. Creativity takes place over time, and most of the creativity occurs while doing the work. The medium is an essential part of the creative process, and creators often get ideas while working with their materials. (p. 88)

Creativity researchers have found evidence that the most successful painters are those who engage in a problem-finding process. This research extends back to a study by psychologists Jacob Getzels and Mihaly Csikszentmihalyi (1976), a 10-year study of MFA students at one of the country's top art schools, the School of the Art Institute of Chicago. In their terms, a *problem-finding* painter is constantly searching for a visual problem while painting—improvising a painting rather than executing one. In contrast, a *problem-solving* style involves starting with a relatively detailed plan for a composition and then simply painting it. The painter defines a visual problem before starting, with the execution of the painting consisting of "solving" the problem.

CHAPTER 8: CREATIVITY IS A PROCESS

Dewey based his aesthetic theory on the distinction between *art product* and *work of art*. His pragmatist framework led him to emphasize action in the world and the practical effects of that action, and he did not associate creativity with what is in the artist's mind.

Contemporary creativity research has moved to a focus on creative process. Prior periods in creativity research emphasized the creative personality or the creative work. With the onset of cognitive psychology, the focus of creativity research has shifted to the creative process, one that is grounded in universally shared mental structures and processes, not in a particular personality type.

CHAPTER 9: ELITE VERSUS POPULAR ARTS

Dewey argued that there is no substantial difference between the "high" arts and the "low," or popular, arts. Both result in an experience that has the same aesthetic characteristics. The belief that high arts are better or more creative is false; it is based on the association between high arts and the elite and upper class in society. Dewey rejected this as irrelevant to the quality of the artwork.

There is no substantial difference in the the creative process between modern, nonrepresentational art and the classics of the European canon. There is no substantial difference in the creative process between the high arts and the low arts. This is consistent with Barnes's collection and curation; his collection includes works from many different historical periods, as well as then-contemporary works. Barnes famously displayed works from different periods side by side, believing that works share properties and communications: they share a view of art as experience.

The claim that both high and low art are equally creative challenges the several creativity conceptions that Dewey rejected as myths. These include the insight view, because one is less likely to believe that a popular work is the result of a brilliant flash of insight; the genius view, because it is harder to maintain that popular works are due to unique geniuses; and the solitary creator view, because popular works are more obviously grounded in collaborative processes and more directly reflect the collective experience of large numbers of people.

Conclusion

Dewey's aesthetic theory, although formulated over 80 years ago, is largely consistent with contemporary empirical studies of creativity, in holding that:

• Creativity does not reside in a moment of insight, but rather is a process through time.
• Creativity is a problem-finding process, where the nature and formulation of the problem is not known at the beginning of the process.

- There is no empirical or theoretical difference between creative processes that lead to fine arts and those that lead to popular arts.
- Creativity is a socially embedded, collaborative endeavor.

Dewey's perspective provides us with a range of productive research questions: What is the nature of the unfolding process of creativity? How can a person begin the creative process, when the problem is not yet fully understood? How do problems and solutions emerge from this process? What can we learn about the fine arts from a study of everyday popular arts? How do social and collaborative groups drive creativity?

Dewey's book is theoretical and philosophical, but it demonstrates a clarity of perception (if not a clarity of prose style). His theory's alignment with contemporary empirical work is astounding. Due to recent developments in creativity research, it's time to return to Dewey's pragmatist theories on the creative process.

References

Beardsley, M. C. (1966). *Aesthetics from classical Greece to the present: A short history.* New York: Macmillan.

Dewey, J. (1934/1980). *Art as experience.* New York, NY: Perigee Books.

Getzels, J. W., & Csikszentmihalyi, M. (1976). *The creative vision.* New York, NY: Wiley.

Hein, George E. (2011). Dewey's debt to Barnes. *Curator: The Museum Journal, 54*(2), 123–139.

Jackson, P. W. (1998). *John Dewey and the lessons of art.* New Haven, CT: Yale University Press.

Kaufman, J. C., & Sternberg, R. J. (Eds.). (2010). *The Cambridge handbook of creativity.* Cambridge, UK: Cambridge University Press.

Runco, M. A. (2014). *Creativity: Theories and themes. Research, development, and practice* (2nd ed.). London: Academic Press.

Sawyer, R. K. (2012). *Explaining creativity: The science of human innovation* (2nd ed.). New York, NY: Oxford.

Weisberg, R. W. (2006). *Creativity: Understanding innovation in problem solving, science, invention, and the arts.* Hoboken, NJ: Wiley.

24

Literary Creative Imagination
Alfred Binet

TODD LUBART AND CHRISTOPHE MOUCHIROUD

Summary

This chapter presents Alfred Binet's work on literary creation. Binet and his colleagues conducted a series of interviews with French playwrights to examine diverse aspects of their creative activity. Binet compared and contrasted authors in terms of their reliance on rational thinking versus instinct and emotions; their different creative processes, some working in bursts of activity and others working in a more regular way; and the different ways that authors generate their literary ideas, some being more auditory and others more visually oriented. These analyses illustrate the focus that Binet placed on individual differences in the study of creativity.

Introduction

Alfred Binet (1857–1911) was a leading French researcher in the emerging field of psychology. He examined "higher" mental functions from a differential and pedagogical perspective. Binet's academic background was quite diverse; he was trained as a lawyer, but then turned to science and studied under the neurologist Charcot. Binet went on to become the director of the Laboratory of Experimental Psychology at the Sorbonne in 1895. Best known for his work on intelligence and early tests used in schools (Binet & Simon, 1905), he was fascinated by the diverse manifestations of cognition, which included creative thinking in his global conception of intelligence. His work included studies of intermodal perceptual ability, reasoning, sensations, hallucinations, and exceptional memory in mental calculators and chess players (Binet, 1894). In terms of cognition and individual differences, Binet (1898, p. 462) noted, "We do not all have intelligence based on the same schemata. Several different kinds of intelligence exist, and the kind that fits one person does not fit another. This is a commonsense truth." He proposed three kinds of abilities or "spirits": literary spirit, scientific spirit, and artistic spirit.

The focus of Binet's papers selected for this chapter are his studies of creative imagination in literary work based on case studies of several dramatists (Binet, 1904; Binet & Passy, 1895). In fact Binet loved the theater, notably the Grand-Guignol Theater in Paris, which presented gory, bloody dramas and horror shows (a precursor to horror movies). He himself contributed to this genre as a playwright (with dramas involving psychiatric disorders), but he tried also to understand the ways that authors got ideas and developed them and how actors could engage in imaginary roles, suspending the realities of their daily lives.

Readings: *La création littéraire: Portrait psychologique de M. Hervieu* and *notes psychologiques sur les auteurs dramatiques*

Sources: Binet, A. (1904). La création littéraire: Portrait psychologique de M. Hervieu. *L'Année Psychologique, 10*, 1–62 (pp. 2–6, 18–21, 26–28, 31–32, 60).

Binet, A., & Passy, J. (1895). Notes psychologiques sur les auteurs dramatiques. *L'Année Psychologique, 1*, 60–118 (pp. 79–81). Works in the public domain. Translations by Todd Lubart and Christophe Mouchiroud.

We had begun, a dozen years ago, [a study] on creative imagination. We had visited the main dramatic authors of the time and asked them to explain their work. The account of these visits appeared first in *Temps*, then, with new developments, in the first volume of the *l'Année Psychologique*. We find there some summary studies on Dumas, Sardou, Valabrègue, F. de Curel, Daudet, Goncourt, Pailleron, Meilhac, Lemaitre, Coppee, etc. These articles are nothing but notes taken after a few hours of conversation; they give the impression experienced by two inquisitive people facing interesting personalities, rather than a scientific explanation of the mechanism by which a work of art is created. . . .

[An example of the interview and observations with Alexandre Dumas the younger]

The work of literary composition is accompanied, for him, by a great sense of enjoyment: while he writes, he is of better humor, he eats, he drinks and sleeps more; it is a kind of physical well-being, resulting from the exercise of a natural function. He does not seek isolation and silence, like those authors whose weakened inspiration disappears at the smallest distraction produced by outside things. At Puys, near Dieppe, where he composed *Denise*, his office was next to the living room where his two daughters played piano throughout the day; he liked to listen to music while he was writing; and it is even this circumstantial accident which gave him the idea of making the public listen to the sound of a piano before the curtain rises on the first act of *Denise*. It is still at Puys that he was often disturbed by a friend in the middle of his work. From dawn he was at his table; he wrote; at eight o'clock, his friend Arago came to call him for a game of billiards; he left his room, went to play, and then returned to his manuscript and began again to write at the precise place where he had been interrupted. No more than his father did he use artificial means, such as coffee, alcohol to stimulate his work; we know that Dumas father whet his verve by drinking a large glass of lemonade; for him too, work was a source of balance and health. We know also that, during the heat of the composition, Dumas (father) experienced a special kind of physiological excitement. Like his father, whom he likes to recall, M. Dumas writes no scenario; he thinks that during the composition of a scenario the verve is spent unnecessarily. When he takes the pen, it is to write his play in the final form. But he does not get to that point until he knows what he wants and where it goes. He carries inside himself a long time, as we have said, the topic of his play, of which he examines all the facets, and which most often contain moral or social problems. After this incubation, he begins to write; he has, as we say, a critical moment for execution. Execution is ordinarily extremely rapid; one of his plays, *Monsieur Alphonse*, was written in 17 days, *La Visite des Noces* in eight days, *Princesse George* in three weeks, *l'Etrangère* in a month. Often he gets to work to obey the pressing request of a barking director who writes to him, "I must absolutely have the play which you have told me about." At this request, M. Dumas replied sometimes with his mixture of good nature and irony: "My dear friend, I started the play at this very moment; you will have it in three weeks and it will be a great success." This happened for *Mr. Alphonse*, for which he had the subject in his head for six or seven years. There was nothing more left than writing it. The difficulty is not to say it; it is to keep one's word. It should be noted that these few facts prove merely a rapidity of execution; the conception of the play, defining the characters and all the adventures require not days and weeks, but months and sometimes years. M. Dumas really only improvises the form, in other words the dialogue. And still this greater or lesser speed of execution depends very much on the subject. Where passion prevails, execution is prompt; when manners, characters, psychology are concerned, it is less easy. He remained on the *Demi-Monde* 11 months pen in hand, with seven to eight hours a day of work. It took him two months to write the second act. On the other hand—and the opposition is very striking—the second act of the *Dame aux Camelias* was written from noon to four o'clock.

This is an interesting confirmation of what he teaches us about his way of working. Never have we seen such clean manuscripts. That of the *Dame aux Camelias* is written on two packets of large pages of different sizes. M. Dumas was in such a hurry that he did not have time to choose his paper, and he took what came into his hands; he has covered the paper with a firm and regular handwriting in which the eye searches in vain for signs of improvisation; whole pages succeed each other without a single erasure. Moreover, M. Dumas has a horror of erasures, spots, overwrites, and corrections. We have shown him—let us hope that this was not an indiscretion—a page detached from the manuscripts of M. Sardou, chopped up by a thousand corrections in all directions, and resembling an obscure undergrowth. M. Dumas, astonished, did not understand how one could find his way there. If we insist on these graphic documents, it is because we consider them not merely as curiosities, good for collectors, we discern there the material trace of two different inspirations; one, that of M. Dumas, is impulsive, and in a certain way explosive; it is the cannon-ball which goes across space; the other, that of M. Sardou, is reflective, made up of an activity which is constantly recursive with auto-examination, corrections and modifications. . . .

I return today to this study of psychology, in order to go deeper. I hope to come out of the period of trial and error, where we are satisfied mainly with anecdotes, and undertake truly the analytic work.

The psychology of imagination in literary authors can have two very different goals:

1. To seek to know what is essential in the person characterized by imagination; to this end, we must either synthesize all the observations made on literary artists, to seek differences which do not concern judgment or practical sense but the lack of imaginative power to create or only to represent themselves. The object pursued will be, in this case, a general theory of imagination.
2. Instead of insisting on similarities between artists, considered as a single natural family, to highlight their differences, seek if the review of their working methods, if their particular psychology does not reveal the existence of distinctive imaginative types then the research goal changes; it is no longer a matter of general psychology but of "individual psychology."

The pages that will follow are mainly a contribution to the latter; by which they are connected as a new link, to the long chain of investigations that I have published for many years, alone or with my pupils, on questions very different in appearance, but whose guiding idea remains the same; whether indeed we measure by a compass the tactile sensitivity of a hand or explore the suggestibility of intelligence of those for whom we set a trap, or enter the orientation of different minds towards observation or idealism, and finally discuss with writers their working methods, all this despite the very clear differences of people, problems, decoration and technique, all this converges on the same goal: to identify individual psychological differences, in order to establish experimentally a classification of the characters. It has even seemed to me that men of talent and genius would serve better than average cases to help us grasp the laws of character, because they present more marked traits.

My naturalistic studies of Mr. Paul Hervieu began in May 1903, and lasted during seven morning visits, of two hours each, which I made at his home; I saw him again several times in January 1904. I did not, so to speak, use any instrument for this research; I limited myself to asking questions as precise as possible, written and prepared in advance, according to a carefully thought-out plan, and with sufficient incoherence to prevent Mr. Hervieu from guessing the nature of my plan; Mr. Hervieu answered orally, and I wrote while listening with an effort to keep the same expression he had used. Ignoring shorthand, and fearing to break the confidential intimacy of a conversation by the presence of a professional stenographer, I had to confine myself to collecting only certain fragments of the words of Mr. Hervieu; I will give these disjointed fragments, surrounding them with quotation marks according to the habits of theatrical style; it must therefore be understood that the lack of connection between the words is my own doing. But the very words are those of my author, and to emphasize their authenticity, I will reproduce them [with quotation marks].

I have begged Mr. Hervieu to listen to the reading of my study, in order to rectify my incomplete shorthand when he deemed it necessary for the truth of his opinions. . . .

Mr. Hervieu made kindly available to me for several months a few of his manuscripts. I have still in hand the complete scenario and the original manuscript of *La course du flambeau*, a copy of *La loi de l'homme* containing many interesting corrections that come from the work of rehearsals, and also the copy of *L'Enigme* in which I've read a lot of revisions made after the reception of the drama, before putting it in repetition. These documents have some-times served as evidence; the study of the author's alterations took me a long time.

I thought it would be good to measure Mr. Hervieu's head with Broca's anthropological methods; I noted also his size, muscle strength, and I even conducted a few psychological tests on suggestibility and ideation; it is the concern to be exact and complete in my report that makes me mention this very special research; they gave me little useful information.

I maintain here what I have always believed, that of the three means of investigation which are offered to us in psychology—survey, observation, and experimentation—it is this last process which gives the most precise, the most certain and the most objective results. Only when one does not wish to be satisfied with obtaining an average truth, when one wishes to know the nuances of a particular personality, when, finally, in this personality one tries to bring to light extremely complex functions, the experimental method, properly speaking, with *tests* and instruments, is applicable only under the condition of being pursued slowly for a long time. A quick experiment gives only very particular and often unusable results. That is why I have used mostly simple conversation, which is a mixed method, based both on survey and observation. I would add that the present study has a new *individual psychology* program underlying it.

It is none the less true that M. Hervieu's method is a curious expression of his personality; if, on the one hand, it excludes the fantasy of those who write, without concern for the next day, works whose beauty has seduced them, on the other hand, it shows us the author's ability to do what he wants when he wants, without feeling paralyzed with nervousness caused by an approaching deadline.

This influence of the will is expressed in all the details of execution. M. Hervieu stays at home. He decides that he will work every day from a certain hour to a certain hour, and he obeys this order for several successive months, without, so to speak, missing a single day. Zola did the same; he devoted his mornings to the novel in progress, and wrote every morning the same number of lines. Mr. Hervieu, who always dines outside his house, who spends his evenings in the world, who goes to bed late and needs a long sleep, does not wake up in the morning with a mind disposed for literary production. He gets up to 8 o'clock, spends his morning doing daily chores, reads newspapers, many newspapers, takes care of the appointments he has made, and thus arrives to his lunch. It's around one o'clock, obeying the order he set himself, that he begins his working session.

This session continues regularly throughout the afternoon until a quarter before six, when a domestic provides an interruption. "They indicate the time, my recreation begins." Sometimes, having made a connection, he works one more hour; but it is quite rare. At seven o'clock Mr. Hervieu dresses and goes out. About five times a week, his day begins again in the same way; the sixth is the day of the Academy; the seventh is Sunday, day of rest.

I thought at first of irony, but it is quite serious. If we believe him, who should we describe as a hard-worker? For there is merit only in effort; one is not a drudge when working by desire and with constant pleasure; it is also necessary to have overcome one's disposition in the opposite sense; and it is precisely the fake lazy ones, like Mr. Hervieu—and also Zola—who are the finest examples of will power.

The regularity of this literary production leads us to be a little astonished; we have learned that many men of letters have a most capricious verve; they write only when they feel "in the mood" and are obliged therefore to wait patiently for the day and the hour of inspiration, the visit of the Muse, as we say for poets. This is not always convenient. But the writers of this category do not complain at all of their fate, and prefer to gloss over others, which is very natural. I have heard some of the instinctive authors, these "inspired" types, mock pleasantly the regular writers; take Edmond de Goncourt who spoke to me of the working habits adopted by Zola, his friend or former friend, I do not know [which], saying: "This is prison literature."

I reminded M. Hervieu of the example of Alphonse Daudet, whom he knew well, and for whom he has tender memories.

Daudet told once Jacques Passy and me about his work: "It is," he said, "like an increase of inner heat which rises to the brain; one is taken, invaded by his subject, and one begins to write with fever. So, nothing stops you; the inkwell is empty, the pencil is broken; regardless, one keeps always going. One gets angry with the falling night, and one's eyes are strained in the twilight, waiting for the lamp that does not come. Time is stolen from sleep and meals. If one has to go, go to the country, make a journey, one can not decide to leave work, one writes still, standing up, on a corner of his trunk."

In the past, when he was young and more robust, he worked in the countryside for 18 hours a day: asleep at midnight, he got up at four in the morning, at the same time as the farmer in the neighboring house. With his mind still numb, he spent two hours recopying the work of the previous day, a mechanical occupation that rekindled his inspiration. During the day he took barely time to eat, having his dessert and his coffee served on his desk.

Today he can no longer afford these splendid follies, but, though fatigued by insomnia, he works by excess, with haste, fever, and quivering fingertips.

At the moment when we are visiting him, he has just been taken by a subject which he had in his mind for 15 years, and which had left him until now perfectly tranquil; then, this subject, one fine day, fascinated him; and now he is constantly working on it; yesterday he suffered horribly; chloral, antipyrine, morphine, he used everything to keep working.

Mr. Hervieu listens to my story with interest, he thinks about it, and then observes that for him this kind of work crisis has always been very slight; he recalls that sometimes when his work session is over and he is putting on his coat to go out, he returned to his table to add a few words to the manuscript which was already locked up. I do not know if Mr. Hervieu realized the difference between his moderate method and Daudet's fever; the contrast is quite striking for those who, like me, have been able to converse with the two men. . . .

I have convinced myself that my precious guide in this maze is the very varied information which other dramatic authors have already furnished me; I have in my memory a gallery of at least fifteen portraits to which I compare M. Hervieu, without him suspecting it: this continuous comparison enables me often to give a meaning to an insignificant detail.

One of the most important questions to ask a literary writer concerns the mental conditions in which ideas come. We are going to find out how ideas, words and phrases move, for Mr. Hervieu, from the unconscious to the conscious when he composes.

Mr. Hervieu speaks his dialogue. A part of the work session occurs while he is standing, walking and smoking in his office and even in the adjoining room which allows a longer walk. In order to find the sentence to be written, he tries to pronounce it; he does not pronounce it aloud, as one does in a conversation between two people, he articulates it above all, in a low and a slightly hoarse voice; however, someone who would be there in his office could hear it. The expression of this voice is rather uniform, and without seeking the means of an actor. "I play it in a very monotonous way in terms of intensity, because I want to tear by force from myself the expression that seems to me true." He observed, surprising himself, a mimicry which appeared to aid him in his effort; it is a parallel movement of the two hands that shake in a gesture of struggle, a sort of abstract gesture of strength. "I have," he says again, "physical movement only for strength. In the scenes of tenderness, I do not have this mimic, this movement of two fists. This mimic is a stimulant, constantly creating the sentence. It is an effort that I make to express what I feel."

The phrase once created, he does not keep it in memory, he sits at his desk, and writes it immediately; at this moment he can amend it, correct it, and cross it out: but what is curious is this instinct which pushes him to put on paper each sentence, successively, immediately after composing it, by writing it, he delivers his mind, he avoids an encumbrance in his head. It is a rule which he follows faithfully. One might say that he ruminates only one sentence at a time, in order to ruminate it with greater care.

But of course, being concentrated on the detail of each phrase, he does not lose sight of the whole. A scene has a step, a rhythm, a conclusion of which he remains conscious; and he sees much further than a sentence, when he is not concerned with direct expression: "I seem," he said, "to have climbed higher, to see a much more extensive landscape, when I conceive; and when I execute, it is going down again; the landscape narrows."

I think this way of composing is very interesting to note. It is the epitome of the voluntary and conscious form. Other authors are graphic, allow me this neologism, it is their penholder that writes and composes, by which I mean that the sentence is constructed by a semi-automatic phenomenon and comes out of their minds by the channel of writing. Others are listeners; they hear the phrase resound in an inner ear; they receive what they hear, and sometimes the voice that speaks is well recognized as their own, sometimes they feel that it is a foreign voice, the voice of their characters, and as Mr. de Curel explained so well, they write almost under the dictation by these fictitious characters, and strangers to their law. I pass over other more or less clear cases. These are sufficient to show by contrast Mr. Hervieu's typical character: I would say that he is a *speaker* if this word, which seems related to chatter, does not apply poorly enough to a man showing discreet and very sober speech; I prefer to use the more technical term articulator. He is articulating, so to speak, always, except for minor and unimportant exceptions. I extract from my notes the following observation which I have written, so to speak, under his dictation: "Yesterday I was putting in a scene a woman who announced that she would take the train in two hours. I hear her mother-in-law saying, 'You are not going to set out at such an hour.' These auditory sentences are very simple phrases." . . .

It seemed to me, by collecting my memories and comparing my observations, that we could divide all the dramatic authors into a classification according to the mode which serves them to realize the collaboration between imagination and critical sense. I do not believe that the classification I am going to give is exhaustive, and that it suffices to assign to it, for example, a literary personality, a precise place for having thus defined all the psychology of this person and to have found his formula. My ambition is less strong. I give what follows as one of the many ways under which writers can be classified; but it is not the only one.

It seemed therefore possible to distinguish three main types of relationships between imagination and critical thinking.

1. A common type, in which these two characters are distinct, independent of each other, and placed on an equal footing. Mr. Sardou seems to me to illustrate perfectly this average type; and as in all he describes, he "makes theater," the analysis he gives us of his mental state assumes a very lively form: "There are two men in me, when I compose: the creator always moves ahead . . . and the critic, who watches him, and from time to time stops him, and shouts to him: 'Hold up there!'" As I have just said, here the two characters are distinct; but this distinction is above all literary; it results from a difference of attitude and orientation; whether it is the critic or the inventor who acts, behind them there is always Mr. Sardou.

2. Here is an extreme type of split personality, and truly so accentuated that it borders on what is observed in nervous and mental pathology, and especially in spiritists. This is the case for Mr. de Curel. I have described him at length, and with his collaboration, in the first volume of the *Année Psychologique*. I do not return to it in detail, I summarize it simply. In Mr. de Curel's case, the distinction between the two parts is more profound. The creator is not only distinct from the critic in literary form, he acquires a personality all the more its own that he is in turn each of the characters; in other words, it is not the author who voluntarily incarnates himself in a borrowed personality and who pulls the strings, it is the character himself who incarnates himself in the author, cohabits with him, dictates to him the words to be written by a phenomenon which I compared formerly to being haunted.

    The distinction between the incubated character and the normal, conscious, and reasoning self of Mr. de Curel becomes so clear that, re-reading with me his plays, Mr. de Curel was able to point out to me the sentence written by himself next to the one that was dictated by the evoked character. This form, so close to a split personality, occurs only in the works in which passion predominates; in the latest plays of the author, plays which by nature of the subject required more intellectual concentration, the role of the division of consciousness was reduced.

3. A third type, as extreme as that of Mr. de Curel, but in the opposite direction, is represented by Mr. Paul Hervieu. His personality, as we have described, experiences an almost absolute repugnance of being split and metamorphosized. It is par excellence a unified type. . . .

There is in each of us a part [that is] instinct and [a] part [that is based on] reasoning; the proportion of the two varies greatly between individuals; and from there one might start to classify individuals by likening them more or less to the two extreme types of instinct and reflection, according to which it is natural force or reasonable force that predominates in them, without forgetting that this predominance of one of the two factors does not go as far as the complete exclusion of the other: the living being is not a schema.

Now, the study we have just made on and with Mr. Paul Hervieu has the principal interest of showing us this opposition between reflection and instinct; and many of the scattered observations in the preceding pages must be considered, in my opinion, as the direct effect of the preponderance of intelligence on the instinctive life of emotions and imagination.

Commentary

In his research, Binet used a case study approach. His contemporary, the psychiatrist Edouard Toulouse (1896, 1910) used a similar methodology and published in-depth studies of Zola and Poincaré. Binet interviewed several famous authors and had them complete questionnaires. His investigation focused on (a) describing the physical characteristics of these creative people (the diameter of the head, weight, motor strength, health, etc.); (b) their biographical details: characteristics of parents, schooling, age of first dramatic work, family support, and date of first theatrical success; and (c) their work processes and conditions. Binet asked questions about the authors' working environment ("Do you prefer to write with or without any sound around you?"), sociological parameters ("Do you prefer to work alone or with another author?"), and physiological information ("At what time of the day do you prefer to write?"). He showed a great deal of interest in qualitative ideation processes used by the authors ("While you are writing a scene, do you hear the character, or do you see him or her as if he or she was in front of your eyes?"). Conscious of the multidimensional nature of creative abilities, Binet notes that "the work of artistic creation . . . lies not only in imagination, but reasoning and common sense" (Binet & Passy, 1895, p. 115).

THE CREATIVE PROCESS AND INDIVIDUAL DIFFERENCES

Binet considered *imagination* (the ability to produce ideas) and *critical thinking* (the ability to select the best of ideas) as central in the study of the creative process. He notes that each of these two aspects of creativity varies widely from one writer to another. Thus Alexandre Dumas worked on only one piece at a time and usually wrote without any correction, unlike Sardou, who made dozens of drafts before setting the final direction of his play. The selection process differs according to the author. For some, imagination and critical thinking function quasi-simultaneously, whereas others operate with two distinct moments. For example, de Curel had an original selection technique that involved, after a draft of his play, rewriting it based on memory in order to keep only what was essential. Binet (1904, p. 31) proposed to establish a typology of the "mode of relation between imagination and critical sense."

The reader will find several useful classifications in Binet's work on the analysis of literary creativity. An example is the observation of very different writing techniques. Binet opposes "graphic" authors (who write very quickly and with a high output, bypassing the auditory mode) with "listeners" (who claim to reproduce the words pronounced by internal voices) and "articulators" (who read aloud their sentences to evaluate them).

AN EARLY MULTIVARIATE APPROACH

Binet's analyses show that he recognized the complexity of the creative act and the many variables that come into play in creativity. The reader can find in Binet's selected texts the roots of a "componential" approach to creativity, which has been developed in many contemporary works on creativity (see Lubart, 1999). Binet attempts to examine the nature of interactions between many predictors of creative behavior, both individual (cognitive, affective, and conative) and environmental. The multiplicity of explanatory psychological variables allows, in turn, the identification of different creative profiles, and Binet addresses the issue of intra-individual variability. In addition, according to the profile of creative skills, a person will be more or less apt for different kinds of creative expression. Thus there are even within the literary domain different forms of creativity (poem, drama, novel, etc.), and they should require combinations of specific abilities. It is the interplay of these variables and their interactive effects that determine the individual's developmental trajectory: "The precocious talent depends not only on the individual but on the environment and the kind of vocation" (Binet, 1904, p. 98).

For Binet, some of the resources are cognitive, others are affective or personality-related. Nevertheless the ability to reason, to articulate efficiently analysis and synthesis, and to sequence these activities are identified as playing a key role in the creative process. This links clearly traditional intellectual ability to creative work. Binet stressed as well the importance of the ability to set a goal, while noting that the goals set at the beginning of a literary composition can significantly change during the writing process (see the case of de Curel): "Sometimes, the image that seduced the author and engaged him to make the piece is not part of the play; it is pushed out" (1895, p. 123). This idea that a creative work is sometimes unrelated to the original idea was also noted by Bergson (1919, p. 175), who compared the dynamics of the creative process to a back-and-forth movement:

> Sometimes there is nothing left of the original pattern in the final image. As the inventor realizes the details of his machine, he gives up some of what he wants to get or gets something else. And, similarly, the characters created by the novelist and the poet react on the idea or the feeling that they are meant to express. There is above all the part of the unexpected.

It is difficult to explain this movement only through cognitive skills or knowledge. Binet made this point and was particularly interested in noncognitive variables. He specifically emphasized the trait of perseverance. The author Hervieu, the subject of one of Binet's case studies, is an example in this regard, as he worked on only one play at a time, until completion, and then he could move on to the next. Like Zola, Hervieu worked daily at his literary task, at regular hours. The personality of Hervieu is characterized by a high emotional stability, in contrast to de Curel or Daudet, who worked in bursts of inspiration and showed a high degree of instability.

The multivariate approach to creativity aims also to identify the personal and the contextual variables, such as access to information, family, and social and societal environment (Lubart, 1999; Lubart, Mouchiroud, Tordjman, & Zenasni, 2015). This aspect of creativity is barely addressed by Binet, except in terms of the family environment. He notes that none of the writers interviewed, except Dumas, come from a literary family, but this information does not allow us to isolate the role (or lack of a role) of environmental factors. Binet insists, nevertheless, as do some contemporary scholars, on the importance of the presence of a mentor in the development of talent.

Once the predictor variables are identified, it is important to understand how these variables interact. Binet raises the question of the relationship between cognitive and personality variables, but remains reserved on the details of their interaction in the creative process. The author de Curel illustrates this point when he writes, "My pessimistic reasoning preaches inaction, my dreamy optimism the force to work" (quoted in Binet, 1895, p. 170), suggesting that the complex interplay of factors involved in creativity may be a personal equation for each playwright, for each individual.

Conclusion

Binet's interviews with writers offer enlightening testimony and set the stage for a differential psychology of creativity. Of course, his work is based in large part on dramatists' introspective self-reports, but Binet's reflections offer some basis for work in the field today. Inspired by Binet's work, current studies using structured interview techniques, discourse analysis, and process-tracing methodologies have begun to offer new insights (see the references in Glăveanu et al., 2013; Bourgeois et al., 2014). The concept of typologies of creative individuals, who may arrive at original ideas in different ways, which are partially idiosyncratic, is also Binet's legacy; the uniqueness of creative acts situates creativity at the heart of Binet's concept of "individual psychology." One issue that continues to concern the field of creativity is the balance between the search for general trends that describe creative work, across individuals and across fields, and more specific, domain-bounded, and even idiosyncratic models of creativity. This is echoed in Binet's typology of domain-related creativity, his typology of creativity within the literary domain, and his work on types of creative process patterns for imagination and critical thinking.

References

Bergson, H. (1919). *L'Energie spirituelle*. Paris: Presses Universitaires de France.

Binet, A. (1894*). Psychologie des grands calculateurs et jouers d'échecs* Paris: Hachette.

Binet, A. (1895). François de Curel, notes psychologiques. *L'Année Psychologique, 1,* 119–173.

Binet, A. (1898). La question des études classiques d'après la psychologie expérimentale. *Revue des Revues, 26,* 461–469.

Binet, A. (1904). La création littéraire: Portrait psychologique de M. Hervieu. *L'Année Psychologique, 10,* 1–62.

Binet, A., & Passy, J. (1895). Notes psychologiques sur les auteurs dramatiques. *Année Psychologique, 1,* 60–118.

Binet, A., & Simon, T. (1905). New methods for the diagnosis of the intellectual level of subnormals. *L'Annee Psychologique, 12,* 191–244.

Bourgeois-Bougrine, S., Glăveanu, V., Botella, M., Guillou, K., De Biasi, P-M., Lubart, T. (2014). The creativity maze: Exploring creativity in screenplay writing. *Psychology of Aesthetics, Creativity, and the Arts, 8*(4), 384–399.

Glăveanu, V. P., Lubart, T., Bonnardel, N., Botella, M., De Biasi, P.-M., De Sainte Catherine, M., . . . & Zenasni, F. (2013). Creativity as action: Findings from five creative domains. *Frontiers in Educational Psychology, 4,* 1–14

Lubart, T. I. (1999). Componential models. In M. A. Runco & S. R. Pritsker (Eds.), *Encyclopedia of creativity* (Vol. 1, pp. 295–300). New York, NY: Academic Press.

Lubart, T. I., Mouchiroud, C., Tordjman, S., & Zenasni, F. (2015). *Psychologie de la créativité [The psychology of creativity]* (2nd ed.). Paris: Armand Colin.

Toulouse, E. (1896). *Enquête medico-psychologique sur les rapports de la supériorité intellectuelle avec la névropathie.* Vol. 1: *Introduction générale: Emile Zola.* Paris: Société d'éditions scientifiques.

Toulouse, H. (1910). *Enquête medico-psychologique sur la supériorité intellectuelle.* Vol. 2: *Henri Poincaré.* Paris: Flammarion.

25

Skinner on Poetry, Fiction, and Design

An Implicit Science of Creativity

Mark A. Runco

Summary

Although B. F. Skinner was one of the key figures in psychology for several decades, his ideas about creativity are often overlooked. This chapter excerpts three of his works that deal with creativity, and in particular with poetry, the writing of fiction, and design. Much of what he had to say was based on his careful analyses of William Shakespeare and Gertrude Stein from before 1950. This chapter also comments on how Skinner's ideas continue to influence several lines of research on creativity and insight.

Introduction

B. F. Skinner was one of the influential psychologists of the 20th century, at least in the US, and perhaps worldwide. Psychology was well on its way to becoming a respectable science when Skinner began his career, but he demonstrated clearly how a highly objective version of the scientific method could be applied to a range of psychological concerns. Some of his work was controversial (e.g., the "baby box"), but even that stimulated debate and contributed to progress. His influence continues still, though he may not be receiving all of the credit he is due. As is the case when a theory is well ingrained in a field, founders and proponents of it are often not cited or named. But the idea of ensuring objectivity by focusing on manifest, observable, measurable behaviors was Skinner's enormous contribution to psychology, and anytime that rationale is used in psychological research, he could and perhaps should be cited.

Very briefly, Skinner focused on observable behaviors and felt that they were controlled by consequences. His view thus differs from earlier learning theories, such as

Pavlov's, in its focus on voluntary behaviors (operants) and his focus on what follow them rather than what elicits them. Skinner did quite a bit of research on reinforcers, punishers, and the schedules and ratios with which they are paired to operants. He himself wrote a novel, *Walden Two*, which describes a utopia. There citizens are aware of the impact of consequences and utilize them for optimal education and even free will.

Skinner may not be given his due often enough in creativity research in part because of an obvious question: How is something as slippery as creativity understood if the focus is on observable, measurable behaviors? Clues to an answer can be found in some of Skinner's early works. Three of them are reviewed in this chapter. They examine poetry, fiction, and design. These are unambiguously creative endeavors, and the fact that Skinner took them on gives some indication that he felt the operant approach could be applied and would be useful. This chapter identifies those indications within the three articles. It identifies a handful of ties between Skinner's thinking and theories of creativity. The conclusion points to some of the more recent evidence that Skinner's approach is still influential for our understanding of creativity. First we will look at Skinner's own words about poetry.

Reading 1: "The Alliteration in Shakespeare's Sonnets: A Study in Literary Behavior"

Source: Skinner, B. F. (1939). The alliteration in Shakespeare's sonnets: A study in literary behavior. *Psychological Record, 3*, 186–192. Selections reproduced with permission from the B. F. Skinner Foundation (http://www.bfskinner.org/).

Alliteration is one of the most familiar forms of sound-patterning in poetry and prose. It is said to exist when two or more syllables beginning with the same consonant occur near each other in a given passage. Examples of alliteration are frequently cited as contributing to the effect of a literary work, and it is usually implied that they represent deliberate acts of arrangement on the part of the writer. If this is true, alliteration should throw some light on the dynamics of verbal behavior and especially upon a process which may be called "formal perseveration" or, better, "formal strengthening." Studies of word-association, latent speech, and so on, have indicated that the appearance of a sound in speech raises the probability of occurrence of that sound for some time thereafter. Stated in a different way: the emission of a verbal response temporarily raises the strength of all responses of similar form. The principal characteristics of poetry (alliteration, assonance, rhyme, and rhythm) seem to be exaggerated cases of the tendency toward formal strengthening, and they should supply useful information with regard to it.

In order to determine the existence or the importance of any process responsible for a characteristic pattern in a sample of speech, it is necessary to allow for the amount of patterning to be expected from chance. We cannot assert, for example, that any one instance of alliteration is due to a special process in the behavior of the writer rather than to an accidental proximity of words beginning with the same sound. Proof that there is a process responsible for alliterative patterning can be obtained only through a statistical analysis of all the arrangements of initial consonants in a reasonably large sample. In the case of alliteration what we want to know is the extent to which the initial consonants are not distributed at random. If the distribution turns out to be random, then no process by virtue of which words come to be arranged on a formal basis can be attributed to the behavior of the writer, even though selected instances still show the grouping commonly called alliteration.

If there is any process in the behavior of the writer by virtue of which the occurrence of an initial consonant raises the probability of occurrence of that sound for a short time thereafter, then the initial consonants in a sample of writing will be grouped. Methods are, of course, available for detecting a tendency toward grouping, but in the case of poetry a more appropriate technique can be based upon the use of the line as a natural unit. In any large sample of poetry certain lines will contain no occurrences of a given initial consonant, and others will contain one, two, three, and so on, occurrences. From the relative frequency of the consonant we may calculate these numbers if we assume that the probability of occurrence remains unchanged and that each occurrence is an independent event. A process of alliteration, if it existed, would violate these assumptions and yield a greater number of lines containing more than one occurrence and also a greater number of empty lines.

This paper presents some facts concerning the alliterative patterns in a block of one hundred Shakespeare sonnets. . . . The sonnets were first scanned according to a set of arbitrary rules, designed to prevent unintentional selection and at the same time to single out the most important syllables in each of the 1,400 lines. The average number of syllables per line thus designated was 5.036, which agrees well with the pentametric form of the poems. The range . . . was from three to eight. A tabulation of initial consonants by line was then made. The results were expressed for each consonant separately in the form of (1) the number of lines containing no occurrences, (2) the number containing one occurrence, (3) the number containing two occurrences, and so on.

The formula for the number of lines containing 0, 1, 2, . . . occurrences of a given initial consonant involves [a] binomial expansion . . . where N is the number of lines examined, n the number of syllables per line, p the probability of occurrence of the consonant under consideration (obtained from its frequency in the whole sample), and q the probability of occurrence of any other sound, or $1 - p$. The successive terms in the expansion give the numbers required. A good approximation could have been obtained by letting $n = 5$, which is close to the average number of important syllables, but a more accurate estimate was obtained by calculating separately for lines of different length according to the lengths in the sample. Calculations were made for 277 lines of four syllables (including a few in the original sample which contained only three), 830 lines of five syllables, 252 of six, and 41 of seven (including a few originally of eight). By adding the occurrences obtained from these separate calculations, the total chance expectancy for that consonant was obtained.

Before the observed and calculated frequencies may legitimately be compared for our present purposes, a spurious alliterative effect in the observed values must be taken into account. Shakespeare, perhaps more than most other English poets, tends to repeat a word (or to use an inflected form) within the space of a line. There are two repetitions, for example, in the line:

Suns of the world may stain when heaven's sun staineth

In tabulating initial consonants, this line must be counted as containing four s's. It is clear . . . that the last two must be attributed not only to formal strengthening but to some thematic source. The line as heard is strongly sibilant, but two of the s's are due to something beyond a simple alliterative process.

In a line containing a repeated word it is at present impossible to determine how the responsibility for the similarity of sound is to be divided between formal and thematic factors. To omit all repeated words from the present tabulation would obviously not be justified; at the same time we cannot accept at full value the instances of alliteration for which they are responsible. . . .

The initial consonants [were] arranged in order according to the frequency with which they occur in the block of 100 sonnets. The numbers of lines containing 0, 1, 2, 3, 4, or 5 occurrences per line observed for Shakespeare [were] calculated as described above. . . . The least frequent sound (qu) occurs only 23 times and never more than once per line, as we should expect from chance. At the other extreme the sound s (which occurs 938 times) fails to occur in 702 lines (the expected number of empty lines being 685) but occurs once in 501 lines (expected: 523), twice in 161 lines (expected: 162), three times in 29 lines (expected: 26), and four times in seven lines (expected: two). If we omit the cases which arise from repeated words, we obtain . . . better agreement. The corrections required in the two-per-line column [were] merely . . . estimated. An examination of every tenth line showing two occurrences indicates that about 19% of such lines are due to repetition. When this correction is made for s, it appears that Shakespeare falls about 30 lines *short* of the expected number of lines containing two s's.

Other consonants . . . show varying degrees of agreement. The estimates of significance (which are in every case based upon the raw data) indicate a possible "use of alliteration" with n, k, h, t, f, b, and l, but these all involve repetition, and the corrected values give very little support to the popular notion. There is possibly a trend in the direction to be expected from a process of alliteration, but the absolute excess of "heavy" lines is very slight. Some indication of this excess may be obtained from the following statements. . . . :

Lines containing four like initial consonants. (Ex.: Borne on the bier with white and bristly beard.)

Of these lines there are only eight more than would be expected from chance, and four of these are due to the repetition of the same word or words. Not more than once in twenty-five sonnets (350 lines) does Shakespeare lengthen a series of three like consonants into four, except when he repeats a word.

Lines containing three like initial consonants. (Ex.: Save that my soul's imaginary sight.)

Of these lines there are 33 too many, but twenty-nine of these are due to repetition of the same word. Only four are, therefore, "pure" alliteration. Except when he repeated a whole word, Shakespeare changed a line of two like consonants into one of three not oftener than once in twenty-five sonnets.

Lines containing two like initial consonants.

There are 92 excess lines of this sort, but the correction for repetition gives a *shortage* of approximately forty lines. Allowing for eight lines extended to contain three or four occurrences, we may say that once in about every three sonnets Shakespeare *discarded* a word because its initial consonant had already been used.

These corrections probably go too far, since a repetition of the same word may in part exemplify an alliterative process. . . . This recalculation would affect chiefly the values for the empty lines and for the lines containing one occurrence.

Shakespeare shows in general an excess of empty lines, but most, if not all, of this difference would disappear under recalculation with a smaller total frequency. Similarly, Shakespeare's shortage of one-occurrence lines would be reduced. These changes cannot be made without an arbitrary estimate of the share contributed by alliteration when a word is repeated, but by taking the raw data as the upper limit and the fully corrected data as the lower, the main question proposed in this study may be answered.

In spite of the seeming richness of alliteration in the sonnets, there is no significant evidence of a process of alliteration in the behavior of the poet to which any serious attention should be given. So far as this aspect of poetry is concerned, Shakespeare might as well have drawn his words out of a hat. The thematic or semantic forces which are responsible for the emission of speech apparently function independently of this particular formal property.

It is scarcely convincing to argue that Shakespeare may have arranged certain alliterative patterns and discarded an equal number due to chance, since it is unlikely that the expected frequencies would be so closely approximated. It is simpler to believe that we have been misled by the selection of instances and that no process of alliteration should ever have been attributed to the poet. If "formal strengthening" proves to be a real characteristic of normal speech, we shall have to look for the key to Shakespeare's genius in his ability to resist it, thereby reversing the usual conception of this kind of poetic activity.

Shakespeare's "philosophy of composition" might well be expressed in the words of the Duchess, who said to Alice, "And the moral of *that* is, 'Take care of the sense, and the sounds will take care of themselves.'"

Commentary on Skinner's View of Poetry

In "The Alliteration in Shakespeare's Sonnets," Skinner (1939) starts with an operational definition of the behavior ("sound patterning") and notes right up front that it is important in poetry and prose and a deliberate act by the artist. Skinner is also explicit about exactly how to test the hypothesis that alliteration is deliberately used by writers: "In the case of alliteration what we want to know is the extent to which the initial consonants are not distributed at random" (p. 186). A tangent here concerns the more recent studies of random (vs. deliberate) processes used by creators (Simonton, 2007; Weisberg & Hass, 2007).

Of some relevance is the fact that Skinner devotes much of this essay to the possibility that there is an important process used by writers. This is noteworthy because processes are not inherently observable, and because it exemplifies Skinner's view that scientific research must focus on operants and observable behaviors—but there may be explanations of behavior that are inferred from these behaviors. In the case of alliteration, what must be inferred is the process used by the writer.

The research on Shakespeare's alliteration might be viewed in the context of Skinner's (1957) broader attempt to explain verbal behavior, as well as other investigations of Shakespeare's creativity (Simonton, 1999). Skinner's attempts to explain verbal behavior were hotly criticized by Chomsky (1967). Contemporary researchers will probably react to Skinner's calculating a large number of statistical tests without a Bonferroni correction, but of course we can't criticize Skinner for using the best methods that were available at that time (even though his findings might be reinterpreted now that new methods are available).

Skinner (1939, p. 188) concluded:

> In spite of the seeming richness of alliteration in the sonnets, there is no significant evidence of a process of alliteration in the behavior of the poet to which any serious attention should given. So far as this aspect of poetry is concerned, Shakespeare might as well have drawn his words out of a hat.

Skinner does acknowledge an alternative explanation for his findings in the last paragraph of this essay, but still true to the scientific method, rejects that alternative because it is not parsimonious.

After dealing with poetry, in 1934 Skinner turned to the writing of fiction, and in particular to the very first published work of Gertrude Stein. This was an essay she wrote about "automism," a label given for doing something (like writing) without attending to it. It may not be far from contemporary concepts such as "automaticity" or "effortless information processing." Below is Skinner's analysis of Stein's fiction.

Reading 2: "Has Gertrude Stein a Secret?"

Source: Skinner, B. F. (1934). Has Gertrude Stein a secret? *Atlantic Monthly, 153,* 50–57. Selections reproduced with permission from the B. F. Skinner Foundation (http://www.bfskinner.org/).

In the *Autobiography of Alice B. Toklas* Gertrude Stein tells in the following way of some psychological experiments made by her at Harvard:

She was one of a group of Harvard men and Radcliffe women and they all lived very closely and very interestingly together. One of them, a young philosopher and mathematician who was doing research work in psychology, left a definite mark on her life. She and he together worked out a series of experiments in automatic writing under the direction of Münsterberg. The result of her own experiments, which Gertrude Stein wrote down and which was printed in the *Harvard Psychological Review*, was the first writing of hers ever to be printed. It is very interesting to read because the method of writing to be afterward developed in *Three Lives* and *The Making of Americans* already shows itself.

There is a great deal more in this early paper than Miss Stein points out. It is, as she says, an anticipation of the prose style of *Three Lives* and is unmistakably the work of Gertrude Stein in spite of the conventional subject matter with which it deals. Many turns of speech, often commonplace, which she has since then in some subtle way made her own are already to be found. But there is much more than this. The paper is concerned with an early interest of Miss Stein's that must have been very important in her later development, and the work that it describes cannot reasonably be over-looked by anyone trying to understand this remarkable person.

Since the paper is hard to obtain, I shall summarize it briefly. It was published in the *Psychological Review* for September 1896 under the title "Normal Motor Automatism," . . . and it attempted to show to what extent the elements of a "second personality" (of the sort to be observed in certain cases of hysteria) were to be found in a normal being. In their experiments the authors investigated the limits of their own normal motor automatism; that is to say, they undertook to see how far they could "split" their own personalities in a deliberate and purely artificial way. They were successful to the extent of being able to perform many acts (such as writing or reading aloud) in an automatic manner, while carrying on at the same time some other activity such as reading an interesting story.

In the experiments with automatic writing, a planchette of the ouija board type was originally used, but as soon as the authors had satisfied themselves that spontaneous writing movements do occur while the attention is directed elsewhere, an ordinary pencil and paper were used instead. The subject usually began by making voluntary random writing movements or by writing the letter m repeatedly. In one experiment this was done while the subject read an interesting story at the same time, and it was found that some of the words read in the story would be written down in an automatic way. At first there was a strong tendency to notice this as soon as it had begun to happen and to stop it, but eventually the words could be written down unconsciously as well as involuntarily. (I shall use Miss Stein's psychological terminology throughout.) "Sometimes the writing of the word was completely unconscious, but more often the subject knew what was going on. His knowledge, however, was obtained by sensations from the arm. He was conscious that he just had written a word, not that he was about to do so."

In other experiments the subject read an interesting story as before, and single words were dictated to him to be written down at the same time. These were difficult experiments, but after considerable practice they were successful. The subject was eventually able to write down "five or six" words spoken by another person, without being conscious of either the heard sounds or the movement of the arm. If his attention were not sufficiently well distracted he might become aware that his hand was writing something. The information came from the arm, not from the sound of the dictated word. "It is never the sound that recalls us. This, of course, may be an individual peculiarity to a certain extent. . . . Yet, Miss Stein has a strong auditory consciousness, and sounds usually determine the direction of her attention."

In a third group of experiments the subject read aloud, preferably from an uninteresting story, while being read to from an interesting one. "If he does not go insane during the first few trials, he will quickly learn to concentrate his attention fully on what is being read to him, yet go on reading just the same. The reading becomes completely unconscious for periods of as much as a page." Automatic reading of this sort is probably part of the experience of everyone.

The fourth and last group brings out the relevance of the experiments to the later work of Gertrude Stein. I shall let Miss Stein describe the result.

"Spontaneous automatic writing . . . became quite easy after a little practice. We had now gained so much control over our habits of attention that distraction by reading was almost unnecessary. Miss Stein found it sufficient distraction often to simply read what her arm wrote, but following three or four words behind her pencil. . . .

A phrase would seem to get into the head and keep repeating itself at every opportunity, and hang over from day to day even. The stuff written was grammatical, and the words and phrases fitted together all right, but there was not much connected thought. The unconsciousness was broken into every six or seven words by flashes of consciousness, so that one cannot be sure but what the slight element of connected thought which occasionally appeared was due to these flashes of consciousness. But the ability to write stuff that sounds all right, without consciousness, was fairly well demonstrated by the experiments. Here are a few specimens:

> Hence there is no possible way of avoiding what I have spoken of, and if this is not believed by the people of whom you have spoken, then it is not possible to prevent the people of whom you have spoken so glibly. . . .

Here is a bit more poetical than intelligible:

> When he could not be the longest and thus to be, and thus to be, the strongest.

And here is one that is neither:

> This long time when he did this best time, and he could thus have been bound, and in this long time, when he could be this to first use of this long time. . . ."

Here is obviously an important document. No one who has read *Tender Buttons* or the later work in the same vein can fail to recognize a familiar note in these examples of automatic writing. They are quite genuinely in the manner that has so commonly been taken as characteristic of Gertrude Stein. Miss Stein's description of her experimental result is exactly that of the average reader confronted with *Tender Buttons* for the first time: "The stuff is grammatical, and the words and phrases fit together all right, but there is not much connected thought." In short, the case is so good, simply on the grounds of style, that we are brought to the swift conclusion that the two products have a common origin, and that the work of Gertrude Stein in the *Tender Buttons* manner is written automatically and unconsciously in some such way as that described in this early paper.

This conclusion grows more plausible as we consider the case. It is necessary, of course, to distinguish between the Gertrude Stein of *Three Lives* and the *Autobiography* and the

Gertrude Stein of *Tender Buttons*, a distinction that is fairly easily made, even though, as we shall see in a moment, there is some of the first Gertrude Stein in the latter work. If we confine ourselves for the present to the second of these two persons, it is clear that the hypothetical author who might be inferred from the writing itself possesses just those characteristics that we should expect to find if a theory of automatic writing were the right answer. Thus there is very little intellectual content discoverable. The reader— the ordinary reader, at least— cannot infer from the writing that its author possesses any consistent point of view. There is seldom any intelligible expression of opinion, and there are enough capricious reversals to destroy the effect of whatever there may be. There are even fewer emotional prejudices. The writing is cold. Strong phrases are almost wholly lacking, and it is so difficult to find a well-rounded emotional complex that if one is found it may as easily be attributed to the ingenuity of the seeker. Similarly, our hypothetical author shows no sign of a personal history or of a cultural background; *Tender Buttons* is the stream of consciousness of a woman without a past. The writing springs from no literary sources. In contrast with the work of Joyce, to whom a superficial resemblance may be found, the borrowed phrase is practically lacking.

When memorized passages occur, they are humdrum—old saws or simple doggerel recovered from childhood and often very loosely paraphrased: "If at first you don't succeed try try again," or "Please pale hot, please cover rose, please acre in the red. . . ." If there is any character in the writing whatsoever, it is due to this savor of the schoolroom, and the one inference about the author that does seem plausible is that she has been to grammar school. Her sentences are often cast as definitions ("What is a spectacle a spectacle is the resemblance . . ." or "A sign is the specimen spoken") or as copy-book aphorisms ("An excuse is not dreariness, a single plate is not butter," or "There is coagulation in cold and there is none in prudence") or as grammatical paradigms ("I begin you begin we begin they began we began you began I began"). This heavy dose of grammar school is especially strongly felt in *An Elucidation*, Miss Stein's first attempt to explain herself, and a piece of writing in which there are many evidences of a struggle on the part of the conscious Gertrude Stein to accept the origin of the *Tender Buttons* manner. Miss Stein wanted the volume *Lucy Church Amiably* to be bound like a schoolbook, but I shall leave it to a more imaginative mind to elaborate this metaphor further.

This is apparently as much of the writing as will help to illuminate the character of the writer. For the rest, it is what Miss Stein describes as sounding all right without making sense. There is no paradox about this, there is no secret about how it is done; but it gives us very little information about the author. Grammar is ever present—that is the main thing. We are presented with sentences ("sentences and always sentences"), but we often recognize them as such only because they show an accepted order of article, substantive, verb, split infinitive, article, substantive, connective, and so on. The framework of a sentence is there, but the words tacked upon it are an odd company. In the simplest type of case we have a nearly intelligible sentence modified by the substitution for a single word of one sounding much the same. This sort of substitution was reported by Miss Stein in connection with her experiments in automatic reading: "Absurd mistakes are occasionally made in the reading of words—substitutions similar in sound but utterly different in sense." The reader will recognize it as the sort of slip that is made when one is very tired. In more complex cases it cannot, of course, be shown that the unintelligibility is due to substitution; if most of the words are replaced, we have nothing to show that a word is a slip. We must be content to characterize it, as Miss Stein herself has done: "We have made excess return to rambling."

From this brief analysis it is apparent that, although it is quite plausible that the work is due to a second personality successfully split off from Miss Stein's conscious self, it is a very flimsy sort of personality indeed. It is intellectually unopinionated, is emotionally cold, and has no past. It is unread and unlearned beyond grammar school. It is as easily influenced as a child; a heard word may force itself into whatever sentence may be under construction at the moment, or it may break the sentence up altogether and irremediably. Its literary materials are the sensory things nearest at hand—objects, sounds, tastes, smells, and so on. The reader may compare, for the sake of the strong contrast, the materials of "Melanctha" in *Three Lives*, a piece of writing of quite another sort. In her experimental work it was Miss Stein's intention to avoid the production of a true second personality, and she considered herself to be successful. The automatism she was able to demonstrate possessed the "elements" of a second personality, it was able to do anything that a second personality could do, but it never became the organized alter ego of the hysteric. The superficial character of the inferential author of *Tender Buttons* consequently adds credibility to the theory of automatic authorship.

The Gertrude Stein enthusiast may feel that I am being cruelly unjust in this estimate. I admit that there are passages in *Tender Buttons* that elude the foregoing analysis. But it must be made clear that the two Gertrude Steins we are considering are not kept apart by the covers of books. There is a good deal of the Gertrude Stein of the *Autobiography* in *Tender Buttons*, in the form of relatively intelligible comment, often parenthetical in spirit. Thus at the end of the section on Mutton (which begins "A letter which can wither, a learning which can suffer and an outrage which is simultaneous is principal") comes this sentence: "A meal in mutton mutton why is lamb cheaper, it is cheaper because so little is more," which is easily recognized as a favorite prejudice of the Gertrude Stein of the *Autobiography*. Similarly such a phrase as "the sad procession of the unkilled bull," in *An Elucidation*, is plainly a reference to another of Miss Stein's interests. But, far from damaging our theory, this occasional appearance of Miss Stein herself is precisely what the theory demands. In her paper in the *Psychological Review* she deals at length with the inevitable alternation of conscious and automatic selves, and in the quotation we have given it will be remembered that she comments upon these "flashes of consciousness." Even though the greater part of *Tender Buttons* is automatic, we should expect an "element of connected thought," and our only problem is that which Miss Stein herself has considered—namely, are we to attribute to conscious flashes all the connected thought that is present?

There is a certain logical difficulty here. It may be argued that, since we dispense with all the intelligible sentences by calling them conscious flashes, we should not be surprised to find that what is left is thin and meaningless. We must therefore restate our theory, in a way that will avoid this criticism. We first divide the writings of Gertrude Stein into two parts on the basis of their ordinary intelligibility. I do not contend that this is a hard and fast line, but it is a sufficiently real one for most persons. It does not, it is to be understood, follow the outlines of her works. We then show that the unintelligible part has the characteristics of the automatic writing produced by Miss Stein in her early psychological experiments, and from this and many other considerations we conclude that our division of the work into two parts is real and valid and that one part is automatic in nature.

I cannot find anything in the *Autobiography* or the other works I have read that will stand against this interpretation. On the contrary, there are many bits of evidence, none of which would be very convincing in itself, that support it. Thus (1) *Tender Buttons* was written on scraps of paper, and no scrap was ever thrown away; (2) Miss Stein likes to write in the presence of distracting noises; (3) her handwriting is often more legible to Miss Toklas than to herself (that is, her writing is "cold" as soon as it is produced); and (4) she is "fond of writing the letter m," with which, the reader will recall, the automatic procedure often began. In *An Elucidation*, her "first effort to realize clearly just what her writing meant and why it was as it was," there are many fitful allusions to the experimental days: "Do you all understand extraneous memory," "In this way my researches are easily read," a suddenly interpolated "I stopped I stopped myself," which recalls the major difficulty in her experiments, and so on.

It is necessary to assume that when Gertrude Stein returned to the practice of automatic writing (about 1912?) she had forgotten or was shortly to forget its origins. I accept as made in perfectly good faith the statement in the *Autobiography* that "Gertrude Stein never had subconscious reactions, nor was she a successful subject for automatic writing," even though the evidence to the contrary in her early paper is incontrovertible. She has forgotten it, just as she forgot her first novel almost immediately after it was completed and did not remember it again for twenty-five years. It is quite possible, moreover, that the manner in which she writes the *Tender Buttons* sort of thing is not unusual enough to remind her of its origins or to be remarked by others. One of the most interesting statements in the excerpt quoted from her early paper is that Gertrude Stein found it sufficient distraction simply to follow what she was writing some few words behind her pencil. If in the course of time she was able to bring her attention nearer and nearer to the pencil, she must eventually have reached a point at which there remained only the finest distinction between "knowing what one is going to write and knowing that one has written it." This is a transitional state to which Miss Stein devotes considerable space in her paper. It is therefore reasonable for us to assume that the artificial character of the experimental procedure has completely worn off, and that there remains only a not-far-from-normal state into which Miss Stein may pass unsuspectingly enough and in which the *Tender Buttons* style is forthcoming.

Having begun to produce stuff of this sort again, however, Miss Stein could not have failed to notice its peculiarities. We have her own opinion that the sentences quoted from her automatic writing do not show much connected thought, and I believe we are fully justified in our characterization of the greater part of *Tender Buttons* as "ordinarily unintelligible." I know that it would be quite possible for an industrious and ingenious person to find any number of meanings in it, just as it is possible to find meanings in any chance arrangement of words. But the conclusion to which we are now led is that the work with which we are dealing is very probably unintelligible in any ordinary sense, not only to other readers, but to Miss Stein herself. Why, then, did she publish?

It is important . . . that between 1896 and 1912 Stein had come to know Picasso and Matisse and was already long in the practice of defending their work against the question, "What does it mean?" With such an experience . . . it is not difficult to accept as art what one has hitherto dismissed as the interesting and rather surprising result of an experiment. It was, I believe, only because Gertrude Stein had already prepared the defense as it applied to Picasso that she could put forth her own unintelligible product as a serious artistic experiment. For a person of the sound intelligence of Stein there is a great natural resistance against the production of nonsense. It was the major problem in her experimental technique: "I stopped I stopped myself." But the writing succeeded in this case, because the resistance had been broken down, first by the procedure of the experiments, which permitted the sustained production of meaningless sentences, and later by the championing of Picasso, which permitted their publication. This was a fortunate combination of circumstances. "I could explain," she says in *An Elucidation*, "how it happened accidentally that fortunately no explanation was necessary."

Stein has not, however, freed herself from the problem of the meaning of the things she writes. She is not above being bothered by criticism on the score of unintelligibility. She often characterizes her work in this vein as experimental, but that is in no sense an explanation. Beyond this her answer seems to be that the writing is its own justification.

It was not a question, she told her Oxford audience, of whether she was right in doing the kind of writing she did. "She had been doing as she did for about twenty years and now they wanted to hear her lecture." And she had previously dealt with the matter in *An Elucidation*:

If it is an event just by itself is there a question
Tulips is there a question
Pets is there a question
Furs is there a question
Folds is there a question
Is there anything in question.

I think we must accept this answer to the ethical question of whether she is doing right by Oxford and the King's English. The final test of whether it is right is whether anyone likes it. But a literary composition is not "an event just by itself," and the answer to Stein's query is that there certainly are questions, of a critical sort, that may legitimately be raised. Meaning is one of them.

One kind of meaning that might be found if our theory is valid is psychological. In noting the presence of verbal slips ("substitutions similar in sound but utterly different in sense") we lay ourselves open to the criticism of the Freudian, who would argue that there are no true slips. According to this view, there is always some reason why the substitution is made, and the substituted word will have a deeper significance if we can find it. But we are here not primarily concerned with such psychological significances.

Of literary significances it may be urged that for the initiated or sympathetic reader there is an intellectual content in this part of Miss Stein's work that we have overlooked. Now, either this will be of such a sort that it could also be expressed normally, or it will be a special kind of content that requires the form given to it by Miss Stein. A partisan could so easily prove the first case by translating a representative passage that we may assume it not to be true. The second case requires a very difficult theory of knowledge in its defense, and we shall not need to inquire into it any more closely. It is quite true that something happens to the conscientious reader of *Tender Buttons*. Part of the effect is certainly due either to repetition or to surprise. These are recognized literary devices, and it may be argued that still a third kind of meaning, which we may designate as emotional, is therefore to be found. But in ordinary practice these devices are supplementary to expressions of another sort. The mere generation of the effects of repetition and surprise is not in itself a literary achievement.

We have allowed for the presence of any or all of these kinds of meaning by speaking only of ordinary intelligibility. I do not think that a case can be made out for any one of them that is not obviously the invention of the analyzer. In any event the present argument is simply that the evidence here offered in support of a theory of automatic writing makes it more probable that meanings are not present, and that we need not bother to look for them. A theory of automatic writing does not, of course, necessarily exclude meanings. It is possible to set up a second personality that will possess all the attributes of a conscious self and whose writings will be equally meaningful. But in the present case it is clear that, as Stein originally intended, a true second personality does not exist. This part of her work is, as she has characterized her experimental result, little more than "what her arm wrote." And it is an arm that has very little to say. This is, I believe, the main importance of the present theory for literary criticism. It enables one to assign an origin to the unintelligible part of Gertrude Stein that puts one at ease about its meanings.

There are certain aspects of prose writing, such as rhythm, that are not particularly dependent upon intelligibility. It is possible to experiment with them with meaningless words, and it may be argued that this is what is happening in the present case. Considering the freedom that Stein has given herself, I do not think the result is very striking, although this is clearly a debatable point. It is a fairer interpretation, however, to suppose, in accordance with our theory, that there is no experimentation at the time the writing is produced. There may be good reason for publishing the material afterward as an experiment. For example, I recognize the possibility of a salutary, though accidental, effect upon Gertrude Stein's conscious prose or upon English prose in general. In "Composition As Explanation," for example, there is an intimate fusion of the two styles, and the conscious passages are imitative of the automatic style. This is also probably true of parts of the *Autobiography*. It is perhaps impossible to tell at present whether the effect upon her conscious prose is anything more than a loss of discipline. The compensating gain is often very great.

We have no reason, of course, to estimate the literary value of this part of Stein's work. It might be considerable, even if our theory is correct. It is apparent that Stein believes it to be important and has accordingly published it. If she is right, if this part of her work is to become historically as significant as she has contended, then the importance of the document with which we began is enormous. For the first time we should then have an account by the author herself of how a literary second personality has been set up.

I do not believe this importance exists, however, because I do not believe in the importance of the part of Stein's writing that does not make sense. On the contrary, I regret the unfortunate effect it has had in obscuring the finer work of a very fine mind. I welcome the present theory because it gives one the freedom to dismiss one part of Gertrude Stein's writing as a probably ill-advised experiment and to enjoy the other and very great part without puzzlement.

Commentary on Gertrude Stein and Fiction

Stein's view was that automism was possible only as a result of deliberately splitting one's personality. The apparatus used by Stein was not unlike a Ouija board, a fact that reminded me of early biographical studies (e.g., Schaefer & Anastasi, 1968) that suggested that creative people tend to be open to far-fetched ideas, including ESP and the like. This always made sense to me because it might indeed be a kind of openness, and openness is probably the personality trait most often empirically associated with creativity (Dollinger, Urban, & James, 2004; McCrae, 1987).

Skinner describes how Stein explained some of the automism as processing on an unconscious level. It would make sense that Stein would recognize the unconscious, both because of what was just said about being open (even to that which is untestable, such as the unconscious) but also because other writers seem to feel strongly that the unconscious plays a role in their work. John Cheever, for example, believed that much of his creativity depended on his being able to tap unconscious (or preconscious) material (Rothenberg, 1990). Interestingly, he also confessed that this sometimes "scared the hell out of him," which in turn may have led to his alcoholism.

Skinner again emphasizes the role of experience, this time in Stein's later fiction. He argues that Stein's writing as part of her research on automism is apparent when reading her later work, especially *Tender Buttons*. At noted earlier, Skinner's interest in experience is apparent throughout his career. One of his later essays suggests that intrinsic motivation, which is so often mentioned in the creativity research, can be explained in terms of experience. Skinner used this reasoning to explain "starving artists": at first blush they seem to do their work without regard for rewards—which is why they are starving! But Skinner argued that these artists had *reinforcement histories* that allowed them to internalize the pleasure associated with reinforcers, the result being that they continued to produce art without new positive consequences. This does make some sense, especially when paired with another Skinnerian idea, namely that of *resistance to extinction*. This supposedly develops when rewards are given frequently, and then less and less frequently. The organism becomes accustomed to rare reinforcement and is willing to maintain behavior even when rewards are not immediately provided.

Skinner referred to Stein's use of "the inevitable alteration of conscious and automatic selves" (1934, p. 54). He did not do much with this, which is unfortunate because there is quite a bit in the literature about creativity resulting from dual processes. These may be conscious and unconscious, divergent and convergent, or, quite similar to Stein's thinking, deliberate and spontaneous. He does mention an intriguing "transitional state" reported by Stein, but again, it would be useful to have more information.

Another intriguing point arises when Skinner brings Stein's friendship with Picasso and Matisse into his thinking. Indeed at this point Skinner (1934, p. 55) revisits the topic of meaning (in art), and he describes "a great natural resistance to the production of nonsense." He relates this resistance to Stein's intelligence, which raises the question of how intelligence is related to creativity. One view is that they are unrelated, though the more common view is of a threshold of intelligence that is required for creative performance (Runco & Albert, 1986). The resistance may also relate to the "cost of expertise," mentioned elsewhere in the present chapter, and certainly it is relevant to the judgments that must be postponed, according to proponents of brainstorming. Another label for resistance is "squelcher," "barrier," or "conceptual block" (e.g., Davis, 1999).

Anyone familiar with the theory of personal creativity will appreciate Skinner's comments on the different kinds of meaning that may be derived from artistic works.

The theory of personal creativity de-emphasizes attributions and social recognition and argues that creativity is the bringing of something new and meaningful into account, where meaning may be personal and is not social (Runco, 2007). Social meaning, in this theory, may follow personal meaning, but there is creativity before social recognition, and social recognition is not vital for creativity. Skinner's ideas about "psychological meaning" and "emotional meaning" are consistent with this theory of personal creativity.

Clearly there is much in Skinner's essay on Gertrude Stein that is relevant to studies of creativity. His work on design is also relevant, in part because it focuses on visual creativity—in contrast to the linguistic creativity of poetry and fiction—and because design has become a very broad and widely cited area of study and education. Not surprisingly, Skinner's work on design was as operational as he could make it. Below is Skinner's 1941 article, "The Psychology of Design."

Reading 3: "The Psychology of Design"

Source: Skinner, B. F. (1941). The psychology of design. In B. Boas (Ed.), *Art education today* (pp. 1–6). New York, NY: Bureau of Publications, Teachers College, Columbia University. Selections reproduced with permission from the B. F. Skinner Foundation (http://www.bfskinner.org/).

Any design, considered as a simple objective thing, can be described in physical mathematical terms, but this will not suffice for an understanding of the place of design in art. The artist is not so much interested in the physical structure of a design as in the effect it has upon the one who looks at it. This happens also to be the concern of the psychologist. We might say that a design is what it *is* only because of what it *does,* and, if this is true, some knowledge of the various kinds of effects which visual patterns have should help us in understanding the nature of design.

THE BEHAVIOR OF LOOKING

One kind of effect of a visual pattern is that which it has on the simple behavior of looking. A uniform surface (so large that some central part need not be regarded as bounded by a frame or border) does not cause the observer to behave in any very definite way. However, if we place upon it a single dot of contrasting color or value, we may be said to have established a rudimentary design, for more or less uniform behavior will be induced when the surface is placed before an observer. It is not likely that the dot will first strike the region of clearest vision, but the eye will turn, almost inevitably, in the direction of the dot and stop there, at least momentarily.

This is a very elementary design, for its possibilities are limited. But if we introduce a second dot, we immediately enhance the effect. The eye now tends to move from one dot to the other, not so inevitably as in the first case, but with considerable uniformity. This movement has certain properties (of which the observer may or may not be aware) which contribute to the total effect: it establishes a "direction" and a "distance." If we add a third or fourth dot, we greatly increase the variety of the resulting activity, although we are less able to predict how or where the eye will move. And, in general, an increase in the number of dots reduces the predictability of the effect and weakens the design, although there are many exceptions to this rule. A number of dots arranged in a line or at the corners of an imaginary regular polygon will yield a more predictable effect than the same number scattered at random.

When we reach the order of complexity exhibited by most of the designs actually used in art, we can say very little about a uniform behavior of looking. . . . We can no longer explain the effect of a design by contending that the eye follows contours, or falls with a rhythmic beat upon the repeated elements of a border, or performs any of the other feats which used to be attributed to it from self-observation. This does not mean that there are no gross differences in the movement of the eye in looking at different pictures. The movement may be localized or scattered, directed or aimless, and so on; and these properties have an obvious bearing upon the character of the picture. But now that something is known about them, eye movements have lost much of their earlier importance in the explanation of design.

What many people think of as eye movements are apparently movements of attention, and this brings us to another kind of effect which a design may have. As everyone knows, it is possible to hold the eye fixed upon some object and at the same time to "attend to" objects in neighboring parts of the field of vision. One may test this with a simple experiment. If the reader will look at the letter at the left end of this line, he will find it possible to examine nearby letters (say, those above or below it) without noticeably moving the eye. This kind of behavior is not clearly understood, but it seems to involve very slight (perhaps merely potential) movements of looking toward or reaching toward other parts of the field. One may be aware of this while performing the experiment. The tendency toward movement may be so strong as to break into a full shift of the center of vision, or into a modified posture of the whole body. We may suppose, then, that while the eye does not actually follow a curved line, there may be a tendency for various other muscles of the body to move as if the line were being followed, and this kind of behavior will contribute to the total effect.

THE PHI PHENOMENON

Our modern knowledge of eye movements, while weakening their explanatory value, compensates for this to some extent by setting up certain new and interesting possibilities. When one is looking at a picture, the eye may be roughly likened to a camera which is taking a number of still photographs of different parts of the canvas. These pictures are thrown upon the eye in rapid succession. Unlike the successive frames of a film, the pictures are usually quite diverse. Under exceptional circumstances, as in looking at a strongly contrasted checkerboard, there may be a noticeable "flicker," but this is fortunately not the usual case. The rapid succession of pictures has, however, a number of effects which make an important contribution to design. The principal example is the production of "apparent movement"—the kind of movement which makes moving pictures move and which is called by psychologists the "Phi phenomenon."

The simplest demonstration of apparent movement is provided by two successive neighboring spots of light projected upon a screen. If one spot is removed just before the

FIGURE 25.1

second one is thrown on the screen, it appears as if a single spot had moved from one position to the other through the intervening space. Traffic lights, if satisfactorily timed, give the effect in spite of the difference in color. Now, a similar effect can be obtained when the successive positions of the light are provided by the movement of the eye itself. In Figure 25.1, a kind of apparent movement is obtained if one looks quickly from one of the birds to the other. The effect is best if the eye falls upon the same relative position (near the beak) in both pictures. The bird on the left appears as if its beak were just being closed, and the one on the right as if its beak were just being opened. By looking very rapidly from one to he other, a lively "movement" is seen.

Many compositions are designed, either intentionally or otherwise, to encourage an effect of this sort. The movement is most obvious if the composition contains two or more principal masses having approximately the same nature but differing slightly in attitude or in the position of minor appendages. In such case the required alternate fixations of the eye are likely to be evoked without explicit instructions, and a considerable similarity to real movement or to a moving picture may result. In Figure 25.2 [see the original publication], when the eye moves from the figure of Sancho Panza, with its inclination to the upper right, to that of Don Quixote, which is inclined to the upper left, a real movement is suggested. The picture appears as if Sancho Panza had just drawn himself back into the position he now holds and as if Don Quixote had just thrown himself forward on his horse. If either half of the picture is covered, this effect is destroyed. Each figure still *represents* a kind of movement; we recognize each figure as in motion but the lively and forceful contribution which is provided by the Phi phenomenon when the figures are viewed alternately is missing.

This picture also exemplifies the related effect of an apparent change of size. If a spot of light is thrown upon the screen and then replaced by a larger spot, it appears as if a single spot had suddenly *grown* larger. If it is replaced by a smaller spot, there is an apparent shrinking in size. In Figure 25.2, when the figures are viewed alternately, this effect makes Sancho Panza appear as if he were moving toward the observer and (what is more important for the effect of the picture as a whole) it makes Don Quixote appear as if he were riding rapidly away. All of this occurs in addition to the regular represented movement of the picture.

The possibility of apparent movement in a still picture has not to my knowledge been pointed out in its bearing upon design. But it will account for a great deal of the animation of many works of art. Some of the dancing girls of Degas (when at least two figures appear) offer excellent examples. Portraits (of two or more people) generally provide interesting cases. If the eyebrows of one face are a little higher than those of another, a peculiar lifting and lowering movement may be generated as one looks from one face to the other. Figure 25.3 [see the original publication], Grant Wood's *Daughters of Revolution*, makes use of this, as well as of a similar apparent stretching and shrinking of the necks of the women portrayed.

Even though apparent movement is not always as pronounced as in these examples, it may nevertheless contribute a good deal to the total effect of a picture. When it supplements a represented movement, the nature of the gain is clear; but a design need not deal with a moving object, and it may even be abstract, while at the same time receiving a considerable contribution from the Phi phenomenon. In any canvas in which all the principal lines lie in approximately the same direction, it is not likely that the successive still pictures taken as the eye moves from one point to another will differ in direction in sufficient magnitude to produce any considerable "Phi." Other things being equal, the painting will be quiet. On the other hand, in a canvas in which there are pronounced curves or an assortment of directions, it is very probable that two successive "still photographs" will contain lines differing in slope in such a way as to produce some movement of this sort. The canvas will be animated—quite apart from any animation inherent in its subject matter.

EFFECT OF LEARNED REACTIONS

One other kind of effect which a design may have arises from various learned or acquired reactions. These constitute the greater part of the "meaning" of the design. It is quite unlikely that any arrangement of lines or areas is wholly unfamiliar to the adult observer, and hence wholly without meaning. No "abstraction" is completely free from a resemblance to previously observed forms, and representative designs are frankly based upon such resemblances. In the latter case, the relation to our previous experience is usually easily identified, but some contribution to the total effect of a design must not be overlooked in the former as well. For example, an architectural painting may, with its converging lines and overlapping surfaces, give an excellent representation of a three-dimensional world. We have moved about in such a world all our lives, and we have come to know that parallel lines converge when they stretch away from us, that the smaller of two similar objects is probably the more distant, that distant colors are usually of lower saturation, and so on. Our response to such a painting cannot escape the influence of this training. This will also be true in an abstraction, since converging lines cannot wholly free themselves from their commonest meaning in the everyday world about us, bright and dull colors are likely to take their characteristic relative positions, and so on. Although some psychologists doubt that our perception of the third dimension is learned, the heightening of this perception through our experiences with similar designs in the practical world about us can scarcely be denied.

EFFECT OF EMOTIONAL REACTIONS

Of greater importance in the field of art than any of these reactions are the emotional reactions with which we respond to many visual patterns. To much of the world about us we are perhaps relatively indifferent, but there are many situations in which more or less vigorous emotional reactions are common. A design may acquire some of its effect through a resemblance to an emotional stimulus, and it is the contention of many psychologists that this may be true of pure design as well, even though we are not aware of the resemblance or do not understand the origin of our reactions.

Figure 25.4 [see the original publication] is a picture of an object to which very few people remain wholly indifferent. Whether there is an inherited fear of snakes is perhaps questionable, but it is nevertheless true that this particular pattern frequently arouses a strong reaction. A snake is not a common subject matter in Western art, perhaps because the reaction is too obvious, but it is an effective subject in the sense that few people would be indifferent to a realistic painting of a snake on the walls of a museum.

The reaction to a picture of this sort is easily attributed to the reaction which would be made to its subject matter in real life. But what are the precise characteristics of the pattern which evoke the reaction? The head of the snake could be concealed without much loss, the scales need not be visible, and a snake of a different marking would give the same effect. The "snake-ness" of the picture is apparently simply the coiling and curving of the main lines. But a picture of a coil of rope, of a cracking whip, or of the tendril of a grapevine would also satisfy this condition. If it is true that we need not recognize the snake as a snake in order to obtain the emotional effect, as many psychologists contend, we must suppose that the reaction made to snakes in real life carries over to many similar designs in art, even of an abstract nature. This example is, of course, an extreme one, but some at least of the otherwise unexplained emotional effect of good design can reasonably be attributed to an overlap with visual patterns to which we have acquired, or at least to which we possess emotional reactions.

This is not an exhaustive list of the kinds of effects which a design may have, but it must suffice. The list is long enough to suggest that complete interpretation of any given design is perhaps impossible. The design itself, as an objective geometrical factor, is only a small part of the story, and we can look for little help from the "formalists," who seek a solution in that direction. A design is a psychological and cultural object of enormous complexity. But if it is idle to attempt to account fully for any one example it is at least important to know the kinds of effects which are involved, and this is all that has been attempted here. It is no paradox that we have a better chance of understanding the nature of design in general than of accounting for the effects of any given example.

There is nothing in what has been said that is not familiar to the practicing artist, even though he does not put it into words. Nor is it likely that an understanding of processes of this sort will supplant the artist by generating a calculated or scientific art. Even though we may eventually achieve an exhaustive list of the processes involved in the practice of design, the production of a work of art will probably still require that mass of unverbalized knowledge which arises from individual experience. Similarly, on the side of the observer, it would be a mistake to identify the understanding of design with its enjoyment. The processes involved in reacting to design seem to operate freely without being recognized; and, although recognition may sharpen their effectiveness, it can hardly act as a substitute for artistic sensitivity.

Commentary on Design and Visual Art

Much of Skinner's thinking implies that he holds what is known in the creativity research as a product perspective. This is suggested by his view that ideas (a common expression of creative thinking, at least according to cognitive theorists) are not appropriate, for Skinner, in a scientific investigation of creativity, yet designs are clearly fair game. Skinner (1979, p. 238) gave a bit of context for this article on design in part 2 of his autobiographical "Shaping of a Behaviorist":

> In the Spring term, I again taught a course in the psychology of aesthetics which I had given two years before, and I began to be interested in the field. An instant authority, I was invited to discuss Picasso on the radio and to write an article on "The Psychology of Design" for *Art Education Today* [1941]. Guy Buswell had published records showing how people looked at a picture, their eyes darting from one point to another, and it occurred to me that successive fixations should produce the apparent movement called the Phi Phenomenon. Pictures with lines at different angles should appear lively, and those with parallel lines quiet. The movement might even be related to the subject.

Skinner's (1941, p. 542) appreciation of design makes sense because, as he points out, a design can be "a simple objective thing." But as was the case in his work on poetry and writing, we see that his thinking was not always and entirely on objective things, even if his theory and methods were. In the two previous readings, Skinner expressed an interest in the processes underlying alliteration, and the same thing is quite obvious in his article on design. Almost immediately he acknowledges that, although designs are objective things which can be described mathematically, such objective description is not useful for understanding design in art. He goes on to say that what is important for design in art is the effect a design has, in "what it does," not just what it is. Most important is his admission that focusing on objective descriptions of design does not tell us about the effect that art has on people. This seems to acknowledge that the subjective world is important! More specifically, it seems to acknowledge that an individual's interpretation of an experience (e.g., a design) is of extreme interest. Thus Skinner seemed to know that operant psychology was useful but limited. It was necessary for objectivity and for psychology to be a science, but it could not explain some things (e.g., interpretations) that are important.

That being said, this article from 1941 was an attempt to use the operant approach with designs. First Skinner discusses eye movements as they are correlated with the patterns of designs. He quickly admits that eye movements are not all that informative and moves on to the role of attention. It is a bit like his interest in the processes underlying alliteration, only here the process is attention as it relates to eye movements. Skinner's thinking about attention is not incompatible with later theories of experimental aesthetics, though they tended to go beyond attention and include emotional reactions, and in particular arousal. Skinner does bring up emotional reactions to certain images and argues that these can be attributed to experience.

In fact Skinner argues that the meaning of designs and art very often depends on what the viewer has previously learned. This is probably not a surprise, given that his theory is often categorized as a learning theory. It can explain how behavior changes as a function of experience (and emphasizes operants emitted in order to obtain a "reinforce" or avoid a "punisher"). In the case of design, Skinner gives the interpretation of converging lines as implying depth as an example of something that probably results from learning and experience. He comes very close to a proposition about rigidity and what in the creativity literature is called "the cost of expertise" when he points out that it is difficult to free ourselves from the "commonness meaning in the everyday world around us" (1941, p. 547). This line of thought has been used to explain why, although expertise can be a good thing for creativity, it sometimes inhibits creative thought, when the individual cannot break away from existing knowledge (Rubenson & Runco, 1992).

Conclusions

Skinner's influence on psychology and education remains obvious. His work has also been extended in a number of ways, several of which relate to the topic of creativity (Runco, 1993). The impact on creativity research is not as obvious as the influence on psychology and education, mostly because "creativity" is, like "idea" and "meaning," not operational in the Skinnerian sense. When detailing the need for an operational psychology Skinner (1945, p. 270) wrote, "The doctrine that words are used to express or convey meanings merely substitutes 'meaning' for 'idea' (in the hope that meaning can somehow be got outside the skin) and is incompatible with modern psychological conceptions of the organism." This implies that science must focus on what is observable and should not attempt to examine internal processes, and it indicates that ideas represent a clear example of an unscientific subject. This is, I believe, incompatible with theories of creativity, or at least those theories that focus on ideation, divergent thinking, brainstorming, and the like.

The need for operational concepts explains why Skinner and Epstein preferred looking to "insight" instead of creativity per se (see Epstein, 1990). Insight may sound like something that is as unoperational as creativity, but actually Skinner and Epstein did an admirable job of explaining insight using operant methods. In one of their early investigations of insight they examined the famous work on insight reported by Kohler (1925), which involved training an ape. Skinner and Epstein tested the possibility that pigeons could be trained such that they would display insightful behavior. Pigeons! They literally have bird brains! But the work was ingenious and successful. The trick was to break down what appeared to be an insightful solution into discrete steps and then train (with the operant method of shaping) each. The actual insight is, then, "the spontaneous integration of previously learned behaviors" rather than some unoperational mystery.

Another interesting contemporary example of operant thinking may reflect more of an independent discovery than linear or historical influence. I am referring to Skinner's idea, mentioned earlier, about motivation sometimes occurring early on but influencing behavior much later. This possibility was raised when I referred to the starving artist. Come to find out a parallel explanation was recently offered by Russ (2016) in her work on creativity and play. Simplifying, the idea is that children may have fun with imaginative play, and they may remember that play is fun, even years later, such that as adults they remain playful (and may very well be creative as a result of it) because they remember that it was a pleasant experience. This is not far from Skinner's concept of *reinforcement histories*.

This is a good point on which to conclude because it underscores the significant point that Skinner was not a radical behaviorist. He was determined to do scientific work, which meant that his emphasis was on operational and objective behaviors and methods, but each of the works reviewed here show clearly that he recognized that human behavior was not fully explained by unrealistically objective science. Many behaviors can be operationalized, including some that are presumed to be unoperational, such as insight, but Skinner did appreciate art, aesthetics, motivation, and a number of human capacities that were—and remain—beyond the scope of extreme objectivity. This strikes me as the only realistic view of what it means to be human (and creative).

References

Chomsky, N. (1967). A review of B. F. Skinner's *Verbal behavior*. In L. A. Jakobovits and M. S. Miron (Eds.), *Readings in the psychology of language* (pp. 142–143). New York, NY: Prentice-Hall.

Davis, G. A. (1999). Barriers to creativity and creative attitudes. In M. A. Runco & S. Pritzker (Eds.), *Encyclopedia of creativity* (pp. 165–174). San Diego, CA: Academic Press.

Dollinger, S. J., Urban, K. K., & James, T. J. (2004). Creativity and openness: Further validation of two creative product measures. *Creativity Research Journal, 16*, 35–48.

Epstein, R. (1990). Generativity theory. In M. A. Runco & R. S. Albert (Eds.), *Theories of creativity* (pp. 116–140). Newbury Park, CA: Sage.

Kohler, W. (1925). *The mentality of apes*. London: Routledge & Kegan Paul.

McCrae, R. R. (1987). Creativity, divergent thinking, and openness to experience. *Journal of Personality and Social Psychology, 52*, 1258–1265.

Rothenberg, A. (1990). Creativity, mental health, and alcoholism. *Creativity Research Journal, 3*, 179–201.

Rubenson, D. L., & Runco, M. A. (1992). The psychoeconomic approach to creativity. *New Ideas in Psychology, 10*, 131–147.

Runco, M. A. (1993). Operant theories of insight, originality, and creativity. *American Behavioral Scientist, 37*, 59–74.

Runco, M. A. (2007). To understand is to create: An epistemological perspective on human nature and personal creativity. In R. Richards (Ed.), *Everyday creativity and new views of human nature: Psychological, social, and spiritual perspectives* (pp. 91–108). Washington, DC: American Psychological Association.

Runco, M. A., & Albert, R. S. (1986). The threshold hypothesis regarding creativity and intelligence: An empirical test with gifted and nongifted children. *Creative Child and Adult Quarterly, 11*, 212–218.

Russ, S. W. (2016). Pretend play: Antecedent of adult creativity. *New Directions*, Spring(151), 21–32.

Schaefer, C., & Anastasi, A. (1968). A biographical inventory for identifying creativity in adolescent boys. *Journal of Applied Psychology, 54*, 42–48.

Simonton, D. K. (1999). William Shakespeare. In M. A. Runco & S. Pritzker (Eds.), *Encyclopedia of creativity* (Vol. 2, pp. 559–563). San Diego, CA: Academic Press.

Simonton, D. K. (2007). The creative process in Picasso's *Guernica* sketches: Monotonic improvements versus nonmonotonic variants. *Creativity Research Journal, 19*, 329–344.

Skinner, B. F. (1934). Has Gertrude Stein a secret? *Atlantic Monthly, 153*, 50–57.

Skinner, B. F. (1939). The alliteration in Shakespeare's sonnets: A study in literary behavior. *Psychological Record, 3*, 186–192.

Skinner, B. F (1941). The psychology of design. In B. Boas (Ed.), *Art education today* (pp. 1–6). New York, NY: Bureau of Publications, Teachers College, Columbia University.

Skinner, B. F. (1945). Operational analysis of psychological terms. *Psychological Review, 52*(5), 270–277.

Skinner, B. F. (1957). *Verbal behavior*. New York, NY: Prentice Hall.

Skinner, B. F. (1979). The shaping of a behaviorist: Part two of an autobiography. New York: Knopf.

Weisberg, R. W., & Hass, R. (2007). We are all partly right: Comment on Simonton. *Creativity Research Journal, 19*, 345–360.

PART NINE

Creativity in Groups and Interactions

26

Social Creativity and the Emergent Self

George Herbert Mead

VLAD P. GLĂVEANU

Summary

George Herbert Mead was a philosopher, social psychologist, and leading figure of American pragmatism together with William James, Charles S. Peirce, and John Dewey. He developed an eminently social account of the human mind by placing perspective taking and reflexivity at the heart of both self and society. His emphasis on agency, temporality, process, novelty, and emergence make Mead's work particularly important for creativity studies. After a brief introduction, this chapter will reproduce his text "Social Creativity and the Emergent Self" and end with a commentary that outlines its main ideas and their relevance for creativity research. Future perspectives will also be discussed toward the end.

Introduction

George Herbert Mead (1863–1931) was a philosopher and social and political theorist who made significant contributions to American pragmatism. His legacy is considered fundamental for a variety of fields, including social psychology (Gillespie, 2005) and sociology (Da Silva, 2006). Moreover, his work has been interpreted and reinterpreted many times since his death and labeled differently by different authors, oftentimes without Mead's having used or identified with any of the terms proposed. Among these are "social behaviorism" (Morris, in Mead, 1934), "social pragmatism" (Cook, 1993), "symbolic interactionism" (Blumer, 1980), "semiotic neopragmatism" (Wiley, 1995), and "symbolically mediated interactionism" (Joas, 1985). The difficulty of finding a definitive formulation for Mead's approach is amplified by the fact that he contributed to a variety of topics: the study of human phylogenesis and ontogenesis, language and interaction, emergence, the theory of the act, the emergence of the self and intersubjectivity, the philosophy of the present, the notion of democracy, and the resolution of moral problems (see Da Silva, 2007). As I argue in this chapter, Mead's conception of creativity, although schematic, is highly relevant for today's field of creativity research.

The chapter reproduced here was included in Mead's best-known book, *Mind, Self, and Society: From the Standpoint of a Social Behaviorist*. This volume, published post-humously, is a compilation of student notes from his Social Psychology course at the University of Chicago and passages from his unpublished manuscripts. The book was edited by Charles Morris, who, notably and controversially (see Gillespie, 2005), used this context to describe Mead's work as that of a "social behaviorist." (In fact Morris seems to be describing both himself and Mead with this term, as he notes, "Our behaviorism is a social behaviorism" [in Mead, 1934, p. 6]). This label did not persist, however, and today this work is remembered much more for its extensive discussion of the human self and its emergence within social interaction.

Mead's account of the self is eminently social. According to him, the self is constituted through relating to others and, in particular, "taking" their perspective or attitude. In other words, the self appears at the moment in which the child is capable of seeing himself or herself the way another person does; in other words, one is capable of becoming other to oneself. How does this relate to the topic of creativity? In the chapter "Social Creativity and the Emergent Self," Mead uses, in part, this argument to shed new light on the creative process, including in the case of genius. The commentary will focus on the wealth of ideas offered in this brief text, as well as discuss other meaningful connections between Mead's general theory and creativity research.

Reading: "Social Creativity of the Emergent Self"

Source: Mead, G. H. (2015). Social creativity of the emergent self. Chapter 28 in *George Herbert Mead: Mind, self & society. Definitive edition* (pp. 214–221). Chicago, IL: University of Chicago Press. Original published in 1934. Reproduced with permission.

We have been discussing the value which gathers about the self, especially that which is involved in the "I" as over against that involved in the "me." The "me" is essentially a member of a social group, and represents, therefore, the value of the group, that sort of experience which the group makes possible. Its values are the values that belong to society. In a sense these values are supreme. They are values which under certain extreme moral and religious conditions call out the sacrifice of the self for the whole. Without this structure of things, the life of the self would become impossible. These are the conditions under which that seeming paradox arises, that the individual sacrifices himself for the whole which makes his own life as a self possible. Just as there could not be individual consciousness except in a social group, so the individual in a certain sense is not willing to live under certain conditions which would involve a sort of suicide of the self in its process of realization. Over against that situation we referred to those values which attach particularly to the "I" rather than to the "me," those values which are found in the immediate attitude of the artist, the inventor, the scientist in his discovery, in general in the action of the "I" which cannot be calculated and which involves a reconstruction of the society, and so of the "me" which belongs to that society. It is that phase of experience which is found in the "I" and the values that attach to it are the values belonging to this type of experience as such. These values are not peculiar to the artist, the inventor, and the scientific discoverer, but belong to the experience of all selves where there is an "I" that answers to the "me."

The response of the "I" involves adaptation, but an adaptation which affects not only the self but also the social environment which helps to constitute the self; that is, it implies a view of evolution in which the individual affects its own environment as well as being affected by it. A statement of evolution that was common in an earlier period assumed simply the effect of an environment on organized living protoplasm, molding it in some sense to the world in which it had to live. On this view the individual is really passive as over against the influences which are affecting it all the time. But what needs now to be recognized is that the character of the organism is a determinant of its environment. We speak of bare sensitivity as existent by itself, forgetting it is always a sensitivity to certain types of stimuli. In terms of its sensitivity the form selects an environment, not selecting exactly in the sense in which a person selects a city or a country or a particular climate in which to live, but selects in the sense that it finds those characteristics to which it can respond, and uses the resulting experiences to gain certain organic results that are essential to its continued life-process. In a sense, therefore, the organism states its environment in terms of means and ends. That sort of a determination of the environment is as real, of course, as the effect of the environment on the form. When a form develops a capacity, however this takes place, to deal with parts of the environment which its progenitors could not deal with, it has to this degree created a new environment for itself. The ox that has a digestive organ capable of treating grass as a food adds a new food, and in adding this it adds a new object. The substance which was not food before becomes food now. The environment of the form has increased. The organism in a real sense is determinative of its environment. The situation is one in which there is action and reaction, and adaptation that changes the form must also change the environment.

As a man adjusts himself to a certain environment he becomes a different individual; but in becoming a different individual he has affected the community in which he lives. It may be a slight effect, but in so far as he has adjusted himself, the adjustments have changed the type of the environment to which he can respond and the world is accordingly a different world. There is always a mutual relationship of the individual and the community in which the individual lives. Our recognition of this under ordinary conditions is confined to relatively small social groups, for here an individual cannot come into the group without in some degree changing the character of the organization. People have to adjust themselves to him as much as he adjusts himself to them. It may seem to be a molding of the individual by the forces about him, but the society likewise changes in this process, and becomes to some degree a different society. The change may be desirable or it may be undesirable, but it inevitably takes place.

This relationship of the individual to the community becomes striking when we get minds that by their advent make the wider society a noticeably different society. Persons of great mind and great character have strikingly changed the communities to which they have responded. We call them leaders, as such, but they are simply carrying to the nth power this change in the community by the individual who makes himself a part of it, who belongs to it.[1] The great characters have been those who, by being what they were in the community, made that community a different one. They have enlarged and enriched the community. Such figures as great religious characters in history have, through their membership, indefinitely increased the possible size of the community itself. Jesus generalized the conception of the community in terms of the family in such a statement as that of the neighbor in the parables. Even the man outside of the community will now take that generalized family attitude toward it, and he makes those that are so brought into relationship with him members of the community to which he belongs, the community of a universal religion. The change of the community through the attitude of the individual becomes, of course, peculiarly impressive and effective in history. It makes separate individuals stand out as symbolic. They represent, in their personal relationships, a new order, and then become representative of the community as it might exist if it were fully developed along the lines that they had started. New conceptions have brought with them, through great individuals, attitudes which enormously enlarge the environment within which these individuals lived. A man who is a neighbor of anybody else in the group is a member of a larger society, and to the extent that he lives in such a community he has helped to create that society.

It is in such reactions of the individual, the "I," over against the situation in which the "I" finds itself, that important social changes take place. We frequently speak of them as expressions of the individual genius of certain persons. We do not know when the great artist, scientist, statesman, religious leader will come—persons who will have a formative effect upon the society to which they belong. The very definition of genius would come back to something of the sort to which I have been referring, to this incalculable quality, this change of the environment on the part of an individual by himself becoming a member of the community.

An individual of the type to which we are referring arises always with reference to a form of society or social order which is implied but not adequately expressed. Take the religious genius, such as Jesus or Buddha, or the reflective type, such as Socrates. What has given them their unique importance is that they have taken the attitude of living with reference to a larger society. That larger state was one which was already more or less implied in the institutions of the community in which they lived. Such an individual is divergent from the point of view of what we would call the prejudices of the community; but in another sense he expresses the principles of the community more completely than any other. Thus arises the situation of an Athenian or a Hebrew stoning the genius who expresses the principles of his own society, one the principle of rationality and the other the principle of complete neighborliness. The type we refer to as the genius is of that sort. There is an analogous situation in the field of artistic creation: the artists also reveal contents which represent a wider emotional expression answering to a wider society. To the degree that we make the community in which we live different we all have what is essential to genius, and which becomes genius when the effects are profound.

The response of the "I" may be a process which involves a degradation of the social state as well as one which involves higher integration. Take the case of the mob in its various expressions. A mob is an organization which has eliminated certain values which have obtained in the interrelation of individuals with each other, has simplified itself, and in doing that has made it possible to allow the individual, especially the repressed individual, to get an expression which otherwise would not be allowed. The individual's response is made possible by the actual degradation of the social structure itself, but that does not take away the immediate value to the individual which arises under those conditions. He gets his emotional response out of that situation because in his expression of violence he is doing what everyone else is doing. The whole community is doing the same thing. The repression which existed has disappeared and he is at one with the community and the community is at one with him. An illustration of a more trivial character is found in our personal relations with those about us. Our manners are methods of not only mediated intercourse between persons but also ways of protecting ourselves against each other. A person may, by manners, isolate himself so that he cannot be touched by anyone else. Manners provide a way in which we keep people at a distance, people that we do not know and do not want to know. We all make use of processes of that sort. But there are occasions in which we can drop off the type of manner which holds people at arm's length. We meet the man in some distant country whom perhaps we would seek to avoid meeting at home, and we almost tear our arms off embracing him. There is a great deal of exhilaration in situations involved in the hostility of other nations; we all seem at one against a common enemy; the barriers drop, and we have a social sense of comradeship to those standing with us in a common undertaking. The same thing takes place in a political campaign. For the time being we extend the glad hand—and a cigar—to anyone who is a member of the particular group to which we belong. We get rid of certain restrictions under those circumstances, restrictions which really keep us from intense social experiences. A person may be a victim of his good manners; they may incase him as well as protect him. But under the conditions to which I have referred, a person does get outside of himself, and by doing so makes himself a definite member of a larger community than that to which he previously belonged.

Such experiences are, of course, of immense importance. We make use of them all the time in the community. We decry the attitude of hostility as a means of carrying on the interrelations between nations. We feel we should get beyond the methods of warfare and diplomacy, and reach some sort of political relation of nations to each other in which they could be regarded as members of a common community, and so be able to express themselves, not in the attitude of hostility, but in terms of their common values. That is what we set up as the ideal of the League of Nations. We have to remember, however, that we are not able to work out our own political institutions without introducing the hostilities of parties. Without parties we could not get a fraction of the voters to come to the polls to express themselves on issues of great public importance, but we can enrol a considerable part of the community in a political party that is fighting some other party. It is the element of the fight that keeps up the interest. We can enlist the interest of a number of people who want to defeat the opposing party, and get them to the polls to do that. The party platform is an abstraction, of course, and does not mean much to us, since we are actually depending psychologically upon the operation of these more barbarous impulses in order to keep our ordinary institutions running. When we object to the organization of corrupt political machines we ought to remember to feel a certain gratitude to people who are able to enlist the interest of people in public affairs.

We are normally dependent upon those situations in which the self is able to express itself in a direct fashion, and there is no situation in which the self can express itself so easily as it can over against the common enemy of the groups to which it is united. The hymn that comes to our minds most frequently as expressive of Christendom is "Onward Christian Soldiers"; Paul organized the church of his time against the world of heathens; and "Revelation" represents the community over against the world of darkness. The idea of Satan has been as essential to the organization of the church as politics has been to the organization of democracy. There has to be something to fight against because the self is most easily able to express itself in joining a definite group.

The value of an ordered society is essential to our existence, but there also has to be room for an expression of the individual himself if there is to be a satisfactorily developed society. A means for such expression must be provided. Until we have such a social structure in which an individual can express himself as the artist and the scientist does, we are thrown back on the sort of structure found in the mob, in which everybody is free to express himself against some hated object of the group.

One difference between primitive human society and civilized human society is that in primitive human society the individual self is much more completely determined, with regard to his thinking and his behavior, by the general pattern of the organized social activity carried on by the particular social group to which he belongs, than he is in civilized human society. In other words, primitive human society offers much less scope for individuality—for original, unique, or creative thinking and behavior on the part of the individual self within it or belonging to it—than does civilized human society; and indeed the evolution of civilized human society from primitive human society has largely depended upon or resulted from a progressive social liberation of the individual self and his conduct, with the modifications and elaborations of the human social process which have followed from and been made possible by that liberation. In primitive society, to a far greater extent than in civilized society, individuality is constituted by the more or less perfect achievement of a given social type, a type already given, indicated, or exemplified in the organized pattern of social conduct, in the integrated relational structure of the social process of experience and behavior which the given social group exhibits and is carrying on; in civilized society individuality is constituted rather by the individual's departure from, or modified realization of, any given social type than by his conformity, and tends to be something much more distinctive and singular and peculiar than it is in primitive human society. But even in the most modern and highly-evolved forms of human civilization the individual, however original and creative he may be in his thinking or behavior, always and necessarily assumes a definite relation to, and reflects in the structure of his self or personality, the general organized pattern of experience and activity exhibited in or characterizing the social life-process in which he is involved, and of which his self or personality is essentially a creative expression or embodiment. No individual has a mind which operates simply in itself, in isolation from the social life-process in which it has arisen or out of which it has emerged, and in which the pattern of organized social behavior has consequently been basically impressed upon it.

---

1. The behavior of a genius is socially conditioned, just as that of an ordinary individual is; and his achievements are the results of, or are responses to, social stimuli, just as those of an ordinary individual are. The genius, like the ordinary individual, comes back at himself from the standpoint of the organized social group to which he belongs, and the attitudes of that group toward any given project in which he becomes involved; and he responds to this generalized attitude of the group with a definite attitude of his own toward the given project, just as the ordinary individual does. But this definite attitude of his own with which he responds to the

generalized attitude of the group is unique and original in the case of the genius, whereas it is not so in the case of the ordinary individual; and it is this uniqueness and originality of his response to a given social situation or problem or project—which nevertheless conditions his behavior no less than it does that of the ordinary individual—that distinguishes the genius from the ordinary individual.

Commentary

George Herbert Mead's work has attracted considerable scholarly attention over the past decades. Notable researchers from various disciplines have offered a reexamination of his thought and, based on it, opened new perspectives for philosophy, sociology, and social psychology (see, e.g., Da Silva, 2006, 2007; Gillespie, 2005; Joas, 1985; Martin, 2005). However, the relevance of this work for the field of creativity studies has rarely been discussed. An important exception is represented by Joas (1990, p. 165), who notes, from a sociological standpoint, that "Mead developed a theory of action in which the creativity of action stands in the foreground." This statement needs to be placed within the author's own concern for building a pragmatist account of creative action (see Joas, 1996) that resonates with the work of Mead as well as that of John Dewey. A pragmatist approach to creativity brings to the fore its social, cultural, and material dimensions. It is in relation to the social expression of creativity and, more generally, the social origins of consciousness and the creative self, that Mead's writings have a lot to offer (see also Perinbanayagam, 1975).

For him, the mind and self are "not initially there at birth, but arise in the process of social experience and activity . . . in the given individual as a result of his relations to that process as a whole and to other individuals within that process" (Mead, 1934, p. 135). At the basis of his philosophy stands the idea that the human self emerges through reflexivity, with the help of language and social interaction. This is because the main unit of analysis for Mead is not the person facing the environment, but the relation between two people within a certain environment. In this sense, Mead is one of the main theorists of the social act (see Gillespie, 2005), in which not only two people but two (or more) perspectives meet, and the actors are capable of each taking the perspective of the other. This is, in a nutshell, Mead's (1934, p. 255) definition of reflexivity, which designates for him those situations in which "the individual becom[es] an object to himself by taking the attitudes of other individuals toward himself within an organized setting of social relationships." In other words, the birth of a specifically human type of consciousness is associated with the capacity of the person—the young child initially—to metaphorically "become other" by understanding his or her own actions from the position of an other. The notion of "an organized setting of social relationships" is important here as well. For Mead, these acts of reflexivity don't occur simply as part of biological development, but are actively scaffolded by a social world that organizes human relations and encourages the self to take the position of an other and adopt the other's attitude or perspective.

This is how, from a Meadean standpoint, the human self develops a dual structure, including an "I" that acts and a "me" that reflects on this action based on social experience. In this way, even if most of our action is habitual and rarely reflected upon, there is always a known and a knower within the self, an initiator and an evaluator of our actions. Importantly, for Mead the "me" should be understood as the internalized responses of others to our immediate actions, either specific other people or our community more generally (what he famously referred to as the "generalized other"). These internalized others become part of the repertoire of the reflective self and make the mind, and our actions, thoroughly social and potentially creative.

What does all of this have to do with creativity? Well, if we consider creativity an action performed by the self, then we can wonder about the interplay between the "I" and the "me" within the creative act and how it relates to the dynamic relation between self and others (both present and absent, external and internalized). But this is a topic I will elaborate a bit later, based on Mead's text on social creativity reproduced here. For the moment, we should note that Mead's work is not widely cited in the creativity literature (except sporadically; see Sawyer, 2000). Likewise, Mead himself rarely discussed creativity as such. In the excerpt, the word "creativity" appears only in the title. And yet, his thoughts on agency and emergence are fundamental for creativity theory. This is why, for instance, Gunter (1990) edited an important collection entitled *Creativity in George Herbert Mead*, in which he brought to the fore Mead's persistent concern for temporality, process, and novelty.

Of particular importance is the notion of emergence (see also Chang, 2004). According to Mead (1938, p. 641), "when things get together, there then arises something that was not there before." Thus, emergence takes place at the encounter between person and world and especially the encounter between people. It is marked by a disruption in experience (Martin, 2006) and, most of all, by those moments in which two or more perspectives intersect (Martin & Gillespie, 2010). This is because meeting the perspective of the other in a specific situation opens up the possibility of gaining a new understanding of that situation and/or of the people acting within it. This conception of emergence is very close to contemporary sociocultural views of creativity. Creativity does take place at the "meeting point" between the person and his or her environment (Glăveanu, 2014), and it leads to emergence through the encounter between people, ideas, or ways of thinking that temporarily create a sense of rupture, followed by curiosity for the new and openness toward different ways of doing things.

In the text "Social Creativity of the Emergent Self," Mead (1934, 2015) outlines the basis for an incipient theory of creativity, one that resonates widely with his ideas about emergence, agency, and the development of the self. At a broader level, he describes human creativity as both acting and being acted upon by the environment, by others, and by society. He associates creativity with individuality, with the actions of the "I" but, at the same time, because of his deeply social conception of the self, this individuality can be understood only in social terms. The creative self emerges only in and through interaction with others. For him "civilized human society" offers individuals many more opportunities to express themselves creatively than "primitive human societies" (p. 221), as they demand much less conformism. Individuality becomes "something much more distinctive and singular and peculiar" (pp. 221–222), in great part due to the changes in human relations and opportunities to know multiple others and get to know multiple points of view. Mead also developed a democratic account of creativity by not restricting this quality to "the artist, the inventor or the scientific discoverer" and making it "belong to the experience of all selves where there is an 'I' that answers to the 'me'" (p. 214). Even more, he believed that "we all have what is essential to genius" (p. 218) because we all live together with others in communities that we are shaped by, but also have an opportunity to shape in return. For him, geniuses resemble leaders who embody creative potential to a great extent, but this creative potential—due to its social underpinning—is something we all possess.

This bidirectional view of the relation between individuality and community, between individual and society, between agency and structure, is specific for Mead and, more broadly, for pragmatist thinkers. In discussing creativity, he emphasizes from the start the fact that "the individual affects its own environment as well as being affected by it" (1934, p. 214). This is not only because interactions always "look" both ways but because, from an evolutionary perspective, person and world shape each other. In acting (creatively), the person not only expresses himself or herself but also effectively creates "a new environment for itself" (p. 215). In his own words: "It may seem to be a molding of the individual by the forces about him, but the society likewise changes in this process, and becomes to some degree a different society" (p. 216). Conversely, the person changes as well in the process of shaping his or her environment. Since "no individual has a mind which operates simply in itself, in isolation from the social life-process in which it has arisen or out of which it has emerged" (p. 222), new social conditions create new social relations that, in turn, impact the "I" and the "me," their interplay and its creative outcomes.

Nowhere is this relational view of creativity more clearly visible than in Mead's discussion of the genius. Traditionally, genius has been seen as an individual quality, grounded within hereditary and reflected by eminence (Galton, 1874). Most of all, geniuses were believed to almost single-handedly revolutionize culture and leave their mark on history. Mead's (1934, p. 217) account recognizes the fact that persons of genius do stand out in society, but at the same time, they "become representative of the community as it might exist if it were fully developed along the lines that they had started." In other words, geniuses are not disconnected from their community and their culture. On the contrary, they come to be their foremost representatives and direct it toward a specific future. How and why do geniuses represent their community, especially since we often think of geniuses as having to fight or rebel against social norms and the conformism of others (see also Montuori & Purser, 1995)? For Mead (1934, p. 217) this apparent paradox is solved by viewing the genius as an individual type who "arises always with reference to a form of society or social order which is implied but not adequately expressed"; the genius comes to embody a certain preexisting attitude within society which was until then implicit or even rejected by certain groups. But, from another perspective, this attitude is often at the core of what constitutes that society at that point in time. In Mead's own words, "such an individual is divergent from the point of view of what we would call the prejudices of the community; but in another sense he expresses the principles of the community more completely than any other" (p. 217). This doesn't mean that the genius goes along with the existing views of his or her society or submits to the perspective of the "generalized other." For Mead, geniuses are in close dialogue with these views and this perspective, but it is a dialogue to which they bring a unique, original position. In this way, Mead himself offers a distinctive take on the relationship between highly creative individuals and the communities and societies they belong to. Instead of standing apart from them, geniuses create from within a society and a culture. They are in close dialogue with important perspectives or attitudes within their social environment, but bring a unique contribution to them. They are different, but, to a great extent, they are also the most representative members of their group and its future.

In order to understand further how novelty comes about—both in the case of geniuses and what he calls ordinary individuals—we need to have a closer look at Mead's concept of agency. As mentioned earlier, one of the main themes of the chapter included here as well as his other works is that of the mutual constitution between person and environment:

> As a man adjusts himself to a certain environment he becomes a different individual; but in becoming a different individual he has affected the community in which he lives. It may be a slight effect, but in so far as he has adjusted himself, the adjustments have changed the type of the environment to which he can respond and the world is accordingly a different world. There is always a mutual relationship of the individual and the community in which the individual lives. (1934, p. 215)

This relationship can be theorized only through the lenses of human agency, and, indeed, there has been a lot written about Mead's understanding of this topic (see Baldwin, 1988; Martin, 2006, 2007). Martin and Gillespie (2010), two neo-Meadean scholars, articulate Mead's theory of agency in terms of taking distance from the here and now of immediate experience by adopting new perspectives on self, others, and world, perspectives that come out of interacting with other people within society. It is because human beings live in a perspectival world, according to Mead, that they develop the capacity to see it differently and choose to act differently within it. This is, for him, the basis of agency and, I would add, of distinctively human forms of creativity (Glăveanu, 2015a). In contrast, non-human animals are "relatively trapped in their immediate activity, responding reflexively to stimuli within their situation" (Martin & Gillespie, 2010, p. 256). Through the use of language and reflexivity, human beings are able to live in an expanded environment, being aware not only of how they perceive or understand it, but also of how others might. This creates a space for agency and creativity as it basically makes people more flexible when it comes to acting in the world, together with others. As the two authors go on to argue, it is not only the ability to take perspectives that is essential for agency, but also that of integrating and coordinating them with others (p. 257).

But what exactly is a perspective? In general terms, "the perspective is the world in its relationship to the individual and the individual in his relationship to the world" (Mead, 1938, p. 115). More concretely, "perspectives may be understood broadly as perceptual and conceptual orientations to a situation with a view to acting within that situation" (Martin, 2005, p. 231). Perspectives are much more than ideas, as they would often be referred to in the creativity literature. They are at once cognitive and affective constructs that relate the person with his or her environment and facilitate certain forms of action while hindering others (see also Glăveanu, 2016). This makes them extremely useful concepts for theorizing creativity. Indeed to create becomes, using Mead's terms, an act of *diversifying, integrating, and generally moving between perspectives in ways that bring about the emergence of novelty within the self and within society*. I have elaborated elsewhere a full perspectival model of creativity built on this basis (for details see Glăveanu, 2015a). For this commentary, it suffices to note that Mead's notion of perspective and its further elaborations, for example position exchange theory (Gillespie & Martin, 2014), are extremely fertile for the field of creativity studies. They argue that, within creative action, the person repositions himself or herself and, in doing so, takes new perspectives on the problem or situation at hand, including the perspective of the community (of the "generalized other"). Mead (1934, p. 222) makes precisely this point within the only note to the chapter reproduced here, a note about the way in which geniuses work:

> The genius, like the ordinary individual, comes back at himself from the standpoint of the organized social group to which he belongs, and the attitudes of that group toward any given project in which he becomes involved, and he responds to this generalized attitude of the group with a definite attitude of his own toward the given project, just as the ordinary individual does.

In other words, creativity is underpinned by perspective taking, including seeing one's work as an entire social group (e.g., the public) might look at it. This theoretical foundation has many conceptual, methodological, and practical implications that should be explored in further research. Among them:

1. The theory of creativity focused primarily on intrapsychological attributes when it came to the study of creativity. These were mainly cognitive functions, even if affect or motivation received some attention in recent decades. However, the social perspective put forward by Mead and others encourages us to reconsider the interpersonal domain and a set of abilities—such as empathy and perspective taking—that are forged within and expressive of social interactions rather than individual characteristics. This kind of expansion would make us sensitive also to the fact that other processes, typically considered and studied at the individual level, have a social origin and dynamic. For instance, divergent thinking is often considered to be related at least to creativity, if not one of the key psychological processes underpinning it. Following a Meadean approach, divergent thinking can be conceptualized in terms of diversifying perspectives (Glăveanu, 2015b) and, as such, grounded firmly within the multiple networks of interactions and organized patterns of relations the creative person belongs to.

2. At a methodological level, it becomes important to develop the necessary tools for studying the networks of relations mentioned earlier. Moreover, we should be able to consider their development in time and the ways in which this development contributes to the constitution of the self. Jack Martin (2016) recently formulated a very interesting method in this regard called life positioning analysis (LPA). This is a "social psychological, biographical method for studying the life projects and creative accomplishments of individuals in interaction with others and objects within socioculturally sanctioned and constituted conventions and traditions" (p. 244). Martin applied LPA to the study of different creative individuals, including Sigmund Freud and B. F. Skinner. It will be important, in the future, to develop new methodological tools that could be applied at not only an ontogenetic (life-course), but also a microgenetic level, i.e., for the study of creative action as it takes place in the here and now.

3. At a practical level, Mead's social perspective encourages us to think about how we can create cultures of creativity by encouraging pro-social values and fostering collaboration rather than conflict. As he notes in the text reproduced here, "until we have such a social structure in which an individual can express himself as the artist and the scientist does, we are thrown back on the sort of structure found in the mob, in which everybody is free to express himself against some hated object of the group" (1934, p. 221). Since creativity depends on taking the perspective of others, we need to develop ways of understanding this perspective and, most of all, of valuing it. Openness toward others and their point of view is a precondition within Mead's democratic and ethical theory of society. It is important to remember, in this context, that totalitarianism is the antithesis of creativity by closing down differences and imposing a unitary mindset (see Montuori, 2005, also Chapter 31 in this volume), in other words, a singular, unitary perspective on the world. Creativity requires and cultivates freedom, but this freedom is also the freedom of others—it is one acquired in and through social relations defined by openness and mutual respect.

In summary, Mead's discussion of creativity relates it to society and the development of the self. The chapter from his work I focused on here is on "social creativity," but a closer reading of the text reveals the fact that this concept is tautological. For Mead, creativity is always social in its origin, process, and consequences. And yet, at the same time, it is also deeply related to individuality, originality, and self-expression. Mead's main contribution to our understanding of creative action stems precisely from addressing (and in my view, solving) this apparent paradox. We are capable of creativity not because we are separate from others and distinct from them; on the contrary, we gain our individuality from being able to engage with the perspective of others and creatively transform it and ourselves in this process. The emergent self is, in this sense, not individual *despite* being social but, rather, *because* of it.

References

Baldwin, J. D. (1988). Mead and Skinner: Agency and determinism. *Cambridge Center for Behavioral Studies, 16*(2), 109–127.

Blumer, H. (1980). Mead and Blumer: The convergent methodological perspectives of social behaviorism and symbolic interactionism. *American Sociological Review, 45*, 409–419.

Chang, J. H.-Y. (2004). Mead's theory of emergence as a framework for multilevel sociological inquiry. *Symbolic Interaction, 27*(3), 405–427.

Cook, G. A. (1993). *George Herbert Mead: The making of a social pragmatist.* Urbana: University of Illinois Press.

Da Silva, F. C. (2006). G. H. Mead in the history of sociological ideas. *Journal of the History of the Behavioral Sciences, 42*(1), 19–39.

Da Silva, F. C. (2007). G. H. Mead: A system in a state of flux. *History of the Human Sciences, 20*(1), 45–65.

Galton, F. (1874). *English men of science: Their nature and nurture.* London: Macmillan.

Gillespie, A. (2005). G. H. Mead: Theorist of the social act. *Journal for the Theory of Social Behaviour, 35*(1), 19–39.

Gillespie, A., & Martin, J. (2014). Position exchange theory: A socio-material basis for discursive and psychological positioning. *New Ideas in Psychology, 32*, 73–79.

Glăveanu, V. P. (2014). *Distributed creativity: Thinking outside the box of the creative individual.* Cham, Switzerland: Springer.

Glăveanu, V. P. (2015a). Creativity as a sociocultural act. *Journal of Creative Behavior, 49*(3), 165–180.

Glăveanu, V. P. (2015b). The status of the social in creativity studies and the pitfalls of dichotomic thinking. *Creativity: Theories—Research—Applications, 2*(1), 102–119.

Glăveanu, V. P. (2016). Perspective. In V. P. Glăveanu, L. Tanggaard, & C. Wegener (Eds.), *Creativity: A new vocabulary* (pp. 104–110). London: Palgrave.

Gunter, P. A. Y. (Ed.) (1990). *Creativity in George Herbert Mead.* Lanham, MD: University Press of America.

Joas, H. (1985). *G. H. Mead: A contemporary re-examination of his thought.* Cambridge, MA: MIT Press.

Joas, H. (1990). The creativity of action and the intersubjectivity of reason: Mead's pragmatism and social theory. *Transactions of the Charles S. Peirce Society, 26*(2), 165–194.

Joas, H. (1996). *The creativity of action.* Cambridge, UK: Polity Press.

Martin, J. (2005). Perspectival selves in interaction with others: Re-reading G. H. Mead's social psychology. *Journal for the Theory of Social Behaviour, 35*(3), 231–253.

Martin, J. (2006). Reinterpreting internalization and agency through G. H. Mead's perspectival realism. *Human Development, 49*, 65–86.

Martin, J. (2007). Interpreting and extending G. H. Mead's "metaphysics" of selfhood and agency. *Philosophical Psychology, 20*(4), 441–456.

Martin, J. (2016). Position exchange, life positioning, and creativity. In V. P. Glăveanu (Ed.), *The Palgrave handbook of creativity and culture research* (pp. 243–262). London: Palgrave.

Martin, J., & Gillespie, A. (2010). A neo-Meadian approach to human agency: Relating the social and the psychological in the ontogenesis of perspective-coordinating persons. *Integrative Psychological and Behavioral Science, 44*, 252–272.

Mead, G. H. (1934). *Mind, self & society from the standpoint of a social behaviorist* (C. W. Morris, Ed.). Chicago, IL: University of Chicago Press.

Mead, G. H. (1938). *The philosophy of the act.* Chicago, IL: University of Chicago Press.

Mead, G. H. (2015). *George Herbert Mead: Mind, self & society. Definitive edition.* (C. W. Morris, Ed.). Annotated edition by D. R. Huebner & H. Joas. Chicago, IL: University of Chicago Press.

Montuori, A. (2005). How to make enemies and influence people: Anatomy of the anti-pluralist, totalitarian mindset. *Futures, 37*(1), 18–38.

Montuori, A., & Purser, R. (1995). Deconstructing the lone genius myth: Toward a contextual view of creativity. *Journal of Humanistic Psychology, 35*(3), 69–112.

Perinbanayagam, R. S. (1975). The significance of others in the thought of Alfred Schutz, G. H. Mead and C. H. Cooley. *Sociological Quarterly, 16*(4), 500–521.

Sawyer, R. K. (2000). Improvisation and the creative process: Dewey, Collingwood, and the aesthetics of spontaneity. *Journal of Aesthetics and Art Criticism, 58*(2), 149–161.

Wiley, N. (1995). *The semiotic self.* Chicago, IL: University of Chicago Press.

27

Group Dynamics and Team Creativity

The Contribution of Kurt Lewin to the Study of Teams, Creativity, and Innovation

RONI REITER-PALMON AND SALVATORE LEONE

Summary

Kurt Lewin's (1947) classic paper "Group Decision and Social Change" provides a review of a number of studies conducted on group decision-making in applied settings. In this paper we discuss the ways Lewin has influenced the work on team creativity and explore which aspects of his work have not been yet been studied and should be incorporated into the study of team creativity. Lewin suggests that change is difficult and that individuals must undergo a series of cognitive processes, unfreezing, moving, and then refreezing, in order to spur changes in behavior. He also suggests that group discussion minimizes resistance to these change efforts. Additionally role conflict and stages of decision-making are factors changing behavior. These topics, as well as future directions, are explored through the lens of creativity research.

Introduction

Kurt Lewin is often considered the father of social psychology and the first to study issues related to group dynamics. He was among the first to argue that group phenomena are more than just the sum of the individuals in the group, a concept that group researchers refer to as emergent states (Marks, Mathieu, & Zaccaro, 2001). It is also important to note that much of his research falls into the category of applied research. As such, he emphasized the significance of understanding psychological phenomena outside of the laboratory setting and using psychological knowledge to address real-world concerns and applications.

His classic paper "Group Decision and Social Change" in *Readings in Social Psychology* (Newcomb & Hartley, 1947) provides a review of a number of studies conducted on group decision-making in applied settings, addressing major concerns related to the US war effort during World War II. As the title of the paper suggests, this collection of studies focuses on the issues that confront researchers when studying group decision-making, specifically issues surrounding decision-making that will lead to changes in behavior. The connection to creativity is clear: change from the status quo is at the heart of creative ideas and solutions. When a creative idea is adopted and implemented, by definition, something has changed.

In this chapter we seek to tie Lewin's seminal work on group decision-making and social change to two specific issues. First, how has his work in this paper influenced the work on team creativity? Second, what aspects of Lewin's work have not been studied yet and should be incorporated into the study of team creativity, and what are some future directions to team creativity based on Lewin's work?

Reading: "Group Decision and Social Change"

Source: Lewin, K. (1947). Group decision and social change. In T. M. Newcomb & E. L. Hartley (Eds.), *Readings in social psychology* (pp. 330–344). Oxford: Henry Holt. © 1947 South-Western, a part of Cengage Learning, Inc. Reproduced by permission. www.ccngage.com/permissions.

Food Habits and Food Channels

The experiment on group decision was part of a larger study on food habits. Its main objective was a comparison of different ethnic and economic groups in a midwestern town. The favorite family food, what food was considered essential, what main frame of reference and values guided the thinking of these groups about foods, and what authorities were seen as standing behind these standards and values. Children at different ages were included to indicate the process of acculturation of the individual in regard to food. Since this study was part of a larger problem of changing food habits in line with war needs, we were interested in including an attempt to bring about some of the desired changes at least on a small scale.

The data acquired give considerable insight into the existing attitudes and practices of the various groups. However in this, as in many other cases, such data about a present state of affairs do not permit many conclusions in regard to how to proceed best to bring about a change. Should one use radio, posters, lectures, or what other means and methods for changing efficiently group ideology and group action? Should one approach the total population of men, women, and children who are to change their food habits or would it suffice and perhaps be more effective to concentrate on a strategic part of the population?

To understand what comes on the table we have to know the forces which determine what food enters a channel. Whether food enters the channel to the family table or not is determined in the buying situation. The buying situation can be characterized as a conflict situation. Food 1 might be attractive, that is, the force toward eating is large but at the same time the food might be very expensive and therefore the opposing force against spending money is large too. Food 2 might be unattractive but cheap. In this case the conflict would be small. The force toward buying might be composed of a number of components, such as the buyer's liking for the food, his knowledge of his family likes and dislikes, or his ideas about what food is "essential." The opposing forces might be due to the lack of readiness to spend a certain amount of money, a dislike of lengthy or disagreeable form of preparation, unattractive taste, lack of fitness for the occasion, etc. Food is bought if the total force toward buying becomes greater than the opposing forces (Food 3) until the food basket is filled. Food of Type 1 can be called conflict food.

The Gate

It is important to know that once food is bought some forces change its direction. Let us assume the housewife has finally decided to buy the high conflict Food 1. The force against spending money, instead of keeping the food out of the channel, will then make the housewife doubly eager not to waste it. In other words, the force against wasting money will have the same direction as the force toward eating this food or will have the character of a force against leaving the channel. This example indicates that a certain area within a channel might function as a "gate": The constellation of the forces before and after the gate region are decisively different in such a way that the passing or not passing of a unit through the whole channel depends to a high degree upon what happens in the gate region.

Lecture Compared to Group Decision

A preliminary experiment in changing food habit was conducted with six Red Cross groups of volunteers organized for home nursing. Groups ranged in size from 13 to 17 members. The objective was to increase the use of beef hearts, sweetbreads, and kidneys. If one considers the psychological forces which kept housewives from using these intestinals [*sic*], one is tempted to think of rather deep-seated aversions requiring something like psychoanalytical treatment. Doubtless a change in this respect is a more difficult task than, for instance, the introduction of a new vegetable.

In three of the groups attractive lectures were given which linked the problem of nutrition with the war effort, emphasized the vitamin and mineral value of the three meats, giving detailed explanations with the aid of charts. Both the health and economic aspects were stressed. The preparation of these meats was discussed in detail as well as techniques for avoiding those characteristics to which aversions were oriented (odor, texture, appearance, etc.). Mimeographed recipes were distributed. The lecturer was able to arouse the interest of the groups by giving hints of her own methods for preparing these "delicious dishes," and her success with her own family.

For the other three groups Mr. Alex Bavelas developed the following procedure of group decision. Again the problem of nutrition was linked with that of the war effort and general health. After a few minutes, a discussion was started to see whether housewives could be induced to participate in a program of change without attempting any high-pressure salesmanship. The group discussion about "housewives like themselves" led to an elaboration of the obstacles which a change in general and particularly change toward sweetbreads, beef hearts, and kidneys would encounter such as the dislike of the husband, the smell during cooking, etc. The nutrition expert offered the same remedies and recipes for preparation which were presented in the lectures to the other groups. But in these groups preparation techniques were offered after the groups [became] interested in knowing whether certain obstacles could be removed. A follow-up showed that only 3 percent of the women who heard the lectures served one of the meats never served before, whereas after group decision 32 percent served one of them.

Degree of Involvement

Lecturing is a procedure by which the audience is chiefly passive. The discussion, if conducted correctly, is likely to lead to a much higher degree of involvement. The procedure of group decision in this experiment follows a step-by-step method designed (a) to secure high involvement and (b) not to impede freedom of decision. The problem of food changes was discussed in regard to "housewives like yourselves" rather than in regard to themselves. This minimized resistance to considering the problems and possibilities in an objective, unprejudiced manner, in much the same way as such resistance has been minimized in interviews which use projective techniques, or in a socio-drama which uses an assumed situation of role playing rather than a real situation.

Motivation and Decision

The prevalent theory in psychology assumes action to be the direct result of motivation. I am inclined to think that we will have to modify this theory. We will have to study the particular conditions under which a motivating constellation leads or does not lead to a decision or to an equivalent process through which a state of "considerations" (indecisiveness) is changed into a state where the individual has "made up his mind" and is ready for action, although he may not act at that moment. The act of decision is one of those transitions. A change from a situation of undecided conflict to decision does not mean merely that the forces toward one alternative become stronger than those toward the other alternative. If this were the case, the resultant force should frequently be extremely small. A decision rather means that the potency of one alternative has become zero or is so decidedly diminished that the other alternative and the corresponding forces dominate the situation. This alternative itself might be a compromise. After the decision people may feel sorry and change their decision. We cannot speak of a real decision, however, before one alternative has become dominant so far as action is concerned. If the opposing forces in a conflict merely change so that the forces in one direction become slightly greater than in the other direction, a state of blockage or extremely inhibited action results rather than that clear one-sided action which follows a real decision. Lecturing may lead to a high degree of interest. It may affect the motivation of the listener. But it seldom brings about a definite decision on the part of the listener to take a certain action at a specific time. A lecture is not often conducive to decision. Evidence from everyday experience and from some preliminary experiments by Bavelas in a factory indicate that even group discussions, although usually leading to a higher degree of involvement, as a rule do not lead to a decision. It is very important to emphasize this point. Although group discussion is in many respects different from lectures, it shows no fundamental difference on this point.

Of course, there is a great difference in asking for a decision after a lecture or after a discussion. Since discussion involves active participation of the audience and a chance to express motivations corresponding to different alternatives, the audience might be more ready "to make up its mind," that is, to make a decision after a group discussion than after a lecture. A group discussion gives the leader a better indication of where the audience stands and what particular obstacles have to be overcome.

In the experiment on hand, we are dealing with a group decision after discussion. The decision, itself, takes but a minute or two. (It was done through raising of hands as an answer to the question: Who would like to serve kidney, sweetbreads, beef hearts next week?) The act of decision, however should be viewed as a very important process of giving dominance to one of the alternatives, serving or not serving. It has an effect of freezing this motivational constellation for action.

The present experiment approaches the individual as a member of a face-to-face group. We know, for instance, from experiments in level of aspiration that goal setting is strongly dependent on group standards. Experience in leadership training and in many areas of re-education, such as re-education regarding alcoholism or delinquency indicates that it is easier to change the ideology and social practice of a small group handled together than of single individuals. One of the reasons why "group-carried changes" are more readily brought about seems to be the unwillingness of the individual to depart too far from group standards; he is likely to change only if the group changes.

One may try to link the greater effectiveness of group decision procedures to the fact that the lecture reaches the individual in a more individualistic fashion than group discussion. If a change of sentiment of the group becomes apparent during the discussion, the individual will be more ready to come along. It should be stressed that in our case the decision which follows the group discussion does not have the character of a decision in regard to a group goal; it is rather a decision about individual goals in a group setting.

Lecture versus Group Decision (Neighborhood Groups)

Dana Klisurich, under the direction of Marian Radke, conducted experiments with 6 groups of housewives composed of 6–9 members per group. She compared the effect of a lecture with that of group decision. The topic for these groups was increasing home consumption of milk, in the form of fresh or evaporated milk or both. Again there was no attempt at high-pressure salesmanship. The group discussion proceeded in a step-by-step way, starting again with "what housewives in general might do" and only then leading to the individuals present. The lecture was kept as interesting as possible. The knowledge transmitted was the same for lecture and group decision.

A check-up was made after two weeks and after four weeks. As in the previous experiments, group decision showed considerably greater effectiveness, both after two weeks and after four weeks and for both fresh and evaporated milk. This experiment permits the following conclusions:

1. It shows that the greater effectiveness of the group decision in the first experiment is not merely the result of the personality or training of the leader. The leader was a lively person, interested in people, but she did not have particular training in group work. She had been carefully advised and had had a tryout in the group decision procedure. As mentioned above, the leader in lecture and group decision was the same person.
2. The experiment shows that the different effectiveness of the two procedures is not limited to the foods considered in the first experiment.
3. It is interesting that the greater effectiveness of group decision was observable not only after one week but after two and four weeks. Consumption after group decision kept constant during that period. After the lecture it showed an insignificant increase from the second to the fourth week. The degree of permanency is obviously a very important aspect of any changes in group life. We will come back to this point.
4. As in the first experiment, the subjects were informed about a future check-up after group decision but not after the lecture. After the second week, however, both groups knew that a check-up had been made and neither of them was informed that a second check-up would follow.
5. It is important to know whether group decision is effective only with tightly knit groups. It should be noticed that in the second experiment the groups were composed of housewives who either lived in the same neighborhood or visited the nutrition information service of the community center. They were not members of a club meeting regularly as were the Red Cross groups in the first experiment. On the other hand, a good proportion of these housewives knew each other. This indicates that decision in a group setting seems to be effective even if the group is not a permanent organization.

Individual Instruction versus Group Decision

For a number of years, the state hospital in Iowa City has given advice to mothers on feeding of their babies. Under this program, farm mothers who have their first child at the hospital meet with a nutritionist for from 20–25 minutes before discharge from the hospital to discuss feeding. The mother receives printed advice on the composition of the formula and is instructed in the importance of orange juice and cod liver oil. There had been indication that [the] effect of this nutrition program was not very satisfactory.

An experiment [was] carried out by Dana Klisurich under the direction of Marian Radke to compare the effectiveness of this procedure with that of group decision. After two weeks and after four weeks, a check was made on the degree to which each mother followed the advice on cod liver oil and orange juice. The group decision method proved far superior to the individual instruction. After 4 weeks every mother who participated in group decision followed exactly the prescribed diet in regard to orange juice. The following specific results might be mentioned:

1. The greater effect of group decision in this experiment is particularly interesting. Individual instruction is a setting [in] which the individual gets more attention from the instructor. Therefore, one might expect the individual to become more deeply involved and the instruction to be fitted more adequately to the need and sentiment of each individual. After all, the instructor devotes the same amount of time to one individual as he does to six in group decision. The result can be interpreted to mean either that the amount of individual involvement is greater in group decision or that the decision in the group setting is itself the decisive factor.

2. Most of the mothers were not acquainted with each other. They returned to farms which were widely separated. Most of them had no contact with each other during the following four weeks. The previous experiment had already indicated that the effectiveness of group decision did not seem to be limited to well-established groups. In this experiment the absence of social relations among the mothers before and after the group meeting is even more clear cut.

3. The data thus far do not permit reliable quantitative, over-all comparisons. However, they point to certain interesting problems and possibilities. In comparing the various experiments concerning the data two weeks after group decision, one finds that the percentage of housewives who served kidneys, beef hearts, or sweetbreads is relatively similar to the percentage of housewives who increased the consumption of fresh milk or evaporated milk or of mothers who followed completely the diet of cod liver oil with their babies. The percentages lie between 32 and 50. The percentage in regard to orange juice for the baby is clearly higher, namely, 85 percent. These results are surprising in several respects. Mothers are usually eager to do all they can for their babies. This may explain why a group decision in regard to orange juice had such a strong effect. Why, however, was this effect not equally strong on cod liver oil? Perhaps, giving the baby cod liver oil is hampered by the mothers' own dislike of this food. Kidneys, beef hearts, and sweetbreads are foods for which the dislike seems to be particularly deep-seated. If the amount of dislike is the main resistance to change, one would expect probably a greater difference between these foods and, for instance, a change in regard to fresh milk. Of course, these meats are particularly cheap and the group decision leader was particularly qualified.

4. The change after lectures is in all cases smaller than after group decision. However, the rank order of the percentage of change after lectures follows the rank order after group decision, namely (from low to high), glandular meat, fresh milk, cod liver oil for the baby, evaporated milk for the family, orange juice for the baby. The constancy of this rank order

may be interpreted to mean that one can ascribe to each of these foods—under the given circumstances and for these particular populations—a specific degree of "resistance to change." The "force toward change" resulting from group decision is greater than the force resulting from lecture. This leads to a difference in the amount (or frequency) of change for the same food without changing the rank order of the various foods. The rank order is determined by the relative strength of their resistance to change.

5. Comparing the second and the fourth week, we notice that the level of consumption remains the same or increases insignificantly after group decision and lecture regarding evaporated or fresh milk. A pronounced increase occurs after group decision and after individual instruction on cod liver oil and orange juice, that is, in all cases regarding infant feeding. This seems to be a perplexing phenomenon if one considers that no additional instruction or group decision was introduced. On the whole, one may be inclined to expect weakening effect of group decision with time and therefore a decrease rather than an increase of the curve.

Two Basic Methods of Changing Levels of Conduct

For any type of social management, it is of great practical importance that levels of quasistationary [sic] equilibria can be changed in either of two ways: by adding forces in the desired direction, or by diminishing opposing forces. If a change from the level L_1 to L_2 is brought about by increasing the forces toward L_2, the secondary effects should be different from the case where the same change of level is brought about by diminishing the opposing forces. In both cases the equilibrium might change to the same new level. The secondary effect should, however, be quite different. In the first case, the process on the new level would be accompanied by a state of relatively high tension; in the second case, by a state of relatively low tension. Since increase of tension above a certain degree is likely to be paralleled by higher aggressiveness, higher emotionality, and lower constructiveness, it is clear that as a rule the second method will be preferable to the high pressure method.

The group decision procedure which is used here attempts to avoid high-pressure methods and is sensitive to resistance to change. In the experiment by Bavelas on changing production in factory work (as noted below), for instance, no attempt was made to set the new production goal by majority vote because a majority vote forces some group members to produce more than they consider appropriate. These individuals are likely to have some inner resistance. Instead a procedure was followed by which a goal was chosen on which everyone could agree fully. It is possible that the success of group decision and particularly the permanency of the effect is, in part, due to the attempt to bring about a favorable decision by removing counterforces within the individuals rather than by applying outside pressure.

The surprising increase from the second to the fourth week in the number of mothers giving cod liver oil and orange juice to the baby can probably be explained by such a decrease of counter-forces. Mothers are likely to handle their first baby during the first weeks of life somewhat cautiously and become more ready for action as the child grows stronger.

Social Habits and Group Standards

Viewing a social stationary process as the result of a quasi-stationary equilibrium, one may expect that any added forces will change the level of the process. The idea of "social habit" seems to imply that, in spite of the application of a force, the level of the social process will not change because of some type of "inner resistance" to change. To overcome this inner resistance, an additional force seems to be required, a force sufficient to "break the habit," to "unfreeze" the custom.

Many social habits are anchored in the relation between the individuals and certain group standards. An individual may differ in his personal level of conduct (L_p) from the level which represented group standards (L_G) by a certain amount. If the individual should try to diverge "too much" from group standards, he would find himself in increasing difficulties. He would be ridiculed, treated severely and finally ousted from the group. Most individuals, therefore, stay pretty close to the standard of the groups they belong to or wish to belong to. In other words, the group level itself acquires value. It becomes a positive valence corresponding to a central force field with the force keeping the individual in line with the standards of the group.

Changing as a Three-Step Procedure: Unfreezing, Moving, and Freezing of a Level

A change toward a higher level of group performance is frequently short-lived: after a "shot in the arm," group life soon returns to the previous level. This indicates that it does not suffice to define the objective of a planned change in group performance as the reaching of a different level. Permanency of the new level, or permanency for a desired period, should be included in the objective. A successful change includes therefore three aspects: unfreezing (if necessary) the present level L_1, moving to the new level L_2, and freezing group life on the new level. Since any level is determined by a force field permanency implies that the new force field is made relatively secure against change. The "unfreezing" of the present level may involve quite different problems in different cases. Allport has described the "catharsis" which seems to be necessary before prejudices can be removed. To break open the shell of complacency and self-righteousness, it is sometimes necessary to bring about deliberately an emotional stir-up.

The experiments on group decision reported here cover but a few of the necessary variations. Although in some cases the procedure is relatively easily executed, in others it requires skill and presupposes certain general conditions. Managers rushing into a factory to raise production by group decisions are likely to encounter failure. In social management as in medicine there are no patent medicines and each case demands careful diagnosis. One reason why group decision facilitates change is illustrated by Willerman. The degree of eagerness to have the members of a students' eating cooperative change from the consumption of white bread to whole wheat [sic]. When the change was simply requested the degree of eagerness varied greatly with the degree of personal preference for whole wheat. In case of group decisions, the eagerness seems to be relatively independent of personal preference; the individual seems to act mainly as a "group member."

Commentary

One important takeaway from Lewin's work to the study of creativity and innovation is the importance of understanding how creative ideas gain acceptance, or innovation implementation. Lewin was concerned with how to get people and groups to change their minds, change their attitudes, and accept change. Many of the studies presented in his paper focus on the very practical issue of how to persuade people to change attitudes and behaviors toward undesired food. Lewin suggests that change is not easy and that individuals would prefer to stay committed to previous attitudes and behaviors. In order to create the desired change, Lewin indicates that we have to a follow a process of cognitive stages, referred to as unfreezing, moving, and refreezing. That is, we need to create a situation where people get "unstuck" and are willing to move toward a new attitude or behavior. Once they have moved, we need to refreeze them, so that the new attitude or behavior will become permanent. In the literature on innovation, the notion that innovation implementation may be difficult due to resistance to change is quite prevalent (Anderson & West, 1998; Damanpour & Gopalakrishnan, 2001). In fact much of the literature on implementation of innovations focuses on what can be done to get people to accept change—unfreezing and moving, in Lewin's terms. For example, research suggests that when there is a champion in the organization who supports the innovation, it is more likely to be implemented (Klein & Sorra, 1996). That is, champions can serve as a mechanism by which organizational members and teams unfreeze and move to accept the change.

Another important factor in determining whether teams can implement innovation is the climate for innovation. One important component of climate for innovation is psychological safety, which is defined as the perception that people are comfortable being themselves on a team where respect and trust exist, and therefore are willing to speak up and share information and ideas (Edmondson, 1999, 2004). Much research has focused on the role of participative or psychological safety (Edmundson, 1999) and on team creativity and innovation. Psychological safety has been linked to team creativity and innovation across multiple studies (Baer & Frese, 2003; Carmeli, Reiter-Palmon, & Ziv, 2010; Carmeli, Carmeli, Sheaffer, Binyamin, Reiter-Palmon, & Sihmoni, 2014; Post, 2012).

Psychological safety is directly related to group discussion, another mechanism by which groups can unfreeze and move. Lewin's work suggests that group discussion, rather than just providing information through instruction, leads to change. He suggests that group discussions minimize the resistance to change. The research on creativity in teams suggests that information sharing is important for the development of creative ideas (Carmeli, Gelbard, & Reiter-Palmon, 2013; Hülsheger, Anderson, & Salgado, 2009). Work on implementation suggests that buy-in, that is, group acceptance of the need for change and implementation, is critical (Klein & Sorra, 1996; Reiter-Palmon, Kennel, Allen, Jones, & Skinner, 2014). In this context it is likely that team discussion may facilitate buy-in, but team discussion is not discussed as one of the common methods to increase buy-in. Among the factors that are covered are psychological safety (discussed above), support for innovation at the team and organizational level, and leadership (Hülsheger et al., 2009; West 2003).

Support for innovation is conceptualized as the expectation and approval of attempts to introduce new ways of doing things or changing the status quo (West, 2003). While not specifically stated, support for innovation in many cases takes the form of verbal discussion and approval of new ideas, akin to Lewin's group discussion notion. Support for innovation has been found to be a strong predictor of the generation of creative ideas and implementation of innovation (Eisenbeiss, van Knippenberg, & Boerner, 2008; West & Anderson, 1996).

An additional aspect of Lewin's work is the role of conflict in decision-making. Lewin discusses the role of internal conflict in comparing desirable food relative to price. In the realm of team creativity and innovation, conflict has been studied extensively. Current conceptualizations of team conflict identify two main types of conflict, task and relational (Jehn, 1997), although sometimes a third type, process conflict, is added. Task conflict focuses on disagreement regarding the task itself, the work that should be carried out by the team (Jehn, 1997), whereas relationship conflict refers to disagreements and difficulties due to personality and interpersonal relationships (Jehn, 1997). Early work suggested that conflict was related to lower creativity (Carnevale & Probst, 1998), but using the more recent conceptualization of task and relationship conflict more nuanced findings emerge. Specifically, relationship conflict may be detrimental to creativity and innovation (Kurtzberg & Amabile, 2001). However, when looking at the relationship between task conflict and creativity, a more complex pattern emerges. Early studies suggested that task conflict may be beneficial to creativity, as team members discuss different viewpoints and resolve any differences (Kurtzberg & Amabile, 2001; Mannix & Neale, 2005). More recent work suggests that the relationship between task conflict and creativity may be curvilinear, with too little and too much task conflict being detrimental to creativity (De Dreu, 2006). De Dreu argues that when task conflict is high, it often becomes more like relationship conflict, a finding supported by Jehn and Mannix (2001). That is, when task conflict is very high, individuals take the disagreement more personally.

Another timely issue discussed by Lewin is the notion that the forces that influence a decision may change depending on the stage in the decision-making process. The effect of time and how specific factors influence creative problem-solving and decision-making based on the timing of the influence is an issue that is currently receiving more attention. Ford and Sullivan (2004) found that novel ideas and novel contributions were helpful for team creative problem-solving in the early stages of the process, that is, during problem identification and construction, information search, and idea generation. However, later in the process, after an idea has been identified and selected and the team works on further development and how to present to stakeholders, novel ideas are disruptive. Similar results have been found when evaluating team membership change on real-world teams. In organizations, teams are rarely static and gain or lose members. Hirst (2009) found that when teams had lower tenure they benefited from membership change, whereas teams with longer tenure showed detrimental results for creativity. Lab studies regarding membership change show similar results, where those that experience membership change generated more ideas compared to teams that did not (Choi & Thompson, 2005). Another area in which the effect of time and phase of the process is related to team creativity is team conflict. Kratzer, Leenders, and van Engelen (2006), studying R&D project teams, found that early in the project, conflict had an inverted U relationship with creativity, such that moderate levels of conflict were beneficial for creativity. However, during later phases of the project, conflict had a negative effect. Taken together these studies suggest that change and conflict can be beneficial while the team is still trying to come up with an idea and is in the early phases of understanding the problem and developing an idea. However, these become more disruptive and negatively influence creativity at later phases of the process, particularly those focusing on innovation—idea selection and implementation.

Going Forward

In this section we address two main issues. The first is aspects of Lewin's work that have not been considered yet in team creativity research as these provide a fertile ground for future research. The second issue focuses on what Lewin has not included in his thinking: How has team creativity research gone beyond the basics outlined by Lewin? With regard to the first issue, Lewin suggests that group discussion is critical for group decision-making and change in behavior and attitudes. While research on team creativity and innovation has addressed the issue of buy-in and its effects on implementation, we know very few specifics of how group discussion influences creative problem-solving in teams. Research on team communication suggests that effective and high-performing teams communicate more effectively (Caldwell & Everhart, 1998). Meta-analyses have found that team communication is indeed related to team creativity (Damanpour, 1991; Hülsheger et al., 2009). However, the relationship between team communication and creativity is not simple. Kratzer, Leenders, and van Engelen (2004) found that communication frequency was in fact negatively related to creativity. Lovelace, Shapiro, and Weingart (2001) suggested that these contradictory findings may be a result of the type of communication, such as whether or not it is collaborative. When team members use collaborative communication they are trying to find common ground and mutually beneficial solutions (win-win), whereas when using contentious communication team members have a more pessimistic attitude and adopt a win-lose framework. Lovelace et al. found that collaborative communication was related to increased creativity, whereas contentious communication was detrimental to creativity, particularly when the frequency of communication was high. Similarly Hoever, van Knippenberg, van Ginkel, and Barkema (2012) indicate that diverse teams are more creative but only when team members share information and elaborate on the information shared. These studies suggest that team communication is important for creativity and innovation; however, our understanding of how team communication influences creativity is somewhat limited and should be further evaluated.

The effect of group member familiarity on decision-making was also studied by Lewin. He found that group member familiarity, that is, whether group members knew each other prior to the group study, did not influence his results regarding group decision-making. This issue, which is an important one, is not really addressed in the team creativity literature. Experimental research in team creativity conducted in lab settings will typically employ teams composed of students, who in most cases are not familiar with each other. Even if students do know each other, they are not likely to work together again, leading to a very different environment compared to long-term teams. Long-term teams are more likely to be found in the workplace (although we do have short-term teams in organizations) and evaluated using case studies, observations, or survey research. These team members not only are familiar with one another; they share both a work history and a future. Both field studies and lab studies are needed to understand team creativity; they provide different strengths and different perspectives by which we can understand the phenomena of interest. However, it is still unclear how team familiarity directly (or indirectly) influences team creativity.

Lewin does not directly address the importance of team and organizational climate and their effect on creative problem-solving. He briefly mentions group norms and standards as influencing group decision-making, but he does not fully align these with team climate. Team and organizational climate have been studied extensively in the creativity literature, both at the individual and the team level. Climate is defined as people's perceptions of or beliefs about environmental characteristics that shape expectations about outcomes, requirements, and interactions in the work environment (James, James, & Ashe, 1990). A climate for creativity, which focuses on perceptions of environmental attributes that signal expectations regarding creative performance, has been identified as critical for creativity and innovation at the individual and team levels (Amabile & Gryskiewicz, 1989; Anderson, De Dreu, & Nijstad, 2004; Hunter, Bedell, & Mumford, 2007; West, 2002). Hunter et al. provide a review and integration of different perspectives and studies regarding climate for creativity and identified 14 different dimensions. Some of these dimensions were discussed earlier (e.g., positive peer relations, positive interpersonal exchange, participative safety). However, other dimensions have not been directly addressed by Lewin, such as resources, autonomy, and job challenge. While some aspects of climate for creativity have been studied extensively (supervisor support, job characteristics), others remain less studied, such as goal clarity, resources, and organizational integration.

A final area that has been studied extensively but has not been explicitly identified by Lewin as critical is leadership and the role that leadership plays in team creativity. Lewin's studies focused on the comparison of group discussion versus individual instruction and the effect of those on decision-making and attitude change. The effect of leadership on creativity has been examined extensively and received much attention in the past two decades (Mumford, Scott, Gaddis, & Strange, 2002; Reiter-Palmon & Royston 2017). In a recent meta-analysis, Rosing, Frese, and Bausch (2011) found that the transformational leadership style was positively related to creativity and innovation; however, there was wide variability in the results, and multiple studies have identified boundary conditions (interactions), suggesting that the relationship is more complex than initially realized. Another leadership approach studied extensively is leader-member exchange (LMX). Rosing et al. found a consistent, significant positive relationship between LMX and creativity. Research on supervisory support has also been found to consistently predict team creativity (Carmeli et al., 2010; Rosing et al., 2011). Less clear are the mechanisms by which leaders and leadership style influence team creativity. A number of moderating and mediating variables have been suggested as important. For example, Rosing et al. suggested that ambidextrous leadership, a style wherein leaders are flexible and switch between opening and closing leader behavior or exploration and exploitation, facilitates creativity. Others have suggested that leaders are key in creating a climate that facilitates creativity, providing support for innovation, team support, and participative safety (Reiter-Palmon, de Vreede, & de Vreede, 2013). Reiter-Palmon and Illies (2004) suggested that leaders play a critical role in facilitating individual and team engagement in the various cognitive processes associated with creative problem-solving. Processes such as problem construction and identification, idea generation, and idea evaluation tend to be resource-intensive and risky. As such, leaders have a great deal of influence on the extent to which these processes are carried out effectively. While some work has been conducted on how leaders can influence team creativity, much more research is necessary to understand the mechanisms by which leadership influences team creativity.

Conclusions

In this chapter we have used early work by Lewin on team dynamics and decision-making to understand his influence on current work on team creativity. Much of the current work being conducted can be traced to concepts first identified by Lewin, such as group discussion, group norms, and implementing change. Future research should capitalize on the direction laid out by Lewin and extend it. For example, a more nuanced understanding of the role of communication and types of communication to support creativity and innovation is needed. Studies regarding organizational climate and leadership are also needed to understand the complex relationships between these constructs and creativity. Lewin provided us with a great roadmap to guide our research on team creativity and innovation, one that is still relevant today, 50 years after its publication.

References

Amabile, T. M., & Gryskiewicz, N. D. (1989). The creative environment scales: Work environment inventory. *Creativity Research Journal, 2*(4), 231–253. doi:10.1080/10400418909534321.

Anderson, N. R., & West, M. A. (1998). Measuring climate for work group innovation: development and validation of the team climate inventory. *Journal of Organizational Behavior, 19*(3), 235-258. doi:10.1002/(SICI)1099-1379(199805)19:3<235::AID-JOB837>3.0.CO;2-C.

Anderson, N., De Dreu, C. K. W., & Nijstad, B. A. (2004). The routinization of innovation research: A constructively critical review of the state-of-the-science. *Journal of Organizational Behavior, 25*(2), 147–173. doi:10.1002/job.236.

Baer, M., & Frese, M. (2003). Innovation is not enough: Climates for initiative and psychological safety, process innovations, and firm performance. *Journal of Organizational Behavior, 24*(1), 45–68. doi:10.1002/job.179.

Caldwell, B. S., & Everhart, N. C. (1998). Information flow and development of coordination in distributed supervisory control teams. *International Journal of Human-Computer Interaction, 10*(1), 51–70. doi:10.1207/s15327590ijhc1001_4.

Carmeli, A., Gelbard, R., & Reiter-Palmon, R. (2013). Leadership, creative problem-solving capacity, and creative performance: The importance of knowledge sharing. *Human Resource Management, 52*(1), 95–121. doi:10.1002/hrm.21514.

Carmeli, A., Reiter-Palmon, R., & Ziv, E. (2010). Inclusive leadership and employee involvement in creative tasks in the workplace: The mediating role of psychological safety. *Creativity Research Journal, 22*(3), 250–260. doi:10.1080/10400419.2010.504654.

Carmeli, A., Sheaffer, Z., Binyamin, G., Reiter-Palmon, R., & Sihmoni, T. (2014). Transformational leadership and creative problem solving: The mediating role of psychological safety and reflexivity. *Journal of Creative Behavior 48*(2), 115–135. doi:10.1002/jocb.43.

Carnevale, P. J., & Probst, T. M. (1998). Social values and social conflict in creative problem solving and categorization. *Journal of Personality and Social Psychology, 74*(5), 1300–1309. doi:10.1037/0022-3514.74.5.1300.

Choi, H. S., & Thompson, L. (2005). Old wine in a new bottle: Impact of membership change on group creativity. *Organizational Behavior and Human Decision Processes, 98*(2), 121–132. doi:10.1016/j.obhdp.2005.06.003.

Damanpour, F. (1991). Organizational innovation: A meta-analysis of effects of determinants and moderators. *Academy of Management Journal, 34*(3), 555–590. doi:10.2307/256406.

Damanpour, F., & Gopalakrishnan, S. (2001). The dynamics of the adoption of product and process innovations in organizations. *Journal of Management Studies, 38*(1), 45–65. doi:10.1111/1467-6486.00227.

De Dreu, C. K. W. (2006). When too little or too much hurts: Evidence for a curvilinear relationship between task conflict and innovation in teams. *Journal of Management, 32*(1), 83–107. doi:10.1177/0149206305277795.

Edmondson, A. (1999). Psychological safety and learning behavior in work teams. *Administrative Science Quarterly, 44*(2), 350. doi:10.2307/2666999.

Edmondson, A. C. (2004). Psychological safety, trust, and learning in organizations: A group-level lens. In R. M. Kramer & K. S. Cook (Eds.), *Trust and distrust in organizations: Dilemmas and approaches* (pp. 239–272). New York, NY: Russell Sage Foundation.

Eisenbeiss, S. A., van Knippenberg, D., & Boerner, S. (2008). Transformational leadership and team innovation: Integrating team climate principles. *Journal of Applied Psychology, 93*(6), 1438–1446. doi:10.1037/a0012716.

Ford, C., & Sullivan, D. M. (2004). A time for everything: How the timing of novel contributions influences project team outcomes. *Journal of Organizational Behavior, 25*(2), 279–292. doi:10.1002/job.241.

Hirst, G. (2009). Effects of membership change on open discussion and team performance: The moderating role of team tenure. *European Journal of Work and Organizational Psychology, 18*(2), 231–249. doi:10.1080/13594320802394202.

Hoever, I. J., van Knippenberg, D., van Ginkel, W. P., & Barkema, H. G. (2012). Fostering team creativity: Perspective taking as key to unlocking diversity's potential. *Journal of Applied Psychology, 97*(5), 982. doi:10.1037/a0029159.

Hülsheger, U. R., Anderson, N., & Salgado, J. F. (2009). Team-level predictors of innovation at work: A comprehensive meta-analysis spanning three decades of research. *Journal of Applied Psychology, 94*(5), 1128–1145. doi:10.1037/a0015978.

Hunter, S. T., Bedell, K. E., & Mumford, M. D. (2007). Climate for creativity: A quantitative review. *Creativity Research Journal, 19*(1), 69–90. doi:10.1080/10400410709336883.

James, L., James, L., & Ashe, D. (1990). The meaning of organizations: The role of cognition and values. In B. Schneider (Ed.), *Organizational climate and culture* (pp. 40–84. San Francisco, CA: Jossey Bass.

Jehn, K. A. (1997). A qualitative analysis of conflict types and dimensions in organizational groups. *Administrative Science Quarterly, 42*(3), 530. doi:10.2307/2393737.

Jehn, K. A., & Mannix, E. A. (2001). The dynamic nature of conflict: A longitudinal study of intragroup conflict and group performance. *Academy of Management Journal, 44*(2), 238–251. doi:10.2307/3069453.

Klein, K. J., & Sorra, J. S. (1996). The challenge of innovation implementation. *Academy of Management Review, 21*(4), 1055–1080. doi:10.2307/259164.

Kratzer, J., Leenders, R. T. A. J., & van Engelen, J. M. L. (2004). Stimulating the potential: Creative performance and communication in innovation teams. *Creativity and Innovation Management, 13*(1), 63–71. doi:10.1111/j.1467-8691.2004.00294.x.

Kratzer, J., Leenders, R. T. A. J., & Van Engelen, J. M. L. (2006). Managing creative team performance in virtual environments: An empirical study in 44 R&D teams. *Technovation, 26*(1), 42–49. doi:10.1016/j.technovation.2004.07.016.

Kurtzberg, T. R., & Amabile, T. M. (2001). From Guilford to creative synergy: Opening the black box of team-level creativity. *Creativity Research Journal, 13*(3–4), 285–294. doi:10.1207/s15326934crj1334_06.

Lewin, K. (1947). Group decision and social change. In T. M. Newcomb & E. L. Hartley (Eds.), *Readings in social psychology* (pp. 330–344). New York, NY: Henry Holt.

Lovelace, K., Shapiro, D. L., & Weingart, L. R. (2001). Maximizing cross-functional new product teams' innovativeness and constraint adherence: A conflict communications perspective. *Academy of Management Journal, 44*(4), 779–793. doi:10.2307/3069415.

Mannix, E., & Neale, M. A. (2005). What differences make a difference? *Psychological Science in the Public Interest, 6*(2), 31–55. doi:10.1111/j.1529-1006.2005.00022.x.

Marks, M. A., Mathieu, J. E., & Zaccaro, S. J. (2001). A temporally based framework and taxonomy of team processes. *Academy of Management Review, 26*(3), 356. doi:10.2307/259182.

Mumford, M. D., Scott, G. M., Gaddis, B., & Strange, J. M. (2002). Leading creative people: Orchestrating expertise and relationships. *Leadership Quarterly, 13*(6), 705–750. doi:10.1016/s1048-9843(02)00158-3.

Newcomb, T. M., & Hartley, E. L. (1947). *Readings in social psychology.* Oxford: Henry Holt.

Post, C. (2012). Deep-level team composition and innovation. *Group & Organization Management, 37*(5), 555–588. doi:10.1177/1059601112456289.

Reiter-Palmon, R., de Vreede, T., & de Vreede, G. J. (2013). Leading creative interdisciplinary teams: Challenges and solutions. In S. Hemlin, C. M. Allwood, B. Martin, & M. D. Mumford (Eds.), *Creativity and leadership in science, Technology and Innovation* (pp. 240–267). New York: Routledge.

Reiter-Palmon, R., & Illies, J. J. (2004). Leadership and creativity: Understanding leadership from a creative problem-solving perspective. *Leadership Quarterly, 15*, 55–77.

Reiter-Palmon, R., Kennel, V., Allen, J. A., Jones, K. J., & Skinner, A. M. (2014). Naturalistic decision-making in after-action review meetings: The implementation of and learning from post-fall huddles. *Journal of Occupational and Organizational Psychology, 88*(2), 322–340. doi:10.1111/joop.12084.

Reiter-Palmon, R., & Royston, R. (2017). Leading for creativity: How leaders manage creative teams. In M. D. Mumford & S. Hemlin (Eds.), *Handbook of research on leadership and creativity* (pp. 159–184). Northampton, MA: Elgar.

Rosing, K., Frese, M., & Bausch, A. (2011). Explaining the heterogeneity of the leadership-innovation relationship: Ambidextrous leadership. *Leadership Quarterly, 22*(5), 956–974. doi:10.1016/j.leaqua.2011.07.014.

West, M. A. (2002). Sparkling fountains or stagnant ponds: An integrative model of creativity and innovation implementation in work groups. *Applied Psychology, 51*(3), 355–387. doi:10.1111/1464-0597.00951.

West, M. (2003). Innovation implementation in work teams. In P. B. Paulus & B. A. Nijstad (Eds.), *Group creativity: Innovation through collaboration* (pp. 245–276). Oxford: Oxford University Press.

West, M. A., & Anderson, N. R. (1996). Innovation in top management teams. *Journal of Applied Psychology, 81*(6), 680–693. doi:10.1037/0021-9010.81.6.680.

28

The Idea of Dialogue
Mikhail Bakhtin

Vlad P. Glăveanu

Summary

Mikhail Bakhtin was a Russian literary theorist and philosopher of language who is widely regarded as the father of dialogism. His work places the dialogue between voices or perspectives at the heart of language, mind, and, last but not least, creativity. While Bakhtin rarely talked about creativity as such, his understanding of "ideas" is essential for developing a dynamic and relational account of creating. This account is vividly illustrated in Bakhtin's analysis of Dostoevsky's novels; the fragment reproduced in this chapter comes from one of his most famous books on this topic, initially published in 1929, updated in 1963, and translated into English in 1984. The final commentary focuses on the importance of Bakhtin's ideas for creativity studies and the impact they (could) have on the field.

Introduction

Mikhail Mikhailovich Bakhtin (1895–1975) was a Russian literary theorist and philosopher of language who left an important mark on cultural history, literary criticism, ethics, aesthetics, linguistics, political science, philosophy, and psychology. He was born in Oryol, in Tsarist Russia, to an old noble family. At the age of nine he fell ill with a bone infection that, years later, would cost him his leg (White, 2015). This physical handicap, however, would also "save" him later in his life from being sent to forced labor in Solovki, an island in the White Sea. Bakhtin ended up living in many places, including Vilnius, Odessa, Leningrad, Kustanai, Saransk, and Moscow, either looking for work, usually in educational institutes, or being forced to move. Following his studies in Odessa, he worked as a schoolteacher in Nevel. In 1920, he left for Vitebsk, where he married Elena Aleksandrovna Okolovich. Toward the end of his life, after often changing jobs and struggling to publish his work,

Bakhtin worked at the Mordov Pedagogical Institute (now University). He died in Moscow at the age of 80.

Bakhtin is widely considered the father of dialogism, a philosophical orientation that goes beyond literary studies and places the open-ended dialogue between perspectives or "voices" at the core of both mind and society. Needless to say, this conception, challenging dominant or hegemonic views, as well as the idea of authority, was not well received by the Soviet establishment. As a consequence, Bakhtin was exiled for many years in Kazakhstan and never received a doctorate (but did earn a lower degree). Moreover, the group of friends and colleagues with whom he developed his ideas—in a highly dialogical manner— known as the Bakhtin Circle, was disbanded and many of its members persecuted. Notable participants in this Circle included Pavel Nikolaevich Medvedev, Valentin Nikolaevich Voloshinov, and Matvei Isaevich Kagan. Nonetheless, his ideas were ultimately discovered, first by Russian scholars after 1960 (when Bakhtin himself was still alive, even if few realized it at the time) and then by scholars in Western countries (initially the French-speaking world through the work of Julia Kristeva and Tzvetan Todorov, then translated into English in the 1980s). Due to these special circumstances and the fact that Bakhtin's collaborators wrote on similar topics, there are ongoing debates regarding the authorship of some texts and especially their interpretation. Paradoxically, such questions would probably be considered secondary if approached from a dialogical perspective. What is uncontested, though, is that Bakhtin's ideas about the carnivalesque, heteroglossia and polyphony, the chronotope, and speech genres are widely read today and built upon in many disciplines, including psychology. They are also present, to a lesser extent, within creativity studies.

This chapter aims to recuperate some of the richness and depth of Bakhtin's conception for an audience interested in creativity. Bakhtin was a highly prolific author and, even if some of his writings are now lost (e.g., a book on the Bildungsroman), his thinking has been popularized through works such as *Toward a Philosophy of the Act*, *Rabelais and His World*, *The Dialogic Imagination*, and *Speech Genres and Other Late Essays*, many of them collected and edited by other people. Most of all, though, Bakhtin is known for his extensive and illuminating analysis of Fyodor Dostoyevsky's novels. This work was initially published in 1929 as *Problems of Dostoevsky's Art* and republished in 1963, in an updated edition, as *Problems of Dostoevsky's Poetics*. The reading included here—a selection from the chapter "The Idea in Dostoevsky"—is the part of this volume in which Bakhtin basically introduced the notion of dialogism and discussed at length issues related to the author, the audience, the hero, the unfinalizable self, and the never-ending dialogue between points of view. His conception of "ideas" and their transformation is particularly important for creativity scholars who examine creative ideation. However, as I will highlight in the commentary, Bakhtin's understanding of ideas is not individual-based but social, and this understanding could be fundamental for a new—and in many ways overdue—branch of dialogical research into creativity.

Reading: "The Idea in Dostoevsky"

Source: Bakhtin, M. (1984). The idea in Dostoevsky. In C. Emerson (Ed. & Trans.), *Problems in Dostoevsky's poetics* (pp. 78–92). Minneapolis: University of Minnesota Press. Reproduced with permission. The author's endnotes and footnotes have been eliminated from the text. The 1984 translation is based on the 1929 text by Bakhtin "Problems of Dostoevsky's Art."

Let us now move on to the next aspect of our thesis—the positioning of the idea in Dostoevsky's artistic world. The polyphonic project is incompatible with a mono-ideational framework of the ordinary sort. In the positioning of the idea, Dostoevsky's originality emerges with special force and clarity. In our analysis we shall avoid matters of content in the ideas introduced by Dostoevsky—what is important for us here is their artistic function in the work.

Dostoevsky's hero is not only a discourse about himself and his immediate environment, but also a discourse about the world; he is not only cognizant, but an ideologist as well.

The "Underground Man" is already an ideologist. But the ideological creativity of Dostoevsky's characters reaches full significance only in the novels; there, the idea really does become almost the hero of the work. Even there, however, the dominant of the hero's representation remains what it had been earlier: self-consciousness.

Thus discourse about the world merges with confessional discourse about oneself. The truth about the world, according to Dostoevsky, is inseparable from the truth of the personality. The categories of self-consciousness that were already determining the life of Devushkin and even more so of Golyadkin—acceptance or nonacceptance, rebellion or reconciliation—now become the basic categories for thinking about the world. Thus the loftiest principles of a worldview are the same principles that govern the most concrete personal experiences. And the result is an artistic fusion, so characteristic for Dostoevsky, of personal life with worldview, of the most intimate experiences with the idea. Personal life becomes uniquely unselfish and principled, and lofty ideological thinking becomes passionate and intimately linked with personality.

This merging of the hero's discourse about himself with his ideological discourse about the world greatly increases the direct signifying power of a self-utterance, strengthens its internal resistance to all sorts of external finalization. The idea helps self-consciousness assert its sovereignty in Dostoevsky's artistic world, and helps it triumph over all fixed, stable, neutral images.

But on the other hand, the idea itself can preserve its power to mean, its full integrity as an idea, only when self-consciousness is the dominant in the artistic representation of the hero. In a monologic artistic world, the idea, once placed in the mouth of a hero who is portrayed as a fixed and finalized image of reality, inevitably loses its direct power to mean, becoming a mere aspect of reality, one more of reality's predetermined features, indistinguishable from any other manifestation of the hero. An idea of this sort might be characteristic of a social type or an individual, or it might ultimately be a simple intellectual gesture on the part of the hero, an intellectual expression of his spiritual face. The idea ceases to be an idea and becomes a simple artistic characterizing feature. As such, as a characteristic, it is combined with the hero's image.

If, in a monologic world, an idea retains its power to signify as an idea, then it is inevitably separated from the fixed image of the hero and is no longer artistically combined with this image: the idea is merely placed in his mouth, but it could with equal success be placed in the mouth of any other character. For the author it is important only that a given true idea be uttered somewhere in the context of a given work; who utters it, and when, is determined by considerations of composition, by what is convenient or appropriate, or by purely negative criteria: it must not jeopardize the verisimilitude of the image of him who utters it. Such an idea, in itself, belongs to *no one*. The hero is merely the carrier of an independently valid idea; as a true signifying idea it gravitates toward some impersonal, systemically monologic context; in other words, it gravitates toward the systemically monologic worldview of the author himself.

A monologic artistic world does not recognize someone else's thought, someone else's idea, as an object of representation. In such a world everything ideological falls into two categories. Certain thoughts—true, signifying thoughts—gravitate toward the author's consciousness, and strive to shape themselves in the purely semantic unity of a worldview; such a thought is not represented, it is affirmed; its affirmation finds objective expression in a special accent of its own, in its special position within the work as a whole, in the very verbal and stylistic form of its utterance and in a whole series of other infinitely varied means for advancing a thought as a signifying, affirmed thought. We can always hear them in the context of the work; an affirmed thought always sounds different from an unaffirmed one. Other thoughts and ideas—untrue or indifferent from the author's point of view, not fitting into his worldview—are not affirmed; they are either polemically repudiated, or else they lose their power to signify directly and become simple elements of characterization, the mental gestures of the hero or his more stable mental qualities.

In the monologic world, *tertium non datur*: a thought is either affirmed or repudiated; otherwise it simply ceases to be a fully valid thought. An unaffirmed thought, if it is to enter into the artistic structure, must be deprived in general of its power to mean, must become a psychical fact. And as for polemically repudiated thoughts, they also are not represented, because denial, whatever form it takes, excludes the possibility of any genuine representation of the idea. Someone else's repudiated thought cannot break out of a monologic context; on the contrary, it is confined all the more harshly and implacably within its own boundaries. Another's repudiated thought is not capable of creating alongside one consciousness another autonomous consciousness, if repudiation remains a purely theoretical repudiation of the thought as such.

The artistic representation of an idea is possible only when the idea is posed in terms beyond affirmation and repudiation, but at the same time not reduced to simple psychical experience deprived of any direct power to signify. In a monologic world, such a status for the idea is impossible: it contradicts the most basic principles of that world. These basic principles go far beyond the boundaries of artistic creativity alone; they are the principles behind the entire ideological culture of recent times. What are these principles?

Ideological monologism found its clearest and theoretically most precise expression in idealistic philosophy. The monistic principle, that is, the affirmation of the unity of *existence*, is, in idealism, transformed into the unity of the *consciousness*.

For us, of course, the important thing is not the philosophical side of the question, but rather something characteristic of ideology in general, something also present here in this idealistic transformation of the monism of existence into the monologism of consciousness. And even this general characteristic of ideology is important to us only from the point of view of its further application in art.

The unity of consciousness, replacing the unity of existence, is inevitably transformed into the unity of a *single* consciousness; when this occurs it makes absolutely no difference what metaphysical form the unity takes: "consciousness in general" (*Bewusstsein überhaupt*), "the absolute I," "the absolute spirit," "the normative consciousness," and so forth. Alongside this unified and inevitably *single* consciousness can be found a multitude of empirical human consciousnesses. From the point of view of "consciousness in general" this plurality of consciousnesses is accidental and, so to speak, superfluous. Everything in them that is essential and true is incorporated into the unified context of "consciousness in general" and deprived of its individuality. That which is individual, that which distinguishes one consciousness from another and from others, is cognitively not essential and belongs to the realm of an individual human being's psychical organization and limitations. From the point of view of truth, there are no individual consciousnesses. Idealism recognizes only one principle of cognitive individualization: *error*. True judgments are not attached to a personality, but correspond to some unified, systemically monologic context. Only error individualizes. Everything that is true finds a place for itself within the boundaries of a single consciousness, and if it does not actually find for itself such a place, this is so for reasons incidental and extraneous to the truth itself. In the ideal a single consciousness and a single mouth are absolutely sufficient for maximally full cognition; there is no need for a multitude of consciousnesses, and no basis for it.

It should be pointed out that the single and unified consciousness is by no means an inevitable consequence of the concept of a unified truth. It is quite possible to imagine and postulate a unified truth that requires a plurality of consciousnesses, one that cannot in principle be fitted into the bounds of a single consciousness, one that is, so to speak, by its very nature *full of event potential* and is born at a point of contact among various consciousnesses. The monologic way of perceiving cognition and truth is only one of the possible ways. It arises only where consciousness is placed above existence, and where the unity of existence is transformed into the unity of consciousness.

In an environment of philosophical monologism the genuine interaction of consciousnesses is impossible, and thus genuine dialogue is impossible as well. In essence idealism knows only a single mode of cognitive interaction among consciousnesses: someone who knows and possesses the truth instructs someone who is ignorant of it and in error; that is, it is the interaction of a teacher and a pupil, which, it follows, can be only a pedagogical dialogue.

A monologic perception of consciousness holds sway in other spheres of ideological creativity as well. All that has the power to mean, all that has value, is everywhere concentrated around one center—the carrier. All ideological creative acts are conceived and perceived as possible expressions of a single consciousness, a single spirit. Even when one is dealing with a collective, with a multiplicity of creating forces, unity is nevertheless illustrated through the image of a single consciousness: the spirit of a nation, the spirit of a people, the spirit of history, and so forth. Everything capable of meaning can be gathered together in one consciousness and subordinated to a unified accent; whatever does not submit to such a reduction is accidental and unessential. The consolidation of monologism and its permeation into all spheres and ideological life was promoted in modern times by European rationalism, with its cult of a unified and exclusive reason, and especially by the Enlightenment, during which time the basic generic forms of European artistic prose took shape. All of European utopianism was likewise built on this monologic principle. Here too belongs utopian socialism, with its faith in the omnipotence of the conviction. Semantic unity of any sort is everywhere represented by a single consciousness and a single point of view.

This faith in the self-sufficiency of a single consciousness in all spheres of ideological life is not a theory created by some specific thinker; no, it is a profound structural characteristic of the creative ideological activity of modern times, determining all its external and internal forms. We are interested only in its manifestations in literary art.

In literature, as we have seen, the statement of an idea is usually thoroughly monologistic. An idea is either confirmed or repudiated. All confirmed ideas are merged in the unity of the author's seeing and representing consciousness; the unconfirmed ideas are distributed among the heroes, no longer as signifying ideas, but rather as socially typical or individually characteristic manifestations of thought. The one who knows, understands, and sees is in the first instance the author himself. He alone is an ideologist. The author's ideas are marked with the stamp of his individuality. Thus the author *combines in his person a direct and fully competent ideological power to mean with individuality, in such a way that they do not weaken one another*. But this occurs in his person alone. In the characters, individuality kills the signifying power of their ideas, or, if these ideas retain their power to mean, then they are detached from the individuality of the character and are merged with that of the author. Hence *the single ideational accent of the work*; the appearance of a second accent would inevitably be perceived as a crude contradiction within the author's worldview.

In a work of the monologic type, a confirmed and fully valid authorial idea can perform a triple function: first, it is the *principle for visualizing and representing the world*, the principle behind the *choice* and unification of material, the principle behind the *ideological single-toned quality* of all the elements of the work; second, the idea can be presented as a more or less distinct or conscious deduction drawn from the represented material; third and finally, an authorial idea can receive direct expression in the *ideological position of the main hero*.

The idea, as a principle of representation, merges with the form. It determines all formal accents, all those ideological evaluations that constitute the formal unity of an artistic style and the unified tone of the work.

The deeper layers of this form-shaping ideology, which determine the basic generic characteristics of artistic works, are traditional; they take shape and develop over the course of centuries. To these deeper layers of form also belongs the very concept we are analyzing here, artistic monologism.

In the presence of the monologic principle, ideology—as a deduction, as a semantic summation of representation—inevitably transforms the represented world into a *voiceless object of that deduction*. The forms of this ideological deduction can themselves be most varied. Depending on these forms, the positioning of represented material changes: it can be a simple illustration to an idea, a simple example, it can be material for ideological generalization (as in the experimental novel), or it can exist in more complex relationship to the final result. Where the representation is oriented entirely toward ideological deduction, we have an ideational philosophical novel (Voltaire's *Candide*, for example) or—in the worst instance—simply a crudely tendentious novel. And even if this direct, straightforward orientation is absent, an element of ideological deduction is nevertheless present in every representation, however modest or concealed the formal functions of that deduction might be. The accents of ideological deduction must not contradict the form-shaping accents of the representation itself. If such a contradiction exists it is felt to be a flaw, for within the limits of a monologic world contradictory accents collide within a single voice. A unity of viewpoint must weld into one both the most formal elements of style and the most abstract philosophical deductions.

In one plane together with form-shaping ideology and ultimate ideological deduction can also be found the semantic position of the hero. The point of view of the hero can be transferred from the objectivized sphere into the sphere of principle. In that case the ideological principles which underlie the construction no longer merely represent the hero, defining the author's point of view toward him, but are expressed by the hero himself, defining his own personal point of view on the world. Such a hero is formally very different from heroes of the ordinary type. There is no need to go beyond the bounds of a given work to seek other documents that attest to a concurrence of the author's ideology with the ideology of the hero. Such a concurrence in matters of content, moreover, established elsewhere than in the work, does not in itself have any persuasive power. Any unity between an author's ideological principles of representation and the hero's ideological position must be revealed in the work itself, *as a single accent common both to the authorial representation and to the speech and experiences of the hero*, and not as some concurrence in the content of the hero's thoughts with the author's ideological views, uttered in some other place. The very discourse of a hero and his experiences are presented differently: they are not turned into objects, but rather they characterize the object toward which they are directed and not only the speaker himself. The discourse of such a hero lies in a single plane with the discourse of the author.

The absence of any distance between the author's position and the hero's position is also manifested in a whole series of other formal characteristics. The hero, for example, is not closed and not internally finalized, like the author himself, and for that reason he does not fit wholly into the procrustean bed of the plot, which is in any case conceived as only one of many possible plots and is consequently in the final analysis merely accidental for a given hero. This open-ended hero is characteristic for Romanticism, for Byron, Chateaubriand; Lermontov's Pechorin is in some ways this sort of hero.

Finally, the ideas of the author can be scattered sporadically throughout the whole work. They can appear in authorial speech as isolated sayings, as maxims, as whole arguments, or they can be placed in the mouth of one or another character—often in quite large and compact chunks—without, however, merging with the character's individual personality (Turgenev's Potugin, for example).

This whole mass of ideology, both organized and unorganized, from the form-shaping principles to the random and removable maxims of the author, must be subordinated to a single accent and must express a single and unified point of view. All else is merely the object of this point of view, "sub-accentual material." Only that idea which has fallen into the rut of the author's point of view can retain its significance without destroying the single-accented unity of the work. Whatever these authorial ideas, whatever function they fulfill, they are *not represented*: they either represent and internally govern a representation, or they shed light on some other represented thing, or, finally, they accompany the representation as a detachable semantic ornament. *They are expressed directly, without distance.* And within the bounds of that monologic world shaped by them, someone else's idea cannot be represented. It is either assimilated, or polemically repudiated, or ceases to be an idea.

Dostoevsky was capable of *representing someone else's idea*, preserving its full capacity to signify as an idea, while at the same time also preserving a distance, neither confirming the idea nor merging it with his own expressed ideology. The idea, in his work, becomes the *subject of artistic representation*, and Dostoevsky himself became a great *artist of the idea*.

It comes as no surprise that the image of an "artist of the idea" had already occurred to Dostoevsky in 1846–47, that is, at the very beginning of his career as a writer. We have in mind the image of Ordynov, the hero in "The Landlady." He is a lonely young scholar. He has his own creative system, his own unusual approach to the scientific idea: He was creating a system for himself, it was being evolved in him over the years; and the dim, vague, but marvellously soothing *image of an idea*, embodied in a *new, clarified form*, was gradually emerging in his soul. And this form craved expression, fretting his soul; he was still timidly aware of its originality, its *truth*, its independence: creative genius was already showing, it was gathering strength and taking shape. (SS I, 425; "The Landlady," Part I, 1) And further, at the end of the story: Possibly a complete, original, independent idea really did exist within him. Perhaps he had been destined to be *the artist in science*. (SS I, 498; "The Landlady," Part II, 3) Dostoevsky was also destined to become just such an artist of the idea, not in science, but in literature.

What are the conditions that make possible in Dostoevsky the artistic expression of an idea?

We must remember first of all that the image of an idea is inseparable from the image of a person, the carrier of that idea. It is not the idea in itself that is the "hero of Dostoevsky's works," as Engelhardt has claimed, but rather the *person born of that idea*. It again must be emphasized that the hero in Dostoevsky is a man of the idea; this is not a character, not a temperament, not a social or psychological type; such externalized and finalized images of persons cannot of course be combined with the image of a *fully valid* idea. It would be absurd, for example, even to attempt to combine Raskolnikov's idea, which we understand and *feel* (according to Dostoevsky an idea can and must not only be understood, but also "felt") with his finalized character or his social typicality as a déclassé intellectual of the '60s: Raskolnikov's idea would immediately lose its direct power to signify as a fully valid idea, and would withdraw from the quarrel where it had *lived* in uninterrupted dialogic interaction with other fully valid ideas—the ideas of Sonya, Porfiry, Svidrigailov, and others. The carrier of a fully valid idea must be the "man in man" about which we spoke in the preceding chapter, with its free unfinalized nature and its indeterminacy. It is precisely to this unfinalized inner core of Raskolnikov's personality that Sonya, Porfiry and the others address themselves dialogically. And the author himself dialogically addresses this same unfinalized core of Raskolnikov's personality, as evidenced by the entire structure of his novel about him.

It follows that only the unfinalized and inexhaustible "man in man" can become a man of the idea, whose image is combined with the image of a fully valid idea. This is the first condition for representing an idea in Dostoevsky.

But this condition has, as it were, retroactive force. We could say that in Dostoevsky man transcends his "thingness" and becomes the "man in man" only by entering the pure and unfinalized realm of the idea, that is, only after he has become an unselfish man of the idea. Such are all the major heroes in Dostoevsky—that is, those who participate in the great dialogue.

In this respect one might apply to all these characters the same definition that Zosima offered of Ivan Karamazov's personality. He offered it, of course, in his own churchly language, that is, within the realm of that Christian idea where he, Zosima, lived. We shall quote the appropriate passage from what is for Dostoevsky a very characteristic *penetrative* dialogue between the Elder Zosima and Ivan Karamazov. "Is that really your conviction as to the consequences of the disappearance of the faith in immortality?" the elder asked Ivan Fyodorovich suddenly.

"Yes. That was my contention. There is no virtue if there is no immortality."

"You are blessed in believing that, or else most unhappy."

"Why unhappy?" Ivan Fyodorovich asked smiling.

"Because, in all probability you don't believe yourself in the immortality of your soul, nor in what you have written yourself in your article on Church jurisdiction."

"Perhaps you are right! . . . But I wasn't altogether joking," Ivan Fyodorovich suddenly and strangely confessed, flushing quickly.

"You were not altogether joking. That's true. The question is still fretting your heart, and not answered. But the martyr likes sometimes to divert himself with his despair, as it were driven to it by despair itself. Meanwhile, in your despair, you, too, divert yourself with magazine articles, and discussions in society, though you don't believe your own arguments, and with an aching heart mock at them inwardly. . . . That question you have not answered, and it is your great grief, for it clamors for an answer."

"But can it be answered by me? Answered in the affirmative?" Ivan Fyodorovich went on asking strangely, still looking at the elder with the same inexplicable smile.

"If it can't be decided in the affirmative, it will never be decided in the negative. You know that that is the peculiarity of your heart, and all its suffering is due to it. But thank the Creator who has given you a lofty heart capable of such suffering; of thinking and seeking higher things, for our dwelling is in the heavens. God grant that your heart will attain the answer on earth, and may God bless your path." (SS IX, 91–92; *The Brothers Karamazov*, Book Two, ch. 6)

Alyosha, in his conversation with Rakitin, gives an analogous definition of Ivan but in more secular language:

"Oh, Misha, his soul [Ivan's] is a stormy one. His mind is a prisoner of it. There is a great and unresolved thought in him. He is one of those who don't need millions, they just need to get a thought straight." (SS IX, 105; *The Brothers Karamazov*, Book Two, ch. 7)

It is given to all of Dostoevsky's characters to "think and seek higher things"; in each of them there is a "great and unresolved thought"; all of them must, before all else, "get a thought straight." And in this resolution of a thought (an idea) lies their entire real life and their own personal unfinalizability. If one were to think away the idea in which they live, their image would be totally destroyed. In other words, the image of the hero is inseparably linked with the image of an idea and cannot be detached from it. We *see* the hero in the idea and through the idea, and we *see* the idea in him and through him.

All of Dostoevsky's major characters, as people of an idea, are absolutely unselfish, insofar as the idea has really taken control of the deepest core of their personality. This unselfishness is neither a trait of their objectivized character nor an external definition of their acts—unselfishness expresses their real life in the realm of the idea (they "don't need millions, they just need to get a thought straight"); idea-ness and unselfishness are, as it were, synonyms. In this sense even Raskolnikov, who killed and robbed the old pawnbroker, is absolutely unselfish, as is the prostitute Sonya, as is Ivan the accomplice in his father's murder; absolutely unselfish also is the *idea* of the Adolescent to become a Rothschild. We repeat again: what is important is not the ordinary qualifications of a person's character or actions, but rather the index of a person's devotion to an idea in the deepest recesses of his personality.

The second condition for creating an image of the idea in Dostoevsky is his profound understanding of the dialogic nature of human thought, the dialogic nature of the idea. Dostoevsky knew how to reveal, to see, to show the true realm of the life of an idea. The idea *lives* not in one person's *isolated* individual consciousness—if it remains there only, it degenerates and dies. The idea begins to live, that is, to take shape, to develop, to find and renew its verbal expression, to give birth to new ideas, only when it enters into genuine dialogic relationships with other ideas, with the ideas of *others*. Human thought becomes genuine thought, that is, an idea, only under conditions of living contact with another and alien thought, a thought embodied in someone else's voice, that is, in someone else's consciousness expressed in discourse. At that point of contact between voice-consciousnesses the idea is born and lives.

The idea—as it was *seen* by Dostoevsky the artist—is not a subjective individual-psychological formation with "permanent resident rights" in a person's head; no, the idea is inter-individual and intersubjective—the realm of its existence is not individual consciousness but dialogic communion *between* consciousnesses. The idea is a *live event*, played out at the point of dialogic meeting between two or several consciousnesses. In this sense the idea is similar to the *word*, with which it is dialogically united. Like the word, the idea wants to be heard, understood, and "answered" by other voices from other positions. Like the word, the idea is by nature dialogic, and monologue is merely the conventional compositional form of its expression, a form that emerged out of the ideological monologism of modern times characterized by us above.

It is precisely as such a live event, playing itself out between consciousness-voices, that Dostoevsky saw and artistically represented the *idea*. It is this artistic discovery of the dialogic nature of the idea of consciousness, of every human life illuminated by consciousness (and therefore to some minimal degree concerned with ideas) that made Dostoevsky a great artist of the idea.

Dostoevsky never expounds prepared ideas in monologic form, but neither does he show their *psychological* evolution within a *single* individual consciousness. In either case, ideas would cease to be living images.

We remember, for example, Raskolnikov's first interior monologue, portions of which we quoted in the preceding chapter. That was not a psychological evolution of an idea within a single self-enclosed consciousness. On the contrary, the consciousness of the solitary Raskolnikov becomes a field of battle for others' voices; the events of recent days (his mother's letter, the meeting with Marmeladov), reflected in his consciousness, take on the form of a most intense dialogue with absentee participants (his sister, his mother, Sonya, and others), and in this dialogue he tries to "get his thoughts straight."

Before the action of the novel begins, Raskolnikov has published a newspaper article expounding the theoretical bases of his idea. Nowhere does Dostoevsky give us this article in its monologic form. We first become acquainted with its content and consequently with Raskolnikov's basic idea in the intense and, for Raskolnikov, terrible dialogue with Porfiry (Razumikhin and Zametov participate in this dialogue as well). Porfiry is the first to give an account of the article, and he does so in a deliberately exaggerated and provocative form. This internally dialogized account is constantly interrupted by questions addressed to Raskolnikov, and by the latter's replies. Then Raskolnikov himself gives an account of the article, and he is constantly interrupted by Porfiry's provocative questions and comments. And Raskolnikov's account is itself shot through with interior polemic, from the point of view of Porfiry and his like. Razumikhin too puts in his replies. As a result, Raskolnikov's idea appears before us in an inter-individual zone of intense struggle among several individual consciousnesses, while the theoretical side of the idea is inseparably linked with the ultimate positions on life taken by the participants in the dialogue.

In the course of this dialogue Raskolnikov's idea reveals its various facets, nuances, possibilities, it enters into various relationships with other life-positions. As it loses its monologic, abstractly theoretical finalized quality, a quality sufficient to a *single* consciousness, it acquires the contradictory complexity and living multi-facedness of an idea-force, being born, living and acting in the great dialogue of the epoch and calling back and forth to kindred ideas of other epochs. Before us rises up an *image of the idea*.

Raskolnikov's very same idea appears before us again in his dialogues with Sonya, no less intense; here it already sounds in a different tonality, it enters into dialogic contact with another very strong and integral life-position, Sonya's, and thus reveals new facets and possibilities inherent in it. Next we hear this idea in Svidrigailov's dialogized exposition of it in his dialogue with Dounia. But here, in the voice of Svidrigailov, who is one of Raskolnikov's parodic doubles, the idea has a completely different sound and turns toward us another of its sides. And finally, Raskolnikov's idea comes into contact with various manifestations of life throughout the entire novel; it is tested, verified, confirmed or repudiated by them. Of this we have already spoken in the preceding chapter.

Let us again recall Ivan Karamazov's idea that "everything is permitted" if there is no immortality for the soul. What an intense dialogic life that idea leads throughout the whole of *The Brothers Karamazov*, what heterogeneous voices relay it along, into what unexpected dialogic contacts it enters!

On both of these ideas (Raskolnikov's and Ivan Karamazov's) the reflections of other ideas fall, similar to what happens in painting when a distinct tone, thanks to the reflections of surrounding tones, loses its abstract purity, and only then begins to live an authentic "painterly" life. If one were to extract these ideas from the dialogic realm of their life and give them a monologically finished theoretical form, what withered and easily refuted ideological constructs would result!

As an artist, Dostoevsky did not create his ideas in the same way philosophers or scholars create theirs – he created images of ideas found, heard, sometimes divined by him *in reality itself*, that is, ideas already living or entering life as idea-forces. Dostoevsky possessed an extraordinary gift for hearing the dialogue of his epoch, or, more precisely, for hearing his epoch as a great dialogue, for detecting in it not only individual voices, but precisely and predominantly the *dialogic relationship* among voices, their dialogic *interaction*. He heard both the loud, recognized, reigning voices of the epoch, that is, the reigning dominant ideas (official and unofficial), as well as voices still weak, ideas not yet fully emerged, latent ideas heard as yet by no one but himself, and ideas that were just beginning to ripen, embryos of future worldviews. "Reality in its entirety," Dostoevsky himself wrote, "is not to be exhausted by what is immediately at hand, for an overwhelming part of this reality is contained in the form of a still *latent, unuttered future Word.*"

In the dialogue of his time Dostoevsky also heard resonances of the voice-ideas of the past—both the most recent past (the '30s and '40s) and the more remote. Also, as we have just said, he attempted to hear the voice-ideas of the future, trying to divine them, so to speak, from the place prepared for them in the dialogue of the present, just as it is possible to divine a future, as yet unuttered response in an already unfolded dialogue. Thus on the plane of the present there came together and quarreled past, present, and future.

We repeat: Dostoevsky never created his idea-images out of nothing, he never "made them up" any more than a visual artist makes up the people he represents—he was able to hear or divine them in the reality at hand. And thus for the idea-images in Dostoevsky's novels, as well as for the images of his heroes, it is possible to locate and indicate specific *prototypes.* Thus the prototypes for Raskolnikov's ideas, for example, were the ideas of Max Stirner as expounded by him in his treatise *Der Einzige und sein Eigentum,* and the ideas of Napoleon III as developed by him in *Histoire de Jules César* (1865); one of the prototypes for Pyotr Verkhovensky's ideas was *The Catechism of a Revolutionary;* the prototypes of Versilov's ideas (*The Adolescent*) were the ideas of Chaadaev and Herzen. By no means have all prototypes for Dostoevsky's idea-images been discovered and clarified. We must emphasize that we are not talking of Dostoevsky's "sources" (that term would be inappropriate here), but precisely about the *prototypes* for his idea-images.

Dostoevsky neither copied nor expounded these prototypes in any way; rather he freely and creatively reworked them into living artistic images of ideas, exactly as an artist approaches his human prototypes. Above all he destroyed the self-enclosed monologic form of idea-prototypes and incorporated them into the great dialogue of his novels, where they began living a new and eventful artistic life.

As an artist, Dostoevsky uncovered in the image of a given idea not only the historically actual features available in the prototype (in Napoleon III's *Histoire de Jules César,* for example), but also its *potentialities,* and precisely this potential is of the utmost importance for the artistic image. As an artist Dostoevsky often divined how a given idea would develop and function under certain changed conditions, what unexpected directions it would take in its further development and transformation. To this end, Dostoevsky placed the idea on the borderline of dialogically intersecting consciousnesses. He brought together ideas and worldviews, which in real life were absolutely estranged and deaf to one another, and forced them to quarrel. He extended, as it were, these distantly separated ideas by means of a dotted line to the point of their dialogic intersection. In so doing he anticipated future dialogic encounters between ideas which in his time were still dissociated. He foresaw new linkages of ideas, the emergence of new voice-ideas and changes in the arrangement of all the voice-ideas in the worldwide dialogue. And thus the Russian, and worldwide, dialogue that resounds in Dostoevsky's novels with voice-ideas already living and just being born, voice-ideas open-ended and fraught with new possibilities, continues to draw into its lofty and tragic game the minds and voices of Dostoevsky's readers, up to the present day.

In such a way, without losing any of their full and essential semantic validity, the idea-prototypes used in Dostoevsky's novels change the form of their existence: they become thoroughly dialogized images of ideas not finalized monologically; that is, they enter into what is for them a new realm of existence, *artistic* existence.

Dostoevsky was not only an artist who wrote novels and stories; he was also a journalist and a thinker who published articles in *Time, Epoch, The Citizen,* and *Diary of a Writer.* In these articles he expressed definite philosophical, religious-philosophical, and sociopolitical ideas; he expressed them there (that is, in the articles) as *his own confirmed* ideas in a *systemically monologic* or rhetorically monologic (*in fact, journalistic*) form. These same ideas were sometimes expressed by him in letters to various correspondents. What we have in the articles and letters are not, of course, images of ideas, but straightforward monologically confirmed ideas.

But we also meet these "Dostoevskian ideas" in his novels. How should we regard them there, that is, in the artistic context of his creative work?

In exactly the same way we regard the ideas of Napoleon III in *Crime and Punishment* (ideas with which Dostoevsky the thinker was in total disagreement), or the ideas of Chaadaev and Herzen in *The Adolescent* (ideas with which Dostoevsky the thinker was in partial agreement): that is, we should regard the ideas of Dostoevsky the thinker as the *idea-prototypes* for certain ideas in his novels (the idea-images of Sonya, Myshkin, Alyosha Karamazov, Zosima).

In fact, the ideas of Dostoevsky the thinker, upon entering his polyphonic novel, change the very form of their existence, they are transformed into artistic images of ideas: they are combined in an indissoluble unity with images of people (Sonya, Myshkin, Zosima), they are liberated from their monologic isolation and finalization, they become thoroughly dialogized and enter the great dialogue of the novel on *completely equal terms* with other idea-images (the ideas of Raskolnikov, Ivan Karamazov, and others). It is absolutely impermissible to ascribe to these ideas the finalizing function of authorial ideas in a monologic novel. Here they fulfill no such function, for they are all equally privileged participants in the great dialogue. If a certain partiality on the part of Dostoevsky the journalist for specific ideas and images is sometimes sensed in his novels, then it is evident only in superficial aspects (for example, in the conventionally monologic epilogue to *Crime and Punishment*) and is not capable of destroying the powerful artistic logic of the polyphonic novel. Dostoevsky the artist always triumphs over Dostoevsky the journalist.

Thus the ideas of Dostoevsky himself, uttered by him in monologic form outside the artistic context of his work (in articles, letters, oral conversations) are merely the prototypes for several of the idea-images in his novels. For this reason it is absolutely impermissible to substitute a critique of these monologic idea-prototypes for genuine analysis of Dostoevsky's polyphonic artistic thought. It is important to investigate the *function* of ideas in Dostoevsky's polyphonic world, and not only their *monologic substance.*

Commentary

On the surface, the reading focuses on Dostoevsky as the "creator of the polyphonic novel" (Bakhtin, 1999, p. 7). At a deeper level, in this text Bakhtin engages with important

questions regarding ideas and dialogue that go beyond the work of Dostoevsky and beyond any literary genre. At the same time, these greater philosophical points are made
with reference to Dostoevsky's novels, and this example allows us to understand what
Bakhtin meant by "monological" and "dialogical" and by calling Dostoevsky a "great *artist
of the idea*" (p. 85). What is particular about these novels is the fact that, reading them,
one notices that there is no overarching "voice" (usually the voice of the author) coming
through and making the characters express the author's own idea or ideas. On the contrary,
as Bakhtin (1984, p. 85) notes in the text reproduced above, "Dostoevsky was capable of
representing someone else's idea, preserving its full capacity to signify as an idea, while at
the same time also preserving a distance, neither confirming the idea nor merging it with
his own expressed ideology." In Dostoevsky, the hero is not "standing in" for the author
or even for himself or herself: every character "stands" for an idea, and this idea is much
more than a discourse about a person; it is at the same time "a discourse about the world"
(p. 78). Dostoevsky had the unique ability to merge the personal life of his characters and
heroes with their most intimate experience of ideas. And, most often, his novels focus on
their developing self-consciousness, their understanding of this idea and of the world they
live in. This comes out of confronting their idea with the ideas of others.

   In order to understand the importance or value of this literary development we need
to consider, as Bakhtin (1984, p. 79) does, the alternative: the monological world and
novel. Within it, ideas are separated from people, for example the hero; "the idea is merely
placed in his mouth, but it could with equal success be placed in the mouth of any other
character." As he goes on, this makes ideas impersonal and seemingly universal. Everyone
in the novel expresses them and yet they belong to no one, except the author. This is a
very common situation in literature, where authors usually build their work by confirming
and rejecting ideas they place within each character in ways that unavoidably take them
toward the one view or vision they hold as "true." The author is the only ideologist, and
the novel expresses a single consciousness: the author's own. It is not hard to see, from this,
how a monological state expands well beyond the context of literature. We experience it in
education and at the workplace, when a single point of view dominates and makes others
impossible; in society, particularly in totalitarian regimes, when only one discourse is accepted as valid and everything else is contested or suppressed; also in science, when the
criteria of truth is used to uphold one perspective and exclude all others.

   This state of affairs is certainly not the case in the work of Dostoevsky, who is praised
by Bakhtin (1999, p. 90) for possessing

> an extraordinary gift for hearing the dialogue of his epoch, or, more precisely, for
> hearing his epoch as a great dialogue, for detecting in it not only individual voices,
> but precisely and predominantly the *dialogic relationship* among voices, their dia-
> logic *interaction*. He heard both the loud, recognized, reigning voices of the epoch,
> that is, the reigning dominant ideas (official and unofficial), as well as voices still
> weak, ideas not yet fully emerged, latent ideas heard as yet by no one but himself,
> and ideas that were just beginning to ripen, embryos of future worldviews.

   What is specific for Dostoevsky and for dialogism as a whole is thus not only the presence of multiple voices, perspectives, or points of view but their interaction, an interaction
that doesn't end with one voice dominating the others or creating a synthesis (as in the
case of dialectics) but that keeps all ideas in (productive and creative) tension with each
other. Important from a creativity perspective, in this dialogue it is not only fully formed
ideas that participate, or ideas that have gained currency in society. It is "weak" ideas,

ideas that are "latent" and express "future worldviews," that give the whole exchange an emergent quality, make it open to difference and oriented toward novelty. In dialogism, such ideas are not living on the sidelines, but are essentially intertwined with the views of others. This is because, as Bakhtin notes elsewhere, every utterance—both in novels and in everyday conversations—represents a response, implicit or explicit, to what has been said before. The use of language is marked by the addressivity of human communication, meaning that "each utterance refutes, affirms, supplements, and relies upon the others, presupposes them to be known, and somehow takes them into account" (Bakhtin, 1986, p. 91). It is thus, metaphorically, "filled" with the responses of others. This characteristic becomes clear when we engage with a second premise of dialogism: the fact that language is not personal (as in belonging to a singular individual), but fundamentally social, shared, contextual. Bakhtin (1981, pp. 273–274) captured this eloquently when he wrote:

> For any individual consciousness living in it, language is not an abstract system of normative forms but rather a concrete heteroglot conception of the world. All words have a "taste" of a profession, a genre, a tendency, a party, a particular work, a particular person, a generation, an age group, the day and hour. Each word tastes of the context and contexts in which it has lived its socially charged life; all words and forms are populated by intentions. . . . Language is not a neutral medium that passes freely and easily into the private property of the speaker's intentions; it is populated, overpopulated—with the intentions of others.

As he explains in this and other writings, language is heteroglot (it involves the speech of others) and polyphonic (it incorporates multiple voices). And these properties are fundamental for creativity, both in the case of Dostoevsky, who masterfully illustrated this dynamic, and in the creativity we engage in on a daily basis. From a dialogical perspective then, to create doesn't mean simply to think divergently or laterally or to combine ideas. It means to engage in a dialogue with the voices of others, whether they are absent or present. It is because we use languages that have a deep social history, on the one hand, and are impregnated also by our own history of interacting with others, on the other, that every act of creativity is a social act. And its "outcomes"—whether ideas, objects, or practices—are always co-created. In fact, Bakhtin's analysis of the nature of ideas is extremely important for creativity scholars, who often study creative ideation. But they do so from the premise that ideas belong to people, are produced by individual minds and located within them. Bakhtin reverses this relationship. For him, based on an analysis of Dostoevsky's heroes, persons are born out of ideas. One might argue that this is always the case in literature, that characters are born out of the ideas of their authors, but this is precisely what Bakhtin contested when it comes to polyphonic novels. Ideas acquire a life of their own and live this life in the space created by dialogue. He writes:

> The idea *lives* not in one person's *isolated* individual consciousness—if it remains there only, it degenerates and dies. The idea begins to live, that is, to take shape, to develop, to find and renew its verbal expression, to give birth to new ideas, only when it enters into genuine dialogic relationships with other ideas, with the ideas of *others*. Human thought becomes genuine thought, that is, an idea, only under conditions of living contact with another and alien thought, a thought embodied in someone else's voice, that is, in someone else's consciousness expressed in discourse. At that point of contact between voice-consciousnesses the idea is born and lives (pp. 87–88).

This reflection is crucial, and it expresses a reality beyond the novel. Ideas, including creative ideas (especially creative ideas), are not what we know in our head but what we share and develop in dialogue. Dialogues are where ideas are born and live, not in isolated minds. This is not an animistic account trying to invest nonhuman entities with human properties: it is the basis of a relational, dynamic, and holistic account of the mind and of creativity as a distributed system (see also Glăveanu, 2014). A thought becomes an idea only when it is communicated, when the consciousness that apprehends it is no longer unitary but multiple. This happens all the time in groups or in collaborative contexts, when ideas are proposed to (and dismissed by) others, but it also takes place "inside" individual minds, populated, because of language, by the ideas and intentions of other people. Instead of things or information units, ideas are defined thus by Bakhtin (1984, p. 88) as lived events, "played out at the point of dialogic meeting between two or several consciousnesses." And it is precisely this gaze of the other that can give ideas their creative quality. It is because they are "outside" of us that other people can more easily see or understand our ideas in a new way, and reveal them to us in a different light. The creative process within this paradigm is far from the mental dynamic we are familiar with from the creativity literature in psychology; quite the opposite, it requires other people and other consciousness to complete itself, to generate a space for dialogue that is the necessary (but not sufficient) condition for creativity.

How have these ideas been represented in creativity studies? Unfortunately, Bakhtin is far from being considered (also) a creativity scholar. If mentioned, his work is referenced in passing (see Rojas-Drummond, Albarrán & Littleton, 2008; Roth, 1997; Sawyer, 2000, 2006) and rarely as the main theoretical basis (see Wesling, 2016). There are, however, a few more or less recent examples of authors who have tried to engage with Bakhtin and his dialogism in relation to creativity within a variety of domains. The most obvious one is education. Matusov and Marjanovic-Shane (2016), for instance, elaborate a dialogical authorial approach to creativity in education defined by four main aspects: addressive, existential, axiological, and cultural (for similar efforts see Wegerif, 2011). Others use Bakhtin to examine concrete educational practices and creativity such as computer-mediated chat use in small groups (Trausan-Matu, 2010), play activities in preschool (Duncan & Tarulli, 2003), or the teaching of English as a form of dialogical communication (Lin & Luk, 2005). Besides education, Bakhtin's approach has been employed to understand the experience of producing art (Sullivan & McCarthy, 2009), of using language (Maybin & Swann, 2007), and even of rethinking sustainable urban regeneration (Evans & Jones, 2008). A notable (Bakhtinian) contribution in the field of collaborative innovation within organizations was recently made by Ness and Søreide (2014), who theorized creativity and knowledge development as entering a "room of opportunity" characterized by polyphonic imagination, alterity, and intersubjectivity.

Recently, I have focused on developing a dialogical understanding of creative processes and of the creative self. Together with Ron Beghetto, I raised the question of what makes a "creative" difference in education (see Glăveanu and Beghetto, 2017). Our answer pointed to the role of openness to difference and perspective taking as ways to creatively engage with diversity in an educational setting. The notion of openness to difference is of Bakhtinian inspiration and it was used to "designate those situations in which differences in perspective are made salient and experienced in ways that lead to the emergence of new ideas, objects, or practices" (p. 45). Notably, we do not approach this concept as a personality trait (similar to the much more popular openness to experience) but in situational terms, as constructed in the encounter between person and world, self and others. How can these encounters be characterized? We proposed the notions of monocular and polyocular situations to designate those contexts in which teachers guide classroom conversations toward singular and preestablished perspectives or, on the contrary, encourage difference and even disagreement in order to foster new understandings. In the text presented here, Bakhtin uses the notions of monological and dialogical to refer to similar phenomena. We wondered too how one can cultivate openness to difference in education and proposed three prerequisites: a plurality of coexisting perspectives, sensitivity to otherness and difference, and, most important, valuing differences of perspective and considering these a resource rather than a nuisance in education.

These differences in a dialogical sense don't "exist" only between people, but also within the self, as noted earlier. This observation led me to use Bakhtin (as well as George Herbert Mead) to conceptualize the creative self as a self in dialogue (Glăveanu, 2017). This internalized dialogue—originating from, reflecting, and contributing to dialogues between people—involves several instances: first, different I-positions within the self, reflecting the multiple social roles we acquire and play in society; second, the voices of others (family members, collaborators, critics, and so on), those who participate in the creative process as "inner others"; third, what Mead called the "generalized other," our dialogue with the norms and conventions of society. In each case, creative action is based on the principles of addressivity, polyphony, and emergence specific for dialogic encounters.

There are many other conceptual and methodological developments possible and worth pursuing in the future. First of all, the notion of dialogue should be included in the vocabulary of creativity, not alongside but in ways that transform our understanding of ideas, divergent thinking, and creative potential. In a Bakhtinian framework, as explained here, not only language, but the human mind itself is intrinsically dialogical (see also Marková, 2003). This understanding encourages us to consider the network of collaborations that creators are part of and try to understand their process in terms of "voices" and perspectives rather than individual knowledge and skills. Important to note, for Bakhtin the person does not disappear within language or society. On the contrary, each individual remains unique because of being placed at the intersection of the personal and the social. This is a "place" where ideas flourish, infused by distinctive life experiences and social encounters. Theorizing further the relation between the personal and the social, the unique and the shared, is essential for dialogical theories of creativity. Also, the notions of heteroglossia and polyphony necessarily play an important part within such theories. This is because they point us to the implicit, less visible layer of sociality that contributes to creative action, above and beyond the social that is embodied in the physical presence of others (see Amabile, 1996). These concepts are also useful in forging a new understanding of creative artifacts as expressive of the multiple voices and perspectives that led to their coming into being. The dialogical properties of creative artifacts bridge their production and appropriation by different audiences, which is not a linear, unambiguous, or uncreative process. Moreover, in a Bakhtinian sense, creative artifacts are never finished, as the dialogues around them—which actively participate in their continuous creation—are ongoing; the opposite state would mean that an artifact had been forgotten and vanished from the sphere of human relations. Finally, there are methodological considerations to pay attention to in the future. The dynamic, social, and holistic theory of language, mind, and creativity presented by Bakhtin cannot be studied with conventional methodologies too eager to operate with static concepts and predetermined categories. A truly dialogical analysis of creativity would, on the contrary, capture the complexity of creative thought and action in a developmental perspective. There are a few examples of analysis trying to achieve this, focused for instance on multivoicedness (Aveling, Gillespie, & Cornish, 2015), but more tools are needed to go beyond social relations within the self and include both materiality and time within a single study.

In the end, Bakhtin's thought goes beyond the realm of aesthetics and into the ethical. This is a great part of the reason why he was persecuted during his life by the Soviet authorities. His message, encouraging freedom, openness, and creativity ran against the propaganda of a totalitarian regime that was fundamentally grounded in monologism: one party, one people, one voice. Bakhtin (1984, p. 92) was a great admirer of Dostoevsky's prose precisely because it offered another vision of the world, what he called "the great dialogue," in which ideas interact "on completely equal terms." This might sound like an idealized version of any human interaction, but it is also a precondition for heightened forms of dialogicality and, implicitly, of creativity. The profoundly ethical call to respect the perspective of others, even if not agreeing with it, is the mark of true forms of collaboration. Creativity involves tension, even conflict, but under conditions of mutual respect and openness. And these conditions are often hard to satisfy.

How to finish a chapter on Bakhtin, the author famous for his fondness for everything unfinished? The author who perhaps understood most about creativity as a phenomenon, as a lived experience, and as a way of being? His words, more polyphonic than ever, suffice:

> Nothing conclusive has yet taken place in the world, the ultimate work of the world and about the world has not yet been spoken, the world is open and free, everything is still in the future and will always be in the future. (Bakhtin, 1984, p. 166)

References

Amabile, T. M. (1996). *Creativity in context.* Boulder, CO: Westview Press.

Aveling, E.-L., Gillespie, A., & Cornish, F. (2015). A qualitative method for analysing multivoicedness. *Qualitative Research, 15*(6), 670–687.

Bakhtin, M. M. (1981). *The dialogic imagination: Four essays by M. M. Bakhtin* (C. Emerson and M. Holquist, Trans.). Austin: University of Texas Press.

Bakhtin, M. (1984). The idea in Dostoevsky. In C. Emerson (Ed. & Trans.), *Problems in Dostoevsky's poetics* (pp. 78–92). Minneapolis: University of Minnesota Press.

Bakhtin, M. (1986). *Speech genres and other late essays* C. Emerson and M. Holquist, Eds.; V. W. McGee, Trans.). Austin: University of Texas Press.

Bakhtin, M. M. (1999). *Problems of Dostoevsky's poetics* (Vol. 8). Minneapolis: University of Minnesota Press.

Duncan, R. M., & Tarulli, D. (2003). Play as the leading activity of the preschool period: Insights from Vygotsky, Leont'ev, and Bakhtin. *Early Education & Development, 14*(3), 271–292.

Evans, J., & Jones, P. (2008). Rethinking sustainable urban regeneration: Ambiguity, creativity, and the shared territory. *Environment and Planning A, 40*(6), 1416–1434.

Glăveanu, V. P. (2014). *Distributed creativity: Thinking outside the box of the creative individual.* Cham, Switzerland: Springer.

Glăveanu, V. P. (2017). The creative self in dialogue. In M. Karwowski & J. C. Kaufman (Eds.), *The creative self: Effect of beliefs, self-efficacy, mindset, and identity* (pp. 117–135). Waltham, MA: Academic Press.

Glăveanu, V. P. & Beghetto, R. A. (2017). The difference that makes a "creative" difference in education. In R. A. Beghetto & B. Sriraman (Eds.), *Creative contradictions in education* (pp. 37–54). Cham, Switzerland: Springer.

Lin, A. M. Y., & Luk, J. C. M. (2005). Local creativity in the face of global domination: Insights of Bakhtin for teaching English for dialogic communication. In J. K. Hall, G. Vitanova, & L. Marchenkova (Eds.), *Contributions of Mikhail Bakhtin to understanding second and foreign language learning* (pp. 77–98). Mahwah, NJ: Lawrence Erlbaum.

Marková, I. (2003). *Dialogicality and social representations. The dynamics of mind.* Cambridge, UK: Cambridge University Press.

Matusov, E., & Marjanovic-Shane, A. (2016). Dialogic authorial approach to creativity in education: Transforming a deadly homework into a creative activity. In V. P. Glăveanu (Ed.), *The Palgrave handbook of creativity and culture research* (pp. 307–325). Hampshire, UK: Palgrave Macmillan.

Maybin, J., & Swann, J. (2007). Everyday creativity in language: Textuality, contextuality, and critique. *Applied Linguistics, 28*(4), 497–517.

Ness, I. J., & Søreide, G. E. (2014). The room of opportunity: Understanding phases of creative knowledge processes in innovation. *Journal of Workplace Learning, 26*(8), 545–560.

Rojas-Drummond, S. M., Albarrán, C. D., & Littleton, K. S. (2008). Collaboration, creativity and the co-construction of oral and written texts. *Thinking Skills and Creativity, 3*(3), 177–191.

Roth, M. (1997). Carnival, creativity, and the sublimation of drunkenness. *Mosaic: A Journal for the Interdisciplinary Study of Literature, 30*(2), 1–18.

Sawyer, R. K. (2000). Improvisational cultures: Collaborative emergence and creativity in improvisation. *Mind, Culture, and Activity, 7*(3), 180–185.

Sawyer, R. K. (2006). Group creativity: Musical performance and collaboration. *Psychology of Music, 34*(2), 148–165.

Sullivan, P., & McCarthy, J. (2009). An experiential account of the psychology of art. *Psychology of Aesthetics, Creativity, and the Arts, 3*(3), 181–187.

Trausan-Matu, S. (2010). Computer support for creativity in small groups using chats. *Annals of the Academy of Romanian Scientists,* Series on Science and Technology of Information, 3(2), 81–90.

Wegerif, R. (2011). Towards a dialogic theory of how children learn to think. *Thinking Skills and Creativity, 6*(3), 179–190.

Wesling, D. (2016). Bakhtin, Pushkin, and the co-creativity of those who understand. *Bakhtiniana: Revista de Estudos do Discurso, 11*(3), 196–212.

White, E. J. (2015). Who is Bakhtin? *International Journal of Early Childhood, 47,* 217–221.

PART TEN

Creativity, Culture, and Society

29

Configurations of Culture Growth
Alfred L. Kroeber

Dean Keith Simonton

Summary

Alfred Kroeber was a cultural anthropologist who was strongly opposed to biological (racial) interpretations of contrasts among human cultures. He applied his cultural perspective to understanding creative genius in human civilizations. In these applications, Kroeber was explicitly opposed to Francis Galton's concept of "hereditary genius." This opposition centered around two main arguments. First, independent and often simultaneous discoveries and inventions prove that the cultural environment provides the basis for creativity without respect to the agency of genius. Second, creative geniuses cluster into specific times and places in a manner inconsistent with the expectation that genius is born rather than made. He also suggested that these configurations reflected an intergenerational process in which the creators of one generation provide the basis for the creators of the next, the successive generations of genius developing the cultural pattern until it is exhausted. Both arguments have received considerable attention for both multiple discovery and role-model availability. This research should inspire future empirical inquiry into the interplay between the creative genius and the sociocultural milieu.

Introduction

Alfred Kroeber (1876–1960) was not only the first to receive a Ph.D. in anthropology from Columbia University, but he was also the first professor of anthropology at the University of California, Berkeley. Yet he was a cultural anthropologist, not a physical anthropologist. As such, he was in the forefront of emphasizing the role of culture in understanding human behavior. He was very much opposed to racial theories of differences among the diverse peoples of the world. Although his primary research interest concerned North American

Native Americans, particularly in the West, he also began to view civilizations across the globe as cultural systems. The cultural nature of civilizations was witnessed in both creativity and discovery. Accordingly he was totally opposed to the complete biological determinism represented by Galton's (1869) *Hereditary Genius*. Creative genius, in particular, was extremely contingent on the prevailing cultural patterns. A person might be born with supreme genetic endowment, but be born at the wrong place and the wrong time. The would-be genius then becomes the "mute inglorious Milton" of Thomas Gray's *Elegy Written in a Country Churchyard*, living and dying in total obscurity. The culture can work in the opposite direction, too. Kroeber (1917) had discussed the phenomenon of simultaneous but independent discovery and invention. At a particular moment in the growth of any given cultural system, certain ideas become so inevitable that the times become ripe for their picking. Anybody willing and able to lift up their hands to grab the low-hanging fruit will become its discoverer or inventor without much regard for personal genius.

In Kroeber's (1944) *Configurations of Culture Growth* he elaborates a much more sophisticated anti-Galton argument. Creative genius is clustered in certain times and places in such a way as to invalidate any reasonable genetic explanation. Only changes in cultural patterns can explain these clusterings. The documentation provided to defend this thesis was amazingly impressive. He systematically collated massive amounts of data regarding the major creative geniuses in world civilizations. The domains of creativity included science, philosophy, literature, music, and the visual arts, while the civilizations included Egyptian, Mesopotamian, Greek, Roman, Indian, Chinese, Japanese, and Islamic (cf. Murray, 2003). After arranging the eminent creators in chronological order within each domain and civilization, he was able to show, using visual representations, how cultural activity fluctuated over many centuries of human history. Creative genius quite visibly clustered into golden ages located in particular historical periods and geographical locations.

Unhappily, Kroeber never went beyond this 882-page monograph, quickly moving back to more mainstream cultural anthropology. He perhaps thought that the book sufficed to establish his main argument.

The selections below are extracted from the second section ("Genius") of the first chapter.

Reading: "Genius"

Source: Kroeber, A. L. (1944). Genius. Chapter 1 in *Configurations of culture growth*. Berkeley: University of California Press. Reprinted with permission from the publisher.

In tracing the historic configuration of the growth of patterns of higher culture, I have used as chief evidence the productions of individuals recognized as superior. This is because there is a strong tendency, ever since there has been history and even before it was written, to associate great cultural products and great men. Whether or not there was a Homer, we invent one. Little as we know of the life and personality of Shakespeare, we use his name to typify a flowering of culture. There is more written about him, probably, than about Elizabethan literature. Most of the readily accessible data of history are attached to personalities.

If the reverse were the case, and history came without names of people, with record only of events and achievements plus their dates and places, the evidential material listed in this book would have had a thoroughly different appearance. And yet it would have shown the same growth configurations, and the culture patterns discussed would have revealed themselves, if anything, more sharply. It is thus clear that while personalities are the medium through which an approach like the present one must largely operate to express itself, they are not of its essence or its goal.

It might be said that what is ordinarily called history deals primarily and cheerfully with persons, though giving their lives the wider illumination of institution and of social or cultural setting; whereas culture history aims consciously to analyze and reëxpress cultural movements, freed so far as possible from the entanglement of individualities. However, culture history has hardly as yet come to be regarded as more than one phase or subdivision of history. The natural or spontaneous procedure is to think of people and events rather than intangibles like social currents or cultural developments. Behind the conventional historian's habits, and reinforcing them, lies the popular assumption that because persons have done whatever is recounted in history, therefore the springs of their actions, and consequently of all historical happenings, must lie in their individualities. That personalities are exceedingly plastic, as all observational psychologists tell us, is partly overlooked in this assumption. So is the fact, most consistently emphasized perhaps by anthropologists, of the tremendous molding power of the cultural environment or social milieu. The more naïve attitude—which the abler historians have pretty well transcended without formally repudiating it—is obviously akin to the view that the human will is free. One can write history without holding this belief, but much history is written as if the will were free. The culture-historical approach, which eliminates individual personalities as much as possible, therewith also eliminates this assumption, and so remains at liberty to consider social or cultural happenings and relations as such and in their own plane. The involved causality therefore tends to become different. Analysis and interpretation proceed without reference to individual human wills.

However, this curious situation results. In analyzing out as many as possible of the principal culture growths of admittedly higher value, I have perforce had to express myself in terms of superior personalities or genius; and I foresee that the main point of my work may be lost, in some quarters, because my recitals of data will be construed all over again as confirmation of the presupposition that personalities are primary and therefore genius produces or "causes" higher cultural values and forms.

I can meet this view only by saying that culture patterns and their values are indeed most fully expressed by genius, but that the subject of this inquiry is not *who* expresses, but *what* is expressed, and *how:* that is, the relations in time, space, and substance of each expression to other expressions of higher culture. Every sophisticated person today will admit that Newton's *Principia* could not have been formulated either in Hottentot culture or even among Newton's Anglo-Saxon ancestors a thousand years earlier. In short, though the *Principia* could have been produced only by a genius like Newton and are the true expression of his personality, it is nevertheless clear that the existence of a certain body of science was needed before his genius could be touched off to realize itself in the *Principia*.

Now if we turn the situation around, so that it can be examined from the other side, it becomes clear that we can just as well focus interest on the growth of science, investigate its development, and look upon Newton as nothing more than the genius that was needed to touch off to its fullest realization the condition to which science had arrived in 1687. This second view point is the one I am occupying; and it will perhaps be conceded to be as legitimate as the first and more spontaneous one.

It has, in fact, this advantage: while understanding of the pattern of seventeenth-century science and knowledge of its growth will never explain the psychology of Newton as a man, it will help understanding of the *Principia* as a cultural product, that is, as a historical phenomenon. On the contrary, the fullest possible understanding of Newton as a personality relates essentially only to the understanding of other personalities, or of genius as a type of personality. It will not explain the *Principia*, which are explainable only in terms of the growth of science. Historically, the work of Newton is a phenomenon inherently related to the phenomena represented by the works of other scientists, in time, place, and cultural substance. But Copernicus, Napier, Galileo, Kepler, *as personalities* or individual aggregations of psychic activity, have of course as good as no specific historical relation to the personality of Newton. And as for the psychological relation which almost certainly exists between them, not alone in type but also in degree or potence of personality, this sort of problem can probably be better studied on living, reëxaminable, or more or less controllable individuals rather than on long-dead ones. At any rate, such seems to be the opinion of psychologists, who as a group are notoriously not historical-minded and presumably see little relation between history and psychology. . . .

At bottom, then, the difference between the two attitudes is one of interest. Each is as legitimate as the other. If we are interested primarily in personalities, we are dealing with psychology, and bring the culture only as a setting which cannot be wholly left out of the picture. If we are interested primarily in culture and how it behaves, we can disregard personalities except as inevitable mechanisms or measures of cultural expression.

It seems that this disregard of personalities, except as symptoms, is justified precisely by the fact that apparently greater, culturally productive individuals appear in history, on the whole, prevailingly in clusters. This makes their appearance a function of sociocultural events. If it were not so, they should appear much more evenly spaced or scattered, except for such minor or mild clusterings as will be produced in a continuous distribution by random accident and can be accounted for by the laws of probability.

It is universally accepted that every human being is the product of two sets of forces: his innate heredity or genetic constitution, and his environment. To attribute the appearance of genius primarily to biological heredity leaves the clusterings or constellations wholly unexplained. The moment we admit these as real, we must admit an important other factor, and it then becomes idle opinion to hold to the primacy of heredity. In fact, the finding of the whole science of genetics is that heredity is normally transmitted according to the laws of chance. Genetics leaves only an infinitesimal possibility for the racial stock occupying England to have given birth to no geniuses at all between 1450 and 1550 and a whole series of geniuses in literature, music, science, philosophy, and politics between 1550 and 1650. Similarly with the Germany of 1550–1650 and 1700–1800, respectively; and innumerable other instances in history.

It was a situation like this which Galton clearly recognized in the difference of genius production between fifth-century Athens and nineteenth-century England. He misinterpreted it by giving the Athenians a hereditary rating as many degrees superior to that of the modern English as these are superior to the African negro. His mathematics is sound—in fact, the greatest tribute is due his insight in applying the laws of probability to problems of this sort. His measurement of genius is probably also reasonably sound; at least, the results of his measurements do not appear to have been seriously challenged. But his explanation in terms of hereditary racial change is simply contrary to all we have learned about heredity since his day. His problem, his method, and his facts stand; it is his conclusions that have collapsed. Why? Evidently because there is a powerful factor of "environment" at work which he ignored in his search for a biological cause. The presence of this environmental factor could be, and was, suspected or taken for granted in some quarters. But cultural evidence and explanation as such could hardly have disproved positively the primacy of hereditary causality. It remained for the geneticists themselves—fellow biologists—to bring the disproof. And therewith the situation to which Galton pointed, which is a situation of the very type that I am examining, was reopened to explanation by the factor—or, better, factors—of environment.

Environment is, in its mechanism, of two kinds: biological, and sociocultural. Biologically operative environment would include selection, as effective ultimately on heredity; and physiological factors, such as malaria, syphilis, hookworm, iodine deficiency, inhibiting or retarding climate, and the like. Ordinary diseases, which either kill or leave the organism essentially unimpaired, hardly come into question, because there is no indication that either their incidence or their mortality is different for genius and the average. There are left, then, diseases which are "hereditary" or which by their prevalence can sap whole populations and bring them down below their normal potentiality of performance. In regard to these, or to genuinely selective factors in the Darwinian sense, no more need be said than that no real evidence has been offered with respect to their being a material influence on cultural productivity, and that in general the efforts in this direction have been naïve. It is legitimate enough for a biologist accustomed to biological thinking to suggest that the decline of Roman civilization was brought about by the introduction of malaria. Almost invariably, however, biologists have thrown off such ideas only in passing, as a possibly fruitless hint. They know their inability to handle historical phenomena with professional competence, and in general they refrain from attempted demonstrations, however strong their convictions may sometimes be. It is half-scientists, scientists who have become propagandists, and above all it is educated laymen, that have pushed such theories; which therefore it is needless to refute. Historians have never taken them seriously. Such theories represent the taking of an opinion, or side, and propping it up with such evidence as can be assembled with convenience or industry, without control of contrary possibilities. It would be dogmatic to say that explanations of this type are wholly unfounded; but it would be a waste of intellectual energy to refute or analyze them until some positive and critical showing shall have been made for them.

This leaves culture as the part of environment giving rise to the uneven distribution or clusterings of the appearance of genius. The type of phenomenon included under the term "culture" in this connection is illustrated by the frequency of simultaneous but independent discoveries and inventions. This simultaneity may now be considered as well established. . . . Familiar examples are the devising of calculus by Newton and Leibnitz, the

discovery of oxygen by Scheele and Priestley, the formulation of the principle of natural selection by Darwin and Wallace in 1858, the discovery of anaesthetics by four separate American
physicians, the invention of the telephone in the same year by Bell and Gray, and innumerable others. Probably a large proportion of the many contested priorities of discovery are due
precisely to this fact: the discoveries were made in genuine independence, so far as relations
of the personalities are concerned; the independence was then stretched into priority by
their partisans, national or other. The same sort of simultaneity obviously occurs in aesthetic
innovations: the first use of blank verse, of a metrical form, of a chord, of an architectural proportion, of a theme in painting such as shadow or atmosphere or a manner of brush handling.

In a world only partly conscious of culture, these contemporary and near-identical
phenomena are apparently attributed to chance, and are noted as dramatic coincidences.
They are, however, far too numerous for that. The explanation now generally given is that
"the times were ripe"—the development of a science or art was sufficiently advanced for a
certain next step to be in order. I have used in this book the concept of pattern growth, saturation, and exhaustion. These are all ways of saying substantially the same thing, however
vaguely we can yet express it: the causal participation of a cultural factor, the intervention of
a superpersonal element in the personal activity of genius. In proportion as a greater number
of sociopolitical innovations can be shown to have begun independently with several persons
at or near the same time, the influence of superpersonal or cultural factors, in distinction
from personal ones, will be construable as greater.

The contemporaneity of inventions is of course one special aspect of cultural "environment" or influence. Any approach that primarily considers patterns of culture as such,
that abstracts them so far as possible from the individual personalities associated with them,
involves the recognition of cultural phenomena or factors as cultural. It is such factors, whatever their specific shape, that we must look for as the principle determinants, not indeed of
the birth or existence of genius, but of its historic appearance, functioning, and productivity.

This view of course does not deny the superiority of certain individuals over others.
It assumes such superiority. It also assumes that the finest flowerings of culture growths are
expressed through such superior personalities. In fact, it assumes that, in general, genius
will be at hand to express the highest manifestations of cultural developments. This belief
in turn almost necessarily involves the assumption that geniuses are presumably being born
at nearly the same rate per thousand or million, century after century—at any rate, within a
given race. Of course in this connection genius means potential, not realized genius: innate,
hereditary, psychological superiority as distinct from manifest, historically expressed superiority. This hypothesis is certainly in agreement with what we know of psychobiological
inheritance: high capacity ought to be born with but little fluctuation from the average rate,
standard for each larger hereditary stock. But inasmuch as historically recognized geniuses
do not ordinarily appear in an even flow, but in clusters separated by intervals, it is evident
that cultural situations or influences must at times allow and at others inhibit the realization
of genius. In short, it would seem that a large proportion, probably a majority, of eminently
superior individuals never get into the reckoning of history. There are long stretches in which
first prizes are not awarded, or at least not recognized by posterity.

In Occidental sculpture, Italy holds preeminence; and in five centuries of Italian preeminence, Michelangelo, born in 1475, is considered as marking the culmination. But can we

be certain that he was inherently, by his innate gifts, a greater sculptor than Ghiberti, born in 1378, Donatello, 1385, Bernini, 1598, or Canova, 1757? Ghiberti had nothing to build on, but he "initiated the Renaissance." Donatello reached higher, but he stood on Ghiberti's shoulders; and Michelangelo on Donatello's. Here the pattern began to strain and wilt; and we rate Bernini much lower. But can we be at all sure that in imagination, sense of form, technical skill, he was inferior to Michelangelo? His themes, his invoking of emotions, and perhaps his taste were on a lower level; but they were the emotions and taste of his age. The same holds for Canova. For sculptural ability we cannot really with certainty rate him one notch below the highest; it is the tepid neoclassicism of his period which we rate below Renaissance intensity. It is true that Michelangelo almost surely remains the greatest personality of the five; but on the extrinsic ground that he was painter, architect, and poet also, the other four are chiefly sculptors only.

What this example shows is that in ranking geniuses we evidently do not rank them according to intrinsic ability, which we have little means of estimating as such; rather, they appear to us as the composite product of personal superiority and cultural influence. If the cultural pattern which they express is still unformed, or is manifestly declining, we tend to evaluate them as lesser individualities than the geniuses at the pattern peak; but it is uncertain that they really are lesser. It does seem somewhat naïve to assume, because Donatello's and Michelangelo's presumptive native endowments plus the known state of art in Florence in 1430 and 1510 come to a higher total than Bernini's and Canova's presumptive native endowments plus the obviously decadent state of Italian art in 1650 and 1800, that Donatello and Michelangelo were therefore the greater men. Yet in our general thinking that is what we do. We veil the imperfect logic of the procedure by assuming that Florentine sculpture of 1450–1500 was made great by some miracle of Donatello's and Michelangelo's ancestral germ plasm.

To this assumption the simplest objection remains that historically such miracles mostly come in clusters, whereas if they were really accidents of the germ plasm they should come scattered.

On the contrary, culture florescences, viewed as such, reveal themselves as tending strongly to come in pattern waves. Hence the inference is justified that it is something in the wavelike character of culture growths which is at the bottom of the otherwise unexplainable clusterings of genius.

It will be clear that I am not denying or minimizing the existence of individual superiority. I am denying it as the cause of cultural superiority. The cause or causes of this latter remain unknown, and constitute a great problem of inquiry: this volume is an attempt to organize data so as to define the problem. Cultural superiority obviously avails itself of individual superiority as an important channel of expression. It therefore helps personally superior individuals to realize themselves as significant historical figures. On the other hand, absence of cultural superiority tends strongly to prevent inherently superior personalities from being realized as such, historically.

Evidently, a majority of born geniuses never come to fruition for the world. If we could keep culture permanently at its best level, the number of productive geniuses would be perhaps three or ten times as great as it actually is on the average in human history. This proposition is aside from the main line of the inquiry into how culture behaves; but it has a deserving interest of its own.

Commentary

In line with other commentaries in the collection of readings, we will first examine the later impact of Kroeber's ideas, as represented in this selection, and then turn to new directions that might be suggested by those ideas.

LATER IMPACT

At the time that Kroeber published his counterargument to Galton's genetic conception of genius, biological determinism was already on the wane in psychology. Indeed the heyday of an almost exclusively environmentalist behaviorism had already begun with the work of such high-impact psychologists as B. F. Skinner and Clark Hull. Moreover after behaviorism was gradually replaced by cognitive psychology in the latter half of the 20th century, the emphasis remained on nurture rather than nature: even the greatest creative genius was just the product of the laborious acquisition of domain-specific expertise (Ericsson, 2014). Genius was made, not born. So, in a sense, any psychologist who might have read Kroeber's book would just have thought it was beating a dead horse. Besides, when interest in creativity finally took off in the 1960s, the focus was more on personality traits and cognitive processes, with little or no curiosity about the cultural basis of creativity. Indeed the first handbook specifically devoted to the latter subject did not appear until very recently (Glăveanu, 2016).

Because of this psychological neglect, Kroeber's most immediate influence was on fellow cultural anthropologists as well as kindred sociologists. Only decades later did his impact on these two social sciences impinge on the psychology of creativity. These influences can be seen in two phenomena: independent discovery and cultural configurations.

Independent discovery. In the extract, Kroeber puts great emphasis on the phenomenon wherein two or more scientists or inventors come up with the same idea independently, and often even simultaneously. He first discussed this phenomenon in more detail in a 1917 article, where he argued that at a particular moment in cultural history certain discoveries become absolutely inevitable, the effects of the "spirit of the times" (or the *Zeitgeist*, to use the German equivalent). This sociocultural determinism was also advocated by two sociologists who offered an affirmative response to the question "Are inventions inevitable?" (Ogburn & Thomas, 1922). A few decades later Robert K. Merton, a pioneer in the sociology of science, rechristened this phenomenon *multiple discovery* (Merton, 1961b) and discussed the severe constraints it imposed on the scientific genius (Merton, 1961a). In effect the genius could discover only what would have been discovered by somebody anyway. Personal creativity became largely irrelevant. Eventually this sociocultural determinism became the standard interpretation (Lamb & Easton, 1984).

In fact when this chapter's author was a graduate student in the early 1970s and mentioned to a sociologist that his main research interest was the psychology of creativity, he was quickly advised that there was no such thing! The sociocultural system can be creative, but not individuals, who are no more than an epiphenomenon with no causal role. Psychology is irrelevant. Provoked by this attack on his chosen discipline, he decided to investigate the phenomenon more closely. It first became clear that many arguments on behalf of the traditional interpretation could not stand up to logical scrutiny. For example, Merton (1961b) made a big deal about how the discovery of the phenomenon of multiples was itself a multiple and thus represents a self-referential proof. Specifically, he named well over a dozen researchers who, between 1828 and 1922, independently discovered the same phenomenon in complete ignorance that it already had been discovered in 1828. If an idea is "in the air" at a precise moment in history, why is it repeatedly rediscovered over a period nearly a century long? Nor is delayed rediscovery rare. Merton himself showed that out of 264 cases he studied, more than one third required a decade or more before an idea was rediscovered. It's a funny kind of "inevitability" that doesn't get it right the first time! Something's amiss.

Derek da Solla Price (1963), a distinguished historian of science and major innovator in scientometrics, noticed another curiosity: if one examines the probability distribution of multiple *grades*—the number of persons who supposedly came up with the same idea—the distribution fits what would be predicted by a Poisson process with a low mean (viz., μ ≈ 1). Contrary to the sociocultural determinists, this distribution is precisely what would be predicted if multiple discovery was generated by chance. Not only do singletons greatly outnumber multiples, but according to this simple model, a very large proportion of potential discoveries would become "nulltons"—ideas that fail to see the light of day! As a result the average grade across a large sample of multiples is just one. Singletons conceived by only one person would represent the most typical case.

This led Simonton (1978a, 1979, 1986a, 2003, 2010, 2015) to conduct a series of logical, empirical, and mathematical investigations into the phenomenon. Other researchers followed suit, most notably the sociologists Brannigan and Wanner (1983a, 1983b; cf. Simonton, 1986b). The upshot is that things are not what they seem. Contrary to what Kroeber and other sociocultural determinists affirm, multiple discovery and invention can be almost entirely ascribed to chance. Stochastic combinatorial models can account for (a) the probability distribution of multiple grades, (b) the temporal separation of multiple discoveries, (c) individual variation in a scientist's participation in multiples, and (d) the degree of multiple similarity (for few multiples are actually identical). The sociocultural milieu is not irrelevant, but rather provides the necessary but not sufficient conditions. Nothing can be discovered or invented unless the prerequisites are first met. The sufficient conditions are found in the creative scientist or inventor. Even then, the individual must often rely on chance, such as serendipity.

Cultural configurations. The main argument in the Kroeber excerpt deals with a different phenomenon to which he devoted the entire book: the clustering of genius into particular times and places. He makes it quite clear that Galton's genetic determinism could not possibly explain this clustering. The clusters must have a cultural rather than biological foundation. Cultural patterns are developed, reach a peak, and then become exhausted. Yet, interestingly, when hypothesizing the underlying mechanism for this cultural development, Kroeber ended up offering what can best be viewed as a psychological process. In particular he quoted at length the views of the Roman historian Velleius Paterculus, who wrote early in the first millennium CE:

Genius is fostered by emulation, and it is now envy, now admiration, which enkindles imitation, and, in the nature of things, that which is cultivated with the highest zeal advances to the highest perfection; but it is difficult to continue at the point of perfection, and naturally that which cannot advance must recede. And as in the beginning we are fired with the ambition to overtake those whom we regard as leaders, so when we have despaired of being able either to surpass or even to equal them, our zeal wanes with our hope; it ceases to follow what it cannot overtake, and abandoning the old field as though preempted, it seeks a new one. Passing over that in which we cannot be preeminent, we seek for some new object of our effort. (in Kroeber, 1944, p. 17)

With less rhetorical flourish, Paterculus argued that each generation of geniuses builds upon the work of prior geniuses until an acme is reached, after which potential genius starts diverting to other forms of creativity, and the geniuses are replaced by epigones of little importance. The historian specifically applied this idea to explain several clusterings of supreme genius, such as the Aeschylus-Sophocles-Euripides triad of Athenian drama and the Socrates-Plato-Aristotle triad of Athenian philosophy—a pair of three-generation sequences that are practically unrivaled in human history.

Nonetheless, unlike Galton before him, Kroeber was not quantitatively inclined and thus made no attempt to test this conjecture empirically. Furthermore, because Kroeber's initial impact was on cultural anthropologists rather than psychologists, subsequent empirical research took a very different direction. Most striking is Charles Gray's (1958, 1961, 1966) attempt to explain the genius clusterings in terms of an "epicyclical" model superficially similar to the epicycles in Ptolemaic astronomy. Major cycles would be synchronized by lesser cycles and the latter synchronized by yet smaller cycles to produce a complex cyclical pattern. This pattern would yield a distinctive rise and fall that Gray tested on both Greco-Roman and Western civilizations. The cycles themselves reflected the ups and downs in social, political, and economic factors. Thus the clusters of creative genius were the upshot of external or extraneous causes rather than internal or intrinsic, as would be implied by the emulation or imitation hypothesis (Simonton, 1981). The problem of explaining the clustering was just swept under the rug because Gray never provided an adequate explanation for the epicycles themselves.

Although Kroeber (1958) gave some tentative support to Gray's (1958) initial work, most other researchers were less appreciative (e.g., Simonton, 1981; Taagepera & Colby, 1979). With one curious exception, Gray's explanatory account left no major imprint on subsequent inquiry. That exception involves the complex scale that Gray (1966) had devised for assessing the differential creativity displayed by the key figures of Western civilization. This scale was later modified by Ludwig (1992b) to become the Creative Achievement Scale (CAS) that Ludwig (1992a, 1995) used to examine the relationship between creativity and psychopathology in a sample of more than 1,000 eminent achievers. Still later the CAS was applied to examine the creative achievement of nearly 300 eminent African Americans (Damian & Simonton, 2015; Simonton, 2008). That said, none of these spinoffs in creativity research addressed the fundamental questions: What causes the clusterings? Could these causes include psychological processes?

These questions were the basis for this author's own doctoral dissertation (Simonton, 1974; see also Simonton, 1975). The thesis was partly inspired by an article titled "Creativity: A Cross-Historical Pilot Survey" (Naroll et al., 1971). The study combined Kroeber's data on cultural configuration with direct measures of sociocultural conditions. Although very crude, the treatment could be vastly improved using more sophisticated measurement techniques and data analyses. In the latter case, the dynamic time-series models used in macroeconomics were adapted to devise a new method called generational time-series analysis (Simonton, 1984b). This method enabled the direct scrutiny of the clusterings of more than 5,000 creative geniuses in the arts and sciences distributed across more than 2,500 years of Western civilization. These clusters were shown to be a positive function of role-model availability, political fragmentation, and revolts against imperial states, but a negative function of political anarchy. The impact of role-model availability constituted a direct test of the emulation hypothesis that Kroeber thought might account for the clusters. In formal terms, the magnitude of creativity activity in generation g was a positive function of the magnitude of creativity in generation $g - 1$ (and sometimes $g - 2$ as well, depending on the creative domain). The autoregressive nature of the fluctuations has been replicated many times for other world civilizations and by other investigators (Murray, 2003; Simonton, 1988, 1992a, 1997, 2018; Simonton & Ting, 2010). These generational analyses have also identified other external influences, such as multiculturalism, ideological diversity, philosophical systems, and demographic changes (for a comprehensive review, see Simonton, in press).

Admittedly a psychologist might object that the foregoing research uses aggregate data: creative geniuses are tabulated into larger units, the 20-year generations. Hence the psychology of creativity would need some research operating at the individual level. That downsizing of the analytical unit has already been accomplished as well. For example, highly eminent scientists or artists are far more likely to have worked with eminent mentors and to have admired distinguished predecessors (Simonton, 1984a, 1992b, 1992c; Zuckerman, 1977). At the same time, links to illustrious contemporaries, whether collaborators or competitors, can also enhance creative achievement (Simonton, 1984a, 1992c). In this respect the notion of the "lone genius" is a pure myth. The greatest creators are embedded in a network of notable contemporaries. Take Isaac Newton, whom the poet William Wordsworth famously described as "a mind forever / Voyaging through strange seas of thought alone." In contrast, Newton was involved with five major rivals and competitors, formed friendships with seven eminent scientists of his time, and had miscellaneous exchanges with 21 distinguished colleagues, correspondents, and similar associates (Simonton, 1992c). He may have been extremely introverted, but he was by no means a social isolate.

These latter results suggest that when genius clusters to form golden ages, the sociocultural event involves more than the emulation or imitation mentioned by the Roman historian. Once the young creative talents launch their careers, they enter into synergistic interactions that accentuate their creative achievements.

NEW DIRECTIONS

A careful reading of the Kroeber excerpt should reveal that the cultural anthropologist was not totally opposed to the influence of psychological and even genetic variables. He was just arguing that they should be placed within the cultural context. Kroeber could even accept that the individual creative genius contributes something unique. This is evident when he says, "Though the *Principia* could have been produced only by a genius like Newton and are the true expression of his personality, it is nevertheless clear that the existence of a certain body of science was needed before his genius could be touched off to realize itself in the *Principia*" (Kroeber, 1944, p. 9). This gets back to what was said earlier about the sociocultural circumstances providing the necessary but not sufficient conditions for the emergence of creative genius. In addition, his point is consistent with what has been learned about so-called multiple discovery and invention: true multiples, in the sense of identical ideas, are extremely rare (Simonton, 2003). Most often each contribution has some unique features that make it identifiably distinct from all others. For instance, although Gottfried Leibniz and Newton carried on a priority dispute about who first invented the calculus, the two versions were far from identical. Each had a different mathematical and philosophical foundation, and even a rather distinct notation. Students who take calculus courses today are very fortunate that Leibniz's version won out over Newton's.

To conclude, what is needed more than anything else right now is further research that articulates the precise ways that individual creative genius interacts with the sociocultural climate. That will require creativity researchers to become cultural psychologists (see also Glăveanu, 2010).

References

Brannigan, A., & Wanner, R. A. (1983a). Historical distributions of multiple discoveries and theories of scientific change. *Social Studies of Science, 13*, 417–435.

Brannigan, A., & Wanner, R. A. (1983b). Multiple discoveries in science: A test of the communication theory. *Canadian Journal of Sociology, 8*, 135–151.

Damian, R. I., & Simonton, D. K. (2015). Psychopathology, adversity, and creativity: Diversifying experiences in the development of eminent African Americans. *Journal of Personality and Social Psychology, 108*, 623–636.

Ericsson, K. A. (2014). Creative genius: A view from the expert-performance approach. In D. K. Simonton (Ed.), *The Wiley handbook of genius* (pp. 321–349). Oxford: Wiley.

Galton, F. (1869). *Hereditary genius: An inquiry into its laws and consequences.* London: Macmillan.

Glăveanu, V. P. (2010). Creativity as cultural participation. *Journal for the Theory of Social Behavior, 41* (1), 0021–8308.

Glăveanu, V. P. (2016). *The Palgrave handbook of creativity and culture research.* London: Palgrave Macmillan.

Gray, C. E. (1958). An analysis of Graeco-Roman development: The epicyclical evolution of Graeco-Roman civilization. *American Anthropologist, 60*, 13–31.

Gray, C. E. (1961). An epicyclical model for Western civilization. *American Anthropologist, 63*, 1014–1037.

Gray, C. E. (1966). A measurement of creativity in Western civilization. *American Anthropologist, 68*, 1384–1417.

Kroeber, A. L. (1917). The superorganic. *American Anthropologist, 19*, 163–214.

Kroeber, A. L. (1944). *Configurations of culture growth.* Berkeley: University of California Press.

Kroeber, A. L. (1958). Gray's epicyclical evolution. *American Anthropologist, 60*, 31–38.

Lamb, D., & Easton, S. M. (1984). *Multiple discovery.* Avebury, UK: Avebury.

Ludwig, A. M. (1992a). Creative achievement and psychopathology: Comparison among professions. *American Journal of Psychotherapy, 46*, 330–356.

Ludwig, A. M. (1992b). The Creative Achievement Scale. *Creativity Research Journal, 5*, 109–124.

Ludwig, A. M. (1995). *The price of greatness: Resolving the creativity and madness controversy.* New York, NY: Guilford Press.

Merton, R. K. (1961a). The role of genius in scientific advance. *New Scientist, 12*, 306–308.

Merton, R. K. (1961b). Singletons and multiples in scientific discovery: A chapter in the sociology of science. *Proceedings of the American Philosophical Society, 105*, 470–486.

Murray, C. (2003). *Human accomplishment: The pursuit of excellence in the arts and sciences, 800 BC to 1950.* New York, NY: HarperCollins.

Naroll, R., Benjamin, E. C., Fohl, F. K., Fried, M. J., Hildreth, R. E., & Schaefer, J. M. (1971). Creativity: A cross-historical pilot survey. *Journal of Cross-Cultural Psychology, 2*, 181–188.

Ogburn, W. K., & Thomas, D. (1922). Are inventions inevitable? A note on social evolution. *Political Science Quarterly, 37*, 83–93.

Price, D. (1963). *Little science, big science.* New York, NY: Columbia University Press.

Simonton, D. K. (1974). *The social psychology of creativity: An archival data analysis.* Unpublished doctoral dissertation, Harvard University.

Simonton, D. K. (1975). Sociocultural context of individual creativity: A transhistorical time-series analysis. *Journal of Personality and Social Psychology, 32*, 1119–1133.

Simonton, D. K. (1978a). Independent discovery in science and technology: A closer look at the Poisson distribution. *Social Studies of Science, 8*, 521–532.

Simonton, D. K. (1979). Multiple discovery and invention: Zeitgeist, genius, or chance? *Journal of Personality and Social Psychology, 37*, 1603–1616.

Simonton, D. K. (1981). Creativity in Western civilization: Extrinsic and intrinsic causes. *American Anthropologist, 83*, 628–630.

Simonton, D. K. (1984a). Artistic creativity and interpersonal relationships across and within generations. *Journal of Personality and Social Psychology, 46*, 1273–1286.

Simonton, D. K. (1984b). Generational time-series analysis: A paradigm for studying sociocultural influences. In K. Gergen & M. Gergen (Eds.), *Historical social psychology* (pp. 141–155). Hillsdale, NJ: Lawrence Erlbaum.

Simonton, D. K. (1986a). Multiple discovery: Some Monte Carlo simulations and Gedanken experiments. *Scientometrics, 9*, 269–280.

Simonton, D. K. (1986b). Multiples, Poisson distributions, and chance: An analysis of the Brannigan-Wanner model. *Scientometrics, 9,* 127–137.

Simonton, D. K. (1988). Galtonian genius, Kroeberian configurations, and emulation: A generational time-series analysis of Chinese civilization. *Journal of Personality and Social Psychology, 55,* 230–238.

Simonton, D. K. (1992a). Gender and genius in Japan: Feminine eminence in masculine culture. *Sex Roles, 27,* 101–119.

Simonton, D. K. (1992b). Leaders of American psychology, 1879–1967: Career development, creative output, and professional achievement. *Journal of Personality and Social Psychology, 62,* 5–17.

Simonton, D. K. (1992c). The social context of career success and course for 2,026 scientists and inventors. *Personality and Social Psychology Bulletin, 18,* 452–463.

Simonton, D. K. (1997). Foreign influence and national achievement: The impact of open milieus on Japanese civilization. *Journal of Personality and Social Psychology, 72,* 86–94.

Simonton, D. K. (2003). Scientific creativity as constrained stochastic behavior: The integration of product, process, and person perspectives. *Psychological Bulletin, 129,* 475–494.

Simonton, D. K. (2008). Childhood giftedness and adulthood genius: A historiometric analysis of 291 eminent African Americans. *Gifted Child Quarterly, 52,* 243–255.

Simonton, D. K. (2010). Creativity as blind-variation and selective-retention: Combinatorial models of exceptional creativity. *Physics of Life Reviews, 7,* 156–179.

Simonton, D. K. (2015). Psychology as a science within Comte's hypothesized hierarchy: Empirical investigations and conceptual implications. *Review of General Psychology, 19,* 334–344.

Simonton, D. K. (2018). Intellectual genius in the Islamic Golden Age: Cross-civilization replications, extensions, and modifications. *Psychology of Aesthetics, Creativity, and the Arts, 12,* 125–135.

Simonton, D. K. (in press). Creativity in sociocultural systems: Cultures, nations, and civilizations. In P. B. Paulus & B. A. Nijstad (Eds.), *The Oxford handbook of group creativity.* New York: Oxford University Press.

Simonton, D. K., & Ting, S.-S. (2010). Creativity in Eastern and Western civilizations: The lessons of historiometry. *Management and Organization Review, 6,* 329–350.

Taagepera, R., & Colby, B. N. (1979). Growth of Western civilization: Epicyclical or exponential? *American Anthropologist, 81,* 907–912.

Zuckerman, H. (1977). *Scientific elite.* New York, NY: Free Press.

30

Sociability and Creativity
The Sociology of Georg Simmel

VLAD P. GLĂVEANU

Summary

Georg Simmel's work on sociability is practically unknown within contemporary creativity research. And yet, his understanding of this phenomenon as the playful, aesthetic nature of human association has deep consequences for how we (could) theorize the relationship between creativity and society. This chapter starts with a brief introduction to Simmel's life and work, reproduces his essay "The Sociology of Sociability" (1949), and ends with a commentary outlining its main ideas and their relevance for creativity research. Future perspectives are discussed in the end, including a consideration of society as a creativity domain, of creativity in interpersonal interactions, and of the creativity and humor involved in protests and demonstrations.

Introduction

Georg Simmel (1858–1918) was a German neo-Kantian philosopher considered by some the first sociologist of modernity (Frisby, 1985). A productive scholar, he authored 25 books and over 300 articles and reviews, among them "On Social Differentiation," "The Philosophy of Money," "The Metropolis and Mental Life," "Sociology: Investigations on the Forms of Sociation," and "Fundamental Questions of Sociology." He had wide interests not only within sociology but also in the fields of ethics and aesthetics, with a particular focus on art (see his book from 1916, *Rembrandt: An Essay in the Philosophy of Art*; Simmel, 2005). Today, his contributions are considered fundamental for a number of fields, including urban sociology, symbolic interactionism, exchange theory, and social network analysis. Appreciated by some as "the most significant and interesting transitional figure in the whole of modern philosophy" (Lukács, 1991, p. 145), Simmel was neglected or received with hostility by critical theorists (Frisby, 1985). Levine, Carter, and Gorman (1976, p. 814), while acknowledging his influence in American sociology, noted "the bewildering variety of topics he treated and the disorganized manner in which he presented his general principle."

True, Simmel made contributions to a variety of domains, not always in a consistent or systematic manner. His essays cover topics as diverse as the metropolis, money, fashion, secrecy, prostitution, and flirtation, and deal with general themes such as history, society, human experience, freedom, exchange, conflict, and sociability. These wide interests draw heavily on his life experience. Simmel was born in Berlin in a Jewish family, the youngest of seven children. His father's death, when Simmel was 16, left him with a considerable inheritance and enabled him to study philosophy and history at the University of Berlin. Despite enjoying the company and support of famous associates—including, among others, Max Weber, Edmund Husserl, Martin Buber, August Rodin, and Rainer Maria Rilke—and being a very popular lecturer, Simmel never managed to obtain a permanent, tenured position in Berlin. It was only toward the end of his life that he obtained a professorship at the University of Strasburg, for which he left behind a much more cosmopolitan and social existence in the capital. His interest in urbanism and sociability certainly built on the fact that Simmel was the center of his own social circle in Berlin, while his marginal position in academia, including as a Jewish member of society, resonates with his reflections on being a stranger (Henricks, 2003).

The essay "Soziologie der Geselligkeit" (translated by E. C. Hughes in 1949 as "The Sociology of Sociability") was Simmel's opening speech at the first meeting of the German Sociological Society in 1910. Here, Simmel "attempted to establish a sociology that had its foundation in aesthetics" (Davis, 1973, p. 328), a theme he became increasingly concerned with toward the end of his life. In this work, Simmel outlines the general principles of his own sociology, taking the literary and intellectual salon and the social relations cultivated within it as a model for the "purest form of sociability" (Gronow, 2011, n.p.). The general disconnection of these types of interaction from the harsher realities of economical and political relations (those that laid the basis, for instance, for the sociology of Marx and to a certain extent of Durkheim) makes Simmel's proposal unique and his discussion important, particularly for the field of creativity research. I explain how and why in the concluding comments.

Reading: "The Sociology of Sociability"

Source: Simmel, G. (1949). The sociology of sociability (E. C. Hughes, Trans.). *American Journal of Sociology*, 55(3), pp. 254–261. Reproduced with permission from Chicago University Press.

Abstract

While all human associations are entered into because of some ulterior interests, there is in all of them a residue of pure sociability or association for its own sake. Sociability is the art or play form of association, related to the content and purposes of association in the same way as art is related to reality. While sociable interaction centers upon persons, it can occur only if the more serious purposes of the individual are kept out, so that it is an interaction not of complete but of symbolic and equal personalities. While it is a departure from reality, there is no deceit in it unless one of the persons involved tries to exploit it.

The Sociology of Sociability

There is an old conflict over the nature of society. One side mystically exaggerates its significance, contending that only through society is human life endowed with reality. The other regards it as a mere abstract concept by means of which the observer draws the realities, which are individual human beings, into a whole, as one calls trees and brooks, houses and meadows, a "landscape." However one decides this conflict, he must allow society to be a reality in a double sense. On the one hand are the individuals in their directly perceptible existence, the bearers of the processes of association, who are united by these processes into the higher unity which one calls "society"; on the other hand, the interests which, living in the individuals, motivate such union: economic and ideal interests, warlike and erotic, religious and charitable. To satisfy such urges and to attain such purposes, arise the innumerable forms of social life, all the with-one-another, for-one-another, in-one-another, against-one-another, and through-one-another, in state and commune, in church and economic associations, in family and clubs. The energy effects of atoms upon each other bring matter into the innumerable forms which we see as "things." Just so the impulses and interests, which a man experiences in himself and which push him out toward other men, bring about all the forms of association by which a mere sum of separate individuals are made into a "society."

Within this constellation, called society, or out of it, there develops a special sociological structure corresponding to those of art and play, which draw their form from these realities but nevertheless leave their reality behind them. It may be an open question whether the concept of a play impulse or an artistic impulse possesses explanatory value; at least it directs attention to the fact that in every play or artistic activity there is contained a common element not affected by their differences of content. Some residue of satisfaction lies in gymnastics, as in card-playing, in music, and in plastic, something which has nothing to do with the peculiarities of music or plastic as such but only with the fact that both of the latter are art and both of the former are play. A common element, a likeness of psychological reaction and need, is found in all these various things—something easily distinguishable from the special interest which gives each its distinction. In the same sense one may speak of an impulse to sociability in man. To be sure, it is for the sake of special needs and interests that men unite in economic associations or blood fraternities, in cult societies or robber bands. But, above and beyond their special content, all these associations are accompanied by a feeling for, by a satisfaction in, the very fact that one is associated with others and that the solitariness of the individual is resolved into togetherness, a union with others. Of course, this feeling can, in individual cases, be nullified by contrary psychological factors; association can be felt as a mere burden, endured for the sake of our objective aims. But typically there is involved in all effective motives for association a feeling of the worth of association as such, a drive which presses toward this form of existence and often only later calls forth that objective content which carries the particular association along. And as that which I have called artistic impulse draws its form from the complexes of perceivable things and builds this form into a special structure corresponding to the artistic impulse, so also the impulse to sociability distils, as it were, out of the realities of social life the pure essence of association, of the associative process as a value and a satisfaction. It thereby constitutes what we call sociability in the narrower sense. It is no mere accident of language that all sociability, even the purely spontaneous, if it is to have meaning and stability, lays such great value on form, on good form. For "good form" is mutual self-definition, interaction of the elements, through which a unity is made; and since in sociability the concrete motives bound up with life-goals fall away, so must the pure form, the free-playing, interacting interdependence of individuals stand out so much the more strongly and operate with so much the greater effect.

And what joins art with play now appears in the likeness of both to sociability. From the realities of life play draws its great, essential themes: the chase and cunning; the proving of physical and mental powers, the contest and reliance on chance and the favor of forces which one cannot influence. Freed of substance, through which these activities make up the seriousness of life, play gets its cheerfulness but also that symbolic significance which distinguishes it from pure pastime. And just this will show itself more and more as the essence of sociability; that it makes up its substance from numerous fundamental forms of serious relationships among men, a substance, however, spared the frictional relations of real life; but out of its formal relations to real life, sociability (and the more so as it approaches pure sociability) takes on a symbolically playing fulness of life and a significance which a superficial rationalism always seeks only in the content. Rationalism, finding no content there, seeks to do away with sociability as empty idleness, as did the savant who asked concerning a work of art, "What does that prove?" It is nevertheless not without significance that in many, perhaps in all, European languages, the word "society" (*Gesellschaft*) indicates literally "together-ness." The political, economic, the society held together by some purpose is, nevertheless, always "society." But only the sociable is a "society" without qualifying adjective, because it alone presents the pure, abstract play of form, all the specific contents of the one-sided and qualified societies being dissolved away.

Sociability is, then, the play-form of association and is related to the content-determined concreteness of association as art is related to reality. Now the great problem of association comes to a solution possible only in sociability. The problem is that of the measure of significance and accent which belongs to the individual as such in and as against the social milieu. Since sociability in its pure form has no ulterior end, no content, and no result outside itself, it is oriented completely about personalities. Since nothing but the satisfaction of the impulse to sociability—although with a resonance left over—is to be gained, the process remains, in its conditions as in its results, strictly limited to its personal bearers; the personal traits of amiability, breeding, cordiality, and attractiveness of all kinds determine the character of purely sociable association. But precisely because all is oriented about them, the personalities must not emphasize themselves too individually. Where real interests, co-operating or clashing, determine the social form, they provide of themselves that the individual shall not present his peculiarities and individuality with too much abandon and aggressiveness. But where this restraint is wanting, if association is to be possible at all, there must prevail another restriction of personal pushing, a restriction springing solely out of the form of the association. It is for this reason that the sense of tact is of such special significance in society, for it guides the self-regulation of the individual in his personal relations to others where no outer or directly egoistic interests provide regulation. And perhaps it is the specific function of tact to mark out for individual impulsiveness, for the ego and for outward demands, those limits which the rights of others require. A very remarkable sociological structure appears at this point. In sociability, whatever the personality has of objective importance, of features which have their orientation toward something outside the circle, must not interfere. Riches and social position, learning and fame, exceptional capacities and merits of the individual have no role in sociability or, at most, as a slight nuance of that immateriality with which alone reality dares penetrate into the artificial structure of sociability. As these objective qualities which gather about the personality, so also must the most purely and deeply personal qualities be excluded from sociability. The most personal things—character, mood, and fate—have thus no place in it. It is tactless to bring in personal humor, good or ill, excitement and depression, the light and shadow of one's inner life. Where a connection, begun on the sociable level— and not necessarily a superficial or conventional one—finally comes to center about personal values, it loses the essential quality of sociability and becomes an association determined by a content—not unlike a business or religious relation, for which contact, exchange, and speech are but instruments for ulterior ends, while for sociability they are the whole meaning and content of the social processes. This exclusion of the personal reaches into even the most external matters; a lady would not want to appear in such extreme *décolletage* in a really personal intimately friendly situation with one or two men as she would in a large company without any embarrassment. In the latter she would not feel herself personally involved in the same measure and could therefore abandon herself to the impersonal freedom of the mask. For she is, in the larger company, herself, to be sure, but not quite completely herself, since she is only an element in a formally constituted gathering.

A man, taken as a whole, is, so to speak, a somewhat unformed complex of contents, powers, potentialities; only according to the motivations and relationships of a changing existence is he articulated into a differentiated, defined structure. As an economic and political agent, as a member of a family or of a profession, he is, so to speak, an *ad hoc* construction; his life-material is ever determined by a special idea, poured into a special mold, whose relatively independent life is, to be sure, nourished from the common but somewhat undefinable source of energy, the ego. In this sense, the man, as a social creature, is also a unique structure, occurring in no other connection. On the one hand, he has removed all the objective qualities of the personality and entered into the structure of sociability with nothing but the capacities, attractions, and interests of his pure humanity. On the other hand, this structure stops short of the purely subjective and inward parts of his personality. That discretion which is one's first demand upon others in sociability is also required of one's own ego, because a breach of it in either direction causes the sociological artifact of sociability to break down into a sociological naturalism. One can therefore speak of an upper and a lower sociability threshold for the individual. At the moment when people direct their association toward objective content and purpose, as well as at the moment when the absolutely personal and subjective matters of the individual enter freely into the phenomenon, sociability is no longer the central and controlling principle but at most a formalistic and outwardly instrumental principle.

From this negative definition of the nature of sociability through boundaries and thresholds, however, one can perhaps find the positive motif. Kant set it up as the principle of law that everyone should have that measure of freedom which could exist along with the freedom of every other person. If one stands by the sociability impulse as the source or also as the substance of sociability, the following is the principle according to which it is constituted: everyone should have as much satisfaction of this impulse as is consonant with the satisfaction of the impulse for all others. If one expresses this not in terms of the impulse but rather in terms of success, the principle of sociability may be formulated thus: everyone should guarantee to the other that maximum of sociable values (joy, relief, vivacity) which is consonant with the maximum of values he himself receives. As justice upon the Kantian basis is thoroughly democratic, so likewise this principle shows the democratic structure of all sociability, which to be sure every social stratum can realize only within itself, and which so often makes sociability between members of different social classes burdensome and painful. But even among social equals the democracy of their sociability is a play. Sociability creates, if one will, an ideal sociological world, for in it—so say the enunciated principles— the pleasure of the individual is always contingent upon the joy of others; here, by definition, no one can have his satisfaction at the cost of contrary experiences on the part of others. In other forms of association such lack of reciprocity is excluded only by the ethical imperative which govern them but not by their own immanent nature. This world of sociability, the only one in which a democracy of equals is possible without friction, is an *artificial* world, made up of beings who have renounced both the objective and the purely personal features of the intensity and extensiveness of life in order to bring about among themselves a pure interaction, free of any disturbing material accent. If we now have the conception that we enter into sociability purely as "human beings," as that which we really are, lacking all the burdens, the agitations, the inequalities with which real life disturbs the purity of our picture, it is because modern life is overburdened with objective content and material demands. Ridding ourselves of this burden in sociable circles, we believe we return to our natural-personal being and overlook the fact that this personal aspect also does not consist in its full uniqueness and natural completeness, but only in a certain reserve and stylizing of the sociable man. In earlier epochs, when a man did not depend so much upon the purposive, objective content of his associations, his "formal personality" stood out more clearly against his personal existence: hence personal bearing in the society of earlier times was much more ceremonially rigidly and impersonally regulated than now. This reduction of the personal periphery of the measure of significance which homogeneous interaction with others allowed the individual has been followed by a swing to the opposite extreme; a specific attitude in society is that courtesy by which the strong, outstanding person not only places himself on a level with the weaker but goes so far as to assume the attitude that the weaker is the more worthy and superior. If association is interaction at all, it appears in its purest and most stylized form when it goes on among *equals*, just as symmetry and balance are the most outstanding forms of artistic stylizing of visible elements. Inasmuch as sociability is the abstraction of association—an abstraction of the character of art or of play—it demands the purest, most transparent, most engaging kind of interaction—that among equals. It must, because of its very nature, posit beings who give up so much of their objective content, who are so modified in both their outward and their inner significance, that they are sociably equal, and every one of them can win sociability values for himself only under the condition that the others, interacting with him, can also win them. It is a game in which one "acts" as though all were equal, as though he especially esteemed everyone. This is just as far from being a lie as is play or art in all their departures from reality. But the instant intentions and events of practical reality enter into the speech and behavior of sociability, it does become a lie—just as a painting does when it attempts, panorama fashion, to be taken for reality. That which is right and proper within the self-contained life of sociability, concerned only with the immediate play of its forms, becomes a lie when this is mere pretense, which in reality is guided by purposes of quite another sort than the sociable or is used to conceal such purposes—and indeed sociability may easily get entangled with real life.

It is an obvious corollary that everything may be subsumed under sociability which one can call sociological play-form; above all, play itself, which assumes a large place in the sociability of all epochs. The expression "social game" is significant in the deeper sense which I have indicated. The entire interactional or associational complex among men: the desire to gain advantage, trade, formation of parties and the desire to win from another, the movement between opposition and co-operation, outwitting and revenge—all this, fraught with purposive content in the serious affairs of reality, in play leads a life carried along only and completely by the stimulus of these functions. For even when play turns about a money prize, it is not the prize, which indeed could be won in many other ways, which is the specific point of the play; but the attraction for the true sportsman lies in the dynamics and in the chances of that sociologically significant form of activity itself. The social game has a deeper double meaning—that it is played not only *in* a society as its outward bearer but that *with* the society actually "society" is played. Further, in the sociology of the sexes, eroticism has elaborated a form of play: coquetry, which finds in sociability its lightest, most playful, and yet its widest realization. If the erotic question between the sexes turns about consent or denial (whose objects are naturally of endless variety and degree and by no means only of strictly physiological nature), so is it the essence of feminine coquetry to play hinted consent and hinted denial against each other to draw the man on without letting matters come to a decision, to rebuff him without making him lose all hope. The coquette brings her attractiveness to its climax by letting the man hang on the verge of getting what he wants without letting it become too serious for herself; her conduct swings between yes and no, without stopping at one or the other. She thus playfully shows the simple and pure form of erotic decision and can bring its polar opposites together in a quite integrated behavior, since the decisive and fateful content, which would bring it to one of the two decisions, by definition does not enter into coquetry. And this freedom from all the weight of firm content and residual reality gives coquetry that character of vacillation, of distance, of the ideal, which allows one to speak with some right of the "art"—not of the "arts"—of coquetry. In order, however, for coquetry to spread as so natural a growth on the soil of sociability, as experience shows it to be, it must be countered by a special attitude on the part of men. So long as the man denies himself the stimulation of coquetry, or so long as he is—on the contrary—merely a victim who is involuntarily carried along by her vacillations from a half-yes to a half-no-so long does coquetry lack the adequate structure of sociability. It lacks that free interaction and equivalence of the elements which is the fundamental condition of sociability. The latter appears only when the man desires nothing more than this free moving play, in which something definitively erotic lurks only as a remote symbol, and when he does not get his pleasure in these gestures and preliminaries from erotic desire or fear of it. Coquetry, as it unfolds its grace on the heights of sociable cultivation, has left behind the reality of erotic desire, of consent or denial, and becomes a play of shadow pictures of these serious matters. Where the latter enter or lurk, the whole process becomes a private affair of the two persons, played out on the level of reality; under the sociological sign of sociability, however, in which the essential orientation of the person to the fulness of life does not enter, coquetry is the teasing or even ironic play with which eroticism has distilled the pure essence of its interaction out from its substantive or individual content. As sociability plays at the forms of society, so coquetry plays out the forms of eroticism.

In what measure sociability realizes to the full the abstraction of the forms of sociological interaction otherwise significant because of their content and gives them—now turning about themselves, so to speak—a shadow body is revealed finally in that most extensive instrument of all human common life, conversation. The decisive point is expressed in the quite banal experience that in the serious affairs of life men talk for the sake of the content which they wish to impart or about which they want to come to an understanding—in sociability talking is an end in itself; in purely sociable conversation the content is merely the indispensable carrier of the stimulation, which the lively exchange of talk as such unfolds. All the forms with which this exchange develops: argument and the appeals to the norms recognized by both parties; the conclusion of peace through compromise and the discovery of common convictions; the thankful acceptance of the new and the parrying-off of that on which no understanding is to be hoped for—all these forms of conversational interaction, otherwise in the service of innumerable contents and purposes of human intercourse, here have their meaning in themselves; that is to say, in the excitement of the play of relations which they establish between individuals, binding and loosening, conquering and being vanquished, giving and taking. In order that this play may retain its self-sufficiency at the level of pure form, the content must receive no weight on its own account; as soon as the discussion gets business-like it is no longer sociable; it turns its compass point around as soon as the verification of a truth becomes its purpose. Its character as sociable converse is disturbed just as when it turns into a serious argument. The form of the common search of the truth, the form of the argument, may occur; but it must not permit the seriousness of the momentary content to become its substance any more than one may put a piece of three-dimensional reality into the perspective of a painting. Not that the content of sociable conversation is a matter of indifference; it must be interesting, gripping, even significant—only it is not the purpose of the conversation that these qualities should square with objective results, which stand by definition outside the conversation. Outwardly, therefore, two conversations may run a similar course, but only that one of them is sociable in which the subject matter, with all its value and stimulation, finds its justification, its place, and its purpose only in the functional play of conversation as such, in the form of repartee with its special unique significance. It therefore inheres in the nature of sociable conversation that its object matter can change lightly and quickly; for, since the matter is only the means, it has an entirely interchangeable and accidental character which inheres in means as against fixed purposes. Thus sociability offers, as was said, perhaps the only case in which talk is a legitimate end in itself. For by the fact that it is two-sided—indeed with the possible exception of looking-each-other-over the purest and most sublimated form of mutuality among all sociological phenomena—it becomes the most adequate fulfilment of a relation, which is, so to speak, nothing but relationship, in which even that which is otherwise pure form of interaction is its own self-sufficient content. It results from this whole complex that also the telling of tales, witticisms, anecdotes, although often a stopgap and evidence of conversational poverty, still can show a fine tact in which all the motives of sociability are apparent. For, in the first place, the conversation is by this means kept above all individual intimacy, beyond everything purely personal which would not fit into the categories of sociability. This objective element is brought in not for the sake of its content but in the interest of sociability; that something is said and accepted is not an end in itself but a mere means to maintain the liveliness, the mutual understanding, the common consciousness of the group. Not only thereby is it given a content which all can share but it is a gift of the individual to the whole, behind which the giver can remain invisible; the finest sociably told story is that in which the narrator allows his own person to remain completely in the background; the most effective story holds itself in the happy balance of the sociable ethic, in which the subjectively individual as well as the objectively substantive have dissolved themselves completely in the service of pure sociability.

It is hereby indicated that sociability is the play-form also for the ethical forces of concrete society. The great problems placed before these forces are that the individual has to fit himself into a whole system and live for it: that, however, out of this system values and enhancement must flow back to him, that the life of the individual is but a means for the ends of the whole, the life of the whole but an instrument for the purposes of the individual. Sociability carries the seriousness, indeed the frequent tragedy of these requirements, over into its shadow world, in which there is no friction, because shadows cannot impinge upon one another. If it is, further, the ethical task of association to make the coming-together and the separation of its elements an exact and just expression of their inner relations, determined by the wholeness of their lives, so within sociability this freedom and adequacy are freed of their concrete and substantively deeper limitations; the manner in which in a "society" groups form and break up, conversation spins itself out, deepens, loosens, cuts itself off purely according to impulse and opportunity, that is a miniature picture of the social ideal that man might call the freedom of bondage.

If all association and separation shall be the strictly appropriate representation of inner realities, so are the latter here fallen by the way, and only the former phenomenon is left, whose play, obedient to its own laws, whose closed charm, represents *aesthetically* that moderation which the seriousness of realities otherwise demands of its ethical decisions.

This total interpretation of sociability is evidently realized by certain historical developments. In the earlier German Middle Ages we find knightly fraternities which were founded by friendly patrician families. The religious and practical ends of these unions seem to have been lost rather early, and in the fourteenth century the chivalrous interests and conduct remain their only specific content. Soon after, this also disappears, and there remain only purely sociable unions of aristocratic strata. Here the sociability apparently develops as the residuum of a society determined by a content—as the residuum which, because the content has been lost, can exist only in form and in the forms of with-one-another and for-one-another. That the essential existence of these forms can have only the inner nature of play or, reaching deeper, of art appears even more clearly in the court society of the *ancien régime*. Here by the falling-off of the concrete life-content, which was sucked away from the French aristocracy in some measure by the monarchy, there developed free-moving forms, toward which the consciousness of this class was crystallized—forms whose force, definitions, and relations were purely sociable and in no way symbols or functions of the real meanings and intensities of persons and institutions. The etiquette of court society became an end in itself; it "etiquette" no content any longer but had elaborated immanent laws, comparable to those of art, which have validity only from the viewpoint of art and do not at all have the purpose of imitating faithfully and strikingly the reality of the model, that is, of things outside art.

With this phenomenon, sociability attains its most sovereign expression but at the same time verges on caricature. To be sure, it is its nature to shut out realities from the interactive relations of men and to build its castle in air according to the formal laws of these relations which move within themselves and recognize no purpose outside themselves. But the deep-running source, from which this empire takes its energies, is nonetheless to be sought not in these self-regulating forms but only in the vitality of real individuals, in their sensitivities and attractions, in the fulness of their impulses and convictions. All sociability is but a symbol of *life*, as it shows itself in the flow of a lightly amusing play; but, even so, a symbol of life, whose likeness it only so far alters as is required by the distance from it gained in the play, exactly as also the freest and most fantastic art, the furthest from all reality, nourishes itself from a deep and true relation to reality, if it is not to be empty and lying. If sociability cuts off completely the threads which bind it to real life and out of which it spins its admittedly stylized web, it turns from play to empty farce, to a lifeless schematization proud of its woodenness.

From this context it becomes apparent that men can complain both justly and unjustly of the superficiality of social intercourse. It is one of the most pregnant facts of mental life that, if we weld certain elements taken from the whole of being into a realm of their own, which is governed by its own laws and not by those of the whole, this realm, if completely cut off from the life of the whole, can display in its inner realization an empty nature suspended in the air; but then, often altered only by imponderables, precisely in this state of removal from all immediate reality, its deeper nature can appear more completely, more integrated and meaningful, than any attempt to comprehend it realistically and without taking distance. According as the former or the latter experience predominates, will one's own life, running its own course according to its own norms, be a formal, meaningless dead thing—or a symbolic play, in whose aesthetic charm all the finest and most highly sublimated dynamics of social existence and its riches are gathered. In all art, in all the symbolism of the religious life, in great measure even in the complex formulations of science, we are thrown back upon this belief, upon this feeling, that autonomies of mere parts of observed reality, that the combinations of certain superficial elements possess a relation to the depth and wholeness of life, which, although often not easy to formulate, makes such a part the bearer and the representative of the fundamental reality. From this we may understand the saving grace and blessing effect of these realms built out of the pure forms of existence, for in them we are released from life but have it still. The sight of the sea frees us inwardly, not in spite of but because of the fact that in its rushing up only to recede, its receding only to rise again, in the play and counterplay of its waves, the whole of life is stylized to the simplest expression of its dynamic, quite free from all reality which one may experience and from all the baggage of individual fate, whose final meaning seems nevertheless to flow into this stark picture. Just so art perhaps reveals the secret of life; that we save ourselves not by simply looking away from it but precisely in that in the apparently self-governing play of its forms we construct and experience the meaning and the forces of its deepest reality but without the reality itself. Sociability would not hold for so many thoughtful men who feel in every moment the pressure of life, this emancipating and saving exhilaration if it were only a flight from life, the mere momentary lifting of its seriousness. It can often enough be only this negative thing, a conventionalism and inwardly lifeless exchange of formulas; so perhaps in the *ancien régime*, where gloomy anxiety over a threatening reality drove men into pure escape, into severance from the powers of actual life. The freeing and lightening, however, that precisely the more thoughtful man finds in sociability is this; that association and exchange of stimulus, in which all the tasks and the whole weight of life are realized, here is consumed in an artistic play, in that simultaneous sublimation and dilution, in which the heavily freighted forces of reality are felt only as from a distance, their weight fleeting in a charm.

"Soziologie der Geselligkeit," being the opening speech at the first meeting of the German Sociological Society, *Verhandlungen des Ersten Deutschen Soziologentages vom 19–12 Oktober, 1910, in Frankfurt A.M.* (Tübingen: J. C. B. Mohr, iglil). Pp. 1–16.

Commentary

Simmel's text on sociability makes a strong case for the existence of a drive toward others and its importance as the foundation for living together. In fact, as he notes, "the word 'society' (*Gesellschaft*) indicates literally 'together-ness'" (1949, p. 255). His text not only vividly reminds us that we are social beings, but also that we rejoice in being with others. Simmel explicitly relates sociability to the feeling of satisfaction one gets from associating and interacting with people in a playful manner, for the sake of the interaction itself. This playfulness is not simply "added" to human relationships on top of their functional, pragmatic aspects; for Simmel there is a *primordiality* of sociability when it comes to building society as well as the self. In his words:

> Typically there is involved in all effective motives for association a feeling of the worth of association as such, a drive which presses toward this form of existence and often only later calls forth that objective content which carries the particular association along. (1949, p. 255)

But what is sociability? The text itself never offers a final or singular definition of the concept. In fact, it refuses the very notion of a definition. There are many statements, however, that help us understand what sociability is, for instance, "association for its own sake" (1949, p. 254), "the art of play form of association" (p. 254), and "the pure form, the free-playing, interacting interdependence of individuals" (p. 255). In a more metaphorical manner, sociability is "a symbolic play, in whose aesthetic charm all the finest and most highly sublimated dynamics of social existence and its riches are gathered" (p. 261). We have already in these fragments some shared characteristics of the phenomenon with association and interaction, play, aesthetics, intrinsic satisfaction, and social existence. Why do we gain from being not only social, but most of all sociable? We get to "maintain the liveliness, the mutual understanding, the common consciousness of the group" (pp. 259–260), above and beyond the "content" of social relations.

The notion of sociability was placed at the basis of Simmel's whole program of formal sociology (Gronow, 2011; also Henricks, 2003). As we will see, he was also criticized because of this, in particular for his specific understanding of sociability. For instance, his discussion is grounded in a basic description between *form* and *content* in social interaction. We interact with others for a variety of practical reasons: in order to learn something, to do things together, to grow personally and professionally, and, at a basic level, to survive. But there is some other element, beyond these particular contents of the interaction, that defines human types of relating. This is their form or the actual way in which we communicate and engage with other people. If we could strip the interaction from all its particular contents and aims (and there is a big "if" about this), we would end up with the pure form, and this is what Simmel calls sociability. This happens when content and form coincide because the person engages in interaction for the sake of the interaction itself. Sociability serves, in this regard, no purpose outside of itself. In order to achieve it, there are a few basic conditions Simmel more or less implicitly postulates: freedom, equal status, reciprocity, and interest in the other. As a basic precondition, Simmel interestingly notes that we need to leave behind (if it is ever possible) both our social roles and scripts and our personal feelings and thoughts. One needs to attend to the other from a position other than that of one's social role or one's egocentric perspective on the world.

What does all of this have to do with creativity? Simmel did not use the term in the text, and, indeed, his work on sociability has been drawn upon in different domains, from the study of massively multiplayer games (Ducheneaut, Moore, & Nickell, 2007), to sports and supporters (Giulianotti, 2005), and driving cabs (Toiskallio, 2000). What Simmel did, however, was to insist on how sociability can "best be compared with art or, even better, with play and games" (Gronow, 2011, p. 1302), both topics closely connected to creative expression. In fact the argument can be made that, by placing sociability at the heart of society and by making the analogy with art, play, and games, Simmel implicitly places creativity at the center of social relations and makes it an indispensable element of living together with others. Has this interpretation been offered within creativity research? More broadly, has sociability as a notion featured at all in creativity studies? The short answer is no or, rather, not really. There are only passing references to Simmel and his work within creativity journals (e.g., Cohen-Shalev & Marcus, 2008; Cohen-Shalev & Raz, 2008). There are more references to sociability as a notion but understood in different terms, often simply as a synonym for being social, and measured in a psychometric manner (see Beach, 1960; Rivlin, 1959). Pachucki, Lena, and Tepper (2010, p. 141) more recently studied "creative sociability" and considered it

> a defining social form in the 21st century, undergirding a range of social experiences in college and beyond, providing students and citizens with the skills and dispositions necessary to navigate a global economy, and serving as a key process whereby individuals negotiate the important balance between conformity and distinction.

But if we follow Simmel's reading, "creative sociability" is a tautological notion. The play and art forms that model his understanding of sociability are *intrinsically creative* (see Davis, 1973; De La Fuente, 2008; Henricks, 2003), if nothing else because they help create society through each and every social interaction. The relation between sociability and aesthetics was particularly discussed in the literature following Simmel. To start with, one of his former students, Arthur Salz (1965, p. 236), once remarked that, since his teacher's discussion focuses on forms and they are a key concern within aesthetics, then for him society "is a work of art." In Simmel's (1968, p. 74) own words, "The social question . . . is not only an ethical question, but also an aesthetic one." And, I would add, a question of creativity. Why is this the case? Because, for Simmel, the relation between the functional and sociable aspects of our social life resembles the relation between art and reality. As De La Fuerte (2008) notes, his whole work unpacks this relationship in a variety of ways: from the art of social forms and the social forms of art to the combination of aesthetic and social factors. De La Fuerte (2008, pp. 348-352) usefully abstracted and discussed six analogical inferences in Simmel's thought:

1. Sociability is like art in that it is an autonomous form.
2. Sociability is like art in that artifice and style are necessary.
3. Sociability is artful but the similarities to art are not literal.
4. Sociability is like art in that content matters—but only as the medium of form.
5. Sociability is like art in that it is a symbol or condensation of reality.
6. Sociability is like art in that it provides relief from life.

Many of these analogies are questionable, in particular the autonomy of art, the priority of form over content, and the separation between art and life or, at least, the concerns of life. In order to understand the origins of these premises we need to place them in their historical context. As Davis (1973, p. 324) reminds us, Simmel was influenced here by the late 19th- and early 20th-century French and English schools of "art for art's sake." The autonomy of art, especially from everyday life, has been rejected, among others, by the pragmatists (see Dewey, 1934). Of course Simmel (1911/1959) recognized in this writing the fact that art builds on life experiences, but he still claimed that, in its final form, it is detached from them and self-sufficient. This assumption becomes problematic for the notion of sociability, which, just like art, is supposed to be in a state of "removal from all immediate reality" (p. 261). The act of distancing oneself from concrete concerns is certainly important for the notion but, when placed at its core, risks undermining its usefulness. It also leads to seemingly paradoxical statements such as, when experiencing sociability and the free association of forms, "We construct and experience the meaning and the forces of its deepest reality but without the reality itself" (p. 261).

A closer reading of Simmel's text shows that he does not oppose sociability and reality but, on the contrary, conceives them as deeply *interrelated*. In his own words, the experience of sociability "makes up its substance from numerous fundamental forms of serious relationships among men, a substance, however, spared the frictional relations of real life" (1949, p. 255). The playful and creative aspects of this phenomenon draw, in many ways, precisely on sociability's relative autonomy. Sociability, in the end, opens up a space of safe and free forms of interaction and association that foster creativity, learning, and togetherness. In the end, it is this simultaneous state of proximity to and distance from reality that enables the creativity of our social life. Simmel warns, "If sociability cuts off completely the threads which bind it to real life and out of which it spins its admittedly stylized web, it turns from play to empty farce, to a lifeless schematization proud of its woodenness" (p. 261).

Regardless of the fact that Simmel's work did not inspire (at least directly) creativity theory, I believe it has a great potential to do so in a number of areas. First of all, his sociology is particularly relevant for highlighting a new dimension within the social study of creativity: the underlying *creative basis of society and of human forms of association*. The past four decades have witnessed an increased interest in the social dynamic of creativity, but only recently have questions concerning the role of creativity within society been formulated (Glăveanu, 2015). There is certainly a great deal of creativity involved in leading groups and communities, imagining collective futures together with others, developing social innovations, and participating in social change. Each one of these collective forms of action requires a "visible" (Big-C or at least Pro-C; Kaufman & Beghetto, 2009) form of creativity. What about the less noticeable and yet pervasive forms of creative expression embedded within everyday human interactions at home, in the school, in organizations, or at the marketplace? How can we account for the creativity embedded within humor, playful exchanges, and the improvisation needed to work collaboratively with others? The notion of sociability, as developed by Simmel, is a great candidate for identifying this level of creativity and, more than this, highlighting its importance for our personal and social existence. Simmel (1949, p. 254) was well aware of the multiple facets of the self-other relation, or what he called "the innumerable forms of social life, all the with-one-another, for-one-another, in-one-another, against-one-another, and through-one-another, in state and commune, in church and economic associations, in family and clubs." Each one of these facets deserves much more attention from creativity scholars, especially those interested in the different nuances of sociability and its creative dynamic. There are clear connections to be made also between sociability and being in flow (Csikszentmihalyi, 1996) since both basically require intrinsic motivation, relinquishing a certain awareness of our social roles and personal concerns, and lead to a certain joy of acting or, in this case, of interacting in the here and now.

When integrating Simmel's work within creativity theory it is important to do so in a reflective manner, in view of its few shortcomings. One of the most obvious comes, as I mentioned before, from Simmel's rather strict separation between sociability and the practical concerns of living. In fact, he goes on to claim that "riches and social position, learning and fame, exceptional capacities and merits of the individual have no role in sociability" (1949, p. 256). This statement needs to be understood in the context of his idea that full or pure sociability can be achieved only between equals, within more or less democratic relationships (see also a similar idealism in describing the public sphere in the case of Habermas, 1991). However, by doing away with the constraints of the social and material realities we inhabit, his notion of sociability is rightfully criticized for being unable to account for *power relations* and, as such, not being fully applicable to the study of ordinary social life, which is full of injustices and inequalities (see Gronow, 2011). Simmel (1949, p. 257) accepted this risk when he admitted, "This world of sociability, the only one in which a democracy of equals is possible without friction, is an *artificial* world." There is nothing intrinsically wrong with describing a concept as an ideal type, recognizing that it is rarely found (in its "pure" form) in reality. But perhaps it would be much better to think of the interplay between sociability and the concrete concerns of living (and the inequalities connected to them) in terms of a *continuum* rather than an *either/or* type of relationship. In the end, the sociability Simmel talks about can be achieved in specific contexts of interaction, even if for a fleeing moment. But its great value comes from being able to inspire us to think, based on these moments, about the nature and value of a world in which people are free to express themselves, challenge the powerful, and find joy in relating with others without any ulterior motives (see also Bakhtin's [1965/1984] notion of the carnival).

A second, related critique has to do with the fact that sociability seems to have only positive consequences. Simmel (1949, p. 257) noted, in this regard, that "sociability creates . . . an ideal sociological world, for in it . . . the pleasure of the individual is always contingent upon the joy of others." The question, though, is: What is the role assigned to *conflict and tension* within sociability? The creativity literature has long emphasized the potentially positive—within limits—effects of conflict for creative expression (see, e.g., Nemeth, Personnaz, Personnaz, & Goncalo, 2004). The social world in particular offers us myriad opportunities to cooperate with but also to contradict or oppose others, and each of these circumstances has associated with it a range of opportunities for creativity. An expanded definition of sociability should be able to account also for tensions, conflicts, and negative emotions.

Considering the future, what would incorporating (and potentially redefining) Simmel's notion of sociability achieve for creativity researchers? There are at least a few directions worth exploring based on his social framework:

1. First of all, becoming aware of sociability turns *society into a creativity domain*. For a long time, this position was occupied by the arts and sciences. (Nowadays the number of creative domains has increased considerably; see Kaufman, Glăveanu, & Baer, 2017.) But when it comes to society, the assumption is either that social relations hinder creativity or that, in this area, the only creative people are those leaders who inspire and achieve social transformation. The most pervasive forms of being creative within the sphere of interpersonal relations remains relatively unexplored (see, however, the notion of social creativity in Mouchiroud & Lubart, 2002; and societal creativity in Glăveanu, 2015);

2. What would a creativity researcher interested in sociability actually study? The improvisational, spontaneous, and playful nature of daily interactions, independent of their actual content or, rather, across different forms of activity. Simmel claimed that sociability concerns the "form" of social interaction and, in this sense, could be seen as a universal characteristic of human relations (even if often not achieved, in practice, in its pure manifestation). Given the growing interest within creativity for domain-specific models and explanations (Kaufman & Baer, 2004), however, it would be interesting to observe the ways in which sociability might be shaped by context, including cultural and historical contexts (see also Henricks, 2003).

3. A particular context that deserves research attention has to do with the expression of sociability within collective action, particularly in protests and demonstrations. There is a growing interest today in the role of humor and creativity, for instance, in political demonstrations (Yalcintas, 2015), but these studies rarely have a strong theoretical framework making the link between social forms of association and creativity. Simmel's work certainly tries to fill this gap, and it could inspire a new line of research on creativity and social change.

4. The description of sociability as having "no ulterior end, no content, and no result outside itself" (Simmel, 1949, p. 255) strongly resembles the definition of intrinsic motivation. And, indeed, there is a long-term interest within creativity studies for unpacking the relationship between intrinsic motivation and creative work (e.g., see the intrinsic motivation principle formulated by Amabile, 1996). Simmel's notion of sociability not only highlights the possibility of talking, in the future, about *social intrinsic motivation* (i.e., the sociability drive) but also questions the assumption that intrinsic motivation is a purely individual property, often diminished due to the intervention of other people (e.g., giving rewards or administrating punishments). Human actions and interactions are plurimotivated, and sociability doesn't have to exclude the need to achieve more than one outcome when associating with others.

In the end, sociability, just like creativity, is a polysemic notion, one that needs to adapt to new historical contexts and social realities. Nonetheless, the core of this concept, as outlined by Simmel, is extremely valuable for creativity researchers working today on the playful, generative nature of social interaction as expressed in play, casual humor, and acts of collective protest, among others. It pushes us to look beyond the content and, in creativity research, the products of human interaction, and pay particular attention to form, process, and experience. Most of all, it can help us theorize further interpersonal relations and place them at the core of our existence as human beings, *at once social and creative*.

In a passage in his diary written toward the end of his life, Simmel (2011, p. xiii) reflected on his legacy:

> I know that I shall die without intellectual heirs, and that is as it should be. My legacy will be like cash, distributed to many heirs, each transforming his part into use according to his nature—a use which will no longer reveal its indebtedness to this heritage.

Creativity scholars working on issues related to society and social relations are necessarily the intellectual heirs of Simmel, even if they are not aware of it. My hope, in writing this chapter, is to make his legacy a little more visible and foreground the notion of sociability for the future—in other words, identify what we did with the "cash" we inherited from Simmel and use it to increase the intellectual and human capital of our discipline, our thinking, and our practice.

References

Amabile, T. M. (1996). *Creativity in context: Update to the social psychology of creativity*. Boulder, CO: Westview Press.

Bakhtin, M. M. (1965/1984). *Rabelais and his world* (H. Iswolsky, Trans.). Bloomington: Indiana University Press.

Beach, L. R. (1960). Sociability and academic achievement in various types of learning situations. *Journal of Educational Psychology, 51*(4), 208–212.

Cohen-Shalev, A., & Marcus, E. L. (2008). Claude Sautet's winter of discontent: The aging of a moviemaker. *Psychology of Aesthetics, Creativity, and the Arts, 2*(4), 213–220.

Cohen-Shalev, A., & Raz, A. (2008). Poetry of unadulterated imagination: The late style of Akira Kurosawa. *Psychology of Aesthetics, Creativity, and the Arts, 2*(1), 34–41.

Csikszentmihalyi, M. (1996). *Flow and the psychology of discovery and invention*. New York, NY: Harper Collins.

Davis, M. S. (1973). Georg Simmel and the aesthetics of social reality. *Social Forces, 51*(3), 320–329.

De La Fuente, E. (2008). The art of social forms and the social forms of art: The sociology-aesthetics nexus in Georg Simmel's thought. *Sociological Theory, 26*(4), 344–362.

Dewey, J. (1934). *Art as experience*. New York, NY: Penguin.

Ducheneaut, N., Moore, R. J., & Nickell, E. (2007). Virtual "third places": A case study of sociability in massively multiplayer games. *Computer Supported Cooperative Work, 16*(1–2), 129–166.

Frisby, D. (1985). Georg Simmel: First sociologist of modernity. *Theory, Culture & Society, 2*(3), 49–67.

Giulianotti, R. (2005). The sociability of sport: Scotland football supporters as interpreted through the sociology of Georg Simmel. *International Review for the Sociology of Sport, 40*(3), 289–306.

Glăveanu, V. P. (2015). Developing society: Reflections on the notion of societal creativity. In A.-G. Tan & C. Perleth (Eds.), *Creativity, culture, and development* (pp. 183–200). Singapore: Springer.

Gronow, J. (2011). Sociability. In D. Southerton (Ed.), *Encyclopedia of consumer culture* (pp. 1302–1305). Thousand Oaks, CA: Sage.

Habermas, J. (1991). *The structural transformation of the public sphere: An inquiry into a category of bourgeois society*. Cambridge, MA: MIT Press.

Henricks, T. S. (2003). Simmel: On sociability as the play-form of human association. *Play and Culture Studies, 5*, 19–32.

Kaufman, J. C., & Baer, J. (2004). The amusement park theoretical (APT) model of creativity. *International Journal of Creativity & Problem Solving, 14*(2), 15–25.

Kaufman, J. C., & Beghetto, R. A. (2009). Beyond big and little: The four c model of creativity. *Review of General Psychology, 13*(1), 1–12.

Kaufman, J. C., Glăveanu, V. P. & Baer, J. (Eds.) (2017). *The Cambridge handbook of creativity across domains*. Cambridge, MA: Cambridge University Press.

Levine, D. N., Carter, E. B., & Gorman, E. M. (1976). Simmel's influence on American sociology. I. *American Journal of Sociology, 81*(4), 813–845.

Lukács, G. (1991). Georg Simmel. *Theory, Culture & Society, 8*(3), 145–150.

Mouchiroud, C., & Lubart, T. (2002). Social creativity: A cross-sectional study of 6- to 11-year-old children. *International Journal of Behavioral Development, 26*(1), 60–69.

Nemeth, C. J., Personnaz, B., Personnaz, M., & Goncalo, J. A. (2004). The liberating role of conflict in group creativity: A study in two countries. *European Journal of Social Psychology, 34*(4), 365–374.

Pachucki, M. A., Lena, J. C., & Tepper, S. J. (2010). Creativity narratives among college students: Sociability and everyday creativity. *Sociological Quarterly, 51*(1), 122–149.

Rivlin, L. G. (1959). Creativity and the self-attitudes and sociability of high school students. *Journal of Educational Psychology, 50*(4), 147–152.

Salz, A. (1965). A note from a student of Simmel's. In K. H. Wolff (Ed.), *Essays on sociology, philosophy and aesthetics* (pp. 233–236). New York, NY: Harper and Row.

Simmel, G. (1911/1959). The adventure. In K. Wolff (Ed.), *Georg Simmel 1858–1918*. Columbus: Ohio State University Press.

Simmel, G. (1949). The sociology of sociability (E. C. Hughes, Trans.). *American Journal of Sociology, 55*(3), pp. 254–261.

Simmel, G. (1968). Sociological aesthetics. In G. Simmel, *The conflict in modern culture and other essays* (P. K. Etzkorn, Ed., pp. 68–80). New York, NY: Teachers College.

Simmel, G. (2005). *Rembrandt: An Essay in the Philosophy of Art* (A. Scott and H. Staubmann, Trans.). New York, NY: Routledge.

Simmel, G. (2011). *Georg Simmel on individuality and social forms*. Chicago, IL: University of Chicago Press.

Toiskallio, K. (2000). Simmel hails a cab: Fleeting sociability in the urban taxi. *Space and Culture, 3*(6), 4–20.

Yalcintas, A. (2015). Intellectual disobedience in Turkey. In A. Yalcintas (Ed.), *Creativity and humour in occupy movements* (pp. 6–29). London: Palgrave.

31

Authoritarianism and Creativity
Else Frenkel-Brunswik and
The Authoritarian Personality

Alfonso Montuori

Summary

The year 1950 saw the publication of a classic study in social science, *The Authoritarian Personality*. The 990-page study by Theodor Adorno, Else Frenkel-Brunswik, Daniel Levinson, and Nevitt Sanford outlined the characteristics of what they called the authoritarian personality in great detail. The study was conducted at the University of California, Berkeley, which also housed the Institute of Personality Assessment and Research, where important research on the creative person was conducted. In fact even though there was some overlap between the researchers of authoritarianism and those of creativity, the connection between the two was never made entirely explicit or studied in depth, despite the fact that the psychological profiles that emerged were mirror images of each other. The study of authoritarianism has taken on new urgency given the current resurgence of authoritarianism in Western Europe and the United States. The connection with creativity research offers intriguing avenues for further research and the potential of education for creativity as an antidote to authoritarianism.

Introduction

The Authoritarian Personality is not usually included or addressed in the literature on creativity. Nevertheless there are interesting connections between authoritarianism and creativity that deserve more attention, and there are potentially important implications in articulating this relationship. This brief excerpt from one of Else Frenkel-Brunswik's contributions to the volume clearly highlights the connection when she compares high scorers with low scorers on authoritarianism. She points to the "generally more creative and imaginative approach of the low scorer both in the cognitive and in the emotional sphere, as compared with a more constricted, conventional, and stereotypical approach in the high scorer" (1950, p. 475). Given this information, and other connections I will point to, it is rather surprising that hardly any research has followed up on the relationship between creativity and authoritarianism or explored its implications (Montuori, 1989, 2005; Rubinstein, 2003).

Starting in the 1940s, social scientists, and psychologists in particular, wanted to understand and contribute to preventing a recurrence of the horrors of fascism and the Second World War. Much important research emerged in the two decades following the war. Researchers wanted to understand how a country like Germany, often considered to be the pinnacle of European culture, could fall into the abyss of fascism and the Holocaust. Much of the research focused on conformity and obedience. It attempted to explain how people could have rallied behind Hitler and followed orders that included committing the most horrendous atrocities. The research was often theoretically and methodologically daring. It included, among others, studies such as the work of Asch (1956) and Crutchfield (1955) on conformity, Milgram's (1963) dramatic research on obedience, Sherif's (1958; Sherif, Harvey, White, Hood, & Sherif, 1961) work on in-groups and out-groups, and later Zimbardo's notorious Stanford Prison experiment (Haney, Banks, & Zimbardo, 1973; Zimbardo, 2007). These studies are still found in almost every introductory work on social psychology.

Erich Fromm's (1941/1994) classic *Escape from Freedom* had already outlined the authoritarian character, and *The Authoritarian Personality* kicked off the empirical study of authoritarianism. The study was conducted by a team of researchers at the University of California, Berkeley: Theodor Adorno, Else Frenkel-Brunswik, Daniel Levinson, and Nevitt Sanford. Frenkel-Brunswik, Sanford, and Levinson brought their background in psychology and statistical research; Adorno was a wide-ranging philosopher from what later came to be known as the Frankfurt School. Alphabetically Adorno's last name made him the first author of the study and the name most closely associated with it, although his contribution was actually the least of the four authors.

One clear connection between research on authoritarianism and creativity can be found in Berkeley, at the Institute for Personality Assessment and Research (IPAR; now the Institute for Personality and Social Research). IPAR was founded in 1949. The first director was Donald MacKinnon (1962), who made important contributions to creativity research, notably through his study of architects (Serraino, 2016). Nevitt Sanford, one of the coauthors of *The Authoritarian Personality*, was IPAR's first associate director. In many ways the Berkeley research on authoritarianism was conducted using the same approach as the Berkeley creativity studies, a combination of assessments and interviews, with the creativity research adding live-in assessment of eminent creatives. Because of this connection, I will draw mainly although not exclusively on the research findings on creativity from the IPAR research, which has been articulated most prominently in IPAR researcher Frank Barron's publications. I hope that revisiting *The Authoritarian Personality* and its connection with creativity will also stimulate a revisiting of IPAR and specifically Barron's (1968, 1969, 1995) important creativity research.

In the reading chosen for this chapter, Frenkel-Brunswik discusses the interviews she conducted and contrasts high and low scorers on prejudice and authoritarianism.

Reading: "Comprehensive Scores and Summaries of the Interview"

Source: Frenkel-Brunswik, E. (1950). Comprehensive scores and summaries of the interview. In T. W. Adorno, E. Frenkel-Brunswik, D. J. Levinson, & R. N. Sanford (Eds.), *The authoritarian personality* (pp. 474–486). New York, NY: Harper & Row. © 1950 by The American Jewish Committee. Reprinted by permission of the publisher.

Among the tendencies which the typical high scorer attempts to keep in a repressed state . . . are mainly fear, weakness, passivity, sex impulses, and aggressive feeling against authoritative figures, especially the parents. Among the rigid defenses against these tendencies there is, above all, the mechanism of projection, by which much of what cannot be accepted as part of one's own ego is externalized. Thus it is not oneself but others that are seen as hostile and threatening. Or else one's own weakness leads to an exaggerated condemnation of everything that is weak; one's own weakness is thus fought outside instead of inside. At the same time there is a compensatory—and therefore often compulsive—drive for power, strength, success, and self-determination. Repression and externalization of the instinctual tendencies mentioned reduces their manageability and the possibility of their control by the individual, since it is now the external world to which the feared qualities of the unconscious are ascribed. . . .

The composite picture of the low scorer . . . not only reveals greater readiness to accept and to face one's impulses and weaknesses, but also to ruminate about them. While for the high scorer possible loss of energy is connected with his tendency toward rigid repressions, the low scorer is apt to waste energies by indulging in often unfruitful introspection and by placing the blame for mishaps too much upon himself. In contrast to the high scorer's tendency toward externalization, the typical low scorer is prone to internalize in an excessive manner, and this in turn may lead to open anxiety, feelings of guilt, and other neurotic features.

The low scorer also tends to be oriented, more than is the high scorer, toward real achievement, toward intellectual or aesthetic goals, and toward the realization of socially productive values. His greater capacity for intensive interpersonal relationships goes hand in hand with greater self-sufficiency. He struggles for the establishment of inner harmony and self-actualization, whereas the high scorer is concentrated on an effort to adjust to the outside world and to gain power and success within it.

One of the results of greater internalization is the generally more creative and imaginative approach of the low scorer both in the cognitive and in the emotional sphere, as compared with a more constricted, conventional, and stereotypical approach in the high scorer. . . .

External criteria, especially social status, are the yardsticks by which the high scorer tends to appraise people in general and the ground on which he either admires and accepts, or rejects them. Such values form the basis of a hierarchical order in which the powerful are seen at the top and the weak at the bottom. . . . The typical low scorer, on the other hand, seems to have developed for himself an image of other people which includes congeniality even with outgroups rather than conceiving of them mainly as a threat or danger. Feeling more secure, he searches in his relations with other people primarily for a realization of positive and individualized values rather than being oriented primarily toward getting support and help from the powerful as is the typical high scorer. . . .

Whereas the striving for status and power, in their purely external aspects, seems to be the major concern of the extremely prejudiced, the unprejudiced individual—though as a rule by no means disinterested in status—still has a greater variety of other resources and pleasures at his disposal.

Though far from being indifferent to recognition, low scorers place comparatively little emphasis on their activities as means to an end; rather, these activities tend to become a source of pleasure and satisfaction in their own right, or else the emphasis lies on their social implications. Activity contributing to the realization of what may be called liberal values may also become important to the low scorer. Finally, interest and liking for art, music, literature, and philosophy are more often found in the low scorer. It may be considered that such interests contribute substantially to the greater resourcefulness, and to the comparative diversion from power and status, that is characteristic of the low scorer. . . .

One of the most pervasive formal aspects of the personality organization of the extremely prejudiced individual is his rigidity. . . . In order to keep unacceptable tendencies and impulses out of consciousness, rigid defenses have to be maintained. Any loosening of the absoluteness of these defenses involves the danger of a breaking through of the repressed tendencies. . . .

Fear of one's own immoral tendencies can be alleviated by exaggerating and condemning the immorality of others, particularly outgroups. . . .

In order to keep the balance under these conditions, a simple, firm, often stereotypical, cognitive structure is required. There is no place for ambivalence or ambiguities. Every attempt is made to eliminate them, but they remain as potentials which might interfere at any time. In the course of these attempts a subtle but profound distortion of reality has to take place, precipitated by the fact that stereotypical categorizations can never do justice to all the aspects of reality. . . .

It is perhaps mainly the readiness to include, accept, and even love differences and diversities, as contrasted with the need to set off clear demarcation lines and to ascertain superiorities and inferiorities, which remains as the most basic distinguishing criterion of the two opposite patterns. Members of an outgroup representing deviations from the cultural norms of the in-group are most threatening to one who must conceive of the cultural norms as absolute in order to be able to feel secure.

Commentary

The Authoritarian Personality is considered a classic of social science, albeit a controversial one. Sixty-eight years after its publication it is still a reference point for political psychology, and more broadly for closed-mindedness, prejudice, anti-Semitism, and ethnocentrism. Ongoing interest in this research and its premises, as well as the continuing controversy, led to a series of retrospective publications around the 40th- and 50th-year anniversaries of the publication (Martin, 2001; Roiser & Willig, 2002; Smith, 1997; Stone, Lederer, & Christie, 1993). Of the retrospective articles, one asserted that the major substantive findings held up well. A second argued that many of the original criticisms were misguided and, while appreciating the purpose and diagnosis of the original research, proposed the term "attitude" would be more appropriate than "personality." A third study argued that there is so much bias in the work that it should be considered the most deeply flawed work in political psychology. Since those publications, interest in *The Authoritarian Personality* only seems to have increased. The political climate in the early 21st century has led to more related research, some of which will be touched upon in these pages. Nevertheless, despite the controversy, the work has seen a considerable rehabilitation in recent years. A consensus seems to be emerging that while some aspects of the study were problematic and indeed flawed, which is perhaps not surprising for a pioneering study, *The Authoritarian Personality* continues to exert its influence and, perhaps more important, it continues to be generative. In these pages I will argue that one finding has been left almost unresearched or certainly vastly underresearched: the relationship between authoritarianism and creativity.

After initial acclaim and the subsequent critique following its publication in 1950, a number of factors militated against *The Authoritarian Personality*, which eventually led to its being largely dismissed and then ignored for several decades. The work is most often remembered for the F-scale (F for "prefascism"), which includes seven personality dimensions: anti-intraception, authoritarian aggression, authoritarian submission, conventionalism, power and toughness, religion and ethics, and superstition. The F scale was indeed the subject of heated methodological criticism (Stone et al., 1993). It's worth noting that in recent years a meta-analysis by Meloen (1993) indicates that while in some respects quite problematic, "the F scale has greater validity for measuring potential and actual fascism than is often assumed" (p. 68) and "the results of authoritarianism research have been strongly underestimated" (p. 69). While the F scale got most of the attention, the 990 pages of the full study contained much other fascinating material. The research involved extensive interviews—Frenkel-Brunswik summarizes them in the extract we have used here—as well as use of the Thematic Apperception Test, the Rorschach test, and "projective questions." Other scales were created besides the F scale, including scales for ethnocentrism, anti-Semitism, and political-economic conservatism.

A further criticism was that the study did not account for left-wing authoritarianism. This was a particularly sensitive issue because the work came out in 1950, in the middle of the McCarthy era. At this point communism was considered the real danger to the United States, not right-wing ideology or fascism. A work that did not address what was considered to be the clear and present danger of communism was consequently rather suspect (Jay, 1996; Wiggershaus, 1995). Rokeach's (1960) work *The Open and Closed Mind* was one significant attempt to address authoritarianism of the left. This was followed by suggestions that authoritarianism was an outdated concept in a postindustrial society, a view that sadly turned out to be mistaken (Roiser & Willig, 2002).

Reading *The Authoritarian Personality* today one is also struck by the now rather quaint-seeming psychoanalytic language and interpretive framework. This makes the work seem particularly dated to readers in the 21st century, perhaps more used to neuroscience as the dominant psychological language and interpretive framework. The use of assessments that have fallen out of favor, such as the Rorschach test, also gives the reader a sense that this research is of a distinctly different era. Nevertheless, in spite of or perhaps even because of this, the volume led to intriguing psychodynamic insights into the deeper psychological roots of authoritarianism.

A further setback for the study was the publication of Walter Mischel's (1968) *Personality and Assessment*, which delivered a powerful critique of personality-trait research and even personality psychology itself. Trait approaches, and even personality psychology as a whole, began to fall out of favor in the early 1970s, and Mischel's critique played a considerable role in this. While the IPAR creativity research addressed traits, the research was actually an attempt at "holistic assessment." Interviews were conducted by, among others, Erik Erikson, and live-in assessment gave the opportunity for observation in a variety of contexts.

It should also be noted that the authors of *The Authoritarian Personality* did not focus on personality to the *exclusion* of social factors. In his reflections on the authoritarian personality, Sanford (1973), one of the authors of the study, wrote:

> Since we assumed that action always depends upon the situation the person is in as well as upon personality, we referred to this structure as a *potential* for fascism, a *susceptibility* to anti-Semitic propaganda, a *readiness* to participate in antidemocratic social movements. (in Adorno et al., 1950, p. 142)

This is a much more nuanced view than the authors are often given credit for. Reviewing the research on authoritarianism and creativity, one may well ask if the quite nuanced perspectives offered by constellations of traits such as tolerance and intolerance of ambiguity, conformity and independence of judgment, and simplicity and complexity of outlook, for example, do not deserve to be revisited in greater depth, as they have been, for example, in recent studies in Italy (Lauriola, Foschi, & Marchegiani, 2015; Lauriola, Foschi, Mosca, & Weller, 2016).

Research on authoritarianism had a period of dormancy following the critiques of the original study of *The Authoritarian Personality*. What interest there was in the study survived in the relatively marginalized subdiscipline of political psychology. Renewed interest in authoritarianism and in the original study emerged in the 1980s, a period that saw a resurgence of ethnocentrism and authoritarianism, particularly in Europe. Since then, research on authoritarianism has once again become part of an attempt to understand the psychology of political events, with Altemeyer's (1981, 1988) work on updating the concept of authoritarianism to right-wing authoritarianism; Stone et al.'s (1993) important review of the original research, *Strength and Weakness: The Authoritarian Personality Today*; Stenner's (2005) *The Authoritarian Dynamic*; Hetherington and Weiler's (2009) *Authoritarianism and Polarization in American Politics*; and a substantial production of articles scattered across any number of journals, including such diverse publications as *Personality and Individual Differences, Assessment, Abstracts on Criminology and Penology, Journal of Mind and Behavior*, and *Futures*.

The important work of Kruglanski (2013; Kruglanski & Boyatzi, 2012) on closed-mindedness and of Jost and colleagues on ideology, conservatism, and system justification (Carney, Jost, Gosling, & Potter, 2008; Jost, Federico, & Napier, 2009; Jost, Glaser, Kruglanski, & Sulloway, 2003) represent just two examples of new research that traces its roots back to *The Authoritarian Personality*, even as they articulate differences. Interestingly, a review of efforts to map political ideology to personality concludes that the "underlying contents identified by diverse theorists and observers converge to a remarkable degree" (Carney et al., 2008, p. 809).

There continue to be many ongoing discussions about specific aspects of the research on authoritarianism, ideology, ethnocentrism, and the topics raised by the original work. One of the most important developments has been a shift toward viewing authoritarianism as a disposition that manifests itself in situation-specific circumstances, where the situation, and especially threat (or the perception of threat), plays a key role (Stenner, 2005). Hetherington and Weiler (2009, p. 110) write that threat can furthermore "actually reduce the difference in preferences between the more and less authoritarian rather than increase it," moving further away from the notion of authoritarianism as "a static personality characteristic" to a disposition that may be present in just about everybody to a greater or lesser degree, and that can be activated by threat.

CREATIVITY

There are still no extensive discussions of creativity in the new works on authoritarianism and the related works on conservatism, although this summary of the differences between liberals and conservatives once again tantalizingly refers to creativity: "In general, liberals are more open-minded, creative, curious, and novelty seeking, whereas conservatives are more orderly, conventional, and better organized" (Carney et al., 2008, pp. 807–808). Surveying the literature on authoritarianism, creativity researchers will also note the conventionalism, rigidity, and intolerance of ambiguity of authoritarians, the focus on order, and the rejection of the inner life and imagination as key characteristics that seem the very opposite of those found in creative individuals (Runco, 2007).

Conventionalism, conformity, and a focus on order are key dimensions of authoritarianism. The connection between conformity, as found in the Asch (1956) studies, and independence of judgment is clear. Barron's (1953) research on independence of judgment drew directly on Asch's research on conformity. In fact Barron contacted Asch to gain access to those 25 percent of Asch's subjects who had resisted the pressure to conform, in order to understand and articulate their independence of judgment. The conventionalism and conformism of authoritarianism, the hostility and punitiveness toward what is different, unconventional, and breaking with established social values is contrasted with the drive toward novelty, complexity, and difference in creative individuals.

Csikszentmihalyi (1997) summarized the creative personality in a series of "paradoxical" characteristics, showing that creative persons are both playful and disciplined, rebellious and conservative, humble and proud, and so on, illustrating what Barron and Harrington (1981) referred to as the integration of opposite or conflicting traits in self-concept found in creative individuals. The characteristics of authoritarian individuals seem to follow a disjunctive (either/or) logic. This leads to a clear split between such terms and the favoring of one term over the other, which in turn reflects a less complex personality and outlook on the world. Disjunctive logic plays a major role in predicting behaviors associated with right-wing radicalism (Lauriola et al., 2015). This was also one of the findings of the original authoritarian personality study, which discussed *stereotypy*, or the "tendency to think in rigid, oversimplified categories, in unambiguous terms of black and white, particularly in the realm of psychological or social matters" (Sanford, 1973).

Also worth noting is the disjunctive, indeed oppositional approach toward gender roles in the prejudiced, authoritarian personality. In another chapter of *The Authoritarian Personality* authored by Frenkel-Brunswik, she states that

> the conception of the masculine and feminine role, by men and women, the rigidity versus flexibility of the conception of these roles, and the intolerance versus tolerance toward tendencies of the opposite sex in oneself are of crucial importance for our problem since these attitudes tend to become generalized and projected into the social sphere. (in Adorno et al., 1950, p. 318)

Here we see two important points. One is viewing gender in terms of fixed oppositional roles in authoritarians and "the intolerance versus tolerance toward tendencies of the opposite sex in oneself," which lead to caricatured images of hypermasculine men and hyperfeminine women. We contrast this with the creative person, where Barron (1972, p. 33) writes:

> Those personality correlates generally ascribed to one sex or the other are much less pronounced in creative people. Creative women have fewer "feminine" traits and more "masculine" interests than noncreative control groups. Sex-specific interests and traits that are descriptive of men and women in general seem to break down when we examine creative people.

The relationship between psychological androgyny and creativity has found further support in more recent research (Hittner & Daniels, 2002; Norlander, Erixon, & Archer, 2000).

The second point is Frenkel-Brunswik's statement that "these attitudes tend to become generalized and projected into the social sphere," which specifically reflects the fact that a clear characteristic of authoritarian social systems is the polarization and hierarchization of gender roles, with women inevitably having subservient roles (Eisler, 1987). More broadly it points to the parallels between personality characteristics and the characteristics of social systems.

The related concept of ambiguity was introduced by Fromm (1941/1994) in his work on the authoritarian character. In 1949 Frenkel-Brunswik published an article on intolerance of ambiguity as an emotional and perceptual personality variable, defining intolerance of ambiguity as a "tendency to resort to black-white solutions, to arrive at premature closure as to valuative aspects, often at the neglect of reality, and to seek for unqualified and unambiguous overall acceptance and rejection of other people" (p. 115). Budner (1962, p. 29) usefully differentiated between intolerance of ambiguity and tolerance of ambiguity:

> Intolerance of ambiguity may be defined as "the tendency to perceive (i.e., interpret) ambiguous situations as sources of threat," tolerance of ambiguity as "the tendency to perceive ambiguous situations as desirable." An ambiguous situation may be defined as one which cannot be adequately structured or categorized by the individual because of the lack of sufficient cues.

Tolerance of ambiguity has long been associated with creativity (Runco, 2007; Sternberg & Lubart, 1991; Zenasni, Besançon, & Lubart, 2008) because creative persons find ambiguity and disorder desirable as a source of potential novelty, providing them with the opportunity to create their own interpretations (Barron, 1995). Piirto (2011) traces tolerance of ambiguity to John Keats's concept of *negative capability* and finds discussions that seem to describe tolerance of ambiguity in numerous writings by creative individuals.

Lauriola et al.'s (2016) research provides a nuanced understanding of what they refer to as "attitude toward ambiguity." This is a multidimensional construct involving affective (discomfort with ambiguity), cognitive (moral absolutism/splitting), and epistemic (need for complexity and novelty) components. The affective dimension reflects Budner's differentiation, with authoritarians perceiving ambiguous situations as a threat, and creatives viewing them as desirable. The cognitive dimension shows up in moral absolutism and black-and-white thinking. This dichotomizing is also a simplification and indicates a loss of nuance and complexity. One cannot, for example, conceive of a person as being both "good" and "bad," hence the frequent use of dramatic language and the use of terms such as "evil"

(Bernstein, 2005). It reduces human beings to a particular (unfavorable) quality which may well be in the eye of the beholder. This disjunctive logic leads to a form of unquestioning absolutism, a willingness to hold on to a specific and simplistic view of "rightness" at whatever cost, to the point that it becomes destructive. Sanford (1973, p. 142) discusses *The Authoritarian Personality*'s finding of *pseudoconservatism*, "in which profession of belief in the tenets of traditional conservatism is combined with a readiness for change of a sort that would destroy the very institutions with which the subject appears to identify himself." The epistemic dimension is also once again the opposite of characteristics found in creative individuals, such as a "need for cognition (e.g., engaging in and enjoying complex problems) and openness to experience (e.g., aesthetic sensitivity, novelty seeking, epistemic curiosity, liberal values)" (Lauriola et al., 2016, p. 15).

The need for cognitive closure is a related construct that has been defined as the desire to have an answer on any topic, any answer rather than confusion and ambiguity. Individuals with a high need for closure want definite order and structure in their lives and cannot bear unconstrained chaos and disorder (Kruglanski, 1990). Contrast this with Barron's (1995, p.63) findings that

> in the individuals whom in retrospect we identify as the bearers of the creative impulse in our generation there appears a positive preference for what we are accustomed to call disorder, but which to them is simply the possibility of a future order whose principle of organization cannot now be told.

Central to the authoritarian personality dynamic is "anti-introception," which involves a rejection of subjectivity, imagination, and self-awareness. Sanford (1973, p. 144) writes of the authoritarian, "Self-awareness might threaten his whole scheme of adjustment. He would be afraid of genuine feeling because his emotions might get out of control, afraid of thinking about human phenomena because he might think 'wrong' thoughts." Compare this with the description of the creative person, who "not only respects the irrational in himself, but courts it as the most promising source of novelty in his own thought" (Barron, 1995, p. 66). One way of describing a key difference is that authoritarians move away from what is new and different and unknown in the world as well as in themselves, whereas creative individuals actively seek out the new, the different, the unknown in themselves and in the world.

IMPLICATIONS

In comparing and contrasting authoritarian and creative persons, we see the emergence of two different personality dynamics and, more broadly, two worldviews. In the brief selection from Frenkel-Brunswik we find a portrait of the high scorer that includes repression, rigidity, a focus on strength versus weakness, social hierarchy, and projection. Frenkel-Brunswik's significant conclusion echoes research on the positive correlation between openness to experience and creativity (Kaufman, 2013; McCrae, 1987), as well as the inverse relationship between creativity and ethnocentrism (Barron, 1963). Frenkel-Brunswik writes:

> It is perhaps mainly the readiness to include, accept, and even love differences and diversities, as contrasted with the need to set off clear demarcation lines and to ascertain superiorities and inferiorities, which remains as the most basic distinguishing criterion of the two opposite patterns. (in Adorno et al., 1950, pp. 485–486)

In an age of increasing complexity and pluralism, with fears of terrorism, economic anxieties, nuclear conflicts, and environmental catastrophes, fear can activate the disposition toward authoritarianism even in those who are low scorers on a measure of authoritarianism. The recently renewed interest in authoritarianism comes in an age that has seen a rise in author-itarian leadership, ethnocentrism, anti-Semitism, xenophobia, and racism. Propaganda and mass media that foster fear and anxiety play a role in activating the authoritarian disposi-tion. There is a long history of the cultivation of an authoritarian response by political and economic interests seeking conformity and obedience through the creation of scapegoat out-groups, the threat of attack, and specific use of dichotomizing language (Lakoff, 2006, 2008; Montuori, 2005; Pratkanis & Aronson, 2001). We are also seeing how authoritari-anism can be activated by threat and how mass media can be used to create the impres-sion of a threat.

While the focus on authoritarianism and related problems is important, it is also nec-essary to understand the characteristics of people who are *not* authoritarian, who are less likely to be prejudiced and intolerant, those whom Frenkel-Brunswik describes as open to "accept, and even love differences and diversities," since we know differences and diversities are essential for creativity (Glăveanu & Beghetto, 2017). If the personal charac-teristics of creativity are generally the opposite of those of authoritarians, creativity research may offer an entry point to address the threat of authoritarianism at the intrapersonal, inter-personal, and more broadly social and political levels.

An obvious question at this point would be how some people who are identified as creative can also be authoritarian. Steve Jobs is a recent example of someone who was considered very creative but was also an authoritarian leader (Isaacson, 2011). The research on authoritarianism may shed some light on this. The original research by Adorno et al. (1950) pointed to the key role of *susceptibility to situational pressures* of authoritarianism, and we recall Sanford's (1973, p. 142) statement:

> Since we assumed that action always depends upon the situation the person is in as well as upon personality, we referred to this structure as a *potential* for fascism, a *sus-ceptibility* to anti-Semitic propaganda, a *readiness* to participate in antidemocratic social movements.

In other words, the role of the situation is part of a fundamental person-situation interac-tion, in which certain situations can trigger authoritarian responses, with certain individuals being more susceptible. The trend toward conceptualizing authoritarianism not as a static personality characteristic but rather as a *disposition* that can be triggered by situations of threat is relevant here (Stenner, 2005). We might view authoritarianism as a disposition on a spectrum of human responses, one that can be triggered by certain situations but might otherwise be dormant, even though some individuals might be more inclined to it than others. In the same way, certain domains as well as certain contexts may facilitate the creative disposition (e.g., during idea-generation in a chosen domain), whereas the imple-mentation and bringing to market of the idea in an organizational context, which may be fraught with problems and threats to success, might as a result be approached in a more authoritarian way. As was the case with many historically eminent creative individuals, there is a quite drastic difference for many in the creativity of their ideas in their specific domain, and the way they engage the world and other people specifically in the process of making that idea a reality, particularly because creative ideas often get pushback or are not under-stood, or because the implementation by others may not conform to the person's vision.

We can imagine a spectrum of human responses that range from authoritarianism to creativity. If we apply the concept of disposition to creativity, we can see how creativity research and the psychology of creativity outline a set of *human possibilities*, pointing to what all humans are potentially capable of but certainly currently not educated for (Robinson, 2001). This also ties in to the larger question of conceptions of human nature and of human capacities and possibilities (Richards, 2007). The findings of creativity research give us a more extended view of what humans are capable of. They defy the more Hobbesian view that human beings are fundamentally driven by a need for social dominance and dread uncertainty, complexity, and pluralism (Burton, 2008; Fine, 2017; Montuori, 2014). It should come as no surprise that Maslow (1959), one of the founders of humanistic psychology, argued that the self-actualized person and the creative person were essentially one and the same, and Barron (1963) titled one of his major works *Creativity and Psychological Health*. From our perspective, we might say that individuals who are mostly on the creative end of the spectrum as a result exhibit characteristics of self-actualization and psychological health.

The new emphasis on the social dimensions of creativity is also particularly relevant here and can counteract criticisms that existing research, centered on individuals, does not address the reality and specificity of *social* conflicts (Brown, 2010). Until fairly recently the social dimensions of creativity had been given less attention in the research. Creativity has also been viewed popularly primarily as an individual function, not as pertaining to the social world (the interpersonal or organizational domains; Glăveanu, 2011, 2014; Montuori, 2011). The challenge of creativity research, particularly in an age of increasing authoritarianism and social polarizations (Hetherington & Weiler, 2009), can also include addressing ways to develop social creativity as a practice of creative collaboration and creative leadership (Montuori & Donnelly, 2017). No longer limited to the generation of products by individuals, the challenge will be to explore the possibility of creating more generative forms of interaction and communication.

As an example, so-called diversity trainings in the US are generally failing because they mostly focus on the problems of racism and prejudice but fail to offer effective alternatives (Dobbin & Kalev, 2016; Montuori & Stephenson, 2010). If we have a good sense of the characteristics associated with authoritarianism and prejudice, would it not make sense to educate for the psychological characteristics of creativity, for openness, tolerance of ambiguity, independence of judgment, complexity of outlook, and so forth? We already know that travel and multicultural experiences can enhance creativity (Leung, Chen, & Chiu, 2011; Leung, Maddux, Galinsky, & Chiu, 2008), and that openness to experience and tolerance of ambiguity can be enhanced (Djikic, Oatley, & Moldoveanu, 2013; Leung & Chiu, 2008). If we can enhance individual creativity and develop the relational skills of creative collaboration, might we in the process also reduce authoritarianism and prejudice? Can we also begin to highlight the many ways in which diversity has creatively contributed to the arts, the sciences, and human culture in general?

We can also see the above-mentioned characteristics of creative individuals as relational. In our interactions with others, do we encourage their independence of judgment, do we approach interactions in a way that fosters mutual openness and tolerance of ambiguity? Do we foster complexity of outlook in our exchanges, do we constructively and creatively engage differences and diversities? Or do we fall back on either/or thinking, impose preexisting schemata and conformity, and remain unwilling to entertain ideas and possibilities? Can we begin to envision the implications and applications of the relational characteristics of creativity?

Could education for relational creativity begin to make different forms of creative contributions, not confined to creative products in the arts and sciences or to innovations in technology, but also developing more generative and less conflictual relationships and organizations (Glăveanu, 2012; Glăveanu, 2017; Montuori, 2011; Montuori & Donnelly, 2017)?

Could ways of increasing creativity not also be used, perhaps indirectly, to contribute to a reduction in authoritarianism, if creativity is viewed in this broader perspective? Could education in creativity and education for creative collaboration foster the development and appreciation of multiple perspectives, the ability to thrive on uncertainty, complexity, and pluralism, to appreciate differences and diversities, all so central to life in the 21st century? My hope is that this commentary will encourage a deeper exploration of these possibilities.

References

Adorno, T. W., Frenkel-Brunswik, E., Levinson, D. J., & Sanford, N. (1950). *The authoritarian personality*. New York: Harper & Row.

Altemeyer, B. (1981). *Right-wing authoritarianism*. Winnipeg: University of Manitoba Press.

Altemeyer, B. (1988). *Enemies of freedom: Understanding right-wing authoritarianism*. San Francisco: Jossey-Bass.

Asch, S. E. (1956). Studies of independence and conformity: A minority of one against a unanimous majority. *Psychological Monographs: General and Applied, 70*(9), 1–70.

Barron, F. (1953). Some personality correlates of independence of judgment. *Journal of Personality, 21*(3), 287–297.

Barron, F. (1963). *Creativity and psychological health: Origins of personal vitality and creative freedom*. Princeton, NJ: Van Nostrand.

Barron, F. (1968). *Creativity and personal freedom*. New York, NY: Van Nostrand.

Barron, F. (1969). *Creative person and creative process*. New York, NY: Holt, Rinehart & Winston.

Barron, F. (1972). *Artists in the making*. New York, NY: Academic.

Barron, F. (1995). *No rootless flower: Towards an ecology of creativity*. Cresskill, NJ: Hampton Press.

Barron, F., & Harrington, D. (1981). Creativity, intelligence, and personality. *Annual Review of Psychology, 32*, 439–476.

Bernstein, R. (2005). *The abuse of evil: Politics and religion after 9/11*. Malden, MA: Polity Press.

Brown, R. (2010). *Prejudice: Its social psychology*. Malden, MA: Wiley-Blackwell.

Budner, S. (1962). Intolerance of ambiguity as a personality variable. *Journal of Personality, 30*(1), 29–50.

Burton, R. A. (2008). *On being certain: Believing you're right even when you're not*. New York, NY: St. Martin's Press.

Carney, D. R., Jost, J. T., Gosling, S. D., & Potter, J. (2008). The secret lives of liberals and conservatives: Personality profiles, interaction styles, and the things they leave behind. *Political Psychology, 29*(6), 807–840.

Crutchfield, R. S. (1955). Conformity and character. *American Psychologist, 10*(5), 191–198.

Csikszentmihalyi, M. (1997). *Creativity: Flow and the psychology of discovery and invention*. New York, NY: Harper Collins.

Djikic, M., Oatley, K., & Moldoveanu, M. C. (2013). Opening the closed mind: The effect of exposure to literature on the need for closure. *Creativity Research Journal, 25*(2), 149–154.

Dobbin, F., & Kalev, A. (2016). Why diversity programs fail and what works better. *Harvard Business Review, 94*(7–8), 52–60.

Eisler, R. (1987). *The chalice and the blade*. San Francisco, CA: Harper Collins.

Fine, C. (2017). *Testosterone Rex: Myths of sex, science, and society*. New York, NY: Norton.

Frenkel-Brunswik, E. (1950). Comprehensive scores and summaries of the interview. In T. W. Adorno, E. Frenkel-Brunswik, D. J. Levinson, & R. N. Sanford (Eds.), *The authoritarian personality* (pp. 474–486). New York, NY: Harper & Row.

Fromm, E. (1941/1994). *Escape from freedom*. New York, NY: Holt.

Glăveanu, V. P. (2011). How are we creative together? Comparing sociocognitive and sociocultural answers. *Theory & Psychology, 21*(4), 473–492.

Glăveanu, V. P. (2012). From dichotomous to relational thinking in the psychology of creativity: A review of great debates. *Creativity and Leisure: An Intercultural and Cross-Disciplinary Journal, 1*(2), 83–96.

Glăveanu, V. P. (2014). *Distributed creativity: Thinking outside the box of the creative individual*. New York, NY: Springer.

Glăveanu, V. P. (2017). A culture-inclusive, socially engaged agenda for creativity research. *Journal of Creative Behavior, 51*(4), 338–340.

Glăveanu, V. P., & Beghetto, R. A. (2017). The difference that makes a "creative" difference in education. In R. A. Beghetto & B. Sriraman (Eds.), *Creative contradictions in education* (pp. 37–54). New York, NY: Springer.

Haney, C., Banks, W. C., & Zimbardo, P. G. (1973). A study of prisoners and guards in a simulated prison. *Naval Research Reviews, 9*, 1–17.

Hetherington, M. J., & Weiler, J. D. (2009). *Authoritarianism and polarization in American politics.* New York, NY: Cambridge University Press.

Hittner, J. B., & Daniels, J. R. (2002). Gender-role orientation, creative accomplishments and cognitive styles. *Journal of Creative Behavior, 36*(1), 62–75.

Isaacson, W. (2011). *Steve Jobs.* New York, NY: Simon & Schuster.

Jay, M. (1996). *The dialectical imagination: A history of the Frankfurt School and the Institute of Social Research, 1923–1950.* Berkeley: University of California Press.

Jost, J. T., Federico, C. M., & Napier, J. L. (2009). Political ideology: Its structure, functions, and elective affinities. *Annual Review of Psychology, 60*, 307–337.

Jost, J. T., Glaser, J., Kruglanski, A. W., & Sulloway, F. J. (2003). Political conservatism as motivated social cognition. *Psychological Bulletin, 129*(3), 339–375.

Kaufman, S. B. (2013). Opening up openness to experience: A four-factor model and relations to creative achievement in the arts and sciences. *Journal of Creative Behavior, 47*(4), 233–255.

Kruglanski, A. W. (1990). Motivations for judging and knowing: Implications for causal attribution. In E. T. Higgins & R. M. Sorrentino (Eds.), *Handbook of motivation and cognition: Foundations of social behavior* (pp. 333–368). New York, NY: Guilford Press.

Kruglanski, A. W. (2013). *The psychology of closed mindedness.* New York, NY: Psychology Press.

Kruglanski, A. W., & Boyatzi, L. M. (2012). The psychology of closed and open mindedness, rationality, and democracy. *Critical Review, 24*(2), 217–232.

Lakoff, G. (2006). *Whose freedom? The battle over America's most important idea.* New York, NY: Farrar, Straus and Giroux.

Lakoff, G. (2008). *The political mind: A cognitive scientist's guide to your brain and its politics.* New York, NY: Penguin.

Lauriola, M., Foschi, R., & Marchegiani, L. (2015). Integrating values and cognitive style in a model of right-wing radicalism. *Personality and Individual Differences, 75*, 147–153.

Lauriola, M., Foschi, R., Mosca, O., & Weller, J. (2016). Attitude toward ambiguity: Empirically robust factors in self-report personality scales. *Assessment, 23*(3), 353–373.

Leung, A. K., Chen, D., & Chiu, C. (2011). Multicultural experience fosters creative cognitive expansion. In A. K. Leung, C. Chiu, & Y. Hong (Eds.), *Cultural process: A social psychological perspective* (pp. 263–285). Cambridge, UK: Cambridge University Press.

Leung, A. K., & Chiu, C. (2008). Interactive effects of multicultural experiences and openness to experience on creative potential. *Creativity Research Journal, 20*(4), 376–382.

Leung, A. K., Maddux, W. W., Galinsky, A. D., & Chiu, C. (2008). Multicultural experience enhances creativity: The when and how. *American Psychologist, 63*(3), 169–181.

MacKinnon, D. W. (1962). The personality correlates of creativity: A study of American architects. In G. Nielson (Ed.), *Proceedings of the XIV International Congress of Applied Psychology.* Vol. 2: *Personality research* (pp. 11–39). Oxford: Munksgaard.

Martin, J. L. (2001). The authoritarian personality, 50 years later: What questions are there for political psychology? *Political Psychology, 22*(1), 1–26.

Maslow, A. (1959). Creativity in self-actualizing people. In H. H. Anderson (Ed.), *Creativity and its cultivation* (pp. 83–95). New York, NY: Harper & Row.

McCrae, R. R. (1987). Creativity, divergent thinking, and openness to experience. *Journal of Personality and Social Psychology, 52*(6), 1258–1265.

Meloen, J. D. (1993). The F scale as a predictor of fascism: An overview of 40 years of authoritarianism research. In W. F. Stone, G. Lederer, & R. Christie (Eds.), *Strength and weakness: The authoritarian personality today* (pp. 47–69). New York, NY: Springer-Verlag.

Milgram, S. (1963). Behavioral study of obedience. *Journal of Abnormal and Social Psychology, 67*(4), 371–378.

Mischel, W. (1968). *Personality and assessment.* New York, NY: Wiley.

Montuori, A. (1989). *Evolutionary competence: Creating the future.* Amsterdam: Gieben.

Montuori, A. (2005). How to make enemies and influence people: Anatomy of totalitarian thinking. *Futures, 37*, 18–38.

Montuori, A. (2011). Beyond postnormal times: The future of creativity and the creativity of the future. *Futures: The Journal of Policy, Planning and Future Studies, 43*(2), 221–227.

Montuori, A. (2014). Créativité et complexité en temps de crise [Creativity and complexity in times of crisis]. *Communications, 95*(2), 179–198.

Montuori, A., & Donnelly, G. (2017). Transformative leadership. In J. Neal (Ed.), *Handbook of personal and organizational transformation* (pp. 1–33). New York, NY: Springer.

Montuori, A., & Stephenson, H. (2010). Creativity, culture contact, and diversity. *World Futures: The Journal of General Evolution, 66*(3), 266–285.

Norlander, T., Erixon, A., & Archer, T. (2000). Psychological androgyny and creativity: Dynamics of gender-role and personality trait. *Social Behavior and Personality, 28*(15), 423–435.

Piirto, J. (2011). *Creativity for 21st century skills.* New York, NY: Springer Science & Business Media.

Pratkanis, A. R., & Aronson, E. (2001). *Age of propaganda: The everyday use and abuse of persuasion.* New York, NY: Macmillan.

Richards, R. (Ed.) (2007). *Everyday creativity and new views of human nature: Psychological, social, and spiritual perspectives.* New York, NY: American Psychological Association Press.

Robinson, K. (2001). *Out of our minds: Learning to be creative.* London: Capstone.

Roiser, M., & Willig, C. (2002). The strange death of the authoritarian personality: 50 years of psychological and political debate. *History of the Human Sciences, 15*(4), 71–96.

Rokeach, M. (1960). *The open and closed mind.* New York, NY: Basic Books.

Rubinstein, G. (2003). Authoritarianism and its relation to creativity: A comparative study among students of design, behavioral sciences and law. *Personality and Individual Differences, 34*(4), 695–705.

Runco, M. (2007). *Creativity. Theories and themes: Research, development, and practice.* Amsterdam: Elsevier.

Sanford, N. (1973). Authoritarian personality in contemporary perspective. In J. Knutson (Ed.), *Handbook of political psychology* (pp. 139–170). San Francisco, CA: Jossey-Bass.

Serraino, P. (2016). *The creative architect: Inside the great midcentury personality study.* New York, NY: Monacelli Press.

Sherif, M. (1958). Superordinate goals in the reduction of intergroup conflict. *American Journal of Sociology, 63,* 349–356.

Sherif, M., Harvey, O. J., White, B. J., Hood, W. R., & Sherif, C. W. (1961). *Intergroup cooperation and conflict: The robbers cave experiment.* Norman: University of Oklahoma Press.

Smith, M. B. (1997). The Authoritarian Personality: A re-review 46 years later. *Political Psychology, 18*(1), 159–163.

Stenner, K. (2005). *The authoritarian dynamic.* Cambridge, UK: Cambridge University Press.

Sternberg, R. J., & Lubart, T. I. (1991). Creating creative minds. *Phi Delta Kappan, 72*(8), 608–614.

Stone, W. F., Lederer, G., & Christie, R. (1993). *Strength and weakness: The authoritarian personality today.* New York, NY: Springer Verlag.

Wiggershaus, R. (1995). *The Frankfurt School: Its history, theories, and political significance.* Cambridge, MA: MIT Press.

Zenasni, F., Besançon, M., & Lubart, T. (2008). Creativity and tolerance of ambiguity: An empirical study. *Journal of Creative Behavior, 42*(1), 61–73.

Zimbardo, P. G. (2007). *Lucifer effect.* New York, NY: Wiley.

PART ELEVEN

Critical Reflections

32

The Recurring Challenge of Nietzsche

MICHAEL HANCHETT HANSON

Summary

Friedrich Nietzsche was a crucial figure in the development of creativity as a psychological, existential, and individualistic concept. In the parable of the madman Nietzsche described the challenge of living in a world without an overarching teleology or the possibility of transcendence, a world of infinite and uncertain potential. He described this challenge as "the death of God." This dramatic passage grounds a larger argument against nihilism within *The Joyful Wisdom* (1882/1910). Developing themes that grew out of his early work on tragedy, Nietzsche's call for joyful engagement with life was not reliant on optimism or on denial of anxiety and fear. The joy was possible *because* of unfathomable stakes, anxiety, and fear. Much has changed in the concept of creativity since Nietzsche wrote. Emerging debates about the ethics of creativity, the dark sides of creativity, and the distribution of creativity run counter to basic Nietzschean themes. Even so, fundamental aspects of Nietzsche's view of life remain relevant. Indeed the overall development of our concepts of creativity, including some of the very "un-Nietzschean" themes, may make his call to joy as a response to nihilism all the *more* relevant.

Introduction

Friedrich Nietzsche's parable of the madman powerfully evokes the uncertainty and urgency that has characterized the history of the concept of creativity. That is no accident. Nietzsche was a crucial figure in the development of creativity as a psychological, existential, and individualistic concept (Cropley, 2010; Hanchett Hanson, 2015; Mason, 2003; Weiner, 2000). That influence is particularly evident in the book in which the parable appears, *The Joyful Wisdom* (1882/1910, translated elsewhere as *The Gay Science*). There Nietzsche presented a paean to life itself. In the process he laid cornerstones for several aspects of today's concept of creativity. *The Joyful Wisdom* begins and ends with poems. There (as elsewhere) Nietzsche held up the artist as an exemplar of human existence. There he advised risk taking: "The secret of realising the largest productivity and the greatest enjoyment of existence is *to live in danger!*" (para. 283). There he encouraged questioning of all certainties, including those of science, while extolling passion in the pursuit of knowledge. There he also described the "death of God."

Some readers may be familiar with the parable of the madman primarily as a description of the death of God. That headline can be misleading, for Nietzsche was not critiquing religion in this passage. He did that with gusto elsewhere, including passages of *The Joyful Wisdom*. In the parable, however, he was describing a related, deep, and psychological phenomenon: the challenge of living in a world without belief in an overarching teleology or the possibility of transcendence. There was no escape from the uncertainties of life to "God's will" or to "progress" or to faith in the ultimate triumph of the "good" or the "true."

This parable grounds a longer line of thinking in *The Joyful Wisdom*. Passages that come before set up the challenges described in the parable. Those that come after respond to anticipated criticism from mystic, religious, and philosophic perspectives. For example, consider just the two passages that immediately precede the parable: "Knowledge More than a Means" (para. 123) and "In the Horizon of the Infinite" (para. 124). As implied by its title, the first argues that the passion for knowledge is an end in itself. Science can continue as merely instrumental problem-solving or even as a kind of leisure, the "scientific impulse" as "ennui." Even in antiquity—often a source of inspiration for Nietzsche—the passion for knowledge was simply a means to virtue. Here Nietzsche argues for "something new in history": passion for knowledge as an intrinsic value. This passage is instructive as a preface to the parable. Living with unlimited potential in a world without a predefined teleology leaves mere human life disoriented at its foundation and without inherent value. Confronting the enormity of the stakes and impossibility of the situation—its association with madness—constitutes the challenge. Nietzsche's response, though, is not can-do optimism about problem-solving (knowledge as means). This is not a problem to be solved at all but a condition to be recognized. And there can be no easy answers, no return to the days of piety. The next passage makes that clear.

"In the Horizon of the Infinite" presents two metaphors: a ship on the ocean and a bird away from land. With both, Nietzsche argues that society has not just left the moorings of solid land, but has also destroyed the land. This irrevocable departure from the beliefs of the past has left us afloat on an ocean of terrifying infinity. Then comes "The Madman" passage, with its uncertainty about who is right and who is wrong, mad or sane, its maelstrom of complex forces and unfathomable challenges, and its long view of the emerging consciousness of the profundity of change that has already taken place.

Reading: "Parable of the Madman"

Source: Nietzsche, F. (1882/1910) *The joyful wisdom (La gaya scienza)* (T. Common, Trans.). In O. Levy (Ed.), *The complete works of Friedrich Nietzsche*. Vol. 10. London: T. N. Foulis. (Original published in German as *Die fröhliche Wissenschaft*.) Work in the public domain.

The Madman.—Have you ever heard of the madman who on a bright morning lighted a lantern and ran to the market-place calling out unceasingly: "I seek God! I seek God!"—As there were many people standing about who did not believe in God, he caused a great deal of amusement. Why! is he lost? said one. Has he strayed away like a child? said another. Or does he keep himself hidden? Is he afraid of us? Has he taken a sea-voyage? Has he emigrated?—the people cried out laughingly, all in a hubbub. The insane man jumped into their midst and transfixed them with his glances. "Where is God gone?" he called out. "I mean to tell you! *We have killed him,*—you and I! We are all his murderers! But how have we done it? How were we able to drink up the sea? Who gave us the sponge to wipe away the whole horizon? What did we do when we loosed this earth from its sun? Whither does it now move? Whither do we move? Away from all suns? Do we not dash on unceasingly? Backwards, sideways, forwards, in all directions? Is there still an above and below? Do we not stray as through infinite nothingness? Does not empty space breathe upon us? Has it not become colder? Does not night come on continually, darker and darker? Shall we not have to light lanterns in the morning? Do we not hear the noise of the grave-diggers who are burying God? Do we not smell the divine putrefaction—for even Gods putrefy! God is dead! God remains dead! And we have killed him! How shall we console ourselves, the most murderous of all murderers? The holiest and the mightiest that the world has hitherto possessed, has bled to death under our knife,—who will wipe the blood from us? With what water could we cleanse ourselves? What lustrums, what sacred games shall we have to devise? Is not the magnitude of this deed too great for us? Shall we not ourselves have to become Gods, merely to seem worthy of it? There never was a greater event,—and on account of it, all who are born after us belong to a higher history than any history hitherto!"—Here the madman was silent and looked again at his hearers; they also were silent and looked at him in surprise. At last he threw his lantern on the ground, so that it broke in pieces and was extinguished. "I come too early," he then said, "I am not yet at the right time. This prodigious event is still on its way, and is traveling—it has not yet reached men's ears. Lightning and thunder need time, the light of the stars needs time, deeds need time, even after they are done, to be seen and heard. This deed is as yet further from them than the furthest star,—*and yet they have done it!*"—It is further stated that the madman made his way into different churches on the same day, and there intoned his *Requiem aeternam deo.* When led out and called to account, he always gave the reply: "What are these churches now, if they are not the tombs and monuments of God?"

Commentary

I teach graduate students in education, many of them already teachers. Most come to my psychology classes on creativity theories with urgent passion, wanting "to make my students creative." Over the years I have learned that their passion is not so much to teach people how to tackle hard problems or to identify what kinds of people do creative work or under what conditions, though they appreciate creativity research on these questions. The teachers in my classes bring more passion to the question of creativity than, say, critical thinking because they want students to have an inherent and resilient sense of their value. Creativity rhetoric has sometimes promised this, and existential questions haunt many branches of creativity research. In practice, though, the psychology of creativity has subjugated the very psychological question of sense of inherent human value to concerns with the outcomes of fame, fortune, social advancement, and economic growth. In this context, I find returning to Nietzsche inspiring and thought-provoking.

The philosopher and Nietzsche scholar Walter Kaufmann (1975) contended that existentialism is unthinkable without Nietzsche. Jaspers, Heidegger, and Sartre built directly and explicitly on Nietzsche. Kaufmann also noted, however, that Nietzsche was not himself an existentialist. Although we cannot imagine Thomism without Aristotle, "to call Nietzsche existentialist is a little like calling Aristotle a Thomist" (p. 22). The same might be said of Nietzsche's relation to current concepts of creativity. It is hard to imagine today's concept of creativity without Nietzsche, but his views were not the same as those that prevail today. In addition, his influence on existential philosophy has been part of his influence on creativity.

Nietzsche wrote during the second industrial revolution in Europe. Communication and travel technologies had shrunk time and space. More and more new material luxuries were available, and belief in progress was widespread. It was an optimistic society (Kaufmann, 1974). But something was amiss. Like Kierkegaard, Dostoyevsky, and, later, Heidegger, Nietzsche diagnosed a crisis of meaning that accompanied Modernity. For the individual subject, uncertainty concerning self, meaning, and value lay in all directions. Along with the supposed signs of progress, science had upended European worldviews in many ways and was advancing at an ever-accelerating pace. Religion, intended to give life meaning, had lost relevance, and industrialization had added social upheaval to the mix. The result was the nihilism that Nietzsche tried to redress throughout his career, a situation he defined as society's highest values devaluating themselves so that "the aim is lacking; 'why?' finds no answer" (1901/1968, para. 1-2). At the heart of Nietzsche's critique of Christianity, for example, was the point that this religion meant to give meaning to life actually rejected life in favor of an imagined hereafter.

Unlike other existentially oriented thinkers (e.g., Kierkegaard 1846/1974), Nietzsche would not return to religious faith as an answer, no matter how existentially conceived. Nor would he replace God with science as a basis of faith. Instead he insisted in continual questioning of beliefs—those of others as well as his own. Nietzsche's imperatives were to *create* our own worldviews and to *become* who we are. He extolled the ability to turn pain and anxiety into art. He concerned himself with the relation between fate and self-creation, and he called for individualism, self-expression, and risk taking. Sound familiar?

Yet Nietzsche's thought cannot be equated to today's views of creativity as the solution to almost all problems: the answer to personal problems, artistic expression, and economic success (see, e.g., Alayarian, 2007; Booth, 2001; Maslow, 1954/1970; Rogers, 1954, 1961/1989); a key to educational policy (e.g., Beghetto & Kaufman 2010; Robinson, 2011); the the driving force of business growth, economic health, and international competition (e.g., Guilford, 1950; Sawyer, 2007; Wright, Woock, & Lichtenberg, 2008). Indeed the psychological endeavor to make creativity a proven solution with predictable outcomes and formulaic processes is just the kind of science-as-faith Nietzsche critiqued. Pick up any article or book on creativity and there will almost always be an opening invocation of our newly minted god: creativity itself. What the author is about to argue is urgently important, necessary, and unquestionably good. We might say, blessed and inspired. Occasionally the invocation is presumed: no one would question the need for change, more new ideas, products, lifestyles, mores, and so on. Usually the invocation is a few paragraphs long. Sometimes it goes on for pages, complete with a hagiography of the luminaries in whose images we hope to remake ourselves and all of humanity. The invocation is a common protocol, reflecting widespread beliefs (Hanchett Hanson, 2015). It is used by serious and interesting thinkers, not just intellectual hacks.

This critique of our unquestioned exuberance for creativity may take a polemical tone but is not original, even within creativity research. Todd Lubart (1999) has noted that across cultures, ideas of creativity tend to be tied to religious mythologies. Arthur Cropley (2010, p. 2) has observed, "This tone of almost religious fervor was already present at the beginning of the creativity era [mid-20th century]."

In a similar vein and with considerable detail, the intellectual historian John Hope Mason (2003) has traced the development of creativity as a value in Europe over the course of the 19th century. He found that this value changed dramatically, as a wholly optimistic view of creativity eclipsed an alternative view of it as dangerous. Mason describes these competing valuations of creativity as outgrowths of two deeply rooted traditions. One reflected the myth of Prometheus bringing fire to humanity, a bold act that would change the course of history but also bring almost certain pain and suffering (the subsequent punishment of Prometheus by Zeus). Mary Shelley's (1818/2008) *Frankenstein: Or, The Modern Prometheus* conveyed that view. Any creativity researcher who has read the original novel must be struck by Shelley's description of Dr. Frankenstein's frenzied drive to achieve his creation, his absolute concentration in the task leading him to neglect other duties and social connections. This absorption in creative work is, in effect, what Csikszentmihalyi (1990) would describe and vigorously promote in the later 20th century as "flow." The creation—the "monster"—was scared and lonely, but its creator rejected and abandoned it. Mason reminds us that a theme running throughout Shelley's novel is the self-absorption of the creator Victor Frankenstein, the results of his lack of social connection and moral compass.

The other tradition that Mason identifies was based on the Christian story of creation and Neo-Platonic philosophy. In contrast to the Promethean tradition, the Neo-Platonic would align creativity unequivocally *with* ethics, an inherent good that, then, would not require ethical critique. One of the most famous uses of the verb *create* is the biblical story of creation at the beginning of the Book of Genesis. There God's creation is declared "good." The Neo-Platonic creative tradition did not need to be explicitly religious, however. It simply and unequivocally aligned the creative with the beautiful, good, harmonious, and spiritual. Mason cites Coleridge, Carlyle, Arnold, and Marx as 19th-century examples of this tradition.

There were many literary, philosophical, and popular culture figures who contributed to the evolution of the idea of creativity in Mason's analysis. Nietzsche, however, plays a particularly important role as the most developed articulation of the Promethean tradition. In Nietzsche the imperative to creativity is not an *answer* to problems but the basis for engaging life itself—an always dangerous achievement of being, not a resolution. This is, after all, a foundation of existential philosophy, not pragmatism, utilitarianism, socialism, or capitalism. In Nietzsche creativity is not the result of happiness or play but the aesthetic product of suffering. And creativity is *not* good but always, necessarily amoral. Mason reminds us that, even today, sections of Nietzsche concerning the necessity of domination, cruelty, and slavery are morally shocking.

Still, it is not hard to imagine how we could get from Nietzsche's writing to today's rhetoric. The study of creativity has been marked by individualism. The idea that creativity is something inside individuals that distinguishes them dominated the field until the later 20th century and is still fundamental to many theories of creativity. Until rather recently the assumption that creativity is *not* an ethical question has dominated the discourse (Moran, 2014). In addition, existential themes run through many psychological theories of creativity (Hanchett Hanson, 2015). Sometimes those links are explicit and sometimes not. For the humanistic psychologists the link was explicit. Carl Rogers (1961/1989) quoted Kierkegaard: "to be that self which one truly is"; his colleague Abraham Maslow (1954/ 1970) quoted Nietzsche: "Become what thou art." Rogers (1954, 1961/1989) placed great emphasis on creativity as part of "becoming a person." Similarly Maslow (1943/2013) linked the pinnacle of his hierarchy of needs, self-actualization, with creativity from the beginning. Maslow also reflected some of Nietzsche's more shocking stances. Nietzsche juxtaposed master morality to slave morality. The latter was constrained by the moral percepts of Christianity, but master morality was not. Maslow (1954/1970) argued that self-actualized people did not conform to the morality of others because the self-actualized were superior, and he called for the general development of a superior form of human, a "Heraclitan" (1971/1993, p. 57), based on creativity. Both Rogers and Maslow cited existential philosophy as inspiration for aspects of their theories, but they drew from many sources. Their colleague Rollo May (1974) built more centrally on existentialism. He described creativity as an anxiety-ridden confrontation with one's worlds, an *encounter* in which the creator and the world come into being.

We see this idea of encounter in other theorists as well with similar existential implications. For example, Howard Gruber (1981, 1989) extended the systemic developmental principles of his mentor Jean Piaget to the lifelong development of creativity. In Gruber's analysis, however, the creator is not following a normative developmental path, as Piaget had identified for children. The creative person is not intrinsically different from other people or simply responding to conditions that foster creativity. Instead the creator purposefully *becomes* who he or she is through work. The painter becomes a painter by painting, the writer by writing, etc. Reflecting Nietzsche's argument that pursuit of knowledge is an end in itself rather than just a means, Gruber and Wallace (1999, p. 109) noted that "the creator sets him- or herself problems in order to think. The creator is not necessarily a better problem solver." Building both on Gruber and on sociocultural theories, Vlad Glăveanu (2014) also uses the idea of the creative encounter in a way very similar to May. In Glăveanu's view of creativity as a form of distributed cognition, the creative encounter is always multidimensional. Creative agency is achieved through material and social interactions over time.

In spite of the existential themes, however, Mason would probably describe all of these creativity theories as variations within the Neo-Platonic tradition. Most of them viewed creativity as an unqualified good, not just existentially but pragmatically and socially. The humanistic idea of self-actualization was not described as dangerous, but seen as wholly and unquestionably positive for individuals and society as a whole. Gruber also saw creativity as inherently good. May's existential framework and Glăveanu's cultural approach recognize dangers inherent in creative work, but their rhetoric still skews positive, emphasizing pragmatic needs for creativity.

In summary, Nietzsche promoted a bold and individualistic view of creativity and helped lay the foundations for existential thought that would then influence creativity theories. In particular, in the parable of the madman he described the challenges of living in a truly unpredictable world, without the assurance of any historical and/or divine teleology. But why go back to read the parable or any of Nietzsche's ideas at this point?

Going back to the roots of our concepts of creativity may inspire deeper thinking and a greater awareness of both the implications and the affordances of those concepts. To that end, Nietzsche is particularly helpful. Although he developed themes across his works, he was not presenting a systemic philosophical view. Instead his aphoristic style was designed to shock the reader into thought. This parable remains thought-provoking. It is uncompromising. The psychological maelstrom described is untenable, and there is no retreat. The one who sees the situation is mad. The rest are blind to the nihilism they have created. To this crisis Nietzsche offers no ultimate solution, no system of philosophy or new god. Instead he simply presents the parable. In reference to it, Kaufmann (1974, p. 110) argued, "Nietzsche believed that to overcome nihilism, we must first of all recognize it." He was raising a question that people of his day and our own may need to ask and want to ask but seldom do. Current concepts of creativity as problem-solving are important—very important—but such instrumental views cannot pretend to answer Nietzsche's question "Why?" When the ultimate fulfillment of human life is linked to creativity as a path to a play-filled life of wealth and fame; when that is the goal of human development, education, and social life—we have stumbled back into the nihilism Nietzsche so feared.

Although Nietzsche may simply have been trying to force recognition of a profound question, he believed that the stance we take in that recognition is crucial. The parable was part of *The Joyful Wisdom*. The challenge was not just to face the terrifying nature of reality and the threat of nihilism. The challenge was to face the unfathomable and intractable with a sense of joy—a joy possible *because* of the extraordinary stakes, not in denial of them. This stance would be developed further in his later work, particularly in his "formula for greatness in a human being": to love one's fate, *amor fati*. That imperative was to "not merely bear what is necessary, still less conceal it—all idealism is mendaciousness in the face of what is necessary—but *love* it" (Nietzsche, 1908/1967, p. 258).

This view of fate was then linked to Nietzsche's call for creativity. As the philosopher and scholar Joan Stambaugh (1994, p. 84) has explained, "Nietzsche, as perhaps no other before him, discovered and expressed the paradox that one can create nothing new unless one affirms what is already there. And this 'already-there-ness,' this given-ness is what he means by fate." The imperative *amor fati* also extended to Nietzsche's famous idea of *eternal recurrence*. He contended that people should so love life in all of its aspects that, if told that they would eternally, again and again, relive their life exactly as it was, it would be joyous news. Eternal recurrence is both an absolute rejection of transcendence and a challenge to every moment lived, an ability to create one's life that can come only from being firmly, unconditionally, and joyfully committed to life as it is in its entirety.

Highlighting Nietzsche's view of the challenge of living with nonteleological change can bring into question our own views and attitudes. This should not be an exercise in nostalgia, however. The point is not to return to origins. At the end of Mason's (2003) book *The Value of Creativity* he describes false assumptions in today's concepts of creativity, including Nietzsche's view of the individual as living in worlds of his or her own making, free of social and natural constraints. We have good reasons to see meaning, including the meaning of the self, as inherently social. Why go back to an extreme individualism when such ideology has produced its own forms of alienation and social disorientation while promoting consumerism and fame (Weiner, 2000), not just the artistic spirits Nietzsche idealized? In addition, the growing discourses around ethics and creativity (e.g., Moran, Cropley, & Kaufman, 2014) and the dark sides of creativity (e.g., Cropley, Cropley, Kaufman, & Runco, 2010) are not likely to roll back. On one hand, so much of the justification for creativity has been based on promises of progress from change, but the impacts of innovations have been far from entirely positive on social class, child development, economic systems, or the ecology. On the other, pointing out the dangers of creativity brings into question the teleology of progress that has been common in creativity rhetoric. Sociocultural views of creativity as a form of social judgment (e.g., Csikszentmihalyi, 1999) are not likely to disappear. Neither are developmental and distributed theories (e.g., Clapp, 2017; Glăveanu,

2014, Gruber & Wallace, 1999; Hanchett Hanson, 2015; Sawyer & DeZutter, 2009) that see creativity as complex and contextual rather than normative or formulaic.

Indeed some of these discourses reflect the very spirit of critique that characterizes Nietzsche. In addition, all of the research and theorizing on creativity since Nietzsche have not changed the central challenge. Relinking creativity to ethics makes the problems of uncertainty *more complex*—much more complex—not less. Once we admit the ethical implications of the many roles people take up in the integration of novelty over long periods of time with continually changing, unpredictable outcomes—as reflected in sociocultural and distributed views of creativity—the lack of moorings that Nietzsche describes gain new immediacy.

Moreover these emerging questions within creativity theory strike at the foundations of the concept of creativity as a problem-solving panacea. Such questions led the creativity researcher and historian Robert Paul Weiner (2000) to ask what comes "beyond creativity." Mason ends his book on the history of the concept with a similar query. Whether we continue our exuberant enthusiasm for creativity or move beyond it, the threat of nihilism is likely to remain. The basic challenge Nietzsche defines will, then, also remain: Can we live in joy without "creativity" as a knee-jerk answer to assuage our anxieties about who we are and what the future holds? The madman said that he had come too soon. The very people who had embraced the uncertainty of living in a world without an overarching teleology did not yet understand the implications of their situation. Since they could not see the current situation, they were in no position to create a future without nihilism. Do we see more clearly now? Or is it still too soon?

References

Alayarian, A. (2007). Trauma, resilience and creativity. In A. Alayarian (Ed.), *Resilience, suffering and creativity: The work of the refugee therapy center* (pp. 1–13). London: Karnac Books.

Beghetto, R. A., & Kaufman, J. C. (Eds.) (2010). *Nurturing creativity in the classroom.* Cambridge, UK: Cambridge University Press.

Booth, E. (2001). *The everyday work of art: Awakening the extraordinary in your daily life.* Lincoln, NE: iUniverse.com.

Clapp, E. P. (2017). *Participatory creativity: Introducing access and equity to the creative classroom.* New York, NY: Routledge.

Cropley, A. J. (2010). The dark side of creativity: What is it? In D. H. Cropley, A. J. Cropley, J. C. Kaufman, and M. A. Runco (Eds.), *The dark side of creativity* (pp. 1–14). Cambridge, UK: Cambridge University Press.

Cropley, D. H., Cropley, A. J., Kaufman, J. C., & Runco M. A. (Eds.) (2010). *The dark side of creativity.* Cambridge, UK: Cambridge University Press.

Csikszentmihalyi, M. (1990). *Flow: The psychology of optimal experience.* New York, NY: Harper & Row.

Csikszentmihalyi, M. (1999). Implications of a systems perspective for the study of creativity. In R. J. Sternberg (Ed.), *Handbook of creativity* (pp. 313–335). Cambridge, UK: Cambridge University Press.

Glăveanu, V. P. (2014). *Distributed creativity: Thinking outside the box of the creative individual.* New York, NY: Springer.

Guilford, J. P. (1950). Creativity. *American Psychologist, 5,* 444–454.

Gruber, H. E. (1981). *Darwin on man: A psychological study of scientific creativity* (2nd ed.). Chicago, IL: University of Chicago Press.

Gruber, H. E. (1989). The evolving systems approach to creative work. In D. B. Wallace & H. E. Gruber (Eds.), *Creative people at work* (pp. 3–22). Oxford: Oxford University Press.

Gruber, H. E., & Wallace, D. B. (1999). The case study method and evolving systems approach for understanding unique creative people at work. In R. J. Sternberg (Ed.), *Handbook of creativity* (pp. 93–115). Cambridge, UK: Cambridge University Press.

Hanchett Hanson, M. (2015) *Worldmaking: Psychology and the ideology of creativity*. London: Palgrave Macmillan.

Kaufmann, W. (1974) *Nietzsche: Philosopher, psychologist, antichrist* (4th ed.). Princeton, NJ: Princeton University Press.

Kaufmann, W. (1975). *Existentialism from Dostoevsky to Sartre*. London: Plume.

Kierkegaard, S. (1846/1974). *Concluding unscientific postscript* (D. F. Swenson and W. Lowrie, Trans.). Princeton, NJ: Princeton University Press.

Lubart, T. I. (1999). Creativity across cultures. In R. J. Sternberg (Ed.), *Handbook of creativity* (pp. 339–350). Cambridge, UK: Cambridge University Press.

Maslow, A. H. (1943/2013). *A theory of human motivation*. Mansfield Centre, CT: Martino.

Maslow, A. H. (1954/1970). *Motivation and personality*. New York, NY: Harper & Row.

Maslow, A. H. (1971/1993). *The farther reaches of human nature*. New York, NY: Penguin Books.

Mason, J. H. (2003). *The value of creativity: The origins and emergence of a modern belief*. Burlington, VT: Ashgate.

May, R. (1974). *The courage to create*. New York, NY: Norton.

Moran, S. (2014). Introduction: The crossroads of creativity and ethics. In S. Moran, D. Cropley, & J. C. Kaufman (Eds.), *The ethics of creativity* (pp. 1–22). New York, NY: Palgrave Macmillan.

Moran, S., Cropley, D., & Kaufman, J. C. (Eds.) (2014). *The ethics of creativity*. New York, NY: Palgrave Macmillan.

Nietzsche, F. (1882/1910) *The joyful wisdom ('La gaya scienza')* (T. Common, Trans.). In O. Levy (Ed.), *The complete works of Friedrich Nietzsche*. Vol. 10. London: T. N. Foulis. (Original published in German as *Die fröhliche Wissenschaft*)

Nietzsche, F. (1901/1968). *The will to power* (W. Kaufmann & R. J. Hollingdale, Trans.). New York, NY: Vintage Books.

Nietzsche, F. (1908/1967). *Ecce homo* (W. Kaufmann, Trans.). In *On the genealogy of morals and Ecce homo*. New York, NY: Vintage Books.

Rogers, C. R. (1954). Toward a theory of creativity. *Review of General Semantics, 11*(4), 249–260.

Rogers, C. R. (1961/1989). *On becoming a person: A therapist's view of psychotherapy*. New York, NY: Houghton Mifflin.

Robinson, K. (2011). *Out of our minds: Learning to be creative* (rev. ed.). Chichester, West Sussex, UK: Capstone.

Sawyer, R. K. (2007). *Group genius: The creative power of collaboration*. New York, NY: Basic Books.

Sawyer, R. K., & DeZutter, S. (2009). Distributed creativity: How collective creations emerge from collaboration. *Psychology of Aesthetics, Creativity, and the Arts, 3*(2), 81–92.

Shelley, M. (1818/2008). *Frankenstein: Or, the modern Prometheus*. Oxford: Oxford World Classics.

Stambaugh, J. (1994). *The other Nietzsche*. Albany: State University of New York Press.

Weiner, R. P. (2000). *Creativity and beyond: Cultures, values and change*. Albany: State University of New York Press.

Wright, M., Woock, C., & Lichtenberg, J. (2008). *Ready to innovate: Are educators and executives aligned on the creative readiness of the U.S. workforce?* New York, NY: Conference Board.

33

Introducing New Voices to the Creativity Studies Conversation

W. E. B. Du Bois, Double-Consciousness, and *The Souls of Black Folk*

Edward P. Clapp

Summary

This chapter makes the case that the development of the field of creativity studies has largely been based on a conversation among educated, middle- and upper-middle-class white people.[1] As a result, the field can best be understood as a scholarly domain (and associated educational practices) that is biased toward the said aspects of dominant white culture. Having made this assertion, this chapter then asks, How can we shift the dominant narrative in the field of creativity studies to better include nondominant voices? By reviewing an excerpt from W. E. B. Du Bois's (1903) landmark book *The Souls of Black Folk*, this chapter aims to do two things: first, to symbolically introduce creativity studies to Du Bois; second, to leverage Du Bois's concept of *double-consciousness* to explore the conflict in meaning making that may be experienced by students from nondominant cultures when they engage with the research, pedagogical frameworks, and policy agendas associated with creativity studies and creativity in education initiatives.

1. The author would like to thank Janine de Novais, Vlad Glăveanu, and Raquel L. Jimenez for their feedback and support on previous drafts of this essay. Correspondence regarding this essay should be addressed to Edward P. Clapp, Project Zero, Harvard Graduate School of Education, Longfellow Hall, Room 431, 13 Appian Way, Cambridge, MA 01238, USA. +1 (617) 496-3859. edward_clapp@gse.harvard.edu.

Introduction

As the editor of this volume has articulated, the goal of this anthology is for contemporary creativity researchers and theorists to draw upon texts written before 1950 and to illustrate how the ideas expressed in those texts have—or could have—influenced our contemporary thinking about the concept of creativity today. While many of my colleagues in this anthology will have drawn upon the work of white Western psychologists and philosophers whose scholarship has served as a foundation for contemporary creativity research, I have chosen to take a different tack.

My choice has to do with the contemporary struggles we face today—both throughout Western culture and as a domain of scholarship. From the perspective of contemporary Western culture, this struggle pertains to issues of access, equity, and inclusion, especially as they relate to race and class, that are pervasive throughout the West, but are perhaps most greatly pronounced by the system of institutional racism that persists within the United States. Our struggles as a domain of scholarship are not quite as exaggerated, but they are no less real.

Historically speaking, there has been an oversaturation of voices from dominant white culture in the syllabi of our creativity studies classes and in the bibliographies of our most influential books and articles.[2] This is not exclusively the case—as there have indeed been important contributions to the field of creativity studies made by people of color—but it is largely the case. Proving this empirically, however, is a challenge. This challenge points to a problem of perspective that we experience within the field of creativity studies. That is a lack of positionality within the scholarly texts that inform the debates and discussions that drive our field forward. Simply put, positionality can be described as "information regarding the researcher(s) which is likely to have influenced shaping and execution of the research" (Atkinson & Sohn, 2013, p. 6). More specifically, one may say that a researcher's positionality *positions* him or her within a particular sociocultural landscape by establishing his or her identity and providing a window into his or her perspective on the world. For example, like so many creativity scholars before me, I identify as a middle-class white man born and raised within the dominant culture of power in the United States. Throughout my life I have benefited from the privilege of that position. When I develop research questions, design inquiries, collect and analyze data, and write books, essays, and articles, I do so from this privileged perspective. In fact my positionality informs everything I do: where I choose to live, what clothes I choose to wear, and where I choose to send my daughter to school. My positionality further brings me to writing this piece. As an educational researcher with a background in creativity and innovation studies, I am deeply interested in understanding how issues of race and class intersect with creativity theory. I am particularly interested in the intersection of issues of race, class, and creativity studies within schools and other formal and informal teaching and learning environments.

Not stating one's positionality within one's creativity studies work suggests that the race of creativity researchers and theorists has no bearing on their critical perspectives. To the degree that the intersection of race and other defining characteristics of identity inform one's values, then lacking positionality suggests a creativity studies dialogue that

---

2. The biases in the field of creativity studies can also be addressed from the perspective of gender, class, sexuality, nationality, ableism, and other important aspects of identity, society, and culture. Here the discussion of the biases of the field is restricted to race, and in particular, dominant white culture. Though other biases in the field of creativity studies are well worth further exploration, a comprehensive discussion of the biases of the field is beyond the scope of this essay.

is both value-free and socioculturally neutral. Glăveanu (2016, p. 106) has referred to this nonperspective as *a view from nowhere*, "something scientific research aims in vain to accomplish, in its pursuit of 'objectivity.'" As Glăveanu rightly suggests, achieving pure objectivity is an impossibility, and as such, suggesting that the creativity studies dialogue is socially and culturally neutral could not be less true. When considering such efforts from the perspective of race, this scenario is highly problematic as it implicitly suggests a color-blind narrative that normalizes whiteness and reinforces its structural dominance and privilege (see Bonilla-Silva, 2010).

All researchers and theorists—whether in the domain of creativity studies or elsewhere—operate and are informed by a set of values and are subject to their own implicit biases (Greenwald & Krieger, 2006; Jolls & Sunstein, 2006), and the dominant narrative in the field of creativity studies (not unlike many other academic domains) has been grossly overinformed by and biased toward the values of dominant white culture.[3] This is not to say that the field of creativity studies is inherently racist, but it is to say that the perspectives of the field are *raced*.

On the most obvious level, the racialized nature of creativity studies is problematic because it privileges the voice of dominant culture over other voices. So long as scholars from the culture of power (including myself, despite the tenor and content of this brief essay) continue to be overrepresented in the discussion, they perpetuate their sociocultural dominance throughout the scholarly narrative. The race problem that we experience in the field of creativity studies is amplified by the concept of *social reproduction*. A popular interpretation of social reproduction suggests that dominant social classes exist to perpetuate themselves by reproducing the structures and conditions that keep them in power over less dominant social classes (for further explanation see, Doob, 2015). Applying the concept of social reproduction to the field of creativity studies would then suggest that the dominant narrative in the field is an expression of the dominant culture of power.

As discussed, the goals of this chapter are twofold. The first goal is to symbolically introduce an important historic voice into the creativity studies conversation. In the pages ahead, I present an excerpt from W. E. B. Du Bois's (1903) groundbreaking text *The Souls of Black Folk* to engage the history of the creativity studies narrative with a significant voice from history that is not ordinarily included in the conversation. By doing so, I recognize that this introduction is symbolic in nature and neither fully levels the playing field between cultural voices in the creativity studies narrative, nor does it sufficiently consider the diverse cultural voices that have managed their way into this broader narrative (of which there are several).

The second goal of this chapter is to focus on Du Bois's concept of *double-consciousness* as it is presented in the excerpt and then to leverage double-consciousness as a means to describe the conflict in meaning making that may be experienced by students

3. Several scholars have described the values and epistemologies that are markers of dominant white and/or Western culture (for an example, see Glăveanu & Sierra, 2015). In the realm of creativity studies, some scholars have argued that the general interest in celebrating individual genius over collaborative and participatory approaches to invention is an expression of dominant white and Western culture's influence on creativity studies (see Glăveanu & Clapp, 2018). This emphasis on individualism over collectivism is reflected in Geert Hofstede's (Hofstede, Hofstede, & Minkov, 2010) Cultural Dimensions Index, which clearly illustrates how Western (mostly white) countries value individualism over collectivism. One may also argue that the personality traits frequently associated with creativity (e.g., openness to new experiences, autonomy, independence, flexibility of thought, etc.; for a complete list with sources from the field of creativity studies see Feist, 1999) can likewise be understood as the values of dominant white culture. However, I hesitate to identify one discrete list of values associated with dominant white culture because the items on any such list will inevitably be valued in different degrees and in different ways by individuals from nondominant cultures.

from nondominant cultures when they engage with the research, pedagogical frameworks, and policy agendas associated with creativity studies and creativity in education initiatives. It is this second goal that will be discussed more fully in the pages that follow the original Du Bois text.

Introduction

The African American scholar William Edward Burghardt Du Bois was born in Great Barrington, Massachusetts, in 1868—a mere five years after the Emancipation Proclamation was issued by President Abraham Lincoln. After traveling extensively and studying abroad in Europe—most notably at the University of Berlin—Du Bois continued his graduate studies at Harvard University, where he became the first African American to earn a doctorate degree. Du Bois was a founding member of the National Association for the Advancement of Colored People (NAACP) and a prolific author who regularly addressed issues of race and racism in his work. After a long career of scholarship and activism, Du Bois died in Accra, Ghana, in 1963 while working on an encyclopedia of the African diaspora.

First published in 1903, *The Souls of Black Folk* serves as a commentary on the African American reality based on Du Bois's own life experiences. *The Souls of Black Folk* stands as a seminal text within the annals of African American history as well as an important work within the field of sociology. Excerpted below is the first chapter, entitled, "Of Our Spiritual Strivings."

Reading: *The Souls of Black Folk: Essays and Sketches*

Source: Du Bois, W. E. B. (1903). *The souls of black folk: Essays and sketches*. Chicago, IL: A. C. McClurg. In the public domain.

1: Of Our Spiritual Strivings

O water, voice of my heart, crying in the sand,
All night long crying with a mournful cry,
As I lie and listen, and cannot understand The voice of my heart in my side or the voice
    of the sea,
O water, crying for rest, is it I, is it I? All night long the water is crying to me.
Unresting water, there shall never be rest Till the last moon droop and the last tide fail,
And the fire of the end begin to burn in the west; And the heart shall be weary and
    wonder and cry like the sea,
All life long crying without avail,
As the water all night long is crying to me.

Arthur Symons

Between me and the other world there is ever an unasked question: unasked by some through feelings of delicacy; by others through the difficulty of rightly framing it. All, nevertheless, flutter round it. They approach me in a half-hesitant sort of way, eye me curiously or compassionately, and then, instead of saying directly, How does it feel to be a problem? they say, I know an excellent colored man in my town; or, I fought at Mechanicsville; or, Do not these Southern outrages make your blood boil? At these I smile, or am interested, or reduce the boiling to a simmer, as the occasion may require. To the real question, How does it feel to be a problem? I answer seldom a word.

And yet, being a problem is a strange experience,—peculiar even for one who has never been anything else, save perhaps in babyhood and in Europe. It is in the early days of rollicking boyhood that the revelation first bursts upon one, all in a day, as it were. I remember well when the shadow swept across me. I was a little thing, away up in the hills of New England, where the dark Housatonic winds between Hoosac and Taghkanic to the sea. In a wee wooden schoolhouse, something put it into the boys' and girls' heads to buy gorgeous visiting-cards—ten cents a package—and exchange. The exchange was merry, till one girl, a tall newcomer, refused my card,—refused it peremptorily, with a glance. Then it dawned upon me with a certain suddenness that I was different from the others; or like, mayhap, in heart and life and longing, but shut out from their world by a vast veil. I had thereafter no desire to tear down that veil, to creep through; I held all beyond it in common contempt, and lived above it in a region of blue sky and great wandering shadows. That sky was bluest when I could beat my mates at examination-time, or beat them at a foot-race, or even beat their stringy heads. Alas, with the years all this fine contempt began to fade; for the words I longed for, and all their dazzling opportunities, were theirs, not mine. But they should not keep these prizes, I said; some, all, I would wrest from them. Just how I would do it I could never decide: by reading law, by healing the sick, by telling the wonderful tales that swam in my head,—some way. With other black boys the strife was not so fiercely sunny: their youth shrunk into tasteless sycophancy, or into silent hatred of the pale world about them and mocking distrust of everything white; or wasted itself in a bitter cry, Why did God make me an outcast and a stranger in mine own house? The shades of the prison-house closed round about us all: walls strait and stubborn to the whitest, but relentlessly narrow, tall, and unscalable to sons of night who must plod darkly on in resignation, or beat unavailing palms against the stone, or steadily, half hopelessly, watch the streak of blue above.

After the Egyptian and Indian, the Greek and Roman, the Teuton and Mongolian, the Negro is a sort of seventh son, born with a veil, and gifted with second-sight in this American world,—a world which yields him no true self-consciousness, but only lets him see himself through the revelation of the other world. It is a peculiar sensation, this double-consciousness, this sense of always looking at one's self through the eyes of others, of measuring one's soul by the tape of a world that looks on in amused contempt and pity. One ever feels his twoness,—an American, a Negro; two souls, two thoughts, two unreconciled strivings; two warring ideals in one dark body, whose dogged strength alone keeps it from being torn asunder.

The history of the American Negro is the history of this strife,—this longing to attain self-conscious manhood, to merge his double self into a better and truer self. In this merging he wishes neither of the older selves to be lost. He would not Africanize America, for America has too much to teach the world and Africa. He would not bleach his Negro soul in a flood of white Americanism, for he knows that Negro blood has a message for the world. He simply wishes to make it possible for a man to be both a Negro and an American, without being cursed and spit upon by his fellows, without having the doors of Opportunity closed roughly in his face.

This, then, is the end of his striving: to be a co-worker in the kingdom of culture, to escape both death and isolation, to husband and use his best powers and his latent genius. These powers of body and mind have in the past been strangely wasted, dispersed, or forgotten. The shadow of a mighty Negro past flits through the tale of Ethiopia the Shadowy and of Egypt the Sphinx. Through history, the powers of single black men flash here and there like falling stars, and die sometimes before the world has rightly gauged their brightness. Here in America, in the few days since Emancipation, the black man's turning hither and thither in hesitant and doubtful striving has often made his very strength to lose effectiveness, to seem like absence of power, like weakness. And yet it is not weakness,—it is the contradiction of double aims. The double-aimed struggle of the black artisan—on the one hand to escape white contempt for a nation of mere hewers of wood and drawers of water, and on the other hand to plough and nail and dig for a poverty-stricken horde—could only result in making him a poor craftsman, for he had but half a heart in either cause. By the poverty and ignorance of his people, the Negro minister or doctor was tempted toward quackery and demagogy; and by the criticism of the other world, toward ideals that made him ashamed of his lowly tasks. The would-be black savant was confronted by the paradox that the knowledge his people needed was a twice-told tale to his white neighbors, while the knowledge which would teach the white world was Greek to his own flesh and blood. The innate love of harmony and beauty that set the ruder souls of his people a-dancing and a-singing raised but confusion and doubt in the soul of the black artist; for the beauty revealed to him was the soul-beauty of a race which his larger audience despised, and he could not articulate the message of another people. This waste of double aims, this seeking to satisfy two unreconciled ideals, has wrought sad havoc with the courage and faith and deeds of ten thousand thousand people,—has sent them often wooing false gods and invoking false means of salvation, and at times has even seemed about to make them ashamed of themselves.

Away back in the days of bondage they thought to see in one divine event the end of all doubt and disappointment; few men ever worshipped Freedom with half such unquestioning faith as did the American Negro for two centuries. To him, so far as he thought and dreamed, slavery was indeed the sum of all villainies, the cause of all sorrow, the root of all prejudice; Emancipation was the key to a promised land of sweeter beauty than ever stretched before the eyes of wearied Israelites. In song and exhortation swelled one refrain— Liberty; in his tears and curses the God he implored had Freedom in his right hand. At last it came,—suddenly, fearfully, like a dream. With one wild carnival of blood and passion came the message in his own plaintive cadences:—

"Shout, O children! Shout, you're free!
For God has bought your liberty!"

Years have passed away since then,—ten, twenty, forty; forty years of national life, forty years of renewal and development, and yet the swarthy spectre sits in its accustomed seat at the Nation's feast. In vain do we cry to this our vastest social problem:—

"Take any shape but that, and my firm nerves
Shall never tremble!"

The Nation has not yet found peace from its sins; the freedman has not yet found in freedom his promised land. Whatever of good may have come in these years of change, the shadow of a deep disappointment rests upon the Negro people,—a disappointment all the more bitter because the unattained ideal was unbounded save by the simple ignorance of a lowly people.

The first decade was merely a prolongation of the vain search for freedom, the boon that seemed ever barely to elude their grasp,—like a tantalizing will-o'-the-wisp, maddening and misleading the headless host. The holocaust of war, the terrors of the Ku-Klux Klan, the lies of carpet-baggers, the disorganization of industry, and the contradictory advice of friends and foes, left the bewildered serf with no new watchword beyond the old cry for freedom. As the time flew, however, he began to grasp a new idea. The ideal of liberty demanded for its attainment powerful means, and these the Fifteenth Amendment gave him. The ballot, which before he had looked upon as a visible sign of freedom, he now regarded as the chief means of gaining and perfecting the liberty with which war had partially endowed him. And why not? Had not votes made war and emancipated millions? Had not votes enfranchised the freedmen? Was anything impossible to a power that had done all this? A million black men started with renewed zeal to vote themselves into the kingdom. So the decade flew away, the revolution of 1876 came, and left the half-free serf weary, wondering, but still inspired. Slowly but steadily, in the following years, a new vision began gradually to replace the dream of political power,—a powerful movement, the rise of another ideal to guide the unguided, another pillar of fire by night after a clouded day. It was the ideal of "book-learning"; the curiosity, born of compulsory ignorance, to know and test the power of the cabalistic letters of the white man, the longing to know. Here at last seemed to have been discovered the mountain path to Canaan; longer than the highway of Emancipation and law, steep and rugged, but straight, leading to heights high enough to overlook life.

Up the new path the advance guard toiled, slowly, heavily, doggedly; only those who have watched and guided the faltering feet, the misty minds, the dull understandings, of the dark pupils of these schools know how faithfully, how piteously, this people strove to learn. It was weary work. The cold statistician wrote down the inches of progress here and there, noted also where here and there a foot had slipped or some one had fallen. To the tired climbers, the horizon was ever dark, the mists were often cold, the Canaan was always dim and far away. If, however, the vistas disclosed as yet no goal, no resting-place, little but flattery and criticism, the journey at least gave leisure for reflection and self-examination; it changed the child of Emancipation to the youth with dawning self-consciousness, self-realization, self-respect. In those sombre forests of his striving his own soul rose before him, and he saw himself,—darkly as through a veil; and yet he saw in himself some faint revelation of his power, of his mission. He began to have a dim feeling that, to attain his place in the world, he must be himself, and not another. For the first time he sought to analyze the burden he bore upon his back, that dead-weight of social degradation partially masked behind a half-named Negro problem. He felt his poverty; without a cent, without a home, without land, tools, or savings, he had entered into competition with rich, landed, skilled neighbors. To be a poor man is hard, but to be a poor race in a land of dollars is the very bottom of hardships. He felt the weight of his ignorance,—not simply of letters, but of life, of business, of the humanities; the accumulated sloth and shirking and awkwardness of decades and centuries shackled his hands and feet. Nor was his burden all poverty and ignorance. The red stain of bastardy, which two centuries of systematic legal defilement of Negro women had stamped upon his race, meant not only the loss of ancient African chastity, but also the hereditary weight of a mass of corruption from white adulterers, threatening almost the obliteration of the Negro home.

A people thus handicapped ought not to be asked to race with the world, but rather allowed to give all its time and thought to its own social problems. But alas! while sociologists gleefully count his bastards and his prostitutes, the very soul of the toiling, sweating black man is darkened by the shadow of a vast despair. Men call the shadow prejudice, and learn-edly explain it as the natural defence of culture against barbarism, learning against ignorance, purity against crime, the "higher" against the "lower" races. To which the Negro cries Amen! and swears that to so much of this strange prejudice as is founded on just homage to civiliza-tion, culture, righteousness, and progress, he humbly bows and meekly does obeisance. But before that nameless prejudice that leaps beyond all this he stands helpless, dismayed, and well-nigh speechless; before that personal disrespect and mockery, the ridicule and system-atic humiliation, the distortion of fact and wanton license of fancy, the cynical ignoring of the better and the boisterous welcoming of the worse, the all-pervading desire to inculcate disdain for everything black, from Toussaint to the devil,—before this there rises a sickening despair that would disarm and discourage any nation save that black host to whom "discour-agement" is an unwritten word.

But the facing of so vast a prejudice could not but bring the inevitable self-questioning, self-disparagement, and lowering of ideals which ever accompany repression and breed in an atmosphere of contempt and hate. Whisperings and portents came home upon the four winds: Lo! we are diseased and dying, cried the dark hosts; we cannot write, our voting is vain; what need of education, since we must always cook and serve? And the Nation echoed and enforced this self-criticism, saying: Be content to be servants, and nothing more; what need of higher culture for half-men? Away with the black man's ballot, by force or fraud,—and behold the suicide of a race! Nevertheless, out of the evil came something of good,—the more careful adjustment of education to real life, the clearer perception of the Negroes' social responsibilities, and the sobering realization of the meaning of progress.

So dawned the time of Sturm und Drang: storm and stress today rocks our little boat on the mad waters of the world-sea; there is within and without the sound of conflict, the burning of body and rending of soul; inspiration strives with doubt, and faith with vain questionings. The bright ideals of the past,—physical freedom, political power, the training of brains and the training of hands,—all these in turn have waxed and waned, until even the last grows dim and overcast. Are they all wrong,—all false? No, not that, but each alone was over-simple and incomplete,—the dreams of a credulous race-childhood, or the fond imaginings of the other world which does not know and does not want to know our power. To be really true, all these ideals must be melted and welded into one. The training of the schools we need today more than ever,—the training of deft hands, quick eyes and ears, and above all the broader, deeper, higher culture of gifted minds and pure hearts. The power of the ballot we need in sheer self-defence,—else what shall save us from a second slavery? Freedom, too, the long-sought, we still seek,—the freedom of life and limb, the freedom to work and think, the freedom to love and aspire. Work, culture, liberty,—all these we need, not singly but together, not successively but together, each growing and aiding each, and all striving toward that vaster ideal that swims before the Negro people, the ideal of human brotherhood, gained through the unifying ideal of Race; the ideal of fostering and developing the traits and talents of the Negro, not in opposition to or contempt for other races, but rather in large conformity to the greater ideals of the American Republic, in order that some day on American soil two world-races may give each to each those characteristics both so sadly lack. We the darker ones come even now not altogether empty-handed: there are today no truer exponents of the pure human spirit of the Declaration of Independence than the American Negroes; there is no true American music but the wild sweet melodies of the Negro slave; the American fairy tales and folklore are Indian and African; and, all in all, we black men seem the sole oasis of simple faith and reverence in a dusty desert of dollars and smartness. Will America be poorer if she replace her brutal dyspeptic blundering with light-hearted but determined Negro humility? or her coarse and cruel wit with loving jovial good-humor? or her vulgar music with the soul of the Sorrow Songs?

Merely a concrete test of the underlying principles of the great republic is the Negro Problem, and the spiritual striving of the freedmen's sons is the travail of souls whose burden is almost beyond the measure of their strength, but who bear it in the name of an historic race, in the name of this the land of their fathers' fathers, and in the name of human opportunity.

And now what I have briefly sketched in large outline let me on coming pages tell again in many ways, with loving emphasis and deeper detail, that men may listen to the striving in the souls of black folk.

Commentary

DOUBLE-CONSCIOUSNESS AND THE CREATIVITY STUDIES EXPERIENCE

By writing *The Souls of Black Folk,* Du Bois planted the seeds for decades' worth of thought, activism, and scholarship. The collection of essays in this book serve as reference points for the civil rights movement, the education of African Americans, the development of the field of African American studies, and the establishment of a black middle class in America. As it concerns the interests of the current volume, I find that one of the most powerful concepts introduced by Du Bois in *The Souls of Black Folk* is the idea of *double-consciousness* as it is presented in chapter 1, "Of Our Spiritual Strivings." In Du Bois's own words:

> It is a peculiar sensation, this double-consciousness, this sense of always looking at one's self through the eyes of others, of measuring one's soul by the tape of a world that looks on in amused contempt and pity. One ever feels his two-ness, an American, a Negro; two souls, two thoughts, two unreconciled strivings; two warring ideals in one dark body, whose dogged strength alone keeps it from being torn asunder.
>
> The history of the American Negro is the history of this strife,—this longing to attain self-conscious manhood, to merge his double self into a better and truer self. In this merging he wishes neither of the older selves to be lost. He would not Africanize America, for America has too much to teach the world and Africa. He would not bleach his Negro soul in a flood of white Americanism, for he knows that Negro blood has a message for the world. He simply wishes to make it possible for a man to be both a Negro and an American, without being cursed and spit upon by his fellows, without having the doors of Opportunity closed roughly in his face.

A great deal has been written about the concept of double-consciousness (see Bruce, 1992; Evans, 2014; Kirkland, 2013; Mocombe, 2009, among others). In the way that Du Bois describes, double-consciousness suggests a tension, a dissonance felt between two experiences, two cultures, two meaning-making structures: one an African American way of knowing and being in the world, and one a white American way of knowing and being in the world.

Central to the concept of Du Bois's double-consciousness is the notion of *the veil*. The veil metaphor describes a duality that separates blackness and whiteness through a physical barrier that "forces blacks to function in both cultures" (Isaksen, 2008, p. 602). While the veil restricts white people's ability to see blacks as equal Americans, "the veil also refers to black people's inability to see themselves beyond the prescripted image projected upon them by whites" (p. 602). As Kirkland (2013, p. 137) has described, the veil "signifies the concealment from white people's comprehension of the legacy and currency of African-American practices and forms of life as shaped by racial hindrance." These practices and forms of life include the hardships faced by African Americans on the one hand—and the promise and richness of black culture on the other. As noted in the *Dictionary of the Social Sciences* (Calhoun, 2002, p. 129), double-consciousness establishes a set of "felt contradicitons" for African Americans: "To be black in America thus implied a range of contradictions between American social ideals, which blacks shared, and the experience of exclusion from American social life."

Through his use of the term double-consciousness and the metaphor of the veil, Du Bois described the cultural code-switching that must take place when individuals move between different cultural contexts. This code-switching may involve a cultural dance between two ways of being in the world that may include moving back and forth between different vocabulary and speech patterns, different traditions and social practices, different cultural reference points, and different social queues. Whereas individuals from dominant culture need to develop a familiarity with only one culture, individuals who juggle their time between dominant and nondominant cultures need to be fluent in both. They must be doubly conscious of the sociocultural *rules* of both cultures and be doubly conscious of how (and when) to engage the rules of each of those cultures.

The concept of double-consciousness pertains to the field of creativity studies in much the same way that Du Bois described it more broadly applying to the African American experience in a white American world (though without the grit of explicit discrimination that Du Bois's prose so dramatically captures). Given the dominance of white voices within the field of creativity studies, the rules at play within the field are biased toward dominant white ways of being. One must therefore live within the consciousness associated with dominant white culture in order to participate. For individuals from nondominant cultures, this may involve the code-switching, the navigating between one consciousness and another, that Du Bois described well over a century ago.

Some may argue that the double-consciousness that Du Bois describes may benefit individuals engaged in creative activity. Previous research has shown that bicultural and mixed-race individuals experienced enhanced creativity when they were able to integrate their dual identities (Cheng, Sanchez-Burks, & Lee, 2008; Tendayi Viki & Williams, 2013). The counterargument may be that the nondominant cultural experience (particularly the African American experience that Du Bois describes)—which is inherently subject to domination and oppression—is markedly different from the bicultural or mixed-race experience, where domination and oppression are experienced in different degrees. Others may argue that from the perspective of dialogical self theory or position exchange theory (Gillespie & Martin, 2014) the code-switching that may be associated with the more metaphysical Du Boisian concept of double-consciousness is a means of moving between different social positions and results in individuals "becoming dialogical beings" (p. 74). While these theories offer insight into the interdependence and exchange of different social positions, they do not take into account the very real issues of power, dominance, and implicit and explicit racism associated with a life doubly lived. Individuals from nondominant cultures, particularly people of color, cannot simply exchange social positions with their more privileged peers (and vice versa). In this way, the oversight, disregard, and short shrift that dialogism and position exchange theories offer to the oppressive social limitations placed upon nondominant cultures act as an expression of white power and privilege.

While there is a great deal more to be discussed (and more research to be done) concerning the relationship between Du Bois's concept of double-consciousness and the experiences of creativity scholars or students of creativity studies who hail from nondominant cultures, I feel that we should also be greatly concerned about how the sociocultural biases of our field impact education.

BIAS IN CREATIVITY STUDIES, BIAS IN CREATIVITY IN EDUCATION

The raced history of creativity studies can be deeply problematic at the level of academia, but when the biases of our field trickle down to educational policy and practice, these problems are greatly amplified. This trickle-down effect can be explained by a simple conditional statement: *If* the field of creativity studies is biased toward the interests of dominant white culture, *and* the field of creativity studies is meant to inform pedagogical frameworks and policy agendas that support creativity in education, *then* the pedagogical frameworks and policy agendas that support creativity in education are likewise biased toward the interests of dominant white culture (see Figure 33.1).

As this conditional logic statement suggests, not only does the dominant white culture skew in the field of creativity studies demand that nonwhite researchers develop a sort of double-consciousness that allows them to culturally code-switch as they

FIGURE 33.1 **The Cultural Biases Inherent in the Field of Creativity Studies and their Conditional Effect on Creativity in Education.**

move from one sociocultural context to the next, it also demands that young people from nondominant cultures who engage in progressive education—rooted in creativity theory—also develop a form of double-consciousness. While this may seem like an extreme argument to some, it is one that has been raised in the past—and one that is quite present today.

In her 1988 article, "The Silenced Dialogue: Power and Pedagogy in Educating Other People's Children," Lisa Delpit put forth the idea that process-based approaches to teaching and learning that lie at the heart of progressive education—and, by association, the creative classroom—are biased toward the needs and interests of dominant white culture. Attributing the development of process-based education to the interests of white culture, Delpit made the case that white culture is the "culture of power" within the process-based classroom. This is problematic, because from its position of power, white culture then becomes dominant over all other cultures. To elaborate on the structural role that power plays within an educational experience, she pointed to five "aspects of power" (p. 282) that are in effect within all learning environments:

1. Issues of power are enacted in classrooms.
2. There are codes or rules for participating in power; that is, there is a "culture of power."
3. The rules of a culture of power are a reflection of the rules of the culture of those who have power.
4. If you are not already a participant in the culture of power, being told explicitly the rules of that culture makes acquiring power easier.
5. Those with power are frequently least aware of—or least willing to acknowledge—its existence. Those with less power are often most aware of its existence. (p. 282)

Here again a connection can be made to Du Bois's concept of double-consciousness. If cultures of power exist within all classrooms, then it is necessary for students from nondominant cultures to learn the rules of the dominant culture of power, to develop a second consciousness that understands and is able to act effectively within this other set of rules and values.

Power, in this sense, is both social and cultural. And as Bourdieu and his colleagues have noted (Bourdieu & Passeron, 1977), education is a vehicle for social and cultural reproduction, as the values of dominant culture are perpetuated through schooling in a way that maintains the social superiority of the dominant culture. It may not be the explicit goal of the field of creativity studies to perpetuate the social status of dominant white culture, but it certainly can be the case that the sociocultural bias toward the interests of dominant white culture that pervades the field of creativity studies then informs creativity in education agendas and pedagogical structures that shape progressive education initiatives. One of the ways this happens is when educators and curriculum designers draw on the findings from creativity research to develop frameworks for teaching and learning that are inspired by creativity theory—which by and large are shaped by dominant white culture—and then apply those frameworks in classrooms that serve young people from nondominant cultures. Another way this happens is when educators apply rubrics and tests developed by creativity researchers, like the Torrance Tests of Creativity Thinking (Torrance, 1972), to these same classrooms.

As Delpit (1988) and others have suggested, progressive education has a race problem (see, e.g., Mehta, 2014), and the field of creativity studies can be understood as being a key player in that problem.

From the perspective of creativity in education, young people from dominant white culture are at an advantage over their classmates from nondominant cultures because they have long been steeped in the rules for engagement that are in effect within the creative classroom. Children from dominant white culture do not need to code-switch in the creative classroom in the same ways that their classmates from nondominant cultures must do, nor must they develop a double-consciousness in any way. The double-consciousness that young people experience and must enact in the creative classroom may be explained by some as an opportunity to engage in perspective taking. From the perspective of Mead (1934, 1938),

> taking the perspectives of others is not so much a matter of simulating their psychological states and attitudes through a combination of empathic resonance and/or analogical reasoning, as it is a matter of recalling previous experience in different phases of action nested within interactive, communicative sequences of exchange. (Martin, 2005, p. 235)

Where race is concerned—as it is in Du Bois's articulation of double-consciousness—it is not possible for one to recall the experience of the other, because the experience of dominance/nondominance is not transferable across the color line. Position exchange and perspective-taking theories that overlook this important social reality normalize whiteness—which, throughout the West, maintains a dominant position that is limited in its experiences of oppression.

The misalignment in meaning making that young people from nondominant cultures experience in the creative classroom is one way in which educational inequity is expressed in many formal and informal learning environments. As Hammond (2015, p. 13) has noted, "for culturally and linguistically diverse students, their opportunities to develop habits of mind and cognitive capacities are limited or non-existent because of education inequity." When students from nondominant cultures experience this lack of opportunity to develop the habits of mind and higher-order cognitive capacities that are valued in the creative classroom they become dependent learners, limiting their ability to excel in creative learning environments that value independence, autonomy, risk taking, cognitive flexibility, and comfort with ambiguity. In this way, what is taught and learned in the creative classroom is more accessible to students from dominant white culture than it is to their peers from nondominant cultural backgrounds (Clapp, 2016). While the goals of many educators within the creative classroom may be to empower all young people (Glăveanu & Clapp, 2018), the biases of the creative classroom—rooted in the field of creativity studies—continue to privilege children from dominant white culture and, as a result, perpetuate the dominance of white culture through the mechanism of the creative classroom.[4]

Conclusion

It is my hope that this chapter has raised more questions than answers. In that regard, and in conclusion, I'd like to highlight a few key questions that emerge from the Du Boisian concept of double-consciousness that I hope have surfaced from this discussion.

The first question is this: *Is the field of creativity studies inherently racist?* No, but I do believe that the field is radically biased toward whites and white American culture. What I mean is that the field of creativity studies is not socially and culturally neutral; it is socially and culturally charged in a way that favors the interests of dominant white culture. The sociocultural biases of the field should not be ignored, but rather be more explicitly addressed.

This first question naturally leads to the next question: *Is creativity just for white people?* Certainly not! But it cannot be denied that the dominant narrative throughout the field of creativity studies has been shaped by individuals who represent dominant white culture. To the degree that the field of creativity studies influences pedagogical frameworks and policy agendas that support creativity in education, the inherent sociocultural biases of the field also express themselves in the creative classroom—where young people from nondominant cultures are further required to code-switch if they are to engage and excel in the work of the traditional creative classroom. In other words, creativity in education is not just for white students, but if the researchers and practitioners in creativity studies and practice are overwhelmingly white, white students will draw greater and more consistent advantage from the creative classroom compared to their classmates from nondominant cultures.

Of course, these questions combined prompt a third set of questions: *As academics in a scholarly domain, what are we to do? How can we strike a greater cultural balance within the field of creativity studies? How can we shift the dominant narrative in the field to better include nondominant voices?* The obvious answer to these questions is quite clear, quite simple: include more people from nondominant cultures in the creativity studies conversation. To paraphrase Du Bois, engaging more voices in the creativity studies conversation is a means of becoming "co-worker[s] in the kingdom of culture." It has certainly been my attempt to symbolically introduce a new voice to the creativity studies conversation by introducing this excerpt from Du Bois. But the simplicity of merely including a wider range of voices in the creativity studies conversation can also be a bit too simplistic (if not tokenistic). Indeed the field of creativity studies demands the inclusion of a greater breadth of sociocultural voices, but even given a radical uptick in racial diversity, the dominant narrative in the field has already been set, the *rules* of participation have already been established, and nearly a century's worth of research and theory will not be rewritten. But no scholarly domain should ever be in the business of rewriting its history anyway. Instead two implications call for our attention. The first is to place greater emphasis on positionality

---

4. Though I speak of students from dominant white culture and those from nondominant cultures as monolithic groups, it should be noted that there are variations of background and experience within these groups. Indeed there are students from nondominant culture who are equipped to excel in the creative classroom, just as there are students from dominant white culture who are ill-prepared to excel in the creative classroom.

throughout the field of creativity studies. By encouraging the sociocultural transparency of our field's scholars, we may be better able to gauge the sociocultural perspectives that shape our domain and become better able to process, synthesize, and apply the findings from the field. The second implication is quite straightforward: if the dominant narrative of the field of creativity studies is racialized in a way that is overly biased toward the interests of a particular culture, then perhaps it is necessary to create a counternarrative that tells a different story.

References

Atkinson, D., & Sohn, J. (2013). Culture from the bottom up. *TESOL Quarterly, 47*(4), 1–25. Retrieved from https://www.researchgate.net/publication/259543272_Culture_from_the_Bottom_Up.

Bonilla-Silva, E. (2010). *Racism without racists: Color-blind racism and the persistence of racial inequality in the United States* (3rd ed.). Lanham, MD: Rowman & Littlefield.

Bourdieu, P., & Passeron, J. (1977). *Reproduction in education, society, and culture.* Beverly Hills, CA: Sage.

Bruce, D. (1992). W. E. B. Du Bois and the idea of double consciousness. *American Literature, 64*(2), 299–309.

Calhoun, C. (Ed.). (2002). *Dictionary of the social sciences.* New York, NY: Oxford University Press.

Cheng, C. Y., Sanchez-Burks, J., & Lee, F. (2008). Connecting the dots within: Creative performance and identity integration. *Psychological Science, 19,* 1177–1183.

Clapp, E. P. (2016). *Participatory creativity: Introducing access and equity to the creative classroom.* New York, NY: Routledge.

Delpit, L. (1988). The silenced dialogue: Power and pedagogy in educating other people's children. *Harvard Educational Review, 58*(3), 280–298.

Doob, C. B. 2015. *Social inequality and social stratification in U.S. society.* New York, NY: Taylor & Francis.

Du Bois, W. E. B. (1903). *The souls of black folk: Essays and sketches.* Chicago: A. C. McClurg.

Evans, J. (2014). *Lifting the veil over Eurocentrism: The Du Boisian hermeneutic of double consciousness.* Trenton, NJ: Africa World Press.

Feist, G. J. (1999). The influence of personality on artistic and scientific creativity. In R. J. Sternberg (Ed.), *Handbook of creativity* (pp. 273–296). Cambridge, UK: Cambridge University Press.

Gillespie, A., & Martin, J. (2014). Position exchange theory: A socio-material basis for discursive and psychological positioning. *New Ideas in Psychology, 32,* 73–79.

Glăveanu, V. P. (2016). Perspectives. In V. P. Glăveanu et al., (Eds.), *Creativity—A new vocabulary.* London: Palgrave MacMillan.

Glăveanu, V. P. & Clapp, E. P. (2018). Leveraging distributed and participatory creativity as a form of cultural empowerment. In A. U. Branco & M. C. Lopes-de-Oliveira (Eds.) *Alterity, values, and socialization,* pp. 51–63. Cham, Switzerland: Springer.

Glăveanu, V. P., & Sierra, Z. (2015). Creativity and epistemologies of the South. *Culture & Psychology, 2*(3), 340–358.

Greenwald, A. G., & Krieger, L. H. (2006). Implicit bias: Scientific foundations. *California Law Review, 94*(4), 945–967.

Hammond, Z. (2015). *Culturally responsive teaching and the brain: Promoting authentic engagement and rigor among culturally and linguistically diverse students.* Thousand Oaks, CA: Corwin.

Hofstede, G., Hofstede, G. J., & Minkov, M. (2010). *Cultures and organizations: Software of the mind.* New York, NY: McGraw-Hill.

Isaksen, J. L. (2008). Veil, in African American culture. In W. A. Darity Jr. (Ed.), *International encyclopedia of the social sciences,* 2nd edition (p. 602). Farmington Hills, MI: Gale, Cenage Learning.

Jolls, C., & Sunstein, C. R. (2006). The laws of implicit bias. Yale Law School faculty scholarship series. Paper 1824. Retrieved from http://digitalcommons.law.yale.edu/fss_papers/1824.

Kirkland, F. M. (2013). On Du Bois's notion of double consciousness. *Philosophy Compass, 8*(2), 137–148.

Martin, J. (2005). Perspectival selves in interaction with others: Re-reading G. H. Mead's social psychology. *Journal for the Theory of Social Behaviour, 35*(3), 231–253.

Mead, G. H. (1934). *Mind, self, and society from the standpoint of a social behaviorist* (C. W. Morris, Ed.). Chicago: University of Chicago Press.

Mead, G. H. (1938). *The philosophy of the act* (C. W. Morris, Ed.). Chicago: University of Chicago Press.

Mehta, J. (2014, June 20). Deeper learning has a race problem. *Education Week.* Retrieved from http://blogs.edweek.org/edweek/learning_deeply/2014/06/deeper_learning_has_a_race_problem.html.

Mocombe, P. (2009). *The soul-less souls of black folk: A sociological reconsideration of black consciousness as Du Boisian double consciousness.* Lanham, MD: University Press of America.

Tendayi Viki, G., & Williams, M. L. J. (2013). The role of identity integration in enhancing creativity among mixed-race individuals. *Journal of Creative Behavior, 48*(3), 198–208.

Torrance, E. P. (1972). Predictive validity of the Torrance tests for creative thinking. *Journal of Creative Behaviour, 6*(4), 236–262.

34

Beyond Creative Destruction
Joseph Schumpeter

VLAD P. GLĂVEANU

Summary

Joseph Schumpeter was an eminent economist of the 20th century, well-known especially for his 1943 book, *Capitalism, Socialism, and Democracy*. In this work, Schumpeter outlines his vision of capitalism as a dynamic, evolutionary system essentially based on incessant acts of creativity. Importantly, the engine of capitalism is not creative production as much as creative destruction, the repeated replacement of the old with the new and, in this process, the periodic crises that mark processes of wealth creation and destruction. His reference to creative destruction—in a short chapter of the book, reproduced here in its entirety—came to inform several theories of the economic cycle, innovation, and entrepreneurship. While not frequently mentioned in the literature on creativity, this notion gives us a powerful depiction of what creativity means for not only individuals but society as a whole, both at its "brightest" and "darkest." The final commentary will offer a critical appraisal of this idea in view of current creativity discourses.

Introduction

Joseph Alois Schumpeter (1883–1950) was an eminent Austrian-born economist and political scientist of the 20th century who later moved to the United States and acquired American citizenship. His father was a factory owner who died when Joseph was very young. Schumpeter went on to study law at the University of Vienna and had as teachers, among others, Friedrich von Wieser and Eugen von Böhm-Bawerk. He worked as a professor of economics at different universities in the Austrian-Hungarian Empire, including the University of Czernowitz and the University of Graz. After Word War I, he was invited to become minister of finance in Austria (in 1919) and became president of Biedermann Bank (in 1921), but the latter venture was not very successful. His academic career was, however; Schumpeter held a chair at the University of Bonn while also lecturing at Harvard University and being a visiting professor in Tokyo. In 1932 he moved to the United States to teach at Harvard, where he remained until the end of his career. In 1947 he became the first immigrant to be elected president of the American Economic Association. Schumpeter died in Connecticut at the age of 66.

The work he is remembered for most is *Capitalism, Socialism, and Democracy* (1943), a book in which he placed innovation and entrepreneurial activities at the heart of economic change in capitalism. This view put him in opposition to traditional, mathematical models of the economy assuming that reaching equilibrium was the ultimate goal of the market system. In contrast, Schumpeter proposed that equilibrium is only a temporary state, at best, and certainly not the natural condition of the free market. Constant innovation and competition instead give capitalism its main feature: the ongoing creation and destruction of knowledge, wealth, and technological means. There are many historical examples of this process at work, for instance, the revolutionary creation of Henry Ford's assembly line, which fundamentally transformed car manufacturing while, at the same time, led to many workers and forms of work becoming obsolete. The internet and the emergence of dot-com companies illustrate a similar dynamic. There is a deep similarity between Schumpeter and Marx in this regard, one acknowledged in the former's seminal work (Elliott, 1980). Marx talked about wealth creation and devaluation as central for capitalism, and, while Schumpeter saw this dynamic as capitalism's engine, he also believed it would lead to the ultimate demise of the entire system. The concept of creative destruction is therefore essential for understanding Schumpeter's view of both innovation and society.

There are many important insights for creativity researchers connected to the notion of creative destruction. It not only establishes a strong, bidirectional link between creativity and society, particularly where the economy and the development of technology are concerned, but it also makes us reflect on the consequences of creativity and innovation. As a community, we often take for granted the idea that creativity is always good, that it leads to personal and societal progress and well-being. Schumpeter agrees that progress is reached through creativity, but also highlights the price we pay for it. The "perennial gale of creative destruction," as he called it, offers multiple rewards but comes at a (high) price. This is a key lesson coming out of the text reproduced here, that there is always a "dark" side to creativity, an element of destruction and disadvantaging others that accompanies "outstanding" creative achievements. It is not only that the new always displaces the old; in doing so, it creates anxiety, frustration, and even misery for people whose lives depended on the old way of doing things. At the same time, as Schumpeter vividly reminds us, this dynamic is the only one possible under capitalism. Or is it? The final commentary will come back to this question and assess the pains and gains of constant creativity.

Reading: "The Process of Creative Destruction"

Source: Schumpeter, J. A. (1943). The process of creative destruction. Chapter 7 in *Capitalism, socialism and democracy* (pp. 81–86). London: Routledge. Copyright © 1943. Reproduced with permission from Taylor & Francis Books UK.

The Process of Creative Destruction

The theories of monopolistic and oligopolistic competition and their popular variants may in two ways be made to serve the view that capitalist reality is unfavorable to maximum performance in production. One may hold that it always has been so and that all along output has been expanding in spite of the secular sabotage perpetrated by the managing bourgeoisie. Advocates of this proposition would have to produce evidence to the effect that the observed rate of increase can be accounted for by a sequence of favorable circumstances unconnected with the mechanism of private enterprise and strong enough to overcome the latter's resistance. . . . However, those who espouse this variant at least avoid the trouble about historical fact that the advocates of the alternative proposition have to face. This avers that capitalist reality once tended to favor maximum productive performance, or at all events productive performance so considerable as to constitute a major element in any serious appraisal of the system; but that the later spread of monopolist structures, killing competition, has by now reversed that tendency.

First, this involves the creation of an entirely imaginary golden age of perfect competition that at some time somehow metamorphosed itself into the monopolistic age, whereas it is quite clear that perfect competition has at no time been more of a reality than it is at present. Secondly, it is necessary to point out that the rate of increase in output did not decrease from the nineties from which, I suppose, the prevalence of the largest-size concerns, at least in manufacturing industry, would have to be dated; that there is nothing in the behavior of the time series of total output to suggest a "break in trend"; and, most important of all, that the modern standard of life of the masses evolved during the period of relatively unfettered "big business." If we list the items that enter the modern workman's budget and from 1899 on observe the course of their prices not in terms of money but in terms of the hours of labor that will buy them—i.e., each year's money prices divided by each year's hourly wage rates—we cannot fail to be struck by the rate of the advance which, considering the spectacular improvement in qualities, seems to have been greater and not smaller than it ever was before. If we economists were given less to wishful thinking and more to the observation of facts, doubts would immediately arise as to the realistic virtues of a theory that would have led us to expect a very different result. Nor is this all. As soon as we go into details and inquire into the individual items in which progress was most conspicuous, the trail leads not to the doors of those firms that work under conditions of comparatively free competition but precisely to the doors of the large concerns—which, as in the case of agricultural machinery, also account for much of the progress in the competitive sector—and a shocking suspicion dawns upon us that big business may have had more to do with creating that standard of life than with keeping it down.

The conclusions alluded to at the end of the preceding chapter are in fact almost completely false. Yet they follow from observations and theorems that are almost completely[1] true. Both economists and popular writers have once more run away with some fragments of reality they happened to grasp. These fragments themselves were mostly seen correctly. Their formal properties were mostly developed correctly. But no conclusions about capitalist reality as a whole follow from such fragmentary analyses. If we draw them nevertheless, we can be right only by accident. That has been done. And the lucky accident did not happen.

The essential point to grasp is that in dealing with capitalism we are dealing with an evolutionary process. It may seem strange that anyone can fail to see so obvious a fact which moreover was long ago emphasized by Karl Marx. Yet that fragmentary analysis which yields the bulk of our propositions about the functioning of modern capitalism persistently neglects it. Let us restate the point and see how it bears upon our problem.

Capitalism, then, is by nature a form or method of economic change and not only never is but never can be stationary. And this evolutionary character of the capitalist process is not merely due to the fact that economic life goes on in a social and natural environment which changes and by its change alters the data of economic action; this fact is important and these changes (wars, revolutions and so on) often condition industrial change, but they are not its prime movers. Nor is this evolutionary character due to a quasi-automatic increase in population and capital or to the vagaries of monetary systems of which exactly the same thing holds true. The fundamental impulse that sets and keeps the capitalist engine in motion comes from the new consumers' goods, the new methods of production or transportation, the new markets, the new forms of industrial organization that capitalist enterprise creates.

As we have seen in the preceding chapter, the contents of the laborer's budget, say from 1760 to 1940, did not simply grow on unchanging lines but they underwent a process of qualitative change. Similarly, the history of the productive apparatus of a typical farm, from the beginnings of the rationalization of crop rotation, plowing and fattening to the mechanized thing of today—linking up with elevators and railroads—is a history of revolutions. So is the history of the productive apparatus of the iron and steel industry from the charcoal furnace to our own type of furnace, or the history of the apparatus of power production from the overshot water wheel to the modern power plant, or the history of transportation from the mail coach to the airplane. The opening up of new markets, foreign or domestic, and the organizational development from the craft shop and factory to such concerns as U.S. Steel illustrate the same process of industrial mutation—if I may use that biological term—that incessantly revolutionizes[2] the economic structure *from within*, incessantly destroying the old one, incessantly creating a new one. This process of Creative Destruction is the essential fact about capitalism. It is what capitalism consists in and what every capitalist concern has got to live in. This fact bears upon our problem in two ways.

First, since we are dealing with a process whose every element takes considerable time in revealing its true features and ultimate effects, there is no point in appraising the performance of that process *ex visu* of a given point of time; we must judge its performance over time, as it unfolds through decades or centuries. A system—any system, economic or other—that at *every* given point of time fully utilizes its possibilities to the best advantage may yet in the long run be inferior to a system that does so at *no* given point of time, because the latter's failure to do so may be a condition for the level or speed of long-run performance.

Second, since we are dealing with an organic process, analysis of what happens in any particular part of it—say, in an individual concern or industry—may indeed clarify details of mechanism but is inconclusive beyond that. Every piece of business strategy acquires its true significance only against the background of that process and within the situation created by it. It must be seen in its role in the perennial gale of creative destruction; it cannot be understood irrespective of it or, in fact, on the hypothesis that there is a perennial lull.

But economists who, *ex visu* of a point of time, look for example at the behavior of an oligopolist industry—an industry which consists of a few big firms—and observe the well-known moves and countermoves within it that seem to aim at nothing but high prices and restrictions of output are making precisely that hypothesis. They accept the data of the momentary situation as if there were no past or future to it and think that they have understood what there is to understand if they interpret the behavior of those firms by means of the principle of maximizing profits with reference to those data. The usual theorist's paper and the usual government commission's report practically never try to see that behavior, on the one hand, as a result of a piece of past history and, on the other hand, as an attempt to deal with a situation that is sure to change presently—as an attempt by those firms to keep on their feet, on ground that is slipping away from under them. In other words, the problem that is usually being visualized is how capitalism administers existing structures, whereas the relevant problem is how it creates and destroys them. As long as this is not recognized, the investigator does a meaningless job. As soon as it is recognized, his outlook on capitalist practice and its social results changes considerably.[3]

The first thing to go is the traditional conception of the *modus operandi* of competition. Economists are at long last emerging from the stage in which price competition was all they saw. As soon as quality competition and sales effort are admitted into the sacred precincts of theory, the price variable is ousted from its dominant position. However, it is still competition within a rigid pattern of invariant conditions, methods of production and forms of industrial organization in particular, that practically monopolizes attention. But in capitalist reality as distinguished from its textbook picture, it is not that kind of competition which counts but the competition from the new commodity, the new technology, the new source of supply, the new type of organization (the largest-scale unit of control for instance)—competition which commands a decisive cost or quality advantage and which strikes not at the margins of the profits and the outputs of the existing firms but at their foundations and their very lives. This kind of competition is as much more effective than the other as a bombardment is in comparison with forcing a door, and so much more important that it becomes a matter of comparative indifference whether competition in the ordinary sense functions more or less promptly; the powerful lever that in the long run expands output and brings down prices is in any case made of other stuff.

It is hardly necessary to point out that competition of the kind we now have in mind acts not only when in being but also when it is merely an ever-present threat. It disciplines before it attacks. The businessman feels himself to be in a competitive situation even if he is alone in his field or if, though not alone, he holds a position such that investigating government experts fail to see any effective competition between him and any other firms in the same or a neighboring field and in consequence conclude that his talk, under examination, about his competitive sorrows is all make-believe. In many cases, though not in all, this will in the long run enforce behavior very similar to the perfectly competitive pattern.

Many theorists take the opposite view which is best conveyed by an example. Let us assume that there is a certain number of retailers in a neighborhood who try to improve their relative position by service and "atmosphere" but avoid price competition and stick as to methods to the local tradition—a picture of stagnating routine. As others drift into the trade that quasi-equilibrium is indeed upset, but in a manner that does not benefit their customers. The economic space around each of the shops having been narrowed, their owners will no longer be able to make a living and they will try to mend the case by raising prices in tacit agreement. This will further reduce their sales and so, by successive pyramiding, a situation will evolve in which increasing potential supply will be attended by increasing instead of decreasing prices and by decreasing instead of increasing sales.

Such cases do occur, and it is right and proper to work them out. But as the practical instances usually given show, they are fringe-end cases to be found mainly in the sectors furthest removed from all that is most characteristic of capitalist activity.[4] Moreover, they are transient by nature. In the case of retail trade the competition that matters arises not from additional shops of the same type, but from the department store, the chain store, the mail-order house and the supermarket which are bound to destroy those pyramids sooner or later.[5]

Now a theoretical construction which neglects this essential element of the case neglects all that is most typically capitalist about it; even if correct in logic as well as in fact, it is like *Hamlet* without the Danish prince.

---

1.   As a matter of fact, those observations and theorems are not completely satisfactory. The usual expositions of the doctrine of imperfect competition fail in particular to give due attention to the many and important cases in which, even as a matter of static theory, imperfect competition approximates the results of perfect competition. There are other cases in which it does not do this, but offers compensations which, while not entering any output index, yet contribute to what the output index is in the last resort intended to measure—the cases in which a firm defends its market by establishing a name for quality and service for instance. However, in order to simplify matters, we will not take issue with that doctrine on its own ground.

2.   Those revolutions are not strictly incessant; they occur in discrete rushes which are separated from each other by spans of comparative quiet. The process as a whole works incessantly however, in the sense that there always is either revolution or absorption of the results of revolution, both together forming what are known as business cycles.

3.   It should be understood that it is only our appraisal of economic performance and not our moral judgment that can be so changed. Owing to its autonomy, moral approval or disapproval is entirely independent of our appraisal of social (or any other) results, unless we happen to adopt a moral system such as utilitarianism which makes moral approval and disapproval turn on them *ex definitions*.

4.   This is also shown by a theorem we frequently meet with in expositions of the theory of imperfect competition, viz., the theorem that, under conditions of imperfect competition, producing or trading businesses tend to be irrationally small. Since imperfect competition is at the same time held to be an outstanding characteristic of modern industry we are set to wondering what world these theorists live in, unless, as stated above, fringe-end cases are all they have in mind.

5.   The mere threat of their attack cannot, in the particular conditions, environmental and personal, of small-scale retail trade, have its usual disciplining influence, for the small man is too much hampered by his cost structure and, however well he may manage within his inescapable limitations, he can never adapt himself to the methods of competitors who can afford to sell at the price at which he buys.

Commentary

Creativity as a concept is widely popular today. We often hear this notion at the workplace, looking to find creative leaders and fight against conformism and passivity; in education, where teachers are asked to educate (for) creativity and students to display more creative and critical skills; in advertisements that want to sell products as innovative and convince potential buyers that they will be touched by the aura of creativity after making the purchase; in politics, when politicians praise the creative or entrepreneurial spirit of the nation or are accused of not displaying enough of this spirit themselves; in public discussions about the economy and economic progress measured in terms of creative potential or achievements. These examples illustrate why we think creativity is important today. But how exactly did we come to believe this?

It is interesting to include a historical reflection at this point (see Glăveanu & Kaufman, 2019; Hanchett Hanson, 2015; Weiner, 2000). It is not only the case that the word "creativity" itself is a rather new addition to our vocabulary, but the emergence of creativity as an all-encompassing "modern value" is even more recent, dating back to the second half of the 20th century. It is the era marked most by authors such as Schumpeter and his belief that economic progress under capitalism—a prevailing system around the world, especially after the end of the Cold War—is tightly linked to innovation and creativity. This is not only because creativity basically constitutes the "fuel" of consumerist societies by fostering the emergence of new and valuable products and services. It is also—or primarily, according to Schumpeter—because creativity and innovation continuously replace the old with the new, constantly change the free market and the nature of competition within it, and, in doing so, bring about progress and wealth. Of course, as we see from the text reproduced in this chapter and discussed further, these are not the sole consequences of creative destruction. What is important to note, for the moment, is the pervasive association nowadays between creativity and economic value (Glăveanu, Tanggaard, & Wegener, 2016). Although there are many other possible discourses about creativity—e.g., those relating it to personal growth and well-being or to community building—what underpins to a great extent the current "creativity era" is the assumed economic value brought about by being creative or innovative.

It is not only the case that an economic logic can be found behind many of today's uses of the word "creativity"—this notion itself has been used to rethink the economy. Indeed, for many the 21st century's "new economy" is all about creativity. Nakamura (2000) made this point clearly when stating that "the growing importance of creative endeavors appears to be what's new in the New Economy" (p. 28), defined by "high-tech innovations and the globalization of world markets" (p. 15). Moreover, the shape of this new economy is intrinsically Schumpeterian. "The New Economy is highly competitive, but creative destruction, not production, is the center of the competition" (p. 28). In order to understand this premise, we need to return to Schumpeter's (1943, p. 82) text, in which he basically states that, when talking about capitalism, "we are dealing with an evolutionary process." Capitalism is, essentially, dynamic (or creative), not static, and this is why static economic models of the old era fall short when it comes to contemporary realities. Here Schumpeter was in dialogue with—and in opposition to—Adam Smith and other economists who trusted that markets naturally reach a state of equilibrium through competition. These models focus, in Schumpeter's view, too much on the present, on the rationality of markets and their agents, and on administrating existing structures. In contrast, if we accept capitalism as dynamic, what we should focus on is competition not with what exists, but with "the new commodity, the new technology, the new source of supply, the new type of organization" (p. 84). In other words, in a creativity- and innovation-driven type of economy, we need to set our sights on the future rather than the present. We also need to understand and engage with the notion of creative destruction.

The practice of creativity destruction seems illogical initially. Why would anyone replace—sometimes totally and radically—existing products and services that still do their job well? Why not simply perfect what already exists and avoid big disturbances in the whole system? Why engage in a kind of competition that "commands a decisive cost or quality advantage and which strikes not at the margins of the profits and the outputs of the existing firms but at their foundations and their very lives" (Schumpeter, 1943, p. 84)? Simply because the "gale" of innovation in different areas of society—most of all in the technological field—necessarily changes the nature of the system for all the actors involved. This gale of creative destruction is thus unstoppable. In 1943, Schumpeter gave the example of how the traditional shop faces competition not only from similar shops but, first and foremost, from "the department store, the chain store, the mail-order house and the supermarket which are bound to destroy those pyramids sooner or later" (p. 85). Seeing what shops and shopping became in the age of the internet, and how these continue to be transformed, would certainly strengthen his view that the history of capitalism is basically one of creativity, a "history of revolutions" (p. 83). Within this history, creative production and destruction are two faces of the same coin. For Schumpeter, the latter designates a process of mutation "that incessantly revolutionizes the economic structure *from within*, incessantly destroying the old one, incessantly creating a new one" (p. 83). And, he continues, creative destruction is the essential fact about capitalism, whose goal is to create new consumer goods, open new markets, and find new ways of doing or new things and deliver services. In this process, the old—its practices, goods, and jobs—disappear to make room for the new.

This vision of creativity as a force of both creation and destruction, at the same time, has deep historical resonances. It goes back to the old gods of mythology who generate and destroy, help and punish, create and take life. It is also inscribed in 19th-century images of the genius who creates out of thin air and manages to, almost singlehandedly, revolutionize society and culture. When it comes to the economy, this logic seems to apply, and many authors support Schumpeter's conclusions (see, e.g., Carayannis & Ziemnowicz, 2007). In fact, his writings have been popular in different fields, including advertising (Zinkhan & Watson, 1996) and the knowledge economy (Bullen, Robb, & Kenway, 2004). They are also important for the growing literature on "disruptive innovation" (Christensen, 1997) and its recent applications (Guttentag & Smith, 2017; Poprawe et al., 2017). Basically, disruptive innovations illustrate one instance of creative destruction in which a product that underperforms but is cheaper, simpler, or more accessible than the old product, is launched, thus changing the market and forcing companies to innovate further. Another literature marked by the notion of creative destruction is the one on entrepreneurship. This is due to the fact that Schumpeter considered innovative entrepreneurs to be the catalysts of the entire process. They are the ones who break with old ways of doing things and are eager to utilize new resources and develop more competitive products and services that effectively change the game for everyone else. This view of entrepreneurs is widely referred to and used to build new theories of corporate (Lassen & Nielsen, 2009) or strategic (Ireland, Hitt, & Sirmon, 2003) entrepreneurship. It has also been contested for turning entrepreneurs into disruptive agents (Kirzner, 1999), and calls for its replacement—in an act of creative destruction—have been made (Gibb, 2002).

Did Schumpeter's work find echoes beyond the innovation and entrepreneurship literature and within creativity studies? Only modestly until now (see, e.g., Potts et al., 2008), and mostly in view of the relation between creativity and the economy. In this regard, for instance, Dubina, Carayannis, and Campbell (2012) argued recently for the need to theorize the "creativity economy" above and beyond existing discussions of the creative economy and creative industries. Building on the work of Schumpeter, they proposed a model that connects creativity, knowledge, and innovation within the economic cycle. In particular, their model focuses on the patterns of cyclical interaction between creativity and crisis, the latter addressed by more creativity. We are back to the starting point of this commentary: creativity seems to be always good and we always need more of it. But is this really the case? Although not directly drawing on Schumpeter, there are more and more discussions today about the "dark side of creativity" (see Cropley, Cropley, Kaufman, & Runco, 2010), and particularly malevolent creativity, intentionally aimed at harming others; think, for example, about innovative ways to commit fraud or to engage in terrorism. There is certainly a big gap between Schumpeter's notion of creative destruction and terrorism. And yet, technological creative destruction, for instance, can have serious negative consequences for many people. But are these consequences intended? And are they unavoidable? These questions are at the core of an important dimension of this debate that we need to address: ethics.

The topic of creativity and ethics started to receive some attention in the literature (see Moran, Cropley, & Kaufman, 2014). What I would like to argue in the end is the fact that Schumpeter's reflections on creative destruction can shed new light on the relation between creativity and society. In Chapter 30 (on sociability) in this reader, I made the case, together with Simmel, that creativity is the foundation of living together and associating with others. What we see in Schumpeter's notion is not only the progress that can come out of these associations, again through the use of creativity, but also the fact that creative acts can dissolve old social bonds and can end up marginalizing or oppressing people. These are, basically, the people whose livelihood depends on the use of "old" goods or technologies. They are the people whose environments are destroyed as part of the quest for new, better products. They are the ones who cannot keep up with rapid technological changes and the fast pace of the new or "creativity economy." We might argue, again drawing on Schumpeter, that this is the cost of progress within capitalism, and, going further, we might be tempted to assume that there is no other way of doing things anymore, that there is no viable alternative to neoliberal understandings of creativity (see Harvey, 2007), that, even if creative destruction became more and more destructive of late (see Komlos, 2014), as the social costs grew exponentially, the cycle of creativity and innovation cannot be stopped. Creativity might be the quick answer today, but we might have forgotten what the question was in the first place.

Critical reflections on the notion of creativity and its consequences for society are long overdue. These reflections cannot, however, be trapped within the same ideological and epistemological framework that led to the notion of creative destruction, but need to step away from it and look at it from new standpoints. Together with Zayda Sierra, I engaged in such an exercise and wrote about creativity seen from the epistemological position of the Global South (see Glăveanu & Sierra, 2015). From this perspective, the neoliberal logic at the core of much creativity research today is replaced by a focus on community, empowerment, collaboration, and sustainability. We questioned the practice of measuring creativity against capitalist and consumerist standards in a world in which the creative actions of some need, necessarily, to reduce the prosperity of others, particularly vulnerable or marginalized communities, playing a zero-sum game with the natural and social resources of the planet. Instead, what a Southern perspective on creativity brings to the fore is "our capacity to create fair and sustainable societies where creativity is not used for more efficient forms of exploitation (of the environment and of other people)" (p. 350). It is as much an epistemological as an ethical perspective that has been recently advanced by Sierra and Fallon (2016), who, again based on case studies coming from the Global South, discussed three forms of creativity: oppressive, of resistance, and transformative. The first one is exemplified by the use of new and innovative means by local, national, or international elites to create new wealth by exploiting the resources of already impoverished communities. The second one captures the innovative responses of these communities aimed at opposing this kind of exploitation and range from creative forms of protest to community mobilization and social action. The third refers to "the efforts made by various populations in the world to reimagine their own realities by breaking unequal conditions and building community well-being" (p. 356).

It is tempting to associate creative destruction with oppressive creativity, in light of its negative social consequences, but this doesn't necessarily have to be the case. There is creative destruction as well in acts of resistance, especially in those of transformation, and this would be an interesting topic for empirical research. What would be particularly useful in future studies is to distinguish between the different forms of creativity proposed by Sierra and Fallon (2016). This is not an easy task given the fact that the pragmatic value of a creative product or process always depends on the group of reference. And yet, here is where engaging with the issue of ethics becomes essential, as difficult as this theme is for creativity researchers used to being detached observers rather than active participants in the phenomenon under investigation. A related interesting question for creativity scholars is whether their field experienced, in the past, processes of creative destruction and how. It is common to assume, for instance, that the area of creativity studies, at least in psychology, started after 1950. And yet, as this *Reader* clearly testifies, there was a tremendous amount of work done before that year, and it was foundational for later scholarship. This work includes that of Schumpeter. Why is there such little recognition of these roots?

Revisiting the work of Schumpeter in light of current creativity research, as well as in the aftermath of a global financial crisis, is both timely and important. It not only offers us an interesting theory of creativity as both a constructive and destructive force. Above all, it makes us aware of the need to have a serious and deep discussion about the consequences of creativity and innovation in society, particularly when it comes to the sharp increase in inequality, discrimination, and disempowerment around the world (see McLean, 2017). For Schumpeter (1943, p. 86), talking about capitalism without mentioning creative destruction is similar to performing *Hamlet* without Hamlet. The question we need to start from is whether we want our societies to enact, economically, a version of *Hamlet* in the first place.

References

Bullen, E., Robb, S., & Kenway, J. (2004). "Creative destruction": Knowledge economy policy and the future of the arts and humanities in the academy. *Journal of Education Policy, 19*(1), 3–22.

Carayannis, E. G., & Ziemnowicz, C. (Eds.) (2007). *Discovering Schumpeter: Creative destruction evolving into "Mode 3."* Hampshire, UK: Palgrave Macmillan.

Christensen, C. M. (1997). *The innovator's dilemma: When new technologies cause great firms to fail.* Boston: Harvard Business School Press.

Cropley, D. H., Cropley, A. J., Kaufman, J. C., & Runco, M. A. (Eds.). (2010). *The dark side of creativity.* Cambridge, UK: Cambridge University Press.

Dubina, I. N., Carayannis, E. G., & Campbell, D. F. (2012). Creativity economy and a crisis of the economy? Coevolution of knowledge, innovation, and creativity, and of the knowledge economy and knowledge society. *Journal of the Knowledge Economy, 3*(1), 1–24.

Elliott, J. E. (1980). Marx and Schumpeter on capitalism's creative destruction: A comparative restatement. *Quarterly Journal of Economics, 95*(1), 45–68.

Gibb, A. (2002). In pursuit of a new "enterprise" and "entrepreneurship" paradigm for learning: Creative destruction, new values, new ways of doing things and new combinations of knowledge. *International Journal of Management Reviews, 4*(3), 233–269.

Glăveanu, V. P., & Kaufman, J. C. (2019). Creativity: A historical perspective. In J. C. Kaufman & R. Sternberg (Eds.), *The Cambridge handbook of creativity*. Cambridge, MA: Cambridge University Press.

Glăveanu, V. P., & Sierra, Z. (2015). Creativity and epistemologies of the South. *Culture & Psychology, 21*(3), 340–358.

Glăveanu, V. P., Tanggaard, L., & Wegener, C. (2016). Why do we need a new vocabulary for creativity? In V. P. Glăveanu, L. Tanggaard, & C. Wegener (Eds.), *Creativity: A new vocabulary* (pp. 1–9). London: Palgrave.

Guttentag, D. A., & Smith, S. L. (2017). Assessing Airbnb as a disruptive innovation relative to hotels: Substitution and comparative performance expectations. *International Journal of Hospitality Management, 64*, 1–10.

Hanchett Hanson, M. (2015). *Worldmaking: Psychology and the ideology of creativity*. London: Palgrave Macmillan.

Harvey, D. (2007). Neoliberalism as creative destruction. *Annals of the American Academy of Political and Social Science, 610*(1), 21–44.

Ireland, R. D., Hitt, M. A., & Sirmon, D. G. (2003). A model of strategic entrepreneurship: The construct and its dimensions. *Journal of Management, 29*(6), 963–989.

Komlos, J. (2014). Has creative destruction become more destructive? *CESifo Working Paper*, No. 4941.

Kirzner, I. M. (1999). Creativity and/or alertness: A reconsideration of the Schumpeterian entrepreneur. *Review of Austrian Economics, 11*(1–2), 5–17.

Lassen, A. H., & Nielsen, S. L. (2009). Corporate entrepreneurship: Innovation at the intersection between creative destruction and controlled adaptation. *Journal of Enterprising Culture, 17*(2), 181–199.

McLean, H. (2017). Hos in the garden: Staging and resisting neoliberal creativity. *Environment and Planning D: Society and Space, 35*(1), 38–56.

Moran, S., Cropley, D. H., & Kaufman, J. C. (Eds.) (2014). *Creativity and ethics*. New York, NY: Palgrave Macmillan.

Nakamura, L. (2000). Economics and the new economy: The invisible hand meets creative destruction. *Business Review, 2000*, 15–30.

Poprawe, R., Hinke, C., Meiners, W., Schrage, J., Bremen, S., Risse, J., & Merkt, S. (2017). Disruptive innovation through 3D printing. In K. Richter & J. Walther (Eds.), *Supply chain integration challenges in commercial aerospace* (pp. 73–87). Cham, Switzerland: Springer.

Potts, J., Hartley, J., Banks, J., Burgess, J., Cobcroft, R., Cunningham, S., & Montgomery, L. (2008). Consumer co-creation and situated creativity. *Industry and Innovation, 15*(5), 459–474.

Schumpeter, J. A. (1943). *Capitalism, socialism and democracy*. London: Routledge.

Sierra, Z., & Fallon, G. (2016). Rethinking creativity from the "South": Alternative horizons toward strengthening community-based well-being. In V. P. Glăveanu (Ed.), *The Palgrave handbook of creativity and culture research* (pp. 355–374). London: Palgrave.

Weiner, R. P. (2000). *Creativity and beyond: Cultures, values, and change*. Albany: State University of New York Press.

Zinkhan, G. M., & Watson, R. T. (1996). Advertising trends: Innovation and the process of creative destruction. *Journal of Business Research, 37*(3), 163–171.

Index

Note: Page references followed by an "*f*" indicate figure.